W9-AXC-253

Frommer's®
Alaska

My Alaska

by Charles Wohlforth

MY FAMILY AND I HAVE LIVED IN ALASKA ALL OUR LIVES, BUT AT times, we feel like visitors. Our house in Anchorage is like a base camp, the place where we pack and prepare, peruse maps and dream, looking to the dark winter sky for inspiration for our next Alaska adventure. We live in this house all winter, working, going to school, and eating dinner around a table like anyone else. But even on school nights, when the sun sets at 3pm, the snow beckons us to strap on our skis. We follow the city's cross-country trails under electric lights, or simply glide in the moonlight, where the smooth landscape gleams a strange lunar color.

As spring nears and the sky lightens, my children strain at the bonds of the city like sled dogs, mad to run. It's not a specific place they want to visit. They yearn for the shock when a whale leaps high next to the boat. The sense of anticipation as a fish we just caught sizzles on the fire. They want to clamber to the top of a mountain in the morning and catch hermit crabs in a sand pail in the afternoon. Then, when we find ourselves awake past midnight under a bright sky, breathing crisp, immaculate air, surrounded by the life of the sea and by fragrant growth on the steep sides of the coastal mountains, we think: "Yes, we're home."

Any visitor can feel that visceral connection—and after looking through the photos in these pages, you'll begin to understand why.

© Charles Wohlforth

We took this **FAMILY PHOTO (left)** in Prince William Sound (South Culross Passage, to be exact) one night in July toward the end of a 16-day camping trip with our little boat. If you ask any of us what we do, who we are—even if you ask little Becky, 3 years old in this picture—you will hear about these summer boating trips in the wilderness. Thoughts of those moments carry us through exams, boring meetings, dead-lines. It's all out there waiting.

When you're camping in the Sound, ice to refill the cooler is never too far away. Dozens of glaciers dump **CENTURIES-OLD ICE (above)** that is as clear and dense as crystal. It's this ice that carved the Sound's long fjords and sheer rock shores, and many extravagant land-forms all along Alaska's southern coast.

Some **FISH (right)** for food, snagging big healthy salmon and grilling them over a fire. Others don't care if they catch anything, contented to feel the breeze and the sun and watch a fly dance over smooth water.

The view at **ALYESKA RESORT (below),** an hour from our home in Anchorage, is a constant source of distraction: You want to stop your skis and gaze at the glistening water of Turnagain Arm stretching from just beyond the base of the mountain.

Ripples around the hull of the canoe. The scent of clean water. A circle of sky bounded by smoothly gliding shores. **CANOEING (above right)** is a favorite summer dream, a memory sustaining itself reliably beneath the ice of winter.

Even in gentle **PRINCE WILLIAM SOUND (below right),** being outdoors in Alaska requires a reliance on machines. You can't get way out there and be safe without them. Most visitors come on tour boats and cruise ships.

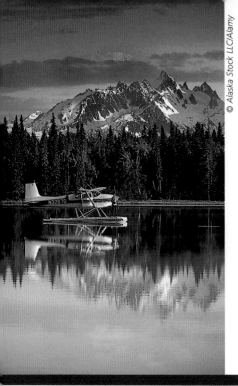

Among the unexpected wonders of the wilderness is the intense sense of privacy that befalls visitors to huge, empty places. A **FLOATPLANE (left)** is a portal to this aloneness. No visitor to Alaska should miss the opportunity to take a small plane either for a remote fishing trip, bear viewing experience, our mountain flightseeing outing. This image comes from the Alaska Range, south of Mt. McKinley.

You don't have to fly or have a boat. You can drive to the wilderness. If you can handle the dust, cracked windshields, and going hundreds of miles between crude services, you can be your own Arctic guide on the **DALTON HIGHWAY (below)**.

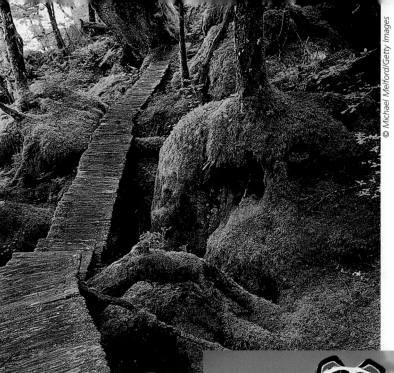

A few yards behind the beach, the sounds and cool colors of the sea disappear and the warmth and earthy dampness of the rainforest envelop your senses in dim greenness. This mysteriously intimate space seems to go on forever. The ecosystem extends unbroken from the Oregon coast to Prince William Sound, a distance greater than from Miami, Florida, to Portland, Maine. Often the land is so thick with mossy life that trails, like this one in **MISTY FJORDS NATIONAL MONUMENT (above)**, can only be built on boardwalks.

The language of carved faces is not lost in Southeast Alaska. Master carvers still work among the huge trees of the rainforest. **TOTEM POLES (right)** were not meant to last; instead, old poles rotted away in the rainy woods over a century or so, inspiring new generations of carvers to follow. Today's carvers use traditional techniques and images, but also tell new stories, recording their peoples' ongoing history.

Running into a bear can be an unwelcome thrill, but more and more visitors come to Alaska in search of bear encounters. The premier site is Katmai National Park's Brooks Camp, where, in season, huge **BROWN BEARS (above)** position themselves at the top of a waterfall to catch salmon heading upstream to spawn.

Children can become jaded by almost anything. I have examples—kids bored with huge waterfalls, spectacular sunsets, even s'mores. *Almost* anything. My children have seen **WHALES BREACHING (right)** often, but their jaws still drop every time.

Opposite page: © Leo Keeler/Alamy

In the fall (late Aug to Sept) it's not unusual to hear the crack and rattle of colliding antlers when **MOOSE FIGHT AT DENALI NATIONAL PARK.** Seeing a moose by design is hard, but it's a rare month that goes by our Anchorage home when we don't run across at least one. Rutting moose do show up in backyards during autumn in Anchorage and other towns.

MILEAGE CHART
Approximate driving distances in miles between cities.

	Anchorage	Circle	Dawson City	Eagle	Fairbanks	Haines	Homer	Prudhoe Bay	Seattle	Seward	Skagway	Tok	Valdez
Anchorage		520	494	501	358	775	226	847	2234	126	832	328	304
Circle	520		530	541	162	815	746	1972	2271	646	872	368	526
Dawson City	494	530		131	379	548	713	868	1843	619	430	189	428
Eagle	501	541	131		379	620	727	868	1974	627	579	173	427
Fairbanks	358	162	379	379		653	584	489	2121	484	710	206	364
Haines	775	815	548	620	653		1001	1142	1774	901	359	447	701
Homer	226	746	713	727	584	1001		1073	2455	173	1058	554	530
Prudhoe Bay	847	1972	868	868	489	1142	1073		2610	973	1199	695	853
Seattle	2243	2271	1843	1974	2121	1774	2455	2610		2493	1577	1931	2169
Seward	126	646	619	627	484	901	173	973	2493		958	454	430
Skagway	832	872	430	579	710	359	1058	1199	1577	958		504	758
Tok	328	368	189	173	206	447	554	695	1931	454	504		254
Valdez	304	526	428	427	364	701	530	853	2169	430	758	254	

Chukchi Sea

RUSSIA

Bering Strait

Little Diomede Island *Bering Land Bridge National Preserve*

Nome

Norton Sound

Yukon Delta National Wildlife Refuge

Kuskokwim River

Bethel

Yukon Delta National Wildlife Refuge

Dillingham

Bering Sea

Pribilof Islands

Bristol Bay

Aniakchak National Monument and Preserve

Cape St. Stephen

Rat Islands

A L E U T I A N   I S L A N D S

Adak

Adak Island

Atka Island

Atka

Dutch Harbor

Unalaska

Unimak Island

Cold Bay

Unimak

ALASKA PENINSULA

Nunivak Island

P A C I F I C

O C E A N

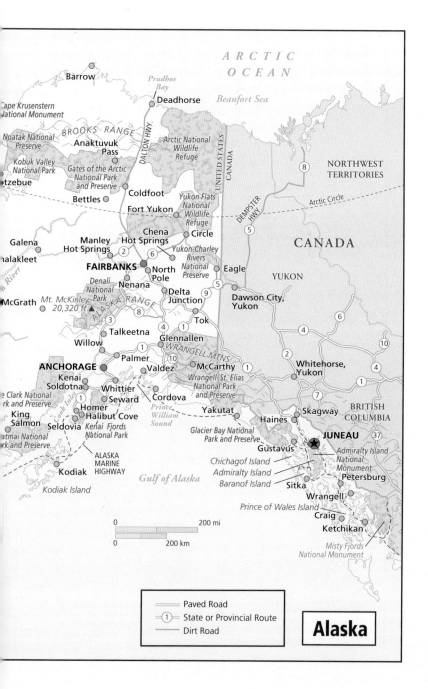

ARCTIC OCEAN

Barrow

Prudhoe Bay

Deadhorse

Beaufort Sea

Cape Krusenstern National Monument

BROOKS RANGE

Noatak National Preserve

Anaktuvuk Pass

Kobuk Valley National Park

Gates of the Arctic National Park and Preserve

Coldfoot

tzebue

Bettles

Fort Yukon

Arctic National Wildlife Refuge

UNITED STATES / CANADA

DALTON HWY.

DEMPSTER HWY.

Arctic Circle

NORTHWEST TERRITORIES

8

Yukon Flats National Wildlife Refuge

Chena Hot Springs

Circle

5

CANADA

Galena

Manley Hot Springs

2

6

Yukon-Charley Rivers National Preserve

YUKON

nalakleet

FAIRBANKS

North Pole

Eagle

5

Dawson City, Yukon

n River

Denali National Park

Nenana

Delta Junction

9

McGrath

Mt. McKinley 20,320 ft.

ALASKA RANGE

8

Tok

6

3

Talkeetna

4

1

4

Willow

Glennallen

WRANGELL MTNS.

2

Whitehorse, Yukon

10

ANCHORAGE

Palmer

10

Valdez

McCarthy

1

4

Kenai

Soldotna

Whittier

Wrangell-St. Elias National Park and Preserve

7

BRITISH COLUMBIA

e Clark National rk and Preserve

Seward

Cordova

Yakutat

Skagway

King Salmon

Homer

Halibut Cove

Prince William Sound

Haines

1

atmai National k and Preserve

Seldovia

Kenai Fjords National Park

JUNEAU

37

Glacier Bay National Park and Preserve

Gustavus

Admiralty Island National Monument

ALASKA MARINE HIGHWAY

Chichagof Island

Petersburg

Kodiak

Gulf of Alaska

Admiralty Island

Baranof Island

Sitka

Kodiak Island

Wrangell

Prince of Wales Island

Craig

Ketchikan

Misty Fjords National Monument

0   200 mi

0   200 km

Paved Road

1 State or Provincial Route

Dirt Road

Alaska

The Kenai Peninsula & Prince William Sound

Alaska

Fairbanks

Anchorage   Juneau
Kenai   Sitka
Ketchikan

Alaska Marine Highway
Railway
Whale Watching

CHUGACH MOUNTAINS

Valdez 4

Columbia Glacier

Cordova

Chugach National Forest

Prince William Sound

Montague Island

Gulf of Alaska

ANCHORAGE 1

Turnagain Arm

Portage

Whittier

Hope

Captain Cook State Recreation Area

KENAI NATIONAL

Cooper Landing

Sterling 1

Moose Pass

Kenai Lake 9

Seward

Sargeant Ice Field

Resurrection Bay

Cook Inlet

Tyonek

Nikiski

Kenai

Soldotna

Kasilof 1

Skilak Lake

WILDLIFE REFUGE

Tustumena Lake

Harding Ice Field

KENAI MOUNTAINS

KENAI FJORDS NATIONAL PARK

LAKE CLARK NATIONAL PARK AND PRESERVE

Clam Gulch

Ninilchik

Sterling Highway

Anchor Point

Homer

KENAI PENINSULA

Kachemak Bay

Halibut Cove

Kachemak Bay State Park

Seldovia

To Kodiak

0   20 Mi
0   20 Km

Frommer's®

Alaska

2007

by Charles Wohlforth

Here's what the critics say about Frommer's:

"Amazingly easy to use. Very portable, very complete."
—*Booklist*

"Detailed, accurate, and easy-to-read information for all price ranges."
—*Glamour Magazine*

"Hotel information is close to encyclopedic."
—*Des Moines Sunday Register*

"Frommer's Guides have a way of giving you a real feel for a place."
—*Knight Ridder Newspapers*

Wiley Publishing, Inc.

About the Author

Charles Wohlforth is a lifelong Alaskan who has been a writer and journalist since 1986. Wohlforth lives in Anchorage with his wife, Barbara, sons Robin and Joseph, and daughters Julia and Rebecca. His book about Eskimos experiencing warming in the Arctic is titled *The Whale and the Supercomputer: On the Northern Front of Climate Change* (North Point Press, $14). Wohlforth can be reached through his website, www.wohlforth.net.

Published by:

Wiley Publishing, Inc.

111 River St.
Hoboken, NJ 07030-5774

ISBN-13: 978-0-471-94554-3
ISBN-10: 0-471-94554-4

Editor: Billy Fox
Production Editor: Michael Brumitt
Cartographer: Andrew Dolan
Photo Editor: Richard Fox
Anniversary Logo Design: Richard Pacifico
Production by Wiley Indianapolis Composition Services

Front cover photo: Juneau Ice Field: Mendenhall Glacier, woman kayaker in foreground.
Back cover photo: Homer, Kachemak Bay: Eagle landing on prey, top of water.

For information on our other products and services or to obtain technical support, please contact our Customer Care Department within the U.S. at 800/762-2974, outside the U.S. at 317/572-3993 or fax 317/572-4002.

Wiley also publishes its books in a variety of electronic formats. Some content that appears in print may not be available in electronic formats.

Manufactured in the United States of America

5 4 3 2 1

Contents

8 The Denali National Park Region   339

9 The Alaskan Interior   379

10 The Bush   433

Appendix: Alaska in Depth   465

Index   489

List of Maps

Acknowledgments

This is my tenth edition of *Frommer's Alaska* and, more than ever, it is the product of teamwork. From the very start I received enormous help from friends, colleagues, and my family. The size and diversity of Alaska would otherwise make the project impossible. I want to acknowledge them all, but I need to give special note to the remarkable professionals who assisted with this 2007 edition. Karen Datko is more than my right hand. She's my life preserver, too. Kathryn Gerlek got the project started by helping with my database. Researchers and writers around the state who contributed brought new life to the book and gave it the insider's insider information that I couldn't have produced alone, even as a life-long Alaskan. They include: Tom Morphet, Eric Troyer, Kris Capps, and Charlotte Glover.

An Invitation to the Reader

In researching this book, we discovered many wonderful places—hotels, restaurants, shops, and more. We're sure you'll find others. Please tell us about them, so we can share the information with your fellow travelers in upcoming editions. If you were disappointed with a recommendation, we'd love to know that, too. Please write to:

Frommer's Alaska 2007
Wiley Publishing, Inc. • 111 River St. • Hoboken, NJ 07030-5774

An Additional Note

Please be advised that travel information is subject to change at any time—and this is especially true of prices. We therefore suggest that you write or call ahead for confirmation when making your travel plans. The authors, editors, and publisher cannot be held responsible for the experiences of readers while traveling. Your safety is important to us, however, so we encourage you to stay alert and be aware of your surroundings. Keep a close eye on cameras, purses, and wallets, all favorite targets of thieves and pickpockets.

Other Great Guides for Your Trip:

Frommer's Alaska Cruises & Ports of Call
Alaska For Dummies

Frommer's Star Ratings, Icons & Abbreviations

Every hotel, restaurant, and attraction listing in this guide has been ranked for quality, value, service, amenities, and special features using a **star-rating system.** In country, state, and regional guides, we also rate towns and regions to help you narrow down your choices and budget your time accordingly. Hotels and restaurants are rated on a scale of zero (recommended) to three stars (exceptional). Attractions, shopping, nightlife, towns, and regions are rated according to the following scale: zero stars (recommended), one star (highly recommended), two stars (very highly recommended), and three stars (must-see).

In addition to the star-rating system, we also use **seven feature icons** that point you to the great deals, in-the-know advice, and unique experiences that separate travelers from tourists. Throughout the book, look for:

Finds	Special finds—those places only insiders know about
Fun Fact	Fun facts—details that make travelers more informed and their trips more fun
Kids	Best bets for kids, and advice for the whole family
Moments	Special moments—those experiences that memories are made of
Overrated	Places or experiences not worth your time or money
Tips	Insider tips—great ways to save time and money
Value	Great values—where to get the best deals

The following **abbreviations** are used for credit cards:

AE	American Express	DISC	Discover	V	Visa
DC	Diners Club	MC	MasterCard		

Frommers.com

Now that you have this guidebook to help you plan a great trip, visit our website at **www. frommers.com** for additional travel information on more than 3,500 destinations. We update features regularly to give you instant access to the most current trip-planning information available. At Frommers.com, you'll find scoops on the best airfares, lodging rates, and car rental bargains. You can even book your travel online through our reliable travel booking partners. Other popular features include:

- Online updates of our most popular guidebooks
- Vacation sweepstakes and contest giveaways
- Newsletters highlighting the hottest travel trends
- Online travel message boards with featured travel discussions

What's New in Alaska

Here are some changes in Alaska travel since the last edition of *Frommer's Alaska*.

PLANNING YOUR TRIP For more planning information, see chapter 2.

Climate information shouldn't be showing up in the "What's New" section, but there's no doubt that Alaska is getting much warmer, as the national media has reported widely in the last year. What this means for visitors is more sunny days, more forest-fire smoke, and shorter, less predictable winters, among other things, but I'm not sure how you can make adjustments for that, since the weather in any particular year could be warm or cold. I've included a brief explanation of Arctic climate change in the appendix on p. 472.

Foreign travelers should prepare for more complicated procedures and delays setting up a visit and entering the United States. Visas now take weeks or months to obtain rather than the days that used to be required. In addition, U.S. citizens will be required to show a passport to reenter the country even from Canada and Mexico. This new rule goes into effect for air and sea entries in 2007 and for land entries in 2008. Rules have changed as well for taking Alaska Native arts and crafts home. It has become essentially impossible to export items made from marine mammals unless they are antique.

The ease of using the Internet while traveling in Alaska has increased dramatically. Free Wi-Fi is becoming the standard in hotels and B&Bs, not the exception, and free hotspots beyond the hotels abound. Some tiny villages that never got telephone service now have broadband Wi-Fi provided by satellite.

THE SOUTHEAST For more, see chapter 5.

The proliferation of large **cruise ships** continues to grow well beyond the carrying capacity of the small-town ports the ships call on. Towns are now receiving more than 10,000 visitors in a day from cruise ships. The towns worst affected are Ketchikan, Juneau, and Skagway. In sections on each, I've given tips for avoiding the crowds.

In **Ketchikan,** the **Best Western Landing Hotel** (© 800/428-8304; www.landinghotel.com) has completed a massive remodel and is quite luxurious. I also can now wholeheartedly recommend the restaurant in the New York Hotel, which is oddly named **That One Place/That Other Place** (© 907/ 225-0246).

In **Sitka,** the aquarium at Sheldon Jackson College is worth a look, as is the museum there. The **Sitka Hotel** (© 907/ 747-3288; www.sitkahotel.com) partially burned over the winter, but the disaster was a blessing in disguise, as the insurance settlement funded a dramatic upgrade of many rooms. One of my favorite B&Bs, **Crescent Harbor Hideaway,** closed, and I've replaced it with a place where you can get a bargain on a room, **Alaska Swan Lake Bed & Breakfast** (© 907/ 747-3917).

One of the most beautiful and historic buildings in Alaska, **Juneau's Holy Trinity Episcopal Church,** burned to the ground in 2006. The cause was arson: A drunk ejected from a party at a nearby house set a boat on fire that was parked next to the church. The century-old wood structure was gone in hours.

Juneau's most famous restaurant, The Fiddlehead, and its sister, DiSopra, closed for good. A fun and inexpensive new restaurant (but hardly a replacement) opened up downtown, **Kenny's Wok & Teriyaki Sushi Bar** (© 907/586-3575). Crondahl's Bed and Breakfast closed because Jay and Judy got tired of running it; instead, try **Alaska Wolf House Bed & Breakfast** (© 888/425-9653 or 907/586-2422; www.alaskawolfhouse.com).

Visits to **Gustavus** and **Glacier Bay National Park** became more difficult in 2006, when the passenger ferry and whale-watching boat from Juneau stopped operating. At this writing, the area is reached conveniently only by air. There is still a good whale watch available from the Gustavus dock, however, with a local company called **Cross Sound Express** (© 888/697-2726 or 907/697-2726; www.gustavus.com/taz).

ANCHORAGE & ENVIRONS   For more, see chapter 6.

I've changed the line-up of hotels to take note of some good new additions and provide more inexpensive choices for families who don't care about staying downtown. My favorite is the remarkable **Dimond Center Hotel** (© 866/770-5002; www.dimondcenterhotel.com).

I can also recommend an exciting new restaurant near the downtown area, **The Bridge** (© 907/677-6771; www.thebridgesalmonbakeandgrill.com), which occupies a building upon an actual bridge. Cuisine is eclectic, drawing on Polynesian influences. **Cafe Savannah** (© 907/646-9121) is the city's first Spanish restaurant. It's a fashionable spot right in the downtown core.

Hockey fans can take in the national champions while visiting Anchorage—the minor-league champions, that is. The **Anchorage Aces** beat a Georgia team for the ECHL crown in 2006.

KENAI PENINSULA & PRINCE WILLIAM SOUND   For more, see chapter 7.

A delightful new restaurant, **Suzie's Place,** in **Sterling** (© 907/260-5751), makes the long drive to the south end of the Kenai Peninsula more pleasant.

Homer has matured as a winter destination. The local ski club has built a terrific network of cross-country trails over spectacular terrain, and the charter fishing fleet has developed a strong wintertime king salmon fishery.

My favorite restaurant in **Valdez,** **Mike's Palace,** closed with the death of its owner. Family members still hope to reopen but hadn't at the date of this writing.

In **Cordova,** the **Reluctant Fisherman Hotel** (© 877/770-3272 or 907/424-3272) is back in business and offering first-class rooms.

DENALI NATIONAL PARK   For more, see chapter 8.

The **Eielson Visitor Center** is being demolished and rebuilt. It won't be completed before 2008. Shuttle buses that formerly turned around there now make their turn at a wayside that has no services at Mile 63 of the park road. Passengers can instead ask questions, use outhouses, buy books, and make bus changes at tents set up at the Toklat River.

Daily educational programs at the **Murie Science and Learning Center** did not take place as predicted in 2006. Exactly what programming visitors will find may vary year to year as the new center finds its feet. The Denali Institute was folded into the center and no longer exists as a separate entity.

The line-up of businesses and hotels on the Parks Highway area nearest the park continues to change rapidly as cruise lines buy everything in sight. More and more, independent travelers without unlimited budgets need to stay in Healy or south of the park, not near the park entrance. A brand new hotel 7 miles to the south, **Cedar Hotel at Denali Grizzly Bear Resort** (© **866/583-2696** or 907/683-2696; www.denaligrizzlybear. com), offers one good choice.

Denali West Lodge stopped operating in 2006 and may or may not revive.

THE INTERIOR   For more, see chapter 9.

Expansion of the **UA Museum of the North** is, at long last, complete. The building is Alaska's most dramatic architectural statement and adds art to the state's best natural history museum.

THE BUSH   For more, see chapter 10.

In **Kodiak,** one of the largest hotels changed hands, got renovated, and brought in a great new restaurant. The Buskin River Inn is now the **Comfort Inn Kodiak** (© **800/544-2202** or 907/487-2700). The restaurant, run by the talented French chef from Mill Bay Coffee, is called **Mill Bay Deux.**

I've dropped the section about **Kotzebue** from this edition, including just a few highlights. With the closure of the NANA Museum of the Arctic and the end of escorted tours, there just is not enough reason for most visitors to go there. I added information for arranging a trip to the **Arctic National Wildlife Refuge.**

1

The Best of Alaska

As a child, when my family traveled outside Alaska for vacations, I often met other children who asked, "Wow, you live in Alaska? What's it like?" I never did well with that question. To me, the place I was visiting was far simpler and easier to describe than the one I was from. The Lower 48 seemed a fairly homogeneous land of freeways and fast food, a well-mapped network of established places. Alaska, on the other hand, wasn't even completely explored. Natural forces of vast scale and subtlety were still shaping the land in their own way, inscribing a different story on each of an infinite number of unexpected places. Each region, whether populated or not, was unique far beyond my ability to explain. Alaska was so large and new, so unconquered and exquisitely real, as to defy summation.

In contrast to many places you might choose to visit, it's Alaska's unformed newness that makes it so interesting and fun. Despite the best efforts of tour planners, the most memorable parts of a visit are unpredictable and often unexpected: a humpback whale leaping clear of the water, the face of a glacier releasing huge ice chunks, a bear feasting on salmon in a river, a huge salmon chomping onto your line. You can look at totem poles and see Alaska Native cultural demonstrations, and you can also get to know indigenous people who still live by traditional ways. And sometimes grand, quiet moments come, and those are the ones that endure most deeply.

As the writer of this guidebook, I aim to help you get to places where you may encounter what's new, real, and unexpected. Opening yourself to those experiences is your job, but it's an effort that's likely to pay off. Although I have lived here all my life, I often envy the stories visitors tell me about the Alaskan places they have gone to and what happened there. No one owns Alaska, and most of us are newcomers here. In all this immensity, a visitor fresh off the boat is just as likely as a lifelong resident to see or do something amazing.

1 The Best Views

- **A First Sight of Alaska:** Flying north from Seattle, you're in clouds, so you concentrate on a book. When you look up, the light from the window has changed. Down below, the clouds are gone, and under the wing, where you're used to seeing roads, cities, and farms on most flights, you see instead only high, snowy mountain peaks, without the slightest mark of human presence, stretching as far as the horizon. Welcome to Alaska.

- **Punchbowl Cove** (Misty Fjords National Monument): A sheer granite cliff rises smooth and implacable 3,150 feet straight up from the water. A pair of bald eagles wheels and soars across its face, providing the only sense of scale. They look the size of gnats. See p. 112.

- **From the Chugach Mountains over Anchorage, at Sunset:** The city sparkles below, on the edge of an orange-reflecting Cook Inlet, far below the mountainside where you stand. Beyond the pink and purple silhouettes of mountains on the other side of the inlet, the sun is spraying warm, dying light into puffs of clouds. And yet it's midnight. See "Getting Outside" in chapter 6.

- **Mount McKinley from the Air** (Denali National Park): Your Bush pilot guides his plane up from the flatlands of Talkeetna into a realm of eternal white, where a profusion of insanely rugged peaks rises in higher relief than any other spot on earth. After circling a 3-mile-high wall and slipping through a mile-deep canyon, you land on a glacier, get out of the plane, and for the first time realize the overwhelming scale of it all. See "Attractions & Activities outside the Park" and "Talkeetna: Back Door to Denali" in chapter 8.

- **The Northern Lights** (Alaska's Interior): Blue, purple, green, and red lines spin from the center of the sky, draping long tendrils of slow-moving light. Bright, flashing, sky-covering waves wash across the dome of stars like ripples driven by a gust of wind on a pond. Looking around, you see that your companions' faces are rosy in a silver, snowy night, all gazing straight up with their mouths open. See p. 389.

2 The Best Alaska Cruises

Cruises provide comfortable, leisurely access to the Inside Passage and the Gulf of Alaska. Here are some of the best bets. See chapter 4 for details.

- **Best Up-Close Alaska Experience:** Glacier Bay Cruiseline's *Wilderness Adventurer* and *Wilderness Explorer* sail itineraries that shun overcrowded port towns in favor of wilderness areas and small fishing villages. Both carry sea kayaks for off-ship exploration, and both feature naturalist-led hikes as central features of the experience. The line is owned by an Alaska Native corporation, and the ships are small (carrying 74 and 36 passengers, respectively) and very casual. They're not fancy, but that's the point—it's where they take you that counts.

- **Most Comfortable Small Ships:** Cruise West's *Spirit of Endeavor* and *Spirit of '98* (a 19th-c. coastal steamer re-creation) and Clipper's *Yorktown Clipper* offer a higher level of comfort than the other small ships in Alaska while still giving you an intimate, casual, up-close small-ship experience.

- **Most Luxurious Big Ships:** If you want a more casual kind of luxury, Radisson Seven Seas' *Seven Seas Mariner* offers just that. Among the mainstream cruise ships, Celebrity's *Infinity* and *Summit* are the big winners, offering cutting-edge modern ships with great service, dining, and design.

- **Best Cruise Tours:** Holland America Line and Princess are the leaders in linking cruises with land tours into the Interior, either before or after your cruise. They own their own hotels, deluxe motorcoaches, and railcars, and after many years in the business, they both really know what they're doing. Princess concentrates more on the Anchorage/Denali/Fairbanks routes, while Holland America has many itineraries that get you to the Yukon Territory's Dawson City and Whitehorse.

Alaska

MILEAGE CHART Approximate driving distances in miles between cities.	Anchorage	Circle	Dawson City	Eagle	Fairbanks	Haines	Homer	Prudhoe Bay	Seattle	Seward	Skagway	Tok	Valdez
Anchorage		520	494	501	358	775	226	847	2234	126	832	328	304
Circle	520		530	541	162	815	746	1972	2271	646	872	368	526
Dawson City	494	530		131	379	548	713	868	1843	619	430	189	428
Eagle	501	541	131		379	620	727	868	1974	627	579	173	427
Fairbanks	358	162	379	379		653	584	489	2121	484	710	206	364
Haines	775	815	548	620	653		1001	1142	1774	901	359	447	701
Homer	226	746	713	727	584	1001		1073	2455	173	1058	554	530
Prudhoe Bay	847	1972	868	868	489	1142	1073		2610	973	1199	695	853
Seattle	2243	2271	1843	1974	2121	1774	2455	2610		2493	1577	1931	2169
Seward	126	646	619	627	484	901	173	973	2493		958	454	430
Skagway	832	872	430	579	710	359	1058	1199	1577	958		504	758
Tok	328	368	189	173	206	447	554	695	1931	454	504		254
Valdez	304	526	428	427	364	701	530	853	2169	430	758	254	

Chukchi Sea

Little Diomede I.

Nome

Norte Soun

Yukon D National Wild Ref

Bethel

Yukon D National Wild Ref

Nunivak Island

Bering Sea

Pribilof Islands

Brista Bay

Attu Island

A l e u t i a n   I s l a n d s

Cape St. Stephen

Rat Islands

Alaska Peninsula

Adak

Adak Island

Atka Island

Atka

Dutch Harbor

Unimak Island

Cold Bay

Unalaska

P A C I F I C

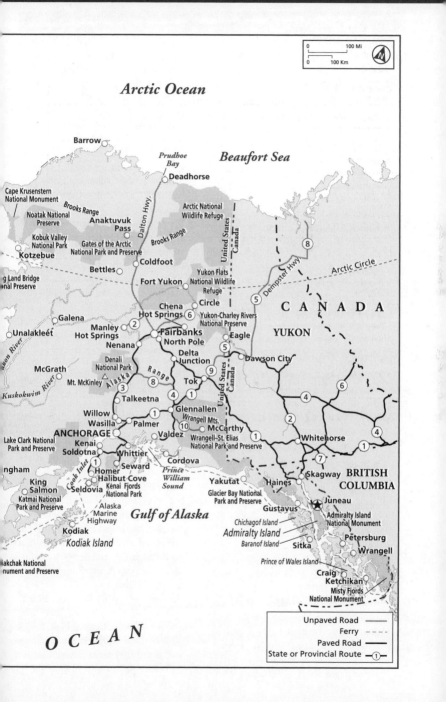

3 The Best Glaciers

More of Alaska—over 100 times more—is covered by glacier ice than is settled by human beings.

- **Grand Pacific Glacier** (Glacier Bay National Park): Two vast glaciers of deep blue meet at the top of an utterly barren fjord. They rubbed and creased the gray rock below for thousands of years before just recently releasing it to the air again. Three intimidating walls of ice surround boats that pull close to the glaciers. See "Glacier Bay National Park" in chapter 5.

- **Childs Glacier** (Cordova): Out the Copper River Highway from Cordova, this is a participatory glacier-viewing experience. The glacier is cut by the Copper River, which is ¼-mile broad; standing on the opposite shore (unless you're up in the viewing tower), you have to be ready to run like hell when the creaking, popping ice gives way and a huge berg falls into the river, potentially swamping the picnic area. Even when the glacier isn't calving, you can feel the ice groaning in your gut. See "Cordova: Hidden Treasure" in chapter 7.

- **Exit Glacier** (Seward): You can drive near the glacier and walk the rest of the way on a gravel path. It towers above like a huge blue sculpture, the spires of broken ice close enough to breathe a freezer-door chill down on watchers. See "Exit Glacier" in section 6 of chapter 7.

- **Western Prince William Sound:** On a boat from Whittier, you can see a couple dozen glaciers in a day. Some of these are the amazing tidewater glaciers that dump huge, office-building-size spires of ice into the ocean, each setting off a terrific splash and outward-radiating sea wave. See "Whittier: Dock on the Sound" in chapter 7.

4 The Most Beautiful Drives & Train Rides

You'll find a description of each road in "Alaska's Highways a la Carte" on p. 382. Here are some highlights:

- **White Pass and Yukon Route Railway** (Skagway to Summit): The narrow-gauge excursion train, sometimes pulled by vintage steam engines, climbs the steep grade that was chiseled into the granite mountains by stampeders to the Klondike gold rush. The train is a sort of mechanical mountain goat, balancing on trestles and steep rock walls far above deep gorges. See p. 199.

- **Seward Highway/Alaska Railroad** (Anchorage to Seward): Just south of Anchorage, the highway and rail line have been chipped into the side of the Chugach Mountains over the surging gray water of Turnagain Arm. Above, Dall sheep and mountain goats pick their way along the cliffs, within easy sight. Below, white beluga whales chase salmon through the turbid water. Farther south, the route splits and climbs through the mountain passes of the Kenai Peninsula. See "Out from Anchorage: Turnagain Arm and Portage Glacier" in chapter 6 and "The Seward Highway: A Road Guide" in chapter 7 for information on the highway, and p. 348 for information on this Alaska Railroad route.

- **Denali Highway:** Leading east-west through the Alaska Range, the highway crosses terrain that could be another Denali National Park, full of wildlife and with views so huge and grand they seem impossible. See p. 344.

- **Richardson Highway:** Just out of Valdez heading north, the Richardson Highway rises quickly from sea level to more than 2,600 feet, switching back and forth on the side of a mountain. With each turn, the drop down the impassable slope becomes more amazing. North of Glennallen, the highway rises again, bursting through the tree line between a series of mountains and tracing the edges of long alpine lakes, before descending, parallel with the silver skein of the Alaska pipeline, to Delta Junction. See "The Richardson Highway & Copper Center," in chapter 9.

- **The Roads Around Nome:** You can't drive to Nome, but 250 miles of gravel roads radiate from the Arctic community into tundra that's populated only by musk oxen, bears, reindeer, birds, and other wildlife. See p. 452.

- **The Dalton Highway:** When you're ready for an expedition—a real wilderness trip by road—the Dalton Highway leads from Fairbanks across northern Alaska to the Arctic Ocean, a mind-blowing drive through 500 miles of spectacular virgin country. See "The Dalton Highway" in chapter 9.

5 The Best Fishing

The quality of salmon fishing in Alaska isn't so much a function of place as of time. See p. 38 for information on how to find the fish when you arrive.

- **Bristol Bay:** This is the world's richest salmon fishery; lodges on the remote rivers of the region are an angler's paradise. See p. 435.

- **Copper River Delta, Cordova:** The Copper itself is silty with glacial runoff, but feeder streams and rivers are rich with trout, Dolly Varden, and salmon, with few other anglers in evidence. See p. 334.

- **The Kenai River:** The biggest king salmon—up to 98 pounds—come from the swift Kenai River. Big fish are so common in the second run of kings that there's a special, higher standard for what makes a trophy. Silvers and reds add to a mad, summer-long fishing frenzy. See p. 294.

- **Homer:** Alaska's largest charter-fishing fleet goes for halibut ranging into the hundreds of pounds. See p. 312.

- **Unalaska:** Beyond the road system, Unalaska has the biggest halibut. See p. 446.

- **Kodiak Island:** The bears are so big here because they live on an island that's crammed with spawning salmon in the summer. Kodiak has the best roadside salmon fishing in Alaska, and the remote fishing, at lodges or fly-in stream banks, is legendary. See p. 436.

6 The Best Tips for Cooking Salmon

Now that you've caught a Pacific salmon, you need to know how to cook it—or order it in a restaurant—to avoid spoiling the rich flavor.

- **Freeze as Little as Possible:** It's a sad fact that salmon loses some of its richness and gets more "fishy" as soon as it's frozen. Eat as much as you can fresh because it'll never be better. Ask if the salmon is fresh when you order it in a restaurant. Don't overlook smoking, the traditional Native way of preserving fish for the winter. See p. 312 for information on getting your salmon frozen and smoked.

- **Choose the Best Fish:** The best restaurants advertise where their salmon comes from on the menu. In early summer, Copper River kings and reds are the richest in flavor; later in the summer, Yukon River salmon are best. The oil in the salmon gives it the rich, meaty flavor; the fish from the Copper and Yukon are high in oil content because the rivers are long and the fish need a lot of stored energy to swim upstream to spawn. King, red, and silver salmon are the only species you should find in a restaurant. Avoid farm-reared salmon, which is mushy and flavorless compared with wild Alaska salmon.

- **Keep It Simple:** When ordering salmon or halibut in a restaurant, avoid anything with cheese or heavy sauces. When salmon is fresh, it's best with light seasoning, perhaps just a little lemon, dill weed, and pepper and salt, or basted with soy sauce; or without anything on it at all, grilled over alder coals.

- **Don't Overcook It:** Salmon should be cooked just until the moment the meat changes color and becomes flaky through to the bone, or slightly before. A minute more, and some of the texture and flavor are lost. That's why those huge barbecue salmon bakes often are not as good as they should be—it's too hard to cook hundreds of pieces of fish just right and serve them all hot.

- **Fillets, Not Steaks:** Salmon is cut two ways in Alaska: lengthwise fillets or crosswise steaks. The fillet is cut with the grain of the flesh, keeping the oil and moisture in the fish. Do not remove the skin before cooking—it holds in the oils and will fall off easily when the fish is done. If you have a large group, consider cooking the salmon bone-in (sometimes called a roast), stuffing seasonings in the body cavity. When it's done, the skin easily peels off and, after eating the first side, you can effortlessly lift out the skeleton.

7 The Best Bear Viewing

There are many places to see bears in Alaska, but if your goal is to make *sure* you see a bear—and potentially lots of bears—these are the best places:

- **Anan Wildlife Observatory:** When the fish are running, you can see many dozens of black bears feeding in a salmon stream from close at hand. Access is easiest from Wrangell. See p. 121.

- **Pack Creek** (Admiralty Island): The brown bears of the island, which is more thickly populated with them than anywhere else on earth, have learned to ignore the daily visitors who stand on the platforms at Pack Creek. Access is by air from Juneau. See p. 167.

- **Katmai National Park:** During the July and September salmon runs, dozens of giant brown bears congregate around Brooks Camp, where, from wooden platforms a few yards away, you can watch the full range of their behaviors. Flight services from Kodiak also bring guests at any time of the summer to see bears dig clams on the park's eastern seashore. See "Katmai National Park" and "Kodiak: Wild Island" in chapter 10.

- **Kodiak Island:** The island's incredible salmon runs nourish the world's largest bears, Kodiak brown bears; pilots know where to find them week to week, landing floatplanes as near as possible. See p. 436.

- **Denali National Park:** The park offers the best and least expensive wildlife-viewing safari in the state.

Passengers on the buses that drive the park road as far as Mile 63 usually see at least some grizzlies. See chapter 8.

8 The Best Marine Mammal Viewing

You've got a good chance of seeing marine mammals almost anywhere you go boating in Alaska, but in some places it's almost guaranteed.

- **Frederick Sound** (Petersburg): A humpback jumped right into the boat with whale-watchers here in 1995. The whales show up reliably for feeding each summer. Small boats from Petersburg have no trouble finding them and watching in intimate circumstances. See p. 130.
- **Icy Strait** (Gustavus) and **Bartlett Cove** (Glacier Bay National Park): Humpback whales show up and often orcas are present off Point Adolphus, in Icy Strait, just a few miles from little Gustavus, a town of luxurious country inns, and in Bartlett Cove within Glacier Bay National Park. See "Glacier Bay National Park" and "Gustavus: Country Inns & Quiet" in chapter 5.

- **Sitka Sound:** Lots of otters and humpback whales show up in the waters near Sitka. In fall, when the town holds its Whale Fest, you can spot them from a city park built for the purpose. See "Sitka: Rich Prize of Russian Conquest" in chapter 5.
- **Kenai Fjords National Park** (near Seward): You don't have to go all the way into the park—you're pretty well assured of sea otters and sea lions in Resurrection Bay, near Seward, and humpbacks and killer whales are often seen in the summer, too. See "Kenai Fjords National Park" in chapter 7.
- **Prince William Sound:** Otters, seals, and sea lions are easy—you'll see them on most trips out of Valdez, Whittier, or Cordova—but you also have a chance of spotting both humpback and killer whales in the Sound. See chapter 7.

9 The Best Encounters with Native Culture

- **Ketchikan Totem Poles:** This Tlingit homeland has three unique places to see totem poles: historic poles indoors at the Totem Heritage Center, faithful reproductions outdoors in a natural setting at Totem Bight State Park, and brand new poles as they are created in a workshop at the Saxman Native Village Totem Pole Park. See p. 104.
- **Sitka:** The Tlingit remain strong where they met Russian invaders in fierce battles 2 centuries ago. The totem poles and ancient Native art you can see here are second to none, and the setting makes them only

more impressive. See section 5 of chapter 5.
- **Alaska Native Heritage Center** (Anchorage): All of Alaska's Native groups joined together to build this grand living museum and gathering place, where dance and music performances, storytelling, art and craft demonstrations, and simple meetings of people happen every day. See p. 234.
- **Iñupiat Heritage Center** (Barrow): A living museum, this is a place to meet and enjoy performances by the Native people who built it, and to see extraordinary artifacts they have made and recovered from digs in frozen ground. See p. 460.

10 The Best Museums & Historic Sites

- **Sitka National Historic Park:** The historic park, its buildings, and other structures in Sitka keep alive an alternate stream in history: one in which a Russian czar ruled Alaska and this little town was one of the most important on the west coast of North America. See p. 138.

- **The Alaska State Museum** (Juneau): This richly endowed museum doesn't just show off its wealth of objects—it also uses them to teach about the state. A visit will put Alaska's Native cultures and pioneer history entirely in context. See p. 152.

- **Anchorage Museum of History and Art:** Alaska's largest museum has the room and expertise to tell the story of Native and white history in Alaska, and to showcase contemporary Alaskan art and culture. See p. 132.

- **The Pratt Museum** (Homer): The Pratt explains natural history (especially the life of the ocean) in a clear and intimate way you'll find nowhere else in Alaska. See p. 307.

- **UA Museum of the North** (Fairbanks): The spectacular renovation of this university museum includes a swooping new gallery to present Alaska's art. Its older gallery contains an extraordinary natural history collection, presented with the help of some of the world's top scientists on Alaskan subjects. See p. 391.

11 The Best Winter Destinations

- **Anchorage:** Anyone can enjoy the Fur Rendezvous and Iditarod sled dog races, which keep a winter-carnival atmosphere going through much of February and March, but winter sports enthusiasts get the most out of winter here. The city has some of the best Nordic and telemark skiing anywhere, close access to three downhill skiing areas, dog mushing, and groomed lake skating. See chapter 6.

- **Alyeska Resort** (Girdwood): Alaska's premier downhill skiing area has lots of snow over a long season, fantastic views, few lift lines, and a luxurious hotel. See "The Best Hotels," below, and p. 252.

- **Chena Hot Springs Resort:** A 90-minute ride from Fairbanks, and you're out in the country, where the northern lights are clear on a starry winter afternoon and night. The resort has lots of activities to get you out into the snowy countryside, or you can just relax in the hot mineral springs. See p. 409.

- **Homer:** In March, you can fish for king salmon in the morning and cross-country ski over a high ridge with limitless ocean views in the afternoon. In the evening, check out Alaska's best art galleries and eat in its best restaurants. See chapter 7, section 10.

- **Barrow:** Go to the shore of the frozen Arctic Ocean, and you have a chance to experience the most extreme winter conditions in the world. It's dark for 65 days except for the aurora blasting across the sky. There's not much to do, but you could run into a polar bear in the street. See "Barrow: Way North" in chapter 10.

12 The Strangest Community Events

- **Cordova Ice Worm Festival** (Cordova): The truth is, ice worms do exist. Really. This winter carnival celebrates them in February. The highlight is the traditional annual march of the ice worm (a costume with dozens of feet sticking out) down the main street. See p. 332.

- **Midnight Sun Baseball Game** (Fairbanks): For more than 100 years they have played a baseball game without lights that doesn't begin until 10:30pm on the longest day of the year. See p. 388.

- **Bering Sea Ice Golf Classic** (Nome): The greens are AstroTurf, as the sea ice won't support a decent lawn in mid-March. Hook a drive and you could end up spending hours wandering among the pressure ridges, but you must play the ball as it lies. See p. 454.

- **Polar Bear Swim** (Nome): This swim in the frigid Bering Sea takes place in late June, but only if the sea ice has opened up sufficiently to provide enough liquid water. See p. 454.

- **Pillar Mountain Golf Classic** (Kodiak): The course is 1 hole, par is 70, and elevation gain is 1,400 feet.

Having a spotter in the deep snow of late March is helpful, but use of two-way radios, dogs, and chain saws is prohibited. Also, there's no cutting down of power poles, and cursing tournament officials carries a $25 fine. See p. 438.

- **Piuraagiaqta** (Barrow): This spring festival, in April, includes lots of strange contests, such as the tea making race—contestants start with solid ice—and the white men vs. Eskimo women tug-of-war contest, which the white men have yet to win after many years of trying. Or the community may have come up with some other silly contest this year. See p. 460.

- **Mountain Mother Contest** (Talkeetna): In this event in the July Moose Dropping Festival, mothers compete in a test of Bush skills, including splitting wood, carrying water, and diapering a baby. See p. 374.

13 The Best Hotels

- **Hotel Captain Cook** (Anchorage; © 800/843-1950): This is the grand old hotel of downtown Anchorage, with a heavy nautical theme, teak paneling, several terrific restaurants, and every possible amenity. It remains the state's standard of service and luxury. See p. 213.

- **Alyeska Prince Hotel** (Girdwood; © 800/880-3880): The first sight of this ski resort hotel—designed in a château style and standing in an undeveloped mountain valley—will make you catch your breath. Wait till you get inside and see the starscape and polar bear diorama in the lobby atrium, or the saltwater swimming pool, with its high-beamed ceiling and windows, looking out on the mountain. A tram carries skiers and diners to the mountaintop. See p. 254.

- **Land's End Resort** (Homer; © 800/478-0400): It's the location: right on the end of Homer Spit, 5 miles out in the middle of Kachemak Bay, where you can fish for salmon from the beach right in front of your room, or watch otters drifting by. The hotel itself is excellent, too, with a tremendous variety of rooms, some extraordinarily luxurious, and a complete spa. See p. 315.

- **Westmark Fairbanks Hotel & Conference Center** (Fairbanks; © 800/544-0970): A tower rises over the flat river city of Fairbanks, a stylish and charming new wing of the city's oldest modern hotel. The owners, the Holland America cruise line, demolished much of the original building, leaping decades from the past to just a little into the future. See p. 399.

14 The Best Websites

Many useful websites are listed throughout the book; some of the best are under "Visitor Information" near the beginning of each town section.

- **www.trollart.com**. Ketchikan artist Ray Troll has created a website that carries you deep into his mind, which is full of odd and resonant humor about the evolution of fish, man, and our common relations. His vibrantly colored art makes it an aesthetic journey.

- **www.adfg.state.ak.us**. The Alaska Department of Fish and Game posts valuable information for anyone interested in fishing, hunting, wildlife watching, or just learning about creatures. Everyone from children to wildlife biologists will find something at their level. Try **www.wildlife.alaska.gov** to go straight to information about where to go and how to see Alaska's wild animals.

- **www.awrta.org**. The Alaska Wilderness Recreation and Tourism Association unites hundreds of small eco-tourism operators. Authentic local guides and lodges can be hard to find, but they are listed here on a comprehensive and easy-to-use site that also delves into current environmental issues and concerns.

- **www.gi.alaska.edu**. The Geophysical Institute at the University of Alaska Fairbanks maintains a fascinating and cool site filled with real-time earth science information about Alaska, such as aurora predictions, volcano watches, earthquake and tsunami updates, rocketry, and space science.

- **www.wohlforth.net**. A bit of self-promotion here, but readers can get something out of it. I've answered hundreds of reader questions on my own website, and I supply links to many of the establishments listed in this book and some of my other writings on Alaska and other subjects. Other travelers have run into the same puzzles you have, and you'll find my advice here.

- **Favorite Small-Town Sites:** Small-town Alaska newspapers, and people in communities too small to have a newspaper, communicate through the Internet; visitors to these sites can vicariously experience the pleasures and pitfalls of remote living, which can be touching and hilarious. The best I've found are: Seldovia's **www.seldovia.com**, Nome's **www.nomenugget.com**, and Kotzebue's **www.cityofkotzebue.com**.

Planning Your Trip to Alaska

Planning a trip to Alaska can be a bit more complicated than getting ready to travel in the rest of the United States. Aside from the vast distances and range of climatic conditions, the best places book up quickly for the high summer season. This chapter provides general orientation information, when to go, and how much it will cost. It then covers how to plan a trip to Alaska, including passport and visa information for international visitors, modes of travel, insurance, safety, and issues to watch out for. I also point you to the best outdoor activities and places and the businesses to get you there. I've included primers on fishing and shopping for Alaska Native art as well.

1 The Regions in Brief

SOUTHEAST ALASKA The Southeast Panhandle is the relatively narrow strip of mountains and islands lying between Canada and the Gulf of Alaska. To Alaskans, it's Southeast, but to the rest of the country, it's more like the northernmost extension of the lush Pacific Northwest. This is a land of huge rainforest trees, glacier-garbed mountains, and countless islands ranging in size from the nation's third largest to tiny one-tree islets strewn like confetti along the channels and fjords. The water is the highway of Southeast Alaska, as the land is generally too steep and rugged to build roads, but there are lots of towns and villages reachable by the ferry system or cruise ships. Southeast contains **Juneau,** Alaska's capital and third-largest city, and **Ketchikan,** next in size to Juneau. Southeast's towns are as quaint and historic as any in Alaska, especially **Sitka,** which preserves the story of Russian America and its conflict with the indigenous Native people. Alaska Native culture—here, Tlingit and Haida—is rich and close at hand. No other region offers more opportunities for boating or seeing marine wildlife. Likewise, no other region is as crowded with tourists. More than 800,000 visitors flood into Southeast annually aboard cruise ships, jamming the little towns all summer. The weather is wet and temperate.

SOUTHCENTRAL ALASKA As a region, Southcentral is something of a catchall. The area is roughly defined by the arc of the Gulf of Alaska from the Canadian border on the east to Cook Inlet and the end of the road network to the west. It's a microcosm of the state, containing **Prince William Sound,** which is similar to the wooded island habitat of Southeast; the **Kenai Peninsula,** a fishing, boating, and outdoor mecca with roads; **Anchorage,** the state's modern, major city; and the **Matanuska and Susitna valleys,** an agricultural and suburban region of broad flatlands between steep mountains. Southcentral dominates Alaska, with most of the state's population and a more highly developed transportation system than elsewhere, including a network of highways and the Alaska Railroad. The ocean influences Southcentral's weather, keeping it from being very hot or very cold. The coastal

Alaska by the Numbers

This chart shows some comparative indicators for 16 of Alaska's most popular destinations. The third column is the best season to visit—months when, during at least part of which, there's enough going on and weather is suitable (that includes weather that's good for winter sports). The fourth column lists modes of transportation to each community—in Alaska you can't drive everywhere.

Place	Population	Season	Transportation	Precip. (in.)	Snow (in.)
Anchorage	274,003	May–Sept/ Jan–Mar	Road, air, rail	16	71
Barrow	4,417	June–Sept	Air	4.5	30
Cordova	2,372	May–Sept	Air, ferry	93	119
Denali National Park	133	June–Sept	Road, rail	15	83
Fairbanks	82,214	May–Sept/ Jan–Mar	Road, air, rail	11	68
Glacier Bay National Park	438	May–Sept	Air, ferry	70	117
Haines	1,715	May–Sept/ Nov	Road, air, ferry	48	123
Homer	4,893	May–Sept/ Mar	Road, air, ferry	25	55
Juneau	31,283	May–Sept	Air, ferry	56	99
Kenai	7,125	May–Sept	Road, air	19	61
Ketchikan	13,548	May–Sept	Air, ferry	151	37
Kodiak Island	13,811	May–Sept	Air, ferry	76	73
Nome	3,448	June–Aug/ Mar	Air	16	61
Petersburg	3,060	May–Sept	Air, ferry	110	67
Seward	2,733	May–Sept	Road, rail	66	81
Sitka	8,891	May–Sept/ Nov	Air, ferry	86	39
Skagway	845	May–Sept	Road, air, ferry	26	50
Unalaska/ Dutch Harbor	4,388	June–Sept	Air, ferry	60	88
Valdez	4,060	May–Sept	Road, air, ferry	62	304

areas are wet, while just behind the coastal mountains the weather is drier.

THE INTERIOR   The vast central part of the state is crossed by highways and by rivers that act as highways. Big river valleys lie between great mountain ranges, the largest of which are the Alaska Range, which contains **Mount McKinley,** North

America's tallest peak, and the Brooks Range, the northern end of the cordillera that includes the Rockies. McKinley is the centerpiece of **Denali National Park,** Alaska's premier road-accessible wildlife-viewing destination. The region's dominant city is **Fairbanks,** Alaska's second largest, which lies on the lazy Chena River, roughly in the middle of the state. The natural environment is drier and less abundant than that in Southeast or Southcentral. The Athabaskans, the Interior's first people, still subsist on this sparse land in tiny villages and river fish camps. Summer days can be hot and winters very cold in the Interior because of the distance from the ocean.

THE BUSH Bush Alaska is linked by lifestyle rather than by geography. One good definition would be that the Bush is the part of the state that's closer to the wilderness than to civilization. It's also the only part of the state where Native people outnumber whites and other relative new-comers. In many Bush villages, readily accessible to the outside world only by small plane, people still live according to age-old subsistence hunting-and-gathering traditions. The Bush region includes the majority of Alaska outside the road and ferry networks, ranging from the north end of the Canadian border all the way around the coast, out to the Aleutians, and the Alaska Peninsula and Kodiak Island, south of Anchorage. But some towns in each of the other regions also could be called "Bush villages." The Bush contains many regions, including the Arctic, Northwest, and Southwest Alaska.

2 When to Go

This section covers one of the questions I am asked most frequently: "What's the best time to visit _____?" Alaska's vast-ness means the seasons change at differ-ent times in different parts of the state. Sports, cultural activities, and visitor facilities also happen at different times in different places.

CLIMATE & SEASONS

The weather in Alaska can be extreme and unpredictable. The state is the first to get whatever Arctic Siberia or the void of the North Pacific have to throw at North America. The extremes of recorded tem-peratures are a high of 100°F (38°C) and low of –80°F (–62°C). At any time of year, your vacation could be enlivened by weeks of unbroken sunny weather or weighed down by weeks of unbroken rain. All you can do is play the averages, hope for the best, and, if you do get bad weather, get out and have fun anyway—that's what Alaskans do. A statistical summary of weather probabilities in various Alaska places is found below in "Alaska's Climate, by Months & Regions." I've summarized the best visitor season in each destination in "Alaska by the Numbers," above.

JUNE, JULY & AUGUST Summer in Alaska is a miraculous time, when the sun refuses to set, the salmon run upriver, and people are energized by limitless daylight. The sun dips below the horizon in Anchorage for only about 4 hours on June 21, the longest day of the year, and the sky is lit all night. The state fills with people coming to visit and to work in the sea-sonal fishing, timber, and construction industries. Weather gets warmer, although how warm depends on where you go (see the chart below). June is the driest of the summer months, July the warmest, and August is generally the rainiest month of the brief summer but warmer than June. In most respects, June is the best summer month to make a visit, but it does have some drawbacks to consider: In the Arc-tic, snow can linger until mid-June; in Southcentral Alaska, trails at high eleva-tions or in the shade may be too muddy or snowy; and not all activities or facilities at Denali National Park open until late June. It's also the worst time for mosquitoes.

Alaska's Climate, by Months & Regions

	Jan	Feb	Mar	Apr	May	June	July	Aug	Sept	Oct	Nov	Dec
Anchorage: Southcentral Alaska												
Average high**	21/-6	26/-3	33/1	44/7	55/13	62/17	65/18	63/17	55/13	40/4	28/-2	22/-6
Average low**	8/-13	11/-12	17/-8	29/-2	39/4	47/8	51/11	49/9	41/5	28/-2	16/-9	10/-12
Hours of light*	6:53	9:41	12:22	15:20	18:00	19:22	18:00	15:15	12:19	9:29	6:46	5:27
Sunny days†	12	10	13	12	11	10	9	9	9	10	10	10
Rainy or snowy days	8	8	8	6	7	8	11	13	14	12	10	11
Precipitation‡	0.8	0.8	0.6	0.6	0.7	1.0	1.9	2.7	2.6	1.9	1.1	1.1
Barrow: Arctic Alaska												
Average high**	8/-13	-12/-24	-8/-22	6/-14	25/-4	39/4	46/8	43/6	34/1	20/-7	5/-15	-6/-21
Average low**	-20/-29	-24/-31	-21/-29	-8/-22	15/-9	30/-1	34/1	34/1	27/-3	10/-12	-6/-21	-17/-27
Hours of light*	0:00	8:05	12:33	17:43	24:00	24:00	24:00	17:34	12:30	7:46	0:00	0:00
Sunny days†	7	18	21	18	8	9	11	5	4	6	8	4
Rainy or snowy days	4	4	4	4	4	5	9	11	11	11	6	5
Precipitation‡	0.2	0.2	0.1	0.2	0.2	0.3	0.9	1.0	0.6	0.5	0.2	0.2
Cold Bay: Aleutian Archipelago												
Average high**	33/1	32/0	35/2	38/3	45/7	50/10	55/13	56/13	52/11	44/7	39/4	35/2
Average low**	24/-4	23/-5	25/-4	29/-2	35/2	41/5	46/8	47/8	43/6	35/2	30/-1	27/-3
Hours of light*	8:05	10:10	12:17	14:36	16:32	17:25	16:33	14:34	12:17	10:04	8:01	7:08
Sunny days†	8	6	8	4	3	3	3	2	4	6	6	7
Rainy or snowy days	19	17	18	16	17	16	17	20	21	23	22	21
Precipitation‡	2.8	2.5	2.3	2.0	2.5	2.3	2.4	3.7	4.3	4.2	4.2	3.3
Fairbanks: Interior Alaska												
Average high**	-2/-18	8/-13	24/-4	42/6	60/16	71/22	73/23	66/19	55/13	32/0	11/-12	1/-17
Average low**	-19/-28	-15/-26	-2/-19	20/-7	38/3	52/11	52/11	47/8	36/2	17/-8	-5/-21	-16/-27
Hours of light*	5:46	9:14	12:22	15:54	19:22	21:48	19:26	15:52	12:24	9:04	5:39	3:43
Sunny days†	15	14	17	14	16	13	12	10	10	9	12	12
Rainy or snowy days	8	7	6	5	7	11	12	12	10	11	11	9
Precipitation‡	0.6	0.4	0.4	0.2	0.6	1.4	1.8	1.8	1.1	0.8	0.7	0.8
Juneau: Southeast Alaska												
Average high**	29/-2	34/1	39/4	48/9	55/13	62/17	64/18	63/17	56/13	47/8	37/3	32/0
Average low**	18/-8	23/-5	27/-3	32/0	39/4	45/7	48/9	48/9	43/6	37/3	28/-2	23/-5
Hours of light*	7:31	9:55	12:18	14:55	17:11	18:17	17:13	14:54	12:20	9:49	7:27	6:22
Sunny days†	8	7	7	8	8	8	8	9	6	4	6	5
Rainy or snowy days	18	17	18	17	17	15	17	17	20	24	20	21
Precipitation‡	4.3	3.9	3.5	2.9	3.5	3.1	4.2	5.3	7.2	7.8	5.4	5.1
Valdez: Prince William Sound												
Average high**	27/-3	30/-1	37/3	45/7	53/12	60/16	63/17	61/16	54/12	43/6	33/1	29/-2
Average low**	18/-8	19/-7	24/-4	31/-1	39/4	45/7	48/9	46/8	41/5	33/1	23/-5	19/-7
Hours of light*	6:54	9:41	12:22	15:19	17:58	19:20	17:57	15:14	12:20	9:30	6:48	5:29
Sunny days†	9	9	11	11	9	8	8	10	8	8	10	7
Rainy or snowy days	17	14	16	14	17	15	17	17	20	20	16	18
Precipitation‡	5.7	5.5	4.7	3.2	3.2	2.8	3.6	6.5	9.3	7.9	5.7	7.6

*Hours of light is sunrise to sunset on the 21st day of each month.

**All temperatures are given in degrees Fahrenheit first, with degrees Celsius after the slash.

†Sunny days include the average observed clear and partly cloudy days per month.

‡Precipitation is the average water equivalent of rain or snow.

Summer also is the season of high prices. Most operators in the visitor industry have only these 90 days to make their year's income, and they charge whatever the market will bear. July is the absolute peak of the tourist season, when you must book well ahead and when crowds are most prevalent. (Of course, crowding depends on where you are. With a population density of roughly one person per square mile, Alaska is never *really* crowded.) Before June 15 and after August 15, the flow of visitors relaxes, providing occasional bargains and more elbow room. Real off-season prices show up before Memorial Day and after Labor Day. But the length and intensity of the visitor season varies widely in different areas: In cruise-ship ports, it's busy from chilly early May into stormy October.

MAY & SEPTEMBER More and more visitors are coming to Alaska during these "shoulder months" to take advantage of the lower prices, reduced crowds, and special beauty.

May is the drier of the 2 months and can be as warm as summer if you're lucky, but as you travel farther north and earlier in the month, your chances of finding cold, mud, and even snow increase. In Alaska, there is no spring—the melt of snow and resultant seas of mud are called **breakup.** Flowers show up with the start of summer. Many outdoor activities aren't possible during breakup, which can extend well into May. Except in cruise-ship towns, most tourist-oriented activities and facilities are still closed before May 15, and a few don't open until Memorial Day or June 1. Where visitor facilities are open, they often have significantly lower prices. Also, the first visitors of the year usually receive an especially warm welcome. The very earliest salmon runs start in May, but for a fishing-oriented trip it's better to come later in the summer. Cruise ships begin calling May 1, and the towns they visit swing into action when they arrive.

Sometime between late August and mid-September, weather patterns change, bringing clouds, frequent rainstorms, and cooling weather, and signaling the trees and tundra to turn bright, vivid colors. For a week or two (what week it is depends on your latitude), the bright yellow birches of the boreal forest and the rich red of the heathery tundra make September the loveliest time of year. But the rain and the nip in the air, similar to late October or November in New England, mean you'll likely have to bundle up, and September is among the wettest months of the year. Most tourist-oriented businesses stay open, with lower prices, till September 15, except in the Arctic. After September 15, it's potluck. Some areas close up tight, but the silver salmon fishing is still active on the Kenai Peninsula, and the season there continues until the end of the month. A lucky visitor can come in September and hit a month of crisp, sunny, perfect weather, and have the state relatively to him- or herself. Or, it can be cold and rainy all month. Cruise ships continue to ply the Inside Passage well into October, while the sky dumps torrential rains: Ketchikan averages 22 inches and 24 rainy days in October.

OCTOBER, NOVEMBER, APRIL I always love Alaska, but I love it least during these transition months between winter and summer. From Southcentral Alaska northward, snow and ice arrive sometime in October; in Southeast Alaska, it is the month of cold, unending rain. Winter starts in November, but you can't count on being able to do winter sports, and darkness is prevalent as the year's shortest day approaches. April is a month of waiting, as winter sports come to an end and summer activities are blocked by melt and mud (although spring skiing can still be great in high-snow years). In-town activities are down in these months, too; with few visitors, many facilities are closed.

DECEMBER THROUGH MARCH
Winter is the whole point of Alaska. For sightseeing, the scenery is at its best (although there are far fewer wildlife viewing opportunities). This is the time to see the aurora borealis. Communities get busy with activities such as sled dog and snowmobile races, theater, music and other performing arts, ice-carving competitions and winter carnivals, and all the rest of the real local culture that takes a break in the summer, when most visitors come. If you enjoy winter and its outdoor activities, an Alaska visit is paradise, with superb downhill, cross-country, and backcountry skiing; snowshoeing; snowmobiling; dog mushing; ice skating—anything that can be done on snow and ice.

By far the best time to come is late winter, from February and March, when the sun is up longer and winter activities hit their peak. Anchorage's Fur Rendezvous is in February; the Iditarod Sled Dog Race is in March. Visiting in late March could mean thin snow at lower elevations for cross-country skiing, but downhill skiing and skiing at backcountry locations keep going strong. At Alyeska Resort, south of Anchorage, some skiing goes on through Memorial Day. In Homer, you can cross-country ski and go salmon fishing on the same day in March.

If you come in winter, you sacrifice some popular Alaska experiences. Some tourism-oriented towns such as Skagway close down almost completely. In places on the ocean, most activities and attractions are closed for the season, but services remain open for business travelers. Inland, where winter sports are better, there is more to do. Hotel prices are often less than half of what you'd pay in the high season. Quite luxurious rooms sometimes go for the cost of a budget motel.

WHAT TO WEAR

You'll find little use for a tie or any formal attire anywhere in Alaska, but you do need to prepare for broad swings in weather.

SUMMER You're not going to the North Pole, and you don't need a down parka or winter boots weighing down your luggage. But you do need to be ready for a variety of weather, from sunny, 80°F (27°C) days to windy, rainy 50°F (10°C) outings on the water. The way Alaskans prepare for such a range is with layers. The content of the layers depends on what you'll be doing, but everyone should bring at least this: warm-weather clothes, heavy long-sleeved shirts and pants, a wool sweater or fleece equivalent, a jacket, and a waterproof raincoat and rain pants. Gloves and wool hats are a good idea, too, especially for boating trips. If you'll be camping, add synthetic thermal long underwear and wool socks, and make your jacket thick synthetic fleece. Combining these items, you'll be ready for any summer conditions. For hiking, bring sturdy shoes or cross trainers.

WINTER You can be warm and comfortable no matter how cold it is. Once you know how to dress, winter is not a time of suffering, and the world of snow opens up to you. First, what not to wear: People don't wear heavy Arctic gear in town, even in the Arctic. To make the dash from car to heated building, all you need is a greatcoat, sweater, hat, gloves, and wool socks. For outdoor pursuits, what to wear depends on how active you will be. The key to warmth and safety during vigorous outdoor activities is to wear layers of breathable clothing that will stay warm when wet, such as wool or synthetics. With the following layers, you can be ready for temperatures well below zero (at which point you won't want to ski or skate anyway): synthetic thermal long underwear, synthetic fleece pants and coat, wool sweater, wind-resistant pants and jacket, wool socks and hat, warm boots with liners or covers, and lined mittens. Remove layers for warmer temperatures. For more sedentary outdoor activities, such as watching the aurora or riding a snowmobile or dog sled, you need warmer clothing. Likewise, drives on rural highways in winter require warm clothing in case of breakdowns. On guided trips or at cold weather resorts, they'll tell you what to bring or provide or rent it to you. A full cold-weather outfit includes synthetic thermal long underwear, the stoutest Sorel-style or Air Force bunny boots, insulated snow pants, a heavy down or fur parka with a hood, thick insulated mittens (not gloves), a wool hat, a face-insulating mask, and ski goggles or quality sunglasses. You don't want any skin showing while riding a snowmobile or standing in a strong wind in below-zero (Fahrenheit) temperatures. Such a get-up costs more than $500. You can buy what you need in Anchorage at **Army Navy Store,** at 320 W. 4th Ave. (© **888/836-3535** or 907/279-2401; www.army-navy-store.com), or in Fairbanks at **Big Ray's Store,** at 507 2nd Ave. (© **800/478-3458** or 907/452-3458; www.bigrays.com).

ALASKA CALENDAR OF EVENTS

Here are some of the biggest community events of the year in Alaska's cities and towns. Event plans can change, so don't set up your vacation around any of these dates without checking for current details. I haven't listed fishing derbies, which go on in almost every coastal town in the summer and are listed in the sections on each town.

February

The Yukon Quest International Sled Dog Race (© **907/452-7954;** www.yukonquest.org). Mushers say this rugged 1,000-mile race is even tougher than the Iditarod. It runs between Fairbanks and Whitehorse, Yukon Territory, trading the direction each year. Starts February 10, 2007, in Fairbanks.

The Anchorage Fur Rendezvous Winter Festival (© **907/274-1177;** www.furrondy.net). The huge, city-wide winter celebration includes all kinds of community events, fireworks, craft fairs, snowshoe softball, dog sled rides, and other fun. The main event has always been the **World Champion Sled Dog Race,** a 3-day sprint event of about 25 miles per heat. The Rondy's end coincides with the start of the Iditarod (see directly below). February 16 to March 4, 2007.

March

The Iditarod Trail Sled Dog Race (© **907/376-5155;** www.iditarod.com). The world's most famous sled dog race starts with fanfare from **Anchorage.** Then the teams are loaded into trucks for the **Iditarod Restart,** north of the city, which is the real beginning of the race; the historic gold-rush trail becomes continuous for the dogs' 1,000-mile run to Nome. The start and the finish in Nome are the biggest sporting and cultural events of Alaska's year, drawing world media attention and turning Nome into a huge party for a few days (they even play golf out on the sea ice). The race solicits volunteers to help, which is a much better way to experience it than just watching. An animal-rights group opposes the race on the grounds that it's cruel to dogs. For more on the issue, see p. 481. In 2007, the race starts March 3.

The Nenana Ice Classic (© **907/832-5446;** www.nenanaakiceclassic.com), Nenana. This is a betting pool on the date of spring breakup that has happened every year for the last 9 decades. The kick-off is Tripod Days, when a "four-legged tripod" that will mark the ice going out on the Tanana River is erected during the first weekend in March, with a celebration of dance performances, dog mushing, and other

Moments Only-in-Alaska Events

By the end of the winter, sports in Alaska can get extreme. The **GCI Arctic Man Ski & Sno-Go Classic** (*©* **907/456-2626;** www.arcticman.com) sounds insane just in the description: A skier goes straight down a steep 1,700-foot slope, then grabs a rope to be pulled up the next slope by a snow machine going as fast as 88 mph, and then skis down the next 1,200-foot slope. Thousands of spectators build a hard-partying city of RVs, snow machines, and a big tent for beer and rock-and-roll in the remote, treeless hills of the Alaska Range near Summit Lake, 10 miles north of Paxson at mile 195 on the Richardson Highway. For a few days, it's the fourth-largest community in Alaska. Parking is $100. The event will be held from April 11 to 15 in 2007 (race day the 13th).

Another kind of insanity occurs in the **Tesoro Iron Dog Snowmachine Race** (*©* **907/563-4414;** www.irondog.org). In mid-February, teams of two racers leave from Wasilla, near Anchorage, take the Iditarod Trail to Nome, and then turn around and ride to Fairbanks in the middle of the state. Racers cover a distance of about 2,000 miles of virgin wilderness at speeds often well in excess of highway driving. In 2006, the winners and second-place team finished in 36 hours, separated by 1 second. The race is by far the longest and toughest in the world.

Muscle-powered sports also have big late-winter events, including the 50km (31-mile) **Tour of Anchorage** Nordic ski race (www.tourof anchorage.com), which winds its way from one side of the city to the other on a Sunday in early March. With as many as 1,800 racers, it has become a major community happening and draws elite skiers, kids, and grandmothers. I ski it every year. Other towns around Alaska have started their own ski marathons during the following weeks, including Homer, Talkeetna, and Fairbanks. For a calendar of events and other Alaska cross-country skiing information, contact the **Nordic Ski Association of Anchorage** (*©* **907/ 276-7609;** www.anchoragenordicski.com).

And don't forget the various human-powered wilderness races that cross Alaska winter and summer, often covering 100 miles or more on skis, snow-shoes, bikes, or foot—or a combination thereof. Sometimes these races have only a few competitors and perhaps only one or two finishers. No one does it for glory, but somehow it makes sense where big, wild land is the dominant theme and trail sports are the primary form of recreation.

activities. The ticket buyer who guesses the minute the tripod will move, usually about 2 months later, wins the jackpot, typically over $300,000.

The World Ice Art Championships (*©* **907/451-8250;** www.icealaska. com), Fairbanks. Carvers from all over the world sculpt immense chunks of clear ice cut from a Fairbanks pond. Among ice carvers, Fairbanks's ice is famous for its clarity and the great size of the chunks. Some spectacular ice sculptures stand as tall as a two-story building. Carving will be February 27 to March 1, and March 4 to 9, with the best viewing of finished works from March 10 to 20, 2007.

April

The Alaska Folk Festival (© 907/ 463-3316; www.alaskafolkfestival.org), Juneau. This is a community-wide celebration, drawing musicians, whether on the bill or not, from all over the state. April 9 to 15, 2007.

May

Copper River Delta Shorebird Festival (© 907/424-7260; www.cordova chamber.com), Cordova. This festival revolves around the coming of dizzying swarms of millions of shorebirds that use the delta and beaches near the town as a migratory stopover in early May. The whole community gets involved to host bird-watchers and put on a schedule of educational and outdoor activities for 3 days. The 2007 festival will be held May 3 to 6.

The Kachemak Bay Shorebird Festival (© 907/235-7740; http://homer alaska.org/shorebird.htm), Homer. Held in early May, this festival includes guided bird-watching hikes and boat excursions, natural-history workshops, art shows, performances, and other events. In 2007, the festival will take place May 10 to 13.

Little Norway Festival (© 907/772-3646; www.petersburg.org), Petersburg. This festival celebrates the May 17, 1814, declaration of the independence of Norway from Sweden. The town has several days of community events. The festival takes place on the third full weekend in May.

Kodiak Crab Festival (© 907/486-5557; www.kodiak.org/crabfest.html), Kodiak. Lasting 5 days over Memorial Day weekend, this is the town's biggest event of the year and includes many fun events, the solemn blessing of the fleet, and a memorial service for lost fishermen and other mariners. May 24 to May 28, 2007.

June

The Sitka Summer Music Festival (© 907/277-4852; www.sitkamusic festival.org), Sitka. Since 1972, this chamber music series has drawn musicians from all over the world for most of June. Performances take place Tuesday and Friday, with other events all week. June 1 to June 22, 2007.

Midnight Sun Baseball Game, Fairbanks. A century-old summer-solstice tradition: a game without artificial lights beginning at 10:30pm. The local semipro baseball team, the Alaska Goldpanners (© 907/451-0095; www. goldpanners.com), has hosted since 1960. Around June 21.

Midnight Sun Festival (© 907/443-5535), Nome. Over the summer solstice, Nome gets more than 22 hours of direct sunlight, ample reason for a parade, softball tournament, raft race, and polar bear swim (so long as sea ice permits). Weekend closest to June 21.

The Last Frontier Theater Conference (© 907/834-1614; www.pwscc. edu), Valdez. The conference brings playwrights and directors from all over the nation to the community for a week of seminars and performances. June 23 to 30, 2007.

July

Independence Day. Most of the small towns in Alaska make a big deal of the Fourth of July. Seward always has a huge celebration, exploding with visitors, primarily from Anchorage. Besides the parade and many small-town festivities, the main attraction is the **Mount Marathon Race,** which goes from the middle of town straight up rocky Mount Marathon to its 3,022-foot peak and down again. **Seldovia, Ketchikan, Skagway,** and **Juneau** also have exceptional Fourth of July events. See the individual town sections for more information.

The Southeast Alaska State Fair (© 907/766-2476; www.seakfair.org), Haines. Held for 4 days in late July, this is a regional small-town get-together music festival, with livestock, cooking, a logging show, a parade, and other entertainment. July 26–29, 2007.

August

The Alaska State Fair (© 907/745-4827; www.alaskastatefair.org), Palmer. The region's biggest event of the year is a typical state fair, except for the huge vegetables. The good soil and long Valley days produce cabbages the size of beanbag chairs. Try to imagine a 19-pound carrot. Held the 12 days before Labor Day.

October

Alaska Day Festival (© 907/747-8806), Sitka. Alaska Day, commemorating the Alaska purchase on October 18, 1867, is a big deal in this former Russian and U.S. territorial capital city.

November

Sitka WhaleFest (© 907/747-7964; www.sitkawhalefest.org), Sitka. Usually held the first weekend in November, during the fall and early winter period when humpback whales congregate in Sitka Sound, experts from around the world present a 3-day symposium, and there are whale-watching tours, concerts, an art show, a run, and community events.

The Alaska Bald Eagle Festival (© 907/766-3094; www.baldeagle festival.org), Haines. Seminars and special events mark an annual congregation of 3,000 eagles near Haines. Mid-November.

The Carrs/Safeway Great Alaska Shootout men's basketball tournament (© 907/786-1250; www.gosea wolves.com/shootout), Anchorage. The University of Alaska Anchorage hosts top-ranked college teams at the Sullivan Arena over Thanksgiving weekend.

3 Cost & Money

Alaska is an expensive destination any way you slice it. With the exception of out-of-the-way spots, standard motel rooms are rarely less than $125 in the high season, and usually over $140. Airfare from Seattle to Anchorage fluctuates wildly with competition among the airlines, but a $350 round-trip, with 14-day advance purchase, is a good deal. (Flying is cheaper than the alternatives, driving or taking the ferry and bus.) You can easily pay twice that to fly to an Alaska Bush community. Even the train is expensive, with a one-way fare from Anchorage to Fairbanks (a 350-mile trip) costing $185.

A couple ordering a good salmon dinner, appetizers, and wine will likely pay $100 in a fine restaurant, plus tip. One reason cruise ships have become such a popular way to visit Alaska is that, for the same quality level, they're less expensive on a daily basis than independent travel, and offer the chance to see remote coastal areas that can be quite costly to get to for land-based visitors. (See chapter 4 for details on cruising.)

To travel at a standard American comfort level, a couple should allow $140 per person per day for room and board. The cost of an activity such as flightseeing, wildlife cruises, or guided fishing typically is $75 to $250 per person. Add ground transportation: A car is the best way to see much of the state, and you won't do much better than $50 a day for an economy model from the major national firms. Weekly rentals generally cost the same as renting for 5 individual days. You also may need train and ferry tickets.

You can trim your costs, however, by cutting your demands. You'll learn more about the real Alaska staying in B&B accommodations than in a standard hotel room. Expect to pay $90 to $120 for a nice room with a shared bathroom, $110 to $140 for a private bathroom (much more in a luxury B&B inn). The free breakfast cuts down on food costs, too. And there are plenty of family restaurants where you can eat a modest dinner for two for $40, with a tip and a glass of beer. Traveling in that style will bring down the cost of room and board to about $100 per person per day for a couple.

You can save the most money by giving up a private room every night and cooking some of your own meals. Camping is a fun way to really see Alaska and costs only $10 to $20 a night in state and federal government campgrounds. Hostels are available in most towns for around $20 a night.

Don't economize, however, when it comes to activities. Unlike other destinations where relatively inexpensive museums or an interesting street scene take up much of your time, a trip to Alaska is all about getting outside and seeing nature. You can hike for nothing, but to go sea kayaking, whale-watching, or flying out to see bears or to fish in a remote stream, you have to pay. Cut those expenses, and you cut much of the reason for going in the first place.

You can save on activities, however, by traveling in the shoulder season, before and after the peak summer season. Hotel and guided activity prices drop significantly, typically 25% or more. May and September are solidly in the shoulder season, and sometimes you get bargains as late as June 15 or as early as August 15. Traveling in the winter is a whole different experience but certainly saves a lot of money—where hotels are open, you'll find their rates typically running half of their high-season levels. For other considerations on off-season and shoulder-season travel, see "When to Go," earlier.

Carrying your money need not be a problem, regardless of your style of travel; those from the United States don't need to make any adjustments in their usual habits. Even Bush hub communities now have ATMs. The only places that don't usually have ATMs these days are remote outdoor destinations such as lodges or parks and tiny Native villages. In the "Fast Facts" section for each town in this book, I'll tell you where to find an ATM.

Every business you'd expect to take credit, charge, or debit cards at home will accept them here. Even bed-and-breakfasts and greasy-spoon diners usually take cards now. Few businesses of any kind will take an out-of-state personal check. Traveler's checks are good just about anywhere, but there's no longer any reason to go through the hassle and expense.

4 Getting There & Getting Around

BY PLANE

CARRIERS Anchorage is Alaska's main point of entry from the outside world (foreign and domestic) and is served by several major carriers to the rest of the United States. A few flights arrive in Anchorage from Japan or Korea, but the vast majority of international travelers arrive in the U.S. in another major city in the contiguous states and then take a domestic flight to Anchorage. It's also possible to fly into Fairbanks or Southeast Alaska. Most passengers come into Anchorage through Seattle, but for a bit more you can fly nonstop to Anchorage from various major cities. There are far more choices in summer than in winter. **Alaska Airlines** (© **800/252-7522;** www.alaskaair.com) has more flights than all other airlines combined, with as many

Native Art: Finding the Real Thing

In a gift shop in Southeast Alaska, I watched as a woman who said she was an artist's assistant sanded a Tlingit-style carving. When I asked who made the carving, the artist said, "It's my work." At the time, that seemed like an odd way of putting it. Only later did I learn from one of the artist's former assistants that his "work" involved ordering the carvings from Southeast Asia and shipping them to Alaska, where he hired locals to pretend to be working on them in the shop. Journalists have repeatedly documented shops fraudulently removing "Made in Taiwan" stickers and the like, and replacing them with "Made in Alaska." One journalist found a whole village in Bali carving Alaska Native designs out of ivory, whalebone, and other materials sent from Alaska.

Good estimates don't exist of the amount of counterfeit Alaska Native art sold annually, but authorities have put it close to $100 million. That's money taken from Alaska Bush economies where jobs in the cash economy are virtually nonexistent and prices for essentials such as fuel and housing are astronomical. Buying fake Native art is cultural and financial theft from subsistence hunters and fishermen who can least afford it. And besides, who wants to come home with an Eskimo mask made in Bali?

You can avoid being scammed if you pay attention. Ask questions before you buy. Any reputable art dealer will provide you with a biography of the artist who created an expensive work. Ask specifically if that artist actually carved the piece: Some Native artists have sold their names and designs to wholesalers who produce knockoffs. Price is another tip-off. An elaborate mask is more likely to cost $1,000 than $100. Another indicator is the choice of materials; most soapstone carvings are not made in Alaska. Even less expensive craftwork should bear the name of the person who made it, and the shop owner should be able to tell you how he or she acquired the item.

as 20 a day to Seattle in summer and summer nonstops to many cities around the country. Alaska Airlines is the only jet carrier with more than token coverage anywhere in the state other than Anchorage and has arrangements with commuter lines that fan out from its network to smaller communities.

Here are the major airlines serving Anchorage at this writing:

Air Canada ℂ **888/247-2262;** www.aircanada.com

Alaska Airlines ℂ **800/252-7522;** www.alaskaair.com

American Airlines ℂ **800/433-7300;** www.aa.com

China Airlines ℂ **800/227-5118;** www.china-airlines.com

Condor Airlines (German) ℂ **800/364-1664;** www4.condor.com

Continental Airlines ℂ **800/523-3273;** www.continental.com

Delta Air Lines ℂ **800/221-1212;** www.delta.com

Frontier Airlines ℂ **800/432-1359;** www.frontierairlines.com

Northwest Airlines ℂ **800/225-2525;** www.nwa.com

Another caution, for international visitors: Do not buy products made from marine mammals, such as walrus ivory, whale bone, or seal skin. Except for antiques, export of these materials is illegal, so you won't be able to take your purchase home. (You may need a permit to export other wildlife items as well. See "What You Can Take Home," p. 44.)

The **Alaska State Council on the Arts** (© 907/269-6610) authenticates Native arts and crafts with a **silver hand** label, which assures you it was made by the hands of an Alaska Native with Alaskan materials. But the program isn't universally used, so the absence of the label doesn't mean the work definitely isn't authentic. Other labels aren't worth much: An item could say ALASKA MADE even if only insignificant assembly work happened here. Of course, in Bush Alaska and in some urban shops, you can buy authentic work directly from craftspeople. Buying in Native-owned co-ops is also safe.

Another program covers any item made within the state, both Native and non-Native. The logo of a mother bear and cub (**www.madeinalaska.org/mia**) indicates that a state contractor has determined that the product was made in Alaska, when possible with Alaskan materials. Non-Natives produce Alaskan crafts of ceramics, wood, or fabric, but not plastic—if it's plastic, it probably wasn't made here. Again, price is an indicator: As with anywhere else in the United States, the cheapest products come from Asia.

You can learn about and buy authentic Alaska Native art from a website made by and for Native people, at **www.alaskanativeartists.com**. Even if you don't buy anything from the site, taking a look will give you an idea of what real Native art looks like and how much it should cost, so you can be a better shopper when you get to Alaska.

Sun Country Airlines © **800/359-6786**; www.suncountry.com

United Airlines © **800/864-8331**; www.ual.com

U.S. Airways © **800-428-4322**; www.usairways.com

The flight line-up (and the existence of the airlines) changes quickly, so all of this is subject to change.

FARES Alaskans fly so much we tend to talk about air fares the way New Yorkers talk about real estate. Fares vary wildly, so watching for sales can pay off. It's almost always cheapest to change planes in Seattle due to the competition on the Seattle-Anchorage route. The competition also makes these fares more volatile than the NASDAQ: You can easily pay more than $400, but it's not unusual to get a ticket for $300, and if you're really alert, you can sometimes snag one for $200. A website maintained by Anchorage travel consultant Scott McMurran (www.alaskatravelgram.com/airfares) monitors the current lowest fares from many cities. Use it for a reference, but don't expect to get those rock-bottom fares without a lot of flexibility and a skilled travel agent. Summer sales

Travel in the Age of Bankruptcy

Airlines go bankrupt, so protect yourself by **buying your tickets with a credit card.** The Fair Credit Billing Act guarantees that you can get your money back from the credit card company if a travel supplier goes under (and if you request the refund within 60 days of the bankruptcy). **Travel insurance** can also help, but make sure it covers against "carrier default" for your specific travel provider (see "Travel & Rental Car Insurance," p. 44). If a U.S. airline goes bust midtrip, federal law requires other carriers to take you to your destination on a space-available basis for a fee of no more than $25, provided you rebook within 60 days of the cancellation.

sometimes hit in April. If you can make a last-minute decision, sign up for Web specials on the Alaska Airlines website and other airline sites, as there often are bargains to be had that you can't get any other way.

BUSH PILOTS   To fly to a roadless village, or to fly between most towns without returning to a hub, you will take a small, prop-driven plane with an Alaska bush pilot at the controls. Small air taxis also charter to fishing sites, lodges, remote cabins, or anywhere else you want to go—even a sand bar in the middle of a river. An authentic Alaskan adventure can be had by taking a Bush mail plane round-trip to a village and back. The ticket price is generally less than that of a flightseeing trip, and you'll have at least a brief chance to look around a Native village, although don't expect to find any visitor facilities without making arrangements in advance. Kodiak, Homer, Nome, Kotzebue, and Barrow are places from which you can do this with a little research. Wait for good weather.

BY SHIP

The most popular way to get to Alaska is on a **cruise ship** (chapter 4, "Cruising Alaska's Coast," provides an in-depth look at your options).

For an affordable, independent trip by sea, with a chance to stop as long as you like along the way, take the **Alaska Marine Highway System** (© 800/642-0066; 800/764-3779 TTY; www.ferry alaska.com). It's my favorite form of public transportation. The big blue, white, and gold ferries ply the Inside Passage from Bellingham, Washington, and Prince Rupert, British Columbia, to the towns of Southeast Alaska, with road links to the rest of the state at Haines and Skagway. In summer, a ferry twice a month connects from that system across the Gulf of Alaska to the central part of the state. From there, smaller ferries connect towns in Prince William Sound and the Kenai Peninsula to Kodiak Island and the Aleutian Archipelago. For a complete discussion of the system and its intricacies, see "Getting Around by Ferry: The Alaska Marine Highway" in chapter 5.

BY RAIL

You can't get to Alaska by train, but you can get close. From the West Coast of the U.S., you can take **Amtrak** (© 800/872-7245; www.amtrak.com) to Bellingham, Washington; the dock for the Alaska ferry is quite close to the railroad station. From the east, it makes more sense to use Canada's **Via Rail** (© 888/842-7245; www.viarail.ca). The transcontinental route starts all the way back in Toronto; you change in Jasper to end up in Prince Rupert, British Columbia, where you can catch the Alaska ferry north.

BY CAR

TIME & DISTANCE Figuring how long it takes to drive between various points in Alaska needn't be complicated, but don't trust your computer. A reader checked three different Internet map sites for one trip and came up with drive times ranging from 4 hours, 27 minutes to 8 hours, 45 minutes. I have included a description of the roads and average speeds you can expect (see "Alaska's Highways a la Carte," p. 382). Get the mileage you plan to drive from the chart on p. 6 or from www.maps.google.com, and then divide the distance by the expected speed to get the time it will take. Add some time for stops. For paved highways, you can count on averaging 50 mph. On some roads you can go faster than 50, but you can't often drive at freeway speeds on these two-lane highways. Even when the surface is smooth—not always a given— the roads aren't designed for high speeds and are often clogged in summer with lumbering RVs. Besides, you need to be on the look-out for moose; hit one of those at 75 mph, and you both die.

DRIVING TO ALASKA Driving from any of the other states to Alaska is a great adventure, but it requires thousands of miles on the road and plenty of time. Allow at least a week each way. By car, Anchorage is 2,250 miles from Seattle and 3,400 miles from Los Angeles. By comparison, New York to L.A. is 2,800 miles. Traveling at an average of 50 mph, few vacationers will want to cover more than 500 or 600 miles a day, and that's a long day of nothing but driving. On such a plan, Seattle is 4 or 5 days from Anchorage without breaks.

Some of the 1,400-mile **Alaska Highway** is dull, but there are spectacular sections of the route, too, and few experiences give you a better feel for the size and personality of Alaska. Putting your car on the ferry cuts the length of the trip considerably but raises the cost; you could rent a car for 2 weeks for the same price as carrying an economy car on the ferry one-way from Bellingham to Haines. I love riding the ferry up the Inside Passage, but I usually rent a car or bike to get around in the towns on the way. Details on the Alaska section of the Alaska Highway, and other highways, are contained in chapter 9. The ferry is described in chapter 5. *The Milepost* (Morris Communications; $27) contains good maps and mile-by-mile logs of all Alaska highways and Canadian approaches; however, it's not interesting to read and is clogged with advertising masquerading as editorial text.

THE RENTAL OPTION Renting a car is the easiest way to see the Interior and Southcentral parts of the state. All the major national car-rental companies are represented in Anchorage, as are many

---

⎛Value The Cheapest Way to Alaska

Flying is the cheapest and by far the simplest way to get to Alaska. Take other means only for the adventure, not for the savings. Round-trip train, ferry, and bus fare between Seattle and Anchorage costs several times as much as a good airfare between the same cities. Driving is expensive, too, when you count rooms, food, and wear and tear on your vehicle. Fuel alone for the 4,500-mile drive from Seattle to Anchorage and back would cost more than $675 in a car that gets 20 miles to the gallon—more than a plane ticket. (Okay, maybe a foursome can do it cheaper than flying if they drive a small car, camp every night, and eat rice and beans.)

local operators, who may have lower prices for older cars. In smaller cities and towns, there is always at least one agency; the town descriptions throughout the book provide details on firms in each town. Base rates for major rental companies are in the range of $50 a day for an economy car. Weekly rentals equate roughly to 5 days' cost.

One-way rentals between Alaska towns are an attractive way to travel, but you generally pay steep drop-off charges, so a more popular plan is to fly into and out of Anchorage and pick up and return the car there. There are two popular circular routes from Anchorage: to Denali and Fairbanks on the Parks Highway and back on the Richardson and Glenn highways, or to Valdez by ferry from Whittier and back on another part of the Richardson Highway and the Glenn Highway. See chapter 3 for more on routes.

BY RV

Touring Alaska in an RV makes a good deal of sense. The home on wheels offers spontaneity by freeing you from hotel reservations (see "Car or RV Camping," in section 6 of this chapter), and it gets you out of town and into the countryside, closer to the natural Alaska most visitors come for. At the same time, an RV is more comfortable than a tent in cool, unpredictable weather conditions.

Many retirees drive to Alaska in their motor homes, park the RV by a salmon stream, and spend the summer fishing. Sounds nice, but for most of the rest of us, with limited time, it makes more sense to rent an RV after flying to Alaska. Rental agencies are listed in Skagway (p. 196) and Anchorage (p. 209). The option of shipping your own RV to Alaska is also covered in the Anchorage chapter. Unless you have a large family, an RV rental saves little over traveling with a rental car, staying in hotels, and eating in restaurants (RVs rent for around $1,400 a week, plus gas and possibly mileage charges), so you make this choice to gain advantages, not avoid costs.

Alaska Highway Cruises (© 800/323-5757; www.bestofalaskatravel.com) offers the unique option of traveling one-way on a Holland America cruise ship and then picking up an RV for a land tour. You can choose a package that ends up back at Seattle by road or by air. The tours follow set itineraries with reservations along the way—the service is designed for first-time Alaska travelers and RV drivers who don't want to worry about the details—so some spontaneity is sacrificed. You get the security and simplicity of a package without being marched around in a group or cooped up in hotels. An 11-day cruise and tour cost around $2,500 per person, double occupancy; a 3-week cruise to Alaska and drive back (or reverse) is around $3,800 per person. There are various discounts, including for third and fourth passengers.

Simple one-way RV rentals to Alaska are available, too, although they add $500 to $1,000, or even more, to the cost. I have listed options from Seattle and Skagway to Anchorage in chapter 5. A large national firm, **Cruise America,** 8850 Runamuck Place (© 800/327-7799 or 907/349-0499; www.cruise america.com) offers one-way rentals between Anchorage and certain rental centers around the country on certain dates.

Generally, availability is best and drop-off rates lowest with any of the firms if you choose the direction of your one-way rental to match their needs. At the beginning and end of the season, the rental companies often find themselves with units in the wrong places. Drive north in the spring or south in the fall to help them, and get the best rate for yourself.

5 Escorted Tour or Do-It-Yourself?

Hundreds of thousands of visitors come to Alaska each year on escorted package tours, leaving virtually all their travel arrangements in the hands of a single company that takes responsibility for ushering them through the state for a single lump-sum fee. Many others cut the apron strings and explore Alaska on their own, in the process discovering a more relaxed, spontaneous experience. Each approach has advantages and disadvantages, of course, and which way you choose to visit depends on how you value those pros and cons. Unfortunately, some people make the choice based on expectations that aren't valid, so it's important to know what you're getting into.

An escorted package tour provides security. You'll know in advance how much everything will cost, you don't have to worry about making hotel and ground-transportation reservations, you're guaranteed to see the highlights of each town you visit, and you'll have someone telling you what you're looking at. Often a package price saves money over traveling at the same level of comfort independently. If there are weather delays or other travel problems, it's the tour company's problem, not yours. Everything happens on schedule, and you never have to touch your baggage other than to unpack when it magically shows up in your room. If you sometimes feel like you're a member of a herd on an escorted tour, you'll also meet new people, a big advantage if you're traveling on your own. Many passengers on these trips are retired, over age 65.

If you're short on time, escorted package tours make the most of it, as they often travel at an exhausting pace. Passengers get up early and cover a lot of ground, with sights and activities scheduled solidly through the day. Stops last only long enough to get a taste of what the sight is about, not to dig in and learn

about a place you're especially interested in. On an escorted trip, you'll meet few, if any, Alaska residents, since most tour companies hire college students from "Outside" (a term Alaskans use to refer to any place other than Alaska) to fill summer jobs. You'll stay in only the largest hotels and eat in the largest, tourist-oriented restaurants—no small, quaint places loaded with local character. For visiting wilderness, such as Denali National Park, the quick and superficial approach can, in my opinion, spoil the whole point of going to a destination that's about an experience, not just seeing a particular object or place.

Studies by Alaska tourism experts have found that many people choose escorted packages to avoid risks that don't really exist. Alaska may still be untamed, but that doesn't mean it's a dangerous or uncomfortable place to travel. Visitors who sign up for a tour to avoid having to spend the night in an igloo or use an outhouse may wish they'd been a bit more adventurous when they arrive and find that Alaska has the same facilities found in any other state. Except for tiny Bush villages that you're unlikely to visit anyway, you'll come across the standard American hotel room almost anywhere you go. The tourism infrastructure is well developed even in small towns—you're never far from help unless you want to be.

It's also possible for an independent traveler to obtain some of the predictability a package tour provides. You can reserve accommodations and activities and control your expenses by using a good travel agent experienced in Alaska travel. Some even offer fixed-price itineraries that allow you to travel on your own (see "Independent Travel Planning," at the end of this section). But independent travelers never have the complete security of those on group tours. Once you're on the road, you'll be on your own to take care of the details, and weather delays and other cancellations can confound the best-laid plans. If you can't relax and enjoy a trip knowing unforeseen difficulties could happen, then an escorted package tour is the way to go.

LARGE TOUR COMPANIES

A single cruise-ship company, Carnival, dominates the Alaska package-tour market operating under various brands. The "vertically integrated" operations allow the company to take care of everything you do while in Alaska with tight quality control. In some popular areas, cruise lines have bought everything in sight, even historic attractions. Holland America and Princess, both now owned by Carnival, developed independently as the primary competitors in Alaska and still operate separately. Each offers tours as short as a couple of hours to independent travelers who want to combine their own exploring with a more structured experience. All can be booked through any travel agent. Other cruise lines also offer land tours but typically only for their own passengers. If you will cruise to Alaska and want to add an escorted land tour, check for deals with your own cruise line first.

Holland America Line Tours   The Holland America cruise line is the giant of Alaska tourism and thousands of visitors do business with no one else when they come. The Alaska/Yukon operation employs more than 2,100 workers operating 225 buses, 14 railcars, and 2 dayboats. Most clients arrive in the state on one of the company's ships (see chapter 4), but even within Alaska, chances are good that a tour you sign up for will put you on a Gray Line coach and exclusively in Westmark hotels, both owned by Holland America. The Westmark hotels are described in the appropriate sections of this book. Some are among the best in town, including those in Juneau (called the Baranof), Fairbanks, and Sitka, while others are unremarkable. But then, on a group tour you don't spend much time in the room, as schedules generally are tightly planned and daily departures are early. You'll find a description of the company's railcars on the Anchorage-Denali-Fairbanks run in chapter 8. Gray Line coaches are first rate, especially several super-luxurious, extra-long vehicles that bend in the middle and have a lounge in the back. And the company goes more places than any other, with a catalog that covers just about anything in the state that could possibly be done with a group. They also have self-drive tours. Some of the tour excursions—on the Yukon River between Dawson City and Eagle, for example—are entirely unique. Prices depend on a variety of factors, but in general a tour of a week is about $1,400 per person.

300 Elliot Ave. W., Seattle, WA 98119. © **800/544-2206.** www.graylineofalaska.com or www.hollandamerica.com.

Beware of Fraud

In 2003, one of the largest trip planners in Alaska went bankrupt, leaving many visitors with worthless vouchers for prepaid reservations. It turned out the owner was using clients' credit cards to keep her business afloat. She took her own trip to federal prison in 2005, but by then, even worse rip-offs had cropped up on the Internet. Use caution. If you prepay large trip expenses to a planner or a provider directly, be certain to use a credit card that will protect you, and buy appropriate travel insurance. Do not buy the insurance from the same entity from whom you bought the trip (see "Travel & Rental Car Insurance," p. 44).

Princess Cruises and Tours Before its sale to Carnival, Princess built its tour operation from the ground up, surpassing Holland America with the consistently outstanding quality of its smaller list of offerings. That advantage persists. The five Princess hotels are all among Alaska's best. Two are near Denali National Park, and one each is in Fairbanks, in Cooper Landing (on the Kenai Peninsula), and in Copper Center, near Wrangell–St. Elias National Park. Princess operates its own coaches and has superb railcars on the Alaska Railroad route to Denali. Descriptions of each hostelry can be found in the appropriate chapter. Most people on the tours come to Alaska on a cruise ship, but tours are for sale separately, too.

2815 2nd Ave., Suite 400, Seattle, WA 98121-1299. © 800/426-0550. www.princesslodges.com.

INDEPENDENT TRAVEL PLANNING

With this guidebook, you can book everything yourself, but for a long trip it can get quite complicated to keep track of all the dates and deposits. If you're using a trusted travel agency to make trip arrangements, our reviews can help you make informed decisions. Read through the book, make your selections, and approach the agent with as detailed a plan as possible, derived from your own research. Then let the agent make the bookings you have chosen. Most agents who don't specialize in Alaska are aware of only the biggest attractions and best-marketed companies. Another option is

to use a travel agency or trip planner based in Alaska. They'll know much more about the place and can help you more in picking out what you want to do. I've listed a few below.

Unfortunately, there are cautions to be offered in using the agencies. They work on commission, which means they're being paid by the establishments you're buying from. A good agent will disregard the size of the commission and really look out for you, but I've encountered too many visitors on poorly planned itineraries not to advise caution. Some travel agents book visitors on trips to far-flung corners of the state in quick succession, so they wind up staying only briefly in expensive places and then zoom off somewhere else, all with little concern for the visitors' true interests. Your best defense is to do enough research so you can actively participate in the planning.

Here I've gathered the names of some agencies that book Alaska trips. Expect to pay booking fees and to have the agent collect commissions from the businesses you use. My knowledge of these agencies is limited to contacting them as a journalist, so a mention here is no guarantee; however, all of these have been around for several years, and I remove agencies from the list when I receive justified complaints.

Alaska Bound This Michigan-based agency is the only one I know of in the Lower 48 that specializes in Alaska, with a staff of former Alaskans. It started as a cruise planner, working primarily with

---

Value **For Coupon Clippers**

A coupon book called **The Great Alaskan Tour Saver** (© 907/278-7600; www.toursaver.com), which costs $100, is well worth the price if you plan on traveling as a couple, especially in the Southcentral region. Among about 150 coupons, there are some freebies and many two-for-one deals on some of the best activities, tours, and lodgings, valuable enough to pay for the book with just a couple of uses. Customers tell me they've saved a lot.

Holland America, but now plans many independent trips, too, charging a per-person fee that depends on the length of the trip ($100 per person would not be exceptional).

116 Cass St., Traverse City, MI 49684. ☎ 888/ALASKA-7 or 231/439-3000. www.alaskabound.com.

Alaska.org This is a deep and well-built website that allows users to shop and customize packaged trips or design their own vacations in the Southcentral-to-Fairbanks region with as much or as little structure and guidance as they choose, and without surcharge. When you've seen enough, call the toll-free number for questions and booking. Or don't. Unique for this kind of site, you can use it just to get information and call the listed operators yourself.

507 E St., Suite 206, Anchorage, AK 99508. ☎ 888/ALASKA-8. www.alaska.org.

Alaska Tour and Travel Started in 1995 and steadily growing, this agency now claims to be the largest custom-vacation company in Alaska. The same folks operate the Park Connection shuttle between Denali and Kenai Fjords national parks, and that central part of the state is what they know best and cover deeply. The website is remarkable, including a search tool that brings up preset itineraries based on criteria you specify, and a live availability-and-rate calendar for a range of Denali hotels.

P.O. Box 221011, Anchorage, AK 99522. ☎ 800/208-0200. www.alaskatravel.com.

Ask Matt Alaskan Adventures & Tours Matthew Lowe is an energetic young concierge at the large Millennium Alaskan Hotel Anchorage who has turned his encyclopedic knowledge of Southcentral Alaska travel into his own business. His strength is in activities, but he happily books travelers into budget B&Bs as well as more expensive lodges and resorts, and charges no up-front fee.

Millennium Alaskan Hotel Anchorage, 4800 Spenard Rd., Anchorage, AK 99517. ☎ 888/355-6288. www.askmatt.com.

Sport Fishing Alaska Choose this company to plan a fishing vacation. The owners, former guides and float, charter, and air-taxi operators, Larry and Sheary Suiter, know where the fish will be week

---

Frommers.com: The Complete Travel Resource

For an excellent travel-planning resource, we highly recommend **Frommers.com** (www.frommers.com), voted Best Travel Site by *PC Magazine*. We're a little biased, of course, but we guarantee that you'll find the travel tips, reviews, monthly vacation giveaways, bookstore, and online-booking capabilities to be thoroughly indispensable. Special features include our popular **Destinations** section, where you can access expert travel tips, hotel and dining recommendations, and advice on the sights to see in more than 3,500 destinations around the globe; the **Frommers.com Newsletter,** with the latest deals, travel trends, and money-saving secrets; and our **Travel Talk** area featuring **Message Boards,** where Frommer's readers post queries and share advice, and where our authors sometimes show up to answer questions. Once you finish your research, the **Book a Trip** area can lead you to Frommer's preferred online partners' websites, where you can book your vacation at affordable prices.

to week. That means they book clients at fly-in fishing lodges when and where the fishing is hot—a critical piece of information that can be difficult to obtain on your own. They charge a $95 up-front fee. (See "Fishing," below.)

9310 Shorecrest Dr., Anchorage, AK 99502. ✆ 888/552-8674 or 907/344-8674. www.alaska tripplanners.com.

Viking Travel   An entrepreneur in the small Southeast Alaska town of Petersburg built this agency, initially specializing in independent outdoor trips in their own area. Today, besides offering all the usual services of a travel agency, they plan trips for the whole state and book all the region's ferries without surcharge. Get on their list, and they will book your cabins and vehicle reservations on the first day the system makes them available.

P.O. Box 787, Petersburg, AK 99833 ✆ 800/327-2571 or 907/772-3818. www.alaskaferry.com.

6 Planning an Outdoor Vacation

Most people visit Alaska to experience wilderness, so it's ironic that so many spend their time in crowded ships, buses, trains, and airplanes, the antithesis of a wilderness experience. You do need technology to get to the wilderness of Alaska, but unless you at least partly let loose of that umbilical cord, you'll never really arrive at your destination.

Every town in Alaska is a threshold to the wild. There's always a way to go hiking, biking, or sea kayaking, or to get on the bank of a stream or the deck of a boat to hook into a furiously fighting wild salmon—and end up in the evening back in a comfortable hotel room. Or take it a step further: Plan to go out overnight, perhaps with a friendly local guide at first, and then go out on your own. I've included lots of details on how to do this throughout the book. Scary? If it weren't a little scary, it would be Disneyland, and that it definitely is not. It's real, and that's why it's worth doing.

Wilderness lodges (which to me means a place you can't drive to) are listed in the following sections: Gustavus in chapter 5, across Kachemak Bay from Homer in chapter 7, and in and around Denali National Park in chapter 8. Remote Forest Service cabins in the Tongass and Chugach national forests are covered in chapters 5 and 7, respectively.

ACTIVITIES

BACKPACKING   Alaska's best country for trail hikes is in **Chugach State Park** near Anchorage (chapter 6), on Chena Hot Springs Road and on the Steese Highway near Fairbanks (chapter 9), and in the **Chugach National Forest** on the Kenai Peninsula (chapter 7). For hiking beyond trails, go to **Denali** or the **Denali Highway** (chapter 8), **Wrangell–St. Elias National Parks,** or the **Dalton Highway** (chapter 9). Alaska trail hikes require the same skills as backpacking anywhere else, plus preparation for cold and damp (see "What to Wear," earlier in this chapter). Hiking beyond the trails is a glorious experience, but you need to know how to cross rivers and find your way—it's best if you have some outdoor experience. Or go with a guide; they're listed later. See section 9, later in this chapter, for some backcountry safety tips.

BIKING   Most every town in Alaska has a bike-rental agency. There are excellent bike routes all over the state and few restrictions on where you can ride. A bike is a great way into Denali National Park (chapter 8), Anchorage has an extensive network of paved trails and many mountain biking routes (chapter 6), and guided biking is available in Haines and Skagway (chapter 5).

> **_Tips_ A Guide to Guide Gratuities**
>
> As a general rule, tip fishing guides and outfitters $10 to $20 per person per day. For outings of less than a day, adjust the tip accordingly. At wilderness lodges, which normally have all-inclusive rates, it's often best to add the tip to your final payment when you leave and let the proprietor distribute it to the staff rather than try to do it at each meal. A blanket tip of $15 per person per day is acceptable.

A couple that built an excellent reputation and a large business for over a decade offering bicycle tours on Alaska's long, rural highways now operates **Alaska Bicycle Adventures** (✆ **907/245-2175;** www.alaskabike.com) on their own from a home office. These are terrific vacations for avid cyclists. The 8-day tour over the spectacular Richardson Highway costs $2,695, inclusive. The schedule includes bike and kayak tours, too.

BIRD-WATCHING In Alaska, birders can encounter birds in greater variety and greater numbers than they have seen before and add many new species to their life lists. I have listed birding groups and best places to go in many of the sections on destinations. Making a "best of" list is difficult because good bird-watching is found in any Alaska town. For example, I could recommend you go to Haines for the eagle sanctuary, but since you are bound to see eagles in every coastal town, I hesitate to send you on a special trip for that purpose. Weeding out the excellent to mention only the truly exceptional, here are the places I would send birders: For marine birding, consider Sitka, Juneau, Seward (Kenai Fjords National Park), Unalaska, and the Pribilof Islands (chapters 5, 7, and 10). Migratory bird festivals happen in May in Homer and Cordova; Homer also has handy sea bird colonies, and Cordova has the wetlands Copper River Delta, an accessible bird paradise of immense proportions (both in chapter 7). Alaska's two largest cities have parks

dedicated to inland birding and other bird resources as well: See chapters 6 and 9 for details on Anchorage and Fairbanks. For Arctic birding, Nome is probably the best choice, thanks to the existence of roads that allow self-guided exploration (chapter 10). The very best bird and wildlife destination in Alaska, and surely among the best in the world, is the Pribilof Islands. You can sign up directly with the island's own Aleut residents for a tour there, described in chapter 10. The Internet makes it easy to network with local birders all over Alaska before your trip to find out what they are seeing and to get tips. Here's a good discussion board where you can get started: http://groups.yahoo.com/group/akbirding.

Serious birders with money to spend can dedicate a trip to some of the world's best and most famous remote bird-watching sites. Find those tours advertised in birding magazines, such as _Bird Watcher's Digest_ (www.birdwatchers digest.com) or _Birders' World_ (www. birdersworld.com). Among the largest and most reputable operators coming to Alaska is Arizona-based **High Lonesome Birdtours** (✆ **800/743-2668** or 520/458-9446; www.hilonesome.com), priding itself on relaxed trips for small groups. All-inclusive tours visit Kenai, Denali, Nome, Gambell, Barrow, Unalaska/Dutch Harbor, Adak, and the Pribilof Islands. Texas-based **Victor Emanuel Nature Tours** (✆ **800/328-8368;** www.ventbird.com) counts well-known authors among its leaders.

CANOEING   Paddling a canoe on a remote Alaska lake or river is the best way to get into the wilderness without a backpack, a guide, or a great deal of expense. For beginners, it's easy to rent a canoe in Fairbanks (chapter 9) for a day trip. If you're ready to go overnight, the choices of routes are extraordinary, including the rivers of the Interior (chapter 9), the bird-watching country of the Copper River Delta near Cordova, or the supreme lake canoe routes of the Kenai National Wildlife Refuge (both in chapter 7).

CAR OR RV CAMPING   Campgrounds are almost everywhere in Alaska, many in extraordinarily beautiful natural places. Public campgrounds outnumber commercial ones. They're usually located where they are because there's something special about the place: a great view or beach, an exceptional fishing stream or trail head. Rarely will you find running water or flush toilets; most are seasonal, with hand pumps for water. (When it's time to wash up, stay at a commercial campground, which I've noted in each town section in the destination chapters throughout this book.) Alaska's public campgrounds fill up only in certain times and places (the Kenai River and Denali National Park campgrounds are among the exceptions), so campers have flexibility other travelers can't share, able to stop when and where they like.

Even if you don't usually consider camping, think about renting a comfortable RV for a tour. One company offers these rentals as add-ons with cruise vacations, taking care of all the details for clients (that and other rental options are under "Getting There & Getting Around," earlier in this chapter).

If you fly to Alaska, car camping can be a bit complicated. Carrying a camp stove on an airplane is forbidden unless there is no attached fuel canister and no odor of fuel (even in that case, keep the unit handy for inspection at check-in). It often makes more sense to buy a new stove in Alaska and then give it away or ship it back to yourself at the end of the trip. Much car-camping equipment is bulky and hard to fit into your limit of two checked bags. Consider renting some of your gear here: Rental agencies are listed with large towns in this book. You can also use the mail, sending packages to yourself care of General Delivery at any post office, or simply invest in compact backpacking equipment that you can fit in your luggage.

I've mentioned some great campgrounds throughout the book, but there are many more than I had space to cover. A free map that lists all the public campgrounds along Alaska's highways is available from the Alaska Public Lands Information Centers (www.nps.gov/aplic). If you are planning to camp the whole way, get a copy of *Traveler's Guide to Alaskan Camping,* by Mike and Terri Church (Rolling Homes Press; $22), which contains detailed reviews of virtually every public and commercial campground in the state.

FISHING   Fishing in Alaska may spoil you for fishing anywhere else. The world's largest salmon and halibut were caught here in recent years, and Pacific salmon are so plentiful that catching and processing them still provides one of the state's largest sources of employment. Fly fishermen also come for thriving wild stocks of steelhead, cutthroat, and rainbow trout; Dolly Varden and Arctic char; and Arctic grayling.

There's no room here to tell you how to fish in Alaska—the best way is to pick it up from other anglers, most conveniently by going with a guide on your first outing. If you can afford it, a day of guided fly-in fishing to a remote stream is the ultimate (you can do it from virtually any town listed in chapters 5, 6, or 7). You can also study with a book; several are available, the best of which focus on

A Salmon Primer

In Alaska, it's not so much where you wet your line, but when. The primary catch, Pacific salmon, lives in salt water but spawns in fresh water, with each fish returning to the stream of its birth during a certain narrow window of time called a "run." When the salmon are running, fishing is hot; when they're not running, it's dead. And the runs change from day to day, typically lasting only a few weeks. (Halibut, on the other hand, are bottom-dwelling ocean fish; you can fish them from a boat every day when the tide is right.) You can fish salmon all over the state in fresh and salt water, but the closer you are to the ocean, the better the fish are. Salmon flesh softens in fresh water and the skin turns dull and red. Salmon right from salt water that haven't started their spawning cycle are called silver bright—when you see one, you'll understand why. No Pacific salmon feeds in fresh water, but kings and silvers, meat eaters at sea, strike out of habit even in the river.

There are five species of Pacific salmon, each preferring its own habitat, and, even when the habitat overlaps, each timing its run differently. Each species has two names.

King (or **chinook**) is the most coveted, best fighting fish, commonly growing to 30 pounds in 5 to 7 years at sea (the sport record, from the Kenai River, was 97 pounds, and the largest ever, taken by commercial fishermen near Petersburg, was 126 pounds). It takes a lot of effort to hook and land a big king, but it's the ultimate in Alaska fishing. You also need a special king stamp on your fishing license from the Alaska Department of Fish and Game, which you can buy at the same time you buy your license. King runs come mostly from late May to early July.

The **silver** (or **coho**) is smaller than the king, typically 6 to 9 pounds, but it fights and jumps ferociously, making it nearly as big a prize. Silvers run mostly in the fall, beginning in August and lasting into October in some streams.

individual areas of the state or particular fishing techniques rather than trying to cover everything.

The best all-around source of information is the **Alaska Department of Fish and Game Sport Fish Division** (www.alaska.gov/adfg; click on "Sport Fisheries"). Browse the website for run timing information and hot spots updated weekly to learn generally about fishing in Alaska and to obtain particulars about where to wet a line in different parts of the state (click "Publications" and then the region you are visiting). You can even buy a fishing license online. If you lack Internet access, the agency also produces printed guides and fields questions from the public, and they record the weekly local updates on telephone hotlines. Contact the office nearest where you will fish; I have listed the phone number for each in the town sections.

If fishing is the primary goal of your trip, think about booking time at a fishing lodge. The remote rivers of the Bristol Bay region have Alaska's most prolific salmon fishing, and the only way out there is to take a floatplane to a remote site. You might find a stream jammed with salmon and with few other anglers around to compete with. But you'll waste your money if you book a date that's not

Red (or **sockeye**) salmon, so named for their tasty red flesh, are the trickiest to catch. They usually weigh 4 to 8 pounds and can run in any of the summer months, depending on the region and stream. Reds feed primarily on plankton at sea, and when they strike a fly, it's out of an instinct that no one really understands; you need perfect river conditions to catch reds legally because snagging anywhere but the mouth generally is not allowed in fresh water.

Pinks (or **humpies**) grow to only a few pounds and aren't as tasty as the other three species; their flesh lacks the fat that makes salmon so meaty in flavor, and it deteriorates quickly once the fish enter fresh water. Pinks are so plentiful that Alaska anglers usually view them as a nuisance to get off the line, but visitors often enjoy catching them: There's nothing wrong with a hard-fighting 4-pound fish, especially if you use light tackle, and a silver-bright pink salmon is tasty if cooked right.

Chum (or **dog**) salmon return plentifully to streams over much of the state but are rarely targeted by anglers. Yet a typical 5- to 10-pound chum hits and fights hard. Chums aren't prized for the table and are mostly used for subsistence by Alaska Natives, who smoke or dry the fish for winter use or freeze it to feed dog teams.

The gear you use depends on the species you are after and the regulations for the area you're fishing. You have to catch the fish in the mouth; snagging is allowed only in special circumstances. On salt water, boats troll for kings and silvers with herring bait and gear to hold it down. Lures, salmon eggs, or flies will work on silvers and kings in the rivers, but regulations vary. Flies work best with reds. Most Alaska fishermen use spinning gear on the larger salmon species—landing such a large fish is iffy with a fly rod.

near the peak of the local salmon run (that does happen, as lodge owners hate to admit slow fishing). Consequently, I've listed few river-fishing lodges in this book (the exceptions: on the Kenai River in Cooper Landing and Kenai-Soldotna in chapter 7, and ocean fishing in Ketchikan in chapter 5). Instead, I recommend booking through **Sport Fishing Alaska,** 9310 Shorecrest Dr., Anchorage, AK 99502 (© **888/552-8674** or 907/344-8674; www.alaskatripplanners.com). The business is run by a couple, Larry and Sheary Suiter, with years of experience on the Kenai River and in Southwest Alaska. After receiving a $95 advance fee, they plan a fishing vacation tailored to your budget that puts you right where fishing is hot at the time when you can travel.

FLIGHTSEEING No one should come to Alaska without seeing the scenery at least once from a small plane. The most spectacular rides of all are the Mount McKinley flights from Talkeetna (chapter 8) and the Glacier Bay National Park flights from Haines or other surrounding communities (chapter 5). But just about anywhere you go is worth seeing from the air; only then can you grasp how huge and complex the land is and how little changed it is by mankind.

Fixed-wing flights give you the most time aloft for your money, with seats starting at around $100 for a brief flight. If you can't afford that, consider taking scheduled prop service between small communities on your itinerary for around the same price, and see almost as much.

RAFTING Letting an Alaskan river pull you through untouched wild country in a raft provides a unique perspective without the sweat and toil of backpacking. Alaska has many great rivers, virtually all undeveloped and, with few exceptions, never crowded. White-water guides operate on rivers all over the state, offering day trips in many towns. Outfitters also lead trips deep into Alaska, using the rivers to visit extraordinary places that can be reached no other way. Many companies offer floats; some are listed below and still others are in the destination chapters throughout this book.

SEA KAYAKING Just about every coastal town, from Kodiak east through Kachemak Bay, Prince William Sound, and the Southeast Panhandle, has at least one kayak outfitter taking visitors on day trips or expeditions. I think it would be a shame for any fit person to come to Alaska and not take a sea-kayaking day trip. It is your best chance to get close enough to really know the wilderness and see whales, sea otters, seabirds, and marine life in an intimate way. Local guides are listed in each town section. Outfitters offering longer trips to a variety of places are listed below.

OUTFITTERS & OUTDOOR PACKAGE TRIPS

Besides the outfitters and tour guides listed below, I've noted other operators in the destination chapters covering the towns where they are based. Browse through those chapters before deciding on a trip, as a trip with a small-town guide service can be wonderful. There are many other larger operators, too; increasingly,

international adventure travel companies bring groups to Alaska, renting equipment or even hiring guides here. Although those trips may be excellent, I've listed mostly homegrown operators who know their territory intimately.

Alaska Discovery A homegrown eco-tourism pioneer, Alaska Discovery was bought out by the famous Mountain Travel Sobek expedition company, but still keeps its local staff in Juneau and offers some of the best guided sea-kayaking trips in Southeast Alaska (sales staff is now in California). Glacier Bay and Admiralty Island outings cater to both beginners and the truly rugged. Their inn-to-inn trips are essentially outdoor-oriented package tours, taking groups to the best spots for day activities such as kayaking, rafting, or watching wildlife. Extended river trips float through the Arctic and on the Tatshenshini and Alsek rivers. They also offer outdoor packages for complete vacations. Check the website. A 3-day kayak expedition near Juneau is $595, while 10 days in the Arctic is around $4,400.

5130 Glacier Hwy., Juneau, AK 99801. ✆ **800/586-1911**. www.akdiscovery.com.

Alaska Wildland Adventures This company specializes in trips for regular folks who may not have done a lot of arduous outdoor activities before. Concentrating on the Kenai Peninsula, where they operate two wilderness lodges, but also going to Denali National Park, most of the company's trips link together a series of outdoor day activities such as rafting, hiking, glacier cruises, or wildlife watching, with beds and indoor plumbing in the evening. A 10-day safari is around $4,725; shorter trips, trips for families with kids, fishing trips, and other choices are available, too.

P.O. Box 389, Girdwood, AK 99587. ✆ **800/334-8730** or 907/783-2928. www.alaskawildland.com.

Equinox Wilderness Expeditions Karen Jettmar, author of *The Alaska River*

ⓘ Tips Make Yourself Useful

You don't have to see Alaska only as an observer—you can be a participant. The **Iditarod Trail Sled Dog Race** (ⓒ **907/376-5155**; www.iditarod.com), the 1,000-mile trek from Anchorage to Nome in March, uses volunteers at the start and finish and, for those who work their way up through the ranks, in the remote villages along the way. Visitors can be part of it and become a part of the real Alaska along the way, contributing only their time and travel to the state. Find the application on the website and act early; they get more volunteers than they can use. Other races and events also use volunteers but don't have a formal program like the Iditarod's. (An animal rights group opposes sled dog racing. A discussion of that issue is on p. 481.)

Two facilities dedicated to study and rehabilitation of wildlife also take volunteers. You might not end up working directly with the creatures, but you can work behind the scenes and get much closer than a casual visitor—while contributing to a good cause. In Seward, the **Alaska SeaLife Center** (ⓒ **800/224-2525**; www.alaskasealife.org) studies, exhibits, and heals marine mammals, birds, and other wildlife and makes extensive use of volunteers (see p. 280). The **Alaska Raptor Center** in Sitka (ⓒ **907/747-8662**; www.alaskaraptor.org) takes in injured eagles, owls, and other birds of prey and nurses them back to health in an impressive facility set along a rainforest stream. Volunteers work side by side with staff, doing everything from selling T-shirts to working with birds (see p. 140).

Guide, the standard guidebook on floating Alaska's rivers, leads challenging rafting, sea-kayaking, and hiking trips and base-camp wildlife viewing each summer in some of the wildest and most exotic places around the state. Her groups are tiny, with five to eight members, and she offers co-ed, family, and women's trips. A 10-day Arctic float trip costs around $3,600.

2440 East Tudor Rd., Suite 1102, Anchorage, AK 99507. ⓒ **604-222-1219** or 604-765-3370. www.equinox expeditions.com.

Nova These guys started commercial rafting on Alaska's rivers in 1975, but as the industry developed, they expanded only slowly, keeping their base in a tiny village on the Matanuska River, northeast of Anchorage, and primarily employing Alaskan guides. I like the fact that they don't minimize the hazards: They make it clear that these fast, cold waters aren't Disneyland rides. Their catalog covers longer expeditions on some of the state's wildest rivers but also includes more

affordable itineraries of 2 or 3 days. Two days on the Matanuska costs $295; 3 days on the Talkeetna, including 14-mile-long, Class IV rapids of the Talkeetna Canyon, costs $1,150. Nova offers trips from Copper Center and Hope as well.

P.O. Box 1129, Chickaloon, AK 99674. ⓒ **800/746-5753** or 907/745-5753. www.novalaska.com.

St. Elias Alpine Guides When you're ready for a real expedition, these are real professionals in real wilderness. Having given up on McKinley years ago as too crowded, they specialize in trekking, climbing, and floating the deep and rugged wilderness of Wrangell–St. Elias National Park. Theirs is the only trip catalog I know of that offers first ascents as part of the product line; so far, they've taken clients to the tops of previously unclimbed mountains more than 45 times. For details, see p. 429.

P.O. Box 92129, Anchorage, AK 99509. ⓒ **888/933-5427** or 907/554-4445. www.steliasguides.com.

7 Entry Requirements

Coming into the U.S. has become more difficult for almost everyone, with new security measures. Even U.S. citizens who pass between the U.S. and Canada must make additional preparations. International visitors can learn of the latest requirements from a travel agent or airline. Another good place to look for help is the U.S. embassy or consulate nearest you, which can be found on the Internet through www.unitedstatesvisas.gov.

PASSPORTS

Under a new requirement, U.S. citizens need passports to re-enter the United States even from other countries in the Western Hemisphere, such as those driving to Alaska through Canada. In Alaska, the rule goes into effect for 2007 for those coming in by air or sea, and for 2008 for those coming in by land—including those driving the Alaska highway. The new regulations are subject to review, so check for the latest at the Customs and Border Patrol website, www.cbp.gov. For information on how to get a passport, go to **"Passports"** in the **"Fast Facts"** section of this chapter—the websites listed provide downloadable passport applications for each nation, as well as the current fees for processing passport applications.

VISAS

A visa is a permit allowing entry to a foreign visitor. Many tourists coming to the United States do not need a visa. Canadian citizens do not need visas to enter the U.S. In addition, the U.S. State Department's **Visa Waiver Program** allows citizens of the following countries (at press time) to enter the United States without a visa for stays of up to 90 days: Andorra, Australia, Austria, Belgium, Brunei, Denmark, Finland, France, Germany, Iceland, Ireland, Italy, Japan, Liechtenstein, Luxembourg, Monaco, the Netherlands, New Zealand, Norway, Portugal, San Marino, Singapore, Slovenia, Spain, Sweden, Switzerland, and the United Kingdom. Citizens of these nations need only a valid passport and a round-trip air or cruise ticket upon arrival. If they first enter the United States, they may also visit Mexico, Canada, Bermuda, and/or the Caribbean islands and return to the United States without a visa. Further information is available from any U.S. embassy or consulate.

Citizens of all other countries or any holder of a passport that is not machine readable must have (1) a valid passport that expires at least 6 months later than the scheduled end of their visit to the United States, and (2) a tourist visa, which may be obtained from any U.S. embassy or consulate. For information on how to get a Visa, go to **"Visas"** in the **"Fast Facts"** section of this chapter. Also check the U.S. State Department website, at **www.travel.state.gov**, where you can download a visa and application.

MEDICAL REQUIREMENTS

Unless you're arriving from an area known to be suffering from an epidemic (particularly cholera or yellow fever), inoculations or vaccinations are not required for entry into the United States. If you have a medical condition that requires syringe-administered medications, carry a signed prescription from your physician. Airline passengers cannot pack syringes in their carry-on baggage without documented proof of medical need. Pack any medication in its original, labeled containers. This is especially important if you need medication that contains narcotics. In that case, also carry documented proof of your need, such as a signed letter from your doctor, and be careful to carry no more than you reasonably could use yourself during your trip. Otherwise, you may risk being accused of smuggling.

People who are **HIV-positive or have AIDS** are barred by an act of Congress from entering the United States unless they have a special waiver. No medical exam is required for entry into the United States, but border officials may stop individuals because they look sick or because they are carrying medicine for HIV/AIDS. In addition, airline passengers are given a form that asks about communicable diseases, including HIV/AIDS. With a "yes" on the form, you are excluded from the U.S. unless you have a waiver. The waivers are granted for "humanitarian" reasons, such as attending a conference, visiting close family members, getting medical treatment, or conducting business. Waivers are for a maximum of 30 days. Applicants must demonstrate that they are not symptomatic, that they have the financial means to obtain medical care if needed, and that they will not pose a danger to public health. You can get more information and a referral to a sympathetic attorney through **Immigration Equality,** 350 W. 31st St., Suite 505, New York, NY 10001 (℗ **212/714-2904;** www.immigrationequality.org), a nonprofit agency advocating for more fairness.

CUSTOMS
WHAT FOREIGN VISITORS CAN BRING IN

Personal effects, which are items you use yourself, such as clothing, cameras, and fishing rods, are exempt from duties. In addition, every visitor over 21 years of age may bring in the following without paying duties: 1 liter of wine, beer, or hard liquor; 200 cigarettes, or 50 cigars for your own use and another 100 as gifts (but not from Cuba), or 2 kilograms (4.4 pounds) of smoking tobacco; and $100 worth of gifts. To claim these exemptions, you must spend at least 72 hours in the United States and cannot have claimed them within the preceding 6 months. The duty on goods exceeding these exemptions is 3% of the value on the first $1,000 (the flat rate); above that amount, it depends on the item. The flat rate applies only to items for your own use or gifts and can be applied only once in 30 days. Importation of most raw food and plant material is prohibited or requires a special license. Foreign visitors may bring in or take out up to $10,000 in U.S. or foreign currency, travelers checks, securities, and so on, with no formalities; larger sums must be declared to U.S. Customs on entering or leaving and paperwork must be filed. A handy brochure called "Visiting the United States: U.S. Customs and Border Protection Regulations for Nonresidents" lays out the rules. It can be downloaded from the U.S. Customs and Border Protection website (www.cbp.gov) by typing the words "Visiting the United States publication" in the search window. Other avenues for information are your nearest U.S. consulate or embassy, or Customs officials at the Anchorage airport (℗ **907/271-6309**).

It is exceedingly complicated for foreign visitors to bring **firearms** into the United States; don't even consider it except for a hunting trip. Unless you are

---

ꞏTips **Prepare to Be Fingerprinted**

International visitors with visas must undergo an instant background check on arrival, be photographed, and have their fingerprints scanned. Exempt from the extra scrutiny are visitors entering from countries not required to have visas for short-term visits (see p. 42). For more information, go to the Department of Homeland Security website at **www.dhs.gov/dhspublic** and look for "US-Visit."

a U.S. citizen or permanent resident alien, you cannot bring in, buy, or even possess a gun without a permit from the **Bureau of Alcohol, Tobacco, Firearms, and Explosives** (© 304/616-4550; www.atf.treas.gov); these take several months to acquire (the application is on the ATF website—look for "Form 6"). The application must be accompanied by a valid hunting license (there are a few narrow exceptions, such as athletes involved in shooting competitions). The **Alaska Department of Fish and Game** (© 907/465-6085; www.alaska. gov/adfg) sells hunting licenses to nonresident aliens for $300; however, aliens can hunt only with a registered guide. First, find the guide; then let him or her help with all the paperwork, but start many months in advance and be ready to pay.

WHAT YOU CAN TAKE HOME

WILDLIFE PRODUCTS Alaska Native art and crafts made from protected marine mammals are perfectly legal in the U.S, even though possessing animal parts is not legal for non-Natives. Alaska Natives have used these materials for thousands of years and their subsistence harvest is not a danger to the species. Generally, however, marine mammal products from any threatened or endangered species cannot be taken out of the country unless they are antiques made prior to the passage of the Marine Mammal Act in 1972. For those items that can legally be taken home, you need a permit under the Convention on International Trade of Endangered Species, known as CITES. These permits can be complicated and time consuming to obtain. For international visitors, this means you should simply avoid buying anything made from marine mammals.

Other species requiring a CITES permit for export include brown or black bear, bobcat, wolf, lynx, bobcat, or river otter. Before you buy an item, make sure you can legally take it home, then have the shop mail it to you insured, and have them take care of the paperwork. If you carry it with you in your baggage, perhaps because you bought it from someone who can't handle the paperwork, you'll need to get your own permits. U.S. residents transiting Canada with wildlife products requiring CITES permits can obtain a Personal Effects Exemption Certificate by calling the **U.S. Fish and Wildlife Service** in Anchorage (© 907/ 271-6198; http://alaska.fws.gov/law). Foreign visitors exporting wildlife may need to contact the agency's **Division of Management Authority** in Washington, D.C. (© 800/358-2104; www. international.fws.gov) regarding permit requirements. Processing time for permits can take from 60 to 90 days.

OTHER GOODS Rules governing what you can bring back duty-free vary from country to country and generally are posted on the Web. For a clear summary of **Canadian** rules, request the booklet *I Declare,* issued by the Canada Border Services Agency (© 800/461-9999 in Canada, or 204/983-3500; www.cbsa-asfc.gc.ca/E/pub/cp/rc4044). **U.K. citizens** should contact HM Customs & Excise at © 0845/010-9000 (from outside the U.K., 020/8929-0152), or consult their website at www.hmce.gov.uk. **Australians** can contact the Australian Customs Service (© 1300/363-263; www.customs.gov.au). **New Zealand** citizens should contact New Zealand Customs (© 04/473-6099 or 0800/428-786; www.customs.govt.nz).

8 Travel & Rental Car Insurance

There are several kinds of travel insurance: for **trip cancellation or interruption,** for **medical costs,** and for **lost**

luggage. Usually they are sold together in a single, comprehensive policy. Insurance for trip cancellation or interruption is a must if you have paid the large cash deposits demanded by many Alaska outfitters, fishing guides, wilderness lodges, package tour operators, and cruise companies. A premium of 5% to 8% of the cost of the trip is well worth the protection against the uncertainty of Alaska weather (most deposits are lost in case of weather delays or cancellations) or unexpected crises that might prevent you from being able to depart as planned. Interruption insurance will get you home under covered circumstances. Major insurers, such as those listed below, offer policy holders access to 24-hour phone assistance to help handle crises. Read the policy carefully to find out when you are covered. Do not buy insurance through the operator holding your deposit, even though the insurer itself is a different entity. Most policies do not cover losses related to the company that originally solicited your business. Instead, buy your insurance directly from the insurance company without the involvement of anyone selling you travel products. Medical insurance is covered below.

Insurance on your baggage will probably come with whatever other insurance you buy; it may not be worthwhile otherwise. Your baggage is probably covered under your homeowners' policy or credit card benefits. If the airline loses or damages your bags, they are usually responsible for up to $2,500 per passenger on domestic flights, or up to approximately $635 per checked bag on international flights. Expensive items such as jewelry and cameras are not included. Carry valuables with you, insuring your baggage only if the worth you are able to prove is more than the airline's responsibility and the limits on your existing policies. That's unlikely because to prove the value of your lost clothing and such, you would need bills of sale or similar documentation for each item. Various companies sell travel insurance online, including **Travel Guard International** (© **800-826-1300;** www.travelguard.com). Or look

---

Tips **Using the Internet on the Road**

If you decide to bring your laptop, you'll find that many hotels and even B&Bs have wireless Internet access for guests, usually for free, and there are numerous other free hotspots all over the state. For a site that lists dozens of free hotspots in Alaska, with maps to get to them, check out www.toursaver.com/alaska-wireless.php. Getting online through dial-up is difficult for visitors to Alaska; national Internet service providers have access numbers only in the largest cities, and dialing up long distance is slow and unreliable from many Alaska communities with antiquated phone connections.

If you leave the computer at home, you can stop in at an Internet cafe or the public library when you want to log on. Alaskans use the Internet heavily, even in tiny villages where people live largely by hunting and gathering, so you can always count on finding a way of getting online with a little effort. I have listed Internet access for each Alaska community in the appropriate sections of the book.

Coverage for wireless Internet technology, such as your Blackberry or other Internet PDA, spread beyond Alaska's two or three largest cities only in 2006. The main provider is an Alaskan firm called ACS (check on roaming with your own provider).

for the best deal around by going to **www.insure.com**; click on the "Travel" tab. The site allows travelers to get instant quotes from many insurance companies at once by providing the dates of the trip, amount and type of coverage, and ages of the travelers.

With **rental cars,** you face a whole different set of insurance considerations. Most of these are the same as when renting a car anywhere, and a few simple preparations will get you through. Before you leave home, check your own auto policy for your liability coverage with a rented car (bringing proof of insurance along is a good idea), and check with your credit card issuer for coverage for damage to a rented car (make sure to use that card when you rent, too). Chances are, you are already covered and don't need to buy the unreasonably priced insurance offered by the rental car company when you rent, but if you are not covered, do buy it: The potential costs you face are even larger than having a crash at home because they include the rental company's lost business.

One special Alaska consideration: Ask the reservation agent or check the rental contract for rules about driving on unpaved roads or other restrictions. I have listed companies that rent for unpaved highways in Fairbanks and Anchorage (chapters 9 and 6, respectively); not many allow it. Cars do get damaged on these roads, and you may be setting yourself up for a real headache if that happens and you violate the rental contract.

9 Health & Safety

CRIME & EMERGENCY SERVICES

CRIME   Sadly, crime rates are not low in Alaska's larger cities, although muggings are rare. Take the normal precautions you'd take at home. You're safe in daylight hours anywhere tourists commonly go, less so late at night leaving a bar or walking in a lonely place. Women need to be especially careful on their own, as Alaska has a disproportionately high rate of rape. This doesn't mean women shouldn't travel alone in Alaska, only that they should be cautious. Most women I know avoid walking by themselves at night, especially in wooded or out-of-the-way areas. The late-night sunlight can be deceiving—just because it's light out doesn't mean it's safe. Sexual assaults occur in towns big and small. Women should never hitchhike alone. If you are a victim of a crime, you can reach police almost anywhere by calling © **911**, or, if it is not an emergency, by using the numbers listed under "Fast Facts" in each community section.

MEDICAL EMERGENCIES   You'll find modern, full-service hospitals in each of Alaska's larger cities, and even in some small towns that act as regional centers. There's some kind of clinic even in the smallest towns, although they often are staffed by physicians' assistants rather than medical doctors. I've listed the addresses and phone numbers for medical facilities in each destination under "Fast Facts." Call those numbers, too, for referrals to a dentist or other health professional. In an emergency, call © **911.**

If health is a particular concern, consider joining **MedicAlert** (© **888/633-4298;** www.medicalert.org) and wearing their engraved bracelet, which will inform emergency medical personnel of a primary preexisting medical condition and provide them with access to the organization's response center for your information on file, such as medications and physician and family contacts. The cost is $35 for the first year, and then $20 a year.

HEALTH INSURANCE

Travelers from within the U.S. are often covered under their regular health insurance as long as they remain in the country.

Take a minute to check your coverage, making sure it adequately covers emergency medical transportation and treatment, especially if you will be adventuring in remote areas. The cost of a MedEvac flight can easily be in the five figures. Check the coverage offered by your credit cards or buy a travel insurance policy to cover you just for the trip (see above).

International visitors should certainly make health insurance arrangements before traveling to the U.S. Doctors and hospitals are expensive and often require proof of coverage before they render services (in an emergency, of course, you'll always get quick treatment, regardless of ability to pay). Good policies will cover the costs of an accident, repatriation, or death. Packages such as **Europ Assistance's Worldwide Healthcare Plan** are sold by European automobile clubs and travel agencies at attractive rates. **Worldwide Assistance Services, Inc.** (© 800/777-8710; www.worldwideassistance.com), is the agent for Europ Assistance in the United States.

INSURANCE FOR BRITISH TRAVELERS Most big travel agents offer their own insurance and will probably try to sell you their package when you book a holiday. Think before you sign. **Britain's Consumers' Association** recommends that you insist on seeing the policy and reading the fine print before buying travel insurance. **The Association of British Insurers** (© 020/7600-3333; www.abi.org.uk) gives advice by phone and publishes *Holiday Insurance,* a free guide to policy provisions and prices. You might also shop around for better deals: Try **Columbus Direct** (© 0870/033-9988; www.columbusdirect.net).

INSURANCE FOR CANADIAN TRAVELERS Canadians should check with their provincial health plan offices or call **Health Canada** (© 866/225-0709; www.hc-sc.gc.ca) to find out the extent of their coverage and what documentation

and receipts they must take home in case they are treated in the United States.

OUTDOOR HEALTH & SAFETY

AVALANCHE When snow sliding down a mountain comes to a stop, it hardens to a consistency that only metal tools can dig through. Avalanche survivors describe the terror of being helplessly locked in this unyielding material while hoping for rescue. Understandably, survivors are in the minority. Victims die if not dug out quickly (well before emergency personnel can arrive at a remote slope). No one should go into the snowy backcountry without training in avalanche avoidance and recovery equipment, including locator beacons, probes, and shovels. Go with a guide if you are unsure.

BEARS & OTHER WILDLIFE Being eaten by a bear is probably the least likely way for your vacation to end. Bear encounters are much less common in Alaska than at the California national parks, where bears are accustomed to people. More people die from dog bites than bear attacks. But it's still wise to be prepared for bears and to know how to avoid being trampled by a moose, which can be fatal.

The first safety rule for bears is to avoid attracting them. Be tidy with your food and trash when you're camping, putting everything away in sealed containers. When backpacking, you can protect your food by hanging it from a long tree branch or, above the tree line, storing it in a bear-resistant canister (for rent or loan in Anchorage, Denali, or Wrangell–St. Elias National Parks; see chapters 6, 8, and 9). Be careful not to spread food odors when you're cooking and cleaning up. Clean fish away from your campsite. Never keep food, pungent items, or clothing that smells like fish in your tent.

When walking through brush or thick trees, make noise to avoid surprising a bear or moose. Bells you can hang on your belt are for sale at sporting-goods shops, or you can sing or carry on conversation. You might not scare a bear away this way, but at least you won't startle it. At all costs, avoid coming between a bear and its cubs or a bear and food (if a bear wants the fish you just caught, that's his food, too). Moose also are strongly defensive of their young. Even a moose on its own can attack if it feels you're getting too close or if it previously has been stressed by contact with people or dogs. People are badly hurt every year trying to sneak by a moose on a trail. I see moose every day when I ski, bike, or run near my house in Anchorage; when the moose wants the trail, I either find a way around or go back the other way.

If you see a bear, stop, wave your arms, make noise, and, if you're with others, group together so you look larger to the bear. Don't run, tempting the bear to chase; depart by slowly backing away, at an angle, if possible. If the bear follows, stop. Once in a great while, the bear may bluff a charge; even less often, it may attack. If you're attacked, fall and play dead, rolling into a ball face down with your hands behind your neck. The bear should lose interest. In extremely rare instances, a bear may not lose interest because it's planning to make a meal of you. If this happens, fight back for all you're worth.

Many Alaskans carry a gun for protection in bear country, but that's not practical for visitors or anyone not practiced in shooting (a few years ago, a greenhorn got flustered and threw his gun at a bear). A better alternative is a bear-deterrent spray. These are canisters that you fire to produce a burning fog of capsaicin pepper between you and a threatening bear. While less deadly than a gun, and with limited effectiveness in wind or rain, research shows they have a better overall track record against bear attacks than guns. The sprays also are legal in national parks and are okay to carry across the Canadian border—two big advantages over firearms. However, you can't bring bear-deterrent spray on an airplane, even in your checked baggage, so if you fly, you will have to buy it on arrival and get rid of it before you leave. The product is easily available at Alaska sporting goods stores for about $45, or order direct from **Counter Assault** (© **800/695-3394;** www.counterassault.com). Be sure to get a holster, too, as the spray is of no use buried in your backpack. If you do take a gun, it had better be a big one, such as a .300-Magnum rifle or 12-gauge shotgun loaded with slugs. No handgun is big enough to stop a large bear bent on attacking.

BOATING SAFETY Because of the cool temperatures, unpredictable weather, and cold water, going out on the ocean or floating a fast river is more hazardous in Alaska than in most other places, and you should go only with an experienced, licensed operator unless you know what you're doing. There's little margin for error if you fall into the water or capsize in this cold water. Many boating deaths occur when good swimmers who are not wearing lifejackets immediately sink— apparently, the shock of falling in is so intense they shut down and fail to swim. With a life jacket on, it takes a few second to get used to the cold water, and then you can concentrate on getting out. You have 15 minutes to half an hour before cold immobilizes you. Equally important, however, is getting warm and dry after you are out of the water. The body temperature of a wet, cold person can easily sink so far he or she cannot get warm without external heating, a deadly condition called hypothermia. If you're sea kayaking or canoeing, always wear a life jacket, stay close to shore, and use plastic dry bags (also called float bags) to pack everything you need to quickly warm a person who gets wet (see "Hypothermia," below). Having a way to get help in an emergency is also important (see "Getting Lost/Wilderness Communications," below).

DANGEROUS PLANTS Two shrubs common in Alaska can cause skin irritation, but there is nothing as bad as poison ivy or poison oak. **Pushki,** also called cow parsnip, is a large-leafed plant growing primarily in open areas, up to shoulder height by late summer, with white flowers. The celery-like stalks break easily, and the sap has the quality of intensifying the burning power of the sun on skin. Wash it off quickly to avoid a rash. **Devil's Club,** a more obviously dangerous plant, grows on steep slopes and has ferocious spines that can pierce through clothing. Also, don't eat anything you can't positively identify, as there are deadly poisonous mushrooms and plants.

DRINKING WATER Unpurified river or lake water may not be safe to drink. Hand-held filters available from sporting-goods stores for around $75 are the most practical way of dealing with the problem. Iodine kits and boiling also work. The danger is a protozoan cyst called *giardia lamblia,* which causes diarrhea and is present in thousands of water bodies all over the United States, even in remote areas, where it may have been carried by waterfowl. It may not show up until a couple of weeks after exposure and could become chronic. If symptoms show up after you get home, tell your doctor you may have been exposed so that you can get tested and cured.

GETTING   LOST/WILDERNESS COMMUNICATIONS Even experienced people get lost outdoors. Hiking off trail or voyaging in a canoe, raft, or kayak, you quickly find that one mountain looks a lot like another. If you are unsure of your navigational skills, maps, or equipment, don't go. Beyond those basics, the most important safety precautions are to go with another person and to make sure someone knows where to look for you if you don't come back. For extended trips (more than a day hike), leave a written trip plan with a person who will call rescuers if you are late. At the very least, leave a note in your car indicating where you are bound. Cellphones sometimes work near towns and highways, but not reliably, and there is little coverage beyond those areas.

For serious outdoors people, technology can add an extra safety backup outdoors. **Personal Locator Beacons** with built-in GPS are the state-of-the-art solution. The beacon is a small device that, when activated, transmits a distress signal and your exact location to an orbiting satellite. Authorities receive the message and find out who you are from a database. After verifying you are really missing, they can then go to the exact spot where the beacon is broadcasting. ACR Electronics' Aquafix or Terrafix PLB (for marine or land use, respectively) cost from $600 to $700 at stores such as West Marine or REI.

If you don't want to shell out that much money, or if you want a device that also allows you to stay in touch in the wilderness, it is possible to rent an Iridium satellite phone that will work outdoors anywhere on earth. The drawback of this approach is that it is less useful in an emergency than a beacon: You need to now where you are and whom to call, and you have to be able to get the phone to work. I rented one for a 2-week wilderness trip and found it rather finicky; I was always able to make a call, but I wouldn't have wanted my life to depend on doing it quickly. I was happy with the customer service of the firm I rented from, a Canadian outfit called **RoadPost** (✆ **888/ 622-7368** or 905/272-5665; www. roadpost.com). Prices start at $89 for the first week and $6 for each additional day, plus around $2 a minute for calls and a $30 delivery fee. They send you the phone by overnight express.

HYPOTHERMIA A potentially fatal lowering of core body temperature can sneak up on you. It's most dangerous when you don't realize how cold you are, perhaps in 50°F (10°C) weather on a damp mountain hike or rainy boating trip. Dress in material (whether wool or synthetic) that keeps its warmth when wet, choosing layers to avoid chilling perspiration. (See "What to Wear," earlier.) Eating well and avoiding exhaustion also are important. Among the symptoms of hypothermia are experiencing cold extremities, being uncommunicative, displaying poor judgment or coordination, and sleepiness. A shivering victim still has the ability to warm up if better dressed; a lack of shivering means the body has gone beyond that point and warmth must be added from the outside or from warm drinks. Get indoors, force the victim to drink hot liquids (except if not fully conscious, which could cause choking), and, if shelter is unavailable, apply body heat from another person, skin on skin, in a sleeping bag.

INSECT BITES The good news is that Alaska has no snakes or poisonous spiders. The bad news is that Alaska makes up for it with mosquitoes and other biting insects. West Nile virus has not arrived here at this writing so the mosquitoes are not dangerous, but they can ruin a trip. Effective insect repellent is a necessity, as is having a place where you can get away from them. We use shirts with hoods of netting when the bugs are at their worst. Mosquitoes can bite through light fabric close to the skin, which is why people in the Bush wear heavy, baggy Carhart pants and jackets (made of canvas), even on the hottest days. Benadryl tablets or other antihistamines will often relieve swelling caused by mosquito bites.

RIVER CROSSINGS Hiking in Alaska's backcountry often requires crossing rivers without bridges. Use great caution: It's easy to get in trouble. Often the water is glacial melt, barely above freezing and heavy with silt that makes it opaque. The silt can fill your pockets and drag you down. If in doubt, don't do it. If you do decide to cross, unbuckle your pack, keep your shoes on, face upstream, use a heavy walking stick if possible, and rig a safety line. Children should go in the eddy behind a larger person or be carried.

SHELLFISH Don't eat mussels, clams, or scallops you pick or dig from the seashore unless you know they're safe to eat. Generally, that means you need some specific and reliable local knowledge. There is a government program to ensure shellfish safety, but the only easily accessible beaches it affects are on the eastern shore of Kachemak Bay. The risk is paralytic shellfish poisoning, a potentially fatal malady caused by a naturally occurring toxin. It causes total paralysis that includes your breathing. A victim may be kept alive with mouth-to-mouth resuscitation until medical help is obtained. For more information, contact the **Alaska Department of Environmental Conservation,** which maintains a hotline and website (© **800/731-1312;** www.alaska. gov/dec/eh/fss/seafood/psphome.htm, or go to www.alaska.gov and search for "psp").

DRIVING SAFETY

ROAD REPORTS The Alaska Department of Transportation has centralized highway reports with a handy toll-free phone and Internet system (© **511;** http://511.alaska.gov). Even in dry summer conditions, it is worthwhile to make the call or check the site before heading on an intercity drive because road construction can cause long delays—at times, workers will close a major highway overnight for work. In winter, checking on conditions is a basic safety essential. Here are more seasonal tips.

SUMMER Alaska's highways are two lane except close to Anchorage and Fairbanks. Keep your headlights on all the time to help oncoming vehicles see you. Drivers are required to pull over at the next pull-out whenever five or more cars are trailing them on a two-lane highway, regardless of how fast they're going. This saves the lives of people who otherwise will try to pass. When passing a truck going the other way on a gravel highway, slow down or stop and pull as far as possible to the side of the road to avoid losing your windshield to a flying rock. Always think about the path of rocks you're kicking up toward others' vehicles. Make sure you've got a good full-size spare tire and jack if you're driving a gravel highway. For remote driving, bring along a first-aid kit, emergency food, a tow rope, and jumper cables, and keep your gas tank full.

WINTER Drivers on Alaska's highways in winter should be prepared for cold-weather emergencies far from help. Take all the items listed for rural summer driving, plus a flashlight, matches and materials to light a fire, chains, a shovel, and an ice scraper. A camp stove to make hot beverages is also a good idea. If you're driving a remote highway (such as the Alaska Hwy.) between December and March, take along gear adequate to keep you safe from the cold even if you have to wait overnight with a dead car at –40°F (–40°C; see "What to Wear," earlier in this chapter, and add blankets and sleeping bags). Never drive a road marked CLOSED or UNMAINTAINED IN WINTER. Even on maintained rural roads, other vehicles rarely come by in winter. All Alaska roads are icy all winter. Studded tires are a necessity. Also, never leave your car's engine stopped for more than 4 hours in temperatures of –10°F (–23°C) or colder. Alaskans generally have electrical head-bolt heaters installed to keep the engine warm overnight; you'll find electrical outlets everywhere in cold, Interior Alaska areas.

10 Specialized Travel Resources

FOR TRAVELERS WITH DISABILITIES

Today it is rare to find a hotel without rooms accessible for people with disabilities, and many B&Bs have made the necessary adjustments as well. The results often are the best rooms in the house. Make sure to ask for the special rooms when making reservations, and question smaller establishments closely about exactly what "accessible" means to them. There are several Alaska agencies for people with disabilities. **Challenge Alaska,** 3350 Commercial Dr., Suite 208, Anchorage, AK 99501 (© **907/344-7399;** www.challengealaska.org), a nonprofit organization, offers therapeutic recreation and education, including outdoor adventures. They operate an adaptive ski school at Alyeska Resort in Girdwood (see p. 252). Summer outings are inexpensive: A 4-day sea-kayaking outing was only $350. Get on the mailing list for current listings. **Alaska Welcomes You! Inc.,** P.O. Box 91333, Anchorage, AK 99509-1333 (© or TTY **800/349-6301** or 907/349-6301), books accessible cruises, tours in Southcentral Alaska, and extended travel packages to Denali National Park and the Kenai Peninsula, and does trip planning for independent travelers with special needs. The operator field-checks the places he books to make sure they really are accessible.

FOR SENIORS

People over age 65 get reduced admission prices to many Alaska attractions, and some accommodations have special senior rates. National parks offer free admission and special camping rates for people over 62 with a Golden Age Passport, which you can obtain at any of the parks for $10 and which never expires. Also mention your age when booking your airfare; most domestic airlines offer senior discounts. Most towns have a senior center where you'll find activities and help with any special needs. The **Anchorage Senior Center** (© **907/258-7823;** www.anchorageseniorcenter.org) offers guidance for visitors; the use of the restaurant, gift shop, and fitness room; and a chance to meet locals. Dances are held Friday nights. **Elderhostel,** 11 Ave. de Lafayette, Boston, MA 02111-1746 (© **877/426-8056** or 978/323-4141, 877/426-2167 TTY; www.elderhostel.org), operates many weeklong Alaska learning vacations for groups of people 55 and older. The catalog of choices is on the website.

FOR GAY & LESBIAN TRAVELERS

Anchorage, Juneau, and Fairbanks have active gay and lesbian communities. In Anchorage, **Identity, Inc.** (www.identityinc.org), offers referrals, publishes a newsletter called *Northview,* sponsors activities throughout the year, and operates a gay and lesbian helpline (© **888/901-9876** or 907/258-4777). The June Pridefest includes a parade and picnic, among other events. Their Gay and Lesbian Community Center of Anchorage is at 2110 E. Northern Lights, Suite A (© **907/929-4528**). Gays and lesbians can find some Alaska B&Bs and tours specifically marketing to them. For example, **Olivia Cruises and Resorts** (© **800/631-6277;** www.olivia.com) typically brings a lesbian cruise to Alaska each summer, with well-known entertainers on board. In Fairbanks, a small company specializes in outdoor tours and backcountry trips for gays and lesbians. It's called **Out In Alaska**

(© **877/347-9958;** www.outinalaska.com). There are plenty of other options. Bob DeLoach specializes in gay and lesbian Alaska travel. His **Apollo Travel** operates with **Whitsett Travel** (© **888/770-0661** or 907/274-0547).

FOR STUDENTS

Many museums offer free or reduced admission for students and anyone under 18, although sometimes you have to ask. Make sure to bring a student ID card.

There are hostels in most towns in Alaska. Except for those in Anchorage, Fairbanks, and Juneau, they tend to be open in the summer only. I have described hostels in the text for each town. They're generally not affiliated with organizations such as **Hostelling International** that provide discounts to members. For a comprehensive listing of hostels, go to **www.hostels.com** and navigate to Alaska by clicking on the maps.

Many students travel to Alaska for summer work. It's usually possible to get a job in a fish cannery in most coastal towns. Work on the slime line is hard and unpleasant and the pay is low, but if the season is good and you work long hours, camping to keep your expenses low (most canneries have tent cities of summer workers nearby), you can take home more money for your summer's work than you would normally earn elsewhere. Hillary Rodham Clinton worked an Alaska slime line when she was in school, and you can, too (George W. Bush worked in Alaska as a young person as well, at a politically connected air service and construction company). Offshore fish processing ships hire many unskilled workers, too, but I wouldn't recommend that for a student; once you're on the ship, you are trapped there, and you may hate it. The work is hazardous (federal worker safety and minimum wage laws do not apply) and medical care may be inadequate. Also, don't come north expecting to make fabulous wages. The stories of college students making huge crew shares on fishing boats are legends— there are experienced deckhands to take lucrative jobs before boats hire raw hands they have to train. Go that way for the adventure (and danger and hard work), but not out of greed. Jobs are always available in the tourism industry, too, although without the extreme flexibility of fish processing. The **Alaska Department of Labor** posts a lot of useful information on its website, including job applications for seafood work and a live database of openings; start at **www.jobs. state.ak.us**.

FOR FAMILIES

When we researched our first edition of this book, my son, Robin, was 3, and my daughter, Julia, was 6 months. As I write this, Robin is 14, Julia is 11, Joseph is 7, and Becky is 5. You might run into us in a campground or on a boat dock anywhere in the state as we travel to research the next edition of "our Alaska book." Robin has surprised people carrying it and introduced himself. Yes, it's a great job, and bringing the family along is the best part.

Alaska's magnificent scenery is something even young children can understand and appreciate. Also, an Alaska vacation is largely spent outdoors, which is where kids like to be. The children never get enough ferry riding, and all four enjoy camping immensely. Our extensive experience camping with babies, even as young as 3 months, has been entirely positive. Having everyone sleep in a tent, at baby level, is an infant's idea of vacation paradise.

There are drawbacks to Alaska as a family destination. The primary one is the expense. We have never gotten a significant break on a child's airplane ticket on the Alaska route. Activities such as flightseeing and tour-boat cruises tend to have less-than-generous children's discounts and cost too much for most families. Often bed-and-breakfast rooms are too small for a family. Hotel rooms and restaurant meals are expensive in Alaska. Car camping solves many of those problems, with stops in a hotel every few days to get everyone cleaned up. I wouldn't take kids over the Alaska Highway, however; instead, I'd fly to Anchorage and rent a car and any bulky camping gear there (see "Car or RV Camping," in section 6 of this chapter).

Be careful in choosing your itinerary and activities with children. The highways in Alaska are long and children will require a gradual approach to covering a lot of ground. They also need time to play, explore, and rest. Frankly, children often don't enjoy activities like wildlife watching. It takes a long time to find the animals, and when you do, they're usually off in the distance—kids younger than 8 often don't have the visual skills or patience to pick out the animals from the landscape. Don't overtax children with walks and hiking trips; we keep track of the longest hike we've managed without excessive whining, and then try to extend that record just a little bit each time out. Short sea-kayaking excursions, on the other hand, are great for children who are old enough, riding in the front of a double-seat boat with a parent in back; we began with Joseph at age 5, and I have friends who have done it with a 3-year-old. In practice, the age limit depends on the outfitter and your child's level of responsibility.

If you're flawed mortals like us, you'll be getting on each other's nerves after a few weeks on the road. We survive by leaving time for low-key kid activities, such as beachcombing or playing in the park, while one grown-up splits off for a museum visit, shopping, or a special, more expensive activity. Of course, if you want to preserve your marriage, you'll have to be scrupulously fair about who gets to go flightseeing and who has to stay behind and change diapers, as you won't have my all-purpose excuse (research).

If you're interested in a package tour with your family, most of the companies listed in this chapter will take children, but research carefully to make sure you will have enough down time and not too much time on the road. **Alaska Wildland Adventures** (© **800/334-8730;** www. alaskawildland.com) has various trips for kids as young as 12 and can take children as young as 6 for a package of day activities based at their Kenai Riverside Lodge. The package, called the Kenai Explorer, is flexible in length and geared to families, offering games and kid-oriented guides. The shortest, 2-night, 3-day version is $895 adults, $825 children. **Alaska Discovery** (© **800/586-1911**) takes children as young as 12 on some of its extended Southeast Alaska sea-kayaking trips, which start at $895 for 3 days and 2 nights, and welcomes younger children on its noncamping trips.

FAST FACTS: Alaska

Area Code All of Alaska is in area code **907.** In the Yukon Territory, the area code is **867.** When placing a toll call within the state, you must dial 1, the area code, and the number.

Automobile Organizations Auto clubs will supply maps, suggested routes, guidebooks, accident and bail-bond insurance, and emergency road service. The **American Automobile Association (AAA)** is the major auto club in the United States. If you belong to an auto club in your home country, inquire about AAA reciprocity before you leave. You may be able to join AAA even if you're not a member of a reciprocal club; the Alaska branch is **AAA Mountain-West** (© **800/332-6119;** www.aaa-mountainwest.com). AAA has a nationwide emergency road service telephone number (© **800/AAA-HELP**).

Banks & ATMs There are banks and automated teller machines everywhere but tiny villages.

Business Hours In the larger cities, major grocery stores are open until late at night and carry a wide range of products (even fishing gear) in addition to food. At a minimum, **stores** are open Monday through Friday from 10am to 6pm, are open on Saturday afternoon, and are closed on Sunday, but many are open much longer hours, especially in summer. **Banks** may close an hour earlier and, if open on Saturday, hours are short. Under state law, **bars** don't have to close until 5am, but many communities have an earlier closing, generally around 2am.

Car Rentals See "Getting There & Getting Around," p. 25.

Cellular Phone Coverage Pretty much every town that can be reached by road or ferry has cellular voice coverage, as well as some of the paved highways. That means the great majority of the people are covered and the great majority of the land is not. The largest provider is an Alaska company called ACS, which posts maps of its coverage area at www.acsalaska.com (click on "Wireless" and then "Resources"). I've found usable coverage is often less than what the companies claim, so don't bet your life on being able to make a call. In any event, if you plan to use your phone, check with your wireless provider to make sure it will work in Alaska and to find out just how badly you will be gouged on roaming charges.

Currency The most common bills are the $1 (a "buck"), $5, $10, and $20 denominations. There are also $2 bills (seldom encountered), $50 bills, and $100 bills (the last two are usually not welcome as payment for small purchases). Coins come in seven denominations: 1¢ (1 cent, or a penny); 5¢ (5 cents, or a nickel); 10¢ (10 cents, or a dime); 25¢ (25 cents, or a quarter); 50¢ (50 cents, or a half-dollar); the gold-colored Sacagawea coin, worth $1; and the rare silver dollar.

Electricity As in Canada, the United States uses 110 to 120 volts AC (60 cycles), compared to 220 to 240 volts AC (50 cycles) in most of Europe, Australia, and New Zealand. Downward converters that change 220 to 240 volts to 110 to 120 volts are difficult to find in the United States, so bring one with you.

Embassies & Consulates All embassies are located in the nation's capital, Washington, D.C. Some consulates are located in major U.S. cities, and most nations have a mission to the United Nations in New York City. If your country isn't listed below, call for directory information in Washington, D.C. (© **202/555-1212**) or log on to **www.embassy.org/embassies**.

Emergencies Generally, you can call © **911** for medical, police, or fire emergencies. On remote highways, there sometimes are gaps in 911 coverage, but dialing 0 will generally get an operator who can connect you to emergency services.

Gasoline (Petrol) The cost of gasoline changes too quickly to make much sense to list in a book. You can find national and state price averages updated online daily at **www.fuelgaugereport.com**. Prices in Alaska vary by location: in Anchorage, they tend to be a little below the national average, while in rural areas they are well above it. As elsewhere in the U.S., taxes are already included in the price quoted or on the pump. One U.S. gallon equals 3.8 liters or .85 imperial gallons. Fill-up locations are known as gas or service stations.

Holidays Besides national holidays, banks and state and local government offices close on two state holidays: Seward's Day (the last Mon in Mar) and Alaska Day (Oct 18, or the nearest Fri or Mon if it falls on a weekend). National holidays, when many stores, restaurants, and museums close as well, include New Year's Day (Jan 1), Martin Luther King, Jr., Day (third Mon in Jan), Presidents' Day (third Mon in Feb), Memorial Day (last Mon in May), Independence Day (July 4th), Labor Day (the first Mon in Sept), Columbus Day (the second Mon in Oct), Veterans' Day (Nov 11), Thanksgiving Day (the fourth Thurs in Nov), and Christmas (Dec 25).

Legal Aid If you are "pulled over" for a minor infraction (such as speeding), never attempt to pay the fine directly to a police officer; this could be construed as attempted bribery, a much more serious crime. Pay fines by mail or directly into the hands of the clerk of the court. If accused of a more serious offense, say and do nothing before consulting a lawyer. Here the burden is on the state to prove a person's guilt beyond a reasonable doubt, and everyone has the right to remain silent, whether he or she is suspected of a crime or actually arrested. Once arrested, a person can make one telephone call to a party of his or her choice. International visitors should call the embassy or consulate.

Information Bureaus The **Alaska Travel Industry Association,** 2600 Cordova St., Suite 201, Anchorage, AK 99503 (✆ **907/929-2842;** www.travelalaska.com), is the state's official visitor agency. It sends out printed information but refers questions to visitor bureaus in individual towns. The largest of these is the Anchorage Convention and Visitor Bureau (see p. 211); otherwise, see the beginning of each town section in this book. For outdoor recreation, the **Alaska Public Lands Information Centers** are centralized sources of information on all government lands, which include some 85% of the state. The centers, located in Anchorage, Fairbanks, Ketchikan, and Tok, are operated cooperatively by many land agencies, including the National Park Service and U.S. Forest Service. The Anchorage center is at 605 W. 4th Ave., Suite 105, Anchorage, AK 99501 (✆ **907/271-2737;** www.nps.gov/aplic); the Fairbanks center is at 250 Cushman St., Suite 1A, Fairbanks, AK 99701 (✆ **907/456-0527**).

Liquor Laws The minimum drinking age in Alaska is 21, and ID is frequently checked. Most restaurants sell beer and wine, while some have full bars that serve hard liquor as well. Packaged alcohol, beer, and wine are sold only in licensed stores, not in grocery stores, but these are common and are open long hours every day. Open containers of alcohol are not allowed in your car or, with few exceptions, in any public place outside a bar or restaurant. Don't even think about driving while intoxicated, which in Alaska carries mandatory jail time for the first offense. More than 100 rural communities have laws prohibiting the importation and possession of alcohol (this is known as being "dry") or prohibiting the sale but not possession of alcohol (known as being "damp"). With a few exceptions, these are tiny Bush communities off the road network; urban areas are all "wet." Of the communities featured in this book, Kotzebue and Barrow are damp, and the rest are wet. Before flying into a Native village with alcohol, ask about the law or check a list online (go to www.dps.state.ak.us/abc and click on "Local Option Restrictions"). Bootlegging is a serious crime, and serious bad manners, in Alaska Native communities that are trying to address the damage of alcohol abuse.

Mail The locations of the post offices in each town in this book are listed in the appropriate "Fast Facts" sections. You can send mail from your hotel or the post office. Mail in the United States must have a five-digit postal code (or zip code) after the two-letter abbreviation of the state to which the mail is addressed. You can receive mail addressed to you at "General Delivery" at the post office.

Maps I've noted the best trail maps in each applicable section throughout this book. For most of the popular areas, I recommend the excellent trail maps published by **Trails Illustrated,** part of *National Geographic* (✆ **800/962-1643;** http://maps.nationalgeographic.com/trails). They're sold in park visitor centers, too. The maps are printed on plastic, so they don't get spoiled by rain; however, they don't cover the whole state. For detailed topographic maps covering all of Alaska, the U.S. Geological Service is still the only place to go. Their maps sales office in Anchorage (a fascinating place for anyone interested in cartography) is on the campus of Alaska Pacific University at the **Earth Science Information Center,** at 4230 University Dr. (*☎* **907/786-7011**).

Newspapers The state's dominant newspaper is the *Anchorage Daily News* (www.adn.com); it's available everywhere but is not always easy to find in Southeast Alaska. Seattle newspapers and *USA Today* are often available, and in Anchorage you can get virtually any newspaper.

Passports **For Residents of Australia:** You can pick up an application from your local post office or any branch of Passports Australia, but you must schedule an interview at the passport office to present your application materials. Call the **Australian Passport Information Service** at *☎* **131-232,** or visit the government website at www.passports.gov.au.

For Residents of Canada: Passport applications are available at travel agencies throughout Canada or from the central **Passport Office,** Department of Foreign Affairs and International Trade, Ottawa, ON K1A 0G3 (*☎* **800/567-6868;** www.ppt.gc.ca). *Note:* Canadian children who travel must have their own passport. However, if you hold a valid Canadian passport issued before December 11, 2001, that bears the name of your child, the passport remains valid for you and your child until it expires.

For Residents of Ireland: You can apply for a 10-year passport at the **Passport Office,** Setanta Centre, Molesworth Street, Dublin 2 (*☎* **01/671-1633;** www.irlgov.ie/iveagh). Those under age 18 and over 65 must apply for a 12€ 3-year passport. You can also apply at 1A South Mall, Cork (*☎* **021/272-525**), or at most main post offices.

For Residents of New Zealand: You can pick up a passport application at any New Zealand Passports Office or download it from their website. Contact the **Passports Office** at *☎* **0800/225-050** in New Zealand or 04/474-8100, or log on to www.passports.govt.nz.

For Residents of the United Kingdom: To pick up an application for a standard 10-year passport (5-yr. passport for children under 16), visit your nearest passport office, major post office, or travel agency, or contact the **United Kingdom Passport Service** at *☎* **0870/521-0410** or search its website at www.ukpa.gov.uk.

For Residents of the United States: Starting in 2008, you will need a passport to re-enter the U.S. from Canada, even by road. You can apply for a passport at many post offices. Before you go, get the requirements at the **U.S. State Department** website (www.travel.state.gov/passport), or call their **National Passport Information Center** (*☎* **877/487-2778**).

Taxes At this writing, there is no state sales tax, but most local governments have a sales tax and a bed tax on accommodations. The tax rates are listed in each town section throughout the book under its "Fast Facts" section.

Telephone I am assured that all major U.S. calling cards will work in Alaska, but this certainly hasn't been the case in the past. To make sure, contact your long-distance company, or buy a by-the-minute card. They are sold in convenience stores and are often the cheapest way to call home for international visitors. **Local calls** made from public pay phones usually cost 25¢. In smaller Alaska communities, you may have to wait for the person you are calling to answer before quickly putting the money in the phone. Pay phones do not accept pennies or anything larger than a quarter.

Most long-distance and international calls can be dialed directly from any phone. For **long-distance calls within Alaska and the United States and to Canada,** dial 1 followed by the three-digit area code and the seven-digit number. An area code of 800, 866, 877, or 888 is toll-free from anywhere in the United States.

For **international calls to places other than Canada,** dial 011 followed by the country code, city code, and telephone number of the person you are calling. U.S. area codes and international country codes are listed in the front of the White Pages telephone directory, or dial 0 to get a country code from the operator. If you're calling the **United States** from another country, the country code is 01.

For **collect, operator-assisted, and person-to-person calls,** dial 0 (the number zero) followed by the area code and number you want; an operator or automated voice will then come on the line, and you should specify that you are calling collect, or person-to-person, or both. If your operator-assisted call is international, ask for the overseas operator.

For **local directory assistance** ("information"), dial 411; for long-distance information, dial 1, then the appropriate area code, and 555-1212. This always carries an extra charge, which may be more than $1.50 on a cellphone.

There are two kinds of telephone directories in the United States. The so-called **White Pages** list private households and business subscribers in alphabetical order; the **Yellow Pages** list businesses and organizations categorized by the services they provide. In Alaska, the two directories are contained in the same book. Look in the front of the White Pages for emergency numbers and instructions on making long-distance calls. Blue pages near the front of the White Pages directory list numbers for government agencies.

Time Zone Although the state naturally spans five time zones, in the 1980s, Alaska's middle time zone was stretched so almost the entire state would lie in one zone, known as Alaska time. It's 1 hour earlier than the U.S. West Coast's Pacific Standard Time, 4 hours earlier than Eastern Standard Time. Crossing over the border from Alaska to Canada adds an hour and puts you at the same time as the West Coast. As with almost everywhere else in the United States, daylight saving time is in effect from 1am on the first Sunday in April (turn your clocks ahead 1 hr.) until 2am on the last Sunday in October (turn clocks back again).

Tipping Tips make up a major part of the compensation for many service workers. To leave no tip in a restaurant is socially unacceptable and leaves your server unpaid. To leave a small tip is a powerful indication of displeasure for bad service; to leave no tip suggests you don't know any better.

In restaurants, bars, and nightclubs, tip your server 15% to 20% of the check, depending on the quality of service. Tip **bartenders** at least 10% to 15% (a dollar or more per drink is customary), tip **checkroom attendants** $1 per garment, and tip **valet-parking attendants** $1 per vehicle. Tipping is not expected in cafeterias or fast-food restaurants where you order at a counter. In hotels, tip **bellhops** $1 per bag and tip the **housekeeper** at least $1 to $2 per day. Tip **cab**

drivers 15% of the fare and tip **hairdressers** and **barbers** 15% to 20%. Do not tip gas-station attendants and ushers at movies and theaters.

See the box "A Guide to Guide Gratuities" on p. 36 for guidelines on tipping outdoor guides and outfitters.

Visas For information about U.S. visas, go to **http://travel.state.gov** and click on "Visas." Or go to one of the following websites:

Australian citizens can obtain up-to-date visa information from the **U.S. Embassy Canberra,** Moonah Place, Yarralumla, ACT 2600 (© 02/6214-5600), or by checking the U.S. Diplomatic Mission's website at **http://usembassy-australia.state.gov/consular**.

British subjects can obtain up-to-date visa information by calling the **U.S. Embassy Visa Information Line** (© 0891/200-290) or by visiting the "Visas to the U.S." section of the American Embassy London's website at **www.us embassy.org.uk**.

Irish citizens can obtain up-to-date visa information through the **Embassy of the USA Dublin,** 42 Elgin Rd., Dublin 4, Ireland (© 353/1-668-8777), or by checking the "Consular Services" section of the website at **http://dublin.us embassy.gov**.

Citizens of **New Zealand** can obtain up-to-date visa information by contacting the **U.S. Embassy New Zealand,** 29 Fitzherbert Terrace, Thorndon, Wellington (© 644/472-2068), or can get the information directly from the "For New Zealanders" section of the website at **http://usembassy.org.nz**.

3

Suggested Alaska Itineraries

Readers ask me about how to fit together their itineraries more frequently than any other travel question. Alaska is unfamiliar territory and the transportation connections are different from those in most places. You can't get to the capital city of Juneau over land, for example, and the distances seem daunting between the towns that do have roads or rails. If you don't even know how to get around, it seems hard to know where to go or how much time to allow. But don't throw in the towel, like so many visitors who think the only way around these complications is to take a cruise or escorted tour. In fact, these travel issues aren't really that hard. Using a map and the list of transportation modes under "Alaska by the Numbers," on p. 16, you can get a good overview. The "Getting There" section for each destination in the book provides the details.

What's really challenging, and where visitors most commonly make mistakes, is in failing to define their interests and not limiting themselves to covering a reasonable area. Some feel compelled to try to see the entire state. Given that Alaska is defined in part by its enormous size, trying to go everywhere is a fool's errand. A version of the same thing is trying to "do" all the famous wilderness parks, which lie far apart in remote regions: You spend too much time and money getting from place to place. Each of Alaska's regions, by itself, has most of what you're

coming to Alaska for—wildlife, mountains, glaciers, historic sites, cute little towns—and you can have a better trip touring one or two regions than spending precious time going from region to region. To be specific, travelers with less than 2 weeks to spend should probably choose to tour either Southeast Alaska or Southcentral and Interior Alaska, but not both.

The other mistake some people make is to focus only on the largest and most famous destinations. Alaska isn't like Europe, with its cathedrals and monuments. Here a goal-oriented style of travel misses the fun and surprises—and may end up missing the whole point. Mount McKinley and Glacier Bay are certainly impressive, but it's perfectly allowed to skip them in favor of memorable places you find on your own that may be just as beautiful, if not as famous. More valuable—and more fundamentally Alaskan—are chance encounters with wildlife or interesting local people, or simply peaceful time alone in the woods.

Finally, remember why you are going to Alaska. Surely it's not to visit museums or tourist attractions, but instead to see one of the most beautiful unspoiled places on earth. To do that, you need to get outside. There's only so much you can see and learn through glass. Take a chance on a sea kayak excursion, a day hike, or a mountain bike ride. You may never have a better chance to try it.

Tips Create Your Own Itinerary

If all travelers had the same interests, needs, abilities, and the same preferences in pacing, they could all follow the same itineraries. Of course, then only the limited number of places that fit on a sample itinerary would receive all the visitors, while the interesting and peculiar places off the beaten path would remain unknown. I hope you use the sample trip plans here as a starting point to design your own individual trip. Substitute different activities or towns, or extend the time in places that are more appealing to you. Do the trips in reverse order or cut and paste portions of two different plans together. Or simply use the itineraries to get a feel for the distances and places and then build your own plan from scratch after browsing through the rest of the book.

1 Southeast Alaska in a Week

This plan takes you to the Southeast's highlights, with whales, glaciers, mountains, totem poles, and Russian American history included. It's fast-paced yet still covers less than half of this diverse and fascinating region. If you have more time, this plan would make a much more relaxing 10-day trip. Add a day each in Sitka, Juneau, and Gustavus. There's plenty to do, or not do, in each town. You can extend this itinerary even more by beginning with a flight into **Petersburg** instead of Sitka. Spend a day or two there sea kayaking, hiking, fishing, or whale-watching before boarding an Alaska Marine Highway System ferry to Sitka and picking up on day 1 of this plan.

Day ❶: Arrive in Sitka 🐾

Fly on an **Alaska Airlines** jet to the historic island city of Sitka, once the capital of Russian America. The town layout you see from the air is little changed from historic photographs and paintings. After settling in, take a walk along winding Lincoln Street, taking in the views from **Castle Hill** (p. 141), where the Russians handed over Alaska to the United States in 1867. Look into stately **St. Michael's Cathedral** (p. 140), and visit **The Russian Bishop's House** (p. 139), making sure to take a National Park Service tour of the extraordinary upstairs section.

Day ❷: Tlingit History & Sitka Wildlife 🐾🐾🐾

Start the day at the **Sitka National Historical Park** (p. 138) to see an extraordinary collection of historic and contemporary totem poles, meeting Tlingit artisans at work and learning about their culture and history. Now walk through the lovely forested totem park and battlefield sites before continuing to the **Alaska Raptor Center** (p. 140) to see eagles being rehabilitated and learning to fly again after injuries. After lunch, join any one of the half-day **wildlife cruises** that go from the boat harbor to see otters, sea lions, and possibly whales and, if conditions permit, the **sea bird colony** at St. Lazaria Island (p. 141).

Day ❸: Juneau by Ferry 🐾🐾

After a final goodbye to Sitka, board a ferry of the **Alaska Marine Highway System** (p. 92) for a spectacular ride to Juneau that will take most of the day. When you arrive, get a cab from the ferry dock to the airport and rent a car there. If you have time enough left in the day, you can now visit **Mendenhall Glacier**

(p. 160) and drive out the road (that's the common local phrase for it) for a lovely and moving walk to the tiny island of **The Shrine of St. Thérèse** (p. 161). Then move into your lodgings.

Day ❹: Juneau 𝒜★★
In the morning, take a **helicopter flight** to the **Juneau Icefield** (p. 165) for a walk or even a dog sled ride and to get a feel for the immensity of the place and to touch glacier ice. If weather isn't promising for that, visit the **Alaska State Museum** (p. 152) or do the **walking tour** downtown (p. 154). In the afternoon, take a **hike** on one of Juneau's beautiful rainforest or mountain trails (p. 162). There are wonderful choices, such as the **Perseverance Trail** near downtown, but since you have a car, you can hike anywhere and get away from any cruise-ship crowds that may wreck the solitude on some of the paths.

Day ❺: To Gustavus/Glacier Bay 𝒜★★
Fly a prop from Juneau to Gustavus, the gateway to **Glacier Bay National Park** (p. 174), to arrive early enough to orient yourself and take a walk on the trails around the park headquarters to enjoy the shoreline and mossy forest trails, or to go bicycling on the country roads or exploring the long sandy beaches in Gustavus. If you're more ambitious, the waters off Gustavus are among Alaska's best for watching humpback whales, and you'll have time today for a half-day viewing trip. You have two lodging choices here. Check in at the **Glacier Bay Lodge** (p. 178), or stay at a wilderness lodge or country inn in Gustavus (your host will pick you up).

Day ❻: Glacier Bay Tour 𝒜★★
The all-day **boat tour ride** (p. 177) leaves from Bartlett Cove and passes through humpback whale areas and other marine mammal grounds far up the bay to where two large glaciers stand like walls at the edge of the water. Be sure to bring binoculars and warm clothing, as the glaciers produce frigid downdrafting winds, even in the height of summer.

Day ❼: Sea Kayaking in Gustavus 𝒜★★★
I've saved some of the best for last. Your Alaska Airlines jet doesn't leave Gustavus until the evening, so you have time today for a **sea kayaking** outing in the lovely waters of **Bartlett Cove,** where whales frequently visit (p. 178), or, if you are staying in Gustavus, kayak from there (p. 179) into an area where whales are virtually always seen. You can connect the flight from Gustavus through Juneau onward to home.

2 Two National Parks in a Week

An itinerary connecting Kenai Fjords National Park, south of Anchorage, and Denali National Park, to the north, is probably Alaska's most popular land trip for first-time visitors. That's because these parks and the area in between offer so much of what visitors come to Alaska to see, and in spectacular places: at Kenai Fjords, waterways full of whales, marine birds, and glaciers; and at Denali, broad swaths of mountain tundra frequented by bears and caribou. This itinerary is set up to do without a car. To save money and have more flexibility, do the same tour with a car rented in Anchorage.

Day ❶: Arrive in Anchorage 𝒜★
Fly to Anchorage and move into a room in the walkable downtown area, which is near the train station, where you will be departing tomorrow. If the weather is nice, do the **walking tour** (p. 228) to find out what the area is like, or rent a bike and ride on the **Tony Knowles Coastal Trail** (p. 238) to see the waterfowl in West Chester Lagoon, the moose

in Earthquake Park, and maybe even the beluga whales of Cook Inlet. You can go as far as you want: Anchorage's paved bike trails weave through the entire city on wooded greenbelts. In bad weather, or if you're not up to the exercise, spend your time at the **Anchorage Museum of History and Art** (p. 232), getting oriented to history and culture in the Alaska Gallery or checking out contemporary Alaskan art.

Day ❷: To Seward and in Kenai Fjords National Park 𝒢𝒢𝒢

Board an **Alaska Railroad** (p. 209) train to Seward to enjoy some of Alaska's most spectacular scenery along the cliffs and surging ocean waters of Turnagain Arm and through the untouched mountains of the Kenai Peninsula; those who choose to drive get to see similar scenery on a slightly different route (see section 8 in chapter 6 and section 2 in chapter 7). In Seward, board a tour boat to **Kenai Fjords National Park** (see section 6 in chapter 7). Make sure to take a vessel headed all the way into the park so you see the best of the wildlife and get close to a tidewater glacier. Make sure also to take a seasickness remedy such as Dramamine or Bonine at least half an hour before getting on board. If the weather is bad, ask to be switched to a boat tomorrow and do tomorrow's activities instead.

Day ❸: In Seward 𝒢𝒢

After a couple of tiring days, this is a good day to relax in a charming little town. In the morning, join a half-day sea-kayaking paddle from Lowell Point with **Sunny Cove Sea Kayaking** (p. 278). You'll likely see sea otters, birds, intertidal creatures, and maybe spawning salmon. By going in the morning, your chances of smooth water are better. In the afternoon, see the marine life and seabirds you encountered yesterday, up close, at the **Alaska SeaLife Center** (p. 280). Consider joining one of

their educational programs to get even closer to the animals.

Day ❹: Denali National Park

Take the comfortable and convenient **Park Connection Motorcoach Service** (p. 276) from Seward straight to Denali National Park, a journey of more than 360 miles that takes all day. The driver does commentary on the highlights along the route. The bus ride takes almost 10 hours with a couple of long stops. If you drive instead, you can do it in under 7 hours. Arriving in Denali, check into your hotel and stretch your legs, but get to bed promptly to be ready for an early start tomorrow.

Day ❺: Exploring Denali National Park 𝒢𝒢𝒢

This is the primary day to see Denali and the bears, caribou, and other wildlife there. The park shuttle bus system is the key to your visit. Reserve as far ahead as possible (the previous December is not too soon) to get a seat on the earliest bus you can manage (reservation details are on p. 373). Wildlife tends to be more active in the morning. Ride deep into the park, taking along all your food and water, a warm jacket and raincoat, and good hiking shoes. Take a look at the suggestions for cross-country hiking in chapter 8, and then make your choice according to how the countryside looks to you. This is a remarkable chance for a low-stress, low-cost wilderness experience. When you're ready to head home, just catch another bus on the way back.

Day ❻: Denali and Back to Anchorage 𝒢

Your train back to Anchorage doesn't leave until late afternoon, giving you most of the day to enjoy the Denali park entrance area. The new **visitor center** and **Murie Science and Learning Center** (both p. 361) should not be missed: The exhibits and programs here will

---

Tips **Itinerary Add-Ons**

This week-long itinerary to two national parks is fast-paced. You can have a more relaxing trip and allow for more spontaneity by adding days to the stops that are already planned.

If you've still got more time after slowing down the pace, extend your trip with a visit to **Fairbanks**: Instead of taking the train back to Anchorage on day 6, take it northward to Fairbanks. There I recommend renting a car to see the sites and perhaps explore the surrounding rural highways for a few days. (See days 1 and 2 of "A 2-Week Grand Loop," below.) When you're finished, fly home from Fairbanks.

Also consider adding on a **Southeast Alaska** sojourn. When you buy your ticket to Alaska, buy it from Seattle to Anchorage on Alaska Airlines and include a stopover, for a reasonable additional cost, in a Southeast Alaska town—Sitka would be my first choice. Spend time seeing the Russian American history and Tlingit culture there, and getting outdoors (see days 1 and 2 of "Southeast Alaska in a Week," above), before flying on to Anchorage and beginning the itinerary listed at day 1.

---

deepen your understanding of the natural places you have already seen. You also have time for a white-water rafting ride on the Nenana River (p. 363) or a relaxing walk on the nature trails and hiking trails near the visitor center (p. 357). Your train arrives in Anchorage in the evening.

Day ❼: Anchorage Activities ✿

If you can arrange for a flight home late in the day, you'll have time for one more activity in Anchorage. Take the free shuttle to the **Alaska Native Heritage Center** (p. 234) to meet indigenous people and learn about their cultures in a magnificent facility they built, own, and manage.

3 A 2-Week Grand Loop

This driving loop includes much of the best of the Interior, Prince William Sound, Anchorage, and Denali National Park. It allows you to end up where you started, saving money on plane tickets and car rental. And you'll see some remote and off-the-beaten-track places. Not many visitors make it to see Childs Glacier on the Copper River Delta, but I think it's the most spectacular accessible glacier in Alaska. Likewise, a trip to Kennecott, in Wrangell–St. Elias National Park, takes you way off the grid, letting you see an amazing historical ghost town and a community of real, backwoods Alaskans.

Day ❶: Starting in Fairbanks ✿

Fly to Fairbanks, rent a car, and then check into your hotel. If time permits, visit the University of Alaska campus and see the magnificent **UA Museum of the North** and, if you are interested in such

topics, the **Large Animal Research Station** or the **Georgeson Botanical Garden** (all p. 391).

Day ❷: Fairbanks ✿

Take the car to explore the Chena Hot Springs Road and the boreal forest of the

Chena River State Recreation Area (see section 3 of chapter 9). There are several wonderful trails here with varying difficulty levels. As an alternative, arrange for a canoeing paddle on the Chena. When you've finished hiking or paddling and start thinking about sore muscles, stop at the Chena Hot Springs Resort (p. 409) for a soak in the natural mineral springs pond there. At the end of the day, return to Fairbanks for dinner and bed.

Day ❸: The Richardson Highway to Copper Center ✿✿

Today you will drive approximately 260 miles (driving time: under 6 hours) through some of Alaska's most spectacular scenery. Drive east from Fairbanks toward Delta Junction; stop there, after about 2 hours, to see the historical park at Rika's Roadhouse and Landing (p. 421), and for lunch in the town (see section 5 in chapter 9). Now drive south on the Richardson Highway. The best part of the drive is here, as the highway rises up and over the Alaska Range on open tundra country, along the silver Alaska pipeline, and at the edge of a series of alpine lakes. Stop for the night in the Athabaskan village of Copper Center, where there is an exceptional hotel, Copper River Princess Wilderness Lodge (p. 425). Be sure to stop in at the Wrangell–St. Elias National Park Visitor Center (p. 428) to get oriented to the park before your visit tomorrow.

Day ❹: Kennecott ✿✿✿

Get up early to drive east about 85 miles on the Edgerton Highway to Chitina, arriving there in time for the 8:30am Backcountry Connection shuttle (p. 427; reserve in advance) for a ride into the park. It's a rough road over an old railroad line deep into the wilderness park to a copper mine that was abandoned in the 1930s and the ghost town it left behind; by taking the van, you save yourself the driving and the planning

necessary for that tough route, and you gain a guide to show you the way (you will have to cross a footbridge at one point). In Kennecott, check into one of two wilderness lodges (see section 8 of chapter 9) and join a guided walking tour through the enormous ghost-town buildings.

Day ❺: Kennecott to Valdez ✿✿

You have time in the morning to relax and wander in the friendly, quiet setting of Kennecott and its funky sister village of McCarthy. If you have the energy, take a half-day guided hike on the glacier that faces the ghost town. In the afternoon, take an air-taxi flight back to Chitina (p. 428) to get to your car (if you ride the van back, you will get in too late; besides, the view from the plane will be fantastic). Drive back to the Richardson and then south to Valdez, about 190 miles total (4 hours). The mountain scenery is spectacular through Thompson Pass nearing the town. Dine and check into lodgings in Valdez (see section 11 of chapter 7).

Day ❻: Valdez to Cordova Ferry ✿

Today you will be taking your car by ferry for a scenic trip across eastern Prince William Sound to the town of Cordova. Depending on when the ferry leaves, you may have time for a day hike, a museum visit, or another activity in Valdez. In the evening, walk around the quaint, forgotten town of Cordova; if time permits, take a look at the two small community museums (see section 12 of chapter 7).

Day ❼: Prince William Sound Sea Kayaking ✿✿✿

Join Cordova Coastal Outfitters (p. 337) for a sea-kayaking excursion, or, if you are staying at the Orca Adventure Lodge (p. 337), you can go with a guide there. Cordova is an exceptional spot for a day's sea kayaking because waters near town are protected and exceptionally rich in marine mammals. You're almost assured of seeing sea otters and sea lions, and very likely to see many other birds and animals as well (see section 12 of chapter 7).

Day ❽: Copper River Delta ⊛⊛

Drive your car east from Cordova over the gravel Copper River Highway through the Copper River Delta, an immense wetland teeming with wildlife, especially trumpeter swans and other waterfowl. There are several excellent and little-used trails and bird-watching areas along the road. The destination at the far end is the Childs Glacier, an incredible wall of ice that is cut by the Copper River. From a viewing area on the other side of the river, you are remarkably close to the glacier, and in warm weather you can see huge chunks falling off and hear the groan of the moving ice (see section 12 of chapter 7). Spend a third night in Cordova.

Day ❾: Across the Sound to Whittier and Anchorage ⊛

Get back on the ferry for a trip across the sound to Whittier. Again, the scenery is incomparable. Hopefully, you aren't too jaded yet! **Whittier** is a strange little port town built by the military during World War II that is reached only by boat or through a one-lane tunnel almost 3 miles long (p. 270). On the far side of the tunnel, you find yourself on Turnagain Arm about 80 miles from Anchorage. Time permitting, stop in Girdwood for a meal and perhaps a hike or visit to a **historic gold mine** (see section 9 of chapter 6). Finish the day in lodgings in Anchorage.

Day ❿: Anchorage ⊛

Take in the **Alaska Native Heritage Center** (p. 234) in the morning to meet indigenous people and learn about their cultures in a magnificent facility they built, own, and manage. In the afternoon, visit the **Anchorage Museum of History and Art** (p. 232) or spend the day outdoors, hiking, mountain biking, fishing,

or bird-watching (see section 5 of chapter 6). At the end of this fairly low-key day, eat in one of Alaska's best **restaurants,** of which Anchorage has the broadest selection (see section 3 of chapter 6).

Day ⓫: Flying over Mount McKinley ⊛⊛⊛

Get an early start for the 112-mile drive to Talkeetna (less than 2 hours) so you can be there in time for a morning flight over Mount McKinley before the clouds build up in the afternoon. The flight services that carry mountain climbers to the flanks of North America's tallest peak can also take you there for a landing on a high-elevation glacier (p. 345). This flight may provide the most memorable hours of your visit; I know I'll never forget any of the times I've done it. After lunch and a walk around hip and historic Talkeetna (see section 10 in chapter 8), drive about 150 miles (roughly 3 hours) to Denali National Park and check in to your lodgings. You should have time to take in the fascinating exhibits at the visitor center, too.

Day ⓬: Exploring Denali National Park ⊛⊛⊛

This is the primary day to see Denali and the bears, caribou, and other wildlife there. The park shuttle bus system is the key to your visit. Reserve as far ahead as possible (the previous December is not too soon) to get a seat on the earliest bus you can manage. Wildlife tends to be more active in the morning. Ride deep into the park, taking along all your food and water, a warm jacket and raincoat, and good hiking shoes. Take a look at the suggestions for cross-country hiking in chapter 8, and then make your choice according to how the countryside looks to you. This is a remarkable chance for a low-stress, low-cost wilderness experience. When you're ready to head home, just catch another bus on the way back.

Day ⑬: Denali and Drive to Fairbanks ⚘

The drive from Denali back to Fairbanks is only a couple of hours, so you can take your time at the park. A white-water rafting ride in the Nenana River would be exciting; a nature walk in the woods from the visitor center might be calming. Also consider an educational program at the **Murie Science and Learning Center.**

(All in chapter 8.) Drive to your lodgings in Fairbanks in the afternoon.

Day ⑭: Fairbanks

Today you get on a plane and fly back home, but if you have time for a relaxing outing before that, stop off for a stroll in **Pioneer Park** (p. 389) to look at the historic paddle wheeler *Nenana* and the other museums and attractions, and to soak up the small-town ambience.

4 A Week in Alaska with Children

Traveling with children means limiting distances and increasing time for casual fun. The best place to do that is on the Kenai Peninsula south of Anchorage. Despite being a relatively contained area, the peninsula is a microcosm of the whole state, with glaciers, mountains, trails, and rugged coastline like that found over the vast span of the state. To make it even easier, I've suggested renting an RV, which takes the stress out of having to keep children quiet in restaurants and hotel rooms. If you prefer to tent, rent a car instead; you can even rent most of your camping equipment in Anchorage. You'll have even more flexibility and opportunities for spontaneous fun. If you can, improve on this itinerary by adding days in Homer or on the Swan Lake Canoe Route.

Day ❶: Arrive in Anchorage

Fly to Anchorage and pick up your rented **RV** (p. 209), or pick up your car and rented **camping gear** (see "Equipment," p. 237). After buying your groceries, you can get on your way south on the Seward Highway, stopping at the **Bird Creek Campground** (p. 220) or the **Williwaw** or **Black Bear** campgrounds (p. 269). The children will need to burn off some energy after your flight and drive, and this stretch of the highway has some of Alaska's best hiking trails. They are all covered, along with other sites, in section 8 of chapter 6.

Day ❷: To Seward and Kenai Fjords National Park ⚘⚘⚘

Drive the rest of the way to Seward on the Seward Highway and get on a tour boat to see **Kenai Fjords National Park** (see section 6 in chapter 7). Every kid enjoys a boat ride, and on this one you're likely to see whales, glaciers, and lots of seabirds. *Note:* These vessels go into the

open ocean and seasickness is common. Everyone in the family should take a seasickness remedy, such as Dramamine, at least 30 minutes before getting on board (for small children, get the right dosage from your doctor before leaving home). Make sure to take a vessel headed all the way into the park so you see the best of the wildlife and get close to a tidewater glacier. After you get back on land, set up your camp at **Miller's Landing** (p. 283) or drive out of Seward to the **Primrose Campground** (p. 269).

Day ❸: Seward ⚘⚘

You have three choices today, depending on the ages of your children and your interests (consider splitting up, as we often do, so everyone can choose what they enjoy most). (1) The **Alaska Sea-Life Center** (p. 280), where you can encounter the marine life and seabirds you saw in the Fjords yesterday up close, and join in educational programs that get you even closer. Allow half a day.

(2) Go sea kayaking for half the day or the whole day with **Sunny Cove Sea Kayaking** (p. 278). You'll likely see sea otters, birds, intertidal creatures, and maybe spawning salmon. (3) Hike the **Caines Head State Recreation Area** (p. 279) to Fort McGilvray to explore the dark corridors of the abandoned World War II installation. (Bring a flashlight, and go halfway by water taxi to make the hike more manageable.)

Day ❹: Homer ✿

Today you'll drive 135 miles from Seward to the end of the road on the southern Kenai Peninsula and the town of **Homer** (see section 10 in chapter 7). Allow 4 hours, with traffic and some stops. In Homer, you can get hookups for the RV on Homer Spit—a fingerlike point into the middle of Kachemak Bay—or in the downtown part of Homer (still near the beach). Tenters have even more choices. Spend the afternoon beachcombing and enjoying relaxed time on the many miles of pebbled shoreline. If it's raining, take in the **Islands and Oceans Visitor Center** (p. 304) or the **Pratt Museum** (p. 307).

Day ❺: Kachemak Bay Natural History ✿✿✿

Join the nonprofit **Alaska Center for Coastal Studies** (p. 313) for a boat ride to the far side of Kachemak Bay. Their all-day natural history outings take visitors through tide pools to see strange little creatures, through a forest of big trees and wildflowers to learn about ecology, and to an ancient Native archeological site. Even without the guides and all their knowledge, this would still be an enchanting place to visit, with wide beaches, caves, and plenty of space for a kid's energy and imagination to run free. Bring your own lunch.

Day ❻: Swan Lakes Canoeing ✿

Now it's time to start heading back toward Anchorage. Drive about 90 miles to Sterling and stop at **Alaska Canoe & Campground** (p. 301) to rent a canoe you can take down the Swanson River Road to the Swan Lake Canoe route in **Kenai National Wildlife Refuge** (see section 9 in chapter 7). Spend the rest of the day paddling in this placid network of connected lakes, where you can fish and explore without seeing other people. There are numerous primitive campgrounds for the RV overnight, or, if you are tent camping, you may want to paddle to a campsite among the hundreds on the lakes. (If you're thinking this plan will leave you too far from the airport when it's time to fly home tomorrow, fair enough. Skip the canoeing and drive on. There are campgrounds all along the highway to Anchorage, so you can stop wherever you feel comfortable and explore there. See sections 2 and 3 of chapter 7.)

Day ❼: Anchorage

From Sterling to Anchorage is about 150 miles and will take more than 3 hours with traffic. You probably won't have extra time after returning the RV or camping equipment before your flight, but if you do, the best way to spend it is at the **Alaska Zoo** (p. 235), where you will be sure of seeing all the most popular Alaska wildlife.

Days ❽, ❾ & ❿ (Optional): Prince William Sound Loop

Another great trip for kids adds 2 or 3 extra days: Instead of returning to Anchorage on day 7, drive to Whittier and take the Alaska Marine Highway ferry to Valdez. Drive north on the Richardson Highway to Glennallen and west on the Glenn Highway back to Anchorage. An overview of these roads is in "Alaska's Highways a la Carte" (p. 382), and details are included in chapters 7 and 9.

5 A Week of Alaska Winter Sports

Winter is when Alaska is at its best. The snow simplifies the scenery and makes it even more beautiful. The outdoor activities are superb: cross-country and downhill skiing, snowmobiling, ice skating, and dog mushing. The people are especially hospitable, since visitors are rare, and the towns are alive with festivals, sled dog races, and authentic cultural events—not just tourist stuff. There's also a very good chance you will see the northern lights. One proviso: It's impossible to make up a real itinerary for winter sports without knowing individual interests. Avid downhill skiers should spend most of their time on the slopes, for example. So take the list below as a starting point for ideas.

Day ❶: Anchorage Festivals & Dog Sled Races ⚜

To enjoy Anchorage fully, rent a car when you arrive. If you have planned your trip for late February or early March, you can be here when Anchorage is alive with the **Fur Rendezvous Winter Festival,** with its dozens of events and World Championship Sled Dog Race, and the **Iditarod Trail Sled Dog Race** (both p. 211), which starts its journey across Alaska to Nome right after the festival. Local cultural institutions will be busy, too: Visit the **Anchorage Museum of History and Art** (p. 232) during the day and catch a performance in the evening at the **Alaska Center for the Performing Arts** (p. 233).

Day ❷: Anchorage Cross-Country Skiing ⚜⚜

If you've never tried cross-country skiing, Anchorage is an excellent place to try. If you do ski, you can enjoy some of the nation's best trails here in many settings and varying difficulty levels and with grooming that's world class—the ski club here sent its groomers to prepare the trails for the winter Olympics in Salt Lake City and Turin. There are no trail fees. The very best trail system is at **Kincaid Park** (p. 243). **Ski rental** is covered under "Equipment," on p. 237. If you don't want to ski, Anchorage also has groomed ice-skating ponds; Westchester Lagoon has more than a kilometer of **skating trails** (p. 243). At the end of the day,

drive 40 miles to the **Alyeska Prince Hotel** (p. 254) in Girdwood for the night. You will find two of Alaska's best restaurants to choose from for dinner, the **Seven Glaciers** (p. 254) and **Double Musky Inn** (p. 254).

Day ❸: Girdwood Downhill Skiing ⚜⚜⚜

Spend the day on the slopes of Alyeska Resort, skiing near sea level, but mostly above the tree line, and with extraordinary ocean views from the slopes and lifts. Those who don't want to ski have enough to do: sliding at the tube park, swimming in the saltwater pool at the hotel, or skating on the outdoor rink at the base of the mountain.

Day ❹: Girdwood to Fairbanks ⚜

Drive to Anchorage and return the car. Your next destination is Fairbanks, 360 miles north, and I don't recommend driving it unless you are experienced on icy highways and prepared for emergencies. The very best way to go is to take the Alaska Railroad, which runs a single-car train once a week from Anchorage to Fairbanks; it's a spectacular and uniquely Alaskan ride, one of America's last flag-stop trains, but it's unlikely that its infrequent schedule will match yours. The most practical route is to fly from Anchorage to Fairbanks and rent another car when you arrive. That will leave you with most of the day to explore the town. Be sure to stop at the **UA Museum of the North** (p. 391).

> *Tips* **Doubling Up the Seasons**
>
> Here's a little-known approach to experiencing the best of Alaska: Arrive in late March and head to Homer, on the south end of the Kenai Peninsula, as an add-on to the above winter itinerary. The community has lengthy and spectacular cross-country ski trails that usually have plenty of snow all month. At the same time, salmon fishing gets started in March in the waters of Kachemak Bay—there's even a fishing derby joined by hundreds of boats. You can go salmon fishing in the morning and ski in the afternoon! (See "Late March Is Perfect," p. 307.)

Day ❺: Fairbanks Ice Carving 🅐
If you have timed your visit to see the Fur Rendezvous and Iditarod in Anchorage, you should also be able to see the **World Ice Art Championships** (p. 387) in Fairbanks. This amazing spectacle brings together the best ice carvers to create sculptures from enormous blocks of crystal-clear ice excavated from a Fairbanks pond. Some of the works are the size of a two-story building. Make a point of going for a dog sled ride while you're here, too, with **Sun Dog Express Dog Sled Tours** (p. 396) or one of the many other operators giving rides; Fairbanks is a center for the sport, with limitless miles of trails in the hilly boreal forest that extends in every direction.

Day ❻: Chena Hot Springs Resort 🅐🅐
Drive a little over an hour into the Bush for a visit to the hot springs, a unique resort that includes them (unique, for example, in that one of the buildings is made entirely of ice), and the rounded mountains of winter in which the resort is nestled. **Chena Hot Springs Resort** (p. 409) has its flaws, but the experience of floating in a pond of hot artesian water on a day when the air around is below zero more than makes up for them. If you want to do more than soak, lots of activities are available, including snowmobiling and dog mushing. After dark, head out for unsurpassed aurora viewing out here, beyond city lights.

Day ❼: Fairbanks
Today you can take one more swim or ski before returning your car in Fairbanks and returning home by air.

4

Cruising Alaska's Coast

by Jerry Brown & Fran Wenograd Golden

Alaska is one of the top cruise destinations in the world, with three-quarters of a million people sailing the state's coast annually, visiting the towns and wilderness areas of the Southeast and the Gulf of Alaska by day, and burrowing into their ships for effortless travel by night. This element of cruise travel—the fact that it's so *easy*—is one of its main drawing cards for visitors to the Southeast, where the lack of roads between towns makes the waters of the Inside Passage the region's de facto highway. You could do the same routes on the Alaska Marine Highway System (the state ferry), but you'd have to be willing to invest more time—both for the actual traveling and for the planning—and be willing to give up the cruise ship's comforts and diversions. (On the other hand, the ferry gives you unlimited stops along the way and a chance to meet Alaskan residents; see "Exploring Southeast Alaska," in chapter 5.)

Now for the bad news: All those cruise ships aren't necessarily good for Alaska and its residents. Alaskans are known for their hospitality, but we all have our limits. The presence of too many cruise passengers has unquestionably spoiled some of Alaska's quaint places. Once-charming streets are transformed into carnival midways jammed wall to wall with people from simultaneous ships landings. Some communities feel that the cultural bulldozing brought by these floating cities is not worth the economic benefit and have placed limits on the number of ships that can come in to port or levied new taxes based on the number of people the ships bring. After years of fast growth, the industry, too, has begun talk of a "carrying capacity."

As a visitor, you can avoid these problems or you can ignore them. To avoid overcrowded port calls, choose a small-ship cruise that spends less time hopping from town to town and more time enjoying the wilderness. Such vessels also call on small towns that the big ships can't get into. On the other hand, riding a mega-ship is a different kind of fun—the ship itself is an attraction, with far more amenities than any of the towns along the way. If you need to relax and leave all stresses of life at home behind—and if seeing Alaska isn't the most important part of your trip—a big ship is the way to go. You can always travel independently after the cruise to find the real Alaska. (For more on the relative benefits of big versus small cruise ships, see "Weighing Your Cruise Options," below.)

In this chapter, we'll go through the cruise options available in the state, focusing primarily on those that give a real in-depth experience. For even more information, pick up a copy of *Frommer's Alaska Cruises & Ports of Call* (Wiley Publishing, Inc.).

1 Weighing Your Cruise Options

Your three main questions in choosing a cruise in Alaska are "When should I go?", "Where do I want to go?", and "How big a ship?"

WHEN TO GO?

Alaska is a seasonal, as opposed to year-round, cruise destination, with the season generally running May through September, although some smaller ships start up in April. May and September are considered the shoulder season, and lower brochure rates are offered during these months (and more aggressive discounts as well). Cruising in May is extremely pleasant—the crowds have yet to arrive and locals are friendlier than they are later in the season, when they're pretty much ready to see the tourists go home for the winter. There is also the statistical fact that May in the Inside Passage ports is the driest month in the season. Late September, though, also offers the advantage of fewer fellow tourists clogging the ports. The warmest months are June, July, and August, with temperatures generally around 50° to 80°F (10°–27°C) during the day, and cooler at night. In the past couple of years, the temperature soared even higher (when temperatures reached 90°F in Juneau in the summer of 2004, there was much local speculation about global warming). You may not need a parka, but you will need to bring along some outerwear. June 21 is the longest day of the year, with the sky lit virtually all night. June tends to be drier than July and August (we have experienced trips in July when it rained nearly every day). April and May are drier than September, although in early April you may encounter freezing rain and other vestiges of winter. If you are considering traveling in a shoulder month, keep in mind that some shops don't open until Memorial Day, and the visitor season is generally considered over on Labor Day (although cruise lines operate well into Sept).

INSIDE PASSAGE OR THE GULF OF ALASKA?

The Inside Passage runs through the area of Alaska known as Southeast (which the locals also call "the Panhandle"), that narrow strip of the state—islands, mainland coastal communities, and mountains—that runs from the Canadian border in the south to the start of the Gulf in the north, just above the Juneau/Haines/Skagway area. The islands on the western side of the area afford cruise ships a welcome degree of protection from the sea and its attendant rough waters (hence the name "Inside Passage"). Because of that shelter, such ports as Ketchikan, Wrangell, Petersburg, and others are reached with less rocking and rolling, and thus less risk of seasickness. Sitka is not on the Inside Passage (it's on the ocean side of Baranof Island) but is included in most Inside Passage cruise itineraries.

Southeast encompasses the capital city, **Juneau,** and townships influenced by the former Russian presence in the state (**Sitka,** for instance), the Tlingit and Haida Native cultures (**Ketchikan**), and the great gold rush of 1898 (**Skagway**). It is a land of rainforests, mountains, inlets, and glaciers (including Margerie, Johns Hopkins, Muir, and the others contained within the boundaries of **Glacier Bay National Park**). The region is rich in wildlife, especially of the marine variety. It is a scenic delight. But then, what part of Alaska isn't?

The other major cruising area is the **Southcentral** region's Gulf of Alaska, usually referred to by the cruise lines as the "Glacier Discovery Route" or the "Voyage of the Glaciers," or some such catchy title. "Gulf of Alaska," after all, sounds pretty bland.

The coastline of the Gulf is that arc of land from just north of Glacier Bay to the Kenai Peninsula. Southcentral also takes in **Prince William Sound;** the **Cook Inlet,** on the northern side of the peninsula; **Anchorage,** Alaska's biggest city; the year-round **Alyeska Resort** at Girdwood, 40 miles from Anchorage; the **Matanuska** and **Susitna** valleys (the "Mat-Su"), a fertile agricultural region renowned for the record size of some of its produce; and part of the Alaska Mountain Range.

The principal Southcentral terminus ports are **Seward** or **Whittier** for Anchorage. No ships in regular Alaska pattern actually head for Anchorage proper, instead carrying passengers from Seward or Whittier to Anchorage by bus or train. However, let us stress that going on a Gulf cruise does not mean that you don't visit any of the Inside Passage. The big difference is that, whereas the more popular Inside Passage cruise itineraries run round-trip to and from Vancouver or Seattle, the Gulf routing is one-way—northbound and southbound—between Vancouver and Seward or Vancouver and Whittier. A typical Gulf itinerary also visits such Inside Passage ports as **Ketchikan, Juneau, Sitka,** and/or **Skagway.**

The Gulf's glaciers are quite dazzling and every bit as spectacular as their counterparts to the south. **College Fjord,** for instance, is lined with glaciers—16 of them, each one grander than the last. On a 2005 cruise, Fran saw incredible calving at **Harvard Glacier** with chunks of 400- and 500-year-old ice falling off and crashing into the water to thunderous sounds every few minutes (any worries about global warming aside, the sight was spectacular). Another favorite part of a Gulf cruise, though, is the visit to the gigantic **Hubbard Glacier**—at 6 miles, Alaska's longest—at the head of Yakutat Bay.

Cruisetours combine a cruise with a land tour, either before or after the cruise. Typical packages link the cruise with a 3- to 5-day Anchorage/Denali/Fairbanks tour, a 7-day Yukon tour (which visits Anchorage, Denali, and Fairbanks on the way), or a 5- to 7-day tour of the Canadian Rockies. Holland America, Princess, and Cruise West (a distant third) are the three leaders in the cruisetour market. Even if you book with another cruise line, chances are your land tour will be through one of these operators.

BIG SHIP OR SMALL?

Imagine an elephant. Now imagine your pet pug dog, Sparky. That's about the size difference between your options in the Alaska market: behemoth modern ships and small, more exploratory coastal vessels.

SMALL SHIPS   Just as big cruise ships are mostly for people who want every resort amenity, **small** or **alternative ships** are best suited for people who prefer a casual, crowd-free cruise experience that gives passengers a chance to get up close and personal with Alaska's natural surroundings and wildlife. Small ships offer little in terms of amenities: They usually have small cabins, only one lounge/bar and dining room, and no exercise facilities, entertainment, or organized activities. There are little or no stabilizers on most of these smaller ships, and the ride can be bumpy in open water—which isn't much of a problem on Inside Passage itineraries, since most of the cruising area is protected from sea waves. They are also difficult for travelers with disabilities, as only four (Cruise West's *Spirit of '98* and *Spirit of Oceanus,* Clipper's *Clipper Odyssey,* and American West Steamboat Company's *Express of the North*) have elevators. Despite all of this, they're universally more expensive than the big ships and offer fewer discounts. That's the minus side.

Thanks to their smaller size, these ships can go places that larger ships can't, such as narrow fjords, uninhabited islands, and smaller ports that cater mostly to small fishing vessels. Due to their shallow draft, they can nose right up to sheer cliff faces, bird rookeries, bobbing icebergs, and cascading waterfalls that you can literally reach out and touch. Also, sea animals are not as intimidated by these ships, so you might find yourself having a rather close encounter with a humpback whale, or watching other sea mammals bobbing in the ship's wake. The decks on these ships are closer to the waterline, too, giving passengers a more intimate view than they would get from the high decks of the large cruise ships. Some of these ships stop at ports on a daily basis, like the larger ships, while some avoid ports almost entirely, exploring natural areas instead. Small ships also have the flexibility to change direction as opportunities arise—say, to go where whales have been sighted and to linger awhile once a sighting's been made.

Visitors aboard large ships may physically be in Alaska, but unless they're reminded of it, they might never know, such is the disjunction between the glitzy modern ships and the real world outside. Visitors aboard small ships, however, get an experience that's many times more intimate, allowing them to really get in touch with the place they've come to see. For all these reasons, our advice to anyone wanting to experience Alaska rather than just get a postcard impression of it is to spend the extra money for a small-ship cruise. As with any product, you get what you pay for, and by paying extra in the short term for a more intimate cruise, you're almost guaranteed to have an Alaska experience that you'll remember your whole life.

BIG SHIPS   The **big ships** in the Alaska market fall generally into two categories: midsize ships and megaships. Carrying as many as 2,670 passengers, the **megaships** look and feel like floating resorts. Big on glitz, they offer loads of activities, attract many families and (especially in Alaska) seniors, offer a large number of public rooms (including fancy casinos and fully equipped gyms), and provide a wide variety of meal and entertainment options. And though they may feature 1 or 2 formal nights per trip, the ambience is generally casual. The Alaska vessels of the Carnival, Celebrity, Princess, and Royal Caribbean fleets all fit in this category, as does Norwegian Cruise Line's *Spirit, Sun and Star* and Holland America's *Oosterdam*. **Midsize ships** in Alaska

---

Tips Sick Ships

Every summer, hundreds of cruise-ship passengers and plenty of visitors on shore come down with vomiting and diarrhea caused by a bug now known as the norovirus. I've had it, and my review is definitely negative. The miserable illness lasts a day or two; it's rarely serious, although some passengers do end up in the hospital because of dehydration. The virus is extremely contagious from the first symptoms until at least 3 days and up to 2 weeks after it clears up. Touching a contaminated handrail and then your face is enough to catch it. To minimize your chances of contracting the virus, wash hands frequently, drink bottled water, and avoid eating raw food on board, especially shellfish. The Centers for Disease Control also recommended in 1998 that passengers 65 and older or those with chronic illnesses check with their doctors before taking a cruise. The CDC website (www.cdc.gov/nceh/vsp) posts sanitation inspection scores for each ship. Type "norovirus" into their search page to find a fact sheet.

fall into two segments: the ultraluxury Regent *Seven Seas Mariner,* and the modern midsize *Veendam, Ryndam, Volendam, Amsterdam, Zaandam,* and *Statendam* of Holland America Line, and the *Norwegian Dream* of Norwegian Cruise Line. In general, the size of these ships is less significant than the general onboard atmosphere. Both the midsize ships and the megaships have a great range of facilities for passengers. Cabins on these ships range from cubbyholes to large suites, depending on the ship and the type of cabin you book. Big dining rooms and a tremendous variety of cuisines are the norm. These ships carry a lot of people and can, at times, feel crowded.

The sizes of these big ships also come with **three major drawbacks** for passengers: (1) They can't sail into narrow passages or shallow-water ports, (2) their size and inflexible schedules limit their ability to stop or even slow down when wildlife is spotted, and (3) when their passengers disembark in a town, they tend to overwhelm that town, limiting your ability to see the real Alaska.

2 The Best Cruise Experiences in Alaska

Cruise lines are in the business of giving their guests a good time, so they've all got something going for them. Here's my pick of Alaska's best, though, in a few different categories.

- **The Best Ships for Luxury:** With Crystal and Silversea out of the market, luxury in Alaska is now defined by Regent Seven Seas, which offers a casual kind of luxury (a really nice ship with a no-tie-required policy). Regent's **Seven Seas Mariner** offers just that, with plush all-suite cabins (most with private balconies); excellent cuisine (which, as of Jan 1, 2007, includes liquor; wine is complimentary at all times). For the ultimate Alaska experience in a small-ship setting, check out the yachts of American Safari Cruises, where soft adventure comes with luxury accoutrements.

- **The Best of the Mainstream Ships:** Every line's most recent ships are beautiful, but Celebrity's *Infinity* is a true stunner, as is sister ship *Summit.* These modern vessels, with their extensive art collections, cushy public rooms, and expanded spa areas, give Celebrity a formidable presence in Alaska. And the late-model *Sapphire Princess* and *Diamond Princess* have raised the art of building big ships to new heights. Both of these vessels will again be in Inside Passage service this year from Vancouver.

- **The Best of the Small Ships:** Clipper Cruise Line's newest vessel, the *Clipper Odyssey,* is a gorgeous little ship, offering a higher level of comfort than most of the other small ships in this category. Plus, it sails some of Alaska's most exotic itineraries.

- **The Best Ships for Families:** All the major lines have well-established kids' programs. **Holland America** and **Norwegian Cruise Line** win points in Alaska for their special shore excursions for kids and teens, and **Carnival** gets a nod for offering shore excursions for teens.

- **The Best Ships for Pampering:** It's a toss-up—Celebrity's *Infinity* and *Summit* offer wonderful AquaSpas complete with thalassotherapy pools and a wealth of soothing and beautifying treatments, and the solariums on **Royal Caribbean's** *Vision of the Seas, Serenade of the Seas,* and *Radiance of the Seas* offer relaxing indoor-pool retreats.

- **The Best Shipboard Cuisine: Regent Seven Seas** is tops in this category. Of the mainstream lines, **Celebrity** is the best, with its cuisine overseen by renowned

French chef Michel Roux. Dinner in the reservations-only specialty restaurants on both the *Infinity* and the *Summit* ($30 service charge per person) is a world-class dining experience. And there are signs of a new and rather surprising challenger for the cuisine award: **Carnival,** which has upgraded both its main dining room and buffet offerings. The line's *Carnival Spirit* in Alaska boasts the Nouveau Supper Club ($30 service charge per person), where you can enjoy just about as fine a meal as you're likely to find anywhere.

- **The Best Ships for Onboard Activities:** The ships operated by **Carnival** and **Royal Caribbean** offer a very full roster of onboard activities that range from the sublime (lectures) to the ridiculous (contests designed to get passengers to do or say outrageous things). **Princess's** ScholarShip@Sea program is a real winner, with excitingly packaged classes in such diverse subjects as photography, personal computers, cooking, and even pottery.

- **The Best Ships for Entertainment:** Look to the big ships here. **Carnival** and **Royal Caribbean** are tops when it comes to an overall package of show productions, nightclub acts, lounge performances, and audience-participation entertainment. **Princess** also offers particularly well-done—if somewhat less lavishly staged—shows.

- **The Best Ships for Whale-Watching:** If the whales come close enough, you can see them from all the ships in Alaska. Smaller ships, though—such as those operated by **Clipper** and **Cruise West**—might actually change course to follow a whale. Get your cameras ready!

- **The Best Ships for Cruisetours: Princess** and **Holland America** are the entrenched market leaders in getting you into the Interior—of Alaska or the Yukon Territory—either before or after your cruise. They own their own hotels, deluxe motorcoaches, and railcars; and after many years in the business, they both really know what they're doing. Some of the other lines actually buy their land products from Princess or HAL. One of Holland America's strengths is its 3- and 4-night cruises combined with an Alaska/Yukon land package. The company offers exclusive entry into the Yukon's Kluane National Park, and they've added another Yukon gem—Tombstone Territorial Park, near Dawson City, a region of staggering wilderness beauty, Native architecture, stunning vistas, and wildlife. Princess is arguably stronger in 7-day Gulf of Alaska cruises in conjunction with Denali/Fairbanks or Kenai Peninsula land arrangements. Princess's Copper River Lodge is by the entrance to Wrangell–St. Elias National Park.

- **The Best Ports:** Juneau and Skagway are our favorites. Juneau is one of the most visually pleasing small cities anywhere and certainly the prettiest capital city in America. It's fronted by the Gastineau Channel and backed by Mount Juneau and Mount Roberts, offers the very accessible Mendenhall Glacier, and is otherwise surrounded by wilderness—and it's a really fun city to visit, too. As for Skagway, no town in Alaska is more historically significant, and the old buildings are so perfect you might think you stepped into a Disney version of what a gold-rush town should look like. If, that is, you can get over the decidedly turn-of-the-millennium Starbucks operation in the Mercantile Center, the pizza parlor at the bottom of Broadway, and all the upscale jewelry shops that have followed cruise passengers from the Caribbean. There are people who will tell you that Skagway is hokey, touristy—and it is. But if you can get yourself into the right frame of mind, and if you can recall the history of the place—the gold-rush frenzy that literally put the town on the map—it's easier to capture the true spirit of Skagway. The residents have made every effort to retain as much as possible of the architecture and historic significance of their community, and they don't mind sharing it with visitors during the cruise season. For a more low-key Alaska experience, take the ferry from Skagway to Haines, which reminds us of the folksy, frontier Alaska depicted on the TV show *Northern Exposure,* and is a great place to spot eagles and other wildlife. Some ships also stop at Haines as a port of call, usually for a few hours after Skagway.

- **The Best Shore Excursions:** Flightseeing and helicopter trips in Alaska are absolutely unforgettable ways to check out the scenery if you can afford them. But airborne tours tend to be pretty pricey—sometimes approaching $500 a head. A helicopter trip to a dog-sled camp at the top of a glacier (usually the priciest of the offerings) affords both incredibly pretty views and a chance to try your hand at the truly Alaskan sport of dog sledding. (Yes, even in summer: The sleds are fitted with wheels.) It's a great way to earn bragging rights with the folks back home. For a less extravagant excursion, nothing beats a ride on a clear day on the White Pass and Yukon Route Railway out of Skagway to the Canadian border at Fraser—the route followed by the gold stampeders of '98. While you're riding the rails, try to imagine what it was like for those gold seekers crossing the same track on foot! And we also like to get active with kayak and mountain-biking excursions offered by most lines at most ports. In addition to affording a chance to work off those shipboard calories, these excursions typically provide optimum opportunities for spotting eagles, bears, seals, and other wildlife. Another, less hectic shore excursion that goes down well with many passengers is a float ride down one of the more placid stretches of Alaska's myriad rivers, such as the Kenai, the Mendenhall, or the Chilkat. These outings don't involve a lot of paddling—which can be hard work—but instead use the natural flow of the river to propel the four- to six-person rubber raft downstream. And they involve little or no white water. Generally, the group will stop for a picnic lunch en route and return to the staging area by motorcoach or automobile.

3 Booking Your Cruise

Every cruise line has a brochure full of beautiful glossy photos. You'll see low starting rates on the charts, but look further and you'll realize those are for tiny inside cubicles; most of the cabins sell for much more. Sometimes the brochures feature published rates that are nothing more than the pie-in-the-sky wish of cruise lines for what they'd like to sell the cruise (most customers will pay less). We strongly suggest you look at the early-bird savings column and book your cruise early (by mid-Feb for average savings of 25%–30% and sometimes as much as 50%). In reality, you may be able to get the cruise for 40% or 50% off at the last minute. But here's the problem with waiting: Alaska right now is hot, hot, hot. Sure, you may be able to save by taking your chances, but if you don't reserve space early, you may also be left out in the cold. Keep in mind the most expensive and cheapest cabins tend to sell out first. Aggressive marketing by the cruise lines to previous passengers is adding to the increase in early bookings.

Over the past 30 years or so, people have booked their cruises through **travel agents** and, though the **Internet** has knocked some of them out of business, most traditional travel agencies have created their own websites in an effort to keep pace.

Shore Excursions: The What, When & Why

Shore excursions offered by the cruise lines provide a chance for you to get off the ship and explore the sights close up, taking in the history, nature, and culture of the region, from exploring gold-rush-era streets to experiencing Native Alaskan traditions such as totem carving.

Some excursions are of the walking-tour or bus-tour variety, but many others are activity oriented: Cruise passengers have the opportunity to go sea kayaking, mountain biking, horseback riding, salmon fishing, and even rock climbing, and to see the sights by seaplane or helicopter—and maybe even to land on a glacier and go for a walk. Occasionally, with some of the smaller cruise lines, you'll find quirky excursions, such as a visit with local artists in their studios. Some lines even offer scuba diving and snorkeling.

With some lines, shore excursions are included in your cruise fare, but with most lines they are an added (though very worthwhile) expense.

So which is the better way to book a cruise these days? The answer can be both. If you're computer savvy, have a good handle on all the elements that go into a cruise, and have narrowed down the choices to a few cruise lines that appeal to you, websites are a great way to trawl the seas at your own pace and check out last-minute deals, which can be dramatic. On the other hand, you'll barely get a stitch of personalized service searching for and booking a cruise online. If you need help getting a refund or arranging special meals or other matters, or deciding which cabin to choose, you're on your own. In addition, agents usually know about cruise and airfare discounts that the lines won't necessarily publicize on their websites.

BOOKING A SMALL-SHIP CRUISE

The small-ship companies in Alaska—American Safari, Clipper Cruise, Cruise West, Lindblad Expeditions, and Majestic America Line/American West Steamboat Company—all offer real niche-oriented cruise experiences, attracting passengers who have a very good idea of the kind of experience they want (usually educational and/or adventurous, and always casual and small scale). In many cases, a large percentage of passengers on any given cruise will have sailed with the line before. Because of all this, and because the passenger capacity of these small ships is so low (12–235), in general you're not going to find the kind of deep discounts you do with the large ships. Still, for the most part, these lines rely on agents to handle their bookings, taking very few reservations directly. (Clipper is the exception to this rule, taking most of their Alaska bookings directly rather than through agents.) All of the lines have a list of agents with whom they do considerable business and can hook you up with one or another of them if you call (or e-mail) and ask for an agent near you.

BOOKING A MAINSTREAM CRUISE

If you don't know a good travel agent already, try to find one through your friends, preferably those who have cruised before. For the most personal service, look for an agent in your local area, and for the most knowledgeable service, look for an agent who has cruising experience. It's perfectly okay to ask an agent questions about his or her personal knowledge of the product, such as whether he or she has ever cruised in Alaska or with one of the lines you're considering. The easiest way to be sure the agent is experienced in booking cruises is to work with an agent at a **cruise-only agency** (meaning that the whole agency specializes in cruises) or to find an agent who is a **cruise specialist** (meaning he or she specializes in cruises). If you are calling a full-service travel agency, ask for the **cruise desk,** which is where you'll find these specialists.

A good and easy rule of thumb to maximize your chances of finding an agent who has cruise experience and who won't rip you off is to book with agencies that are members of the **Cruise Lines International Association** (CLIA; *℟* 212/921-0066; www.cruising.org) or the **National Association of Cruise Oriented Agencies** (NACOA; *℟* 305/663-5626; www.nacoaonline.com). Members of both groups are cruise specialists. Membership in the **American Society of Travel Agents** (ASTA; *℟* 800/275-2782; www.astanet.com) assures that the agency is monitored for ethical practices, although it does not designate cruise experience.

You can tap into the Internet sites of these organizations for easy access to agents in your area.

THE COST: WHAT'S INCLUDED & WHAT'S NOT

However you arrange to buy your cruise, what you basically have in hand at the end is a contract for transportation, lodging, dining, entertainment, housekeeping, and assorted other miscellaneous services that will be provided to you over the course of your vacation. It's important, though, to remember what extras are *not* included in your cruise fare. Are you getting a price that includes port charges, taxes, fees, and insurance, or are you getting a cruise-only fare? Are airfare and airport transfers included, or do you have to book them separately (either as an add-on to the cruise fare or on your own)? Make sure you're comparing apples with apples when making price comparisons. Read the fine print!

Aside from **airfare,** which is usually not included in your cruise fare (see more on air arrangements below), the priciest addition to your cruise fare, particularly in Alaska, will likely be **shore excursions.** Ranging from about $30 for a bus tour to $299 and up (sometimes as high as $600) for a lengthy helicopter or seaplane flight-seeing excursion, these sightseeing tours are designed to help cruise passengers make the most of their time at the ports the ship visits, but they can add a hefty sum to your vacation costs.

You'll also want to add to your calculations **tips for the ship's crew.** Tips are given at the end of the cruise, and passengers should reserve at least $10 per passenger per day for tips for the room steward, waiter, and busperson. (In practice, we find that most people tend to give a little more.) Additional tips to other personnel, such as the head waiter or maitre d', are at your discretion. On the small ships, all tips often go into one pot, which the crew divides up after the cruise.

Most ships charge extra for **alcoholic beverages** (including wine at dinner) and for soda. Nonbubbly soft drinks, such as lemonade and iced tea, are included in your cruise fare.

MONEY-SAVING STRATEGIES

Cruise pricing is a fluid medium, and there are a number of strategies you can use to save money off the booking price.

EARLY & LATE BOOKING

The best way to save on an Alaska cruise is to **book in advance.** In a typical year, lines offer early-bird rates, usually 25% to 30% off the brochure rate, to those who book their Alaska cruise by mid- to late February of the year of the cruise. If the cabins do not fill up by the cutoff date, the early-bird rate may be extended, but it may be slightly lower—say, a 15% or 20% savings.

If the cabins are still not full as the cruise season begins, cruise lines typically start marketing special deals, usually through their top-producing travel agents. It's our feeling that in 2007, these last-minute discounts, which can run as high as 50%, will be less common than in some previous years. And keep in mind that last-minute deals are usually for a very limited selection of cabins. Planning your Alaska cruise vacation well in advance and taking advantage of early booking discounts is still the best way to go.

SHOULDER SEASON DISCOUNTS

You can save by booking a cruise in the **shoulder months of May or September,** when cruise pricing is lower than during the high summer months. Typically, Alaska cruises are divided into budget, low, economy, value, standard, and peak seasons, but since these overlap quite a bit from cruise line to cruise line, we can lump them into three basic periods:

1. **Budget/Low/Economy Season:** May and September
2. **Value/Standard Season:** Early June and late August
3. **Peak Season:** Late June, July, and early to mid-August

DISCOUNTS FOR THIRD & FOURTH PASSENGERS & GROUPS

Most ships offer highly discounted rates for third and fourth passengers sharing a cabin with two full-fare passengers, even if those two have booked at a discounted rate. It may mean a tight squeeze, but it'll save you a bundle. Some lines offer **special rates for kids,** usually on a seasonal or select-sailings basis, that may include free or discounted airfare.

One of the best ways to get a cruise deal is to book as a **group** of at least 16 people in at least eight cabins. The savings include a discounted rate, and at least the cruise portion of the 16th ticket will be free. Ask your travel agent about any group deals they may offer.

SENIOR DISCOUNTS

Seniors may be able to get extra savings on their cruise. Some lines will take 5% off the top for those 55 and up, and the senior rate applies even if the second person in the cabin is younger. Membership in groups such as AARP is not required, but such membership may bring additional savings.

BOOKING AIR TRAVEL THROUGH THE CRUISE LINE

Except during special promotions, airfare to the port of embarkation is rarely included in the cruise rates, so you'll have to purchase airfare on your own or take advantage of the cruise lines' air add-ons, which is usually a better option. Why? First of all, as frequent customers of the airlines, cruise lines tend to get decent (if not the best) discounts on airfare, which they pass on to their customers. Second, booking air with the cruise line also allows the line to keep track of you. If your plane is late, for instance, they may hold the boat, though not always. When you book air travel with your cruise line, most lines will include **transfers** from the airport to the ship, saving you the hassle of getting a cab. (If you do book the air travel on your own, you may still be able to get the transfers separately—ask your agent about this.) Be aware that once the air ticket is issued by the cruise line, you usually aren't allowed to make changes. The only times it may pay to book your own air transportation are if you are using frequent-flier miles and can get your air travel for free, or if you are particular about which carrier you fly or which route you take.

CHOOSING YOUR CABIN

Cruise-ship cabins run from tiny boxes with accordion doors and bunk beds to palatial multiroom suites with hot tubs on the balcony. Which is right for you? Price will likely be a big factor here, but so should the vacation style you prefer. If, for instance, you plan to spend a lot of quiet time in your cabin, you should probably consider booking the biggest room you can afford. If, conversely, you plan to be out on deck all the time checking out the glaciers and wildlife, you might be just as happy with a smaller (and cheaper) cabin to crash in at the end of the day. Cabins are either **inside** (without a window or porthole) or **outside** (with), the latter being more expensive. On the big ships, the more deluxe outside cabins may also come with **private verandas.** The cabins are usually described by price (highest to lowest), category (suite, deluxe, superior, standard, economy, and others), and furniture configuration ("sitting area with two lower beds," for example).

SPECIAL MENU REQUESTS

The cruise line should be informed at the time you make your reservations about any special dietary requests you have. Some lines offer kosher menus, and all will have vegetarian, low-fat, low-salt, and sugar-free options available.

4 The Small-Ship Cruise Lines

Small ships allow you to see Alaska from sea level, without the kind of distractions you get aboard the big ships—no glitzy interiors, no big shows or loud music, no casinos, no spas, and no crowds, as the largest of these ships carries only 235 passengers. You're immersed in the 49th state from the minute you wake up to the minute you fall asleep, and, for the most part, you're left alone to form your own opinions. Personally, we feel that despite these ships' higher cost, they provide, by far, the better cruise experience for those who really want to get the feel of Alaska.

Small-ship itineraries can be categorized as **port-to-port,** meaning they mimic the larger ships in simply sailing between port towns; **soft-adventure,** meaning they provide some outdoors experiences such as hiking and kayaking, while not requiring participants to be trained athletes; and **active-adventure,** meaning the hiking and kayaking will be the real focus of the trip, and may be strenuous.

On all of these types of cruises, the small-ship experience tends toward education rather than glitzy entertainment. You'll likely get **informal and informative lectures** and sometimes video presentations on Alaska wildlife, history, and Native culture. Meals are served in open seatings, so you can sit where and with whom you like, and time spent huddled on the outside decks scanning for whales fosters great camaraderie among passengers.

Cabins on these ships don't generally offer TVs or telephones, and they tend to be very small and sometimes spartan (see the individual reviews for exceptions). There are no stabilizers on most of these smaller ships, so the ride can be bumpy in rough seas. Alaska Sightseeing's *Spirit of '98* and *Spirit of Oceanus,* Clipper Cruise Line's *Clipper Odyssey,* and American West Steamboat Company's *Empress of the North* have elevators, but in general the small ships are not good choices for travelers who require the use of wheelchairs or have other mobility problems.

AMERICAN SAFARI CRUISES

19101 36th Ave. W., Suite 201, Lynnwood, WA 98036. ℂ 888/862-8881. Fax 425/776-8889. www.amsafari.com.

American Safari Cruises promises an intimate, all-inclusive yacht cruise to some of the more out-of-the-way stretches of the Inside Passage—and it succeeds admirably. The price is considerable—but so is the pampering. The vessels carry between 12 and 22 guests, guaranteeing unparalleled flexibility, intimacy, and privacy. Once passenger interests become apparent, the expedition leader shapes the cruise around them. Black-bear aficionados can chug off in a Zodiac boat for a better look, active adventurers can explore the shoreline in one of the yacht's four kayaks, and slacker travelers can relax aboard ship. A crew-to-passenger ratio of about one to two ensures that a cold drink, a good meal, or a sharp eagle-spotting eye is always nearby on the line's comfortable 120-foot ships.

PASSENGER PROFILE   Passengers, almost always couples, tend to be more than comfortably wealthy and range from 45 to 65 years of age. Most hope to get close to nature without sacrificing luxury. Dress is always casual, with comfort being the prime goal.

SHIPS   More private yachts than cruise ships, the 22-passenger *Safari Quest,* the 12-passenger *Safari Spirit,* and the 12-passenger *Safari Escape* look like Ferraris—all sleek, contoured lines and dark glass. Cabins are comfortable, and sitting rooms are intimate and luxurious, almost as if they had been transported whole from a spacious suburban home. A big-screen TV in the main lounge forms a natural center for impromptu lectures during the day and movie-watching at night. A shipboard chef assails guests with multiple-course meals and clever snacks, barters with nearby fishing boats for the catch of the day, and raids local markets for the freshest fruits and vegetables—say, strawberries the size of a cub's paw and potent strains of basil and cilantro. **Sample rates per person:** Lowest-price outside cabins start at $624 per day for the *Safari Escape;* no inside cabins or suites.

CLIPPER CRUISE LINE

11969 Westline Industrial Dr., St. Louis, MO 63146. ℂ 800/325-0010 or 314/655-6700. Fax 314/655-6670. www.clippercruise.com.

The *Clipper Odyssey* is a down-to-earth, comfortable small ship with a focus on offbeat ports of call, learning, and mingling with your fellow passengers. It's the ideal small-ship cruise for people who've tried Holland America or Princess and now want a more intimate cruise experience. Its ships sail port-to-port itineraries. As aboard Alaska's other small-ship lines, the onboard atmosphere is casual; what lies out there beyond the ship's rail is most passengers' real focus. Throughout the cruise, onboard naturalists offer a series of informal lectures and accompany passengers on shore excursions. Organized shore excursions are offered at each port (the tours cost extra), including flightseeing, sportfishing, and city tours with commentary by local residents. No need to dress up here—everything's casual.

The *Clipper Odyssey* sails a **13-night Inside Passage** between Anchorage/Seward and Seattle visiting Prince William Sound, Valdez, Kayak Island, Point Adolphus, Haines, Tracy Arm, Juneau, Petersburg, Wrangell and Prince Rupert, B.C. and a **14-night Alaska/Russia** visiting Nome, the Bering Sea, Big Diomede Island, Naukan and Uelin (Russia), St Lawrence Island, St Paul Island, St George Island, the Aleutians and Kodiak Island.

PASSENGER PROFILE   The majority of Clipper passengers are well-traveled, 50-and-older couples. Most are well educated though not academic, casual though not sloppily so, and adventurous in the sense that they're up for a little hiking but are happy to be able to get back to their comfortable cabins or have a drink in the lounge afterward.

SHIPS   Along with Cruise West's *Spirit of Endeavor* and *Spirit of Oceanus,* and Glacier Bay's *Executive Explorer,* the 120-passenger **Clipper Odyssey** is one of the best choices in Alaska for someone who wants small-ship intimacy and flexibility but doesn't want to skimp on comfort. Their public rooms are larger and more appealing than those aboard competing ships, and all cabins are outside. Except for those at the lowest level (which have portholes), all cabins have picture windows. Although relatively simple in ingredients and presentation, the cuisine is easily the equal of all but the best that is served aboard mainstream megaships. **Sample rates per person:** Lowest-price outside cabins on *Odyssey,* $543 per day for 14-night cruise. No inside cabins.

CRUISE WEST

2301 5th Avenue, Suite 401, Seattle, WA 98121. ℰ **800/426-7702** or 206/441-8687. Fax 206/441-4757. www.cruisewest.com.

Cruise West is the largest operator of small ships in Alaska, offering port-to-port itineraries in various areas of Alaska, friendly service, and a casual onboard atmosphere. Like all small ships, Cruise West's ships can navigate in tight areas such as Misty Fjords and Desolation Sound, visit tiny ports such as Petersburg and Haines, and scoot up close to shore for wildlife-watching. But these are not adventure cruises. These vacations are for people who want to visit Alaska's coastal communities and see its wilderness areas up close and in a relaxed, comfortable, small-scale environment without big-ship distractions.

The operative words here are casual, relaxed, and friendly. At sea, the lack of organized activities on the line's port-to-port itineraries leaves you free to scan for wildlife, peruse the natural sights, or read a book. In port—whether one of the large, popular ports or a less visited one—the line arranges some novel, intimate shore excursions, such as a visit with local artists at their homes outside Haines or an educational walking tour led by a Native guide in Ketchikan. All excursions are included in the price.

Ships sail a 4-night Glacier Bay, between Juneau and Glacier Bay; an 8-night Inside Passage itinerary, an 11-night Coastal Odyssey between Vancouver and Whittier, and a 13-night Bering Sea Cruise between Anchorage and Yanrakynnot (Russia).

PASSENGER PROFILE   Cruise West passengers tend to be older (typically around 60–75), financially stable, well educated, and independent-minded—folks who want to visit Alaska's ports and see its natural wonders in a relaxed, dress-down atmosphere.

SHIPS   The 96-passenger **Spirit of '98,** a replica of a 19th-century steamship, carries its Victorian flavor so well that fully two-thirds of the people we met on board thought the ship had been a private yacht at the turn of the 20th century. If you use a wheelchair or otherwise have mobility problems, note that the *'98* is one of only four small ships in Alaska that has an elevator. (The line's *Spirit of Oceanus,* American West Steamboat Company's *Empress of the North,* and Clipper's *Clipper Odyssey* are the others.) The 78-passenger **Spirit of Alaska** and **Spirit of Columbia,** and 84-passenger

Spirit of Discovery are all spartan ships designed to get passengers into small ports and allow them to see the state up close. The 102-passenger *Spirit of Endeavour,* on the other hand, offers among the highest levels of small-ship comfort of any small ship in Alaska, comparable to Clipper's *Yorktown Clipper* and Glacier Bay's *Executive Explorer.* The line's new 114-passenger *Spirit of Oceanus,* the former *Renaissance V* of Renaissance Cruises, is the line's most luxurious ship, able to sail more far-flung itineraries. **Sample rates per person:** Lowest-price inside cabins $387 for a 4-night cruise, lowest-price outside $522 for an 8-night cruise.

LINDBLAD EXPEDITIONS

96 Morton St., 9th Floor, New York, NY 10014. (�C) **800/397-3348** or 212/765-7740. Fax 212/265-3770. www. expeditions.com.

Lindblad Expeditions specializes in environmentally sensitive, soft-adventure vacations that are explorative and informal in nature, designed to appeal to the intellectually curious traveler seeking a cruise that's educational as well as relaxing. Days aboard are spent learning about the Alaskan outdoors from high-caliber expedition leaders trained in botany, anthropology, biology, and geology, and observing the world around you either from the ship or during shore excursions, which are included in the cruise package. Educational films and slide presentations aboard ship precede nature hikes and quick jaunts aboard Zodiac boats. Flexibility and spontaneity are keys to the experience, as the route may be altered at any time to follow a pod of whales or school of dolphins.

The ships cruise an 11-night itinerary between Juneau and Seattle and a 7-night trip between Juneau and Sitka.

PASSENGER PROFILE   Lindblad Expeditions tends to attract well-traveled and well-educated, professional, 55-and-older couples who have "been there, done that" and are looking for something completely different in a cruise experience.

SHIPS   The 62-passenger *Sea Lion* and *Sea Bird* (built in 1981 and 1982, respectively) are nearly identical and are, in fact, very similar to many of the other small ships in the Alaska market. All are basic vessels built to get you to beautiful spots, and feature a minimum of public rooms and conveniences: one dining room, one bar/lounge, and lots of deck space for wildlife and glacier viewing. Cabins are small and functional. **Sample rates per person:** Lowest-price outside cabins $626 per day for an 11-night cruise; no inside cabins or suites.

MAJESTIC AMERICA LINE/AMERICAN WEST STEAMBOAT COMPANY

2101 4th Avenue, Suite 1150, Seattle, WA 98121. (℃) **800/434-1232** or 206/292-9606. Fax 206/340-0975. www.americaweststeamboat.com.

Carrying 235 passengers, this company's ship, *Empress of the North,* belongs in a whole new, separate category—stern-wheelers. Clearly, the appeal here is the nostalgia. Pure Americana—that's what the *Empress of the North* represents. There is not much in the way of organized fun and games. A lecturer accompanies each cruise, offering insights into the passing scenery and cultures. Shore excursions are included in the price, but don't look for kayaks off the back of the vessel, or scuba diving or anything of that nature.

The line offers 7- and 11-night Inside Passage cruises.

PASSENGER PROFILE   Not necessarily filthy rich, but probably comfortably off. And they are experienced cruisers.

SHIPS   *Empress of the North,* built in 2003, carries 235 passengers. It has four decks, two lounges, and elevators. The cabins are large by small-ship standards, all have views of the ocean, and 105 out of 112 of the cabins have verandas. Elegance is the byword in public rooms. **Sample rates per person:** Outside cabins start at $441 per day for 11-night cruise, suites start at $533 for 11-night cruise; no inside cabins.

5 The Big-Ship Cruise Lines

The ships featured in this section vary in size, age, and offerings, but share the common thread of having more activities and entertainment options than any one person can possibly take in over the course of a cruise. You'll find swimming pools, health clubs, spas, nightclubs, movie theaters, shops, casinos, multiple restaurants, bars, and special kids' playrooms, and, in some cases, sports decks, virtual golf, computer rooms, martini bars, and cigar clubs, as well as quiet spaces where you can get away from it all. In most cases, you'll find lots and lots of onboard activities, including games, contests, classes, and lectures, plus a variety of entertainment options and show productions, some very sophisticated.

CARNIVAL CRUISE LINES

Carnival Place, 3655 NW 87th Ave., Miami, FL 33178-2428. ℂ **800/CARNIVAL.** Fax 305/471-4740. www.carnival.com.

Translating the line's warm-weather experience to Alaska has meant combining the "24-hour orgy of good times" philosophy to include the natural wonders, so you may find yourself bellying up to the rail with a multicolored party drink to gawk at a glacier. Drinking and R-rated comedians are part of the scene, as are "hairy-chest contests" and the like.

Entertainment is among the industry's best, with each ship boasting a dozen dancers, a 10-piece orchestra, comedians, jugglers, and numerous live bands, as well as a big casino. Activity is nonstop. Cocktails begin to flow before lunch, and through the course of the day you can learn to country line-dance or ballroom dance, take cooking lessons, learn to play bridge, watch first-run movies, practice your golf swing by smashing balls into a net, or just eat, drink, shop, and then eat again. Alaska-specific naturalist lectures are delivered daily. In port, Carnival offers **nearly 100 shore excursions,** divided into categories of easy, moderate, and adventure. For kids, the line offers Camp Carnival, an expertly run children's program with activities that include Native arts and crafts sessions, lectures conducted by wildlife experts, and special shore excursions for teens.

Ships cruise the Gulf of Alaska route. In May and September, Inside Passage cruises that visit Glacier Bay are offered.

PASSENGER PROFILE   Overall, Carnival has some of the youngest demographics in the industry: mostly under 50, including couples, lots and lots of singles, and a good share of families. It's the same Middle America crowd that can be found in Las Vegas and Atlantic City and at Florida's megaresorts. This is not a sedate, bird-watching crowd. They may want to see whales and icebergs, but they will also dance the Macarena on cue.

SHIPS   The 2,124-passenger megaship *Carnival Spirit* returned to Alaska in 2006. It offers plenty of activities, great pool and hot-tub spaces (some covered for use in chillier weather), a big oceanview gym and spa, and more dining options than your doctor would say is advisable. **Sample rates per person:** Lowest-price inside cabins $107, lowest outside $142, lowest suite $257 per night for an Inside Passage cruise.

CELEBRITY CRUISES

1050 Caribbean Way, Miami, FL 33132. ℰ **800/437-3111** or 305/262-8322. Fax 800/437-5111. www.celebrity cruises.com.

Celebrity Cruises offers a great combination: a classy, tasteful, and luxurious cruise experience at a moderate price—it's definitely the best in the midpriced category. The line's ships are real works of art; its cuisine—guided by Michel Roux, one of the top French chefs in Britain—is outstanding; its service first-class, friendly, and unobtrusive; and its spa facilities among the best in the business.

A typical day might offer bridge, darts, a culinary art demonstration, a trapshooting competition, a fitness-fashion show, an art auction, a volleyball tournament, and a not-too-shabby stage show. Resident experts give lectures on the various ports of call, the Alaskan environment, glaciers, and Alaskan culture. For children, Celebrity ships employ a group of counselors who direct and supervise a camp-style children's program. Activities are geared toward different age groups. There's an impressive kids' play area and a lounge area for teens.

Last year Celebrity began visiting the tiny port of Icy Straight Point between Juneau and Glacier Bay; the port offers a prime vantage point for whale- and wildlife-watching and easier access to the Alaskan wilderness.

The company offers 7-night Inside Passage and 7-night Gulf of Alaska itineraries.

PASSENGER PROFILE   The typical Celebrity guest is one who prefers to pursue his or her R&R at a relatively relaxed pace, with a minimum of aggressively promoted group activities. The overall impression leans more toward sophistication and less to the kind of orgiastic Technicolor whoopee that you'll find, say, aboard a Carnival ship. You'll find everyone from kids to retirees.

SHIPS   Sleek, modern, and stunningly designed, the 1,896-passenger *Mercury* and the larger, 1,950-passenger *Infinity* and *Summit* have a lot of open deck space and lots of large windows that provide access to the wide skies and the grand Alaskan vistas. All the ships (but especially *Mercury*) feature incredible spas with hydrotherapy pools, steam rooms, and saunas, plus health and beauty services and exceptionally large fitness areas. **Sample rates per person:** Lowest-price inside cabins $107, lowest outside $149, lowest suite $271 per night for a 7-night cruise.

HOLLAND AMERICA LINE

300 Elliott Ave. W., Seattle, WA 98119. ℰ **800/426-0327** or 206/281-3535. Fax 206/286-7110. www.holland america.com.

Holland America can be summed up in one word: *tradition.* The company was formed way back in 1873 as the Netherlands-America Steamship Company, and its ships today strive to present an aura of history and dignity, like a European hotel where they never let rock stars register. And thanks to its acquisition over the years of numerous land-based tour operators, Holland America has positioned itself as Alaska's most experienced and comprehensive cruise company.

Though most of the line's Alaskan fleet is relatively young, the ships are designed with a decidedly "classic" feel—no flashing neon lights here. Similarly, Holland America's ships are heavy on more mature, less frenetic kinds of activities. You'll find good bridge programs and music to dance (or just listen) to in the bars and lounges, plus health spas and the other amenities found on most large ships. The line has improved its nightly show-lounge entertainment. In 2006, the line will continue its Artists in Residence Program, arranged through the Alaska Native Heritage Center in Anchorage, with Alaska Native artists accompanying all 7-night cruises and demonstrating traditional art forms such as ivory and soapstone carving, basket weaving, and mask making. Club HAL is one of the industry's more creative children's programs, though the children's playrooms (often no more than a meeting room stocked with toys) are no match for what you find on the latest Princess or Celebrity megaships.

Alaska itineraries include 7-night Inside Passage cruises and 7-night Gulf of Alaska cruises.

PASSENGER PROFILE   Holland America's passenger profile used to reflect a much older crowd. Now the average age is dropping, partly thanks to an increased emphasis on its Club HAL program for children and partly due to some updating of its onboard entertainment. Still, HAL's passengers in Alaska include a large percentage of middle-aged-and-up vacationers.

SHIPS   The 1,266-passenger *Maasdam, Ryndam, Statendam,* and *Veendam* are more or less identical. All cabins have a sitting area and lots of closet and drawer space, and even the least expensive inside cabins run almost 190 square feet, quite large by industry standards. Outside doubles have either picture windows or verandas. The striking dining rooms, two-tiered showrooms, and Crow's Nest forward bar/lounges are among these ships' best features. The newer, 1,440-passenger *Volendam* and *Zaandam* are larger and fancier, with triple-decked oval atriums, 197 suites and deluxe staterooms with private verandas, five showrooms and lounges, and an alternative restaurant designed as an artist's bistro, featuring drawings and etchings. The smallest cabin is a comfortable 190 square feet. The *Oosterdam, Westerdam,* and *Zuiderdam,* the newest vessels in the fleet, weigh 85,000 tons and carry 1,848 passengers. These are sophisticated, spacious yet intimate ships well equipped to support HAL's position as a force in the Alaska market. **Sample rates per person:** Lowest-price inside cabins $121 per diem, lowest outside $164, lowest suite $205 for a 7-night cruise.

NORWEGIAN CRUISE LINE

7665 Corporate Center Dr., Miami, FL 33126. ℭ 800/327-7030 or 305/436-4000. Fax 305/436-4120. www.ncl.com.

Norwegian Cruise Line (NCL) offers an informal and upbeat onboard atmosphere on the *Norwegian Sun,* sailing from Vancouver, and the *Norwegian Sky* and *Norwegian Star,* both sailing from Seattle. The line excels at activities, and its recreational and fitness programs are among the best in the industry. Though the onboard food has been described as unmemorable, NCL recently inaugurated what has become a very popular casual-dining policy that allows passengers to dine when they want pretty much any time between 5:30pm and midnight, with whomever they want, dressed however they want.

In Alaska, NCL offers an Alaskan lecturer, wine tastings, art auctions, trapshooting, cooking demonstrations, craft and dance classes, an incentive fitness program, and bingo, among other activities. Passengers can choose from a good selection of soft-adventure shore excursions, including hiking, biking, and kayaking. Entertainment is generally strong and includes Vegas-style musical productions. The top-notch kids' program includes an activity room, video games, an ice-cream bar, and guaranteed babysitting aboard, plus sessions with park rangers and escorted shore excursions.

The line offers 7-night Inside Passage cruises.

PASSENGER PROFILE   In Alaska, the demographic tends more toward retirees than on the line's warmer-climate sailings, but you'll find families as well, including grandparents bringing along the grandkids.

SHIPS   The 2,050-passenger *Norwegian Sun* is the first ship built with NCL's new "freestyle" dining policy in mind, as evidenced by the nine separate onboard restaurants. An airy eight-story glass atrium welcomes visitors in the lobby. More than two-thirds of the guest rooms (about 650 in all) have ocean views, and closet space is more generous than on other NCL ships. The 2,240-passenger *Norwegian Star* has no fewer than 11 rooms in which people can eat—depending on the time of day. The *Star* is well equipped for the sports-minded and active vacationer—in addition to the fitness center, there are three heated pools, a jogging/walking track, and a wide array of sports facilities. The 2,466-passenger *Norwegian Pearl* is getting lots of attention from the company, and it shows. **Sample rates per person:** Lowest-price inside cabins $129 a night, lowest outside $154, lowest suite from $209 for a 7-night cruise.

PRINCESS CRUISES

24305 Town Center Dr., Santa Clarita, CA 91355. © **800/LOVE-BOAT** or 661/753-0000. Fax 661/753-1535. www.princess.com.

Consistency is Princess's strength. With new ships joining its fleet like so many cars off a Detroit assembly line, you'd think that maintaining acceptable service standards could be a problem. All things considered, though, Princess accomplishes this rather well. Throughout the fleet, the service in all areas—dining room, lounge, cabin maintenance, and so on—tends to be of consistently high quality. Aboard Princess, you get a lot of bang for your buck, attractively packaged and well executed. Although its ships serve every corner of the globe, nowhere is the Princess presence more visible than in Alaska. Through its affiliate, Princess Tours, it owns wilderness lodges, motorcoaches, and railcars in the 49th state, making it one of the major players in the Alaska cruise market, alongside Holland America.

The *Dawn* and the *Sun Princesses* are older vessels—the *Sun* is all of 11 years old and the *Dawn* is 2 years younger. (The *Regal,* the oldest in the Alaska fleet, built in 1991, was in Inside Passage rotation out of San Francisco in 2006; it will not sail Alaska this year.) As a function of their age, the *Dawn* and *Sun Princesses* lack some of the pizzazz of their newer fleet mates.

Princess passengers can expect enough onboard activities to keep them going morning to night, if they've a mind to, and enough nooks and crannies to allow them to do absolutely nothing, if that's their thing. Kids are well taken care of, with especially large children's playrooms. On shore, the line's shore-excursion staffs get big points for efficiency.

Princess offers 7-night Inside Passage cruises, 7-night Gulf of Alaska cruises, and a special 10-night round-trip Inside Passage cruise that departs from San Francisco.

PASSENGER PROFILE   Typical Princess passengers are likely to be between, say, 50 and 65, and are experienced cruisers who know what they want and are prepared to pay for it. Recent additional emphasis on its youth and children's facilities has begun to attract a bigger share of the family market.

SHIPS   Princess's diverse fleet in Alaska essentially comprises eight ships, five of which entered service since the millennium. The fleet includes the *Diamond* and *Sapphire,* which were completed in 2004; the *Coral* and *Island,* of 2002/2003 vintage and the *Golden* (2001), not to mention the *Pacific Princess,* which was built in

1999 and extensively refurbished in 2002 when it was purchased from Renaissance Cruises. The *Sun* (1995) and the *Dawn* (1997) complete Princess's Alaska complement this year. The ships generally are pretty but not stunning, bright but not gaudy, spacious but not overwhelmingly so, and decorated in a comfortable, restrained style that's a combination of classic and modern. They're a great choice when you want a step up from Carnival, Royal Caribbean, and NCL but aren't interested in the slightly more chic ambience of Celebrity or the luxury of Seven Seas. **Sample rates per person:** Lowest-price inside cabins $114 per diem, lowest outside $157, lowest suite $214 for a 7-night cruise.

REGENT SEVEN SEAS CRUISES

1000 Corporate Dr., Suite 500, Fort Lauderdale, FL 33334. © 800/285-1835. www.TheRegentExperience.com.

Regent's guests travel in style and extreme comfort. Its brand of luxury is casually elegant and subtle; its cuisine among the best in the industry. The line assumes, for the most part, that passengers want to entertain themselves on board, so organized activities are limited, but they do include lectures by local experts, well-known authors, and the like, plus facilities for card and board games, blackjack and Ping-Pong tournaments, bingo, big-screen movies with popcorn, and instruction in the fine arts of pompom making, juggling, and such. Bridge instructors are on board on select sailings. The line has a no-tipping policy and offers creative shore excursions. Room service is about the best you'll find on any ship, and the cuisine is excellent. As of January 1, 2007, Regent switches to a fleetwide liquor-inclusive policy on all departures.

The Seven Seas Mariner sails a 7-night Gulf of Alaska itinerary.

PASSENGER PROFILE   Regent tends to attract passengers in their 40s to 60s who have a household income of more than $200,000 and don't like to flaunt their wealth. The typical passenger is well educated, well traveled, and inquisitive.

SHIPS   Cabins on the 700-passenger *Seven Seas Mariner* are all oceanview suites, and all have private verandas. The standard suite is a large 301 square feet; some suites can interconnect if you want to book two for additional space. The Constellation Theater is two-tiered and designed to resemble a 1930s nightclub. There are two additional lounges, plus a casino and the Connoisseur Club, a cushy venue for predinner drinks and after-dinner fine brandy and cigars. The ship's spa offers Judith Jackson European spa treatments using a variety of herbal and water-based therapies. **Sample rates per person:** Lowest-price suite $528 a night for 7-night cruise; no inside or standard outside cabins.

ROYAL CARIBBEAN INTERNATIONAL

1050 Caribbean Way, Miami, FL 33132. © 800/327-6700 or 305/379-2601. www.royalcaribbean.com

Royal Caribbean sells a mass-market style of cruising that's reasonably priced and offered aboard informal, well-run ships with nearly every diversion imaginable—craft classes, horse racing, bingo, shuffleboard, deck games, line-dancing lessons, wine-and-cheese tastings, cooking demonstrations, art auctions, and the like—plus elaborate health clubs and spas, covered swimming pools, large open sun deck areas, and innumerable bars, lounges, and other entertainment centers. The Viking Crown Lounge and other glassed-in areas make excellent observation rooms from which to see the Alaska sights. Royal Caribbean spends big bucks on entertainment, which includes high-tech show productions. Headliners are often featured. Port lectures are offered on topics such as Alaska wildlife, and the line offers some 65 shore excursions. The line's children's activities are some of the most extensive afloat.

The line offers 7-night Inside Passage and Gulf of Alaska cruises.

PASSENGER PROFILE   The crowd on Royal Caribbean ships, like the decor, rates pretty high on the party scale, though not quite at the Carnival level. Passengers represent an age mix from 30 to 60, and a good number of families are attracted by the line's well-established and fine-tuned kids' programs. In Alaska, Royal Caribbean is focusing more on international sales than the entrenched market leaders, Princess and Holland America, which often results in sailings populated by a good many international passengers, especially travelers from Asia and Europe.

SHIPS   Royal Caribbean owns the largest ship in the world, the new *Freedom of the Seas* at 158,000 tons, and four 142,000-ton Voyager-class vessels. Although these 3,000-plus-passenger ships—which introduced such cruise-ship design features as ice-skating rinks, rock-climbing walls, and cabins overlooking interior atrium areas—are not in Alaska this year, Royal Caribbean does offer the very up-to-date 2,500-passenger *Radiance of the Seas.* The ship is joined in Alaska for the second year by its sister ship, the similarly dimensioned *Serenade of the Seas.* The *Radiance* is in Gulf of Alaska service between Vancouver, B.C., and Seward, the *Serenade* in Inside Passage service out of Vancouver. Also returning to Alaska in 2007 is the 2,435-guest *Vision of the Seas.* **Sample rates per person:** Lowest-price inside cabins $100 per diem, lowest outside $128, lowest suite $221 for a 7-night cruise.

5

Southeast Alaska

Rich, proud people have lived in Southeast Alaska for thousands of years, fishing the region's salmon and hunting in its primeval forests, where the tree trunks grow up to 10 feet thick. In canoes, they explored the hundreds of misty, mossy, enchanted islands where animals, trees, and even ice had living spirits. The salmon lived under the sea in human form, becoming fish in the summer to swim in seething masses up the rivers and streams as a gift of food to feed their kin, the people. In return, the people treated the salmon with respect and ceremony, allowing their spirits to return to human form under the sea to live another year. So blessed, the Tlingit and Haida built great carved houses and poles, fought wars, owned slaves, traded with faraway tribes, and held rich contests of giving called potlatches, where they passed on the stories that still help explain their mysterious world. Even for a modern non-Native walking in the grand quiet of the old-growth rainforest, it's easy to find yourself listening for the spirits of the trees speaking their mysteries.

Discovery subsists on mystery, and Southeast Alaska is still being discovered. A honeycomb of limestone caves under Prince of Wales Island wasn't found until 1987. Explorers continue to map its endless miles of caverns, finding the bones of extinct animals, the artifacts of some of North America's earliest prehistoric people, bear dens, strange eyeless shrimp that live nowhere else, and even underground streams that host spawning salmon. The caves network at every step into passages that lead straight up or down or off to either side, some only wide enough to allow a cool wind to pass through. The unfathomable intricacy is exhilarating but also a bit disquieting, like a breath of the supernatural, for it is proof of the unknowable.

Southeast Alaska unfolds like this intricate, hidden world below the tree roots. On a map, this land of ice and forest may not look as large as other parts of Alaska, but the better you know it, the bigger it becomes, until you have to surrender to its immensity. You don't need to go underground to experience the sensation—you can feel it by gazing from a boat at the fractal geometry of the endlessly folded, rocky shoreline. On a cruise through the Inside Passage, you'll marvel at all the little beaches and rocky outcroppings you pass, hundreds of inviting spots each day. If you were to stop at random on any one of those uninhabited beaches in a skiff or kayak, you'd find you could spend a day surveying just a few acres of rocks, the overhanging forest, and the tiny pools of water left behind by the tide. And if you gazed down into any one of those pools, you'd find a complex world all its own, where tiny predators and prey live out their own drama of life in the space of a few square feet. The discoveries you make in Southeast Alaska depend only on how closely you look.

The region stands apart from the rest of Alaska, and not only because most of it can't be reached by road. No other part of the state shares the mysterious, spirit-laden quality of the coastal rainforest. No other area has such mild weather, more akin to the climate of the Pacific Northwest than to the heart of Alaska. Certainly, no other area in Alaska gets as much rain, nor do many other places on earth. The traditional Native people here differed from other Alaska Natives, too: They were far richer and left behind more physical artifacts. The Tlingit, Haida, and Tsimshian exploited the wealth nature gave them and amplified it by successfully trading with tribes to the south and over the mountains in today's British Columbia and Yukon Territory. In their early contact, the Tlingits even briefly defeated the Russian invaders in the Battle of Sitka

and, after white dominance was established, managed to save many of their cultural artifacts and stories.

Along with its other riches and complexities, Southeast Alaska has many charming small towns and villages that seem to have grown organically from the mountainsides bordering the fjords and channels of the islands. With economies that predate Alaska's oil boom, they developed slowly, their fishermen building houses to hand down to their children. The smaller towns remain completely exempt from the American blight of corporate sameness. Real, old-fashioned main streets are prosperous with family businesses where the proprietors know their customers by first name.

1 Exploring Southeast Alaska

A unique and inviting aspect of travel in Southeast Alaska is that no roads connect most of the communities. People are forced to get out of their speeding cars and ride on boats, where they can meet their fellow travelers and see what's passing by—slowly. The islands of the region form a protected waterway called the **Inside Passage,** along which almost all of the region's towns are arrayed. Thanks to the **Alaska Marine Highway** ferry system, it's inexpensive to travel the entire passage, hopping from town to town and spending as much time in each place as you like. And if you're short on time, air service is frequent, with jets to the major towns and commuter planes to the villages.

GETTING AROUND BY FERRY: THE ALASKA MARINE HIGHWAY

The state-run **Alaska Marine Highway System** (© **800/642-0066** or 907/465-3941, 800/764-3779 TTY; www.ferryalaska.com) is a subsidized fleet of big, blue-hulled ferries whose mission is to connect the roadless coastal towns of Alaska for roughly the same cost you'd pay if there were roads and you were driving. Call for a free schedule or download it from the website.

PROS & CONS   The ferry system's strengths are its low cost, frequent summer sailings, inexpensive stopovers, exceptional safety, and the fact that kids love it. In the summer, Forest Service guides offer interpretive talks on board in Southeast's Inside Passage and in Prince William Sound. The system's weaknesses are crowding during the July peak season; the fact that if they're late, they can be many hours late (although they're usually on time); and a shortage of cabins, which means that most people have to camp on deck or in chairs during overnight passages.

ROUTES   The system mostly serves Southeast Alaska, though it does cover most of coastal Alaska, with two sailings a month (the *Kennicott*) connecting Southeast Alaska with the Southcentral region nearer Anchorage. The smaller Southcentral ferries link communities all the way out the Aleutian chain (see chapters 7 and 10).

Southeast Alaska

▲ Mt. Hubbard

Yakutat Bay

Yakutat
← to
Whittier

**YUKON
TERRITORY**

▲ Mt. Fairweather

Skagway

**Glacier Bay
National
Park**

Haines

*Glacier
Bay*

*Lynn
Canal*

Cross Sound

*Gulf of
Alaska*

Gustavus

*Icy
Strait*

Mendenhall Glacier

Pelican

★ Juneau

*Chicagof
Is.*

**Admiralty
Island**

*Baranof
Is.*

Angoon

*Tracy
Arm*

*Stephens
Passage*

**Cassiar
Mountains**

Sitka

Alexander Archipelago

Kake

▲ Mt. Ratz

*Frederick
Sound*

Kupreandf
Is.

▲ Kates Needle

*Kuiu
Is.*

Petersburg

*Chatham
Strait*

Wrangell

*Prince of
Wales Is.*

*Clarence
Strait*

Mt.
Pattullo ▲

Craig

*Revillagigedo
Is.*

Hyder

Hydaburg

Ketchikan

■ Misty Fjords
National
Monument

Metlakatla

Prince
Rupert

**Queen
Charlotte
Islands**

*Graham
Is.*

*Moresby
Is.*

Hecate Strait

*Banks
Is.*

*Pitt
Is.*

*Pacific
Ocean*

Butedale

*Princess
Royal Is.*

**BRITISH
COLUMBIA**

Inside Passage	– –
Ferry Route	- - -
Whale-watching	

Bella Bella

Bella Coola

Queen Charlotte Strait

0   50 Miles

0   50 Kilometers

↓ to
Bellingham

Coast   Mountains

Rocky   Mountains

Area of
Coverage

YUKON
TERRITORY

BRITISH
COLUMBIA

VANCOUVER
ISLAND

Vancouver

Victoria

Seattle

⌒*Tips* Ferry System Booking

The **Alaska Marine Highway** (www.ferryalaska.com) has an online booking system that makes figuring out a trip far easier than using its inscrutable timetables. Just be sure to make vehicle and cabin reservations as early as possible. If you need to talk to a real person for advice or to change reservations, the system has a toll-free number (℃ **800/642-0066**), but it can be understaffed, with waits of half an hour for an operator. Try instead the staff at the ferry office in Anchorage, where they have less to do, at ℃ **907/272-7116.** That office is staffed for walk-ins, too, and is located in the Alaska Public Lands Information Center, at 4th and F streets in Anchorage. Or call **Viking Travel,** in Petersburg (℃ **800/327-2571** or 907/772-3818; www.alaskaferry.com), which will accept your booking before the official reservation system opens and then reserve it the first day the system becomes available. They can also take care of all your air and tour connections, lodgings, activities, travel insurance, and so on.

You can sometimes avoid crowds on the boats with careful scheduling. Ferries are crowded northbound in June and southbound in August and both ways in July. If you're planning to fly one way and take the ferry the other, go against the flow.

In Southeast, five large mainline ferries serve the Inside Passage. Two begin their run in British Columbia's Prince Rupert and travel about 30 hours north to Haines and Skagway. Two more start in Bellingham, Washington; travel 37 hours nonstop to Ketchikan; and then continue up to Skagway and Haines. Each of these four towns is connected to the rest of the world by roads, but none of the towns in between are. In the summer, the large ships stop at least daily (although sometimes in the middle of the night) in Ketchikan, Wrangell, Petersburg, Juneau, Haines, and Skagway. Some make a side trip to Sitka on the way. Juneau is the hub, with many extra sailings north from Juneau on the Lynn Canal to Haines and Skagway. These are offered by a newer fast ferry, the *Fairweather,* which travels at up to 45 mph. It cuts travel times in half, connecting Juneau with Haines 5 days a week, Skagway 4 days a week, and Sitka 2 days a week.

Smaller ferries connect the larger towns to tiny villages up and down the coast. They mostly take local residents back and forth to their villages, so they're rarely crowded. Those routes are definitely off the beaten track, offering the cheapest and easiest way to absorb the real wilderness of the Alaska Bush. The feeder ferries have food service but no cabins.

CONNECTING TO THE FERRY   From the south: The appeal of taking the Alaskan Marine Highway ferry to Alaska from Bellingham, Washington, is obvious, but it is not cheaper than flying and it takes 2 days just to get to Ketchikan. The popular alternative is to board the ferry in Prince Rupert, British Columbia. You can get to Prince Rupert by rail or road (this is covered under "Getting There & Getting Around" in chapter 2).

Another option is to get to Prince Rupert by riding the **BC Ferries** system, 1112 Fort St., Victoria, B.C., Canada V8V 4V2 (℃ **888/223-3779** or 250/386-3431; www. bcferries.bc.ca). This is quite a trek and requires that you have a car. First, you have to take a ferry to the southern end of British Columbia's Vancouver Island, then drive the island's length to its northern end, and then take another ferry from Port Hardy to Prince Rupert. That ferry docks next to the Alaska ferry.

You can get to Vancouver Island's southern end from the mainland from two directions. BC Ferries goes to Nanaimo from near the city of Vancouver. **Black Ball Transport** (© 360/457-4491; www.cohoferry.com) operates a ferry from Port Angeles, Washington, to Victoria.

To the north: The northern end of the Inside Passage Alaska ferry system rejoins the road system in Skagway and Haines. Haines is a bit closer to the rest of the state but has just one independent car-rental agency. Skagway has more transportation options, including car and RV rental and a bus that connects Skagway to Whitehorse, Yukon, where you can catch another bus onward on the Alaska Highway. See the Skagway and Haines sections, later, for details.

By air: By flying to your starting point, you can save time and reduce the chance of having to spend the night sleeping in a chair on board. Long hauls on the ferry can be uncomfortable and don't save you much money over flying, but the ferry is much less expensive and more appealing for connecting nearby towns within the Southeast region. Fly into Juneau, Sitka, or another sizable town and plan a ferry trip from there, stopping at various places before returning to catch your plane home.

STOPPING OVER   Buying ahead or booking round-trip tickets saves you nothing on the ferry, and stopovers of any length add little to the cost of your passage. Use the ferry system to explore the towns along the way, grabbing the next ferry through to continue your journey. If you travel without a vehicle, you generally don't need reservations (with the possible exceptions of the Bellingham sailings and passages across the Gulf of Alaska). Bring along a bike, or even a sea kayak, to have total freedom in exploring Southeast. Port calls usually are not long enough to see the towns; if the boat is running late, they may not let you off at all.

WALK-ON FARES   Fares change every year, so don't count on these, but they may help for planning. The adult walk-on fare from Prince Rupert to Skagway is $184. Bellingham to Ketchikan is $232, Bellingham to Skagway $352. Juneau to Sitka is $44. All fares for children 6 to 11 are roughly half-price, and children 5 and under ride free. Off season only, October through April, the driver of a vehicle does not need a separate walk-on ticket, and other fare sales sometimes go in effect.

BRINGING VEHICLES   In the summer, you often need a reservation for any chance of taking your vehicle on the ferry, and reserving 3 to 6 months early is wise. The vehicle spots on the ferries from Bellingham and Prince Rupert are particularly coveted. Fares vary according to the size of the car as well as your destination; a passage from Prince Rupert to Haines for a typical 15-foot car is $383, the passage from Bellingham to Haines is $772. You also have to buy a separate ticket for each person on the ferry, including, in summer, the driver. Renting a car at your destination will probably save money and enhance your trip because you will have more flexibility in your stopovers. You can carry a kayak, canoe, or bike on the ferry (without a car) quite inexpensively.

CABIN RESERVATIONS   Sometimes you can snag a cabin from the standby list when you sail (board quickly and approach the purser immediately), but generally you must reserve ahead for the summer season. Cabins from Bellingham book many months ahead. A two-berth outside cabin (one with a window) with a bathroom is under $75 on most town-to-town hops, $172 from Prince Rupert to Haines, and $381 from Bellingham to Haines, plus the cost of your ticket. The great majority of the cabins are small and spartan, coming in two- and four-bunk configurations, but for a premium you can reserve a more comfortable sitting-room unit on some vessels. Most cabins have tiny private bathrooms with showers. Try to get an outside cabin so that you can watch the world go by. Cabins can be stuffy, and the windowless units can be claustrophobic as well.

DO YOU NEED A CABIN? If you do a lot of layovers in Southeast's towns, you can arrange to do most of your ferry travel during the day, but you'll probably have to sleep on board at least once (unless you make that hop by air). You can't sleep in your vehicle. One of the adventures of ferry travel is finding a chair to sleep in or setting up a tent on deck with everyone else. The patio-furniture lounge chairs on the covered outdoor solarium, on the top deck, are the best public sleeping spot on board, in part because the noise of the ship covers other sounds. If you're tenting, the best place is behind the solarium, where it's not too windy. On the *Columbia,* that space is small, so grab it early. Bring duct tape to secure your tent to the deck in case you can't find a sheltered spot, as the wind over the deck of a ship in motion blows like an endless gale. The recliner lounges are comfortable, too, but can be stuffy. Bring a pillow. If the ship looks crowded, grab your spot fast to get a choice location. **Showers** are available, although there may be lines. Lock any valuables and luggage you don't need in the **coin-operated lockers.** If all that sounds too rugged, or if you have small children and no tent, reserve a cabin. It offers a safe and private home base and a good night's rest, and there's a certain romance to having your own compartment on a public conveyance.

FERRY FOOD If you can, bring at least some of your own food on the ferry. Ferry food can get boring after several meals in a row and, during peak season, lines are sometimes unreasonably long. We usually bring a cooler or picnic basket. Even if you're traveling light, you can pick up some bagels and deli sandwiches on a stopover or long port call.

THE BEST RUNS Going to Sitka through **Peril Straits,** the ferry fits through extraordinarily narrow passages where no other vessel of its size ventures; the smooth, reflective water is lovely, and you may see deer along the shore. The **Wrangell Narrows,** between Petersburg and Wrangell, is also an incredible ride, day or night, as the ship accomplishes a slalom between shores that seem so close you could touch them, in water so shallow the schedules must be timed for high tide. **Frederick Sound,** between the Narrows and Wrangell, is prime for whale sightings. Approaching Skagway through the towering mountains of the **Lynn Canal** fjord also is impressive.

GETTING AROUND BY AIR & ROAD

BY AIR Air travel is the primary link between Southeast's towns and the rest of the world. Several towns without road access have jet service, provided by **Alaska Airlines** (© **800/252-7522;** www.alaskaair.com), the region's only major airline. Juneau is Southeast Alaska's travel hub. Ketchikan and Sitka each have a few flights a day, while Wrangell, Petersburg, and Yakutat each have one flight going each direction daily. Gustavus is served from Juneau once daily during the summer. Some of these "milk runs" never get very far off the ground on hops between small towns: On the 31-mile Wrangell-to-Petersburg flight, the cabin attendants never have time to unbuckle. Haines and Skagway, which have highway connections, don't receive visits from jets, but all the towns and even the tiny villages have scheduled prop service.

Tips Seeing Southeast from Above

If you can possibly afford it, take a **flightseeing** trip at some point during your trip. The poor man's way of doing this is to fly a small prop plane on a scheduled run between two of your destinations instead of taking the ferry. If you ask, the pilot may even go out of his or her way to show you the sights; if not, you'll still gain an appreciation for the richness and extreme topography of the region. Each flight service also offers flightseeing tours in addition to scheduled runs between destinations. Flightseeing costs as little as $100 for a brief spin. Flight services are listed in each town section.

Like the ferries, the planes can be quite late. Each of the airports in Southeast has its own challenges caused by the steep, mountainous terrain and the water. In bad weather, even jet flights are delayed or they "overhead"—they can't land at the intended destination and leave their passengers somewhere else. Your only protection against these contingencies is travel insurance, a schedule that allows plenty of slack in case you're significantly delayed, and low blood pressure.

BY ROAD   Three Southeast Alaska communities are accessible by road: Haines, Skagway, and the village of Hyder, which lies on the British Columbia border east of Ketchikan and is accessible from the gravel Cassiar Highway through Canada. If you're driving the Alaska Highway, passing through Haines and Skagway adds 160 miles of very scenic driving to the trip, as well as a 15-mile ferry ride between the two towns (they're separated by 362 road miles). This ferry route is not as heavily booked as the routes heading between either town and Juneau, but it's still a good idea to reserve ahead. You also can rent a car from Haines or Skagway for travel to the rest of the state at the end of a ferry journey (Haines saves just 60 miles over Skagway), and buses serve Skagway. Details are listed in the sections on each of those towns. If you're driving the highway in winter, you should be prepared for weather as cold as 40°F below zero (–40°C). Alaska winter driving information is under "Health & Safety" in chapter 2.

Bikes make a lot of sense for getting around Southeast's small towns, which tend to be compact. You can rent one almost anywhere you go, or bring your own on the ferry. The networks of abandoned or little-used logging roads on some islands offer limitless routes for mountain biking. Elsewhere, Forest Service hiking trails are often open for riding.

GETTING OUTSIDE IN THE TONGASS NATIONAL FOREST

Nearly all of Southeast Alaska, stretching 500 miles from Ketchikan to Yakutat, is in Tongass National Forest. The towns sit in small pockets of private land surrounded by 17 million acres of land controlled by the U.S. Forest Service—an area nearly as large as the state of Maine and considerably larger than any other national forest or national park in the United States. The majority of this land has never been logged, and the rate of logging has dropped dramatically in recent years, preserving one of the world's great temperate rainforests in its virgin state. It's an intact ecosystem full of wildlife and mostly free of human development. Indeed, you quickly forget it *is* the Tongass National Forest. Since it always surrounds you when you're in this region, it's simply the land.

(Fun Fact Why There Are No Highways

A tectonic plate under the Pacific Ocean brought the islands of the Southeast Alaska Panhandle from across the globe and squished them up against the plate that carries the landmass of Canada. Along the line of this glancing collision, large glacial mountains thrust up and islands were stretched and torn into the fractured geography that makes the area so interesting. In short, it has been too expensive to build roads through those icy mountains and across the steep, jumbled terrain of the islands. But Alaska's current leaders are pursuing various transportation projects, regardless of the price. A plan approved by Governor Frank Murkowski calls for a road from Juneau almost to Skagway, with a short ferry ride at the end. The project is extremely controversial, and its completion now depends on the changing winds of politics as much as the geography.

FOREST SERVICE CABINS

One of the best ways to get into Southeast's wilderness is by staying at one of the scores of remote Forest Service Public Recreation Cabins. These are simple cabins without electricity or running water where you can lay your sleeping bag on a bunk and sit by a warm woodstove out of the rain. You need to bring everything with you, as if camping, but it's a good deal more comfortable than a tent. And you will probably find yourself in a stunningly beautiful spot, perhaps with your own lake and a boat for fishing. Cabins are located along canoe trails, on beaches best reached by sea kayak, on high mountain lakes accessible only by floatplane, and along hiking trails. We do this with our family every summer by boat or canoe or on foot. I've learned three critical lessons to pass on: Do your research, pack carefully (take all the essentials but little more), and spend at least 3 nights, preferably a week, to make all the effort pay off with real relaxation.

GETTING CABIN INFORMATION   In this chapter, I've listed a few of the cabins in the sections devoted to the town that they're closest to, but for complete information, check the Tongass website (www.fs.fed.us/r10/tongass) or contact the visitor centers and ranger offices listed with each town section in this chapter. The main contact point for recreation information for the whole forest is the **Southeast Alaska Discovery Center,** 50 Main St., Ketchikan, AK 99901 (© **907/228-6220** or 907/288-6237 TTY; fax 907/228-6234). You'll need a good map to figure out where the cabins are, and an idea of how to get there and how much travel will cost—generally, the cost of transportation will be many times larger than the cabin-rental fee of $25 to $45 a night. Few cabins can be reached without a boat or aircraft, and for all but large groups, flying is the economical way to go. A flight service can help you choose a cabin according to your interests and how far you can afford to fly. You may be able to rent the gear you need, but you'll have to reserve that ahead, too. The solution to these puzzles is different for each town; I've listed where to find help in the town sections later in this chapter.

RESERVING A CABIN OR CAMPSITE   The cabins and some campgrounds are reserved through a national system. Don't rely on the reservations operators or website for advice or cabin information—they're in upstate New York—instead, pose your questions to the ranger station nearest where you plan to go. The rangers are friendly and have probably stayed in the cabin you're interested in. Use the reservations system when you're ready to book; you can check cabin availability dates and reserve on the Internet (www.reserveusa.com). By telephone, contact the **National Recreation Reservations Service (NRRS),** operated by **Reserve America,** at © **877/444-6777,** 877/833-6777 TTY, or 518/885-3639 from overseas. The phone lines are open April 1 through Labor Day, Monday through Friday from 8am to midnight EST, Saturday and Sunday 8am to 9pm; off season Monday through Friday 10am to 7pm, Saturday and Sunday 10am to 5pm. They take American Express, Discover, MasterCard, and Visa, or you can reserve on the phone and then pay by certified check or money order. Cabins are available for reservation on a first-come, first-served basis, starting 180 days ahead, and campsites are available 240 days ahead. For the most popular cabins, you need to be online the minute reservations become available to have a chance.

2 Ketchikan: On the Waterfront

Had they known about it, the film noir directors of the 1950s would have chosen the Ketchikan (*ketch*-e-kan) waterfront for Humphrey Bogart to sleuth. The black-and-white montage: A pelting rain drains from the brim of his hat, suspicious figures dart through saloon doors and into the lobbies of concrete-faced hotels, a forest of workboat masts fades into the midsummer twilight along a shore where the sea and land seem to merge in miles of floating docks. Along Creek Street, salmon on their way to spawn swim under houses chaotically perched on pilings beside a narrow boardwalk; inside, men are spawning, too, in the arms of legal prostitutes. Meanwhile, the faces of totem poles gaze down on the scene disapprovingly, mute holders of their own ancient secrets.

Today, the director hoping to re-create that scene would have his work cut out for him removing the T-shirt shops and bright street-front signs that seek to draw in throngs of cruise passengers to buy plastic gewgaws. Not so long ago, Ketchikan was a rugged and exotic intersection of cultures built on the profits of logging Southeast's rainforest, but in a decade, it has transformed itself into a tourist center, softening its rough edges while selling their charm to visitors. And the changes can only accelerate. More and bigger ships are coming, and Southeast Alaska's last major timber mill—the Louisiana Pacific–owned pulp plant in Ward Cove, north of town—closed in 1997, due in part to environmental concerns. A major portion of the mill was blown up in 1999; they sold tickets to see who would get to press the button on the explosives, but the occasion was less than festive, as former employees saw the scene of their work lives disappear into dust. The idea of a smaller, more labor-intensive operation, intended to replace the lost pulp mill jobs with jobs sawing lumber and making veneer, has had a rocky time getting off the ground. In the meantime, the economy had moved on.

On summer days, the white cruise ships tower above the town like huge new buildings on the dock facing Front Street, the downtown's main drag. Each morning their gangways disgorge thousands of visitors, clogging the streets and, for a few hours, transforming the town into a teeming carnival. On their short visits, the passengers explore the closest of the twisting streets, see the museum at the Southeast Alaska Discovery Center, or take a tour to one of the totem pole parks. Then evening comes, the streets empty, and the cruise ships slide off quietly on the way to their next port.

That is when a sense of the old, misty, mysterious Ketchikan starts to return. Visitors with a little more time to spend, and the willingness to explore beyond the core tourist areas, can drink in the history and atmosphere of the place. Stay in a quaint old hotel, hike a boardwalk path through the primeval rainforest, and visit the museums, clan house replicas, and totem pole parks that make Ketchikan a center of Tlingit and Haida culture.

Ketchikan also makes a great jumping-off point for some spectacular outdoor experiences, including a trip to **Misty Fjords National Monument** (p. 112). As the state's fourth-largest city, Ketchikan is the transportation hub for the southern portion of Southeast Alaska. (The nicknames Gateway City and First City refer to its geographical location and transportation function.) Seaplanes based on docks along the waterfront are the taxis of the region, and a big interagency visitor center can get you started on your explorations of the area. Ketchikan is one of the wettest spots on earth, with rain measured in the hundreds of inches; quality rain gear is requisite for any activity, in the wilds or in the streets of town.

ESSENTIALS

GETTING THERE

BY AIR   **Alaska Airlines** (© 800/252-7522; www.alaskaair.com) jet service connects Ketchikan south to Seattle nonstop and north to Petersburg, Wrangell, Sitka, Juneau, and Anchorage. Commuter lines run wheeled planes and floatplanes from Ketchikan to the neighboring communities and also offer fishing packages and flightseeing.

The airport is on Gravina Island, to which there is no bridge (perhaps you've heard of the famous "Bridge to Nowhere" Congressional scandal—the Ketchikan airport is its destination). A ferry runs each way every half-hour (more frequently at peak times). Believe the airline when it tells you when to catch the ferry for your plane. The fare is $5 for adults, $2 ages 6 to 12, and free for children under 6. Returning the same day is free. The fare for cars is $6 each way, no matter how soon you come back. See "Getting Around," below, for how to get from the airport ferry dock to town and for a water taxi right from the airport (a fun option).

BY FERRY   The dock is 2½ miles north of downtown. **Alaska Marine Highway** ferries (© 800/642-0066; www.ferryalaska.com) run 6 hours north to Wrangell and 6 hours south to Prince Rupert, British Columbia. The walk-on fare from Prince Rupert is $58; from Wrangell, it's $36. Call the local terminal at © 907/225-6181 or 907/225-6182 for a recording of updated arrival and departure times.

ORIENTATION

Ketchikan is on huge **Revillagigedo Island,** popularly known as **Revilla Island.** The downtown area, pretty much taken over by tourism, is quite compact and walkable, but the whole of Ketchikan, including a second commercial area used by locals, is long, strung out between the Tongass Narrows and the mountains. A waterfront road goes under various names through town (it's Water St. on our map), becoming North Tongass Highway as it stretches about 16 miles to the north. Saxman is 2½ miles to the south of downtown on the 14-mile South Tongass Highway.

GETTING AROUND

You can spend a day seeing the downtown sights on foot, but you will need transportation to get to the totem pole parks or airport.

BY SHUTTLE OR BUS   The **Airporter Shuttle** (© 907/225-5429) meets each flight and picks up at the major hotels according to a schedule you can get at the front desk. They'll pick up anywhere else by arrangement. The $20 fare downtown includes

Ketchikan

Fair St.
To Deer Mountain Trail →

Church ⛪
Post Office ⊠
Information ⓘ
Stairs ▮▮▮

0   1/8 Mi
0   1/8 Km

Ketchikan Creek
Park Ave.
Woodland Ave.
Deermount St.
Harris St.
Funicular
Creek St.
Stedman St.
Thomas St.
Bawden St.
Revilla St.
Pine St.
Grant St.
Edmond St.
Mission St.
Mill St.
Main St.
Pine St.
Dock St.
Front St.
Tunnel
Water St.
Ketchikan Visitors Bureau ⓘ
To Airport, Ferry Dock, Totem Bight, and Salmon Falls Resort ←
Cruise Ship Docks
Tongass Narrows
Thomas Basin

Alaska
Fairbanks ○
Anchorage ○ Cordova ○ Juneau ○
Kenai ○ Sitka ○
Ketchikan

ACCOMMODATIONS ■
Cape Fox Lodge **13**
First United Methodist Church Hostel **1**
New York Hotel **17**

DINING ◆
Diaz Café **19**
Good Fortune Chinese Restaurant **10**
Halibut Hole **10**
Luna's **5**
Steamers **3**

ATTRACTIONS ●
Cape Fox Hill-Creek Street Funicular **14**
City Park **21**
Creek Street **15**
Deer Mountain Tribal Hatchery and Eagle Center **20**

Dolly's House **16**
Fish Ladder **11**
Married Men's Trail **12**
Southeast Alaska Discovery Center **4**
Tongass Historical Museum **7**
Totem Heritage Center **22**

SHOPPING ●
Alaska Eagle Arts **10**
Blue Heron Gallery and Gifts **8**
Eagle Spirit Gallery **2**
Exploration Gallery **6**
Herring Cove Originals **17**
Hide-A-Way Gifts **16**
Main Stay Gallery **9**
Market Place Cape Fox **5**
Salmon Landing/Dockside Gallery **3**
Soho Coho **10**

the cost of the airport ferry, a good deal for a single passenger, but a couple would save money taking the ferry and then getting a cab. Since the shuttle drives right to the terminal, however, it's still the best way to go for a couple with a lot of luggage. The least costly way to the airport or ferry dock is the **Ketchikan Gateway Borough bus** (ⓒ **907/225-8726**). To get downtown or to points south from the airport costs $1.50. Buses come every half-hour. Your luggage must fit under the seat.

BY TAXI   The local taxis, mostly minivans, are convenient and usually easy to flag down on the single main road through town. Try **Sourdough Cab** (© **907/225-5544**). Taking a cab to the airport terminal is costly because of time that runs up on the meter waiting for and riding the ferry to Gravina Island. Take the cab just to the airport ferry dock and walk on. If you have a lot of luggage, take the Airporter Shuttle (see above), which goes to the terminal, or take a water taxi from downtown.

BY WATER TAXI   Only in Ketchikan could you take a boat from the airport to your hotel. **Tongass Water Taxi** (© **907/225-8294**) also happens to be reasonably priced and quick. The six-passenger boat runs back and forth from near the airport ferry dock to downtown all day. The first person is $18 and each additional person $7. It also crosses the same route as the airport ferry (without going on to downtown) for $6. Several hotels are right on the water, so the water taxi can take you almost to your door. The operator holds up a sign in the baggage claim area to meet arriving flights, or you can call to arrange a pick-up.

BY RENTAL CAR   **Budget** has locations at the airport or in town (© **800/527-0700** reservations, 907/225-6004 at the airport, 907/225-8383 in town; www.budget.com). **Alaska Car Rental** (© **800/662-0007** or 907/225-5000; www.akcarrental.com) also has offices at the airport or in town.

BY BIKE   A bike is a good way to get around Ketchikan. A 2½-mile bike trail runs along the water to Saxman, stopping a few blocks short of the totem pole park there, and another goes north 6 miles to the Ward Lake Recreation Area. Bikes are for rent at the **Great Alaska Lumberjack Show,** on Main Street near the cruise-ship dock (© **888/320-9049;** www.lumberjacksports.com). The cost is $8 an hour, $25 half-day.

VISITOR INFORMATION

The **Southeast Alaska Discovery Center,** 50 Main St., Ketchikan, AK 99901 (© **907/228-6220** or 907/288-6237 TTY; fax 907/228-6234; www.fs.fed.us/r10/tongass), is much more than a visitor center. Housed in a large, attractive building of big timbers and cedar, and located a block from the cruise-ship dock, the center is the best museum in the region when it comes to illustrating the interaction of the region's ecology and human society, including both traditional Native and contemporary uses. An auditorium here shows a high-tech slide show. Admission to these facilities in summer costs $5, free ages 15 and under, with a $15 family maximum; in winter it's free. Without paying, you can get guidance about planning your time and activities in the outdoors. An information kiosk is located near the entrance, and downstairs you'll find a luxurious bookstore decorated like an explorer's private den with room to relax. The center is open May through September daily from 8am to 5pm, October through April Tuesday through Friday noon to 4pm and Saturday 10:30am to 4:30pm.

The **Ketchikan Visitors Bureau,** 131 Front St., Ketchikan, AK 99901 (© **800/770-3300** or 907/225-6166; fax 907/225-4250; www.visit-ketchikan.com), stands right on the cruise-ship dock, offering town information and desks where tourism businesses sell their wares, including tickets for tours. The center is open daily in the summer from 8am to 5pm and when cruise ships are in town; weekdays only in winter.

SPECIAL EVENTS

There's a detailed events calendar at **www.visit-ketchikan.com**.

The **Festival of the North** brings art to Ketchikan audiences for the entire month of February, including theater, ballet, live music, poetry readings, and a wearable-art show the first weekend of the month that is a highlight of the winter. The festival is sponsored by the Ketchikan Area Arts and Humanities Council, 716 Totem Way (© **907/225-2211**; www.ketchikanarts.org).

King Salmon Derby, a nearly 60-year-old tradition, takes place at the end of May and the beginning of June.

The Fourth of July celebration is huge, with a long parade on Front Street attended by mobs of locals and visitors. After the parade, there's a **Timber Carnival** with an all-afternoon loggers' competition at the baseball field near City Park on Park Avenue; admission is free. Don't miss the legendary **pie sale** at St. John's Church at 423 Mission St., where a slice, ice cream, and beverage is $5. Fireworks are at 11pm on Gravina Island, best viewed from the cruise ship dock.

The crowd-pleasing **Great Alaskan Lumberjack Show** goes on all summer behind the Alaska Discovery Center (© **888/320-9049** or 907/225-9050; www.lumberjack sports.com). Canadian and U.S. professional teams of lumberjacks—highly skilled and cute, too, according to my friend Charlotte—compete three or more times daily, mostly to an audience of cruise-ship passengers. The show is charming and intentionally a little goofy. The setting is attractive and comfortable. Tickets are $30 adults, half-price ages 5 to 12—expensive for a show than lasts 1 hour, but the great majority of clients leave happy.

The Blueberry Arts Festival, held the first weekend of August, has booths, music, and food, and is put on by the Ketchikan Area Arts and Humanities Council, mentioned just above as the sponsor of the Festival of the North. Check with the council for the **Monthly Grind** coffeehouse variety show as well, which happens in the Saxman Tribal House every third Saturday from September to May.

FAST FACTS: Ketchikan

Banks A bank with an ATM is at 306 Main St.; grocery stores and the visitor center also have ATMs.

Hospital Ketchikan General Hospital is at 3100 Tongass Ave. (© **907/225-5171**).

Internet Access SeaPort Cyberstations (© **907/247-4615**; www.seaportel.com) is at the ship dock on the second floor at 5 Salmon Landing.

Police Call © **907/225-6631** for nonemergencies.

Post Office The main post office is at 3609 Tongass Ave.; a more convenient downtown substation is 2 blocks from the cruise ship dock at the Barnaby's Old time Curios, 422 Mission St.

Taxes Sales tax is 6%. Room taxes total 13%.

EXPLORING KETCHIKAN

Pick up a copy of the **Official Historic Ketchikan Walking Tour Map,** available all over town, which has three ways through town to follow and loads of information about sites of both great and modest interest on the way.

Many motorized tours of the town vie for customers, getting the majority of their clients from the cruise ships but welcoming independent travelers when space is available. Tickets are for sale at the visitor center on the dock. Besides riding a tour bus through town, you can go into the woods in a Hummer or on a motorcycle, or even drive from the streets into the harbor in an amphibious vehicle. That one, called **The Duck** (© **866/341-DUCK** or 907/225-9899), is a favorite of kids. It costs $36 adults and $22 children, and lasts 90 minutes.

One of the longest-established tour guides caters only to five visitors at a time—not ships full of clients. Schoolteacher Lois Munch, of **Classic Tours** (© **907/225-3091;** www.classictours.com), has a fun personality and neat concept: She wears a poodle skirt to drive visitors around in her '55 Chevy. A 2-hour tour to the Saxman totem poles is $84; a 3-hour tour adds a natural history stop and costs $99. Rates are per person and include the admission to Saxman.

TLINGIT, HAIDA & TSIMSHIAN CULTURAL HERITAGE

The Ketchikan area has two totem pole parks and a totem pole museum, as well as a wealth of contemporary Native art displayed all over town. Notable pieces stand at Whale Park at Mission and Bawden streets and at the Cape Fox Lodge. Most of what you see in Southeast Alaska is Tlingit—the Haida and Tsimshian generally live to the south and east in British Columbia—but Ketchikan is near the boundary between the three peoples' areas, so their similar cultures mix here.

Totem Heritage Center 🐾🐾 Located near City Park, the center contains the largest collection of original 19th-century totem poles in existence. The poles, up to 160 years old, are displayed indoors, mostly unpainted, many with the grass and moss still attached from when they were rescued from the elements in villages. Totem poles were never meant to be maintained or repainted—they generally disintegrate after about 70 years and were constantly replaced—but these were preserved to help keep the culture alive. A high ceiling and muted lighting highlight the spirituality of the art. Well-trained guides are on hand to explain what you're looking at, and there are good interpretive signs. The gift shop, open during the summer, carries authentic Native crafts.

601 Deermount St. © **907/225-5900.** Admission $5 in summer, free in winter. Summer daily 8am–5pm; winter Mon–Fri 1–5pm.

Totem Bight State Historical Park 🐾🐾🐾 The park presents poles and a clan house carved beginning in 1938 by Natives working with traditional tools to copy fragments of historic poles that had mostly rotted away. The project, funded by the New Deal's Civilian Conservation Corps, helped save a Tlingit and Haida culture that had been essentially outlawed until that time. The setting, purportedly the site of a traditional fishing camp, is a peaceful spot on the edge of Tongass Narrows, at the end of a short walk through the woods, so the experience is both aesthetic and educational. The park also stands out for its excellent interpretive signs, a printed guide, and an interpretive website. There's a small park bookstore.

Ketchikan Area State Park Office, 9883 N. Tongass Hwy. (10 miles out of town.) © **907/247-8574.** www.alaska stateparks.org (click on "Individual Parks"). Free admission. Park always open.

Saxman Native Village Totem Pole Park 🐾 Saxman's park has artifacts similar to those at Totem Bight park, but with an added attraction: You can see carvers at work in the building to the right of the park. It's possible to see the studio and the poles without joining a tour, using a pamphlet that costs $1.50, but Totem Bight is better for that kind of visit—it has a more inspiring location and better interpretive materials. Cape Fox Corp., which operates the tours, caters mainly to cruise-ship passengers with its 2-hour

---

Tips Avoiding the Crowds

Ketchikan is overrun with as many as 10,000 cruise-ship passengers every day May through September, far more than the small visitor attractions or even the streets can comfortably handle. Independent travelers can avoid the crush by planning to visit popular spots in the afternoon. Spend the morning on an outdoors activity instead. Ships usually leave the town in early evening.

---

tour, which includes entry to the clan house and a demonstration of traditional dance and song by the Cape Fox Dancers. The tour schedule is different each day, depending on the ships. Buy tour tickets in the gift store on the right as you enter the park.

In Saxman, 2½ miles south of Ketchikan on the S. Tongass Hwy. ℰ **907/225-4846** for tour times and tickets. www.capefoxtours.com. Free admission. Guided tour $35 adults, $18 children 12 and under (no tours Oct–Apr). Park always open.

DOWNTOWN ATTRACTIONS

Ketchikan's best downtown attractions are all within walking distance of one another. See Creek Street, walk up Park Avenue past the Ketchikan Creek fish ladder, and then up to lovely **City Park,** site of the Totem Heritage Center, described above. The park is among my favorite places in Ketchikan. The creek splits into a maze of ornamental pools and streams once used as a hatchery, with footbridges, a fountain, and large trees with creeping roots.

The Creek Street boardwalk starts at the Stedman Street bridge, running over the tidal creek. It was Ketchikan's red-light district until not that long ago; now it's a quaint tourist mall. Prostitution was semilegal in Alaska until 1952, recent enough to survive in local memories but distant enough to have made Creek Street historic and to transform the women who worked there from outcasts to icons. Dolly Arthur, who started in business for herself on the creek in 1919 and died in 1975, lived through both eras, and her home became a commercial museum not long after her death. **Dolly's House** (ℰ **907/225-6329**) is amusing, mildly racy, and a little sad. Admission is $5; it's open from 8am to 4pm during the summer and when cruise ships are in town.

Creek Street has some interesting shops, described below, but it's also fun just to walk on the creekside boardwalk, into the forest above, and over the "Married Men's Trail"—once a discreet way for married men to reach the red-light district. **The Cape Fox Hill–Creek Street Funicular** (known as "the tram"), a sort of diagonal elevator, runs 211 feet from the boardwalk up to the Cape Fox Lodge on top of the hill. Take it up and then enjoy the walk down through the woods. The summertime fare is $2, but if no one is around, just press the "up" button and go.

Deer Mountain Tribal Hatchery and Eagle Center ℰℰ   This remarkable nonprofit center combines one of Alaska's best hatchery tours and a great place to see a bald eagle close up. The wooden buildings stand over Ketchikan Creek. You can see fish climbing against the current up into pools where they are sorted before being cut open to complete their biological purpose (salmon die when they spawn anyway). The hatchery tours are special for letting you get so close, right in the action, where you can feed the growing salmon fry yourself. The hatchery produces king and silver salmon and steelhead trout. Visitors can also walk right through the eagle enclosure. Remarkably, the resident pair of injured, flightless bald eagles have mated for life and built a nest where they lay eggs each year. They hunt salmon swimming naturally through their enclosure. No glass stands between you and this activity, only a few feet away.

1158 Salmon Rd. (© **800/252-5158** or 907/225-6760. Admission $9 adults, free for children 12 and under. May–Sept daily 8am–4:30pm; winter by arrangement.

Tongass Historical Museum This one-room museum is where Ketchikan talks back to itself, with well-executed revolving exhibits that have always held my interest. A small permanent area shows Native artifacts. In the same building, the attractive Ketchikan Public Library is a great place to recharge, especially in the children's section downstairs, where big windows look out on Ketchikan Creek's falls.

629 Dock St. (© **907/225-5600**. Admission $2 summer; free winter. Summer daily 8am–5pm; winter Wed–Fri 1–5pm, Sat 10am–4pm, Sun 1–4pm.

SHOPPING

The Ketchikan art scene is one of Alaska's liveliest, thanks in part to the Ketchikan Arts and Humanities Council, whose helpful staff operates the **Main Stay Gallery,** near Creek Street at 716 Totem Way (www.ketchikanarts.org). Shows change monthly.

Ray Troll is Alaska's leading fish-obsessed artist. His small gallery, **Soho Coho,** at 5 Creek St., is worth a visit even if you aren't a shopper. It shows Troll's own work and that of other Ketchikan artists from the same school of surreal rainforest humor. In Troll's art, subtle ironies and silly puns coexist in a solidly decorated interior world. T-shirts are his most popular canvas; "Spawn Till You Die" is a classic. Troll's incredible work-of-art website delves far into his strange mind (and sells shirts), at www.troll art.com. The gallery is open summer daily from 9am to 6pm; winter Wednesday through Saturday from noon to 5:30pm; or order at (© **800/888-4070.**

Adjacent to Soho Coho, **Alaska Eagle Arts** is a serious gallery featuring the bold yet traditional work of Native artist Marvin Oliver. Upstairs, **Parnassus Books** is a pleasing little cubbyhole with Alaskana, art, cooking, and popular fiction. Down the boardwalk at 18 Creek St., craftspeople carve and interact with visitors at **Hide-A-Way Gifts.** At 123 Stedman St., across the creek, **Blue Heron Gallery and Gifts** carries Alaska arts and crafts that appeal to locals as well as visitors: jewelry, stained glass, clothing, jam, prints, and so on. Nearby, at 633 Mission St., **Exploration Gallery** is owned by local artist Diane Naab and shows original work from all over the region. Stop for kettlecorn popcorn on your shopping trip at **Ocra Corn,** at 602 Dock St., an addictive local favorite that you can get in the usual movie theater style, or with such flavors as blueberry or maple.

Moving back toward the waterfront, **Eagle Spirit Gallery of Ketchikan,** at 310 Mission St., shows some very impressive Alaska Native art, including large carved pieces from this region. At 500 Mission, look into the **Market Place Cape Fox,** which contains three distinctive shops carrying jewelry, art, and gifts with Alaska Native and Northwest themes, and **Luna's,** where you can stop in for an espresso, ice cream, or snack.

At the waterfront, the building that stands right over the dock is Salmon Landing Market Place, at 5 Salmon Landing. Of particular interest here is the **Dockside Gallery,** which shows work of several local artists. Next to Dockside Gallery, hobby-ists should check out **The Bead and Yarn Shoppe,** which has an astonishingly diverse selection, and handcrafted jewelry.

Note: Ketchikan is a shopping and art destination, but if you want something authentically Alaskan, you have to be careful. For some important tips, see "Native Art: Finding the Real Thing," in chapter 2.

GETTING OUTSIDE

There's a lot to do outdoors around Ketchikan, but most of it will require a boat or plane; drive-by attractions are limited. In any event, your first stop should be the trip-planning room at the Southeast Alaska Discovery Center (see "Visitor Information," near the beginning of the Ketchikan section), for details on trails, fishing, and dozens of U.S. Forest Service cabins.

BEAR VIEWING Salmon returning to a fish hatchery on a creek south of town have long attracted black bears. A local business, **Alaska Rainforest Sanctuary** (© 907/225-5503), takes advantage of the viewing opportunity by hosting visitors on well-made trails with guides. It's an excellent program; however, the firm is solely focused on cruise ship passengers and wouldn't even disclose a price for individuals to join the tours. As a passenger, you can book on board. Otherwise, call, but I cannot speak to schedule, availability, or price. On the other hand, you can watch the same bears from public property for free, without a guide. Drive about 10 miles south of town, beyond Saxman on the South Tongass Highway, to the Herring Cove Bridge. From here you have a viewpoint of the same estuary owned by the sanctuary and just as good a chance of seeing black bears. Bears may be present June through September, and sightings are most likely in July and August.

For more of a wilderness experience, Ketchikan is a good place to get on a float plane, soar over water and wooded islands, and land where bears are gathering at streams where the salmon are running. Depending on where the bears are, it costs $250 to $400 per person. **Promech Air** (© 800/860-3845 or 907/225-3845; www.promechair.com) and **Island Wings Air Service** (© 888/854-2444 or 907/225-2444; www.islandwings.com) offer this service; both are described in "Majestic Misty Fjords," p. 112.

CABIN TRIPS The U.S. Forest Service maintains more than 50 **cabins** around Ketchikan; all are remote and primitive, but at $25 to $45 a night, you can't beat the price or the settings. This is a chance to be utterly alone in the wilderness; many of the lake cabins come with a boat for fishing and exploring. For details and descriptions of all the cabins, contact the **Southeast Alaska Discovery Center** (© 907/228-6220; www.fs.fed.us/r10/tongass). The reservations system to use when you're actually ready to book a cabin is described in "Getting Outside in the Tongass National Forest," on p. 97. If you stay in a cabin, you'll need all your camping gear (except a tent), including sleeping bags, a camp stove, your own cooking outfit and food, a lantern, and so on. The easy way to handle this is to contact **Alaska Wilderness Outfitting and Camping Rentals,** 3857 Fairview St. (© 907/225-7335; www.latitude 56.com/camping/index.html), which has been supplying cabin trips for more than 15 years. They rent almost everything you need, including small outboards and life jackets for the skiffs, and deliver directly to the air taxi or water taxi. The cabins are remote. You can hike or take a boat to some of them, but most are accessible only by floatplane (and unless you have loads of stuff, flying is probably the cheapest way to go). Expect to pay around $1,000 round-trip for three passengers. Obviously, it makes sense only if you will stay for a while—we never go for less than 3 nights. For recommended carriers, see "Majestic Misty Fjords," p. 112.

FISHING The **Alaska Department of Fish and Game** produces a 24-page fishing guide to Ketchikan with details on where to find fish in both fresh and salt water, including a list of 17 fishing spots accessible from the roads. Get it from the local office of the **Alaska Department of Fish and Game,** at 2030 Sea Level Dr., Suite 205, Ketchikan, AK 99901 (ⓒ **907/225-2859;** www.alaska.gov/adfg, click "Sport Fisheries" and then on the Southeast region on the map). More fishing ideas are under "Hiking" and "Cabin Trips." Guided fishing charters can take you out on the water for salmon and halibut. **Ketchikan Charter Boats** (ⓒ **800/272-7291** or 907/225-7291; www.ketchikancharterboats.com) has a lot of experience in these waters. You can also get a referral from the visitor center. The going rate for a day-long guided charter is around $300 per person, half-day about $160.

HIKING   Eight miles out the North Tongass Highway, the **Ward Lake Recreation Area** covers a lovely patch of rainforest and lake and stream habitat, and has a picnic area, several trails, and campgrounds. Ward Creek has steelhead and cutthroat trout, Dolly Varden char, and silver salmon; check current regulations before fishing. The wide gravel **Ward Lake Nature Trail** circles the placid lake for a mile among old-growth Sitka spruce large enough to put you in your place. For a more challenging hike, **Perseverance Lake Trail** climbs through forest with steps and boardwalks from the Three Cs Campground, across the road from Ward Lake, to a lake 2 miles away that can be reached no other way. There's a good bit of climbing to get there, but the trail is extraordinarily well maintained, without mud even in wet weather. To reach the recreation area, turn right off the highway on Revilla Road and follow the signs.

   Deer Mountain Trail, right behind downtown, is a steep but rewarding climb through big, mossy trees up to great views. You can walk from City Park to the trail head, half a mile and 500 feet higher on steep Fair Street and Ketchikan Lakes Road, but if you take a cab, you will save energy for the trail. The first mile rises 1,000 feet to a great ocean view south of Tongass Narrows, and the next mile and 1,000 feet to another great view, this time of Ketchikan. The alpine summit, at 3,000 feet, comes near the 3-mile mark. A public shelter (first come, first served) is a bit farther, and the trail continues to another trail head 10 miles away. Pick up a trail guide sheet from the Forest Service at the Southeast Alaska Discovery Center (p. 98).

SEA KAYAKING   The islands, coves, and channels around Ketchikan create protected waters rich with life and welcoming for exploration by kayak. **Southeast Sea Kayaks** (ⓒ **800/287-1607** or 907/225-1258; www.kayakketchikan.com), rents kayaks and guides day trips and overnights. They specialize in taking small groups of independent travelers, not big mobs from the cruise ships, and have half-day trips that start with a boat ride to real wilderness with only six paddlers along. Those are $149 adults, $119 children, including food and drink. A 2½-hour paddle is $79 adults, $59 children as young as 6. They have multiday Misty Fjords expeditions, too.

WHERE TO STAY

In addition to the hotels and B&Bs listed below, the **Ketchikan Reservation Service,** 412 D-1 Loop Rd., Ketchikan, AK 99901 (ⓒ **800/987-5337** or phone/fax 907/247-5337; www.ketchikan-lodging.com), books many bed-and-breakfasts and outfitted apartments, and has online availability and reservations. **Alaska Travelers Accommodations** (ⓒ **800/928-3308** or 907/247-7117; www.alaskatravelers.com) is a Ketchikan-based service of long standing that handles lodgings here, in Juneau, and scattered in other Southeast communities.

EXPENSIVE

Best Western Landing 🏵🏵   This hotel already boasted newly furnished rooms, done in bright colors and with granite bathroom counters, when 45 brand new rooms opened in 2006. They're terrific: built with 9-foot ceilings and big opening windows, and equipped with high-quality beds, cherrywood furniture, flatscreen TVs, and, in nine premium-view rooms, fireplaces and covered decks. Every room is loaded with amenities, including both Wi-Fi and wired broadband. Service is professional. The hotel's competition wins only in the category of charm, as an excellent corporate-feeling hotel may not be what you want in Ketchikan. The location, right across from the ferry dock, is distant from the downtown sights, so you'll need to rent a car or use the courtesy van that the hotel offers.

The **Landing Restaurant,** a fountain and grill with lots of chrome, is a local favorite and very kid friendly. Try the fresh halibut sandwich. Lunch and dinner range from $7.25 to $25. You can order from that same steak-and-seafood menu upstairs, at **Jeremiah's** bar, which also serves sandwiches, pizza, and good pasta in a sumptuous room; the nonsmoking area is glassed off and not smoky.

3434 Tongass Ave., Ketchikan, AK 99901. © **800/428-8304** or 907/225-5166. Fax 907/225-6900. www.landinghotel. com. 76 units. High season $190–$200 double, $210 suite; low season $137–$147 double, $175 suite. AE, DC, DISC, MC, V. **Amenities:** 2 restaurants; bar; exercise room; courtesy van; covered parking; limited room service; laundry service; dry cleaning. *In room:* TV, high-speed Internet, Wi-Fi, microwave, fridge, coffeemaker, hair dryer, iron.

Cape Fox Lodge 🐾🐾 This is Alaska's most beautiful hotel. It stands on a wooded pinnacle above downtown, reached from Creek Street by a funicular. The sheer drop-off and tall rainforest trees create the lofty feeling of a treehouse in the rooms and restaurant. Perfectly proportioned buildings are executed in extraordinarily good taste. Warm wood frames complement the stunning views out of the double-hung windows. The Cape Fox Native Corporation built the hotel, and the lobby and parking area are a museum of Tlingit art masterpieces, adding to the peace and rainforest spirit. Rooms are large and airy, appointed in rich-toned wood, and all but a dozen share a view of Ketchikan and the sea and islands beyond (rooms on the opposite side are $10 less). Each room has an attractively tiled bathroom. On our latest visit, we found flaws in the housekeeping and a need for a general sprucing up.

The **Heen Kahidi** restaurant has one of Alaska's most attractive dining rooms, a tall, narrow rectangle of windows with a fireplace. It is a beautiful, calming place to eat. The food, especially at breakfast and brunch, shows the hand of a talented chef and is well worth taking time for. The service, however, can be slow and unresponsive. Lunch ranges from $7 to $20; dinner main courses range from $17 to $37, with most around $25. The dining room is open from 7am to 9pm daily.

800 Venetia Way, Ketchikan, AK 99901. © **800/325-4000** or 907/225-8001. Fax 907/225-8286. www.westcoast hotels.com. 72 units. High season $190–$200 double; low season $140–$150 double; year-round $251 suite. AE, DC, DISC, MC, V. **Amenities:** Restaurant; bar; limited room service; dry cleaning. *In room:* TV w/pay movies and Nintendo rental, dataport, Wi-Fi (with fee), coffeemaker, hair dryer, iron.

Salmon Falls Resort 🐾🐾 If fishing is your goal, a stay at this huge on-island lodge has several advantages. First, there's the incredible setting, on island-dotted Clover Pass next to a waterfall where 10,000 pink salmon spawn. Next is the cost savings of a road-accessible lodge, since you don't have to fly there. Finally, you're not trapped in the middle of nowhere if one of you doesn't want to fish—the attractions of Ketchikan are a 17-mile drive down the road. The facilities are quite good: large, up-to-date, white-walled motel rooms with phones, TVs, and small bathrooms. Those in the upper building are slightly preferable and cost the same. Some 40 lodge-operated boats tie at the dock. Inclusive fishing packages start at $1,100 per person, double occupancy, for a 3-day stay with 2 days on the water, self-guided. With a guide, the price is $1,550 per person. Without fishing, room and board are $675.

The **restaurant** and bar are in a massive log octagon held up in the center by a section of the Alaska pipeline, with great views and a menu of steak and seafood ranging from $18 to $40. It's worth a drive out the road for dinner, even if you aren't staying here (the restaurant doesn't open until May 26).

16707 N. Tongass Hwy. (P.O. Box 5700), Ketchikan, AK 99901. ℂ 800/247-9059 (reservations) or 907/225-2752. Fax 907/225-2710. www.salmonfallsresort.com. 52 units. See rates in description above. AE, MC, V. Closed Sept 15–May 15. **Amenities:** Restaurant; bar; inclusive guided fishing. *In room:* TV, no phone.

MODERATE

The Narrows Inn ⊕ The motel buildings sit above the water, where fishing charters and floatplanes collect guests for outings. The rooms, done in an outdoors theme, are fresh and nicely decorated, with wallpaper borders. My only complaint is that they are too small—the TV is mounted on the wall. The bathrooms are large. Rooms with balconies rent for $10 more. The location is 4 miles from downtown; they have a shuttle that takes guests to the airport, ferry terminal, and sites within city limits. For flexibility, however, you may want to rent a car if staying here.

The **Narrows Inn Restaurant** (ℂ **907/247-5900**) is a quiet, comfortable place to eat, with a water view. The food is consistently good enough to bring locals out for dates, celebrations, or brunch with family. For lunch, try a half order of one of the rich pasta dishes. Best choices for dinner include the crispy chicken cordon bleu or flavorful Tequila pork.

4871 N. Tongass Hwy. (P.O. Box 8296), Ketchikan, AK 99901. ℂ 888/686-2600 or 907/247-2600. Fax 907/247-2602. www.narrowsinn.com. 46 units. High season $130–$145 double, $220–$235 suite; low season $89–$99 double, $150 suite. Extra person $10. AE, DC, DISC, MC, V. **Amenities:** Restaurant; bar; courtesy shuttle; marina. *In room:* TV, Wi-Fi, microwave, fridge, coffeemaker, hair dryer.

INEXPENSIVE

Captain's Quarters Bed & Breakfast ⊕⊕ *Value* The rooms here rival the best in Ketchikan but cost half as much. They are large, quiet, and immaculate, with sweeping views of the city and ocean, and share a self-contained, self-service breakfast room. Little things are done right, such as each room having a private phone with its own outside line and number. A light nautical theme carries through the building. One room has a full kitchen. The setup allows as much privacy as you want—socialize with hostess Toni Bass, a gregarious school secretary, or come and go without seeing anyone. The house is perched in a mountainside neighborhood just north of the tunnel, where half the streets are stairs or wooden ramps. It's a significant but doable walk from downtown. There's no smoking in the house.

325 Lund St., Ketchikan, AK 99901. ℂ 907/225-4912. www.ptialaska.net/~captbnb. 3 units. High season $100–$110 double; low season $69 double. Extra person $15. Rates include continental breakfast. MC, V. *In room:* TV, hair dryer.

Eagle Heights Bed & Breakfast ⊕⊕ *Finds* A house with treetop views of the waterfront was recently remodeled with exceptional craftsmanship and taste into large, airy guest rooms and a comfortable common room. Two of the units are large suites, and all three are equipped with many amenities, including refrigerators stuffed with food and goodies. Hostess Cherry Ferry keeps the place as immaculate as the day it was built and brings the generous continental breakfast to the room. She even washes guests' laundry. Every room has a private entrance, there's plenty of parking, and the downtown sites are about 20 minutes away on foot.

1626 Water St., Ketchikan, AK 99901. ℂ **800/928-3308** or 907/2251760. www.eagleheightsbb.com. 3 units. $95–$125 double. Extra adult $25. MC, V. **Amenities:** Laundry service. *In room:* TV/VCR, stocked fridge, microwave, coffeemaker, hair dryer, iron.

New York Hotel/The Inn at Creek Street ★★ ⓥₐₗᵤₑ   The same family operates two sets of lodgings in the center of the most historic area. The original portion is the hotel, a funny little 1924 building with a tiny lobby and charming antique-furnished rooms. It is on the National Register of Historic Places, and the owners have done a good job of adding modern comfort while keeping the essentially funky feel. Four rooms look out on a small boat harbor, while five with less street noise face the garden. They're not large, but all are a great value—more attractive than other hotel rooms in town that cost much more. To create the new part of the business—the inn—the owners have bought apartments above the shops on the Creek Street boardwalk and renovated them into spacious modern suites. These units are downright luxurious, with kitchens, excellent amenities, and great privacy, and they sit on pilings over the flowing creek. The hotel offers a courtesy van to the airport, ferries, and hiking trails. Note that those who have trouble with stairs shouldn't consider either of these properties.

A small, casual restaurant called **That One Place** during the day and **That Other Place** in the evening is attached to the hotel. Run by the same family as the outstanding Bar Harbor Restaurant (see below), the food here is remarkable: Items such as seared yellow fin tuna, mussels in red chile sauce, pear and parmesan salad, or baconwrapped scallops are presented in generous portions for low prices. Breakfast and lunch choices are memorable, too. The desserts are the best in town. The hours are a little bit up in the air at this writing, but the restaurant should be open for three meals a day through the summer.

207 Stedman St., Ketchikan, AK 99901. ℂ **866/225-0246** or 907/225-0246. Fax 907/225-1803. www.thenewyork hotel.com. 12 units. High season $99–$119 double, $159–$179 suite; low season $79–$89 double, $109 suite. DISC, MC, V. **Amenities:** Restaurant; courtesy van. *In room:* TV, high-speed Internet.

A HOSTEL & CAMPING

Three Forest Service campgrounds with a total of 47 sites are located at **Ward Lake** (see "Special Places," p. 128). A salmon stream runs through the middle of the lakeside Signal Creek Campground, which, along with the Last Chance Campground, can be reserved through the national system described in "Getting Outside in the Tongass National Forest," on p. 97. The camping fee at either place is $10.

Eighteen miles out North Tongass Highway, the **Settler's Cove State Park** includes a sandy beach (a good place to watch whales, beachcomb, or even swim), a disabilities-accessible path to a spectacular waterfall, and a short coastal trail. There are 14 campsites, half of which will take rigs of up to 30 feet, without hookups. Camping costs $10 a night. For information, contact the **Alaska Division of Parks** (ℂ **907/247-8574**), 9883 N. Tongass Hwy.

If you need hookups for an RV, try **Clover Pass Resort,** about 15 miles north of the ferry terminal on North Point Higgins Road (ℂ **800/410-2234** or 907/247-2234; www.cloverpassresort.com). They charge $29 to $31 a night.

First United Methodist Church   This downtown church hostel offers utilitarian male and female dorms, and guests have use of the church kitchen. Bring a sleeping bag. It is open only June through August; office hours are Monday through Saturday 7 to 9am and 6 to 11pm, Sunday 7am to 8:30am and 6 to 11pm.

400 Main St. (P.O. Box 8515), Ketchikan, AK 99901. ℂ **907/225-3319**. 19 beds. $15 per person. Closed Sept–May.

Majestic Misty Fjords

In Punchbowl Cove, south of Ketchikan in Misty Fjords National Monument, sheer cliffs rise 3,150 feet straight up from calm water, as high and smooth as those in the Yosemite Valley. Misty is well over twice Yosemite's size, but there isn't a single car here. There isn't so much as a mile of road; in fact, there are hardly any trails. It's something like a great national park before the people arrived. Visits to the monument are by tour boat, float plane, or, for the hardy, sea kayak. It isn't a cheap place to go, and you don't see much wildlife. By boat, you don't see glaciers, although glaciated mountains are a spectacular feature of the flights. Unlike Glacier Bay, Tracy Arm, Kenai Fjords, or Resurrection Bay—all places with more wildlife and more glaciers at sea level—the experience at Misty is pure geology. You go for the scenery.

Two companies currently offer boat tours to Misty's Punchbowl Cove, Rudyerd Bay, and back, and both offer meals in the price. Sitka-based **Allen Marine** ((*C* 877/686-8100 or 907/747-8100; www.allenmarinetours.com) has some distinct advantages. The fast, quiet boat makes the round-trip in 4½ hours. All seats face forward. A knowledgeable naturalist interprets the scenery. Adult passengers can peruse regional books, while children work with crafts boxes and activities. Tickets are $144 adults, $99 children ages 3 to 12, free 2 and under. Sailings every day in the summer coordinate with the cruise ships' dockings. The Misty tour with the most longevity is run by **Alaska Cruises,** owned by Juneau's Goldbelt Native corporation, 57 Main St., Suite 201, Ketchikan ((*C* 800/228-1905 or 907/225-6044; www.goldbelttours. com). The company offers the opportunity see the fjords from above by float plane and return to Ketchikan by water; the price of $150 adults, $125 children 2 to 10, free 1 and under, is a bargain with the inclusion of the flightseeing.

I prefer seeing the fjords on an extended floatplane flight (and I certainly recommend it for those susceptible to seasickness). Flying over the scenery

WHERE TO DINE

Besides these restaurants, see the New York Hotel, Cape Fox Lodge, Narrows Inn, Salmon Falls Resort, and Best Western Landing, all above, for other choices. There are several good stops for light meals or snacks. The Smith family's **Fish and Chips** booth comes back to the dock every summer, to the delight of locals and cruise-ship crew members who line up at lunchtime. The fish is halibut with beer batter, and they also serve shrimp and great seafood chowder. Picnic tables are handy for seating on a sunny day. **Halibut Hole,** at 7 Creek St., on the deck of the Eagles Club ((*C* **907/225-5162**), serves some of the best fried fish in town, including halibut, salmon, clams, and shrimp in crispy batter, with fries and hush puppies. It's open daily 11am to 4pm in the summer and accepts cash only.

Bar Harbor Restaurant *斧斧* SEAFOOD/ECLECTIC   The wonderful food and attentive service here are the result of a family's commitment to bringing a new class of dining to Ketchikan. They know they're in a small town, so you still find fish and is amazing, but it's the floatplane landing that really blows your mind because then you get a sudden sense of the scale of everything you've seen from the air. The cliffs are magnified while you shrink to a speck. Go in the late afternoon when the light is pretty and the swarms of planes carrying cruise-ship passengers are gone. Several air-taxi operators in Ketchikan take flightseeing day trips to Misty Fjords or drop clients at remote cabins. **Promech Air** (✆ **800/860-3845** or 907/225-3845; www.promechair.com) is a large one, charging about $200 for a 75-minute flight, including about 10 minutes on the ground. But I like best a smaller company, **Island Wings Air Service** (✆ **888/854-2444** or 907/225-2444; www.islandwings.com). The owner and pilot is Michelle Madsen, and my flight with her was among the most memorable of the many I've taken around Alaska. She flew the plane with her long blond hair flowing and her little white dog Perro at her side (although she offered to leave him behind), offering a choice of music on the iPod as background to her impromptu commentary about the fjords. We soared with Van Morrison while Michelle told us about her favorite places down below. The landing was as long as anyone needed to soak in the awesome surroundings. It felt like an outing with old friends. Madsen charges $199 for a seat on a six-passenger DeHavilland Beaver for a 2-hour flight that includes 45 minutes on the ground at the fjords. She also flies guests to Forest Service cabins (many of them in Misty), places she knows intimately, and she will take the time to help you choose one that suits your interests and budget. Take a look at her informative website for a good start.

Visiting the fjords by kayak is a real expedition, advisable only for those who already know they enjoy this mode of travel, but I can think of few more spectacular places to paddle. **Southeast Exposure** (✆ **907/225-8829**; www.southeastexposure.com) has done guided paddles there for 20 years, earning a good reputation. Their 6-day trip is $950 per person.

chips and other basics on the menu, but the best of the seafood selections are as good as you find anywhere in Alaska. I was especially impressed by the crab cakes and the clam appetizer. The crab and corn chowder is spicy and satisfying. They also do many specials, both to allow the chef-owner to stretch and to educate their audience. Prices are reasonable—usually around $18 for a seafood special. Be ready to settle in, as a meal here can take time. The restaurant operates in an old house over the water a short drive from the downtown tourist area, and the dining room consists of a series of partly connected small rooms, all decorated in a cozy fashion with bric-a-brac and white Christmas lights. The name derives from the boat basin that the restaurant overlooks. Given the few seats, reservations are essential.

The same family operates a restaurant downtown at the New York Hotel (p. 111), a sort of Bar Harbor–lite that serves three meals a day in the summer.

2813 Tongass Ave. ✆ **907/225-2813**. www.barharborketchikan.com. Reservations recommended. Dinner main courses $13–$30. DC, DISC, MC, V. Tues–Sat 4:30–9pm.

Burger Queen _(Finds)_ BURGERS   Restaurants with the word _burger_ in the name don't often get full write-ups in travel guidebooks, and this place looks unlikely for special treatment as well, but Debbie and Shawn Rahr have turned their four-table restaurant into a Ketchikan institution by doing simple food right. You certainly won't go wrong ordering a burger and milkshake here, but also consider the grilled chicken (teriyaki or barbecue), the cornmeal-breaded halibut, or the colorful salads, which are fresh and satisfying and have homemade dressings on the side. The portions are so large most adults will get plenty to eat ordering from the children's section of the menu. Since the dining room is so small, having your meal delivered for no extra charge makes sense, or get takeout and eat in the park across the street.

518 Water St. (C) **907/225-6060.** Lunch and dinner $4–$13. MC, V. High season Mon–Sat 11am–7pm; low season Wed–Sat 11am–6pm.

Diaz Cafe _(Kids) (Finds)_ FILIPINO   Many Alaskan towns have strong, cohesive Filipino communities, created over decades by large, close families drawn across the ocean one by one for cannery work. In Ketchikan, the heartbeat of the Filipino community has beat in this bright little diner since the early 1950s as ownership passes generation to generation in the same family. The place is so well loved among all ethnicities in Ketchikan that its current owner is unable to change the slightest detail—she even faced an insurrection when she tried to change the color of the menus—so everything remains today as it was half a century ago: the Formica, worn from wiping, the yellow and red walls, and the nondescript street front (which could scare you off, although the restaurant inside is immaculate). If you haven't had Filipino food, this is the place to try it. The spicy chicken adobo, a huge, delicious half-chicken bathed in gravy with rice, is $12. The sweet and sour halibut is memorable, too. Regulars order the "Large Guy," a bowl of sweet-and-sour rice mixed with meat, which arrives instantly and costs $5.25. You can also get sandwiches, burgers (also served with rice), and Chinese food.

335 Stedman St. (C) **907/225-2257.** Lunch and dinner $5.25–$14. No credit cards. Tues–Sat 11:30am–2pm, 4–8pm; Sun noon–7:30pm.

Good Fortune Chinese Restaurant CHINESE   This restaurant stands on pilings in Creek Street, with small upstairs and downstairs dining rooms. The food is consistently good year after year, with a long and varied menu that allows you to choose by style of cuisine—Cantonese, Szechuan, and so on.

4 Creek St. (C) **907/225-1818.** Lunch $6.25; dinner $12–$19. DISC, MC, V. Mon–Sat 11am–9pm; Sun noon–9pm. Closed Mon in winter.

Ocean View Restaurante _(Kids) (Finds)_ MEXICAN/ITALIAN   Everyone in Ketchikan already knows how good the food is at this family restaurant, which is why the place is so lively and festive even on an off-season weeknight—in fact, the dining room can be deafening. Few tourists know about it or make the drive a mile from downtown. The menu is long and reasonably priced, with separate columns of Mexican and Italian cuisine (and an occasional Greek item slipped into the Italian column), a page of seafood and sautéed entrees, plus chicken, veal, steak, pasta, and pizza. Variety is a common technique used by small-town restaurants to make it through the winter; the difference here is remarkably good cooking. They serve beer and wine. The pizza, delivered free, is the best in town.

1831 Tongass Ave. (C) **907/225-7566.** Reservations recommended. Lunch $7–$9; dinner $6–$16. MC, V. Daily 11am–11pm.

3 Wrangell

Wrangell, valued for its position near the mouth of the Stikine River, began as a Tlingit stronghold and trading post and became the site of a Russian fort built in 1834. The British leased the area from the Russians in 1840, and their flag flew until the U.S. purchase of Alaska in 1867. Over the balance of the 19th century, Wrangell experienced three gold rushes and the construction of a cannery and sawmill.

Then time pretty much stopped.

While the world outside changed, Wrangell stayed the same from the mid–20th century on. It even moved backward. Elsewhere, Wal-Marts and shopping malls were invented and small-town main streets deflated. Then people noticed what they had lost and tried to bring back their communities. Not out here, beyond the road system. With little incentive for anyone to visit, Wrangell stayed as it was after a 1952 fire burned the downtown: a burly, blue-collar American logging town, simple and conservative. Wrangell cut trees, processed them, and shipped them. The bars stayed busy, and no one thought of opening a health-food restaurant. As long as there were trees to saw into lumber, the future was safe in the past.

Or so it seemed until environmental and economic issues closed the mill in 1994. Some feared the town would die, too. Sawing lumber had sustained the local economy for more than 100 years, and a third of the paychecks in town came from that one plant. But it hasn't been so simple. The logging industry survived, off and on, and on a much smaller scale. The town grew quieter. Some trailer houses disappeared and stores closed, but the lights didn't go out, although the population declined.

But Wrangell is working to improve on its positive qualities. Residents show an endearing eagerness to please. A new museum was completed in 2005, and ecotourism operators started offering kayaking, hiking, biking, and the like. Tour boats now take guests up the wild Stikine River, out on the water for Southeast's great salmon fishing, and over to the mainland to see hordes of black bears at the Anan Wildlife Observatory. The U.S. Forest Service maintains gravel roads that lead to some spectacular places.

The town has a nonthreatening, small-scale feel that allows a family to wander comfortably and make friends. We were invited home to dinner by another family we had just met. With so little crime, there is no fear of strangers. We picnicked in a totem pole park, hiked in the rainforest, and looked at ancient art strewn across Petroglyph Beach. We were sorry to have to leave. On the ferry back to Juneau, a class of Wrangell sixth-graders sat next to us. They talked with excited innocence of all the new things they hoped to experience in the state capital, the most electrifying of which seemed to be the prospect of eating for the first time at McDonald's. Wrangell, I thought, still has a long way to go to catch up with the rest of the world, and that is a condition much to be envied.

ESSENTIALS

GETTING THERE   **Alaska Airlines** (℃ **800/252-7522;** www.alaskaair.com) serves Wrangell once daily with a jet flying 28 minutes north from Ketchikan and another 19 minutes south from Petersburg, a flight that skims treetops the entire way.

Wrangell is on the main line of the **Alaska Marine Highway System** (℃ **800/642-0066;** www.ferryalaska.com). The voyage through the narrow, winding **Wrangell Narrows** north to Petersburg is one of the most beautiful and fascinating in Southeast Alaska. It's quite a navigational feat to watch as the 400-foot ships squeeze through a passage so slender and shallow the vessel's own displacement changes the water level onshore as it passes. The route, not taken by cruise ships, which approach through larger waterways, is also a source of delays, as the narrows are deep enough for passage only at high tide. The walk-on fare is $33 from Ketchikan, $28 from Petersburg. The terminal is downtown ((C) **907/874-3711**) a block from the Stikine Inn.

VISITOR INFORMATION   The city's **Wrangell Visitor Center** is in the new Nolan Center, along with the Wrangell Museum, on the water in the heart of town at 296 Outer Dr. ((C) **800/367-9745;** www.wrangell.com). Staff from both the Nolan Center and the U.S. Forest Service are on hand to answer questions May 1 to September 30 Monday through Saturday 10am to 5pm, the rest of the year Tuesday through Saturday 1 to 5pm.

The Forest Service's **Wrangell Ranger District Office** is at 525 Bennett St. (P.O. Box 51), Wrangell, AK 99929 ((C) **907/874-2323;** www.fs.fed.us/r10/tongass), located on the hill behind town. Forest Service personnel here or at the visitor center have local knowledge of the logging roads and fishing holes, offer printed information on each Forest Service cabin and path, and, for $7, sell a detailed Wrangell Island Road Guide topographic map, which is printed on waterproof material. The district office is open Monday through Friday from 8am to 4:30pm.

ORIENTATION   The main part of town is laid out north to south along the waterfront on the northern point of Wrangell Island. **Front Street** is the main business street, leading from the small-boat harbor and **Chief Shakes Island** at the south to the city dock and the ferry dock at the north. Most of the rest of the town is along **Church Street,** which runs parallel to Front Street a block higher up the hill. **Evergreen Avenue** and **Bennett Street** form a loop to the north that goes to the airport. The only road to the rest of the island, the **Zimovia Highway,** heads out of town to the south, paved for about 12 miles, and then connects to over 100 miles of gravel logging roads built and maintained by the Forest Service, most of which are usable by two-wheel-drive vehicles in the summer.

GETTING AROUND   You can do the town on foot, but you will need wheels for the airport or Zimovia Highway. **Practical Rent A Car** is located at the Wrangell airport ((C) **907/874-3975**). **Northern Lights Taxi** can be reached at (C) **907/874-4646.** Rent **bikes, canoes,** or **kayaks** from Rainwalker Expeditions ((C) **907/874-2549;** www.rainwalkerexpeditions.com) at the city dock, described under "Gearing Up," below.

FAST FACTS: Wrangell

Bank **Wells Fargo** is at 115 Front St., with an ATM. There's also an ATM across from the Stikine Inn.

Hospital **Wrangell Medical Center** is at 310 Bennett St. ((C) **907/874-7000**).

Internet Access You can surf the Web at the public library on Church Street ((C) **907/874-3535**).

Police For nonemergency calls, dial (C) **907/874-3304.**

Post Office Buy stamps for postcards home at 105 Federal Way, across from the Stikine Inn.

Taxes Sales tax is 7%. Rooms are taxed at 13% starting in 2007.

Wrangell

ACCOMMODATIONS ■
Harding's Old
  Sourdough Lodge **8**
Rooney's Roost
  Bed & Breakfast **2**
Stikine Inn **1**
Wrangell Hostel **3**

DINING ◆
Diamond C Cafe **5**
Zak's Cafe **6**

ATTRACTIONS ●
Grave of Chief Shakes **7**
Nolan Center
  Museum & Visitor Center **4**

0   1/8 Mi
0   1/8 Km

Information ⓘ
Post Office ✉

To Petroglyph Beach
Evergreen
Bevier St.
Ferry Terminal
Stikine Ave.
2nd St.
Reid St.
McKinnon
Cruise Ship Dock
Brueger St.
Front St.
Church St.
Outer Dr.
St. Michael's St.
Zimovia Strait
Episcopal Ave.
Seaplane Dock
Shakes St.
Case Ave.
To Airport
Peninsula St.
Chief Shakes Island
Boat Harbor
Case Ave.

Alaska
Fairbanks ○
Anchorage ○ Cordova ○ ○ Juneau
Kenai ○ Sitka ○
Wrangell ○
Ketchikan ○

SPECIAL EVENTS   **The Garnet Festival,** held the third week of April, marks the arrival of the sea lions, hooligans, shorebirds, and a great concentration of bald eagles on the Stikine River Delta, a spring tornado of wildlife in the region's largest coastal marshes. Community activities take place in town while jet boat tours traverse the delta. **The Wrangell King Salmon Derby,** the last half of May and first half of June, started in 1953. Contact the Wrangell Chamber of Commerce for details (© **907/ 874-3901;** www.wrangellchamber.org). Wrangell also puts on a classic small-town **Independence Day** celebration.

EXPLORING WRANGELL & ENVIRONS

Before white settlers arrived, the Tlingit had already warred for centuries over this strategic trading location near the mouth of the Stikine River. The first Chief Shakes was a successful conqueror who enslaved his enemies, and then handed down power through the female line, in the Tlingit tradition, for seven generations. Charlie Jones was recognized as Chief Shakes VII, the last of the line, at a potlatch in 1940, but the position had long since lost most of its status. The decline began after the Alaska purchase, in 1867. Word came of the Emancipation Proclamation, which theoretically freed a third of the residents of the coast's Tlingit villages. Chief Shakes VI sent his slaves in canoes to dry halibut; they kept paddling home to Puget Sound, never looking back. (An excellent pamphlet, *Authentic History of Shakes Island and Clan,* by E. L. Keithhahn, sells for $4 at the Nolan Center Museum, described below.)

Chief Shakes Island, a tiny islet in the middle of the small-boat harbor, is the site of a Tlingit clan house and collection of totem poles constructed by Native workers, using traditional tools, in the Civilian Conservation Corps during the 1930s. Unlike some CCC clan house replicas in the region, which mix Tlingit styles, this house is an exact, scaled-down copy of the house in which Chief Shakes VI lay in state in 1916. The inside of the clan house is fascinating, both in the sense that it gives an insight to the people's ways and displays some extraordinary artifacts. Unfortunately, it takes some effort to get inside, as it is open mostly only when the cruise ships are in town, a few times a week in the summer. These times are posted around town or at the clan house. Only then can you get in for the single admission of $3 (an increase is under consideration). Otherwise, you can pay a $25 minimum to have someone come down and show you around. Call Nora Rinehart at © **907/874-2023** (norarinehart@yahoo. com), or, if you can't reach Nora, Margret Sturdevant at © **907/874-3747.** Nora can give you the cruise-ship schedule before you come, too. Even if you can't manage that, visit the island to see the totem poles and the charming setting (and, with extra time, visit the overgrown grave of Chief Shakes V, on Case Ave. just across the harbor). You can often see an otter near the island's footbridge.

The carved house posts in the clan house are replicas of the mid-18th-century originals protected by the local museum. These are probably the oldest and certainly the best-preserved Tlingit house posts in existence, still bearing the original fish egg and mineral paints, and a gash where, during a potlatch, a chief hacked off an image that a visitor admired and gave it to him—a gesture that demonstrated the extent of his wealth then, and still does.

The **Nolan Center Museum,** at 296 Campbell Dr. (© **907/874-3770**), opened in 2004. It's an impressive building, with galleries devoted to natural history, logging and fishing, and Native culture. The museum owns many important early Alaska Native pieces and a lot of just plain old stuff telling the story of Wrangell, one of Alaska's most historic towns. Admission is $5 adults, $3 seniors, $2 children ages 6 to 12; family admission is $12. The museum is open May 1 to September 30 Monday through Saturday 10am to 5pm, the rest of the year Tuesday through Saturday 1 to 5pm.

The museum helped preserve an impressive set of petroglyphs that lie on the beach a mile north of town. The 50 carvings at **Wrangell Petroglyph Beach State Historic Park** probably represent the work of forgotten indigenous people predating the Tlingit and were made over a long period of time. The images, chipped into rocks, are of animals and geometric forms. Their purpose is lost to time. Walk north on Evergreen Avenue and follow the signs down to the beach (don't go within an hour of high tide). Replicas of the petroglyphs were recently carved so that visitors who want to take rubbings will not destroy the originals; also try not to step on them. The great pleasure here is simply to search for the carvings—they're just lying out there, and it takes some looking—and to wonder at their meaning and age.

GETTING OUTSIDE

ON THE ISLAND   Wrangell Island's network of gravel roads, maintained by the Forest Service, leads to places of awesome beauty rarely visited by non-Alaskans. There are a few day-hike trails, some lovely campsites, and paths to remote shelters and fishing lakes you can have to yourself. There are also a couple of calm and scenic places to start a kayak paddle.

THE TRAVELOCITY GUARANTEE

...THAT SAYS EVERYTHING YOU BOOK WILL BE RIGHT, OR WE'LL WORK WITH OUR TRAVEL PARTNERS TO MAKE IT RIGHT, RIGHT AWAY.

*To drive home the point,
we're going to use the word "right" in every single sentence.*

Let's get right to it. Right to the meat! Only Travelocity guarantees everything about your booking will be right, or we'll work with our travel partners to make it right, right away. Right on!

Here's a picture taken smack dab right in the middle of Antigua, where the Guarantee also covers you.

The Guarantee covers all but one of the items pictured to the right.

Now, you may be thinking, "Yeah, right, I'm so sure." That's OK; you have the right to remain skeptical. That is until we mention help is always right around the corner. Call us right off the bat, knowing our customer service reps are there for you 24/7. Righting wrongs. Left and right.

For example, what if the ocean view you booked actually looks out at a downright ugly parking lot? You'd be right to call – we're there for you. And no one in their right mind would be pleased to learn the rental car place has closed and left them stranded. Call Travelocity and we'll help get you back on the right track.

Now if you're guessing there are some things we can't control, like the weather, well you're right. But we can help you with most things – to get all the details in righting,* visit travelocity.com/guarantee.

*Sorry, spelling things right is one of the few things not covered under the Guarantee.

I'd give my right arm for a guarantee like this, although I'm glad I don't have to.

travelocity
You'll never roam alone.

There's only one way out of town: south on the Zimovia Highway along narrow Zimovia Strait. The Forest Service map (see "Visitor Information," above) is helpful for anything you might want to do along this route.

The first potential stop is **City Park,** just south of town. Besides having a picnic area on the shore among big trees, it's a fine **tide pooling** spot. Check a tide book or ask a local to find the time of a low tide of at least average magnitude, and start your expedition an hour or two before. Five miles out Zimovia Highway you reach the **Shoemaker Bay Recreation Area,** with a small boat harbor, campground, and picnic sites (see "A Hostel & Camping," later).

Continuing south, **Eight Mile Beach** is a good stop for a ramble, and don't miss **Nemo Point,** a high oceanside overlook from which you can see more than 13 miles along Zimovia Strait all the way back to town. There are eight gorgeous campsites, and a plank walk trail (described under "Hiking") along the road leads down to the beach.

All the way across the island, about 45 minutes from town, **Earl West Cove** gives access to the protected wilderness waters on the Eastern Passage. There's a campsite there, too.

OFF THE ISLAND   Wrangell provides a stepping-off point for vast, rich wild lands and remote fishing, rafting, sea kayaking, or wildlife watching. I've described two of the main off-island destinations below—the Stikine River and the Anan Wildlife Observatory—but there are many more, too many to mention. The guides I've listed can give ideas, or look into the Forest Service cabins for rent to the public, many of which provide exclusive access to exceptional fishing. To get beyond the island, you need a boat or floatplane. You can go independently, hiring a water taxi for $200 to $260 an hour; it costs over $500 one-way to get to a remote Forest Service cabin by boat. That service is offered by various operators (see "Gearing Up," below). If you prefer to go by air, **Sunrise Aviation** (② **800/874-2311** or 907/874-2319) is a Wrangell-based operator.

GEARING UP   For a lift over the water, a guide, or rental equipment, there are several long-established businesses. **Alaska Waters,** with a desk in the Stikine Inn, 107 Stikine Ave. (② **800/347-4462** or 907/874-2378; www.alaskawaters.com), rents equipment and offers various marine services, including fishing and tours. **Alaska Vistas,** at the city dock where the cruise ships land (② **866/874-3006** or 907/874-3006; www.alaskavistas.com), started as a sea-kayaking business but now offers water taxis, guided hiking, and other services. You can stop in at their office on the dock for advice, books and maps, gear, and espresso. Both companies are listed below under the appropriate headings.

Marie Oboczky's **Rainwalker Expeditions** (② **888/276-2549** or 907/874-2549; www.rainwalkerexpeditions.com) rents bikes, sea kayaks, and canoes. She also leads guided activities and offers accommodations on a houseboat in Wrangell or afield (all covered below). Among her choices, Oboczky takes clients for a full day of guided hiking, biking, and sea kayaking for $99 per person—quite a bargain. Her van tour of the island is $75, including lunch. She also has teamed up with other outdoor businesses in town to offer joint booking and trip planning. Check her website for advice or stop in at the office near the city dock (the sign says "Tour Reservations & Information"), next door to the Stikine Inn.

OUTDOOR ACTIVITIES NEAR WRANGELL

BIKING   A paved 6-mile bike trail along the water next to the Zimovia Highway leads all the way from town to the Shoemaker Bay Loop Road. There are many more miles of appealing mountain-bike routes on Forest Service roads all over the island. See "Gearing Up," above, for rental information.

FISHING   Anglers can dip a line in various streams and lakes on Wrangell Island, reachable by car or a drive and short hike. The Forest Service provides a list, and the **Alaska Department of Fish and Game** (© **907/874-3822;** www.adfg.state.ak.us, click "Sport Fisheries" and then the Southeast region) publishes an extensive *Petersburg/ Wrangell Sport Fishing Guide*. May and June are the prime months for king salmon fishing, silvers start in July, and halibut are available all summer. The well-run **Alaska Waters** (see "Gearing Up," above) offers a long day of saltwater fishing for $250 per person; they're professional and knowledgeable. They also rent skiffs with outboard motors for self-guided fishing. Many other charter boats are available at the harbor; ask at the visitor center. You can often arrange to use part of the day on the boat for sightseeing and wildlife watching, too.

HIKING   Across the road from the Shoemaker Bay Recreation Area, the **Rainbow Falls Trail** climbs steeply for just under a mile (and 500 ft. in elevation gain) on a boardwalk with steps, up a ridge between two creeks, forested with big, mossy Sitka spruce and western hemlock. The falls seem to tumble down between the branches. From that point, you can continue another 2.5 miles and another 1,100 feet higher into open alpine terrain on the **Institute Creek Trail** to the Shoemaker Overlook, where there are great views, a picnic area, and a shelter. An additional section of the trail continues from there another 8 miles across the island. **Rainwalker Expeditions** (see "Gearing Up," above) leads nature walks on the lower part of the trail, and longer hikes all over the island, starting at $35 for a 2-hour outing. The advantage of going with guide Marie Oboczky is that she is a skilled naturalist and teacher and knows all the best places to go.

   The Rainbow Falls Trail is sometimes visited by groups from cruise ships. If you want to be sure you won't see anyone, take one of the less-developed walks reachable along the logging roads—the Forest Service can point the way. The new **Nemo Saltwater Access Trail** is a well-built half-mile plank walk leading to the beach near Turn Island, near a wonderful stand of red cedar and the Turn Island Campsite, with two wooden platforms, picnic tables, and dry firewood. Another good choice is the **Salamander Ridge Trail,** which leads a mile to subalpine terrain, where you can go off-trail hiking. The trail begins 27 miles from Wrangell on Salamander Road, also known as Forest Road 50050. The **Long Lake Trail** leads over a half-mile boardwalk to a public shelter and rowboat on the lake, on Forest Road 6271 (you'll need a map).

SEA KAYAKING   **Alaska Vistas** (see "Gearing Up," above) offers kayaking day-trip paddles starting from the boat harbor, longer day tours to lovely Earl West Cove on the east side of the island, or guided trips of many days. A 5-day trip starts with a jet-boat trip on the Stikine River to Shakes Lake and then paddles back to Wrangell with stops at the natural hot springs and other sites along the way.

THE STIKINE RIVER

The Stikine's gray glacial waters rush all the way from the dry Interior of British Columbia to a broad, shallow delta in the rainforest a few miles from Wrangell. It's among the fastest free-flowing navigable rivers in North America and in early gold-rush years was a route through the Coastal Range. Tours that sometimes go as far as Telegraph Creek, British Columbia, speed against the current with the roar of high-powered engines that send a jet of water out from under their shallow, metal bottoms. On still water, the jet boats can go as fast as a car on the highway.

The shallow delta is an exceptionally rich wildlife-viewing area, a habitat of grasslands, braided channels, and marshes populated by sea lions, eagles, and many other species of birds. In late April and early May, when the hooligans run, more than 1,500 bald eagles congregate, and some two million other birds rest on their West Coast migration. Later in the year, when summer's salmon are running, you can see them thrashing in their spawning pools. Farther upriver, tours encounter Sitka black-tailed deer, moose, brown and black bears, mountain goats, river otters, and beavers.

Traveling upriver, tours usually stop at the **Shakes Glacier** and **Shakes Lake,** where there are 3,000-foot cliffs and some 50 waterfalls. Bring a swimsuit for a dip in the Forest Service–owned **Chief Shakes Hot Springs,** where there's an indoor and an outdoor tub for public bathing. The temperature is adjustable up to 120°F (49°C). Alaska Waters and Alaska Vistas offer these tours (see "Gearing Up," above). Alaska Waters goes all the way to Telegraph, British Columbia, 160 miles upriver, bringing travelers to a remote homestead lodge. Commentary on all their trips includes natural history and Tlingit cultural traditions and legends. A 3-day, 2-night package is $1,399. The going rate for a 6-hour jet-boat tour from Wrangell to the glacier, delta, and hot springs is around $180.

Rafting the Stikine offers fast water, expansive scenery, and the potential for a remote, many-day journey. Alaska Vistas offers these guided trips, lasting about 10 days to 2 weeks, for an inclusive price of around $2,500 per person. Alaska Vistas rents rafts and other gear for floating the Stikine. A raft rents for about $100 a day. (See "Gearing Up," above.)

ANAN WILDLIFE OBSERVATORY

When the pink salmon are running in July and August (peak is mid-July to Aug 20), a population of more than 40 **black bears** and a few brown bears gathers near a waterfall on Anan Creek, on the mainland southeast of Wrangell Island, often walking close to a platform where visitors stand watching. Don't visit outside the time of this salmon run, however, unless you have it on good authority that bears are actively using the creek. Forest Service interpreters are on duty during the bear months; visitors must

---

⎛Fun Fact⎞ Why the Garnet Stands?

In the streets of Wrangell, you sometimes encounter kids selling garnets the way children other places sell lemonade. The gems come from the Garnet Ledge, near the mouth of the Stikine River, a mine that is still productive recreationally 130 years after its discovery. A visit to the mine isn't worth the effort for most travelers, but the story is interesting. The ledge was mined commercially from 1907 to 1936 by the first all-woman corporation in the nation, a group of investors from Minneapolis. Its current ownership is unusual, too: A 1962 deed gave the mine to the Boy Scouts and all the children of Wrangell, which is interpreted to mean that only children have the right to remove the stones. You can get a water taxi out there, but take a Wrangell child along if you intend to take garnets. Of course, it's easier simply to buy garnets from a kid at a card table in the street.

also follow safe bear behavior (they'll brief you when you arrive; also see "Outdoor Health & Safety," in chapter 2). Most visitors will enjoy a guided day trip from Wrangell more than going on their own. Both **Alaska Waters** and **Alaska Vistas** go by boat (see "Gearing Up," above). Expect to pay $200 to $250 per person for the hour-long run from Wrangell and a few hours with the bears.

It's also possible to go without a guide, but you will need a pass issued by the Forest Service **Wrangell Ranger District Office,** at 525 Bennett St. (P.O. Box 51), Wrangell, AK 99929 (© **907/874-2323;** fax 907/874-7595; www.fs.fed.us/r10/tongass/districts/wrangell). Check the website for an explanation of the system, a calendar showing the number of permits available each day, and application forms. A total of 60 passes are allocated for each day of the period from July 5 through August 25, with 12 held back until 3 days before the visit. Passes are given out first come, first served by mail, fax, e-mail, or in person and cost $10. There's a Forest Service cabin for rent, too, in very high demand during the bear-viewing season. The walk to the observatory is a half-mile from the shore where you land, on a good trail. **Sunrise Aviation** (© **800/874-2311** or 907/874-2319) offers charters to Anan for prices competitive with going by boat.

WHERE TO STAY

Besides the places listed below, you will find good, inexpensive rooms at **Grand View Bed and Breakfast,** Mile 2, Zimovia Highway (P.O. Box 927), Wrangell, AK 99929 (©/fax **907/874-3225;** www.grandviewbnb.com).

Harding's Old Sourdough Lodge ✦ Former mayor Bruce Harding runs this hotel in the style of a fishing lodge, renting the rooms alone or as packages with trips to the Anan Bear Observatory, Stikine River tours, fishing, kayaking, rafting, and other outdoor activities. The attractive building with a wraparound porch is in a waterfront area about a mile from the ferry dock, but Harding will drive you there or wherever else you want to go. The lodge is decorated with an outdoors theme. Most rooms are small and they generally have only shower stalls, not tubs. Some lack TVs, but all have high-speed Internet access. The suite is huge and has a Jacuzzi tub. Fresh seafood dinners are served nightly, family style (you eat what they cook). Dinner prices are $19 to $24 per person; nonguests by reservation only.

1104 Peninsula (P.O. Box 1062), Wrangell, AK 99929. © **800/874-3613** or 907/874-3613. Fax 907/874-3455. www.akgetaway.com. 16 units. $99 double; $149 triple or quad; $179 suite. Rates include continental breakfast. AE, DC, DISC, MC, V. **Amenities:** Sauna; bike rental; tour desk; courtesy car; coin-op laundry; fish freezing. *In room:* TV (in some), high-speed Internet, Jacuzzi (in some).

Rooney's Roost Bed & Breakfast ✦✦ Located downtown, this attractive old house with dormer windows was restored by a new generation of the family that has operated the place for years. They didn't miss a detail, adding antiques on the hardwood floors for an elegance otherwise unknown in Wrangell. The rooms, while small, are decorated according to themes (the Moose Room features outdoorsy decor, the Princess Room is all roses, and so on). All rooms have fans and four-poster beds with thick mattresses, comforters, and oversize pillows. The bathrooms attached to two of the rooms have showers only, not tubs. The other three rooms share a bathroom. Elaborate breakfasts with local ingredients, such as seafood or berries, are served in a sunny dining room at the guests' convenience. The rooms with private bathrooms also have TVs with VCRs.

Rent a Houseboat

Marie Oboczky, the naturalist who owns Rainwalker Expeditions (© **907/874-2549**; www.rainwalkerexpeditions.com), offers a cute and cozy old wooden houseboat as a summer accommodation. Early in summer, it sits in Shoemaker Harbor; then July through September, Oboczky keeps it tied up in remote Bradford Canal, 35 miles from town. This is a chance to stay in relative comfort in the wilderness, and for a bargain price. At the dock, the boat rents for $85 a night, including bikes for getting around. In its remote setting, she offers 3- and 5-day packages, including transportation and canoes, starting at $550. The boat isn't large, but a couple or family of three who enjoy kayaking and being outdoors could be very content here, while still able to cook and use the shower and bathroom on board. You can put the stay together with an outfitter for guided activities, too.

206 McKinnon (P.O. Box 552), Wrangell, AK 99929. © **907/874-2026.** Fax 907/874-4404. www.rooneysroost.com. 5 units, 2 with private bathroom. $100 double private bathroom; $80 double shared bathroom. Extra person $25. Rates include full breakfast. MC, V. **Amenities:** Courtesy car; laundry service. *In room:* No phone.

Stikine Inn   The town's main hotel is close to the ferry dock and stands right on the water's edge, a center of community activity for decades. It's a convenient place to stay, but it got a bit rough around the edges until new management initiated much-needed improvements prior to a recent sale to new owners in 2006. At this writing, it's too early to review the new ownership. What I've always liked best are the superb waterside views; you can watch the sunset on the ocean and hear the water lapping the shore. The restaurant shares the views.

107 Stikine Ave. (P.O. Box 662), Wrangell, AK 99929. © **888/874-3388** or 907/874-3388. Fax 907/874-3923. www.stikine.com. 34 units. High season $111–$122 double; low season $100–$111 double. Extra person over age 12 $10. AE, DC, DISC, MC, V. **Amenities:** Restaurant. *In room:* TV, dataport.

A HOSTEL & CAMPING

Wrangell Hostel is at the First Presbyterian Church, 220 Church St. (P.O. Box 439), Wrangell, AK 99929 (© **907/874-3534**). They're open Memorial Day through Labor Day, and the rate is $18 a night.

There are several attractive campgrounds in Wrangell. I've never seen another campground in a spot like the mountaintop **Nemo Point Forest Service Campground** (see "Getting Outside," earlier), but it's more than a dozen miles out of town. Five miles south of town, the **Shoemaker Bay Recreation Area** has sites by the road overlooking the boat harbor, right across from the Rainbow Falls Trail. There are free tent sites and RV sites with electric hookups for $25 a night, $15 without electric; the camping fee includes use of the town pool and its showers. Contact the **Wrangell Recreation and Parks Department** (© **907/874-2444**) for information. They also manage **City Park,** right at the edge of town on Zimovia Highway, where camping is permitted with a 1-night limit.

For a full hookup RV site, try **Alaska Waters'** small park, at 241 Berger St. (© **800/347-4462**). They charge $25 a night for rigs up to 35 feet, $30 a night for rigs over that length.

WHERE TO DINE

There's just one really good restaurant in Wrangell: Zak's, described below. Otherwise, the **Diamond C Cafe,** 215 Front St. (© **907/874-3677**), is a good diner, open daily 6am to 3pm in summer. **Harding's Old Sourdough Lodge** (see "Where to Stay," above) serves meals to guests, and to others by reservation. It's a family-style dinner without a menu.

Zak's Café 𝒢𝒢 STEAK/SEAFOOD   It's a surprising treat to find food like this in Wrangell, but there's a good explanation: The owners got tired of the lack of good dining options and decided to do something about it. For lunch, they serve salads, wraps, burgers, and sandwiches; and for dinner, a short but diverse menu of steak, seafood, pasta, and chicken. The stir-fry was seasoned just right, and the steak béarnaise melted in the mouth. The dining room is small, light, and spare; it doesn't live up to the food. Take the time to talk with the fascinating owners, James and Katherine, who staff the kitchen and dining room, respectively.

Front St. © 907/874-3355. Reservations recommended for dinner. Lunch $6.25–$10, dinner $13–$25. MC, V. Mon–Sat 11am–8pm.

4 Petersburg: Unvarnished Threshold to the Outdoors

Petersburg is the perfect small town, the sort of prosperous, picturesque, quirky place that used to be mythologized in Disney films. Except that Petersburg would never let Disney in the door. People here are too smart for that, and too protective of a place they know would be spoiled by too much attention. For the same reason, Petersburg's residents are just as glad the big cruise ships can't enter their narrow harbor. The town is unspoiled by the ships' throngs of tourists and seasonal gift shops. Instead, locals spend the money that keeps Nordic Drive, the main street, thriving with family-owned grocery and hardware stores, a fish market, and other businesses. Wooden streets over Hammer Slough still serve utilitarian purposes, making them far more appealing than if they were prettied up as tourist areas. As you walk along Sing Lee Alley and check out the stylish little bookstore, you rarely see others like yourselves—instead, you see Norwegian fishermen in pickup trucks and blond-haired kids on bikes.

Because Petersburg is insular and authentic, the sublime outdoor opportunities nearby remain little used. There are wonderful trails, mountain-biking routes, and secret places. On the water, the humpback whale-watching is as reliable as anywhere in Alaska and largely undiscovered. There's a glacier to visit, terrific fishing, and limitless sea-kayaking waters. The in-town attractions are few—a day is plenty for simple sightseeing—and little attempt has been made to accommodate lazy gawkers. But Alaska's best is waiting for those willing to spend the effort to look.

Petersburg is named for its founder, Peter Buschmann, who killed himself after living here for only 4 years. But that shouldn't be a reflection on the town, which is in an ideal location and has flourished since that inauspicious beginning. In 1898, or thereabouts (historians differ), Buschmann founded a cannery on Mitkof Island facing the slender, peaceful Wrangell Narrows in what was to become Petersburg. The stunning abundance of salmon and halibut and a nearby source of ice—the LeConte Glacier—made the site a natural. Buschmann had emigrated from Norway in 1891 and, as a proud old Son of Norway told me, he always hired Norwegians. Any Norwegian who came to him, he hired. In a few years, the cannery failed. Perhaps an excessive payroll? My suggestion was met with an icy glance and a change of subject.

Petersburg

Teasing aside, Buschmann's mistake was merging his cannery with a firm trying to challenge a monopolistic canning operation, and they went down together.

Buschmann's suicide followed his financial reverses, but the promise of Petersburg remained. The Norwegians stayed and slowly built a charming town of white clapboard houses with steeply pitched roofs, hugging the water. Their living came from the sea, as it still does. Appropriately, the downtown area doesn't stop at water's edge. Roads, boardwalks, and buildings continue over the smooth waters of Wrangell Narrows, out to the cannery buildings that survive on long wooden piers, and into the boat harbors, which branch out in a network far more extensive than the city's streets.

Today, the town's economy is based on fishing and government work. The Stikine Ranger District of the Tongass National Forest is headquartered here. That makes for a wealthy, sophisticated, and stable population.

ESSENTIALS

GETTING THERE   Petersburg has the most welcoming **ferry terminal** in the system (© **907/772-3855**), with a grassy lawn and a pier from which to watch the boats and marine animals. It's about a mile to the town center. The **Alaska Marine Highway**

(© **800/642-0066;** www.ferryalaska.com) connects to Juneau directly (an 8-hr. run), or by way of Sitka, far to the west (10 hr. to Sitka from Juneau, and then 9 more from Sitka to Petersburg). The fare is $28 from Wrangell (3 hr.), $39 from Sitka, and $58 from Juneau.

Petersburg is served by **Alaska Airlines** jets (© **800/252-7522;** www.alaskaair.com) once north and once south each day, with the nearest stops on the puddle jumper being Juneau and Wrangell. From the airport, call **Metro Cab** (© **907/772-2700**) for a taxi into town.

VISITOR INFORMATION   The Petersburg Chamber of Commerce **Visitor Information Center,** at the corner of 1st and Fram streets (P.O. Box 649), Petersburg, AK 99833 (© **907/772-4636;** www.petersburg.org), offers guidance on outdoor opportunities, boats, and lodgings, and distributes trail guides and natural history publications. The center is open in summer Monday through Saturday from 9am to 5pm, Sunday from noon to 4pm; winter Monday through Friday from 10am to 2pm.

The full-service **Viking Travel** agency, corner of Nordic Drive and Sing Lee Alley (© **800/327-2571** or 907/772-3818; www.alaskaferry.com), also specializes in booking local guides for tours, kayaks, whale-watching, flights, fishing charters, and other activities. Owners Dave and Nancy Berg are knowledgeable and helpful.

ORIENTATION   Petersburg is on Mitkof Island, divided from the much larger Kupreanof Island by the long, slender channel of the Wrangell Narrows. There are three small-boat harbors and so many docks, boardwalks, and wooden streets that the town seems to sit on the ocean. **Nordic Drive** is the main street, running from the ferry dock through town, and then becoming **Sandy Beach Road** as it rounds Hungry Point to the north. At Sandy Beach, you can circle back past the airport, which stands above the town, to **Haugen Drive,** which meets Nordic again near **Hammer Slough,** right in town. To the south, Nordic becomes the **Mitkof Highway,** which runs to the undeveloped balance of the island.

GETTING AROUND   You can walk downtown Petersburg, but you'll need wheels or a boat to get to most outdoor activities. The **Tides Inn Motel** and **Scandia House** (see "Where to Stay," later) both rent cars, but not many are available in town, so book well in advance for summer. The Scandia House also rents small boats, a wonderful way to explore Wrangell Narrows and get to trails across on the other side, or to go fishing inexpensively. An 18-footer with a 40-horsepower outboard rents for $160 a day, gas included; $25 less for guests of the hotel. They don't provide fishing gear.

FAST FACTS: Petersburg

Banks There are two banks, both with ATMs, at the intersection of Nordic Drive and Fram Street.

Hospital **Petersburg Medical Center** is at 2nd and Fram streets (© **907/772-4291**).

Internet Access Use is free at the public library, at Nordic and Haugen drives.

Police Find them on Nordic Drive near Haugen; nonemergencies © **907/772-3838.**

Post Office You can find the post office near the airport on Haugen Street.

Taxes Sales tax is 6%. The tax on accommodations totals 10%.

SPECIAL EVENTS   The Little Norway Festival, which celebrates the May 17, 1814, declaration of independence of Norway from Sweden, is an occasion for Petersburg to go wild. The 4-day schedule of events includes a street fair, food and crafts booths, a parade, and a salmon bake on the beach. The celebration is held on the third full weekend of May. The King Salmon Derby offers $30,000 in prizes over Memorial Day weekend. July 4th is a very big deal in Petersburg. The Canned Salmon Classic lasts from July 1 to August 15, with a first prize of up to $4,000 going to the person who guesses how many cans of salmon will be packed in Petersburg during the season. The Festival of Lights begins the day after Thanksgiving with an evening candlelight parade, the lighting of the Community Christmas Tree, and caroling. Julebukking, a Norwegian tradition, happens on Christmas Eve, when merchants offer food and drink to their customers and the streets fill with people.

For information on any of the above events, contact the Petersburg Chamber of Commerce (© 907/772-3646; www.petersburg.org).

EXPLORING PETERSBURG

A walk around Petersburg should include the boardwalk streets of Hammer Slough, the tidal mouth of a creek that feeds into the waterfront. Sing Lee Alley leads from North Nordic Drive at the charming center of town, passing by several interesting little shops, including Sing Lee Alley Books, at no. 11 (© 907/772-4440), where there's a good collection on natural history and local culture. Petersburg has so many thriving little shops because of its isolation and healthy economy—so far, it's been too small to attract the predation of Wal-Mart and other chains.

Sing Lee Alley turns from solid ground to wooden dock before you reach the Sons of Norway Hall, a town center where a large model Viking ship used in the Little Norway Festival is often parked. Next door, also on pilings, is the Fishermen's Memorial Park. Plaques memorialize Petersburg mariners lost at sea, under a bronze statue of Bojer Wikan, a fisherman and lifelong resident. Across the street, on the outboard side, Tonka Seafoods (© 888/560-3662 or 907/772-3662; www.tonkaseafoods.com) is a specialty fish processor with a shop and mail-order operation; they will process your sport-caught fish, too. They offer 1-hour tours for $5 during the summer at 1 and 3pm Monday through Saturday.

Continue on to Nordic Drive and turn left, crossing back over the slough to Birch Street, which follows the slough's bank on pilings upstream past old, weathered houses that hang over the placid channel. Many have one door for the road and another for the water. It's a charming, authentic place. Step out of the way of cars on the one-lane dock/street.

Back down at the waterfront, stroll the harbor floats to see the frenetic activity of the huge commercial fishing fleet in the summer, and then continue north on Nordic Drive to Eagle's Roost Park, where there is a grassy area to sit and a stairway that leads down to the water. At low tide an interesting but rugged beach walk starts here. You're almost guaranteed to see eagles, which congregate for the fish waste from the nearby cannery. Look in the tops of the trees. (In fact, you can see eagles almost anytime and anywhere along the water in Petersburg.) Another nice walk leads you on a boardwalk a third of a mile over muskeg swamp from the uphill side of the elementary school, at 4th Street.

The Clausen Memorial Museum, at 2nd and Fram streets (© 907/772-3598; www.clausenmuseum.alaska.net), interprets Petersburg and its history for the people who live here. It has a living, community feel. On one visit a portfolio of old photographs was on display with notes for visitors to write down the names of anyone they could identify and other memories. No doubt the local fishermen are fascinated by the obsolete fishing gear, rugged old nautical equipment, and a model fish trap, outlawed in 1959 when Alaska became a state. It's like being invited into the town's collective memory. The museum is open in summer Monday through Saturday from 10am to 5pm; call for hours in the winter. Admission is $3 for adults, free for children 12 and under.

GETTING OUTSIDE

I have listed only a few highlights from Petersburg's wealth of outdoor opportunities. For other choices, many of them just as good as those I've written about here, or for the detailed trail and backcountry information you'll need, contact the U.S. Forest Service at the **Petersburg Ranger District** offices at 12 N. Nordic Dr. (P.O. Box 1328), Petersburg, AK 99833 (© **907/772-3871;** www.fs.fed.us/r10/tongass/districts/petersburg).

Some of the best places to go around Petersburg require a boat. **Viking Travel** (see "Visitor Information," above) books most of the dozen or so small charter boats that operate from the harbor at any one time, allowing them to consolidate small groups into 6- to 15-person boatloads for whale-watching, sightseeing, glacier viewing, or fishing.

Some operators have made a specialty of natural history and environmentally responsible tours. Barry Bracken, a marine biologist, offers these kinds of trips on his 28-foot vessel. Contact **Kaleidoscope Cruises** (© **800/TO-THE-SEA** or 907/772-3736; www.petersburglodgingandtours.com).

SPECIAL PLACES

SANDY BEACH   The beach at City Park is an easy bike ride or a longish walk 1½ miles up Nordic Drive, around Hungry Point at the northern tip of the island, and then along Sandy Beach Road to the beach and picnic area. Return by way of the airport, coming back into town on Haugen Drive. The beach itself is coarse sand and fine gravel, and you can't swim in the frigid water, but it's a lovely spot, facing Frederick Sound on the east side of Mitkof Island.

If you go at high tide, you can beachcomb and bird-watch—a great blue heron was hanging around on one visit—but a better plan is to time your visit at low tide (free tide books are widely available, or ask at the visitor center). At tides of 1 foot or lower, you can see the outlines of ancient fish traps built on the beach beginning 2,000 years ago. They look like V-shaped rows of rocks, and at times you can see stakes. The indigenous people who built them knew how to create channels that would corral salmon at high tide, leaving them stranded to be gathered up when the water receded. These ancient people presumably also created the petroglyphs on rocks near the traps, which may depict the traps or could have something to do with the sun. Finding the traps and petroglyphs isn't easy—it's best if you can get someone to lead you, perhaps by joining the occasional Forest Service walks that you can ask about at the Ranger District office. But if you have the time and inclination to explore, walk out to the left from the picnic area, to the edge of the lagoon near the house with the greenhouse. A major petroglyph is on a black bedrock face, visible when you are looking back toward the picnic area, and the traps are just offshore from there. Please be sensitive to the delicate artifacts so they can last another 2,000 years.

RAVEN TRAIL & RAVEN'S ROOST CABIN   About 4 miles up the steep but spectacular Raven Trail, which begins behind the airport off Haugen Drive roughly a mile from town, the Raven's Roost Forest Service cabin sits atop a mountain with a sweeping view of the town and surrounding waters and islands. It's the sort of place that inspires artists and poets. Allow half a day for the climb along a boardwalk, then up a steep muddy slope, and then along a ridge, with an elevation gain of over 1,000 feet. It's possible to continue hiking over the steep, subalpine terrain of the Twin Ridge Ski Trail another 5 miles to the Twin Creek Road, and then get a ride 11 miles back to town. Ask your lodging host about options, or arrange for a pick-up by taxi cab. Check with the visitor center for trail conditions. You'll need sleeping bags, cooking gear, lights, and food. Reserve the cabin through the national system described in "Getting Outside in the Tongass National Forest" (p. 97), and check there for information sources on the other 19 cabins in the area, most of which are reached by plane or boat.

MITKOF ISLAND   The Mitkof Highway, leading south from Petersburg, opens access to most of Mitkof Island, with its king salmon fishing; views of swans, fish, and glaciers; salmon hatchery; hiking trails; lakes; and many miles of remote roads for mountain biking. The town's swimming hole and ice-skating pond are out the road, too. Anyone can enjoy a day's sightseeing drive over the island, and if you like hiking and the outdoors, you'll find days of fun. Pick up the $4 *Forest Service Mitkof Island Road Guide* map at the visitor center or ranger office; it shows what you'll find along the way.

The **Three Lakes Loop Road** intersects with the highway twice, once 10 miles from Petersburg and again 20 miles from town. From the north intersection, the one closest to town, it's 15 more miles to the level 4½-mile boardwalk **Three Lakes Trail,** which circles four small lakes, each of which contains trout, and three of which have Forest Service rowboats for public use. Besides the fish, it's a place of abundant wildflowers and berries, where you may see deer, beavers, bear, and many birds, including seasonal sandhill cranes.

Fourteen miles down Mitkof Highway from Petersburg, a quarter-mile wheelchair-accessible boardwalk leads across the damp, hummocky ground of the rainforest muskeg to **Blind River Rapids,** a peaceful spot with a three-sided shelter where you can watch and fish for king salmon in June and silvers in September, and sometimes see eagles and bears feeding on the fish. A half-mile-long loop leads farther into the forest and muskeg.

At 17 miles, somewhat hidden in the trees on the right, a bird-watching blind looks out on **Blind Slough,** where trumpeter swans winter. Swans normally will be gone by mid-March.

At 18 miles, at the end of the pavement, you'll reach the **Blind Slough Recreation Area,** where locals go to swim in amber water in the summer. Water warms in the narrow slough, more than 5 miles from Wrangell Narrows. In the winter much of the town congregates here for ice-skating and bonfires.

Finds Takeout Lunch & Take-Home Fish

Stop in at **Coastal Cold Storage,** at Excel Street and Nordic Drive (© **907/772-4177**), where they sell seafood from freezers and live from tanks. They'll freeze and ship seafood home for you. It's also a good shop for burgers, sandwiches, fish specials, and ice-cream cones at the counter.

At 20½ miles from Petersburg, the popular **Man Made Hole** picnic area and swimming pond has foot bridges and a pathway; it is accessible to people with disabilities.

At 22 miles, you reach the **Ohmer Creek campground,** with a 1-mile trail, a floating bridge over a beaver pond, and trout and some salmon in late summer. The road continues from here along the south shore of Mitkof Island, with great ocean views, to its end at Mile 32.

PETERSBURG CREEK   The lovely, grassy Petersburg Creek area either could offer an afternoon frolic among the meadows of wildflowers that meet the water or the start to a challenging 21-mile, multiday hike into the **Petersburg Creek-Duncan Salt Chuck Wilderness.** The fishing is exceptional: The creek contains four species of salmon and two of trout. You'll need a skiff or sea kayak, or get a charter to drop you off, as the creek is on Kupreanof Island, across Wrangell Narrows from town; the state maintains a dock there. Sea kayaking up the creek makes a wonderful day trip, which you can do on your own or with a guide (see "Sea Kayaking," below). A trail reaches two Forest Service cabins, at Petersburg Lake and East Salt Chuck, each with a boat for public use (reservations are required). The trail to the lake is not difficult, but continuing on to East Salt Chuck is tougher going, including wading some beaver ponds. At the lake you can fish for trout, and odds are good of seeing ducks, geese, loons, trumpeter swans, bald eagles, or black bears. The Kupreanof dock also provides access to the 3-mile, 3,000-foot trail that climbs Petersburg Mountain, a challenging hike that has spectacular views from the top.

ACTIVITIES

FISHING   There are various fishing streams and lakes that you can reach on the roads—several are mentioned above, under "Mitkof Island"—and many more accessible by boat or plane. Check at the visitor center, or contact the **Alaska Department of Fish and Game** (© 907/772-5231; www.alaska.gov/adfg). They produce the informative *Petersburg/Wrangell Sport Fishing Guide,* available on paper or on the website (click on "Sport Fisheries" and then the Southeast region). The boat harbor has a couple dozen licensed charter fishing boats, mostly six-passenger vessels. As elsewhere, halibut and salmon are usually the target. You can get a list of operators at the visitor center, or book through **Viking Travel** (see "Visitor Information," earlier). Half-day salmon charters cost around $175 per person, while halibut charters or longer salmon charters are $225 to $280 per day.

SEA KAYAKING   The waters of Wrangell Narrows are protected and interesting, with plenty to see. On longer trips of 3 days to a week, you can get out among the glaciers, Stikine River Delta, and even the whales—there's as much variety here, among these rainforest islands, as anywhere in the region. It's possible to set up a kayak trip linking some of the Forest Service cabins, too, or to use one as a base camp for a few days of exploration. (Get a copy of the free handout *Paddling the Petersburg Ranger District* from the district office.) **Tongass Kayak Adventures** (© 907/772-4600; www.tongasskayak.com) offers guided and unguided versions of each of these adventures (they rent equipment, too). Their 4-hour paddle crosses Wrangell Narrows from the harbor and penetrates Petersburg Creek, where they stop for a snack and often see bear and deer. No experience is required; they charge $70. A 3-night base-camp tour costs $790 per person; an 8-night version begins at $1,390.

WHALE-WATCHING   Most summers, Petersburg's **Frederick Sound** is one of the best places in the state to see humpbacks feeding. Whale-watching charters can go any day from May 15 to September 15, but the height is midsummer. You may see stunning bubble-net feeding, when the whales confine a school of fish in a circle of bubbles and then lunge upward to scoop them up, bursting through the surface in a great swoosh. Whales have even been known to spy hop, poking their heads as high above the surface as possible in order to look down into the boats that are watching them. In summer 1995, a humpback jumped right into one of these boats, presumably accidentally. (No one was injured, but a few people fell into the water.) Several charter operators offer trips in small six-passenger boats. Some, including Kaleidoscope Cruises (see p. 128), have hydrophones on board, so you may be able to hear the whales' vocalizations while waiting for them to surface, if their feeding behavior and the water conditions are right. Book trips through Viking Travel or directly with one of the operators. Trips usually leave around 8am and stay out 6 to 10 hours, with several hours among the whales. Prices are $150 to $210 per person. Viking Travel's conference room (at the corner of Nordic Drive and Sing Lee Alley) houses the **Petersburg Marine Mammal Center,** where you can use a computer to learn more about whales (www.psgmmc.org).

WHERE TO STAY

Bumbershoot Bed & Breakfast ☆ (Finds)   The industrious Gloria Ohmer, who also owns the Tides Inn Motel (see below), has opened her extraordinary waterfront home on Frederick Sound to guests as well. The rooms are large, decorated with quilts she made, and Gloria also will happily show off beadwork, woodwork, sewing, stained glass, stone cutting and engraving, a music room, fish-cleaning room, and deck barbecue. The place is brimming with the hosts' enthusiasm for life. Some rooms have water views, and the water is only barely beyond your reach. For $165 a night, you can rent the entire downstairs apartment, with two bedrooms, a kitchen, and a large living room with a fireplace. They also lend bicycles, offer free use of the laundry machines, and arrange transportation from the ferry dock or airport.

901 Sandy Beach Rd. (P.O. Box 372), Petersburg, AK 99833. ☎ **907/772-4683.** Fax 907/772-4627. glohmer@ pobox.aptalaska.net. 4 units, 2 with shared bathroom. $80–$90 double. Rates include continental breakfast. No credit cards. **Amenities:** Free bicycle loan; courtesy car; free laundry machines. *In room:* TV/VCR, hair dryer, iron.

Scandia House ☆☆   Rebuilt in the town's distinctive Norwegian style, this building's solid simplicity puts it in a class by itself. White rooms with blonde-wood trim are blessed with natural light. You have a choice: front rooms with king-size beds, rooms with kitchenettes, twin-bedded rooms, or a magnificent fourth-floor suite with towering ceilings. Most rooms have only one bed and a few have shower stalls, not tubs. Book well in advance for the busy summer season. The owners offer skiff rentals and car rentals.

110 Nordic Dr. (P.O. Box 689), Petersburg, AK 99833. ☎ **800/722-5006** or 907/772-4281. Fax 907/772-4301. http:// scandiahousehotel.com. 33 units. $90–$110 double, $130 double with kitchenette; $185 suite. Extra person over age 12 $10. Rates include continental breakfast. AE, DC, DISC, MC, V. **Amenities:** Car rental; courtesy van. *In room:* TV.

Tides Inn Motel ☆ (Value)   Few hotels in Alaska have such good rooms at such affordable prices. The kitchenette rooms, which rent for the same rate as the standard rooms, are an incredible bargain. The biggest difference among the rooms is the views, as all are well maintained. Those in the older part of the motel face the other building, while nonsmoking units in the front of the new section get a sweeping view. I watched bald eagles doing aerobatics less than 50 feet from my front window. The management is efficient and committed to quality, and they keep the motel in clean,

attractive condition. The hotel has an Avis car-rental franchise and serves a continental breakfast in the lobby.

307 N. 1st St. (P.O. Box 1048), Petersburg, AK 99833. © **800/665-8433** or 907/772-4288. Fax 907/772-4286. tidesinn@alaska.net. $95 double. Extra person $10. Rates include continental breakfast. AE, DC, DISC, MC, V. **Amenities:** Car rental; courtesy van. *In room:* TV.

Waterfront Bed & Breakfast   This building, designed as a bed-and-breakfast as well as a family home, sits on pilings over the Wrangell Narrows near the ferry dock. Rooms are decorated with Mission-style oak furniture and down comforters; they have shower stalls, not tubs. Four of the rooms have one bed—two with a queen and two with a double—and one has two double beds. With notice, they'll drive guests to or from the airport, harbor, or ferry dock. The family even cooks seafood dinners for those who make arrangements. Smoking is allowed only on the large deck.

1004 S. Nordic Dr. (P.O. Box 1613), Petersburg, AK 99833. © **866/772-9301** or 907/772-9300. Fax 907/772-9308. www.waterfrontbedandbreakfast.com. 5 units. $95–$105 double, $10 each additional adult. Rates include full breakfast. MC, V. **Amenities:** Covered outdoor Jacuzzi; free laundry machines. *In room:* No phone.

Water's Edge Bed & Breakfast 🏖 *(Finds*   Barry and Kathy Bracken's house sits right on the beach on Frederick Sound, about 2 miles from town center, with a creek running next to one room. You can sit in the large common room and watch waterfowl, boats, and icebergs through big windows. Probably the best thing to do here is to book a package combining a stay at the B&B and an excursion on Barry's 28-foot boat. A marine biologist, he leads natural history glacier- and whale-watching excursions. His knowledge of the area is deep and his enthusiasm infectious. Book well ahead, as it's a rare and popular opportunity. No smoking is permitted.

705 Sandy Beach Rd. (P.O. Box 1201), Petersburg, AK 99833. © **800/868-4373** or phone/fax 907/772-3736. www.petersburglodgingandtours.com. 2 units. High season $100 double; low season $70 double. Extra person $10. 2-night minimum stay. Rates include continental breakfast. No credit cards. No children under 12. **Amenities:** Free bike loan; courtesy car; free laundry machines; kitchenette. *In room:* Hair dryer.

A HOSTEL & CAMPING
Friendly little **Alaska Island Hostel,** at 805 Gjoa St. (© **907/772-3632** or 907/723-5340; www.alaskaislandhostel.com), has male and female dorm rooms with four beds in each. The $22 nightly rate includes room tax and Internet access. They're open regularly from April 15 to September 15; call for the winter schedule. Check-in and office hours are 5 to 7pm or by arrangement.

The closest natural camping is found 22 miles out the Mitkof Highway at **Ohmer Creek** (see "Mitkof Island," above). **Twin Creek RV Park** is 7½ miles out the highway (© **907/772-3244**), charging $25 for full hookups.

WHERE TO DINE
The lack of a really good restaurant is one of Petersburg's main drawbacks. There are some acceptable family restaurants typical of a small town, but that's about the best of it. For takeout pizza or calzone, burgers, fried fish, or other casual choices, try **Papa Bear's Pizza** (© **907/772-3727;** www.papabearspizza.com), across from the ferry terminal, open in summer Monday through Saturday 10am to 9pm, Saturday and Sunday 3 to 8pm (in winter Mon–Sat 10am–8pm, closed Sun). It is one of the better bets in town.

Joan Mei Restaurant 🏖 CHINESE   This would be my first choice for dinner. The whole family works together in a large, bright dining room, serving flaky egg rolls and entrees with vegetables that remain crisp and flavorful rather than being smothered or overcooked. The American food is better than elsewhere in town, too. Locals come here for a nice dinner out, and we saw many happy faces. They also have a karaoke room.

1103 S. Nordic, across from the ferry dock. (**C**) **907/772-4222**. Lunch $6.25–$13; dinner $8–$22. MC, V. Mon–Tues and Thurs–Fri 11am–9pm; Sat–Sun 7am–9pm. Closed mid-Jan to mid-Feb.

Rooney's Northern Lights SEAFOOD/DINER   You couldn't find a much better site for a restaurant than this one, sitting on pilings in Hammer Slough, overlooking a boat harbor. Call ahead to reserve one of the tables at the window or on the deck, where you can see Kupreanof Island, the fishermen working in the harbor, a cannery, and often waterfowl or seals or a sea lion. The evening menu includes steaks and several ways of having halibut or shrimp, or you can order from inexpensive Mexican selections or burgers, sandwiches, and salads. The food is generally good, attracting locals as well as tourists. (This is the place to see the morning crowd rolling dice to see who pays for coffee.)

203 Sing Lee Alley. (**C**) **907/772-2900**. Lunch $7–$12; dinner $7–$30. MC, V. Daily 6am–10pm.

5 Sitka: Rich Prize of Russian Conquest

If I could visit only one Alaska town, it would probably be Sitka.

Sitka preserves the Russian legacy of Alaska's initial European invasion and, more deeply, the story of the conflict between Alaska Natives and the newcomers, and the Natives' resistance and ultimate accommodation to the new ways. Here, 18th-century Russian conquerors who had successfully enslaved Aleuts to the west met their match in battle against the rich, powerful, and sophisticated Tlingit. A visit to Sitka reveals the story of that war and also the cultural blending that occurred in the uneasy peace that followed under the influence of the Russian Orthodox church—an influence that remained even after the Russians sold Alaska to the U.S. in 1867 (that exchange also happened here) and continues today.

Sitka's history is Alaska's richest, and there's more of real interest in this town than any other you might visit. The fact is, most Alaska towns haven't been on the map long enough to have accumulated much history. Those that have been around for a while often have been wiped out a time or two, leaving little to remind you of the distant past. There's usually a small museum and a few gold-rush sites that can be seen in half a day. Not so in Sitka. Historic photographs bear a surprising resemblance to today's city. The National Park Service protects buildings and grounds of major historic significance—places where the pioneers spoke Russian, with ways much more European than those of the rest of the American West. Even a superficial exploration of the attractions takes a day, and that's without time for the out-of-the-way points of interest or the outdoors.

In 1799, the Russians chose these protected waters on Sitka Sound, on the ocean side of Baranof Island, for a new fort as part of a strategy of pushing their sea otter–hunting operations and territorial claims east and south along the west coast of North America. The Tlingit understandably considered this to be an invasion and in 1802 they attacked the Russian's redoubt and killed almost everyone inside. The Russians counterattacked in 1804 with the cannons of the ship *Neva* and a swarm of Aleut warriors, eventually forcing the Tlingit battle leader, Katlian, to withdraw. But the

---

Fun Fact **Thank You. No, Thank *You*.**

In 1867, Russia's Czar Alexander feared that he couldn't hold the unprofitable colony of Alaska and saw a political advantage in doing his American allies the favor of selling it to them. Ironically, the Americans thought they were doing Russia a favor by buying it. Congress balked at paying the $7 million price that Secretary of State William Seward had negotiated for this worthless waste, relenting more than a year later partly out of fear of offending the czar. Americans didn't change their dim view of "Seward's Folly" until gold discoveries decades later.

Russians never rested easy in their new capital, named New Archangel, and the hostility of the proud and dangerous Tlingit long remained. Some Russian laborers intermarried and essentially adopted Tlingit culture, but the bureaucrats and naval officers sent to run the colony for the czar tended to view Alaska as purgatory and left as soon as they could. Under their ineffective and uninterested control, the Russians made surprisingly little impression on the great mass of Alaska. They failed to explore the Interior and held only tenuous control of the vast coastline.

The departing Russians rushed home, leaving only three significant towns—Unalaska, Kodiak, and Sitka—of which only Sitka retains more than a single Russian building. During their century of rule, the Russians had nearly wiped out the sea otter and the culture of the Aleuts, but both would eventually bounce back. The Russian Orthodox church stood as Russia's only lasting cultural gift to Alaska. Thanks to the efforts of one extraordinary cleric, Bishop Innocent Veniaminov, Alaska Natives were able to worship in their own languages, winning for the Russian Orthodox church many villages' continuing loyalty over less tolerant Protestant churches that came under American rule.

Besides its historic significance, Sitka is also fun to visit. Somehow it has retained a friendly, authentic feel, despite the crush of thousands of visitors. Perhaps because cruise-ship travelers must ride shuttle boats to shore, or because Sitka is a slightly inconvenient, out-of-the-way stop on the Alaska Marine Highway's main-line ferry routes, the city's streets haven't been choked by solid rows of seasonal gift shops, as has occurred in Ketchikan, Skagway, and a large part of Juneau. It remains picturesque, facing Sitka Sound, which is dotted with islands and populated by feeding eagles. Tourism is important here, but Sitka's own residents remain the center of the business and cultural world. The process of being "spoiled" hasn't begun. (The town currently is debating its future, however, with a proposal to build a new cruise-ship dock.)

Even beyond the town and its rich history, Sitka is a gateway to a large, remote portion of Southeast Alaska, in the western coastal islands. This area contains some of Tongass National Forest's least-used outdoor opportunities. The ocean halibut and salmon fishing are excellent and not overexploited, and the bird- and wildlife-watching is exceptional.

ESSENTIALS

GETTING THERE　Sitka sits on the west side of Baranof Island, a detour from the Inside Passage for the **Alaska Marine Highway System** (✆ **800/642-0066;** www.ferry alaska.com). Three kinds of ferries come here: the big, main-line ferries, the fast ferry

Sitka

N

Church ✝
Post Office ⊠
Information ⓘ
Whale-watching ✈

1/8 Mi
1/8 Km

Indian River Rd.

Sawmill Creek Rd.

To Whale Park, Green Lake, and Pulp Mill

College St.

Jeff Davis St.

De Groff St.

Biorka St.

Etolin St.

Oja St.

Finn St.

Lincoln St.

Baranoff St.

Monastery St.

Crescent Harbor

Sitka Sound

Lake St.

Seward St.

Halibut Point Rd.

Erler St.

Observatory St.

American St.

Barracks St.

Marine St.

Kogwanton St.

Katlian St.

Sitka Harbor

Alaska Native Brotherhood Harbor

O'Connell Bridge

To Airport

To Ferry Terminal and Old Sitka State Historic site

Visitors Dock

Alaska

Fairbanks ○
Anchorage ○ Cordova Juneau
Kenai   **Sitka**
        Ketchikan

ACCOMMODATIONS ■

Alaska Ocean View Bed & Breakfast **1**
Alaska Swan Lake Bed & Breakfast **1**
Cascade Inn **1**
Finn Alley Inn **15**
Sitka Hotel **6**
Super 8 Sitka **14**
Westmark Sitka **10**

DINING ◆

Backdoor Café **7**
Bayview Restaurant **11**
Channel Club **1**
Highliner Coffee **13**
Ludvig's Bistro **3**
Pizza Express **20**

ATTRACTIONS ●

Alaska Raptor Center **19**
Castle Hill **5**
Harrigan Centennial Hall
  Visitor Center **9**
The Russian Bishop's House **12**
Russian Blockhouse **2**
Sheldon Jackson Museum **17**
Sheldon Jackson College
  Aquarium **16**
Sitka National Historical
  Park **18**
Sitka Tribe of Alaska's
  Community House **4**
St. Michael's Cathedral **8**

Fairweather, and most often the little *LeConte,* which is like a local bus, stopping at all the tiny outlying villages and giving visitors an insight into their island lifestyle. The *Fairweather* cuts a 9-hour journey from Juneau to less than 5 but runs only Monday and Wednesday. On any of the ships, the ride through narrow Peril Straits into Sitka is definitely worth the trip. The shore seems close enough to touch, and if you look closely, you can sometimes see deer. The fare from either Juneau or Petersburg (10 hr. away by conventional ferry) is $44. The ferry dock (© **907/747-3300**) is 7 miles out of town.

Alaska Airlines (© **800/252-7522;** www.alaskaair.com) links Sitka daily to Juneau and Ketchikan with flights that then continue nonstop to Seattle and Anchorage.

To get to town from the airport or ferry dock, the **Sitka Tours** bus charges $6 one-way, $8 round-trip. No reservations are needed; just climb aboard and pay the driver. **Sitka Cab,** at © **907/747-5001,** is among three taxi companies in town; the ride from the ferry dock is around $15.

VISITOR INFORMATION   A kiosk in the city-operated **Harrigan Centennial Hall,** 330 Harbor Dr., next to the Crescent Boat Harbor (© **907/747-3225**), is the only walk-in information stop. It is staffed by volunteers only when cruise ships are in town, although you may be able to ask questions of hall staff other times. The hall is open Monday through Friday from 8am to 10pm, Saturday 8am to 5pm, and sometimes Sunday. The town's professional visitor organization is the **Sitka Convention and Visitors Bureau,** at P.O. Box 1226, Sitka, AK 99835 (© **907/747-5940;** fax 907/747-3739). They maintain a very useful website at **www.sitka.org**.

The **Sitka National Historical Park Visitor Center,** 106 Metlakatla St., Sitka, AK 99835 (© **907/747-0110;** www.nps.gov/sitk), run by the National Park Service, which maintains key historic sites in Sitka, is an essential stop to gather information and learn about what happened here. The center is open daily from 8am to 5pm in summer, Monday through Saturday from 8am to 5pm in winter. Also see "Exploring Sitka," below, for more on the park.

ORIENTATION   Sitka, on the west side of Baranof Island, has only a few miles of road. The **ferry terminal** is located at its north end, 7 miles out, on **Halibut Point Road;** the site of an abandoned pulp mill is at the south end, roughly the same distance out **Sawmill Creek Road.** The town faces Sitka Sound. Across Sitka Channel is **Japonski Island,** with the **airport** (don't worry, it only looks as if your plane is going to land in the water). **Lincoln Street** contains most of the tourist attractions.

GETTING AROUND   The airport has branches of **Avis** (© **800/230-4898** or 907/966-2404; www.avis.com) and **North Star Rent-a-Car** (© **800/722-6927** or 907/966-2552; www.northstarrentacar.com).

The Visitor Transit Bus operated by the **Sitka Tribe** (see "Exploring Sitka," below) makes a continuous circuit of the sites from May to September, Monday through Friday from 12:30 to 4:30pm, with added morning hours when cruise ships are in. The fare is $7 all day.

Bike rental makes a good deal of sense in Sitka. **Yellow Jersey Cycles,** at 329 Harbor Dr., right across from the Centennial Hall downtown (© **907/747-6317;** www. yellowjerseycycles.com), rents quality bikes for $25 a day.

FAST FACTS: Sitka

Banks Three banks are at the center of downtown, around 300 Lincoln St., with ATMs, which are also found at local grocery stores.

Hospital Sitka Community (© 907/747-3241) is at 209 Moller Dr.

Internet Access Seaport Cyber, across the hall from the Bayview Restaurant near the boat harbor, charges $5 an hour. Or try **Highliner Coffee**, on Lake Street near Seward Street, or the downtown post office.

Police Call © 907/747-3245 for nonemergency business.

Post Office Open on Saturday, the post office is at 338 Lincoln St.

Taxes Sales tax is 5% October through March, 6% April through September. The tax on rooms totals 11% and 12%, respectively.

SPECIAL EVENTS   The **Starring Ceremony,** January 7, marks Russian Orthodox Christmas with a procession through the streets and song and prayer at the doors of the faithful. Call St. Michael's Cathedral for information (© **907/747-8120**).

The **Sitka Salmon Derby** occurs at the end of May and beginning of June, when the kings are running; contact the Sitka Sportsman's Association (© **907/966-2281**) for information.

The **Sitka Summer Music Festival,** a chamber-music series that began in 1972, is one of Alaska's most important cultural events, drawing musicians from all over the world for 3 weeks in early summer (June 1–22, 2007). Performances take place Tuesday and Friday, and other events all week. Contact the festival office for information (© **907/277-4852;** www.sitkamusicfestival.org).

Alaska Day, October 18, commemorating the Alaska Purchase, is a big deal in this former Russian capital city; the **Alaska Day Festival** lasts 4 days leading up to the big event. The Convention and Visitors Bureau has information. The **Sitka Grind,** a music and arts celebration at varying sites around town, takes place the third Saturday of each month from October to March.

The **Sitka WhaleFest** (© **907/747-7964;** www.sitkawhalefest.org) takes place over a weekend in early November, during the fall and early winter period when humpback whales congregate in Sitka Sound. Experts come from around the world to present a 3-day symposium, and there are whale-watching tours, concerts, an art show, a run, and community events. Consider combining it with the Alaska Bald Eagle Festival in Haines, coordinated to follow (see section 9 of this chapter, on Haines).

EXPLORING SITKA

The **Sitka Tribe of Alaska's Community House** is a good starting point, where you can watch dance performances (see below), join walking or bus tours, or sign up for kayaking or other outdoor activities, including trail hikes. A 2-hour walking tour includes the town, a national historic park, and a marine science facility at Sheldon Jackson College. The house is at 200 Katlian St. (© **888/270-8687** or 907/747-7290; www.sitkatribe.org). **Sitka Tours** (© **907/747-8443**) also offers tours, taking more of the Russian perspective. Prices for each choice of tour range from about $12 for a brief downtown tour to $57 for a longer town tour that includes most of the attractions and dancing; the type of dancing—Native or Russian—depends on which firm you go with. See "Sitka Tribe Dance Performances," p. 140, for a description of the Alaska Native choice. Russian folk dance is performed by the women of the **New Archangel Dancers** (© 907/747-5516) in the Harrigan Centennial Hall at 330 Harbor Dr., next to the Crescent Boat Harbor. Performances are scheduled when cruise ships are in town, and most of the audience comes from Sitka Tours. Admission is $8 at the door.

SITKA'S TLINGIT & RUSSIAN HERITAGE

Sitka National Historical Park ୧୧୧   In 1799, the Russian American Company, led by Alexander Baranof, landed from their base in Kodiak, established Redoubt St. Michael (today the **Old Sitka State Historic Site,** 7½ miles north of town—just a grassy picnic area with interpretive signs), and claimed the Pacific Northwest of America for Russia. The Tlingit, sophisticated traders who had already acquired flintlocks, attacked with knives, spears, and guns, and destroyed the redoubt in mid-June 1802, killing almost all of the Russians. The Natives immediately began building fortifications on the site now within the national historical park, anticipating a Russian counterattack, which came in 1804. Baranof returned with an attacking force of a Russian gunship and a swarm of Aleut kayaks, which towed the becalmed vessel into position to begin the bombardment. The Tlingits withstood the siege for 6 days and then vacated their fort at night after a canoe delivering gunpowder exploded, leaving them short of ammunition. The Russians founded and heavily fortified the town of New Archangel, and in 1808, it became their administrative capital. But the Tlingit name is the one that stuck: Shee Atika, since contracted to Sitka.

The historic significance of the battle site was recognized early. President Benjamin Harrison, a friend of Alaska missionary Sheldon Jackson, set the land aside as a public park in 1890. In 1902 and 1905, a collection of totem poles from around Southeast was brought here, and in 1910, the site was designated a national monument. The park visitor center and grounds emphasize the Native perspective. There is no better place to learn about Tlingit art and history. A naturally lit hall with a 30-foot ceiling displays the original poles (reproductions stand outside) in startlingly good condition despite their age. The artistic power of these poles is overwhelming, and their age and critical value for the Tlingit and Haida cultures only add to the impact. Moreover, the art still lives. Extraordinary poles by current Native artists stand outside, and within the building artisans of the Southeast Alaska Indian Cultural Center work in a series of windowed workshops creating traditional crafts of metal, wood, beads, textiles, and woven grass. Visitors are invited to enter the workshops and ask questions. A free 12-minute video provides a good historical overview.

The outdoor totem loop trail and the site of the battle and of the fort also must not be missed. The totems stand tall and forbidding along a pathway through massive spruce and hemlock, where misty rain often wanders down from an unseen sky somewhere above the trees. The shoreside battle site and the nearby fort site—only a grassy area now—are along the trail. While plenty of imagination is needed to place a desperate fight in this peaceful setting, it is easy to feel deep down what the Tlingits were fighting for when you stand among the trees and totems and hear the lapping sea and raven's call.

Though they lost the battle for this ground, the Tlingit won the war—they're still here. In 1996, a gathering of clans erected a major new pole in front of the center to explain their story back to mankind's arrival in North America. It took quite a bit of debate to settle the story the pole would tell. For example, the crests of the eagle and raven tribal moieties are traditionally never shown on the same pole, but they had to be to tell the whole history of the Tlingits. In 1999, another new pole rose at the site of the battle to commemorate that story. At the bottom of the pole is a carving of the raven helmet worn by Katlian, the Tlingit's leader in the battle of Sitka. You can see the helmet itself in the Sheldon Jackson Museum (see below). Contrary to the popular phrase "low man on the totem pole," the position shows the strength with which Katlian led and supported his people.

106 Metlakatla St. ℂ 907/747-0110. Admission $4. Visitor center open summer daily 8am–5pm; winter Mon–Sat 8am–5pm. Park open summer daily 6am–10pm; winter daily 7am–8pm.

The Russian Bishop's House 🐾🐾🐾

Bishop Innocent Veniaminov, born in 1797, translated scriptures into Tlingit and other Native languages and trained deacons to carry Russian Orthodoxy back to their Native villages. Unlike most of the later Protestant missionaries led by Sitka's other historic religious figure, Sheldon Jackson, Veniaminov and his followers allowed parishioners to use their own language, a key element to saving Native cultures. When the United States bought Alaska in 1867, few Russians stayed behind, but thanks to Veniaminov's work, the Russian Orthodox faith remains strong in Native Alaska; today there are 89 parishes, primarily in tiny Native villages. In 1977, Veniaminov was canonized as St. Innocent in the Orthodox faith.

In 1842–43, the Russian American Company constructed this extraordinary house for Veniaminov as a residence, school, and chapel. It may have survived many years of neglect in part because its huge beams fit together like a ship's. In 1972, the National Park Service bought and began restoring the building, which is the best of only three surviving from all of Russian America (the others are in Kodiak and at 206 Lincoln St. in Sitka, today occupied by the Log Cache Gifts). The Bishop's House is Alaska's most interesting historic site. Downstairs is a self-guided museum; upstairs, rangers lead tours of the bishop's quarters, which are furnished with original and period pieces. It's an extraordinary window into an alternate stream of American history, from a time before the founding of Seattle or San Francisco, when Sitka was the most important city on North America's Pacific Coast. The tour concludes with a visit to a beautiful little chapel with many of the original icons Innocent imported from Russia.

Lincoln and Monastery sts. No phone; call Sitka National Historical Park Visitor Center (ℂ 907/747-0110). Admission $4 per person or $15 per family (family admission covers both facilities). Summer daily 9am–5pm; by appointment in winter.

Sheldon Jackson Museum 🐾🐾

Sheldon Jackson, a Presbyterian missionary with powerful friends in Washington, was Alaska's first General Agent for Education, a paternal guardian of the welfare, schooling, and spiritual lives of Alaska's Natives. His benevolent aim was to defend Natives from exploitation and abuse and bring them into American civilization as equals. Tragically, his strategy to accomplish this goal was to erase indigenous cultures and replace them with Protestantism, causing incalculable, lasting harm to peoples over a broad swath of Alaska. As a side hobby during his travels from 1888 to 1898, Jackson gathered an omnivorous 5,000-piece collection of Native art, cultural, and everyday objects. That collection, the best in Alaska, has been displayed for more than a century in a concrete building on the college campus that bears Jackson's name. It's a jewel box; the overwhelming wealth is displayed by Alaska State Museum curators in ingenious ways that avoids a feeling of clutter. Many drawers open to reveal more displays. Despite the age of many of the pieces, they appear new, as if just made. Don't miss Katlian's helmet, worn by the Kiksadi clan's war leader in the Battle of Sitka in 1804; raven-shaped, it is that rare piece of great history that's also great art. Native artists demonstrate their skill on summer days, and the gift shop contains almost exclusively authentic Native arts and crafts. Authentic Native art pieces cost more than tourist trinkets: Plan to spend over $100 except for small, simple items. (If you're already here, take time for the college aquarium, mentioned under "Walking Downtown," below.)

104 College Dr. © 907/747-8981. www.museums.state.ak.us. Admission $4 adults, free for ages 18 and under. Mid-May to mid-Sept daily 9am–5pm; mid-Sept to mid-May Tues–Sat 10am–4pm.

St. Michael's Cathedral ⚔   The first Orthodox cathedral in the New World stands grandly in the middle of Sitka's principal street, where it was completed in 1848. Bishop Veniaminov (see "The Russian Bishop's House," above) designed it and oversaw construction. The cathedral contains several miraculous icons, some dating from the 17th century. The St. Michael, the farthest right of six on the front screen, was bound for Sitka aboard the *Neva* in 1813 when the ship went down some 30 miles from Sitka. Thirty days later, the icon, in its crate, washed ashore undamaged and was recovered by Sitka's townspeople. The original building burned down in a 1966 fire that started elsewhere and took much of Sitka's downtown, but almost all the contents were saved by a human chain in the 30 minutes before the building was destroyed. One man lifted down the huge central chandelier, which later took six men to carry. Orthodox Christians all over the United States raised the money to rebuild the cathedral exactly as it had been, using a Russian architect who could interpret Veniaminov's original plans. It was completed in 1976. A knowledgeable guide is on hand to answer questions or give talks when large groups congregate. Sunday services are sung in English, Church Slavonic, Tlingit, Aleut, and Yupik. Right across Lincoln Street, stop in at the cathedral's well-stocked Archangel Michael Icons, Books and Gift Shop for souvenirs, music CDs, books, and even children's books.

Lincoln and Cathedral sts. © 907/747-8120. $2 donation requested. Summer Mon–Fri 9am–4pm. Call for weekend and winter hours.

Sitka Tribe Dance Performances ⚔   The Sheet'ka Kwaán Naá Kahidi, Sitka's community house, standing on the north side of the downtown parade ground, is a modern version of a Tlingit clan house, with an air handling system that pulls smoke from the central fire pit straight up to the chimney. The magnificent house screen, a carved wall at the front of the hall, installed in 2000, is the largest in the Pacific Northwest. Performances last 30 minutes, including three dances and a story. It's entirely traditional and put on by members of the tribe. You can also sign up for tours and activities in the lobby.

200 Katlian St. © 888/270-8687 or 907/747-7290. www.sitkatribe.org. Admission $7 adults, $5 children. Call for times.

OTHER ATTRACTIONS IN TOWN
Alaska Raptor Center ⚔⚔   This nonprofit center takes in injured birds of prey (mainly bald eagles, but also owls, hawks, and other species) for veterinary treatment and release or, if too badly injured, for placement in a zoo or as part of the collection of 25 that live on-site. Visitors get to see the impressive birds up close in a lecture setting, through the glass wall of the veterinary clinic, and in outdoor enclosures, but the highlight is an extraordinary flight-training center, built in 2003 at a cost of $3 million. This enormous aviary is where recuperating birds learn to fly again, and visitors can

walk its length behind one-way glass, watching them preen, feed, and take to the air in a peaceful setting simulating their natural habitat. Watching these giant birds fly from so close is awesome. The center's grounds also include a pleasant nature trail (accessible for traveler's with disabilities) that leads down to a river with four species of salmon, where healthy eagles sometimes can be seen feeding.

1000 Raptor Way (off Sawmill Creek Blvd.) (C) **800/643-9425** or 907/747-8662. www.alaskaraptor.org. Admission $12 adults, $6 ages 12 and under. Summer daily 8am–4pm. Call for winter hours.

WALKING DOWNTOWN   The grassy park at Lincoln and Katlian was the site of the Russians' barracks and parade ground. Just north on Marine Street is a replica of a **Russian Blockhouse;** across Lincoln Street to the south and up the stairs is **Castle Hill,** a site of historic significance for the ancient Tlingits, for the Russians, and for contemporary Alaskans. The first American flag raised in Alaska was hoisted here in 1867. There are historic markers and cannons. As you walk east past the cathedral and Crescent Harbor, several quaint historic buildings are on the left. My favorite is **St. Peter's by-the-Sea Episcopal Church,** a lovely stone-and-timber chapel with a pipe organ, consecrated in 1899.

At the east end of the harbor is a **public playground** and the **Sheldon Jackson College Aquarium,** in the Sage Building on the ocean side of Lincoln Street. All the tanks contain local marine life (a king crab had just been dismembered by an octopus on our visit), and it's eye opening to realize what's down below. Best of all are the large touch tanks where visitors can handle animals from three different seafloor habitats. Admission is free. The aquarium is open to the public May to September Monday through Friday 8am to 5pm and weekends when large cruise ships are in town.

SHOPPING

There are some good shops and galleries in Sitka, mostly on Lincoln and Harbor streets. Several are across the street from St. Michael's Cathedral. **Artist Cove Gallery,** at 241 Lincoln St., shows art and contains a small but interesting section of used and out-of-print books about Alaska. **Fishermen's Eye Fine Art Gallery and Graphic,** at 239 Lincoln St., is owned by an artist who shows only work by Alaskans, most of it created in Sitka. **Fairweather Prints,** at 209 Lincoln St., has a fun, youthful feel; it is large and has a diverse selection, including wearable art (including T-shirts), watercolors, prints, ceramics, and cute, inexpensive crafts. Continue west on Lincoln to **Baranov's Russian and American Store** on the right, and, on the left, **Log Cache Gifts,** a typical gift store housed in an 1835 Russian cabin. **Old Harbor Books,** at 201 Lincoln St., is a good browsing store with an excellent selection of Alaska books. Back in the other direction, near the Crescent Harbor dock, the **Sitka Rose Gallery** occupies a Victorian house at 419 Lincoln St., featuring higher-end work, mostly local: sculpture, original paintings, engraving, and jewelry. The **Sheldon Jackson Museum Gift Shop,** 104 College Dr., is an excellent place to buy Alaska Native arts and crafts with assurance of their authenticity.

GETTING OUTSIDE: ON THE WATER

The little islands and rocks that dot Sitka Sound are an invitation to the sea otter in all of us; you must get out on the water.

SIGHTSEEING & WILDLIFE TOURS

When conditions allow, tour boats visit **St. Lazaria Island,** a bird rookery where you can expect to see tufted puffins, murres, rhinoceros auklets, and other pelagic birds.

Storm petrels show up by the hundreds of thousands at dawn and dusk for those who charter a boat to stay overnight at the rookery. The volcanic rock drops straight down into deep water, so even big boats can come close, but in rough weather even they won't go to the exposed location of the island. Even then, there's plenty to see. Humpback whales show up in large groups in the fall and are often seen by the half-dozen in the summer. There are so many bald eagles that you're pretty well guaranteed to see them even from shore. But the lowly sea otter is the most common and, in my experience, most amusing and endearing of marine mammals, and you'll certainly see them from a tour boat. The public tubs at **Goddard Hot Springs,** 17 miles south of town, are another possible stop for charters.

The **Sitka Wildlife Quest,** operated by Allen Marine Tours (© **888/747-8101** or 907/747-8100; www.allenmarinetours.com), runs a popular marine tour with well-trained naturalists to explain the wildlife. You have a good chance of encountering humpback whales and sea otters. Tours visit St. Lazaria Island when sea conditions permit. A 2-hour cruise Tuesday and Thursday at 6pm costs $59 adults, $39 children ages 3 to 12, free 2 and under. A 3-hour cruise Saturday and Sunday at 8:30am costs $79 adults, $49 children ages 3 to 12, free 2 and under. The boat leaves from the Crescent Harbor Visitors Dock late May through early September. Buy tickets on board. These are different excursions from the ones offered cruise-ship passengers. Allen Marine, which also builds vessels, has a long-standing reputation for the quality of its offerings.

For $100 per person, you can charter a six-passenger boat for a 3-hour tour to St. Lazaria Island, for whale-watching, and to learn about the Sound with a married couple who are both former wildlife biologists, Kent Hall and Beverly Minn, at **Sitka's Secrets** (© **907/747-5089;** www.sitkasecret.com). They do fishing charters, too.

Sea Life Discovery Tours (© **877/966-2301** or 907/966-2301; www.sealifediscovery tours.com) offers a chance to see the rich underwater life of Sitka Sound from an extraordinary boat with big windows 4 feet below the waterline; it's really cool. They charge $79 for a 2-hour tour; call for times.

SALTWATER FISHING
Many charter boats are available for salmon or halibut. The Sitka Convention and Visitors Bureau (see "Visitor Information," earlier) keeps a detailed charter boat list online. Using the grid view (www.sitka.org/grid.html), you can compare boats, rates, and services, and link to the vessel's own home page. Or book through **Alaska Adventures Unlimited** (© **907/747-5576;** akfish@gci.net), which has been setting up charters in Sitka since 1982. If you can handle your own boat, **Sitka Ocean Adventures** (© **907/ 747-6375;** www.ssoceanadventures.com) rents skiffs for $95 per half-day and up.

SEA KAYAKING
Sitka's protected waters and intricate shorelines are perfect for sea kayaking. You're almost sure to see sea otters, seals, sea lions, and eagles, and could see whales. **Sitka Ocean Adventures,** mentioned in the previous paragraph, offers tours for beginners every day in the summer when they have at least two customers to go along. Guides don't follow regular routes, seeking wildlife wherever animals have recently been seen. A 2-hour paddle (plus a half-hour for instruction and gearing up) takes kayakers into the islands around Sitka and costs $63. A half-day paddle could also go to a historic World War II fort, where you can walk through the abandoned bunkers; that's $85. The firm offers all day paddles, too.

GETTING OUTSIDE: ONSHORE
FRESHWATER FISHING

Anglers should pick up the *Sitka Area Sport Fishing Guide,* which has lots of tips on streams, lakes, and fishing methods in the area. You can download the guide from the **Alaska Department of Fish and Game** at www.alaska.gov/adfg (click on "Sport Fisheries" and then the Southeast region). The site also has weekly fishing updates. The local Fish and Game office is at 304 Lake St., Room 103, Sitka, AK 99835 (*©* 907/747-5355).

FOREST SERVICE CABINS

The **Sitka Ranger District,** 204 Siginaka Way, Sitka, AK 99835 (*©* **907/747-6671;** www.fs.fed.us/r10/tongass/districts/sitka), maintains two dozen wilderness cabins on Baranof, Chichagof, and Kruzof islands, in sea-kayaking coves and on remote fishing lakes, where rowing skiffs generally are provided. The cabins and their facilities are described in a Forest Service handout or on their website. You will need camping gear and a boat or floatplane to get there, a much greater cost than the nightly rental of $35 to $45. For cabins on salt water near Sitka, the most affordable way is a water taxi, such as **Esther G Sea Taxi** (*©* **907/747-6481** or 907/738-6481; www.puffinsand whales.com). Operator Davey Lubin also offers marine wildlife tours and kayak drop-offs to remote shores. **Harris Aircraft Services,** 400 Airport Rd. (*©* **877/966-3050** Alaska only, or 907/966-3050; www.harrisaircraft.com), offers floatplane charters to cabins or anywhere else. Either way, allow time in your schedule in case bad weather prevents backcountry travel. Information on researching and reserving a cabin is under "Getting Outside in the Tongass National Forest," on p. 97. Another remote cabin option is the Camp Coogan Bay Hideaway, listed below, under "Rent a Floathouse."

HIKING

Sitka is a great hiking area, with trails threading all over the mountains behind the town. There are a dozen U.S. Forest Service hiking trails accessible from the roads around Sitka and another 20 rough trails you can get to by plane or boat. A beauti-fully made little book, *Sitka Trails* (Alaska Natural History Association, $8), covers each trail with a detailed description and fine-scale color topographic map. If you need further advice, contact the ranger district office (see the preceding paragraph).

From downtown, the 4-mile (one-way) **Indian River Trail** is a relaxing rainforest walk rising gradually up the river valley to a small waterfall. Take Indian River Road off Sawmill Creek Road just east of the downtown. For a steeper mountain-climbing trail to alpine terrain and great views, the **Gavan Hill-Harbor Mountain Trail** is near the end of Baranof Street, which starts near the Russian Bishop's House. It gains 2,500 feet over 3 miles to the peak of Gavan Hill and then continues another 3 miles along a ridge to meet Harbor Mountain Road. The **Sitka Cross Trail** connects these trails and neighborhood streets, allowing you to start almost anywhere.

At the north end of Halibut Point Road, 7½ miles from downtown, several wonder-ful trails loop through the **Starrigavan Recreation Area.** On the right, the **Estuary Life Trail** and **Forest Muskeg Trail,** totaling about a mile, are exquisitely developed and accessible to anyone, circling a grassy estuary rich with birds and fish. The well-built **Mosquito Cove Trail,** starting from the far end of the campground loop on the left, loops 1.25 miles along the shore to the secluded gravel beach of the cove, returning over boardwalk steps through the old-growth forest. Camping here is covered below.

TIDE POOLING & SHORE WALKS

Halibut Point State Recreation Area, 4½ miles north of town on Halibut Point Road, is a great place for a picnic, shore ramble, and tide pooling. The Mosquito Cove Trail (see above) is also promising. To find the best low tides, check a tide book, available all over town. It's best to go at the lowest tide possible, arriving on the shore an hour before the low. To identify the little creatures you'll see, pick up a plastic-covered field guide at a bookstore.

WHALE-WATCHING

Humpback whales stop to feed in Sitka Sound on their way south in the winter migration. During October, November, December, and March, you can watch from shore—the local government has even built a special park for the purpose. At **Whale Park,** just south of town on Sawmill Creek Road, spotting scopes are mounted on platforms along a boardwalk and at the end of staircases that descend the dramatic, wooded cliffs. Excellent interpretive signs, located near surfacing concrete whales in the parking lot, explain the whales. The Sitka WhaleFest, in November (see "Special Events," earlier), is the best time for whale enthusiasts, as then you can watch whales in the company of cetacean scientists.

WHERE TO STAY

In addition to the places below, you'll find superclean rooms with many amenities in a quiet building downtown at the **Super 8 Sitka,** 404 Sawmill Creek Blvd. (✆ 800/800-8000 for reservations, or 907/747-8804; www.super8.com). You'll find comfortable B&B rooms in a quiet subdivision a half-hour walk from town at **Sitka Woodside Lodging,** 411 Wortman Loop (✆ 907/747-8287; www.woodsidelodging.com). A nice single-unit B&B, **Finn Alley Inn** (✆ 907/747-3655; www.finnalleybedand breakfast.com), is at 711 Lincoln St. Also, the **Sitka Convention and Visitors Bureau** (✆ 907/747-5940; www.sitka.org) has links to many B&Bs on its website and can send you a printed list as well.

Alaska Ocean View Bed & Breakfast ✿✿✿   Ebullient Carole Denkinger and her husband, Bill, have a passion for making their bed-and-breakfast one you'll remember. They've thought of everything—the covered outdoor Jacuzzi where you can watch the eagles, toys and games for the kids, a laptop to borrow, thick robes and slippers, an open snack counter, a big and delicious full breakfast, and even wildflower seeds to take home. Rooms are soft and plush, and guests are pampered with unique extras such as DVD players and a media library and HEPA air cleaners in each room for people with allergies. The hospitality is exceptional, too. For example, Carole has stocked her kitchen with Atkins-approved food for low-carb dieters and cooks special meals for those sensitive to gluten or lactose. Moreover, she doesn't charge extra for any of her exceptional amenities. The B&B is on a residential street with a view of the water about a mile from the historic district. No smoking is permitted.

1101 Edgecumbe Dr., Sitka, AK 99835. ✆ 907/747-8310. Fax 907/747-3440. www.sitka-alaska-lodging.com. 3 units. High season $129–$229 double; low season $89–$169 double. Extra person free–$30, depending on circumstances. Rates include full breakfast. AE, DC, DISC, MC, V. **Amenities:** Outdoor Jacuzzi; business center. *In room:* TV/VCR/DVD, CD player, Wi-Fi, fridge, coffeemaker, hair dryer, iron, microwave, free videos and CDs.

Alaska Swan Lake Bed & Breakfast (*Value*   This economical B&B is in a big, white house above the lake just a mile from the downtown area. Rooms, decorated on Alaskana and bird themes, are well equipped with extras such as bathrobes. All have private bathrooms with shower stalls. They are situated in two pairs, upstairs and downstairs, each pair capable of being combined into a suite by a single party. The upper rooms are larger and brighter. The phone is in the common area, which also has a kitchen available for guest use. The breakfast, although classified as continental, includes an egg main course.

206½ Lakeview Dr., Sitka, AK 99835. © **907/747-3917.** Fax 907/747-3915. www.sitka.org/swanlake/index.htm. 4 units. High season $95 double; low season $85 double. Extra person 13 and over $50. Rates include continental breakfast. MC, V. *In room:* TV, microwave, hair dryer, iron.

Cascade Inn ¦ Two and a half miles from downtown, this family-operated waterfront hotel puts you in a trim standard room with a balcony over Sitka Sound and a spectacular view. The red building is fronted by gas pumps and a liquor store, but don't let that fool you. The rooms, although small, are an oasis of ocean light where you can fall asleep to the sound of the sea. Each has one or two queen-size beds, and some include handy kitchenette units, which cost $15 more. The sauna has a glass front to take advantage of the view. *Note:* Stay elsewhere if you have trouble with stairs, and plan on having wheels to get around.

2035 Halibut Point Rd., Sitka, AK 99835. © **800/532-0908** or 907/747-6804. www.cascadeinnsitka.com. 10 units. High season $115–$140 double; low season $85–$105 double. Extra person $20. MC, V. **Amenities:** Sauna; coin-op laundry. *In room:* TV, coffeemaker, hair dryer, iron.

Sitka Hotel *Value*   After a major fire hit this family-owned budget hotel early in 2006, it blossomed from the ashes (thanks to an insurance settlement) with 15 brand new rooms and complete redecorating, upgrading what had always been a good deal in a fairly rickety wooden building into a very good deal in a relatively modern building. The smaller rooms will never be luxurious, but the owners keep them clean and comfortable. Fourteen lack private bathrooms, but there are plenty of shared facilities to prevent waits. The location is prime, right across from the Russian parade grounds. The brand new rooms, in the back of the building, have private bathrooms and added amenities, such as coffee makers.

Victoria's Restaurant, with about a dozen tables in the storefront downstairs, tries for a high Victorian feel, but in actuality it's more of a friendly small-town diner, with hearty breakfasts and lunches in winter and an inexpensive fine-dining dinner menu added in the summer.

118 Lincoln St., Sitka, AK 99835. © **907/747-3288.** Fax 907/747-8499. www.sitkahotel.com. 60 units, 14 with shared bathroom. High season $70 double with shared bathroom, $90 double with private bathroom; low season $60 double with shared bathroom, $75 double with private bathroom. Extra person $7. AE, DISC, MC, V. **Amenities:** Restaurant; coin-op laundry. *In room:* TV, Wi-Fi, iron/ironing board.

Westmark Sitka ¦¦ The community's main upscale hotel, above Crescent Harbor in the heart of the historic district, contains many comfortable rooms with sweeping views of Sitka Sound. The lobby suggests the building style of Northwest Native Americans, but the more anonymous rooms will be familiar to any business traveler, with furniture of warm wood and all the expected amenities. Service likewise comes with a professionalism you won't find elsewhere in town.

The **Raven Dining Room** restaurant shares the hotel's view and is one of the best places in town for an evening meal, with a quiet dining room that, while far from formal, is a bit more refined than the other choices in town. Service was careful and respectful at my last meal. There's a long menu of seafood and beef in the evening, and even the more challenging entrees are expertly prepared.

Finds **Rent a Floathouse**

Southeast Alaska has a unique kind of dwelling called a floathouse, a house on a barge, permanently anchored in some quiet, forgotten cove. There have even been float-towns, with houses, schools, and other buildings tied together, usually at remote logging sites. **Camp Coogan Bay Hideaway** (© **907/747-6375;** www.ssoceanadventures.com) is a floathouse you can rent for $175 a day. It floats in a narrow, placid bay out of a wilderness fantasy, 20 minutes from Sitka by boat (it's also the best place in the area to see bears). A charming, peeling old bunkhouse from town was stuck on a 1940s barge and anchored here, with a rainwater system, a woodstove for heat, propane appliances, and a diesel generator if you want light. A wood-fired sauna and a gas barbecue are out on deck. Don't expect the Hilton: It's primitive and a little grubby. You'll want to rent a boat or sea kayaks for mobility; owners John and Barbara DeLong offer those services, too.

---

330 Seward St., Sitka, AK 99835-7523. © **800/544-0970** for reservations, or 907/747-6241. Fax 907/747-5486. www.westmarkhotels.com. 101 units. High season $149–$159 double; low season $139–$149 double. Extra person 14 and over $15. AE, DC, DISC, MC, V. **Amenities:** Restaurant; bar. *In room:* TV, high-speed Internet, coffeemaker, hair dryer, iron.

A HOSTEL & CAMPING

Hostelling International–Sitka is contemplating a move but currently is located at 303 Kimsham St., in the United Methodist Church (P.O. Box 2645, Sitka, AK 99835; © **907/747-8661**), more than a mile from downtown. The 18 beds are $19 per night for members, $22 for nonmembers. Guests need to bring their own sleeping bags. It's open June through August; office hours and dorm access are from 8 to 10am and 6 to 10pm. Reservations are recommended, but advance payment is not accepted: Simply call or write to tell them when you will need a bed.

The Forest Service's **Starrigavan Campground,** at the north end of Halibut Point Road, 7½ miles from town and ¾ mile from the ferry dock, is one of the loveliest in Alaska. There are three loops. The Backpackers' Loop has six hike-in sites. The Estuary Loop (which joins the Estuary Life Trail), on the right, has 26 sites for RVs or tents, which are widely separated under huge trees. The Bayside Loop, at the water's edge, is the last left on the highway. Three of its sites are situated on the edge of Starrigavan Bay, creating the feeling that you're way out in the wilderness. Fees are $12 to $30 a night. Fourteen sites are available on a first-come, first-served basis, but all the rest must be reserved on the national system (see "Reserving a Cabin or Campsite," p. 98). The campground is open all year, but vehicle access is restricted in the winter. May through mid-September, access gates are locked from 10pm to 7am.

There are two RV parks, each with water and electric hookups only and each charging under $22: City-run **Sealing Cove RV Park** (© **907/747-3439**) is near the airport and a free dump station, and **Sitka Sportsman's Association RV Park** (© **907/747-6033**) is near the ferry dock.

WHERE TO DINE

See other good restaurant choices at the Westmark Sitka and Sitka Hotel above, under "Where to Stay." A **Subway sandwich shop** is at Seward and Lake streets, behind the Westmark.

Bayview Restaurant 𝄐 BURGERS/PASTA/SEAFOOD   The view of the boat harbor and good food make this small second-story restaurant popular year-round, although it's sometimes noisy and slightly cramped. Everything I've tried from the extensive menu has been well prepared and quickly served by friendly staff. I was quite satisfied with a lunch of a tasty Cajun halibut taco, which came with a salad and the always wonderful clam chowder for $9.75. Dinner prices also are competitive with other places in Sitka, and even then you have the option of simple fare or fancier seafood selections. It's a great spot for breakfast, too.

407 Lincoln St. 𝄐 **907/747-5440.** Main courses $9–$30. DISC, MC, V. High season Mon–Sat 5am–9pm, Sun 5am–3pm; low season Mon–Sat 7am–8pm, Sun 7am–3pm.

Channel Club 𝄐 STEAK/SEAFOOD   Occupying one big room where the cigarette smoke floats freely, the restaurant is like a manly club for fish slayers to let loose, laughing loud and drinking after a day on the water. A swordfish decorates one wall, the grill is on the other, and the dominant fashion is T-shirts and baseball caps. They grill a good steak here, and the salad bar, which comes with every meal, is something like a potluck dinner all by itself, with a wide and wonderful array of unfamiliar flavors. The service is as casual as in a greasy-spoon diner: On each of my visits, I've been expected already to know I should load up a plate from the salad bar before someone would come to ask what kind of steak I wanted from the list up on the wall—I've never seen a printed menu. Channel Club is several miles out Halibut Point Road, but a courtesy van will come get you and take you home at the end of the evening. They have a full bar, which stays open an hour after the restaurant closes (hours below are just for the restaurant).

2906 Halibut Point Rd. 𝄐 **907/747-9916.** Reservations recommended. Main courses $12–$42. AE, DC, DISC, MC, V. Sun–Thurs 5–10pm; Fri–Sat 5–11pm.

Ludvig's Bistro 𝄐𝄐 MEDITERRANEAN/OYSTER BAR   This tiny dining room and its young proprietors offer Sitka's only first-rate cuisine, and it's a very pleasant

---

⌒Tips Hip Eats & Coffee in Sitka

A cool couple owns **The Backdoor Café**, in the back half of Old Harbor Books at 104 Barracks St. (𝄐 **907/747-8856**), the kind of place that develops a following among local poets, musicians, and the like. Besides coffee and the owners' own homemade bagels, the cafe serves fresh pastries for breakfast and a single special for lunch (which can run out). It's open Monday through Saturday from 6:30am to 5pm, Sunday 9am to 2pm. Credit cards are not accepted.

   Highliner Coffee, on Lake Street just above Seward Street (𝄐 **907/747-4924**), is a fancier place, with free Wi-Fi (or use their computer for $3 for the first 15 minutes). A "highliner" is a top commercial fisherman; the name here is a bit of a boast for its fisherpeople owners, who hope to educate customers about their way of life as well as roasting Sitka's coffee. It's open Monday through Saturday from 5:30am to 5pm, Sunday from 8am to 4pm.

place for a meal. They've taken a formerly grungy concrete space and filled it with charm and warmth, with Mediterranean colors, wine bottles, and nice clutter. They can't serve many meals a night here, so each one is carefully crafted, coming from a changing menu intended to stretch the chef and introduce the small-town clientele to new tastes. A recent menu included grilled marinated lamb chops, a wild mushroom ragu, and calamari. Or snack in the afternoon on tapas or local oysters in the $13 to $17 price range. Best of all, they're not pretentious—the owners, Colette and Lisa, create a sense of friendship with diners; at times the whole place feels like a big dinner party.

256 Katlian St. ✆ 907/966-3663. Reservations recommended. Lunch $5–$15; dinner main courses $17–$27. MC, V. Tues–Sat 2–9pm.

Pizza Express *(Value* MEXICAN/PIZZA   Come here when you want a filling, inexpensive meal or to order in for a good pizza. The dining room is a strip mall a little outside the downtown, near the Raptor Center and across from the historical park. The owners are Mexican and produce yummy homemade tortilla chips among other national cuisine.

1321 Sawmill Creek Rd. ✆ 907/966-2428. Main courses $7–$13. MC, V. Mon–Sat 11am–10pm; Sun noon–10pm; closes at 9pm Sun in winter.

6 Juneau: Forest Capital

Juneau (*June*-oh) hustles and bustles like no other city in Alaska. The steep downtown streets echo with the mad shopping sprees of cruise-ship passengers in the summer tourist season and the whispered intrigues of politicians during the winter legislative session. Miners, loggers, and eco-tourism operators come to lobby for their share of Southeast's forest. Lunch hour arrives, and well-to-do state and federal bureaucrats burst from the office buildings to try the latest restaurant or brown-bag on one of the waterfront wharves, the sparkling water before them and gift store malls behind. The center of town becomes an ad hoc pedestrian mall as the crush of people forces cars to creep.

My Juneau is close at hand, but very different. As a child, at a magical age, I lived here with my family in a house on the side of the mountains above downtown. My Juneau is up the 99 steps that lead from the cemetery to the bottom of Pine Street— the way I walked home from school—and then to the top of residential Evergreen Avenue, where the pavement gives way to a forest trail among fiddlehead ferns and massive rainforest spruces. That trail leads to the flume (a wooden aqueduct that used to bring water down from the mountains), upon which we would walk into the land of bears and salmon, the rumbling water at our feet. It's still a short walk from the rackety downtown streets to a misty forest quiet, where you can listen for the voices of trees.

Juneau is Alaska's third-largest city (Anchorage and Fairbanks are larger), with a population of 30,000, but it feels like a small town that's just been stuffed with people. Splattered on the sides of Mount Juneau and Mount Roberts along Gastineau Channel, where there isn't room for much of a town, its setting is picturesque but impractical. Further development up the mountains is hemmed in by avalanche danger; beyond is the 1,500-square-mile **Juneau Icefield,** an impenetrable barrier. Goldmine tailings dumped into the Gastineau created the flat land near the water where much of the downtown area now stands. The Native village that originally stood on the waterfront is today a little pocket of mobile homes several blocks from the shore. There's no road to the outside world, and the terrain discourages building one. Jets are the main way in and out, threading down through the mountains to the airport.

Gold was responsible for the location; it was found here in 1880 by Joe Juneau and Richard Harris, assisted by the Tlingit chief Kowee, who told them where to look. All three men are buried in the Evergreen Cemetery. Their find started Alaska's development. The territory's first significant roads and bridges and its first electrical plant were built in the mountains here, which were carved with miles of hard rock tunnels well before the Klondike gold rush began. In a few years, these mines removed more gold than the United States paid for all of Alaska, as attested to by a photograph in the State Museum showing comparative piles. There's plenty of gold left, but mining died out with World War II; efforts to start again have repeatedly faltered in the face of environmental controls and economics. There are several interesting gold-mining sites to visit.

In 1900, Congress moved the territorial capital here from Sitka, which had fallen behind in the flurry of gold-rush development. Alaskans have been fighting over whether or not to keep it here for many decades since, but Juneau's economy is heavily dependent on government jobs, and it has successfully fought off a series of challenges to its capital status. In 2002, voters turned down a petition initiative to move the legislature by a two-to-one margin. In 2005, Juneau attempted to cement its place as the capital city by launching a drive to build a new capitol building, but the ploy backfired when the public panned the futuristic design city leaders selected. As a result, the legislature started talking about moving again. The closest the issue came was in the 1970s, when voters approved moving the capital but then balked at the cost of building a whole new city to house it—a necessity since neither Anchorage nor Fairbanks, which have their own rivalry, would support the move if it meant the other city got to have the capital nearby.

There's plenty to see in Juneau, and it's a good town to visit because the population of government workers supports restaurants and amenities of a quality not found elsewhere in Southeast. Alaska's most accessible glacier, the Mendenhall, is in Juneau, and many businesses have set up tours, including visits to the fish hatchery, the brewery, and an abandoned mine. Juneau is also a starting point and travel hub for outdoor activities all over the northern Panhandle: You'll likely pass through on your way to Glacier Bay or virtually anywhere else in the region. The outdoors is always close at hand in Juneau. You can start from the capitol building for a hike to the top of Mount Juneau or Mount Roberts, or up the Perseverance Trail that leads in between. Sea-kayaking and whale-watching excursions are nearby, as well as some of Alaska's most scenic tide pooling and beach walking.

Downtown the crush of visitors can be overwhelming when many cruise ships are in port at once. The streets around the docks have been entirely taken over by shops and other touristy businesses. Many of these are owned by people from outside Alaska who come to the state for the summer to sell gifts made outside Alaska. But only a few blocks away are quiet mountainside neighborhoods of houses with mossy roofs, and only a few blocks farther are the woods and the mountains, populated by bear, eagles, and salmon.

ESSENTIALS
GETTING THERE

BY AIR   Jet service is available only from **Alaska Airlines** (✆ **800/252-7522;** www.alaskaair.com), with several daily nonstop flights from Seattle and Anchorage and from the smaller Southeast Alaska towns. Many of the region's commuter and air-taxi operators also maintain desks at the airport and have flights out of Juneau. Among

---

⌒Tips Flying to Juneau

Juneau's mist-shrouded airport, wedged between ocean and mountain, has a special verb: *to overhead*. That means that when you try to fly to Juneau on a foggy day, you could end up somewhere else instead (although this now happens less frequently, thanks to new navigational technology). Planes overhead other Southeast towns, too, but more frequently in Juneau, since it is the region's travel hub, with many flights a day. The airline will put you on the next flight back to Juneau when the weather clears, but they won't pay for hotel rooms or give you a refund. Your only protection is travel insurance and a loose itinerary. This situation is such an ingrained part of Juneau's way of life that a channel on the cable TV system broadcasts the view from the airport 24 hours a day, showing the weather over the Gastineau Channel (it's called the Channel Channel, 23 on the dial). Residents know the view so well they can tell from the silent image if they'll get out that day.

---

the best, with many flights to surrounding communities and an active flightseeing operation, is **Wings of Alaska** (✆ **907/789-0790;** www.ichoosewings.com).

BY FERRY   All the main-line ferries of Southeast's **Alaska Marine Highway System** (✆ **800/642-0066;** www.ferryalaska.com) stop at the terminal in Auke Bay (✆ **907/789-7453** or 907/465-3940 for a recording), 14 miles from downtown, and the fast ferry, *Fairweather,* is based here, too. It cuts off half the 5 hours to Haines or Skagway, with four and five sailings there a week, respectively. The passenger fare is $36 to Haines, $48 to Skagway.

GETTING INTO TOWN FROM THE AIRPORT & FERRY TERMINAL   Airport shuttle businesses have been starting up and going out of business regularly for years; rather than list a number here that may change, I recommend you ask at the visitor desk in the baggage claim area. An express **Capital Transit city bus** (✆ **907/789-6901**) comes to the airport at 11 minutes past the hour on weekdays from 7:11am to 5:11pm and costs $1.50; your luggage has to fit under your seat or at your feet. Ask the driver for the stop closest to your hotel; you may need a short cab ride from there. Shuttles sometimes operate from the ferry dock downtown in the summer, but the arrangements are changeable. Ask when you arrive, or call ahead to the visitor center (below). A cab downtown from the airport will cost you $20, from the ferry dock $30. One taxi company is **Capital Cab** (✆ **907/586-2772** or 907/789-2772), which also offers tours for $55 an hour.

ORIENTATION

Juneau has three main parts: downtown, the Mendenhall Valley, and Douglas. Downtown Juneau is a numbered grid of streets overlying the uneven topography like a patterned quilt over a pile of pillows. As you look at Juneau from the water, Mount Juneau is on the left and Mount Roberts on the right; Mount Roberts is a few hundred feet taller, at 3,819 feet. **Franklin Street** extends south of town 5½ miles to good hiking trails and the hamlet of Thane. When the city outgrew its original site downtown, housing spread to the suburban **Mendenhall Valley,** about a dozen miles north out the Egan Expressway or the parallel, two-lane Glacier Highway. The glacial valley also contains the Juneau International Airport, University of Alaska Southeast, and

Auke Bay area, where the ferry terminal is located. The road continues 40 miles to a place known as **"The End of the Road."** Across a bridge over the Gastineau Channel from downtown Juneau is Douglas Island. Turn left for the town of **Douglas,** mostly a bedroom community for Juneau, and turn right for the North Douglas Highway, which leads to the ski area and some beautiful rocky beaches.

GETTING AROUND

BY RENTAL CAR   A car is a hindrance in compact downtown Juneau, but if you're going to the Mendenhall Glacier or to any of the attractions out the road or on Douglas Island, renting a car for a day or two is a good idea. Hertz, Avis, Budget, Alamo, and National are based at the airport.

BY BIKE   If you can handle hills, bikes make good sense in Juneau, where separated paths parallel many of the main roads and downtown traffic is slow. The 24-mile round-trip to Mendenhall Glacier keeps you on a bike path almost all the way. Bikes are for rent at the **Driftwood Lodge,** 435 Willoughby Ave. (© **800/544-2239** or 907/586-2280; www.driftwoodalaska.com) for $25 a day, $15 for a half-day.

VISITOR INFORMATION

The **Visitor Information Center** is in the Centennial Hall at 101 Egan Dr., near the State Museum (© **888/581-2201** or 907/586-2201; fax 907/586-6304; www.travel juneau.com). Operated by the Juneau Convention and Visitors Bureau, the center distributes a *Juneau Travel Planner,* online or on paper, that contains exhaustive listings of hotels and B&Bs, charter boats, tours, and other services. The center is open in summer Monday through Friday from 8:30am to 5pm, and Saturday and Sunday from 9am to 5pm; in winter Monday through Friday from 9am to 4pm. A ticket desk for the Alaska Marine Highway System is staffed by an agent Monday through Friday year round. Visitors Bureau volunteers also operate **information desks** at the airport, near the door in the baggage-claim area, and at the Auke Bay ferry terminal. During the summer, centers are staffed at the cruise ship terminal and at Marine Park.

The offices of the **Tongass National Forest Juneau Ranger District** were expected to move by the time of publication, to 8510 Mendenhall Loop Rd., Juneau, AK 99801. The telephone numbers remain unchanged (© **907/586-8800,** 907/790-7444 TTY; fax 907/586-8808; www.fs.fed.us/r10/tongass).

FAST FACTS: Juneau

Banks **Wells Fargo,** at 123 Seward St. (© **907/586-3324**), is one of the many banks and stores that have ATMs.

Hospital **Bartlett Regional,** at 3260 Hospital Dr. (© **907/796-8900**), is 3 miles out the Glacier Highway from downtown.

Internet Access Computers are easy to find downtown at coffeehouses and businesses such as **Copy Express,** at 233 Seward St. (© **907/586-2174**). In the Mendenhall Valley, try **Electronic Adventures,** 9109 Mendenhall Mall Rd. (© **907/790-3658**).

Police The police station is at 6255 Alaway Ave. (© **907/586-0600** for nonemergencies).

Post Office You'll find them downtown in the federal building, 709 W. 9th St.; and in the Mendenhall Valley at 9491 Vintage Blvd., by Carr's supermarket. A postal contract station handier to the cruise-ship dock is at 225 Front St., Suite 103, in the mall across the street from the movie theater.

Taxes Sales tax is 5%. You pay 12% tax on rooms.

SPECIAL EVENTS

An event calendar is posted on the Visitors Bureau website: www.traveljuneau.com/discover.

The Alaska Folk Festival (© 907/463-3316; www.alaskafolkfestival.org) is the state's biggest annual coming together of musicians, at Centennial Hall. Musicians take over the town and can be found jamming in every bar, coffeehouse, or wherever a crowd gathers. The 33rd annual festival is April 9 to 15, 2007.

The Juneau Jazz & Classics Festival (© 907/463-3378; www.jazzandclassics.org), in late May, includes 9 days of concerts and workshops in many styles of music at various venues, even on a boat, and at many prices—free to $60 a ticket. Most evening performances are around $20.

Gold Rush Days (© 907/790-1998; www.juneaugoldrush.com) includes logging and mining events and competitions that anyone can join, the last weekend in June. Check the website for the latest.

The Golden North Salmon Derby (© 907/463-3830; www.salmonderby.org), held annually since 1947, targets kings and silvers August 3 to 5, 2007. Unlike some other such fishing contests around the state, this isn't just a tourist thing—it brings out as many as 3,000 local fishermen and is even covered live on the radio.

EXPLORING DOWNTOWN

Alaska-Gastineau Mill and Gold Mine Tour 🐟
A half-day tour visits the ruins of a hard-rock gold operation that operated from 1915 to 1921, and then goes 360 feet into one tunnel for a mining demonstration. Guests also get to pan for gold from the mine's tailings. Although Princess Tours provides the buses and sells the tickets, the tour is the work of people who came to Juneau to reopen the A.J. mine (of which this was a part) and stayed to turn it into a tourist attraction when that project failed; their fascination is infectious. The mine site is south of town, but buses pick up visitors at the state museum downtown and at the Mt. Roberts Tram. The tour is quite in-depth; those without interest in mining history or mechanical matters may get bored. Dress warmly.

Book though Princess Tours, 151 Mill St. © 907/463-3900. $59 adults, $39 children 12 and under. Daily departures during summer; call ahead to reserve.

Alaska State Museum 🐟🐟🐟
The museum contains a large collection of art and historical artifacts, but it doesn't seem like a storehouse at all because the objects' presentation is based on their meaning, not their value. Come here to put the rest of your visit in context. A clan house in the Alaska Native Gallery contains authentic art in the functional places where it would have been used in a memorial potlatch. The Lincoln Totem Pole is here, carved by an artist who used a picture of the president as his model to represent his clan's first encounter with whites. Superb artifacts from Native

cultures from around the state are presented to illustrate the lifestyle of those who made them. The ramp to the second floor wraps around the natural history display, with an eagle nesting tree, and at the top a state history gallery uses significant pieces to tell Alaska's story. The children's area is exceptionally fun, with a ship that the kids can play in. Allow at least 2 hours for the museum; half a day would not be out of line. The shop off the lobby is also well worth a look. Although small, it carries lots of quality Alaska Native art, books, and no junk at all.

395 Whittier St. ✆ 907/465-2901. www.museums.state.ak.us. Admission mid-May to mid-Sept $5 adults, free for ages 18 and under; mid-Sept to mid-May $3 adults, free for ages 18 and under. Mid-May to mid-Sept daily 8:30am–5:30pm; mid-Sept to mid-May Tues–Sat 10am–4pm.

The Juneau-Douglas City Museum ⟨↸⟩   This fun little museum displays artifacts and photographs from the city's pioneer and mining history and Tlingit culture, with special exhibits that change annually. It's quite well done and holds real interest. There are gorgeous stained-glass windows, a large topographical model of the Juneau area, and a 600-year-old fish trap found near a local river. A 26-minute video on Juneau's gold-mining history shows each half hour. The tiny bookshop is stocked with handy information for your visit to Juneau, including the historic hike guide booklet, free historic walking-tour map, and maps of the Evergreen Cemetery and the old Tread-well Mine. The plaza in front is where the 49-star U.S. flag was first raised in 1959—they didn't make many of those, as Hawaii was admitted as the 50th within a year, but you'll still find one flying here.

At the corner of 4th and Main sts. ✆ 907/586-3572. www.juneau.org/parksrec/museum. Admission $4 adults (free in winter), free for ages 18 and under. Summer Mon–Fri 9am–5pm, Sat–Sun 10am–5pm. Winter Tues–Sat noon–4pm.

The Last Chance Mining Museum and Historic Park ⟨↸⟩ ⟨Finds⟩   On the site on forested Gold Creek where gold was first discovered in Juneau, the museum preserves old mining buildings and some of their original equipment, including an immense 1912 air compressor and a layered glass map of the tunnels. This was once a nerve center for one of the world's biggest hard-rock mines. The highlight is its energetic and learned guide, Renee Hughes, who lives above the compressor with her husband, Gary Gillette. Both are leaders of the Gastineau Channel Historical Society. Ask Renee about the cave-in of the Treadwell Mine to hear her riveting storytelling. The entrance to the site—which contains relics and buildings spread over several acres—is a bridge across the creek, which leads to a steep trail up to the buildings.

⟨Tips⟩ **The Cruise Ship Dock: Where Do You Get Off?**

Cruise-ship passengers disembark in Juneau's attractive **Marine Park** waterfront area, where a kiosk dispenses information and tour operators sell their services. Downtown shops and attractions are close by. Among the most popular sights is one right at the dock, the statue of a small dog facing the ships as they come in. This is *Patsy Ann,* a bull terrier that, in the 1930s, always seemed to know when a steamer was arriving and faithfully stationed herself on the dock to meet the disembarking passengers. There's also a spotting scope in the park for watching mountain goats on Mt. Juneau. For a quiet break, visit the beautiful library at the top of the parking garage at the south end of the dock.

1001 Basin Rd. ℂ **907/586-5338**. Admission $4. Daily 9:30am–12:30pm and 3:30–6:30pm. Closed Oct to mid-May. From downtown, take Gold St. up the hill to its end, and then join Basin Rd., continuing 1 mile up the valley to the end of the road.

Mount Roberts Tramway 🌲 The tram takes only 6 minutes to whisk passengers from tourist-clogged Franklin Street to the clear air and overwhelming views at the tree line (1,760 ft.), a destination that used to require a day of huffing and puffing to witness. The tram can be crowded; it's once you're up there that the beauty hits you. The Alaska Native owners seem to understand that, and they have done a good job of building a network of paths that take advantage of the views as you pass through a fascinating alpine ecosystem; the owners have even carved clan crests into the living trunks of some of the trees. If you're energetic, you can start a 6-mile round-trip hike to Mount Roberts's summit (at 3,819 ft.), or you can hike the 2.5 miles back to downtown. There's an auditorium at the top tram station showing a film on Tlingit culture, a shop where Native artisans are often at work, and a bald eagle enclosure. The bar and grill serves lunch and dinner. I would choose something else to do on a day when fog or low overcast obscures the view, especially considering the price; however, I am told it is sometimes sunny up top while rainy down on Franklin Street—it can't hurt to ask.

490 S. Franklin St., at the waterfront near the cruise-ship dock. ℂ **888/461-8726** or 907/463-3412. www.goldbelt tours.com. Full-day pass $24 adults, $13 children ages 6–12, free ages 5 and under; tax included. May–Sept daily 9am–9pm. Closed Oct–Apr.

A JUNEAU WALKING TOUR

Start & Finish: Alaska State Capitol, 4th and Seward streets.
Time: 1 to 1½ hours for standard tour; 2½ hours for the extended tour, with minimal stops.

---

❶ Alaska State Capitol

This structure fills the block between 4th and 5th and Main and Seward streets. Except for the marble portico on the 4th Street side, it is a nondescript brick box, probably the least impressive state capitol in the most beautiful setting in the nation. Legislators hanker for a larger, grander building, but since they can barely agree on the time of day, that's unlikely to happen anytime soon. The federal government built the structure in 1931, when Alaska was still a territory. Inside, some of the old-fashioned woodwork and decorative details are interesting, and the public is free to walk through. During the summer, free tours are offered Monday through Saturday from 9am to 4:30pm; other times, pick up a self-guided tour brochure in the lobby. Call ℂ **907/465-3800** for information. The legislature is in session from January to early May.

Across 4th is the:

❷ State Courthouse

The statue of a bear in front defines official Alaskan taste in art: It replaced a hated abstract steel sculpture called *Nimbus* that was removed by an act of the legislature and that finally came to rest in front of the state museum a few blocks away.

On the opposite, northwest corner is the:

❸ Juneau-Douglas City Museum

Stop in here now to buy the Evergreen Cemetery map if you plan to include that in your walk, or get the *Historic Downtown Juneau Guide* to learn more on the whole walk.

Downtown Juneau Walking Tour

1 Alaska State Capitol
2 State Courthouse
3 Juneau-Douglas City Museum
4 State Office Building
5 Governor's Mansion
6 Gold Creek
7 The Wickersham House State Historic Site
8 St. Nicholas Orthodox Church
9 The Evergreen Cemetery
10 Abandoned wooden flume
11 The Last Chance Mining Museum

Church ✝
Information ⓘ
Post Office ✉

On the southwest corner of Main and 4th is the:

❹ State Office Building

This building is built into the edge of a cliff that forms a major barrier through the downtown area; if you're headed for the lower land, where the State Museum and Centennial Hall are located, you can avoid eight flights of steps in between by taking the building's elevator down. In any event, visit the towering atrium, with its great views and a 1928 movie theater pipe organ that's played on Friday at noon. The state library historical collections off the lobby contain historic photographs and artifacts, some of which are often on exhibit. On sunny days, the patio off the atrium is a warm place for a picnic, with a fabulous view.

Leaving again through the door that you entered, turn left and follow Calhoun Street around the curve. An outdoor staircase here leads down to the flat area of town below (but you know about taking the elevator). Those lowlands originally were mostly underwater and

this embankment stood just above the shore-line, which continued along Front and South Franklin streets. The land you see below you is made of mine tailings that were dumped in the Channel. Continue on Calhoun; the governor uses the pedestrian overpass (which we walk under) to cross Calhoun to get to the Capitol from the white, neoclassical:

❺ Governor's Mansion

Located on the left, the mansion was built by the federal government in 1912 for $40,000. It isn't normally open for public tours. Gov. Frank Murkowski, a Republican, became the eighth to hold the office when he was sworn in on December 2, 2002, returning from 22 years as a U.S. Senator. He then appointed his own daughter, Lisa Murkowski, to fill out his term in the Senate. She retained that seat in 2004 against a challenge from former Governor Tony Knowles, who had handed the keys to the mansion to her father. By the time you read this, we'll have seen the next step in this game of musical chairs, as the gubernatorial election was held in November 2006.

Shortcut: If you don't mind missing the next stop (Gold Creek), you can save yourself some hill-climbing by continuing on Calhoun, turning right on Gold-belt Street, climbing past some beautiful houses to 7th, and then picking up the tour at the Wickersham House.

Continuing down Calhoun, you'll come to:

❻ Gold Creek

Juneau's founders made their gold strike in this stream in 1880. Trace it upstream through peaceful **Cope Park,** past the playground and tennis courts to the unique ball field, which is bounded by the stream's forested canyon walls. (To continue this walk to Evergreen Cemetery and up to the top of the town and through the woods on the flume—a long, strenuous hike—return to Calhoun Street and continue in the direction you were going. That route is covered below under "The Extended Walk.")

Go all the way to the right side (that's left field, on your right) of the baseball diamond to find a lovely path and public stairway through the woods steeply up to 7th Street, which runs along a narrow ridge between downtown Juneau and the creek. Across the street from the top of the stairway is:

❼ The Wickersham House State Historic Site

This white 1898 frame house, at 213 7th St. (© **907/586-9001;** www.alaskastate parks.org, click "Individual Parks"), was the retirement home of Judge James Wickersham, who was revered by Alaskans for bringing law to the gold rush in Eagle, Nome, and Fairbanks; for exploring the Denali area and helping to make it a national park; for convincing the federal government to build the Alaska railroad and found the state university; and for winning Alaska's right to make its own laws when he represented the territory in Congress. The house was in the family from 1928 until the state bought it in 1984, so it still contains Wickersham's belongings, including an Edison cylinder gramophone he took to Fairbanks and his assignment to go to Alaska, which is signed by Theodore Roosevelt. The house badly needed repair when a renovation project funded in part by the National Park Service began several years ago. Although work is behind schedule, chances are good the house will be open by 2007. During normal operations, the house has been open from mid-May to the end of September from 10am to noon and 1 to 5pm, winter by appointment. The site requests a $2 donation.

Continue on 7th to Gold Street, turn right and follow it downhill to 5th, site of the:

❽ St. Nicholas Orthodox Church

This small structure is a significant architectural and historic landmark. The octagonal building was built in 1893–94 by Serbian miners and Tlingits. Many Tlingits chose the Russian Orthodox faith in the late 19th century when government-sponsored Protestant missionaries arrived with authority to force Christianity on Alaska Natives. The Protestants' civilizing program entailed wiping out Native languages and culture, but the Orthodox allowed people to worship in Tlingit and to continue more of their own customs. Bishop Innocent Veniaminov had translated sacred texts into Tlingit 50 years earlier when the Russians were still in Sitka (learn more under "The Russian Bishop's House," p. 139). Today, Alaska Natives make up the bulk of Russian Orthodox congregations in Alaska, and St. Nicholas still has an active Tlingit parish. Lengthy services are sung in English, Tlingit, and Church Slavonic for Saturday vespers at 6pm and on Sunday morning at 9am; the congregation stands throughout the service. Visitors are welcome for service, or come during the tourist season Monday through Friday from 9am to 5pm, Saturday 10am to 4pm, and Sunday 1pm to 5pm. Admission is $2. There is a small gift shop.

Walk 1 block down and 2 blocks to the right to the start/finish point.

THE EXTENDED WALK

This walk of roughly 3 miles includes some steep stairways and streets. Follow the walking tour until you reach Gold Creek (see number 6, above).

Cross the creek and stay on the same road (which goes under various names), bearing right as it becomes Martin Street. On the left is:

❾ The Evergreen Cemetery

The cemetery slopes toward the ocean, opening a wonderful vista over the clear green lawn. One reason the view is so broad and open is that the markers are flush with the ground. The old Alaska Native graves are in the wooded portion on the far side. Joe Juneau and Richard Harris, the city's founders, are buried near the cross at the top end of the cemetery, near where you arrive on the walk.

Across the road from the cross, Hermit Street reaches a little way into the mountainside. Follow the steep public stairs next to house no. 430 up to the bottom of Pine Street. This is the walk I described in the introduction. The views get better and better as you rise to the top of Pine Street; then go right on Evergreen Street, following the road to where it dissipates into a trail among shadowy spruce and western hemlock.

Continue on the peaceful forest trail among the ferns and evergreens up the valley, coming to the:

❿ Abandoned Wooden Flume

Once the town's aqueduct, the flume now is maintained as a boardwalk into the forest. Since it carried water, it's nearly level, but watch your step in wet weather, as it crosses some high trestles over gullies.

At the end of the flume, cross over the valley to Basin Road. Stop here to see:

⓫ The Last Chance Mining Museum

The museum is described on p. 153. To the left is the Perseverance Trail, which continues up between the mountains; the Perseverance also leads to the trail head for a challenging hike up Mount Juneau (both hikes are covered later).

To get back to town, follow Basin Road 1 mile back down the valley. Taking the first right will put you at the top of Gold Street. Descend a block to 7th and pick up the walking tour at stop 7 (the Wickersham House is a block down 7th), or continue down Gold to St. Nicholas Orthodox Church, stop 8 on the tour.

Avoiding Cruise-Ship Crowds

On the busiest days of the summer, cruise ships bring more than 10,000 passengers and another 4,000 crew members to the docks on Juneau's Franklin Street. That's simply too many for these narrow old streets; downtown becomes a solid crush of people and attractions are packed, spoiling the experience for everyone. The crush worsens every year and is largely unavoidable, with a minimum of three ships tying up on the light days. In recent years, those lighter days have been Friday and Sunday. If you can plan your Juneau sightseeing then, you may find somewhat less crowding.

SHOPPING

The shops near the dock cater primarily to cruise-ship passengers. After almost 500 summer port calls, many close their doors. The year-round community and more local shops tend to be farther up the hill. If you're looking for authentic Alaska Native arts and crafts, be warned that counterfeiting is widespread. For buying tips, read "Native Art: Finding the Real Thing" in chapter 2.

The Raven's Journey, 435 S. Franklin (© **907/463-4686**), shows Tlingit and other Northwest Indian carvings and masks, and whalebone, ivory, basketry, and fossil ivory carvings and jewelry from the Yup'ik and Iñupiat of western and northern Alaska. Works are displayed with biographical placards of the artists.

Juneau Artists Gallery, in the Senate Building at 175 S. Franklin (© **907/586-9891;** www.juneauartistsgallery.com), is staffed by a co-op of local artists and shows only the members' work: paintings, etchings, photography, jewelry, fabrics, ceramics, and other media. Much of it is good and inexpensive, and the way it is displayed creates a panorama of artistic visions.

Juneau's Rie Muñoz is one of Alaskans' favorite artists for her simple, graphic, generally cheerful watercolors of coastal Alaskan communities and Native people. Her prints and tapestries are shown downtown at the **Decker Gallery,** 233 S. Franklin (© **907/463-5536**), and in the Mendenhall Valley at the **Rie Muñoz Gallery,** at 2101 Jordan Ave. (© **800/247-3151** or 907/789-7449; www.riemunoz.com).

For gifts, try **Annie Kaill's** fine arts and crafts gallery at 244 Front St. It's a little out of the cruise-ship shopping area and gets business from locals. The shop has a rich, homey feeling, with local work at various price levels. The long-established **Ad Lib,** at 231 S. Franklin St., also is a fun little shop.

Hearthside Books (www.hearthsidebooks.com) is a cubbyhole of a bookstore at the corner of Franklin and Front streets, but has a good selection for its size, especially of Alaskan books. (A larger branch, with a good toy department, is in the Mendenhall Valley's Nugget Mall, at 8745 Glacier Hwy., a 5-min. walk from the airport.) Also downtown, at 113 Seward St., **Rainy Day Books** has more than 10,000 new, used, and rare books.

The most remarkable shop in Juneau is **The Observatory,** at 200 N. Franklin St. (© **907/586-9676;** www.observatorybooks.com). This browser's paradise specializes in rare maps and books about Alaska. The collection of antique etchings is mind-blowing in its comprehensiveness. Among the items I've seen here were huge charts drawn by the first 18th-century explorers to trace Alaska's coastline. The shop's greatest treasure is its owner, Dee Longenbaugh, who created this collection and knows its history. Her expertise is certified: She is a fellow of the Royal Geographical Society and the only Alaskan member of the Antiquarian Booksellers Association. Just ask her a question to begin a fascinating tour of Alaska history.

Bill Spear sells his own brightly colored enamel pins and zipper pulls from his studio, hidden upstairs at 174 S. Franklin (© **907/586-2209;** www.wmspear.com). Alaskans collect the vividly executed fish, birds, airplanes, dinosaurs, vegetables, and many other witty, provocative, or beautiful pins, which cost from $4 to $20 each.

Taku Store, at 550 S. Franklin, across the parking lot from the tram station (© **800/582-5122** or 907/463-3474; www.takustore.com), is worth a stop if you're nearby, even if you're not in the market for the pricey seafood in the case: It's interesting to watch workers fillet, smoke, and pack salmon through large windows, and to read the explanatory signs about what they're doing. They'll ship fish anywhere in the U.S.

ATTRACTIONS BEYOND WALKING DISTANCE

Mendenhall Glacier Transport (© **907/789-5460;** www.mightygreattrips.com) does a 2½-hour town and Mendenhall Glacier tour for $22, or you can ride their "Blue Bus Express" to the glacier for $12. Generally, it runs every half-hour both directions, from the waterfront visitor center to the glacier and back, daily 9am to 6pm in summer. Otherwise, take a rented car or, for vigorous people, bike 24 miles out to the Mendenhall Glacier and back. I've listed these sites by distance from downtown, with directions starting from there.

Alaskan Brewing Company   Beer lovers and aspiring capitalists will enjoy the tour of Alaska's most popular craft brewery. Now too big to be called "micro," the brewery started small in 1986 when Geoff and Marcy Larson had the idea of bringing a local gold rush–era brew back to life. It worked, and now Alaskan Amber and several other brews are everywhere in Alaska and many places down the West Coast, and the brewery has won a long list of national and international awards for its brews. The short, free tour, which starts every half-hour, is fairly interesting, with views of the brewing equipment behind glass, but it's the tasting that makes it fun. They serve free samples of half a dozen beers, often creating an impromptu party in the lobby. Identification is required.

5429 Shaune Dr. © 907/780-5866. www.alaskanbeer.com. Daily 11am–5pm (last tour starts at 4:30pm). Turn right from Egan Dr. on Vanderbilt Hill Rd., which becomes Glacier Hwy., then right on Anka St., and right again on Shaune Dr.

Glacier Gardens   This is the place to see the rainforest if you have mobility problems. The heart of the hour-long tour is a ride in vehicles similar to golf carts up a steep mountainside, past a stream and pools, to a platform with a view of the Mendenhall Valley. They cater to the cruise ships, but the staff will take groups of just a few visitors for a ride, explaining the forest flora in as much detail as you wish. Gardeners will especially enjoy the extraordinary hanging baskets and other bright and ingenious plantings in the lower area—weddings of cruise-ship passengers are held here almost every day in the summer. The gardens' trademark is upside-down trees whose roots, way up in the air, are planted with trailing flowers. All good—but if you're planning a hike in the area, the ride will hold less interest, and, as much as I like the place, I have to point out it is priced as a guided tour, not a botanical garden. More vigorous visitors, who don't want to ride in the golf carts, may find the admission price too high.

7600 Glacier Hwy. © 907/790-3377. www.glaciergardens.com. Admission $20 adults, $16 ages 6–12. Summer daily 9am–6pm. Closed Oct–Apr. Near the Fred Meyer store about 1 mile from the airport.

Macaulay Salmon Hatchery ☏ The hatchery, known by locals as DIPAC (Douglas Island Pink and Chum, Inc.), was ingeniously designed to allow visitors to watch the whole process of harvesting and fertilizing eggs from outdoor decks. From mid-June to October, salmon swim up a 450-foot fish ladder, visible through a window, into a sorting mechanism, and then are "unzipped" by workers who remove the eggs. Guides and exhibits explain what's happening. During that period you can often see seals and other wildlife feeding on the returning salmon just offshore from the hatchery. Inside, large and realistic saltwater aquariums show off the area's marine life as it looks in the natural environment. The tour is less impressive in May and June, before the fish are running. At that time, visitors see the immature salmon before their release and sometimes get to feed them. The tours don't take long; allow 45 minutes for your entire visit.

2697 Channel Dr. ☏ 877/463-2486 or 907/463-4810. www.dipac.net. Admission $3.25 adults, $1.75 children ages 12 and under. Summer Mon–Fri 10am–6pm, Sat–Sun 10am–5pm; winter call ahead. 3 miles from downtown, turn left at the first group of buildings on Egan Dr.

Mendenhall Glacier ☏☏ At the head of Mendenhall Valley, the Mendenhall Glacier glows bluish white, looming above the suburbs like an Ice Age monster that missed the general extinction. Besides being a truly impressive sight, Mendenhall is the most easily accessible glacier in Alaska and the state's third-most-visited attraction. The parking and an adjacent shelter have a great view across the lake to the glacier's face, and a wheelchair-accessible trail leads close to the water's edge. The land near the parking lot shows signs of the glacier's recent passage, with little topsoil, stunted vegetation, and, in many places bare rock that shows the scratch marks of the glacier's movement. Atop a bedrock hill, reached by stairs, a ramp, or an elevator, the Forest Service visitor center contains a glacier museum with excellent explanatory models, computerized displays, spotting scopes, and ranger talks. Admission is $3 for adults, free for children under 16. In late summer, you can watch red and silver salmon spawning in **Steep Creek,** just short of the visitor center on the road.

There are several trails at the glacier, ranging from a half-mile nature trail loop to two fairly steep 3.5-mile hikes approaching each side of the glacier. At the visitor center and a booth near the parking lot, the Forest Service distributes a brochure that includes a trail map. The **East Glacier Loop Trail** is a beautiful day hike leading through the forest to a view of a waterfall near the glacier's face and to parts of an abandoned rail tram and an abandoned dam on Nugget Creek; the trail has steep parts but is doable for school-age children. You can park at the visitor center and start from there. The **West Glacier Trail** is more challenging, leaving from 300 yards beyond the Skater's Cabin and following the edge of the lake and glacier, providing access to the ice itself for experienced climbers with the right equipment. You will need wheels to get to the trailhead. Take the Mendenhall Loop Road to Montana Creek Road, turn right, and then turn right again on Skater's Cabin Road.

The Skater's Cabin is also the starting point for a groomed cross-country-ski loop on Mendenhall Lake in front of the glacier. Don't go beyond the orange safety markers near the glacier's face. Other trails weave through the pothole lakes across from the glacier.

At the head of Glacier Spur Rd. (right from Egan Dr. on Mendenhall Loop to Glacier Spur). Visitor center admission $3 adults, free children under 16. Visitor center (☏ 907/789-0097) open daily in summer 8am–7:30pm; winter Thurs–Sun 10am–4pm.

Juneau Beyond Downtown

ACCOMMODATIONS ■
Alaska Wolf House Bed &
   Breakfast **9**
Extended Stay Deluxe **5**
Pearson's Pond Luxury Inn
   and Adventure Spa **3**

DINING ◆
Chan's Thai Kitchen **1**
Hot Bite **2**

ATTRACTIONS ●
Glacier Gardens **6**
Macaulay Salmon Hatchery **8**
Mendenhall Glacier
   Visitor Center **4**
Mendenhall Wetlands
   State Game Refuge **7**

WHAT TO SEE & DO "OUT THE ROAD"

On sunny summer weekends, Juneau families get in the car and drive "out the road" (northwest along the Glacier Hwy., as it's officially known). The views of island-stippled water from the paved two-lane highway are worth the trip, and there are also several good places to stop. To use this road guide, set your trip odometer to zero at the ferry dock (which is 14 miles from downtown Juneau).

The **Auke Village Recreation Area** is a mile beyond the ferry dock and is a good place for picnics and beach walks. Less than a mile farther is a Forest Service campground.

The **Shrine of St. Thérèse** ⊛ (© **907/780-6112;** www.shrineofsainttherese.org), 9 miles beyond the ferry dock, rests on a tiny island reached by a foot-trail causeway. The wonderfully simple chapel of rounded beach stones, circled by markers of the 15 stations of the cross, stands peaceful and mysterious amid trees, rock, water, and the cries of the raven and eagle. It is the most spiritual place I know. The vaguely Gothic structure was built in the late 1930s of stone picked up from these shores and dedicated by Alaska's first Catholic bishop to St. Thérèse of Lisieux, who died in 1897 at the age of 24. Sunday liturgy services are held from June to September at 1:30pm. The shrine is part of a large retreat maintained by the Juneau Catholic Diocese, which includes a log lodge on the shore facing the island, as well as several cabins for rent as lodgings. The shrine's island is a good vantage from which to look upon **Lynn Canal** for marine mammals or, at low tide, to go tide pooling among the rocks. The website covers the shrine's history and gives information on the facilities, gardens, and trails.

Eagle Beach, 14 miles beyond the ferry dock, makes a good picnic area in nice weather, when you can walk among the tall beach grass or out on the sandy tidal flats, watch the eagles, or go north along the beach to look for fossils in the rock outcroppings.

The road turns to gravel and then comes to **Point Bridget State Park,** 24 miles beyond the ferry dock (② 907/465-4563; www.alaskastateparks.org, click on "Individual Parks"). A flat 3.5-mile path leads through forest, meadow, and marsh to the shore, where you may see sea lions and possibly humpback whales. Two public-use cabins rent for $35 a night. See "State Parks Cabin Reservations," p. 262. The road ends 26 miles from the ferry dock at pretty **Echo Cove.**

GETTING OUTSIDE: ONSHORE

BIRDWATCHING   Bald eagles are as common as pigeons in Juneau. Years ago, one of them made off with a tourist's Chihuahua, starting a statewide debate about whether it was funny or horrible. Eagles are most common on the shoreline, especially where fish are plentiful, such as at the hatchery. For more variety, visit the **Mendenhall Wetlands State Game Refuge,** which encompasses 3,800 acres of tidal estuaries in the Gastineau Channel near the airport. More than 100 species of birds use the refuge, mainly during the April and May migrations. Access points are on either side of the channel, including a viewing platform on the downtown-bound side of Egan Drive, at Mile 6.

FRESHWATER FISHING   Juneau isn't known particularly for its stream fishing, but there are a few places on the roads where you can put in a line. The advice you need is in the free printed **Juneau Sportfishing Guide** available from the Alaska Department of Fish and Game, 1255 W. 8th St. (P.O. Box 25526), Juneau, AK 99802-5526 (② **907/465-4180;** www.alaska.gov/adfg, click on "Sport Fisheries," and then on the Southeast region on the map). For a remote fly-in experience with fly or spinning gear, contact **Alaska Fly 'N' Fish Charters,** 9604 Kelly Court (② **907/790-2120;** www.alaskabyair.com). A guided 5-hour trip is $450 per person, with a two-person minimum. The same reputable guy (Butch Laughlin) also does flightseeing and bear-viewing flights.

HIKING   I've mentioned several good hikes at Mendenhall Glacier and out the road, above. More than two dozen are described in a nicely made book with detailed topographic maps of each, *Juneau Trails* (www.alaskanha.org), which you can find at visitor centers for $8. *In the Miner's Footsteps,* a guide to the history behind 14 Juneau trails, is available for a nominal price from the Juneau-Douglas City Museum. The Juneau city **Department of Parks and Recreation** (② **907/586-5226;** www.juneau.org/parksrec) leads hikes (and other activities) through the year; check the website or call the 24-hour hike line at ② **907/586-0428.**

The **Perseverance Trail** climbs up the valley behind Juneau and into the mining history of the area it accesses. It can be busy in summer. The trail head is about 1.5 miles from town on Basin Road. The trail is 4 miles of easy walking on the mountainside above Gold Creek to the Perseverance Mine, at the Silverbow Basin, a mining community from 1885 to 1921. Use caution on icy patches, as there are steep drop-offs. A well-documented historic pamphlet is for sale at the Juneau-Douglas City Museum.

Two trails start from points along the Perseverance Trail. The challenging **Mount Juneau Trail** rises more than 3,500 feet over about 2 miles from a point 1 mile from the Perseverance trail head. Go only in dry weather to avoid disastrous falls. The **Granite Creek Trail,** starting 2 miles in on the Perseverance Trail, climbs 1,200 feet over 1.5 miles to an alpine basin. Both are quieter than the Perseverance Trail.

Another hike right from downtown climbs **Mount Roberts**—just follow the stairway from the top of 6th Street in a neighborhood called Star Hill. The summit is 4.5 miles and 3,819 vertical feet away, but you don't have to go all the way to the top for incredible views and alpine terrain. At the 1,760-foot level, you come to the restaurant at the top of the Mount Roberts tram, mentioned on p. 154 (the ride down is free with a $5 purchase if you walk up). Of course, it's easier to take the tram up and hike down. A third choice: Start from the tram and hike to the summit.

The **Treadwell Mine Historic Trail,** on Douglas Island, is a fascinating hour's stroll through the ruins of a massive hard-rock mine complex that once employed and housed 2,000 men. Since its abandonment in 1922, big trees have grown up through the foundations, intertwining their roots through rails and machinery and adding to the site's exceptional power over the imagination. A well-written guide to numbered posts on the trail is available from the Juneau–Douglas City Museum. This is a great hike for kids. To find the trailhead, take 3rd Street in Douglas, bearing left at the Y onto Savikko Street, which leads to Savikko Park, also known as Sandy Beach Park. The trail starts at the far end of the park.

Another great family outing is to the **Outer Point Trail,** 1.5 miles on a forest boardwalk to a beach with good tide pooling, lots of eagles, and possible whale sightings. Nowhere else I know do so many different kinds of lovely spots present themselves in such a short walk: the mossy rainforest, the stunted muskeg swamp, a glassy little creek, and the pebbled beach and bedrock ocean pools. From there, on the western point of Douglas Island—the opposite side from Juneau—you can see Auke Bay to the east, Admiralty Island to the west, and the tiny islands of Stephens Passage before you. The trail's only drawback is crowding, especially when tour groups tromp

---

⌒ Tips Gearing Up for Juneau's Outdoors

You can rent the gear you need for outings on the water or to equip Forest Service cabin visits from **Alaska Boat and Kayak,** at the Auke Bay Harbor (© 907/ 789-6886; www.juneaukayak.com). They rent sea kayaks ($45 a day for a single, $60 double), camping gear, and skiffs with outboard motors ($130–$300 a day) that you can use for fishing or exploring, and they offer guidance in planning where and how to go. They will deliver a sea kayak anywhere on Juneau's road system, to outlying areas, or to Admiralty Island. See "Getting Around," earlier in this section, for bike rentals.

Finds   **Remote Cabins on Foot**

Five U.S. Forest Service cabins and three Alaska State Parks cabins are accessible by hikes of less than a day on trails connected to Juneau's road system. That means that you can get to these cabins without an expensive plane or boat charter, and that's a rarity. The three Alaska State Parks cabins are at Point Bridget State Park (see "What to See & Do 'Out the Road,'" above). The Forest Service cabins include: **Peterson Lake,** with lake and stream fishing for Dolly Varden char and cutthroat trout; **John Muir,** on a 1,500-foot ridge top above Auke Bay, up the Auk Nu Trail; **Dan Moller,** on Douglas Island right across from town; **Eagle Glacier,** overlooking the glacier upriver from Eagle Beach and reached by the Amalga Trail; and beautiful **Windfall Lake,** with fishing. Each cabin rents for $35 a night, and generally there's a 2-night maximum stay. All are popular and must be reserved well in advance (it's wise to book as soon as your dates become available 6 months earlier). If you can afford a charter, or if you are an expert sea kayaker, there are many more choices farther afield, especially on Admiralty Island (see below). You'll need camping gear to stay at these primitive cabins (see "Gearing Up for Juneau's Outdoors," p. 163). Get information on cabins from the Ranger District (see "Visitor Information," p. 116) and then reserve through the national system described in "Getting Outside in the Tongass National Forest" on p. 97.

through; avoid them by going early or late. To get there, drive over the bridge to Douglas, and then right on North Douglas Highway 12 miles to the trail head.

RAFTING   The Mendenhall River isn't a wild or scary ride, so the guides on the Native-owned **Auk Ta Shaa Discovery,** 76 Egan Dr. (© **800/820-2628** or 907/586-8687; www.goldbelttours.com), offer commentary on Native legends and natural history. The 4-hour rides cost $99 for adults, $66 ages 16 and under (no kids under 70 lbs. allowed). Transportation from downtown is included in the price, but even with that considered, the cost is higher than similar rafting outings at other Alaska destinations.

SKIING   For **downhill skiing,** the city-owned **Eaglecrest Ski Area** (© **907/790-2000;** www.skijuneau.com) is the large, steep home hill of Olympic silver medalist Hillary Lindh, Juneau's favorite daughter (her father helped choose the site in the 1970s). A chair goes almost to the top of Douglas Island, with expansive views and 640 acres of skiing terrain. The three lifts serve 31 runs with a total vertical drop of 1,400 feet, rated 40% expert, 40% intermediate, and 20% novice. There's also a hill for inner-tubing. It's only 12 miles from downtown on North Douglas Highway. An all-day lift ticket is $34 for adults, $26 for seniors and children grades 6 to 12, and $20 for children grades 5 and under; inner-tubing is $10 for all ages. Even among Alaskans, Eaglecrest is little known, despite being second in size and ski lift development only to Alyeska Resort, near Anchorage.

Eaglecrest has 8km of **cross-country-skiing** trail, offering the most reliable track skiing in town. Generally, Juneau's warm, damp winters don't provide enough snow for good cross-country skiing at lower elevations. Many of the hiking trails into the mountains become winter backcountry routes, however, and snow does stick up there. Before going out, always check with the Forest Service (see "Visitor Information," earlier in this section) for advice on your route and on avalanche conditions. Several of the Forest Service cabins also serve as winter warm-up houses during the day and make good skiing destinations. If conditions permit, a network of trails is set around the Mendenhall Glacier (see above).

GETTING OUTSIDE: ON THE WATER

SALTWATER FISHING & WHALE-WATCHING The closest I ever came to a humpback whale—I almost touched it—was on the way back from king salmon fishing out of Juneau on a friend's boat. More than two dozen companies offer charters from Juneau and Auke Bay; you can go to watch whales or fish, or both. Juneau is well protected behind layers of islands, so the water generally is calm. A lot of companies offer trips. The Juneau Convention and Visitors Bureau maintains a list of businesses, and their website has links to each. **Juneau Sportfishing and Sightseeing,** 2 Marine Way, Suite 230 (✆ **907/586-1887;** www.juneausportfishing.com), is one of the largest operators, and their rates are typical: $240 per person for a full day fishing for salmon, $275 for halibut; or $150 for 4 hours fishing salmon. They charge $110 for a 2½-hour whale-watching trip.

SEA KAYAKING The protected waters around Juneau appeal to sea kayakers, and the city is a popular hub for trips on the water farther afield. Besides the sublime scenery, you'll almost certainly see eagles, sea birds, and seals, and possibly humpback whales.

There are many operators offering sea-kayaking excursions, but the area's most established eco-tourism operator is **Alaska Discovery,** 5310 Glacier Hwy. (✆ **800/586-1911;** www.alaskadiscovery.com), with trips all over Southeast and beyond. A multiday kayak trip is your chance to really know the Alaska wilderness. If you haven't spent much time in the outdoors but would like to see real Alaska wilderness, an excellent introductory trip is the Coastal Escape, a 3-day, 2-night camping trip to Berner's Bay, on Lynn Canal north of the end of the road. Besides paddling, groups spend plenty of time exploring the beaches and rainforest shorelines. Fit beginners will do fine, with teens as young as 14 normally invited; some trips may include kids as young as 10. No whiners, however: There's a good chance of rain, you'll sleep in a two-person tent, and paddling is work. The cost is $595 per person.

If you don't have that kind of time, **Alaska Travel Adventures** (✆ **800/791-2673** outside Alaska, or 907/789-0052 in Alaska; www.bestofalaskatravel.com) offers 3½-hour kayak trips from an unspoiled spot on north Douglas Island for $85 adults, $57 children 6 to 12. The tour includes orientation for beginners, transportation from downtown, and a snack.

A business that rents and delivers kayaks is listed under "Gearing Up for Juneau's Outdoors" (p. 163).

GETTING OUTSIDE: ON THE ICE

More than 36 major glaciers around Juneau flow from a single ocean of ice behind the mountains, the 1,500-square-mile **Juneau Icefield.** You can land on it in a helicopter just to touch the ice or to take a nature hike or dog sled ride. It's expensive, but there are few other places to see, let alone explore, the kind of ice sheet that carved North America in the last ice age. From the air, glaciers look unreal, like creations by a graphic artist, their sinuous lines of blue and white ice striped with darker gray gravel

A Day Trip to Tracy Arm

The fjords of the Tracy Arm–Fords Terror Wilderness (part of Tongass National Forest) are relatively unknown outside the area, but the scenery and wildlife viewing easily rival those of Glacier Bay National Park. And for those not riding a cruise ship, Tracy Arm has a significant advantage over Glacier Bay: It costs less than half as much and is easier to get to. A Tracy Arm tour takes about 8 hours; going to Glacier Bay from Juneau is an exhausting day trip—it's wiser to overnight there, though that adds more to the cost.

The Tracy Arm fjord is a long, narrow, twisting passageway into the coastal mountains, with peaks up to a mile high that jut straight out of the water, waterfalls tumbling down thousands of feet down their sides. At its head, Sawyer Glacier and South Sawyer Glacier calve ice into the water with a rumble and a splash. Whales and other wildlife usually show up along the way. And, as at Glacier Bay, John Muir paid a visit. No second-best here!

The largest operator is the Native-owned **Goldbelt**, 76 Egan Dr., Juneau (© **800/820-2628** or 907/586-8687; www.goldbelttours.com), which owns many of the big tourism businesses in town. They offer day-long glacier trips to Tracy Arm Fjord daily, with the exact destination somewhat contingent on tides; at times they go to Fords Terror and Dawes Glacier. Tours start at 8am in the summer (check for schedule changes). A naturalist provides commentary on the high-speed catamaran. Light meals are for sale, and the use of binoculars is included in the adult price of $139, $90 children ages 2 to 10, free under 2. Other large boats compete with Goldbelt, and you can shop around. **Adventure Bound Alaska**, at 215 Ferry Way, Juneau (© **800/228-3875** or 907/463-2509; www.adventureboundalaska.com), is a family business operating a 56-foot single-hull boat with deck space all the way around. They charge $120 adults, $80 ages 17 and younger.

Another way to go to Tracy Arm is to charter your own boat. Although it may cost twice as much or more per person, you can decide when and where to linger with the animals or ice. Check with the visitor center for a referral, or with **Juneau Sportfishing and Sightseeing** (© **907/586-1887**), listed above under "Saltwater Fishing & Whale-Watching."

debris. Only standing on the ice, which on closer inspection resembles the crusty compressed snow of springtime snow berms, do you get a clear sense of this entirely unfamiliar kind of terrain.

It's worth noting that these tours have had some major mishaps. While the accidents represent a tiny fraction of all the safe flights, they're a reminder that flying a helicopter to a glacier is not like flying an airliner.

Era Helicopters (© **800/843-1947** or 907/586-2030; www.flightseeingtours.com) is a respected operator. Their 1-hour flight over four glaciers with a 15-minute landing on Norris Glacier costs $254 per person. They also offer a program of **dogsled rides** on the ice, a chance to try a winter sport in the summer. That excursion includes the 4-glacier overflight and adds about an hour at a sled-dog camp on a glacier with a ride behind the dogs. It costs $450 per person. *One caveat:* Poor or even overcast weather makes it difficult to see the ice clearly, but if you wait for a sunny morning, all seats will likely be booked. They have a 48-hour cancellation policy, so you have to gamble to some extent on good viewing conditions. Of course, they don't fly in unsafe conditions.

NorthStar Trekking (© 907/790-4530; www.northstartrekking.com), another company with its own helicopters, specializes in hiking and teaching about glaciers. Their small groups (a maximum of 12, with two guides) go on ice-hiking excursions of up to a few miles, with the speed determined by the group. The 4-hour trip, which includes 2 hours on the ice and half an hour in the air (the balance is getting to the helicopter and gearing up), costs $359 per person. They offer longer, more expensive options, overnights, and less expensive options, too.

Wings of Alaska (© 907/586-6275; www.ichoosewings.com) offers glacier overflights by floatplane and flightseeing tours to the remote Taku Lodge, where they land for salmon for brunch, lunch, or dinner.

GETTING OUTSIDE: ON ADMIRALTY ISLAND

Beyond Douglas Island from Juneau, near the entrance to Gastineau Channel, is 1 million–acre Admiralty Island, one of the largest virgin blocks of old-growth forest in the country. The vast majority of the island is the protected **Kootznoowoo Wilderness.** Kootznoowoo, Tlingit for "fortress of bears," is said to have the highest concentration of brown bears on earth. Despite the town of Angoon on the western side of the island, there are more bears than people on Admiralty. The island's **Pack Creek Bear Viewing Area** is the most famous and surefire place to see bears in Southeast. The area has been managed for bear viewing since the 1930s, when hunting was outlawed. There's a platform for watching the bears up close as they feed on salmon spawning in the creek in July and August. Peak viewing occurs in the middle of that period. The bears generally pay no attention to the people watching them from a safe viewing platform.

Only 25 miles from Juneau, Pack Creek is so popular that the Forest Service uses a permit system to keep it from being overrun during the day (no humans are allowed 9pm–9am). The great majority of people go for only a few hours. There are no facilities in this wilderness area, and you can't even camp without some kind of watercraft to get to a designated area. The easiest way to go is with a tour operator who has permits. The Forest Service District Ranger Office can give you a list of guides. **Alaska Discovery,** 5310 Glacier Hwy. (© 800/586-1911; www.alaskadiscovery.com), has many permits for Pack Creek sea-kayak trips. Their 1-day excursion flies out and then paddles to the creek; no experience is necessary, but you must be physically capable of hiking and paddling. It costs $595 per person. A 2-night campout and sea-kayak near the creek offers more time to see the bears and appreciate the scenery. It costs $1,095 per person. **Alaska Fly 'N' Fish Charters,** 9604 Kelly Court (© 907/790-2120; www.alaskabyair.com), also has permits for its naturalist-guided 5½-hour fly-in Pack Creek visits, which cost $495 per person, with everything you need included.

Twelve permits per day go to the commercial operators, and 12 to people who go without any guide; 8 of those 12 private permits can be booked in advance with the Forest Service, and the other 4 are available in person at the Juneau Ranger District Office at 9am 3 days before the date on which they're good, or on the previous Friday for Tuesday and Wednesday. In the peak season, July 5 to August 25, permits cost $50 for adults, $25 for those ages 16 or under or 62 and over. Lower prices and easier availability prevail outside the peak, but then you might not see any bears. After you have the permit, you'll still need a way to get there, plus your own gear (including rubber boots and binoculars). The Forest Service lists air taxi operators on its website (www.fs.fed.us/r10/tongass/districts/admiralty). Among the best is **Alaska Fly 'N' Fish Charters,** which charges $350 per person, round-trip, to drop off customers with their own permits; the per-person price drops for groups of three or more.

Protected **Seymour Canal,** on the east side of the island, is good for canoeing and kayaking, and has two other sites besides Pack Creek where bears often show up: Swan Cove and Windfall Harbor. For information on the island, its 15 Forest Service cabins, and an excellent $4 map, contact the **Admiralty Island National Monument,** 8461 Old Dairy Rd., Juneau (© **907/586-8800;** www.fs.fed.us/r10/tongass/districts/admiralty).

WHERE TO STAY

Hotel rooms can be tight in the summer, so book ahead. Bed-and-breakfasts are a good way to get a better deal and have more fun. Lodging rates are high and room reservations tight in Juneau. The Juneau Convention and Visitors Bureau's *Juneau Travel Planner* and website contain listings of the hotels and B&Bs with links (© **888/581-2201;** www.traveljuneau.com).

EXPENSIVE

Besides the lodgings listed in full below, Juneau has a first-rate business hotel downtown: **Goldbelt Hotel Juneau,** 51 W. Egan Dr., (© **888/478-6909** or 907/586-6900; www.goldbelttours.com). The large bedrooms, with either two full-size or one king-size bed, are nicely furnished and noticeably quiet and immaculate. The views are good, and there is wireless Internet throughout. Summer rates are $169 to $179 double.

Alaska's Capital Inn 🐾🐾🐾 This scrupulously restored 1906 mansion offers constant surprises in its fascinating detail: the shining potbellied stove and 1879 pump organ in the parlor, the Alaskan artwork and Persian rugs, the original (electrified) gas lamps, period wallpaper, and even those old-fashioned push-button light switches. It took owners Linda Wendeborn and Mark Thorson 2½ years to bring the house back to this former glory, and they never would have done it without a driving vision, for they poured effort and expense into making details authentic that no one will ever notice. Fortunately, the house was worth it, with many large rooms with high ceilings, good views, fireplaces, claw-foot tubs, and real elegance. The best asset of all, however, may be the warmth and fun of the inn. The common rooms are conducive to socializing, and the hosts love to connect with guests and strive to accommodate their needs. For this reason, and the location just steps from the state Capitol Building, the inn fills with affluent lobbyists in the winter. There are some lower-priced rooms, allowing those on midrange budgets to enjoy the ambience, but the real showplaces carry luxury rates. Scottie dogs named Riley and Brodie patrol the place. An elaborate breakfast is served at 8am. Smoking is not allowed, and they don't take children under 11.

113 W. 5th St., Juneau, AK 99801. © 888/588-6507 or 907/586-6507. Fax 907/586-6508. www.alaskacapitalinn.com. 7 units. High season $134–$285 double; low season $109–$235 double. Extra person $15. Rates include full breakfast. AE, DC, DISC, MC, V. Children under 11 are not permitted. **Amenities:** Jacuzzi; shared computer w/Internet access; off-street parking. *In room:* TV/VCR, Wi-Fi.

Downtown Juneau

ACCOMMODATIONS ■
Alaska's Capital Inn **4**
Baranof Hotel **11**
The Driftwood Lodge **1**
The Historic Silverbow Inn **10**
Goldbelt Hotel Juneau **14**
Gold Street Inn **8**
Juneau International Hostel **6**
Prospector Hotel **3**

DINING ◆
The Hangar **15**

Heritage Coffee Co.
  and Café **16**
Kenny's Wok & Teriyaki
  Sushi Bar **13**
Pizzeria Roma **15**
Rainbow Food **9**
Red Dog Saloon **17**
Silverbow Bakery **10**
Twisted Fish Co.
  Alaskan Grill **20**
Valentine's Coffee House
  and Pizzeria **13**

ATTRACTIONS ●
Alaska State Museum **2**
The Juneau-Douglas
  City Museum **5**
The Last Chance
  Mining Museum **7**
Mount Roberts Tramway **19**
Patsy Ann Statue **18**

See *"Juneau Walking Tour"*
map for other attractions

Alaska Wolf House Bed & Breakfast 🦶 This huge cedar log house stands like a fortress in the woods overlooking Gastineau Channel and Douglas Island just off the Glacier Highway a half-mile beyond the edge of Juneau's core area. The abundance of dark wood and the views contribute to a wilderness lodge atmosphere despite the urban setting. The warm, manly hospitality of the innkeeper, a fishing guide, also fits in: He is known to hand guests a Guinness beer and a bag of popcorn on arrival. Rooms are crammed with amenities such as video games and DVD players, and there's a huge movie library. Breakfasts are likewise extravagant: King salmon soufflé and king crab quiche have made the menu. Two of the four units are suites, and all four are priced differently.

1900 Wickersham Dr., Juneau, AK 99801. ☎ **888/425-9653** or 907/586-2422. Fax 907/586-9053. www.alaskawolf house.com. 4 units. High season $129–$179 double; low season $109–$149. Additional person 13 and over $35. MC,

V. **Amenities:** Car rental; business center; Internet access. *In room:* A/C, TV/DVD, Wi-Fi, video games, fridge, coffee-maker, hair dryer, iron.

Baranof Hotel 𝒦𝒦 The Baranof is the only lodging in Alaska with the pedigree and style to pull off the role of the old-fashioned grand hotel. Built of concrete in 1939, it served for decades as an informal branch of the state capitol. Legislators and lobbyists still confer amid the overstuffed furniture and dark wood of the opulent lobby. The structure itself constrains modernization—the bathrooms and many rooms tend to be small—but features such as glass doorknobs and pressed-tin ceilings remain to show that it comes by its faults honestly. The management appreciates the building's ambience, and they have kept the style intact while lightening and updating rooms over the years. The upper-floor rooms have great views on the water side, while lower rooms were redone most recently, in 2003. Most bathrooms were remodeled with period tile and porcelain pedestal sinks and tubs. There are many appealing suites.

The Art Deco **Gold Room** 𝒦 restaurant is Juneau's most traditional fine-dining establishment. The dining room combines intimacy and grandeur in a showplace of shining brass, frosted glass, and rich wood. Most entrees are $23 to $30.

127 N. Franklin St., Juneau, AK 99801. © **800/544-0970** or 907/586-2660. Fax 907/586-8315. www.westmarkhotels.com. 196 units. High season $139–$169 double; low season $129–$139 double. Extra person 13 and over $15. AE, DC, DISC, MC, V. **Amenities:** 2 restaurants; bar; tour desk; salon; limited room service; fitness room; laundry service; dry cleaning. *In room:* TV, dataport, high-speed Internet (in some), kitchenette (in some), coffeemaker, hair dryer, iron.

The Historic Silverbow Inn 𝒦 There is an oddly pleasing style to this quirky little downtown hotel. The 1914 building, with wood floors, bare brick, and stained glass, is decorated with family pictures and weird postcards, mismatched furniture, and varied fabrics. The cozy little rooms come with extras such as lollipops and popcorn, among the original and considerate touches that show up repeatedly—for example, the shelf of supplies you may have forgotten, the answering machines on the direct-line phones, and the sack breakfast if you have to leave too early for the free breakfast in the bakery. The proprietors and staff and the scene they have created with their popular Silverbow Bakery and their cinema give the whole place a communal feel. With six small rooms and bathrooms, the place is more reminiscent of a European pension than a standard hotel; five more rooms were due to be added after our visit. The on-site cinema is an opportunity to watch independent and classic movies while tossing down a few pints of beer and scarfing up free popcorn. The restaurant, Silverbow Bakery, is described below.

120 2nd St., Juneau, AK 99801. © **800/586-4146** or 907/586-4146. Fax 907/586-4242. www.silverbowinn.com. 11 units. High season $154 double; low season $94 double. Extra person $20. $20 surcharge for 1-night stays in high season. Rates include continental breakfast. AE, DISC, MC, V. **Amenities:** Restaurant; cinema. *In room:* TV, Wi-Fi, hair dryer.

Pearson's Pond Luxury Inn and Adventure Spa 𝒦𝒦𝒦 Diane Pearson found a vocation when she opened her bed and breakfast years ago in a suburban house near the Mendenhall Glacier, and she pursued it with a zeal that's still startling to encounter after all the years I have known her. The result is an extraordinary, sensual retreat of superbly appointed rooms, packed with every conceivable amenity, in a building and on grounds that create the illusion of being in a fairyland somewhere in the Alaska wilderness—there's even a private pond with a rowboat. Diane herself remains the wizard behind the curtain, putting out her husband's freshly baked bread with the wine that greets new guests. On overhearing visitors wish they could have fish for dinner, she has been known to grab her rod, ride her bike down to the Mendenhall River,

---

---

catch a salmon, and light the barbecue in time for the evening meal. As the place has grown, she has added well-trained staff, so you can get a massage or join twice-daily yoga classes, and, of course, the palaces (I mean rooms) are always immaculate. She hosts business travelers—there's a well-stocked snack room and all units have Ethernet ports and access to a wireless LAN (and she'll lend you a laptop, too)—but it's really a place for couples. Diane plans weddings and even officiates on-site; some rooms have wonderful bathing facilities, and all are heavily sound-proofed for nights of passion. She also plans custom tour packages if you want her to set up your whole vacation (see the sample itineraries on the website), and she has more conventional condo-like lodgings downtown.

4541 Sawa Circle, Juneau, AK 99801. © 888/658-6328 or 907/789-3772. Fax 907/789-6722. www.pearsonspond.com. 5 units. High season $179–$329 double; low season $99–$219 double. Extra person $50. AE, DC, DISC, MC, V. **Amenities:** Health club; 2 outdoor Jacuzzis; concierge; business center; massage; free laundry service; free loan of rowboat, paddleboat, fishing gear, bike, or laptop computer. *In room:* TV/VCR/DVD, CD player, high-speed Internet, Wi-Fi, kitchenette, coffeemaker, hair dryer, iron.

Prospector Hotel 🐾   If you want a standard American hotel room, this place is a good choice. Situated just across the road from the water, it has nice views and proximity to the state museum and other attractions. Parking is easy, too. The rooms are spacious and well furnished with two queen-size beds each; one I saw had sleigh beds, while another had Shaker-style pieces in gorgeous wood. Colors are rich but calming, and the housekeeping seemed to be flawless. The standard room upstairs had a walk-in closet and facilities for snacks. But rooms are not all the same: Those on upper floors and facing the water are the best (the water view carries a $10 premium), but there is noticeable road noise on that side. The elevator runs only from the lobby level upward (floors 2–5); an entire floor of rooms below (floor 1) is half-basement and can be reached only by stairs. The attached restaurant, **TK McGuire's,** is comfortable and consistent.

375 Whittier St., Juneau, AK 99801-1781. © 800/331-2711 outside Alaska, 800/478-5866 inside Alaska, or 907/586-3737. Fax 907/586-1204. www.prospectorhotel.com. 63 units. High season $149–$155 double; low season $109–$129 double. AE, DC, DISC, MC, V. **Amenities:** Restaurant; bar; limited room service; laundry service; dry cleaning. *In room:* TV, Wi-Fi, fridge, coffeemaker, hair dryer.

INEXPENSIVE

In addition to the inexpensive places listed in full below, you'll find comfortable, private rooms in a house right downtown at **Gold Street Inn,** (© **907/586-9863;** www. juneauinn.com). The five rooms, all with full kitchens, range in price from $95 double for a small unit to $155 for a large two-bedroom suite. A continental breakfast is supplied.

The Driftwood Lodge *(Value)* This downtown motel, next door to the State Museum, is popular with families, and houses legislators and aides in the winter in its apartment-like kitchenette suites. Although the building can't hide its cinderblock construction and old-fashioned motel exterior, small bathrooms, or lack of elevators, the rooms are remarkably comfortable and well kept. The management has held prices low while making continuous improvements, so for a rate that won't get you in the door at other Juneau hotels ($119), you can put four people in a two-bedroom suite with a full kitchen. The round-the-clock courtesy van saves big money to the airport or ferry, and the rental bikes will cover your transportation needs downtown.

435 Willoughby Ave., Juneau, AK 99801. © 800/544-2239 or 907/586-2280. Fax 907/586-1034. www.driftwood alaska.com. 63 units. High season $94 double, $102–$125 suite; low season $66 double, $89 suite. Extra person $10. AE, DC, DISC, MC, V. **Amenities:** Bike rental; courtesy van; coin-op laundry. *In room:* TV, coffeemaker.

A HOSTEL

Juneau International Hostel *(Finds)* The historic yellow house among the downtown sights is a showplace of custom cabinetry and big, light common rooms. The shared kitchen was squeaky-clean when I visited (everyone has to pitch in with a chore). Men and women sleep in a number of small separate dorm rooms, and there is one private room for families with children, which is in high demand. Office hours are from 7 to 9am and 5pm to midnight in the summer, 8 to 9am and 5 to 10:30pm in the winter, with lockout during the day. There's a coin-op laundry, free Internet access and Wi-Fi, lockers, and free local calls. Reservations must be prepaid by mail or phone for a 5-night maximum stay; if there is space available, you can stay up to 7 days. Alcohol, drugs, and pets are not allowed and shoes are removed at the door.

614 Harris St., Juneau, AK 99801. © 907/586-9559. www.juneauhostel.org. 47 beds. $10 per adult; $5 children ages 6–17 with adult; free ages 5 and under. $2 premium for credit card payment. MC, V. Closed 2 weeks during winter holidays. **Amenities:** Free Internet access; coin-op laundry. *In room:* No phone.

CAMPING

Juneau has two exceptional Forest Service campgrounds open from mid-May to mid-September. For information, call the Juneau Ranger District at © **907/586-8800** or contact them at www.fs.fed.us/r10/tongass. **The Mendenhall Glacier Campground,** overlooking the lake and glacier and next to the Mendenhall River, is the best-built public campground in the state, with granite block construction. The bathrooms have showers and flush toilets, and there is a half-mile nature trail accessible to travelers with disabilities. The 69 sites are huge and broadly separated; 9 have full RV hookups and another 9 have electricity and water. Tents and RVs are segregated. To get there, turn right on Montana Creek Road from Mendenhall Loop Road. Tent sites are $10, RV sites $26 and $28. The 12-site **Auke Village Campground,** 1¾ miles north of the ferry dock, is in an extraordinary place, with sites among large trees along an ocean beach, looking out on the islands of Auke Bay. The campground has pit toilets and running water. Sites are $10 per night. **Spruce Meadow RV Park,** at 10200 Mendenhall Loop Rd. (© **907/789-1990;** www.juneaurv.com), has full hookups in a natural setting with many amenities. Full hookups are $27, plus $2.50 for cable.

WHERE TO DINE

Besides these restaurants, see the **Gold Room,** in the Baranof Hotel, on p. 170. For a beer and simple fare, try crossing the bridge to Douglas and **The Island Pub,** 1102 2nd St. (© **907/364-1595**), a warm, modern remake of a waterfront restaurant dating to the 1930s. The cuisine is pizza and bar food. Try the apple pie pizza for dessert.

Chan's Thai Kitchen 𝒜𝒜 *Finds* THAI   The small, overlit dining room in a half-basement sees few tourists, but I've heard locals brag about how long they were willing to stand in the small entrance area to get a table. When I went, I became a believer, too—the authentic Thai food is that good and the atmosphere, if lacking in polish, is conducive to a good time. You will need a car, as the location is 20 minutes from town across from the Auke Bay boat harbor. Reservations are not accepted and they do not have a liquor license.

11820 Glacier Hwy. ℭ **907/789-9777**. Reservations not accepted. Main courses $9–$13. MC, V. Tues–Fri 11:30am–2pm and 4:30–8:30pm; Sat 4:30–8:30pm.

The Hangar 𝒜 STEAK/SEAFOOD/PASTA   Situated in a converted airplane hangar on a wooden pier with large windows, this bar and grill has great views and a fun atmosphere; even off-season, it's packed. It's a fine place to drink beer (with 24 brews on tap), listen to live music, or play at one of the three pool tables. What's surprising is that the food is good, too. The seared ahi sashimi appetizer, raw inside, had a pleasant texture and taste, and the jambalaya, a huge portion for $12, was spicy but balanced.

2 Marine Way. ℭ **907/586-5018**. Reservations recommended. Main courses $15–$25. AE, MC, V. Daily 11am–10pm.

Kenny's Wok & Teriyaki Sushi Bar *Value* CHINESE/JAPANESE   Kenny is an old hand in the restaurant business, going all the way back to his first restaurant in Nome in 1976. This relatively new place in Juneau quickly became a favorite of cruise-ship crews for its reasonable prices and seemingly endless menu ranging from familiar pot stickers or teriyaki chicken to exotic selections such as seaweed salad or sashimi. The light downtown dining room has a 10-seat sushi bar and 11 well-separated tables on a hardwood floor—all good except for the annoying television. Service is fast and professional. Our veggies and rice and "Alaska roll" sushi (smoked salmon, asparagus, avocado, crab, and hot sauce) were fresh, tasty, and filling, and set us back only $15 for two. The restaurant delivers in the downtown area. It does not serve alcohol.

126 Front St. ℭ **907/586-3575**. Reservations not accepted. Lunch $6–$9, dinner main courses $9–$16. MC, V. Mon–Fri 11am–9:30pm, Sat–Sun noon–9:30pm.

Finds **Quick Bites in Juneau**

The **Silverbow Bakery,** at 120 2nd St. (ℭ **907/586-4146;** www.silverbowinn. com), is a happening spot for bagels or hearty sandwiches. It's open daily 6am to 8pm. The **Rainbow Food** health-food grocery at 224 4th St. (ℭ **907/586-6476**) is the best picnic-packing place downtown, making sandwiches and salads at the deli. **Hot Bite,** at the Auke Bay boat harbor, is a local secret, serving charcoal-broiled hamburgers and halibut burgers and mind-blowing milkshakes. Take out or sit at one of six indoor tables. Downtown Juneau's young, professional population supports several good coffeehouses. **Valentine's Coffee House and Pizzeria,** 111 Seward St. (ℭ **907/463-5144**), serves light, hot meals in an authentic old-fashioned storefront. **Heritage Coffee Co. and Café,** at 174 S. Franklin St. (ℭ **907/586-1087;** www.heritagecoffee.com) and 216 2nd St. (ℭ **907/ 586-1752**), has two trendy, comfortable coffeehouses good for watching people or using the Internet, either wireless or on their terminals. They also roast famous coffee.

Pizzeria Roma ⚄ PIZZA   The pizza here is fantastic—the best in Southeast Alaska. They also serve tasty calzones, pasta, many focaccia sandwiches, and terrific salads, and have a good wine list. The dining room is small, can be hot, and gets quite crowded, but it's a good place if you can slip in. The location is on the water, across the hall from the Hangar.

2 Marine Way (In the Wharf Building). ℂ 907/463-5020. Reservations not accepted. All items $7–$22. AE, DISC, MC, V. Summer daily 11am–10pm; winter daily 11am–9:30pm.

Twisted Fish Co. Alaskan Grill ⚄ SEAFOOD/PIZZA/BURGERS   Overlooking the water at the cruise ship dock, in the same building as Taku Smokeries, the dining room is magnificent, with high ceilings and an entire wall of windows on the Gastineau Channel, a fireplace of beach rock, lots of hardwood, and, to keep it from being too grand, cartoonlike fish hanging down. The quality and range of the food brings locals to a tourist zone they would otherwise avoid: items like salmon on a cedar plank or in pastry, halibut or salmon tacos, and also little pizzas, burgers, and terrific desserts. The service is fast and attentive, but the dining room makes you want to stay long after you are done eating.

550 S. Franklin St. ℂ 907/463-5033. Reservations recommended. Lunch $7–$15, dinner main courses $18–$30. AE, DISC, MC, V. Summer daily 11am–10pm. Closed Oct–Apr.

NIGHTLIFE

Alaska Travel Adventures has offered its **Gold Creek Salmon Bake** (ℂ 907/789-0052) for more than 30 years. It's touristy, yes, but fun, with marshmallow roasting, music, and other entertainment—great for families. (I'd avoid it in the rain, however.) The cost is $34 for adults, $22 for children 12 and under. For more substantial performances, try to catch a show by Juneau's **Perseverance Theatre,** Alaska's largest professional theater. The winter season, starting in September and lasting until early June, includes Alaska's best cutting-edge dramas, including serious homegrown work. Paula Vogel was here when she wrote *How I Learned to Drive,* which later won the Pulitzer Prize. Summer offerings are limited to youth theater and workshops. To find out what's playing, contact the theater's office at 914 3rd St., Douglas (ℂ 907/364-2421), or check the website at www.perseverancetheatre.org.

A political scandal or two put a damper on some of the infamous legislative partying that once occurred in Juneau, far away from home districts, but good places to go out drinking and dancing still exist. The **Red Dog Saloon,** at 278 S. Franklin St., is the town's most famous bar, with a sawdust-strewn floor, a slightly contrived but nonetheless infectious frontier atmosphere, and walls covered with Alaska memorabilia. Locals hang across the street, at **The Alaskan Bar,** 167 S. Franklin, which occupies an authentic gold-rush hotel with a two-story Victorian barroom. Boisterous parties and music go on there all year. **The Hangar,** listed above under "Where to Dine," is the place for beer drinkers. They have a big-screen TV and live music Friday and Saturday nights, as well as pool and darts.

7 Glacier Bay National Park

Glacier Bay is a work in progress; the boat ride to its head is a chance to see creation unfolding. The bay John Muir discovered in a canoe in 1879 didn't exist a century earlier. Eighteenth-century explorers found instead a wall of ice a mile thick where the entrance to the branching, 65-mile-long fjord now opens to the sea. Receding faster

Glacier Bay National Park

than any other glacier on earth, the ice melted into the ocean and opened a spectacular and still-unfinished land. The land itself is rising 1½ inches a year as it rebounds from the weight of now-melted glaciers. As your vessel retraces Muir's path—and then probes northward in deep water where ice stood in his day—the story of this new world unravels in reverse. The trees on the shore get smaller and then disappear; then all vegetation disappears, and finally, at the head of the bay, the ice stands at the water's edge surrounded by barren rock, rounded and scored by the passage of the ice but not yet marked by the waterfalls cascading from the clouds above. And there, still doing their landscape-shaping work, are the great blue glaciers, the largest among them the awesome Grand Pacific Glacier.

Glacier Bay, first set aside as a national monument by Calvin Coolidge in 1925, is managed by the National Park Service, which has the difficult job of protecting the wilderness, the whales, and the other wildlife while serving the huge public visiting the park. This rugged land the size of Connecticut cannot be seen by car, only by boat or plane, and the presence of too many boats threatens the wilderness experience and may disturb the wildlife. The whales appear to be sensitive to the noise of vessels, and, since the 1970s, when in some years hardly any whales returned, the park service has used a permit system to limit the number of ships that can enter the bay. Any boat sees several other ships on a day's journey up the bay, but how much the vessels bother the whales and other wildlife is difficult to measure precisely, and political pressure always pushes for more huge ships. In response to legislation passed by Alaska's pro-development Congressional delegation, the park service increased the number of cruise ships entering the bay, but in 2001, environmentalists won a court ruling that briefly reduced the number and held off a further increase pending study. In 2003, the Park Service completed an Environmental Impact Statement on the issue. It allows an increase from 139 cruise ships a year to 184 per year, but only if recommended by a science advisory board. Currently, a 10% increase is proposed starting in 2007—more than environmentalists support, but fewer than the cruise industry could use. To read more about the park's vessel-management plan, go to **www.nps.gov/glba**.

On my longest visit, I saw humpback whales breaching (leaping all the way out of the water) every day. I saw orcas, too. One day, while fishing for halibut from a small boat in foggy Icy Strait, just outside the park, I heard a sound like thunder not far off. Like thunder, the sound was repeated, growing closer, but its source remained hidden behind the white circle of fog that surrounded us. Then the smooth water suddenly bulged and a huge barnacled creature shot upward and crashed down with a sharp clap and a splash that rocked the boat. And then it happened again. The whale went on performing for most of an hour. A day later, I encountered the same spectacle while sea-kayaking in the park's Bartlett Cove.

Leaping whales and falling glaciers are hard to beat. But the park also has major drawbacks to consider. Sightings aren't guaranteed, so there's a risk that you'll spend a lot of money and not see any whales. And even though this is a huge wilderness, the ways to see it are limited, so most people never get away from crowds. The lone concessionaire-operated tour boat into the bay costs $170 per person and is usually full of people. The large cruise ships that bring most visitors to the park view the scenery without getting up close to the shore or wildlife and miss the shore-based attractions. Smaller ships see more, with smaller groups and more chances to get outdoors. Independent travelers can spend a few days in some of Alaska's most attractive remote accommodations, in Gustavus, with great fishing, hiking, sea kayaking, and tour boat rides into the park. But the only way to see the heart of the park in true solitude is on a boat you charter for yourself (out of range of most budgets) or on a rugged overnight sea-kayaking adventure.

As an alternative, consider the other places to see Alaska's glaciers and whales that are easier and less expensive to visit. If you're in Juneau, consider a day trip to Tracy Arm instead. In Southcentral Alaska, plan a day trip from Whittier to see the glaciers of western Prince William Sound or from Seward to see Kenai Fjords National Park. There are other places in Southeast rich with marine wildlife as well. Still, Glacier Bay beats them all—and just about any place on Earth—for the combination of lots of whales and lots of big glaciers.

ESSENTIALS
GETTING THERE

Gustavus, covered in the next section of this chapter, is the gateway to Glacier Bay National Park, lying 10 miles by road from the park headquarters at Bartlett Cove. Visitors get to the park either on a cruise ship or by air through Gustavus and then by road to Bartlett Cove. (A third excellent option of coming on a daily passenger ferry from Juneau is not currently offered, but check with the visitor information sources below in case that service has been reinstituted when you visit.) Cruise ships generally pass through the bay without landing, so those visitors can skip the material below (although you may be interested in the introduction, above). Information about flying to Gustavus is covered in the next section. Getting from the airstrip to Bartlett Cove is easy. Vans meet planes, charging $12 to make the 10-mile trip to the park, plus $2 for baggage. It's free if you are traveling with a package tour; also, most of the inns and lodges in Gustavus offer free transfers to the park. Once you're at Bartlett Cove, you're only at the edge of a park with no roads. To go from there to the rest of the park you need some kind of boat. That's covered below under "Activities at the Park."

The **Alaska Marine Highway System** (© **800/642-0066;** www.ferryalaska.com) has experimented with offering service to Bartlett Cove from Juneau. In 2006, sailings were scheduled once every 2 weeks during the summer—not practical, unless you fly one way and take the boat the other way.

VISITOR INFORMATION

Contact the **Glacier Bay National Park and Preserve** at P.O. Box 140, Gustavus, AK 99826 (© **907/697-2230;** www.nps.gov/glba). The park service interprets the park mainly by placing well-prepared rangers on board most cruise and tour vessels entering the bay. The park also maintains a modest visitor center with displays on the park on the second floor of the lodge at wooded Bartlett Cove. Pick up the park map and handy guide, *The Fairweather.* Nearby are the park's offices, a free campground, a backcountry office, a few short hiking trails, a dock, sea kayak rental, and other park facilities. Rangers lead a daily nature walk and present an evening program.

ACTIVITIES AT THE PARK

HIKING AT BARTLETT COVE   There are three short hiking trails through the rainforest of Sitka spruce and western hemlock at Bartlett Cove. Each weaves through the cool, damp quiet created by these huge trees and the moss on the forest floor. Wet spots are often crossed by boardwalks with railings. A map is included in the *Fairweather* visitor guide.

The **Forest Loop** is an easy trail about 1 mile long, beginning at the lodge and passing through the woods and past some park buildings to the cove's pebble beach. The **Bartlett River Trail** is a 4-mile round-trip leading to the Bartlett River Estuary, a good bird-watching spot, especially during migrations. The **Bartlett Lake Trail** branches off the Bartlett River Trail after about a quarter mile for a one-way forest hike to the lake of 3.75-miles.

BOAT TOURS   Bartlett Cove is nowhere near the park's highlights. Most independent travelers take a day boat to see the vast majority of Glacier Bay. The boat is operated by the park concessionaire, a joint venture of ARAMARK and Huna Totem, with offices at 241 W. Ship Creek Ave., Anchorage, AK 99501 (© **888/229-8687** or 907/264-4600; fax 907/258-3668; www.visitglacierbay.com), or, locally, in the summer only, at P.O. Box 179, Gustavus, AK 99826 (© **907/697-4000;** fax 907/697-4001). The boat leaves from the dock in Bartlett Cove and sails to the fjords' very head and the Grand Pacific Glacier. The 8-hour voyage is too long for many children. There's a snack bar, and a simple lunch is provided. Bring binoculars, good rain gear, and layers of warm clothing. A park service employee does the commentary, so you can count on accuracy and a didactic approach missing from most commercial tours. The fare is $170 for adults ($182 with tax), half-price for children ages 2 to 12, free under 2. The company also offers an overnight package that includes the boat ride, meals, and lodging for $399, plus airfare.

CHARTERING A BOAT   Local family operators based in Gustavus take visitors up the bay in comfort, with the spontaneity and intimacy of boating with friends. If you have a group, you can have a boat and guide to yourself. Mike Nigro, a former backcountry ranger and longtime resident, takes groups of four to six for $1,800 per day on a 42-foot yacht, the Kahsteen. His **Gustavus Marine Charters** can be reached at ℂ **907/697-2233** or www.gustavusmarinecharters.com.

KAYAKING IN THE PARK   You won't forget seeing a breaching humpback whale from a sea kayak, sitting just inches off the water. It happens around here. When we breathlessly told our innkeepers about the experience, they smiled politely. They hear the same descriptions all the time.

Inexperienced paddlers should choose a guided trip. **Alaska Discovery,** 5310 Glacier Hwy., Juneau (ℂ **800/586-1911;** www.alaskadiscovery.com), is Alaska's best large sea-kayak guide organization. They offer paddles ranging from 6 hours to 8 days in Glacier Bay. A 6-hour guided paddle from Bartlett Cove is the best choice for beginners. Although the trip goes nowhere near the glaciers, the paddlers stand a good chance of seeing whales, sometimes quite close up. The guides are well trained and know how to teach and make the trip an adventure. Any fit person can enjoy the trip. It costs $140, including a tasty lunch and a ride from your lodgings or the airport. The longer tours also are well guided and outfitted, but I wouldn't recommend a week of sea kayaking to anyone who hasn't tried it before (what if you find out the first day that you don't like kayaking?). If you're up to it, however, this is the most intimate and authentic way to experience this wilderness, with almost unlimited time to see the glaciers and wildlife. A 5-day trip to the bay's more visited west arm, geared to novices, is $1,995; a more strenuous 8 days in the spectacular but forgotten east arm is $2,395. The company also has a simple bed-and-breakfast in Gustavus, for 1- or 2-night stays at the beginning or end of a sea-kayaking excursion.

It's also possible to paddle around Bartlett Cove or near Gustavus without a guide. Raw beginners can try it, but a safer course is to take a guided outing first. **Glacier Bay Sea Kayaks,** based in Gustavus (ℂ **907/697-2257;** www.glacierbayseakayaks.com), is the park service rental concessionaire, operating from May 1 to September 30. They offer rentals, which begin with an instructional briefing, for $60 half-day, $80 full day. Experienced kayakers ready for an overnight in the wilderness up the bay can rent equipment, too, and get dropped near the glaciers for $214 round-trip. Do your planning and decide what to bring before you leave for the park, as you may not be able to buy or rent what you need once there. Check the gear list and other advice on the Glacier Bay Sea Kayaks website. Before starting off on an overnight, you also will have to attend a park service briefing and get a backcountry permit from the headquarters.

FLIGHTSEEING   One spectacular way to get into the park is by flightseeing. Gustavus-based **Air Excursions** (ℂ **907/697-2375**) offers air tours in float or wheeled planes. Other operators fly from various nearby towns, including Haines and Skagway (covered later in this chapter). You'll see the incredible rivers of ice that flow down into the bay, and you may even see wildlife. What you give up is the sense of scale from ground level.

WHERE TO STAY, CAMP & DINE

Glacier Bay Lodge ✿   This is the only place to stay in the park (although Gustavus, 10 miles down the road, has some of the most attractive accommodations in Alaska; see the next section). A new concessionaire has upgraded the rooms, starting in 2005; they have new curtains, phones, and hair dryers. In general, they are comfortable but unmemorable, although the setting is pleasant. The buildings are set amid the soothing quiet of large rainforest trees and are reached from the main lodge by boardwalks and steps. Laundry facilities and rental of bikes and fishing gear are available. The company offers all-inclusive packages starting at $399 per person, which include lodging, meals, activities, and transfers from the airport.

The **restaurant** has huge windows looking onto Bartlett Cove. The menu includes a wide variety of dishes, including fresh fish. I have always enjoyed dining on the deck and watching for whales. The restaurant serves breakfast as early as 6am and dinner as late as 10pm. Drinks are served in the restaurant or on the deck over the cove from 4 to 11pm; on rainy days, visitors congregate around the fire in the comfortable lobby.

The lodge also provides public showers and a convenience store for the free park service **campground.** About ¼ mile from the dock, the campground lacks running water but has a warming hut, firewood, and bear-resistant food caches. You have to cook in a fire ring in the intertidal zone and observe other bear-avoidance rules the rangers will explain. Get a camping permit at the ranger station when you arrive; the campground is almost never full.

Bartlett Cove (P.O. Box 179), Gustavus, AK 99826. ℂ **888/229-8687** or 907/697-4000. Fax 907/258-3668 or 907/697-4001. www.visitglacierbay.com. 56 units. $185 double. Extra person $10. AE, DC, DISC, MC, V. Closed mid-Sept to mid-May. **Amenities:** Restaurant; bike rental; coin-op laundry. *In room:* Hair dryers.

8 Gustavus: Country Inns & Quiet

Gustavus (gus-*tave*-us) remains an undiscovered treasure—or, at least, it succeeds in making itself feel that way. It's wonderfully remote, easily accessible only by air, but has a selection of comfortable and even luxurious inns and lodges, plus several days' worth of outdoor activities, excellent salmon and halibut fishing, nearly surefire whale-watching, close access to sea kayaking and other activities at Glacier Bay National Park, and places for casual hiking and bicycle outings. Large cruise ships cannot land here, leaving the roads free of their throngs of shoppers. Miraculously, the 450 townspeople have been smart enough to value what they've got and build on it. Even the gas station is a work of art. Walking, biking, or driving down the quiet roads, everyone you pass—every single person—waves to you.

The buildings, mostly clapboard houses and log cabins, are scattered widely across an oceanfront alluvial plain. Several of the founding homesteads were farms, and the broad clearings of sandy soil wave with hay and wildflowers. The setting is unique in Alaska, and when I had a choice to go anywhere in the state for a 4-day trip with extended family, this is the place I chose. Each of us took something lasting from the trip. My older son, then 8, learned what it was like to be able to bike anywhere at will, making discoveries in the woods and friends on the quiet lanes without his parents reining him in. My parents, in their 60s, glowed when they returned from kayaking among the breaching humpback whales in the park's Bartlett Cove. I often reminisce about a day at the beach when I built dams and sand castles with the children, looking up to see a family of orcas romping just offshore. My cousin won't forget the huge platters of Dungeness crab that came for dinner one night at the inn.

The problem with Gustavus is the expense (and the dampness, but you get used to that). The best outdoor activities involve charters or rentals, which can add more than $200 a day per person to the cost of your trip. Most accommodations have all-inclusive plans, which include great meals but come with price tags of $175 per person per

---

Tips Town without a Downtown

This town looks like the country: houses, cabins, and a few businesses spread far apart along quiet roads. Services are limited. On Dock Road you will find an ATM outside Gusto Building Supply, and the Bear Track Mercantile, which sells necessities. Bring your own booze and whatever else you will want with you, and reserve all accommodations in advance. The local government, founded in 2004, imposes a 2% sales tax and an added 4% tax on accommodations.

---

night or more. Less expensive B&Bs exist, but the choice of restaurants for dinner is limited.

ESSENTIALS

GETTING THERE   For years, Gustavus was served by private passenger ferries, and may be again when you read this. At the time of writing, however, the service was not running. The **Alaska Marine Highway System** (② **800/642-0066;** www.ferryalaska. com) occasionally runs vessels to Gustavus; check with them for the latest on the changing schedule.

During the summer, **Alaska Airlines** (② **800/252-7522;** www.alaskaair.com) flies a jet once a day from Juneau to Gustavus and back in the early evening. An advance fare is around $180 round-trip. For more frequent service by prop from Juneau to Gustavus, at roughly the same fare as with Alaska Airlines, use **Wings of Alaska** (② **907/ 789-0790** reservations, or 907/697-2201 in Gustavus; www.ichoosewings.com),

VISITOR INFORMATION   The traditional way to plan a trip to Gustavus is to contact a lodge and, once you're comfortable with them, allow them to advise you and book your activities. The **Gustavus Visitors Association** (www.gustavusak.com) is a cooperative website of local businesses, with links and community information; there is no staffed center. Messages sent through the site and calls to an answering machine (② **907/697-2454**) are distributed to members for response. Reach them by mail at P.O. Box 167, Gustavus, AK 99826. A local travel agency, **Alaska's Glacier Bay Travel** (② **907/697-2475;** www.glacierbaytravel.com), run by the same folks as the TLC Taxi (see below), also can help with choices and reservations. Be certain to reserve a place to stay before showing up in Gustavus.

GETTING AROUND   There are just a few roads. The main one starts at the airport and runs about 10 miles to **Bartlett Cove,** the Glacier Bay National Park base of operations. **Dock Road** branches off to the left, at the gas station, and leads to the ocean dock. There's a map and list of businesses posted near the gas station, and most businesses will give you one to take along for exploration by bicycle. Many inns and B&Bs have courtesy vans and free bicycles; ask about transportation when you reserve. **TLC Taxi** (② **907/697-2239;** tlctaxi@glacierbaytravel.com) offers transportation between the airport, Bartlett Cove, and points in between, with flat fees depending on the destination. Reserve ahead. A van can accommodate groups, gear, and kayaks. **Bud's Rent a Car** is at ② **907/697-2403.**

EXPLORING GUSTAVUS

Everything to do in Gustavus involves the outdoors. I've listed the activities here in priority order.

WHALE-WATCHING & FISHING   Whales keep their own schedule, but you're almost certain to see them on a whale-watching excursion here, where the swirling current of Icy Strait creates such a rich feeding ground that humpbacks come back every summer without fail. The big tour boat in the national park (see the previous section) frequently sees whales, but Icy Strait, outside the park, is even more prolific and is served by smaller operators. **Cross Sound Express** (𝄞 **888/697-2726** or 907/ 697-2726; www.gustavus.com/taz) takes two viewing trips a day with 16 passengers aboard the *TAZ,* which is also used for kayak drop-offs and other marine transportation. It's a substantial vessel, and the outings are highly rated. The cost is $95 per person (no discount for children). That's about half the cost of the park tours, and the experience is more intimate, getting you closer to the whales—but, of course, you don't see the glaciers.

Gustavus has superb charter-boat fishing for halibut and salmon (if salmon are running). The waters are protected and seasickness generally is not a concern. Your inn host in Gustavus can make the arrangements. A boat typically charters for $250 to $300 per person for a full day, plus the cost of having your fish professionally packed and shipped home to you. Half-days are rarely available because the boats are fully booked. If you do a fishing charter and the others on board agree, you can take some of the time for whale-watching.

SEA KAYAKING   Gustavus-based **Spirit Walker Expeditions** (𝄞 **800/KAYAKER** or 907/697-2266; www.seakayakalaska.com) has a good reputation locally. They lead guided day trips to the whale-watching grounds, and overnight expeditions as long as a week. **Alaska Discovery,** 5310 Glacier Hwy., Juneau (𝄞 **800/586-1911;** www.alaska discovery.com), offers an easy 3-day, 2-night kayaking expedition among the whales for $895 per person. They take a boat to a base camp and then kayak among the whales from there. The outing is suitable for fit beginners and older children. **Sea Otter Kayak Glacier Bay,** on Dock Road (𝄞 **907/697-3007;** www.he.net/~seaotter), rents kayaks and gear for Gustavus or Glacier Bay waters and provides basic training (although I recommend beginners go with a guide). They also help with trip planning.

HIKING & BICYCLING   There are few cars in Gustavus, but most inns provide bikes. The roads are fun to explore, and the sandy beaches, accessed from the town dock, are great for a walk and a picnic, and to watch eagles and other birds and wildlife. You can go many miles, if you are of a mind, for a run or long walk, but we saw little reason to go far before stopping to play and picnic on a broad sand beach undisturbed by any other human footprint.

WHERE TO STAY

Gustavus contains some of Alaska's best remote accommodations, more than I have room to describe here. Most accommodations are "Gustavus style," which means they charge a daily per-person price for rooms, breakfast and dinner served family style, brown-bag lunches, bicycles and some other outdoor equipment and transfers, and they book and charge for fishing, sea kayaking, hiking, and Glacier Bay tours. It's expensive, but it's a carefree way to visit. Another set of accommodations charges less but leaves you on your own for lunch and dinner. Before choosing that less costly, a la carte approach, consider your dining options, which are covered below. Except as noted, rooms in Gustavus don't have phones. Some of the inns do not have licenses to serve alcohol; if that's a consideration, be sure to ask before you book your stay, and consider bringing it with you.

Blue Heron Bed and Breakfast at Glacier Bay ✸   Stay here if your budget doesn't allow a pricey all-inclusive package, and you'll still get many of the same comforts in fresh, attractive rooms with features such as VCRs, comforters, and superior linens. The hosts, longtime residents, are enthusiastic about their guests and serve large breakfasts. If you rent one of the cottages, you can cook your own evening meal; the rooms have access to microwaves and refrigerators in the sunroom dining area, and a country store and deli are a few minutes' walk away. The location is among the wild-flowers and marshland near the Gustavus waterfront.

Off Dock Rd. (P.O. Box 77), Gustavus, AK 99826. ✆ **907-697-2337.** Fax 907/697-2293. www.blueheronbnb.net. 2 units, 2 cottages. $143 double, $175 double cottage. Extra adult $80. Discounts for children. Rates include full break-fast. No credit cards. **Amenities:** Free bike loan; courtesy van; laundry machines ($6 per load). *In room:* TV/VCR.

Glacier Bay Country Inn ✸✸✸   This inn has more of the feel of a wilderness lodge. It sits on 160 acres of unspoiled forest looking out on its own airstrip where a plane waits to take guests out to fish in even more remote spots (the inn has its own charter fishing boat, too). The buildings are quirky and charming, with log beams, strange angles, and an authentically rough-hewn look. Guests make no sacrifices in comfort, however; each of the five rooms and five cabins has its own bathroom, and there is ample room to relax and while away the day if you stay home from the day's activities. Meals are ample, with two main courses offered at the evening family-style service. As at other Gustavus inns, bicycles and rides in the van are free, but most activities off the property are paid for separately.

35 Tong Rd. (P.O. Box 5), Gustavus, AK 99826. ✆ **800/628-0912** or 907/697-2288. Fax 907/697-2289. www.glacier bayalaska.com. 5 units, 5 cabins. $185 per person, double occupancy, rooms; $215 per person, double occupancy, cab-ins. Extra adult (after 2) $100; extra child ages 3–11 $50. Rates include all meals. DISC, MC, V. Closed mid-Sept to mid-May. **Amenities:** Free bike loans; activity desk; courtesy van; Internet access in common room; laundry; fish cleaning/freezing. *In room:* Coffeemaker, hair dryer.

Glacier Bay's Bear Track Inn ✸✸✸   Six miles from Gustavus, this extraordinary log building faces its own field of wildflowers, which, if you walk half a mile across, leads to the shore. You look out on this scene from a lobby with a huge fireplace, a ceiling 28 feet high, and a wall of windows. The immense logs of the walls and the isolation give the place the feeling of a wilderness lodge, but the rooms are as good as those of any upscale hotel and have the advantage of large dormer windows with sweeping views. Objectively, it's the best place in Gustavus and one of the best remote lodges in Alaska, but which place you prefer depends on your taste: What the Bear Track gains from perfection it loses in the funky, quaint atmosphere I like about the area. One major advantage over the other lodges and inns: Meals here are cooked to order from a varied menu. Those not staying here can buy dinner, too. The inn serves beer and wine.

255 Rink Rd., Gustavus, AK 99826. ✆ **888/697-2284** or 907/697-3017. Fax 907/697-2284. www.beartrackinn.com. 14 units. $465 per person, double occupancy. Discounts for additional nights. Rates include round-trip air from Juneau, transfers, and all meals. DISC, MC, V. Closed Oct–Apr. **Amenities:** Restaurant; free bike loan; children's pro-grams; concierge; tour desk; courtesy van; business center; limited room service; massage; babysitting; laundry serv-ice. *In room:* Hair dryer.

Gustavus Inn at Glacier Bay ✸✸✸   This is the original and still my favorite of the Gustavus full-service inns. By objective standards of modern luxury, imitators have surpassed the old homestead farmhouse, but no one could duplicate the extraordinary hospitality of the Lesh family, honed over 40 years of running the inn. Dave and

JoAnn know how to make guests feel immediately a part of the place. The site is unsurpassed, too, standing at the center of the community amid blowing grass and with a huge vegetable garden that provides much of the dining room's wonderful food. Dave, the chef, has published a cookbook and his ginger sablefish is now widely copied. The seasonings he uses on seafood are a revelation He serves big, inexhaustible platters in the dining room, where there's also a beer and wine bar and sushi appetizers. Before going, talk over what you want to do with JoAnn, Dave, or Dave's father, Jack, and let them book everything.

1 Gustavus Rd. (P.O. Box 60), Gustavus, AK 99826. ℂ 800/649-5220 or 907/697-2254. Fax 907/697-2255. www. gustavusinn.com. 13 units. $175 per person per night based on double or triple occupancy. Half-price for children under 12. Rates include all meals. AE, MC, V. Closed Sept 16–May 15. **Amenities:** Restaurant; bike loan; courtesy car; Wi-Fi; laundry service; fishing rods (bring your own tackle).

WHERE TO DINE

Even if you do not stay at one of the full-service inns, I recommend taking at least some of your meals there. Some of the best chefs in Alaska cook at these places (I still try to copy some of the flavors prepared by Dave Lesh of the Gustavus Inn at Glacier Bay). Make reservations; you can't just show up and eat. The other choice for fine dining is The Glacier Bay Lodge, which serves three meals a day—but it's 10 miles away at the park's Bartlett Cove headquarters. Otherwise, the dining choices in Gustavus are few and fairly basic.

One free-standing restaurant that's been going strong for years is **A Bear's Nest Cafe,** less than half a mile from the main intersection on Wilson Road (ℂ 907/697-2440; www.gustavus.com/bearsnest), where the often braided Lynne Morrow serves organic dishes, homemade bread, local seafood, soup, sandwiches, and dessert in a homey dining room with baskets hanging from the open beam ceiling. You can check your e-mail here, too. The cafe is open in summer daily 11am to 8pm and accepts Amex, Discover, MasterCard, and Visa. Lynne has a room and a couple of cabins for rent, too.

The other choice is **Homeshore Cafe,** at Gustavus's central intersection on Wilson Road (ℂ 907/697-2822), where a young family serves meals all year in a dining with about 40 seats next door to an art gallery. The menu includes pizza, calzones, sandwiches, salad, and the like; a large pizza is $24, sandwiches $10. Summer hours are Monday through Saturday 11:30am to 2pm and 5 to 8pm; winter Tuesday through Saturday 11:30am to 1:30pm and 4 to 6pm, staying open Friday until 7pm. The cafe accepts Visa and MasterCard.

9 Haines: Eagles & the Unexpected

For years we always just passed through Haines on the way from the ferry up the highway. I didn't know what I was missing until I stopped and took a couple of days to really investigate. Now Haines is one of my favorite Alaska towns.

Haines is casual, happy, and slightly odd. It waits for you to find it, but, once found, it unveils wonderful charms. If you're looking for the mythical town of Cicely from television's *Northern Exposure,* you'll get closer in Haines than anyplace else I know (in fact, the producers scouted here before choosing to shoot in Roslyn, Washington). As I walked down a sidewalk, I saw a sign in a storefront that said to look in the big tree across the street. I looked, and there was an eagle peering back at me. At the Alaska Indian Arts Native cultural center, seeking an office or a ticket window or someone in charge, I wandered into a totem pole studio where a carver was completing a major commission. He gladly stopped to talk. It turned out there wasn't anyone in charge. Issues that are a big deal in some other towns just aren't in Haines.

Haines's dominant feature, the 1904 **Fort William H. Seward,** gives the town a pastoral atmosphere. The fort is a collection of grand white-clapboard buildings arranged around a 9-acre parade ground, in the middle of which stands a Tlingit clan house—out of place, yes, but wonderfully symbolic of Haines. The town is a friendly, accessible center of Tlingit culture, as well as a retired outpost of seemingly pointless military activity.

And Haines has **bald eagles**—always plenty of bald eagles and, in the fall, a ridiculous number of bald eagles. More, in fact, than anywhere else on earth. The chance to see the birds draws people into the outdoors here. There are well-established guides for any activity you might want to pursue, all cooperating and located together. There are some excellent hiking trails right from town, as well as protected sea-kayaking waters. Also, it's worth noting that, because of its location in the flow of weather (adjacent to the drier Interior), Haines is not quite as rainy as towns farther south.

The big controversy of local politics concerns how firmly Haines should embrace tourism. Some want Haines to remain friendly, funky, and forgotten, while others hope new recognition the town has recently received for its attraction to visitors will help start an economic boom. In 2004, two national magazines listed Haines as one of the best places to go. Having written for travel magazines, I can assure you most of those "best of" lists are entirely bogus, made up off the top of the head over doughnuts in the conference room—but in this case, they got it right, either letting the cat out of the bag or exposing a suppressed truth, depending on your point of view. Even as tourism growth divides residents, however, another laurel has united them, one that really makes Haines people beam with pride: In 2005, *Library Journal* and the Bill and Melinda Gates Foundation cited Haines's library as the best small library in America. Maybe it's just me, but I think a town that's proudest of its library must have a good heart.

ESSENTIALS

GETTING THERE   The **Alaska Marine Highway System** (② **800/642-0066,** or 907/766-2111; www.ferryalaska.com), is how most people get to Haines, and the cruise on the Lynn Canal fjord from Juneau or Skagway is among the most beautiful in the Inside Passage. The conventional ferry takes almost 5 hours from Juneau, the fast ferry about half that. The Juneau-Haines fare is $36. The trip to Skagway takes an hour and the fare is $30. The dock is 5 miles north of town. There is currently only one van service meeting the ferry, **Haines Shuttle and Tours** (② **907/766-3138**), which charges a pricey $20 for the short ride.

If you're just going to or from Skagway without a car, a good alternative is the Haines-Skagway Fast Ferry, operated by **Chilkat Cruises and Tours** (② **888/766-2103** or 907/766-2100; www.chilkatcruises.com). The company's *Fairweather Express,* a 150-passenger catamaran, makes at least three daily 35-minute round-trips Monday through Friday and two a day Saturday through Sunday. The catamaran leaves from the Port Chilkoot dock, below Fort William Seward. Adult round-trips are $45, one-way $25; children 12 and under pay half-price.

If you're driving, the **Haines Highway** leads 155 miles to Haines Junction, Yukon Territory, an intersection with the Alaska Highway (you must pass through Canadian Customs—see "The Alaska Highway" section in chapter 9 for rules). The road runs

Haines

ACCOMMODATIONS ▪
A Sheltered Harbor B&B **12**
Captain's Choice Motel **3**
Fort Seward Bed and Breakfast **14**
Fort Seward Lodge,
   Restaurant & Saloon **9**
Hotel Hälsingland **11**
The Summer Inn Bed & Breakfast **2**

DINING ◆
The Bamboo Room **4**
Commander's Room **11**

Fort Seward Lodge,
   Restaurant & Saloon **10**
The Lighthouse **7**
Mountain Market & Café **8**

ATTRACTIONS ●
Alaska Indian Arts Cultural Center **13**
American Bald Eagle Foundation
   Natural History Museum **9**
Hammer Museum **5**
Sheldon Museum
   and Cultural Center **6**
Tsirku Canning Co. **1**

To Mt. Ripinski Trail

Information (i)
Post Office ✉

along the Chilkat River and the bald eagle preserve, and then climbs into spectacular alpine terrain. Anchorage is 760 driving miles from Haines, and Fairbanks is 644.

Several air services offer scheduled prop service, air taxis, and flightseeing tours to surrounding communities from Haines. **Wings of Alaska** (𝒞 **907/789-0790** reservations, or 907/766-2030 in Haines; www.ichoosewings.com) has plenty of flights, charging $186 round-trip from Juneau.

VISITOR INFORMATION   The small but well-staffed and -stocked **Haines Convention and Visitors Bureau Visitor Information Center,** 2nd Avenue near Willard (P.O. Box 530), Haines, AK 99827 (𝒞 **800/458-3579** or 907/766-2234; www.haines. ak.us), is operated by the local government, which also sends out a vacation-planning packet. It's open summer Monday through Friday from 8am to 7pm, Saturday and Sunday from 9am to 6pm; in winter, hours are Monday through Friday from 8am to 5pm.

ORIENTATION   Haines sits on the narrow Chilkat Peninsula near the north end of the Southeast Alaska Panhandle. Highways run north and east on either side of the peninsula; the one on the east side goes to the ferry dock, 5 miles out, and ends after 11 miles at **Chilkoot Lake.** The other is the **Haines Highway,** which leads to the Canadian border, the Alaska Highway, and the rest of the world. The town has two parts: the sparsely built downtown grid and, a short walk to the west down Front Street or 2nd Avenue, the Fort William Seward area.

GETTING AROUND   Bikes are available from **Sockeye Cycle,** just uphill from the Port Chilkoot Dock on Portage Street in the Fort William Seward area ((C) **907/766-2869;** www.cyclealaska.com), for $12 for 2 hours or $30 a day. **Haines Shuttle and Tours** is a taxi and shuttle service. It can be reached at (C) **907/766-3138.** Rent at **Affordable Cars,** in the Captain's Choice Motel (see "Where to Stay," below).

FAST FACTS: Haines

Bank **First National Bank of Alaska,** which has an ATM, is at Main Street and 2nd Avenue.

Hospital The **Haines Medical Clinic** ((C) **907/766-2521**) is on 1st Avenue, near the visitor center.

Internet Access The gorgeous **Haines Borough Library,** 111 3rd Ave. S. ((C) **907/766-2545;** www.haineslibrary.org), has eight public terminals.

Police Reach city police in nonemergencies at (C) **907/766-2121.** Outside city limits, call the **Alaska State Troopers** at (C) **907/766-2552.**

Post Office It's located at 55 Haines Hwy., just west of Fort Seward.

Taxes The local sales tax is 5.5%. Tax on accommodations totals 9.5%.

SPECIAL EVENTS   The 160-mile **Kluane to Chilkat International Bike Relay** ((C) **907/766-2202;** www.kcibr.org) is held the third Saturday in June, heading steeply down the Haines Highway from Haines Junction, with more than 1,000 entrants riding in teams of two, four, or eight.

The **Southeast Alaska State Fair** ((C) **907/766-2476;** www.seakfair.org) is the biggest event of the summer, held for 4 days in late July; it's a regional small-town get-together, with livestock, cooking, a logging show, a parade, music, and other entertainment. Buildings constructed for the filming of the movie *White Fang* in 1990 were donated to the fair and form the nucleus of a retail area. (One stop of interest here, at any time, is the local microbrewery, **Haines Brewing Co.,** which offers samples and informal tours.)

The **Alaska Bald Eagle Festival** ((C) **907/766-3094;** www.baldeaglefestival.org) offers seminars and special events to mark the annual eagle congregation. Held over 5 days in mid-November.

EXPLORING HAINES

It seems that each year Haines further cements its position as Alaska's center of odd or unusual museums. In the spirit of this distinction, I've described these attractions in the order of their creation, beginning with the Tlingit art center in an old military hospital and ending with the newest addition, a collection of more than 1,400 hammers.

You can't miss **Fort William H. Seward National Historic Site,** the collection of large, white, wood-frame buildings around sloping parade grounds overlooking the magnificent Lynn Canal fjord. (Get the informative *History Walking Tour* brochure of the National Historic Site from the Haines Convention and Visitors Bureau to learn about each building.)

The fort led a peaceful life, for a military installation. By the time the U.S. Army built it, in 1904, the Klondike gold rush was over, and there's no evidence it ever deterred any attack on this little peninsula at the north end of the Inside Passage. It was deactivated at the end of World War II, when it was used for training.

In 1947, a group of five veterans from the Lower 48 bought the fort as surplus with the idea of forming a planned community. That idea didn't quite work out, but one of the new white families helped spark a Chilkat Tlingit cultural renaissance in the 1950s. The Heinmillers, who still own a majority of the shares in the fort, formed a youth group that evolved into the Chilkat Dancers. A pair of elders led the group in construction of a Tlingit tribal house on the parade grounds. The **Alaska Indian Arts Cultural Center** grew from the same movement. Lee Heinmiller, a member of the family's second generation, still manages the arts center, where you can see totem carving and silversmithing practiced. It is open from 9am to 5pm Monday through Friday. The center occupies the old fort hospital on the south side of the parade grounds.

In the downtown area, the **Sheldon Museum and Cultural Center,** 11 Main St. (© **907/766-2366;** www.sheldonmuseum.org), contains an upstairs gallery of well-presented Tlingit art and cultural artifacts; downstairs is a collection on the pioneer history of the town. There's a uniquely personal feel to the Tlingit objects, some of which are displayed with pictures of the artisans who made them and the history of their relationship with the Sheldons, for whom the museum is named. It's open in summer Monday through Friday 10am to 5pm, Saturday and Sunday 1 to 4pm; in winter, it's open Monday through Friday from 1 to 4pm. Admission is $3 for adults, free for children under 12.

The entirely unique **American Bald Eagle Foundation Natural History Museum,** at 2nd Avenue and Haines Highway (© **907/766-3094;** www.baldeagles.org), is essentially a huge, hair-raising diorama of more than 180 eagles and other mounts of Alaska wildlife. Often, Dave Olerud sits behind the desk in a wheelchair and talks your ear off about the museum if you let him—he worked on it for many years and was paralyzed in a fall during construction. Admission is $3 adults, $1 ages 8 to 12; children need to be with an adult. It's open summer Monday through Friday from 9am to 6pm, Saturday and Sunday from 1 to 4pm; closed during the winter.

The **Tsirku Canning Co.,** at 5th Avenue and Main Street (© **907/766-3474;** www.cannerytour.com), is a museum of Alaska salmon canning, full of 80-year-old machinery salvaged from abandoned canneries around the state, including a 120-foot line that goes through the process of canning imaginary fish, including making the can. The fishing industry remains among the state's largest employers and was long its largest industry by any measure. In 1929, 157 canneries stood all along the coast, teeming with summer workers and served by frequent steamer service, many in places where nothing remains today but broken dock pilings. Haines had nine. The hour-long museum tour, including a 10-minute video, costs $10 adults, free ages 12 and under. Call for a recorded message of the time of the next tour, which is changeable.

The newest addition to Haines' lineup of the unusual is the **Hammer Museum,** at 108 Main St., across from the bank (℗ **907/766-2374**). Longshoreman Dave Pahl created his collection of hammers over a couple of decades of building a homestead. He found the prize of his collection, an 800-year-old Tlingit war hammer, while digging up the foundation of the museum itself. More than 1,400 hammers from all over the world, old and new, exotic and ordinary, fill a tiny space. The fun part is guessing what each is for. It is open summer Monday through Friday 10am to 5pm, closed off season. Admission is $3 adults, free for children 12 and under.

GETTING OUTSIDE

EAGLE VIEWING Haines is probably the best place on earth to see bald eagles. The **Chilkat Bald Eagle Preserve** protects 48,000 acres of river bottom along the Chilkat River. From October to mid-December, peaking around Thanksgiving, up to 3,000 eagles gather in the cottonwood trees (also known as western poplar) on a small section of the river, a phenomenon known as the Fall Congregation. (A healthy 200–400 are resident the rest of the year.) The eagles come for easy winter food: A very late salmon run spawns here into December in a 5-mile stretch of open water known as the Council Grounds. During the Congregation, dozens of eagles stand in each of the gnarled, leafless cottonwoods on the riverbanks, occasionally diving for a fish. The best places to see them are pull-outs, paths, and viewing areas along the Haines Highway from Miles 18 to 21. Don't walk on the flats, as that disturbs the eagles. The preserve is managed by **Alaska State Parks** (www.alaskastateparks.org, click on "Individual Parks"). Contact the local ranger at ℗ **907/766-2292;** the headquarters is at 400 Willoughby, 3rd Floor, Juneau, AK 99801.

Local guides offer trips to see the eagles by raft, bicycle, or bus—mostly in the summer, when the eagles are fewer but visitors more numerous. **Chilkat Guides,** based at 1 Mile Haines Hwy. along Sawmill Road (℗ **888/282-7789** or 907/766-2491; www.raftalaska.com), does a rafting trip several times a day during the summer down the Chilkat to watch the eagles. The water is gentle—if it's too low, there's a chance you'll be asked to get out and push—and you'll see lots of eagles, mostly at a distance. The company is run by young people who create a sense of fellowship with their clients. The 3½-hour trip, with a snack, costs $79 for adults, $62 for children ages 7 to 12. **Sockeye Cycle** (see "Biking," below) has guided bike tours to see eagles and Fort Seward on a 90-minute trip that costs $42. Serious bird watchers and others who want an in-depth tour should join **Alaska Nature Tours** (℗ **907/766-2876;** www.alaskanaturetours.net), which leads 3-hour wildlife viewing tours by bus for $60 year-round. The company also offers longer tours, such as all-day guided hikes, for $100, and cross-country skiing in and around the preserve.

BIKING **Sockeye Cycle,** at 24 Portage St., near the dock (℗ **907/766-2869;** www.cyclealaska.com), leads a variety of guided trips—a couple of hours, half or full days, or even a 9-day trek along gold-rush routes. A 3-hour ride along Chilkoot Lake costs $80. Or you can rent your own bicycle for $30 a day. The area is quite conducive to biking.

FISHING There are several charter operators in Haines for halibut and salmon fishing, and guided freshwater fishing for silver or sockeye salmon, Dolly Varden, and cutthroat trout. The **Haines Convention and Visitors Bureau,** 2nd Street near Willard (P.O. Box 530), Haines, AK 99827 (℗ **800/458-3579** or 907/766-2234; www.haines.ak.us), can help you find a guide or fishing lodge through the links on their website or the list of operators they keep at the office. For self-guided fishing advice and weekly updates of what's running, contact the local office of the Alaska Department of Fish and Game (© 907/766-2625; www.alaska.gov/adfg, click on "Sport Fisheries," and then the Southeast region on the state map). See "Sea Kayaking," below, for self-guided boat rental.

FLIGHTSEEING This is one of Alaska's best places to go flightseeing. The Inside Passage is beautiful, and one mountain away is Glacier Bay National Park; the ice field and the glaciers spilling through to the sea are a sight you won't forget. It's possible to land on an immense glacial ice field and see the sun slicing between the craggy peaks. **Alaska Mountain Flying and Travel,** 132 2nd Ave. (© 800/954-8747 or 907/766-3007; www.flyglacierbay.com), offers these flights—or, as owner Paul Swanstrom says, adventures. He is known for his glacier and beach landings. Prices range from $125 to $299 per person, and reservations are recommended. Other flight services offer these tours, too; ask at the visitor center.

HIKING There are several good trails near Haines, ranging from an easy beach walk to a 10-mile, 3,650-foot climb of **Mount Ripinsky,** north of town (it starts at the top of Young St.). Get the *Haines Is for Hikers* trail guide from the visitors' bureau. The easiest for families is the 2-mile **Battery Point Trail,** which goes along a beach decorated with wild iris. The trail starts at the end of Beach Road, which leads southeast from the Port Chilkoot cruise-ship dock. **Mount Riley** is south of town, with three trail routes to a 1,760-foot summit that features great views and feels much higher than it is; get the trail guide or ask directions to one of the trail heads. **Seduction Point Trail** is 7 miles long, starting at Chilkat State Park at the end of Mud Bay Road south of town and leading to the end of the Chilkat Peninsula. It's a beach walk, so check the tides; they'll give you a tide table at the visitors bureau.

SEA KAYAKING **Chilkat Cruises and Tours,** 121 Beach Rd. (© 888/766-2103 or 907/766-2100; www.chilkatcruises.com), offers instruction, short guided trips, longer expeditions, and rentals ($35 a day for a single, plus $25 for drop-off and pickup anywhere on the Haines Rd. system; or paddle right from the shop). A half-day guided paddle is $85, including a snack; a full day, including lunch, is $125.

WHERE TO STAY

Besides the hotels I've listed below, you'll find good economy rooms at these other places: **A Sheltered Harbor B&B,** 57 Beach Rd. (© 907/766-2741, 616/780-1128 in winter; www.sheltered-harbor.com), and **Fort Seward Lodge, Restaurant & Saloon,** in the old fort exchange (© 800/478-7772 or 907/766-2009; www.ftseward lodge.com).

Captain's Choice Motel ✦ Many towns have a lot of chainlike hotels and only one or two unique places with character. In Haines, the situation is reversed, and these trim, red-roofed buildings are the one exception to the general eccentricity. The standard rooms contain all the anticipated amenities, yet the motel still has a certain amount of charm, making it—objectively, anyway—probably the best hotel in town. The room decor is on the dark side, with paneling, and is somewhat out-of-date, but it's quite clean, and many of the rooms have good views on a large sun deck.

108 2nd St. N. at Dalton St. (P.O. Box 392), Haines, AK 99827. © 800/478-2345 or 907/766-3111. Fax 907/766-3332. www.capchoice.com. 39 units. High season $117 double; low season $86 double; year-round $128–$168 suite. Extra person $5. Rates include continental breakfast. AE, DC, DISC, MC, V. **Amenities:** Tour desk; car rental; courtesy van; limited room service; coin-op laundry. *In room:* TV, Wi-Fi, microwave, fridge, coffeemaker, hair dryer.

Fort Seward Bed and Breakfast *(Finds* The fort surgeon's quarters overlook the parade grounds and the Lynn Canal with a big wraparound porch. The inn has an unspoiled historic feel. Norm Smith has lived in this house most of his life and in 1981 started the B&B with his wife, Suzanne, a gifted hostess who instantly makes you feel like an old friend. The rooms have high ceilings, fireplaces, wonderful cabinetry—all kinds of authentic charm. It's a social place, with a barbecue on the porch, and guests are welcome to use the kitchen, where Norm produces a fine full breakfast of sourdough pancakes. Smoking is not allowed.

1 Fort Seward Dr. (P.O. Box 5), Haines, AK 99827. (C) 800/615-6676 or phone/fax 907/766-2856. www.fortseward bnb.com. 7 units, 3 with shared bathroom. High season $99–$135 double; low season $79–$105 double. Extra person $25. Rates include full breakfast. DISC, MC, V. Closed Oct 15–Easter. **Amenities:** Bike loan; kayak rental; courtesy car. *In room:* TV/VCR/DVD.

Hotel Hälsingland *(★* This grandly rambling hotel fell on hard times after more than 50 years in the same family until new owners Jeff and Shannon Butcher took over in 2002 and started putting in a lot of work, as well as new carpeting, furniture, drapes, paint, and beds. The hotel has always been the most interesting place in town to stay. The group of buildings, designated a National Historic Landmark, served as the Commanding Officer's Quarters for Fort William Seward during both World Wars. You can almost hear well-shined boots on the wood floors, echoing off high ceilings and old-fashioned woodwork. Rooms vary widely, so it's a good idea to take a look before checking in. Some share bathrooms, and some of those with private bathrooms have only shower stalls, while others have claw-foot tubs. The hotel also books tours and has an RV park out back.

The remodeled **Commander's Room** restaurant, open for dinner only, offers a short menu of well-prepared dishes, with prices for main courses in the $19 to $30 range. The small bar has craft brews on tap. This is a friendly, low-key place in the evening.

Fort William Seward parade grounds (P.O. Box 1649), Haines, AK 99827. (C) 800/542-6363 or 907/766-2000. Fax 907/766-2060. www.hotelhalsingland.com. 50 units, 5 with shared bathroom. $69 double with shared bathroom, $89–$109 double with private bathroom. AE, DC, DISC, MC, V. Closed mid-Nov to mid-Mar. **Amenities:** Restaurant; bar; tour desk; courtesy van; coin-op laundry. *In room:* TV, Wi-Fi.

The Summer Inn Bed & Breakfast *(Value* This lovely old clapboard house downtown has a big porch and a living room decorated in whites and pale, lacy fabrics, like Grandma's house. The five rooms are cozy but small and share three bathrooms among them (bathrooms were immaculate when we visited). The house was built by a reputed former member of Soapy Smith's gang in 1912 (see the Skagway section for more on Soapy), and the great big claw-foot tub is said to be the first in the history of Haines upstairs bathtubs. No smoking or drinking is allowed.

117 2nd Ave. (P.O. Box 1198), Haines, AK 99827. (C) and fax 907/766-2970. www.summerinnbnb.com. 5 units, all with shared bathroom. High season $90 double, $105 suite; low season $80 double, $95 suite. Extra person $20. Rates include full breakfast. MC, V.

WHERE TO DINE

Haines has a few consistently good restaurants—which is a few more than most other Alaska towns this size—and you can also eat well during the summer at the Hotel Hälsingland (see "Where to Stay," above). There are lots of places for a casual meal as well. Among the best lunch places is the **Mountain Market & Café** *(★*, a natural-food and grocery store at 3rd Avenue and the Haines Highway ((C) 907/766-3340). The main town hangout and the best espresso stop, it serves hearty and reasonably priced sandwiches, tortilla wraps, and soups, and many fresh-baked goods. Pick up a picnic, or stop by for coffee, roasted in-house, or breakfast. The liquor store carries organic wine.

The Bamboo Room ☞ DINER/SEAFOOD   This small restaurant, in the same family for more than 50 years, was rescued from being a smoky adjunct to the bar. It has been divided off by attractive etched glass and made into a first-class diner serving burgers, salads, pasta, and lots of seafood. Many light and healthful items are on the menu along with the solid fried foods. The building started as a French restaurant during the gold-rush era and then became a brothel and speakeasy before the Tengs family got it in 1953. The history is on the back of the menu. Get the halibut and chips.

2nd Ave. near Main St. ☎ 907/766-2474. www.bamboopioneer.net. Lunch $6–$13; dinner $8–$25. AE, DISC, DC, MC, V. Summer daily 6am–11pm; winter daily 6am–8pm.

Fort Seward Lodge, Restaurant & Saloon ☞ STEAK/SEAFOOD   A favorite of the locals, the restaurant resides in a tall room in the old Post Exchange of the historic fort, where patrons have long speared dollar bills to the ceiling, which is now papered with money. This is a fun place, with a friendly and gregarious staff and a partying tradition (although the bar is in a separate room). The food brings people back: simple seafood, meat, and vegetables. The prime rib is especially famous, and in midsummer there is all-you-can-eat Dungeness crab. The full bar has Alaska microbrews on tap.

Mile 0 Haines Hwy., in Fort William Seward. ☎ 907/766-2009. www.ftsewardlodge.com. Dinner $8–$25. DISC, MC, V. Summer daily 5:30–9pm. Closed Oct–Apr.

The Lighthouse ☞☞ SEAFOOD/HAWAIIAN   Chef Song Nash, who grew up in Haines, was avoiding returning to his job cooking at a private resort in Hawaii when he suggested to the owner of a local supermarket buying this threadbare waterfront restaurant to see what he could do with it. The result is a style of dining Haines has never seen before. Nash remodeled completely, updating the interior by 50 years to make it light and stylish, and putting in new windows to take good advantage of the spectacular water view (don't let the saloon exterior scare you away). Drawing on his experience as a chef with flavors from the South Pacific and his experience as a hand on his family's commercial fishing boat, Nash created a style of cuisine fusing the two. Main courses include ginger Alaskan sable fish with coconut wasabi sauce, which was terrific, and blackened Lynn Canal sockeye salmon with Hawaiian relish; there are also many conventional seafood restaurant staples—steaks and such. The lunch menu is extensive, too. Service is quick and professional.

Main and Front sts. ☎ 907/766-2442. Lunch $9–$12, dinner $10–$23. AE, DC, DISC, MC, V. High season daily 8am–10pm; low season daily 11:30am–9pm.

⌐Tips A Quick Side Trip to Juneau from Haines or Skagway

Without changing your lodgings, you can travel from Skagway or Haines for a tour of Juneau's highlights and a sightseeing day cruise of the Lynn Canal. **Alaska Fjordlines'** high-speed catamaran (☎ **800-320-0146** or 907/766-3395; www.alaskafjordlines.com) carries passengers for half a day in Juneau, with wildlife sightings on the way. The fare is $139, including a narrated bus tour of Juneau and Mendenhall Glacier. The whole excursion is about 12 hours.

10 Skagway: After the Gold Rush

It's only been 100 years since white civilization came to Alaska. There were a few scattered towns in Southeast before that—Juneau, Sitka, and Wrangell, for example—but until the Klondike gold rush, the great mass of Alaska was populated only by Natives who had never seen a white face. Then, in a single year, 1898, the population exploded. That year still stands as the greatest in Alaska's short but eventful history, for the influx of those people set the patterns of development ever since.

In the rush years of 1897 and 1898, Skagway and its ghost-town twin city of Dyea were the logical places to get off the boat to head off on the trek to the gold fields near the new city of Dawson City, Yukon Territories. (See "Dawson City & Eagle: Detour into History," p. 416.) Skagway instantly grew from a single homestead to a population of between 15,000 and 25,000. No one knows exactly how many, partly because the people were flowing through too quickly to count and partly because there was no civil authority to count them. This was a wide-open boomtown, a true Wild West outpost that in its biggest years was completely without law other than the survival of the meanest. Then, almost as quickly as it started, the rush ended and the town deflated.

But Skagway survived by showing off where it all happened. In 1896, there was a single log cabin in Skagway, in 1897 the word of the Klondike strike made it to the outside world, and in 1898 Skagway was a huge gold-rush boomtown. In 1899, the gold rush was ending, and 300 tourists arrived in a single day in 1903 to see where the gold rush happened. By 1908, local businessmen had started developing tourist attractions, moving picturesque gold-rush buildings to Broadway, the main street, to create a more unified image when visitors arrived on the steamers. By 1920, tourism had become an important part of the economy. By 1933, historic preservation efforts had started. Today, more money and more than 20 times as many visitors come through in a year as made the trip to the Klondike during the gold rush.

With 862 residents and more than half a million visitors annually, the "real" town has all but disappeared, and most of the people you'll meet are either fellow visitors or summer workers brought north to serve them. Most of the tourists are from cruise ships—it's not unusual for several ships to hit town in a single morning, unleashing as many as 9,000 people at once up the wharf and into the one historic street. There are plenty of highway and ferry travelers, too, and outdoor enthusiasts come to do the Chilkoot Trail, just as the stampeders did.

Is it worth all those visits? Skagway, spared from fire and recognized so long ago for its history, may be the best-preserved gold-rush town in the United States. What happened here in a 2-year period was certainly extraordinary, even if the phenomenon the town celebrates is one of mass insanity based on greed, inhumanity, thuggery, prostitution, waste, and, for most, abject failure. While Canada was well policed by the Mounties, Skagway was truly lawless—a hell on earth, as one Mountie described it. Soapy Smith ruled this scam-pire with a team of con artists and toughs who milked the suckers for every dollar available. Half of the stories about Soapy are probably lies, but this one is too good not to repeat: He set up a telegraph office for suckers to wire their money home, but with no telegraph line. Such was his influence and high repute in the newspapers he controlled that the governor offered to put Smith officially in charge as a territorial marshal and rode with him in the 1898 Independence Day parade. Four days later, Smith was shot dead in a gunfight with Frank Reid, who led a vigilante committee upset over one of Smith's thefts. Reid died of wounds sustained

ACCOMMODATIONS ■
At the White House **4**
Chilkoot Trail Outpost **1**
Mile Zero Bed & Breakfast **3**
Sgt. Preston's Lodge **6**
Skagway Home Hostel **13**

DINING ◆
Haven Cafe **5**
Red Onion Saloon **17**
Sabrosa's **7**
The Stowaway Cafe **20**
Sweet Tooth Café **14**

ATTRACTIONS ●
Corrington Museum
    of Alaska History **12**
Days of '98 Show (in Eagles Hall) **11**
Klondike Gold Dredge Tours **2**
Mascot Saloon **15**
Mollie Walsh Park **8**
Moore House **10**
National Park Service Visitor Center **18**
Skagway Museum and Archives **9**
Skagway Streetcar Company **16**
The White Pass
    and Yukon Route Depot **19**

in the shootout, too, but Soapy Smith's gang was broken. Of course, the gold rush was about to end anyway.

In 1976, the National Park Service began buying many of Skagway's best old buildings for the **Klondike Gold Rush National Historic District,** and now it owns about 15, having completed restoration in 1999. Broadway is a prosperous, freshly painted 6-block strip of gold rush–era buildings. A few that look like real businesses turn out to be displays showing how it was back then. Other buildings restored by the park service are under lease to gift shops and such. Sadly, those historic businesses not preserved by the Park Service have been lost to the onslaught of cruise ship–oriented shopping: A curio shop operating since the gold rush was converted a few years ago, and in 2002, the longest-operating hotel in Alaska, which dated from the earliest days, became a T-shirt shop.

But there's a much bigger and safer business in mining the tourist trade. The rush of visitors each summer dwarfs the number who came in 1898, and, in the true spirit of the event whose history they celebrate, the gold-rush towns of Skagway, Dawson City, Fairbanks, and Nome know there's more money to be made from people than from gold.

ESSENTIALS
GETTING THERE   The **Alaska Marine Highway System** (© **800/642-0066** or 907/983-2941; www.ferryalaska.com) connects Skagway daily with Haines and Juneau.

The Gold Rush in Context

The 1898 Klondike Gold Rush was the single biggest event in Alaska history. You'll be hearing a lot about it. Here's some of the context for the barrage of anecdotes you can expect.

Prospectors sought gold in small numbers even before Russia sold Alaska to the United States in 1867, but the Russians' main interest in Alaska was sea otter pelts, and they made few forays beyond the coast, leaving the great mass of the North and Interior unexplored. When the United States took over, Alaska had virtually no white population, and what it had was concentrated in Southeast—in Sitka, the Russian capital; in a few other Russian settlements; and at the trading post of Wrangell, which miners used as a jumping-off point for gold fields up the Stikine River in British Columbia.

After the American flag went up over Sitka, prospectors slowly worked their way into Alaska's vastness, often led by or in partnership with Natives who knew the country. Called **sourdoughs** for the live yeast-and-flour mixture they carried to make their bread, these were tough wilderness men living way beyond the law or communication with the outside world. A few of them struck it rich. In 1880, a major find on the Gastineau Channel started the city of Juneau and decades of industrial, hard-rock mining there. Finds followed on the Fortymile River in 1886 (on the Taylor Hwy.), near Circle in 1893 (on the Steese Hwy.), and near Hope on the Kenai Peninsula in 1895 (on the Seward Hwy.). Gold slowly brought more people to Alaska, but not enough to catch the nation's attention.

In 1896, white prospector George Carmack and his Native partners, Tagish Charlie and Skookum Jim, found gold on the Klondike River, a tributary to the Yukon in Canada. Word traveled downriver to the gold fields in the Fortymile Country, and within 48 hours that area was empty and claims on the Klondike were being staked. The miners dug gravel from the creek that winter, and when they washed it in the spring, it yielded big hunks of solid gold, a massive discovery. They were instant millionaires in a time when a million dollars meant something.

It's hard to grasp today the impact of the news on the outside world. The U.S. economy was deeply in depression. The dollar was on a gold standard and the scarcity of gold had caused a deflationary vise that in 1893 brought a banking collapse and national unemployment of 18%. Suddenly, in 1897, a steamer arrived in Seattle bearing men from a place called the Klondike with trunks and gunny sacks full of gold. The supply of money suddenly grew and economic confidence returned. The national economy turned around on the news, and some 100,000 people set off for Alaska to get rich, too, plunging off into a trackless wilderness for which most were completely unprepared.

Contemporary Alaska marks the Klondike Gold Rush as the start of its history. Before the gold rush, Alaska largely remained as it had been for thousands of years, ruled and inhabited by its indigenous people. As late as the

1880 census, the territory had fewer than 500 white residents, and only 4,000 by 1890—it was virtually empty from the point of view of those who discounted the Alaska Natives. In 1898, the stampede began, bringing an instant population. Even the mayor of Seattle left for Alaska. Within a few years, Alaska had cities, telegraph lines, riverboats, and sled-dog mail routes. About 30,000 made it all the way to Dawson City. Few of that number struck it rich, but those who built the towns and businesses to serve them did—there were suddenly saloons and brothels, dress shops, and photo studios. Promoters sold a credulous public newly laid-out towns on supposed routes to the gold fields, including routes that were essentially impassable.

The White Pass above Skagway and the Chilkoot Pass above Dyea carried the most stampeders. Gold seekers arrived in the crazily lawless settlements by steamer from Seattle, got robbed and cheated, and then ferried their goods over the passes to Lake Bennett. (Upon completion of the railroad through the White Pass in 1901, Dyea and the Chilkoot Pass were abandoned, but Skagway lives on.) The Canadian authorities wisely required each stampeder to bring a ton of supplies, a rule that undoubtedly prevented famine but made the single-file journey over the passes a miserable ordeal. Prospectors sometimes had to make dozens of trips up the trail to get their supplies over the pass. At Lake Bennett, the stampeders built boats, crossed the lake, and floated down the Yukon River, through the dangerous Five Finger Rapids, to Dawson City, a 500-mile journey from the sea.

Imagine their disappointment when they found, on their arrival, that the gold claims had all been staked and big companies were taking over. Prospectors looking to strike it rich had humbling choices. The smart ones started businesses to make money off the other stampeders, and some of them did quite well. Others worked for wages or went home. But many continued in pursuit of the next find. Their wild chase for gold drew the modern map of Alaska, founding dozens of towns. Many of these towns disappeared as soon as the frenzy cooled and now are entirely forgotten or live on only as place names, but some became real cities. Nome came in 1899; Fairbanks in 1902; Kantishna, now within Denali National Park, in 1905; Iditarod in 1908; and many others, until the rush finally ended with the start of World War I in 1914.

Even without a rush, there's still gold to be dug. Ever larger and more sophisticated machinery worked the Klondike claims and washed the gravel until the 1960s, and gold mining remains an important part of that area's economy to this day. Small-time prospectors are still looking all over Alaska and working their claims, and sometimes someone does make a significant new strike. A 1987 find north of Fairbanks, developed at a cost of $400 million, today brings out more than 1,000 ounces a day.

The fare is $30 from Haines, $48 from Juneau. If you're headed to Haines without a vehicle, consider the private passenger ferry listed under "Getting There" in the Haines section. Haines is 15 miles away by boat but more than 350 miles by road.

Since 1978, **Klondike Highway 2** has traced the route of the stampeders through the White Pass into Canada, a parallel route to the Chilkoot Trail. The road runs 99 miles and then meets the Alaska Highway a dozen miles southeast of the Yukon capital of Whitehorse. The border is at the top of the pass, 14 miles from Skagway. (Information on Customs is in chapter 9 in the Alaska Highway section, p. 382.) This is one of the most spectacular drives anywhere in Alaska, and the road is a well-maintained two-lane highway with wide shoulders. The views are basically equivalent to those from the White Pass and Yukon Route railway, but a lot cheaper. Do it in clear weather, if possible, as in cloudy weather all you'll see is whiteout. Car rentals in Skagway are available from **Avis,** in the Westmark Hotel at 3rd and Spring streets (✆ **800/230-4898** or 907/983-2247; www.avis.com).

Riding the ferry or a cruise ship to Skagway and then heading inland in a rented RV is an attractive option. Expect to pay around $200 a day, plus many required extras (it's not a cheap option). **Alaska Motorhome Rentals** (✆ **800/254-9929;** www.bestofalaskatravel.com) also rents RVs one-way to Anchorage with a $695 drop-off fee, plus the cost of the rental, mileage, and gas. The same company, under a different name, also offers structured RV tours from Skagway as add-ons to cruise vacations; that's covered in chapter 2 under "Getting There & Getting Around."

It takes 2 days to travel by bus between Skagway and Anchorage or Fairbanks; you have to spend the night and change buses in Whitehorse, Yukon. The only operator is **Alaska Direct Bus Line** (✆ **800/770-6652** or 907/277-6652 in Anchorage; to book while in Skagway, call the Whitehorse office, ✆ 867-668-4833). The bus operates year-round from the ferry terminal, charging $253 one-way to Anchorage, $220 to Fairbanks. Call ahead to learn the frequency of service and departure times at the time you plan to travel.

Several air taxi operators serve Skagway. A round-trip from Juneau costs $200 on **Wings of Alaska** (✆ **907/789-0790** reservations, or 907/983-2442 in Skagway; www.ichoosewings.com).

VISITOR INFORMATION   Located in the restored railroad depot, the **National Park Service Visitor Center,** 2nd Avenue and Broadway (P.O. Box 517), Skagway, AK 99840 (✆ **907/983-9223;** www.nps.gov/klgo), is the focal point for activities in Skagway. Rangers answer questions, give lectures and show films, and five times a day lead an excellent guided walking tour. The building houses a small museum that lays the groundwork for the rest of what you'll see. The park service's programs are free. The visitor center is open early May through late September daily from 8am to 6pm; the rest of the year the museum is open Monday through Friday from 8am to 5pm.

The **Skagway Convention and Visitors Bureau Center,** 245 Broadway (P.O. Box 1029), Skagway, AK 99840 (✆ **907/983-2854,** fax 907/983-3854; www.skagway.com), occupies the historic Arctic Brotherhood Hall, the building with the driftwood facade. The website contains links to lodgings and activities, or you can request the same information on paper (order at ✆ **888/762-1898**). Stop in especially for the handy and informative **Skagway Walking Tour Map** of historic sites. The center is open summer daily from 8am to 6pm, winter Monday through Friday from 8am to 5pm.

GETTING AROUND   Skagway is laid out on a simple grid, with streets branching off from Broadway. The main sights can be reached on foot. For places you can't walk, try **Klondike Taxi** (© **907/983-2400**). A bike is fun and practical transportation in Skagway. **Sockeye Cycle,** on 5th Avenue off Broadway (© **907/983-2851;** www.cycle alaska.com), rents good mountain bikes for $12 for 2 hours and leads guided day trips (see "Getting Outside," below).

FAST FACTS: Skagway

Bank **Wells Fargo,** at Broadway at 6th Avenue, has an ATM.

Hospital The **Dahl Medical Clinic,** staffed by a physician's assistant, can be reached at © **907/983-2255** during business hours.

Internet Access **Alaska Cruiseship Services,** charging $6 an hour, at 2nd Avenue and State Street (© **907/983-3398**).

Police For nonemergency business, call © **907/983-2232.** The station is located at State Street, just south of First Avenue.

Post Office The post office is on Broadway between 6th and 7th avenues.

Taxes Sales tax is 4%. The bed tax totals 8%.

SPECIAL EVENTS   The springtime **Buckwheat Ski Classic,** in the deep snow of the White Pass, is as much for fun as it is for Nordic skiing competition. Various events for adults and kids range from 5km to 50km. Racers often wear costumes and carry libations, and spectators carve villages from the snow to drink beer and soak up the warm spring sun. A dinner and dance follow. It happens March 24, 2007. **Skagway's July 4th Parade and Celebration,** organized by the chamber of commerce and featuring lots of small-town events, has been a big deal since Soapy Smith led the parade in 1898. **The Klondike Road Relay,** a 110-mile overnight footrace over the pass, brings hundreds of runners in teams of 10 from all over the state. It's held in early September. Call the visitor center for information on any of these events.

EXPLORING SKAGWAY

You can see most of Skagway on foot, and everything by bike. Many companies also offer car, van, or bus tours. No one goes to greater lengths to give visitors a unique experience than the **Skagway Street Car Company,** 270 2nd Ave. (© **907/983-2908;** www.skagwaystreetcar.com), which uses antique touring vehicles and costumed guides performing "theater without walls." The very personal and amusing 2-hour streetcar tour, based on a tour originally given to President Harding in 1923, is $42 for adults and $20 for children 12 and under. The company operates out of a big gift shop with an espresso counter and a theater, where the tour finishes. Book the tour at least 2 weeks in advance, as they're always sold out.

TOURING THE HISTORIC PARK

The main thing to do in Skagway is to see the old buildings and historic gold-rush places. Do it with the *Skagway Walking Tour Map* or join a fascinating National Park Service guided walking tour (see "Visitor Information," above).

Start with a visit to the **museum** at the National Park Service Visitor Center and in the building next door. It helps put everything else in context. Of greatest interest is a collection of food and gear similar to the ton of supplies each prospector was required to carry over the pass in order to gain entry into Canada, a requirement that prevented famine among the stampeders but made the job of getting to Dawson City an epic struggle.

While they prepared to go over the pass, gold-rush greenhorns spent their time in Skagway drinking and getting fleeced in the many gambling dens and brothels. Nothing was against the law in the town's heyday because there was no civil authority. It's hard to picture at times because everything looks so orderly now, but the park service has tried. For example, the **Mascot Saloon,** at Broadway and 3rd Avenue, has statues bellying up to the bar. It's open daily from 8am to 6pm; admission is free.

The Park Service walking tour ends at the 1897 **Moore House,** near 5th Avenue and Spring Street, open from 10am to 5pm during the summer. Ten years before the gold rush happened, Capt. William Moore brilliantly predicted it and homesteaded the land that would become Skagway, knowing that this would be a key staging area. He built a cabin in 1887, which stands nearby and is open for inspection. But when the rush hit, the stampeders simply ignored his property claims and built the city on his land without offering compensation. Years later, he won in court.

A block east, on 6th Avenue, is **Mollie Walsh Park,** with a good children's play area, public restrooms, and phones. A sign tells the sad story of one of Skagway's first respectable women, a lady who chose to marry the wrong man among two suitors and was killed by him in a drunken rage. The other suitor—who'd previously killed another rival for her affections—commissioned the bust of Walsh that stands at the park.

The **Gold Rush Cemetery** is 1½ miles from town, up State Street. Used until 1908, it's small and overgrown with spruce trees, but some of the charm and mystery of the place is lost because of the number of visitors and the shiny new paint and maintenance of the wooden markers. The graves of Soapy Smith and Frank Reid are the big attractions, but don't miss the short walk up to Reid Falls. The closely spaced dates on many of the markers attest to the epidemics that swept through mobs of stampeders living in squalid conditions. Remember, there was little sanitation for the tens of thousands who passed this way in 1898.

About 9 miles northwest of Skagway is the ghost town of **Dyea,** where stampeders started climbing the Chilkoot Trail. It's a lovely coastal drive or bike ride: From Skagway, go 2 miles up Klondike Highway 2 and then turn left, continuing 8 miles on gravel road. Dyea is a lot more ghost than town. All that remains are a few boards, broken dock pilings, and miscellaneous iron trash. On a sunny day, however, the protected historical site is a perfect place for a picnic, among beach grasses, fields of wild iris, and the occasional reminder that a city once stood here. The National Park Service leads an interesting guided history and nature walk here daily in summer at 2pm; check at the visitor center. (See "Getting Outside," below, for more on going to Dyea.)

The little-visited **Slide Cemetery,** in the woods near Dyea, is the last resting place of many of the 60 to 70 who died in an avalanche on the Chilkoot Trail on Palm Sunday, April 3, 1898. No one knows how many are here, or exactly who died, or how accurate the wooden markers are. In 1960, when the state reopened the Chilkoot Trail, the cemetery had been completely overgrown and the markers were replaced. Somehow the mystery and forgetting make it an even more ghostly place, and the sense of anonymous, hopeless hardship and death it conveys is as authentic a gold-rush souvenir as anything in Skagway.

MUSEUMS & ATTRACTIONS

The White Pass and Yukon Route 🦉🦉 A narrow-gauge railroad line that origi-
nally ran to Whitehorse, the White Pass was completed after only 2 years in 1900. It's
an engineering marvel and a fun way to see spectacular, historic scenery. The excursion begins at a depot with the spine-tingling whistle of a working steam engine. The
steamer pulls the train a couple of miles and then diesels take the cars—some of them
originals more than 100 years old—up steep tracks that were chipped out of the side
of the mountains. They "recommend" you don't get out of your seat, but it's a long
ride on a slow train, and most people get up and socialize; however, you cannot move
from car to car while the train is moving. The trick is to go in clear weather. When
the pass is socked in, all you see is white clouds. Tickets are expensive, however, and
you have to reserve ahead. Take the gamble: Cancellation carries only a 10% penalty
and you can change dates for no charge. Also try to go on a weekend, when fewer
cruise ships are in town taking up all the seats; weekend trains can be booked as little
as a week ahead, while midweek excursions can book up months ahead. The summit
excursion—which travels 20 miles with an elevation gain of 2,865 feet and then turns
back—takes about 3 hours and costs $89 to $95 for adults. All fares are half-price for
ages 3 to 12 (except for Chilkoot Pass hiker's fares; see "Backpacking," below).

The biggest treat for train lovers is the steam-powered trips. An all-day round-trip
to Lake Bennett, where the stampeders launched their boats for the trip to Dawson
City, leaves each Saturday morning June through August. The fare is $180, including
lunch and a walking tour at Lake Bennett. Four-hour summit rides on Sunday afternoons are $125. Either of those trains takes you into Canada, so proof of citizenship
is required (a passport or notarized birth certificate).

These days, the line operates only as a tourist attraction May through September.

2nd Ave. depot (P.O. Box 435), Skagway, AK 99840. ☎ 800/343-7373 or 907/983-2217. www.wpyr.com. For the
entire schedule and fares, see the website.

Skagway Museum and Archives 🦉 The museum contains a fine collection of
gold-rush artifacts and other items reflecting Skagway's colorful history. The building
is the town's most impressive and one of the state's most dignified architectural landmarks, with crisp granite walls and a high-pitched roof standing among tall shade trees
on the edge of town. It began life as a short-lived gold rush–era college and later
became a federal courthouse and jail. The city hall and museum have occupied the
building since 1961 except for a brief hiatus for renovations.

7th and Spring sts. ☎ 907/983-2420. Admission $2 adults, $1 students, free for children 12 and under. Summer
Mon–Fri 9am–5pm, Sat 10am–5pm, Sun 10am–4pm. Winter hours vary, call ahead.

Corrington Museum of Alaska History The eclectic exhibit that leads into the
gift shop is well worth a brief stop. Alaska's history is told in 32 tusks of walrus
scrimshaw. Besides owning some rare and interesting items, they've done a good job
of putting it all together in an understandable way.

5th Ave. and Broadway, in Corrington's Alaska Ivory Co. ☎ 907/983-2580. Free admission. Mid-May to mid-Sept
9am–7pm. Closed winter.

Klondike Gold Dredge Tours Gold mining never happened in Skagway; it was
only a transit point. But more gold-rush tourists come here than anywhere else, so
promoters brought a dredge to where the people are. The 1937 rig, weighing 350 tons,
dug up and sorted gravel to remove gold first in Idaho, then near Dawson City, and

finally near the border on the Top of the World Highway. A 2-hour visit includes a 10-minute video, costumed guides who spice up the tour with humor, and gold panning in heated water. If you will visit Dawson City or Fairbanks, you can see larger dredges in authentic historic settings for less money, but if not, this stop can satisfy your mechanical curiosity and fever to pan for gold.

Mile 1.7 Klondike Hwy. **©** **907/983-3175.** www.klondikegolddredge.com. $39 adults, $22 children under 12. Add $5 for transfer from Skagway. Summer Sun–Fri 8:30am–4:30pm; full tours 9:30am and 1:30pm.

GETTING OUTSIDE

The **Mountain Shop,** 355 4th Ave. (**© 907/983-2544;** www.packerexpeditions.com), rents and sells the equipment you need for backpacking or other outdoor activities in Skagway. The owner, who is also the mayor, leads guided day hikes, backpacking trips, and float trips under the name Packer Expeditions, at the same address.

BACKPACKING   The National Park Service and Parks Canada jointly manage the famous **Chilkoot Pass Trail,** publishing a trail guide and offering information at their offices in Skagway and Whitehorse. Some 20,000 stampeders used the trail to get from Dyea—9 miles from Skagway—to Lake Bennett, 33 miles away, where they could build and launch boats bound for Dawson City. Today, about 3,000 people a year make the challenging hike, taking 3 to 5 days. The Chilkoot is not so much a wilderness trail as an outdoor museum, but don't underestimate its difficulty, as so many did during the gold rush.

To control the numbers, **Parks Canada,** 205–300 Main St., Whitehorse, Yukon Y1A 2B5 Canada (**© 800/661-0486** or 867/667-3910; fax 867/393-6701; www.pc. gc.ca/chilkoot), allows only 50 hikers with permits per day to cross the summit. To buy the permits, call with a Visa, American Express, or MasterCard; the date you plan to start; and the campsites you will use each night. Permits are C$55 for adults, C$28 ages 16 and under, plus a C$12 per-person reservation fee. You pick up the permit at the Trail Centre in Skagway; that's also where 8 of the 50 daily permits are held for walk-ins, to be distributed along with any no-shows. The reservation fee is nonrefundable, and the permit fee is refundable only until a month before the hike.

Once over the pass, you're on Lake Bennett, on the rail line 8 miles short of the road. You can walk to the road, or get back to Skagway on the White Pass and Yukon Route railway (see p. 199), at 1pm Friday, Saturday, and Sunday. The one-way fare to Frasier, British Columbia, is $40 to $50, and the scenic 3-hour ride to Skagway is $65 ($80 on the steam train). There is a $15 surcharge per person if you buy your tickets at Bennett. Be sure to make your reservations well in advance; you will need proof of citizenship, such as a passport or notarized birth certificate.

There are two **U.S. Forest Service cabins** near Skagway, and official access to both is by the White Pass and Yukon Route railway. Both are on trails described in the *Skagway Trail Map,* mentioned below. The **Denver Caboose** is an old, red White Pass caboose parked next to the tracks 6 miles up the line at the trail head for the 4.5-mile **Denver Glacier Trail.** Another cabin is 1½ miles off the track, 14 miles up on the spectacular **Laughton Glacier Trail.** For either, you need a $35 cabin permit (see "Getting Outside in the Tongass National Forest," on p. 97, for reservations information) and a train ticket from the railroad. For details, contact the National Park Service visitor center (see above), or the **Juneau Ranger District,** 8510 Mendenhall Loop Road, Juneau, AK 99801 (**© 907/586-8800;** www.fs.fed.us/r10/tongass).

BIKING   Sockeye Cycle, on 5th Avenue off Broadway (℗ **907/983-2851;** www. cyclealaska.com), leads bike tours, including one that takes clients to the top of the White Pass in a van and lets them coast down on bikes; the 2½-hour trip is $75. Going up on White Pass and Yukon Route railroad and riding back down brings the price to $165. Riders must be at least 14 years old. The company also leads a 3-hour tour of the quiet ghost town site of Dyea for $75, going over in a van. I rode to Dyea from Skagway on my own over the hilly 10-mile coastal road, one of the most pleasant, scenic rides I can remember.

FLIGHTSEEING   Skagway, like Haines, is a good place to choose for a flightseeing trip, as Glacier Bay National Park is just to the west. The flightseeing operators listed in the Haines section offer flights from Skagway, too (p. 189). **Temsco Helicopters** (℗ **866/683-2900** or 907/983-2900; www.temscoair.com) takes 55-minute tours near Skagway with a 25-minute landing on a glacier (not in Glacier Bay); those flights cost $219. A helicopter and dogsled tour on Denver Glacier is $419.

HIKING   A *Skagway Trail Map* is available from the visitor center, listing 10 hikes around Skagway. An easy evening walk starts at the footbridge at the west end of the airport parking lot, crossing the Skagway River to **Yakutania Point Park,** where pine trees grow from cracks in the rounded granite of the shoreline. Across the park is a shortcut taking a couple of miles off the trip to Dyea and to the **Skyline Trail and A.B. Mountain,** a strenuous climb to a 5,000-foot summit with great views. On the southeast side of town, across the railroad tracks, a network of trails heads up from Spring Street between 3rd and 4th avenues to a series of mountain lakes, the closest of which is **Lower Dewey Lake,** less than a mile up the trail.

WHERE TO STAY

The accommodations in Skagway are within close walking distance of the historic district, except as noted.

At The White House 🐾   The Tronrud family essentially rebuilt a burned 1902 gable-roofed inn, which has dormer and bow windows and two porticos with small Doric columns. They made the rooms comfortable and modern while retaining the authentic gold-rush style of the original owner, Lee Guthrie, a successful gambler and saloon owner of the early years. The inn has hardwood floors and fine woodwork. Bedrooms vary in size, but all have quilts and other nice touches, including ceiling fans.

Corner of 8th and Main sts. (P.O. Box 41), Skagway, AK 99840-0041. ℗ **907/983-9000.** Fax 907/983-9010. www. atthewhitehouse.com. 10 units. High season $115 double; low season $85 double. Extra person $10. Rates include continental breakfast. AE, DISC, MC, V. *In room:* TV, Wi-Fi, fridge.

Chilkoot Trail Outpost 🐾   These beautifully crafted log cabins built in 2002 by long-time residents contain comfortable, modern lodgings with carpeted floors and log interior walls, some in the form of two-room suites, with many amenities (but no phones). The hiker's suite consists of two rooms in a duplex with bunkbeds that rent for $125 double, including breakfast but without linens. The location, in Dyea near the Chilkoot Trail and Taiya River, puts you in quiet, natural surroundings away from the carnival atmosphere created by the crush of tourists in Skagway proper. In good weather, the hosts have a nightly campfire and provide supplies for s'mores. You can also cook your own food at a barbecue and sink in a screened gazebo. Breakfast, served in a remarkable log building with a vaulted ceiling, consists of a buffet with various choices, including one hot selection, such as eggs or pancakes. Computers are available for guests' use.

7 Mile Dyea Rd. (P.O. Box 286), Skagway, AK 99840. ℂ **907/983-3799.** Fax 907/983-3599. www.chilkoottrailoutpost. com. 10 units. $125 double in duplex; $150 double-occupancy cabin. Extra adult $25, extra child ages 2–11 $13. MC, V. Rates include full breakfast. **Amenities:** Bike loan. *In room:* TV/VCR, Wi-Fi, fridge, microwave, coffeemaker, hair dryer, no phone.

Mile Zero Bed & Breakfast 🗲   This building was designed to be a B&B, and it shows in details such as the soundproofing and the back doors to every room—guests can access the common rooms through one door or go outside through French doors leading to the porch. The idea is to offer the privacy and convenience of a motel and the warmth and character of a B&B, and it works. All units are accessible to people with disabilities. The site is a few blocks from the historic area. Smoking is not allowed. There are barbecue facilities on-site and wireless Internet throughout.

9th Ave. and Main St. (P.O. Box 165), Skagway, AK 99840. ℂ **907/983-3045.** Fax 907/983-3046. www.mile-zero. com. 6 units. High season $125 double; low season $75 double. Extra person $25. Rates include continental breakfast. MC, V. **Amenities:** Wi-Fi; rooms for traveler's w/disabilities; barbecue.

Sgt. Preston's Lodge   Three buildings sit on a landscaped lawn just steps off Broadway, Skagway's main historic street, at 6th Avenue and State Street. U.S., Canada, and Alaska flags fly out front, underlining the theme, along with the trim tan, red, and green paint scheme, of the tidy image of the Royal Canadian Mounted Police. Once inside, however, you will find typical modern motel rooms, familiar accommodations for those who simply want a comfortable place to sleep. A pair of two-bedroom apartments costs more for the additional space and both have vaulted ceilings. Ten rooms have only shower stalls—no tubs. Rooms were clean but the lobby a bit unkempt on our last early season visit.

370 Sixth Ave. (P.O. Box 538), Skagway, AK 99840. ℂ **866/983-2521** or 907/983-2521. Fax 907/983-3500. www.sgt prestonslodge.com. 39 units. High season $97–$123 double, $162 apartment; low season $76 double, $140 apartment. Extra person 13 and over $10. AE, DISC, MC, V. **Amenities:** Courtesy car. *In room:* TV.

A HOSTEL & CAMPING

A primitive **National Park Service Dyea Campground** has 22 well-separated sites near the water at the ghost town 9 miles from Skagway. The campground has pit toilets and no water. RVs over 27 feet are not allowed. The fee is $6. The **Pullen Creek RV Park** (ℂ **800/936-3731** or 907/983-2768) is near the small-boat harbor, with coin-operated showers. RV sites with power, water, and dump station use are $30; car camping sites are $20; tenting with no vehicle $14.

Skagway Home Hostel   Frank Wasmer and Nancy Schave open up their historic home to hostellers, sharing their meals, refrigerator, bathrooms, laundry machines, bicycles, and hospitality side by side with guests. The atmosphere is like off-campus shared housing at college, except the house is nicer and better kept. Bunks are in separate male and female dorm rooms except for the single private room. To reserve, use the website, as they don't return long-distance calls. In winter, reservations are required, as Frank and Nancy might otherwise not be there. Summer registration hours are from 5:30 to 10:30pm. No pets, alcohol, or smoking.

3rd Ave. near Main St. (P.O. Box 231), Skagway, AK 99840. ℂ **907/983-2131.** www.skagwayhostel.com. 1 private room, 3 dorms. $15 per bunk; $50 double private room. MC, V. **Amenities:** Bike loan; laundry machines $3. *In room:* No phone.

WHERE TO DINE

Restaurants go out of business and open up faster in Skagway's entirely seasonal economy than anywhere else I know. There were more than 20 at last count, and a third of these were brand new. The choices listed here have been good for years and remain among the best, but even these could change. Asking around for a current recommendation may pay off. Restaurants that stay open year-round tend to be better for two reasons: They can keep their staff, and they have to be good or they wouldn't make it through the winter in a town with fewer than 1,000 residents. The **Sweet Tooth Café,** at 315 Broadway (© **907/ 983-2405**), is a good year-round diner, open for breakfast and lunch.

Haven Cafe 𝒓 ESPRESSO/SANDWICHES   The stand-out selections here are the espresso and the milkshakes, but it's also a good choice for breakfast or bagels or, for lunch or a light dinner, panini sandwiches or salads. Diners order at a counter and then sit in the fashionable wooden-floored dining room at one of 11 small tables, a single larger table, or outdoors on an uncovered deck.

9th and State St. © **907/983-3553**. www.haven-cafe.com. All items $4–$9. MC, V. High season daily 6am–8pm; low season daily 6:30am–4pm.

Sabrosa's 𝒓 *Finds* DELI/MEXICAN/VEGETARIAN   This tiny sidewalk cafe down an alley across from the post office feeds locals. Seating is either indoors or in a pleasant fenced area, a sort of patio arrangement. It's an island of intimacy out of the stream of the tourist rush. Our meals were tasty, wholesome, filling, and inexpensive, a rare combination in Skagway. They also serve Mexican specials and fresh baked goods, espresso beer, and wine, and a healthy breakfast is on the menu all day. Service is quick and friendly.

6th and Broadway. © **907/983-2469**. Lunch $5–$10. MC, V. Summer daily 6am–4pm. Closed winter.

The Stowaway Cafe 𝒓𝒓 SEAFOOD/CAJUN   Housed in a small, gray clapboard house overlooking the boat harbor, a 5-minute walk from the historic sites, this little restaurant has for several years turned out many of Skagway's best meals. Grilled and blackened salmon and halibut anchor the menu; there's also beef, pasta, Thai and French cuisine, and all the usual waterfront restaurant items. Part of the attraction is the restaurant's handmade charm. It was founded and operated by a local couple who put their heart into the place, and the tiny dining room is decorated on a mermaid theme that will keep your attention almost as well as the harbor view. They have a beer and wine license.

End of Congress Way near the small-boat harbor. © **907/983-3463**. Reservations recommended. Dinner $13–$29. V. Summer daily 4pm–10pm. Closed winter.

NIGHTLIFE

Incredibly, the ***Days of '98 Show*** has been playing since 1927 in the Fraternal Order of Eagles Hall No. 25, at 6th Avenue and Broadway (© **907/983-2545**). Jim Richards carries on the tradition each summer with actors imported from all over the United States, doing four shows a day (10:30am, 12:30pm, 2:30pm, and 7pm). The evening shows begin with an hour of mock gambling at a casino run by the actors. The actual performance, which lasts an hour, includes singing, cancan dancing, a Robert Service reading, and the story of the shooting of Soapy Smith. All shows are $16. Children 15 and under are charged half-price.

The **Red Onion Saloon,** at 2nd Avenue and Broadway, plays up its gold-rush history, with costumed waitresses wearing corsets. It was a brothel originally—what wasn't in this town?—and mock madams offer $5 tours of a "brothel museum" upstairs. The saloon often has live acoustic music. It closes in winter.

Moe's Frontier Bar, at 5th Avenue and Broadway, is more of a gritty local hangout, open year-round.

6

Anchorage & Environs

As teenagers living in Anchorage, my cousin and I got a job from a family friend painting his lake cabin. He flew us out on his floatplane and left us there, with paint, food, and a little beer. A creek that ran past the lake was so full of salmon that we caught one on every cast until we got bored and started thinking of ways to make it more difficult. We cooked the salmon over a fire and then floated in a boat on the lake under the endless sunshine of a summer night, talking and diving naked into the clear, green water. We met some guys building another cabin one day, but otherwise we saw no other human beings. When the week was over, the cabin was painted—it didn't take long—and the floatplane came back to get us. As we lifted off and cleared the trees, Anchorage opened in front of us, barely 10 minutes away.

The state's largest city, Anchorage—where 40% of Alaska's population resides—is accused, crushingly, of being just like a city "Outside," not really part of Alaska at all. It's true that the closer you get to Anchorage, the more the human development reminds you of the outskirts of Anytown, USA, with fast-food franchises, occasional traffic jams, and the ugly big-box retail development inflicted everywhere by relentless corporate logic. You often hear the joke, "Anchorage isn't Alaska, but you can see it from there," and writers piously warn visitors to land in

Anchorage but move on as soon as possible, as if it's catching.

When I hear that advice, I think of the many great experiences I've had here—such as painting that cabin years ago. Anyone in Anchorage with a few hundred dollars for a floatplane can be on a lake or river with the bears and salmon in a matter of minutes, in wilderness deeper than any you could find in the Lower 48. **Chugach State Park** is largely within the city limits, but it's the size of Rocky Mountain National Park and has similar alpine terrain, with the critical difference that most of it is virtually never visited. Yet you can be climbing those mountains in half an hour's journey from your downtown hotel. **Chugach National Forest,** the nation's second largest, is less than an hour down the road. In downtown's **Ship Creek,** people catch 40-pound salmon from under a freeway bridge. Even within the city, you can bike dozens of miles along the coast or through wooded greenbelts, or ski in one of the nation's best Nordic skiing parks.

Anchorage is indeed a big American city, with big-city problems of crime and pollution, but it's also entirely unique for being surrounded by pristine and spectacular wild lands. Anywhere else, Anchorage would be known not for its shortcomings, but as one of America's greatest cities for outdoor enthusiasts.

ANCHORAGE YESTERDAY & TODAY

Anchorage isn't old enough to have a sharp identity as a city. The first mayor to be born here was elected only in 2003 (and he was barely 40). The city started as a tent camp for workers mobilized to build the Alaska Railroad in 1915. A few houses and businesses went up to serve the federal employees who were building and later running the railroad, as Steve McCutcheon's father was. McCutcheon, who died in 1998, remembered a remote, sleepy railroad town enlivened by a couple of large World War II military bases, but never more than strictly functional. As one visitor who came in the early 1940s wrote, the entire town looked like it was built on the wrong side of the tracks.

McCutcheon looked out the picture window from his living room on a placid lake surrounded by huge million-dollar houses, each with a floatplane pulled up on the green front lawn, and he recalled the year people started to take Anchorage seriously. It was the year, he said, when they started thinking it would be a permanent city, not just an encampment where you went for a few years to make money before moving on—the year they started building Anchorage to last. That year was 1957. Oil was discovered on the Kenai Peninsula's Swanson River, south of here. It was around that time that McCutcheon built his own house all by itself on a lake, far out in the country. At that time, you could homestead in the Anchorage bowl. Those who had the opportunity but chose not to—my wife's family, for example—gave it a pass only because it seemed too improbable that the flat, wet acreage way out of town would ever be worth anything.

Oil fueled Anchorage's growth like nitrogen fertilizer poured on a shooting weed. Those homesteads that went begging in the 1950s and early 1960s now have shopping malls and high-rise office buildings on them. Fortunes came fast, development was haphazard, and a lot was built that we'd all soon regret. I had the bizarre experience of coming home from college to the town I'd grown up in and getting completely lost in a large area of the city that had been nothing but moose browse the last time I'd seen it. Visitors found a city full of life but empty of charm.

In the last 20 years, that has started to change. Anchorage is slowly outgrowing its gawky adolescence. It's still young, prosperous, and vibrant—and exhausting when the summer sun refuses to set—but now it also has some excellent restaurants, a good museum, a large Native cultural center, a nice little zoo, and culture in the evening besides the tourist melodramas you'll find in every Alaska town. People still complain that Anchorage isn't really Alaska—in Fairbanks, they call it "Los Anchorage" (and in Anchorage, Fairbanks is known as "Squarebanks")—yet the great wilderness around the city remains intertwined with its streets. Along with a quarter-million people, Anchorage is full of moose—so many, they're considered pests and wintertime hazards, inspiring debate about hunting them within the city limits. Bears and bald eagles also show up regularly on the system of greenbelts and bike trails that brings the woods into almost every neighborhood.

Anchorage stands on broad, flat sediment between the Chugach Mountains and the silt-laden waters of upper Cook Inlet. At water's edge, mud flats not yet made into land stretch far offshore when the tide is at its low point, up to 38 vertical feet below high water. There's a **downtown area** of about 8 by 20 blocks, near Ship Creek where it all started, but most of the city lies on long commercial strips. Like many urban centers built since the arrival of the automobile, the layout is not particularly conducive to any other form of transportation. But the roads go only so far. Just beyond, wilds

Anchorage

Alaska

Fairbanks
Anchorage Cordova
Kenai Sitka Juneau
Ketchikan

0   1 Mi
0   1 Km

Bike Trails •••••
Railway ┄┄┄

Knik Arm

Point
Woronzof

Earthquake
Park
10

11

*Westchester
Lagoon*

14

12

Postmark Dr.

Aircraft Dr.

Wisconsin St.

Spenard Rd.

*Lake
Hood*

8
7
6
3 **5**
4

9

Fish Creek

*Lake
Spenard*

International Airport Rd.

Coastal Trail

Anchorage
International
Airport

**Connors Lake
Park**

*Connors
Lake*

Point
Campbell

Kincaid
Park

1

Sand Lake Rd.

Raspberry Rd.

*Sand
Lake*

Minnesota Dr.

2

*Jewel
Lake*

Jewel Lake Rd.

Dimond Blvd.

*Campbell
Lake*

W. 166th Ave.

Turnagain Arm

Klatt Rd

ACCOMMODATIONS ■
Anchorage Downtown B&B **14**
Anchorage RV Park **42**
Centennial Camper Park **40**
Courtyard by Marriott **5**
Diamond Center Hotel **30**
Elderberry Bed and Breakfast **2**
Holiday Inn-Express **9**
Lake Hood Inn **3**
Lakeshore Motor Inn **7**
Mahogany Manor **19**
Millennium Alaskan
   Hotel Anchorage **6**
Parkwood Inn **28**
Residence Inn by Marriott **27**
Sheraton Anchorage **16**
Spenard Hostel International **8**

DINING ◆
Arctic Roadrunner **21, 29**
Bear Tooth Grill & Theater Pub **12**
Cafe del Mundo **23**
Campobello Bistro **26**
The Greek Corner **22**

Jens' Restaurant **25**
Kaladi Brothers **13**
The Lucky Wishbone **17**
The Moose's Tooth Pub
   and Pizzeria **24**
New Sagaya's City Market **15**
Noble's Diner **38**

ATTRACTIONS ●
Alaska Aviation Heritage Museum **4**
Alaska Botanical Garden **36**
Alaska Museum of Natural History **39**
Alaska Native Heritage Center **41**
The Alaska Zoo **32**
Campbell Creek Science Center **35**
Earthquake Park **10**
Glen Alps Trailhead **33**
Goose Lake **37**
H2Oasis **31**
Hilltop Ski Area **32**
Kincaid Park **1**
Mulcahy Stadium **18**
Sullivan Arena **20**
Westchester Lagoon **11**

Bluff Rd.

Davis
Park

Ship Creek

Glenn Hwy.

To Eagle River
and Eklutna

see
Downtown
Anchorage"
map
4th Ave.

3rd Ave.

Merrill
Field

Mt. View Dr.

Russian Jack
Spring Park

Turpin St.

15th Ave.

Chester Creek Trail

Chester Creek

Debarr Ave.

Bragaw St.

Muldoon Rd.

Ingra St.

Karluk St.

A St.

Fireweed Lane

Northern Lights Blvd.

Goose
Lake

Boniface Pkwy.

Baxter Rd.

Benson Blvd.

36th Ave.

Tudor Rd.

C St.

Far North
Bicentennial
Park

Campbell Airstrip Rd.

Dowling Rd.

Campbell Creek

E. 68th Ave.

Campbell
Field

Abbott Loop Rd.

Hillside
Park

Old Seward Hwy.

New Seward Hwy.

Abbott Rd.

Lake Otis Pkwy.

O'Malley Rd.

Upper
O'Malley Rd.

Johns Rd.

Birch Rd.

Hillside Dr.

Huffman Rd.

Upper Huffman Rd.

207

beckon in the Chugach, along the trails of Turnagain Arm, at Alyeska Ski Resort in Gird-wood, in Prince William Sound, and in the Matanuska and Susitna valleys. You'll find ways to that wilderness, and the urban pleasures by its side, throughout this chapter.

1 Essentials

GETTING THERE

BY PLANE   You'll probably get to Anchorage at the start of your trip by air, as it has by far the most flights linking Alaska to the rest of the world on many airlines. The **Ted Stevens Anchorage International Airport** is a major hub. Seattle has the most frequent flights connecting to Anchorage, with numerous domestic carriers flying nonstop all day. (See "Getting There & Getting Around" in chapter 2 for more details.) Within Alaska, most flights route through here, even for communities that are much closer to each other than they are to Anchorage. **Alaska Airlines** (© 800/252-7522; www.alaskaair.com) is the dominant carrier for Alaska destinations and the only jet operator to most Alaska cities. Various commuter carriers link Anchorage to rural destinations not served by jet. **Era Aviation** (© 800/866-8394 or 907/266-8394; www.flyera.com) is one of the largest for Southcentral Alaska destinations and can be booked directly or through Alaska Airlines. Era ran into financial problems early in 2006 and went through bankruptcy court, but continued flying. Always use a credit card when buying an airline ticket and consider travel insurance (p. 44).

Unless your hotel has a courtesy van or you rent a car, a taxi is probably the best way to get downtown from the airport. A **taxi ride** downtown from the airport runs $18 to $20. Try **Yellow Cab** (© 907/563-5353). Shuttle vans serve the airport, with arrangements changing frequently. Ask as the visitor information desk in the baggage claim area. **The People Mover** city bus connects the airport and the downtown transit center hourly. Take Spenard Route 7A (every other Route 7 bus on weekdays). For finding schedules and other details on using the People Mover see "Getting Around," below.

BY CAR   There's only one road to the rest of the world: the Glenn Highway. It leads through the Mat-Su Valley area and Glennallen to Tok, where it meets the Alaska Highway, 330 miles from Anchorage. Thirty miles out of Anchorage the Glenn meets the Parks Highway, which leads to Denali National Park and Fairbanks. The only other road out of town, the Seward Highway, leads south to the Kenai Peninsula. See "Alaska's Highways a la Carte" in chapter 9 for a review of all the roads. For more on driving to Alaska, see chapter 2.

BY BUS   **Alaska/Yukon Trails** (© 800/770-7275; www.alaskashuttle.com), a van and minibus service, runs between Anchorage and Fairbanks, with stops in Talkeetna and Denali National Park. From Fairbanks, they run to Dawson City and Whitehorse and offer rural highway tours. In Anchorage, they stop at various points, including the airport and the downtown Egan Civic and Convention Center. A one-way ticket to Talkeetna is $45, Denali $65, and Fairbanks $91. Various other van and bus services offer transportation to and from Seward, Homer, Talkeetna, Denali National Park, and Skagway (via Whitehorse); see the sections on each of those places for details.

BY RV   A recreational vehicle is a popular way to explore the region. Renting an RV in Anchorage for a tour is covered below under "Getting Around." Driving an RV to Alaska is covered in chapter 2. It's also possible to come to Alaska with your own RV without making the time-consuming return trip by shipping your RV back from

Anchorage and Tacoma, Washington, and flying to meet it (since southbound ships are relatively empty, you get a special rate). Contact **Totem Ocean Trailer Express** (© 800/234-8683 in Anchorage, 800/426-0074 in the Lower 48; www.totemocean.com).

In addition, several firms offer one-way rentals between Anchorage and Skagway (the ferry terminus) or cities around the U.S. **Alaska Motorhome Rentals** (© 800/254-9929; www.bestofalaskatravel.com) offers Skagway one-way rentals to Anchorage with a drop-off fee of $295 to $695, Anchorage to Seattle for $495 to $895, and Anchorage to Fairbanks for $195 to $495; plus the cost of the rental, $195 to $225 a day in the high season; plus mileage (or pay $30 a day for unlimited mileage) and gas (budget generously). AAA and AARP members can get 5% off. The same company has another operation, **Alaska Highway Cruises** (© 800/323-5757), that provides packages to cruise one-way, tour Alaska in an RV, and fly home. For more on that option and on one-way rentals from the balance of the Lower 48, see chapter 2.

BY RAIL   The **Alaska Railroad** (© 800/544-0552, 907/265-2494, or 907/265-2620 TTY; www.alaskarailroad.com) connects Anchorage with Seward and Whittier to the south, and Fairbanks and Denali National Park to the north. It's a fun way to travel, with expert commentary in the summer, good food, and clean, comfortable cars. However, the train is priced as a tourism excursion and costs much more than ordinary transportation. For example, the spectacular Seward run, only about 120 miles, costs $124 round-trip. Most trains run only in the summer, but a snowy 12-hour odyssey to Fairbanks runs once a week all winter. The summer fare to Fairbanks is $185 one-way; the winter fare is $130 one-way ($105 for Alaska residents). See chapter 8 on Denali National Park, and sections on other destinations for fares and service details.

ORIENTATION

Many visitors never make it beyond the **downtown** area, the old-fashioned grid of streets at the northwest corner of town where the large hotels and gift shops are located. Street numbers and letters work on a simple pattern, and navigation is easy. Beyond downtown, most of Anchorage is oriented to commercial strips, and you'll need a map to find your way. The map on p. 206 will suffice for major thoroughfares, but to find anything on smaller streets, pick up a detailed map at the visitor centers, at a grocery store, or on the Internet. Some parts of greater Anchorage are in distinct communities outside the bowl formed by the Chugach Mountains, including **Eagle River** and **Eklutna,** within a half-hour on the Glenn Highway to the northeast, and **Girdwood** and **Portage,** on the Seward Highway, 45 minutes to the south. The suburban **Matanuska and Susitna valleys** (known as Mat-Su) lie an hour north of the city on the Glenn and Parks highways.

GETTING AROUND

BY RENTAL CAR   Driving is the most practical way for most independent travelers to tour the main part of Alaska, and the location of Anchorage at the hub of transportation networks makes it the handiest place to start. A car improves a visit to Anchorage, too, as the city is spread out and public transportation and taxi service are poor. Most major car-rental companies operate in Anchorage, largely from desks at the airport in a tunnel off the domestic baggage-claim area. A compact car for $50 a day, with unlimited mileage, is a fair deal. The airport adds a 10% concession fee plus a $4-a-day facility fee, which you can avoid by renting off-site from **Avis**, at 5th Avenue and B Street (© 800/230-4898 or 907/277-4567; www.avis.com) or several other

---

Tips Car Wheels on Gravel Roads

Most car-rental contracts prohibit drivers from going on Alaska's unpaved highways, such as the Denali Highway (p. 344), the McCarthy Road to Kennecott (p. 427), or the Dalton Highway (p. 412). What this means, as a practical matter, is that you are responsible for any damage that occurs when you are off pavement, even if you buy the expensive "collision damage waiver" coverage. **Enterprise Rent-A-Car** (© 800/261-7331 or 907/277-1600; www.enterprise.com) allows its cars to be driven anywhere, but under the same conditions; with them you aren't violating your contract, but you are still assuming the risk. If you prefer not to take that risk, one Anchorage company allows its vehicles to go anywhere and sells insurance to cover damage on gravel highways. **ABC Motorhome Rentals** (© 800/421-7456 or 907/279-2000; www.abcmotorhome.com) rents mostly older cars and minivans as well as its main line in late-model RVs. Customers are responsible for any damage up to $2,500, but the company sells a $10-a-day policy that brings the deductible down to $500, and another $10-a-day policy that covers windshield damage (the most likely risk on gravel highway). Note, however, that these kinds of arrangements are changeable, so you may still need to do some research. Two Fairbanks firms that allow gravel-road driving are under "Equipped for the Back Roads" (p. 393).

---

firms. The city charges an 8% rental car tax and the state adds an additional 10% tax. Including the airport fees, taxes total well over a third of the rental price. Sorry about that! Cars can sell out in summer, so reserve ahead.

BY RENTAL RV Several large RV-rental agencies operate in Anchorage (see "Getting There," above). High-season rates are around $1,400 a week, plus the cost of the large amount of fuel RVs use. **ABC Motorhome Rentals,** 3875 Old International Airport Rd. (© **800/421-7456** or 907/279-2000; www.abcmotorhome.com), charges no mileage fee. See "Getting There & Getting Around" in chapter 2 for more on this option.

BY BUS It takes patience to go a long way on the **People Mover** buses (© **907/343-6543;** www.peoplemover.org), especially if you have to transfer, but if you have the time, the system is inexpensive and safe, and covers most of the city. Bus fares all over town are $1.75 for adults; $1 for ages 5 to 18; 50¢ for those over age 60, with disabilities, or with a valid Medicare card; free ages 4 and under. The transit center bus depot is at 6th Avenue and G Street. Buses generally come every half-hour, hourly on weekends, but to use the system conveniently, go online and figure out your route and schedule in advance.

BY BIKE The network of bike trails is a great way to see the best side of Anchorage, but not a practical means of point-to-point transportation for most people. The **Tony Knowles Coastal Trail** starts right downtown (see "Getting Outside," later in this chapter). Good street bikes are usually for rent near Elderberry Park downtown, at the start of the Coastal Trail, from **Pablo's Bike Rental,** a booth at the corner of 5th and L (© **907/250-2871**). Rates are $20 for 4 hours, $40 for a day. An established bike-rental shop with a wider choice of equipment is in the brown shopping mall at 4th and C: **Downtown Bicycle Rental** (© **907/279-5293;** www.alaska-bike-rentals.com).

Rates start at $15 for 3 hours, $2.50 each additional hour, max $29 per day. The shop also carries tandems, kids' bikes, and trailers, and offers a shuttle to the Glen Alps parking lot—the trail head for Flattop Mountain—which is also the start of a good mountain-biking route. For a rental outfit specializing in mountain biking, see "Equipment," later in this chapter.

VISITOR INFORMATION

The **Anchorage Convention and Visitor Bureau,** 524 W. 4th Ave., Anchorage, AK 99501-2212 (© **907/276-4118;** fax 907/278-5559; www.anchorage.net), offers information on the city and the entire state at its centers and extensive website. The main location is the **Log Cabin Visitor Information Center,** downtown at 4th Avenue and F Street (© **907/274-3531;** daily June–Aug 7:30am–7pm, May and Sept 8am–6pm, Oct–Apr 9am–4pm). If it's crowded, go to the storefront office right behind it. You'll also find visitor information desks at the airport: one in the baggage-claim area in the C concourse and one in the international terminal.

The **Alaska Public Lands Information Center,** located at 605 W. 4th Ave. (across the intersection from the log cabin at 4th and F), Suite 105, Anchorage, AK 99501 (© **866/869-6887** or 907/271-2737, or 907/271-2738 TTY; www.nps.gov/aplic; daily 9am–5pm in summer, Mon–Fri 10am–5pm in winter), can help anyone planning to spend time outdoors anywhere in Alaska. Exhibits in the grand room with high ceilings—the building was a 1930s post office and federal courthouse—orient visitors to Alaska's geography and outdoor activities and make an excellent starting point for your trip. When you're ready for details, you will find all the land agencies represented by rangers whose advice is based on personal experience. Be sure to pick up the free booklets they distribute on the highways and parks you will be visiting. You can buy ferry tickets for the Alaska Marine Highway System, and at the bookstore pick from an excellent selection of trail and field guides. Even if you have no need for information, stop in for free films, presentations, and children's programs. The center is well worth passing through the federal security checkpoint at the entrance.

SPECIAL EVENTS

For more events, and online calendars, see "The Performing Arts," later.

The **Anchorage Folk Festival** (© **907/566-2334;** www.anchoragefolkfestival.org), from January 18 through 28, 2007, imports musicians and shows off local talent in free concerts, workshops, and jam sessions, as well as four guest-musician dances that raise money for the festival. They have other events through the year, including an August fiddle camp and a Novemberfest; check the website for the latest.

The **Fur Rendezvous Winter Festival** (© **907/274-1177;** www.furrondy.net; Feb 16–Mar 4, 2007) is the city's big winter celebration, with many community events, a parade, fireworks, a carnival, craft fairs, snowshoe softball, dog sled rides, and other fun. The Rondy's traditional centerpiece is the **World Champion Sled Dog Race,** a 3-day sprint event of about 25 miles per heat. In addition, the last weekend of the festival coincides with the start of the **Iditarod Trail Sled Dog Race** (© **907/376-5155;** www.iditarod.com). The Iditarod, long Alaska's biggest winter event, has recently dramatically grown as a tourist attraction, bringing in a flood of visitors who link seeing the race with winter sports and festivals in Anchorage and Fairbanks. On the weekend of the start, the streets of Anchorage fill with foreign languages, as European visitors come in disproportionate numbers. The Iditarod begins from Anchorage the first Saturday in March (in 2007, Mar 3) and then proceeds in trucks to the re-start the next day in the Mat-Su Valley for the 1,000-mile run to Nome (see the section on Nome in chapter 10 for more details).

The **Native Youth Olympics** (© 907/793-3267), held by the Cook Inlet Tribal Council in late April at the Sullivan Arena, is a tough competition in traditional Alaska Native sports such as the seal hop (done on the knuckles) and the spectacular high kick, in which young men kick a ball suspended as high as 9 feet off the floor.

The **Saturday Market** and **Sunday Market,** known collectively as Anchorage Market & Festival, are big street fairs and farmers' markets held every weekend from mid-May through mid-September at 3rd Avenue and E Street (© **907/272-5634;** www.anchoragemarkets.com).

The stocked salmon runs in Ship Creek, which runs right through downtown Anchorage, produce one of the town's most popular summer activities (see "Roadside Fishing," p. 241). The **Slam'n Salm'n Derbies** (© **907/646-4877**) add the possibility of winning money and prizes for fishing. The derby for kings is June 1 to 10, 2007, and another for silvers is August 3 to 12. One-day tickets are $10 and benefit the Downtown Soup Kitchen; they are available at the derby headquarters in the Alaska Railroad plaza near the creek.

The **Blues on the Green** music festival, the second Saturday in June, takes place under the sky in the natural amphitheater at Kincaid Park. It is an all-day, all-evening blues concert. Headliners in the past have included Taj Mahal, Bo Diddley, and Buddy Guy.

The **Alaska State Fair** (© **907/745-4827;** www.alaskastatefair.org), which culminates a 12-day run on Labor Day each year, is the biggest event in the area. It takes place in Palmer, 40 miles north of Anchorage on the Glenn Highway. In most ways, it's a typical state fair, with rides, booths, exhibits, contests, fireworks, and live music. Not typical are the vegetables. The good soil and long days in the Matanuska Valley around Palmer boost their growth to massive size, the stuff of childhood nightmares. Cabbages are the size of bean-bag chairs. A mere beach ball–size cabbage would be laughed off the stage. And it's not just the 100-pound cabbages. Imagine a 19-pound carrot, 35-pound broccoli, 42-pound beet, or 75-pound rutabaga (all world records from the fair, among others you can check out on the website). The flower gardens are amazing too, although not in the same way. Note that on the weekends the fair ties up traffic between Palmer and Anchorage, so it's wise to go midweek, if possible.

The **Carrs/Safeway Great Alaska Shootout basketball tournament** (© **907/786-1250;** www.goseawolves.com/shootout), hosted by the University of Alaska Anchorage, brings top-ranked college men's and women's teams to the Sullivan Arena over Thanksgiving weekend and the preceding week.

FAST FACTS: Anchorage

Banks A bank is rarely far away, and all grocery stores and gas stations also have **ATMs.** Downtown, **Wells Fargo** (© 907/263-2016) has a branch in the 5th Avenue Mall (5th Ave. and D St.), with a foreign exchange desk and wire-transfer services.

Hospitals Alaska Regional Hospital is at 2801 DeBarr Rd. (© **907/276-1131;** www.alaskaregional.com), and **Providence Alaska Medical Center** is at 3200 Providence Dr. (© **907/562-2211;** www.providence.org).

Internet Access and Business Services Downtown, the **UPS Store,** at 645 G St., next to City Hall (© **907/276-7888**), has computers with high-speed connections as well as other services.

Police The **Anchorage Police Department** has main offices at 4501 S. Bragaw Rd., south of Tudor Road; for a nonemergency, call © **907/786-8500.** For non-emergency police business outside the city, call the **Alaska State Troopers,** 5700 E. Tudor Rd. (© **907/269-5511**).

Post Office It's downtown, downstairs in the brown building at 4th Avenue and D Street.

Taxes There's no **sales tax** in Anchorage. The **bed tax** is 12%. **Car rental taxes** amount to over a third of the price between the state, local, and airport taxes and fees.

2 Where to Stay

Hotel rooms are overpriced in Anchorage, so this is a good place to choose a B&B or small inn. I've searched for such places, choosing those with character and reasonable prices. There are hundreds more, many of them just as good. About 50 B&Bs link through a website maintained by the cooperative **Anchorage Alaska Bed and Breakfast Association** (www.anchorage-bnb.com). Rates, amenities, and location are listed in a grid with links to each business's own website. Another page shows availability at member B&Bs on a calendar. Without a computer, call their hotline (© **888/584-5147** or 907/272-5909), which is answered by hosts at member properties to offer referrals to places that meet callers' requirements.

DOWNTOWN
VERY EXPENSIVE

Besides the Hotel Captain Cook, described in full below, three other high-rise hotels downtown offer a similar level of service without as much character or quite as many amenities. **Hilton Anchorage,** 500 W. 3rd Ave. (© **800/445-8667** or 907/272-7411; www.hilton.com), is a large conference hotel right at the center of downtown activities. The **Sheraton Anchorage,** 401 E. 6th Ave. (© **800/478-8700** or 907/276-8700; www.sheratonanchoragehotel.com), is comparable to the Hilton, but in a slightly less attractive area a few blocks away. The newer **Anchorage Marriott Downtown,** 820 W. 7th Ave. (© **800/228-9290** or 907/279-8000; www.marriotthotels.com), has a nice pool and fabulous views from rooms with wall-size picture windows.

Hotel Captain Cook ✿✿✿   This is Alaska's great, grand hotel, where royalty and rock stars stay. Former governor Wally Hickel built the first of the three towers after the 1964 earthquake, and now the hotel fills a city block and anchors the downtown skyline. Inside, the earth tones and dark wood decor contribute to a fully realized (maybe a little excessive) nautical theme, with art memorializing Cook's voyages and enough teak to build a square-rigger. The regularly renewed rooms are decorated in a rich, sumptuous style using exquisite fabrics, unique pieces of custom-built furniture, and lots of varnished trim. The hotel never abandoned the deep colors that are now returning to fashion—not a scrap of pale wood or generic beige ever came in. Rooms are comfortable in size, but not as large as those in modern upscale chains, and all have a choice only of a king or two twin beds. Lots of custom tile and mirrors make up for the relatively small size of the bathrooms. There are great views from all sides, and you don't pay more to be on a higher floor. The pool, spa, and fitness facilities in the below-ground lower lobby are among the best in town.

Sophisticated food and elaborately formal service justify the high prices at **The Crow's Nest** ❀❀❀, the city's most traditional fine-dining restaurant, on the hotel's top floor. Most tables have stupendous views, and high-backed booths lend intimacy for a romantic dinner. No other restaurant in Anchorage makes its patrons feel as special and important. The cuisine draws on many influences without being trendy and all our food looked wonderful on the plate. Everything was prepared perfectly as well. Main courses range from $26 to $50. The wine list is huge, with few bottles under $40. **Fletcher's,** off the lobby, is an English pub serving good Italian-style pizza, pasta, and sandwiches. **The Pantry** is far better than the typical hotel cafe, with excellent service and interesting entrees mixed in with more predictable choices. The **Whale's Tail** serves light meals, coffee, and cocktails amid overstuffed chairs and big TVs. It's a place for a drink without feeling like you're in a bar.

4th Ave. and K St. (P.O. Box 102280), Anchorage, AK 99510-2280. ☎ **800/843-1950** or 907/276-6000. Fax 907/343-2298. www.captaincook.com. 547 units. High season $240–$250 double, $260–$1,500 suite; low season $135–$145 double, $150–$1,500 suite. Extra person $20. AE, DISC, MC, V. **Amenities:** 3 restaurants; 3 bars; indoor pool; separate men's and women's health clubs with racquetball, Jacuzzi, steam room and sauna; concierge; car-rental desk; business center; shopping arcade; salon; 24-hr. room service; massage; dry cleaning; concierge-level rooms. *In room:* TV w/pay movies, Wi-Fi, hair dryer, iron.

EXPENSIVE

Here are a few chain-hotel options downtown for those who prefer national brands: The **Days Inn,** 321 E. 5th Ave. (☎ **800/329-7466** or 907/276-7226; www.daysinnalaska.com), which has a courtesy van to the airport and rail depot; the **Clarion Suites,** 325 W. 8th Avenue (☎ **888/389-6575** or 907/274-1000; www.clarionsuites.com), an all-suite building across from the Federal Building, with a small pool; and the **Hawthorn Suites,** 1110 W. 8th Avenue (☎ **888/469-6575** or 907/222-5005; www.hawthorn.com), with similar facilities as the Clarion Suites, plus a Benihana Restaurant on-site.

Anchorage Grand Hotel ❀❀   This all-suite hotel has a rare combination of advantages: a superb central location; solid, quiet, freshly remodeled rooms; fully equipped kitchens in every unit, full of housewares and with dishwashers and automatic ice makers; generous amenities such as free high-speed Internet in the bedroom and living room; and rates that beat the competition in this area of town by $10 to $30 a night or more. The hotel lacks much of a lobby, as the main entrance and entrance for travelers with disabilities lead directly into a stairway or hallway; that's because it is a reincarnation of an old, concrete apartment building. But the rooms and tiled bathrooms are quite large, decorated in a trim, subdued style with fine cabinetry, and they are immaculate. Despite the full kitchens, I noticed no odors in the several rooms I checked. Also despite the kitchen, they serve a free continental breakfast in the morning (and deliver the newspaper). Every unit has a bedroom and a queen-size sofa sleeper in the living room.

505 W. 2nd Ave., Anchorage, AK 99501. ☎ **888/800-0640** or 907/929-8888. Fax 907/929-8899. www.anchorage grandhotel.com. 31 units. Summer $169 double; winter $89 double. Extra person 14 and over $10. Rates include continental breakfast. AE, DISC, MC, V. **Amenities:** Business center. *In room:* TV, high-speed Internet, kitchen, hair dryer, iron, voice mail.

Downtown Anchorage

ACCOMMODATIONS ■
Anchorage Grand Hotel **13**
Anchorage International Hostel **27**
Anchorage Marriott Downtown **30**
Caribou Inn **4**
Clarion Suites **20**
Copper Whale Inn **2**
Days Inn **18**
G Street House **29**
Hawthorn Suites **30**
Hilton Anchorage **14**
Hotel Captain Cook **7**
The Oscar Gill House Bed
  & Breakfast **32**
Susitna Place **31**
The Voyager Hotel **6**

DINING ◆
The Bridge **33**
Cafe Savannah **22**
Club Paris **23**
Dianne's Restaurant **21**
Downtown Deli and Cafe **16**
Glacier Brewhouse **8**
Kumagoro **15**
The Marx Brothers Cafe **12**
The Muffin Man **26**
Orso **9**
Sacks Cafe **11**
Side Street Espresso **10**
Simon and Seafort's
  Saloon and Grill **3**
Snow City Cafe **5**

ATTRACTIONS ●
Alaska Center for the
  Performing Arts **24**
The Alaska Experience
  Theatre **25**
Alaska State Troopers
  Museum **17**
Anchorage Museum
  of History and Art **19**
The Imaginarium **9**
The Oscar Anderson
  House Museum **1**

Copper Whale Inn 🐾🐾   A pair of clapboard houses overlook the water and Elderberry Park right on the Coastal Trail downtown, with attractive rooms of various shapes and sizes. New ownership in 2006 took the historic main building, which was growing worn, and redecorated in fashionable tans and browns with comfortable new beds, huge nature photographs, and even granite countertops around the sinks. The small upstairs rooms still have wonderful views and funny angles, and now have a style that requires no excuses for the high rates. Two of those rooms have shared bathrooms. Lower-level rooms in the original building open onto a patio but lack a view. The rooms in the newer building are larger (although none is very large) and have cherry wood furniture and high ceilings. The common area in the old building is a comfortable place to gather or to check e-mail. The staff serves a large continental breakfast. Rooms also have free Wi-Fi and telephones, but the inn has no TVs, by design.

440 L St., Anchorage, AK 99501. © 866/258-7999 or 907/258-7999. Fax 888/WHALE-IN or 907/258-6213. www.
copperwhale.com. 15 units, 2 with shared bathroom. High season $165 double with shared bathroom, $165–$195
double with private bathroom; low season $69 double with shared bathroom, $110 double with private bathroom.
Extra person $10. Rates include continental breakfast. AE, DISC, MC, V. **Amenities:** Access to health club; bike rental;
concierge. *In room:* Wi-Fi, iron.

The Voyager Hotel ⊀⊀   Thanks to its exacting proprietor, Stan Williams, The Voyager
is just right, down to the high quality of the linen and mattresses. The size is small, the
location central, the rooms large and light, all with well-designed kitchenettes, and the
housekeeping is exceptional. The whole place has a feel of crisp professionalism. Remodeling projects have been moving through the building for several years, most recently
updating the facade and adding big, opening windows that bring in light and air (the hotel
also has central air-conditioning). The hotel is best for business travelers. The desks have
speaker phones, free high-speed Internet ports (Wi-Fi is available in the lobby), and extra
electrical outlets. The pick of the rooms are those on the northwest corner, which have an
added meeting or sitting room but cost the same as the units that have only the bedroom.
There's nothing ostentatious or outwardly remarkable about the hotel, yet experienced
travelers return again and again. Smoking is not permitted on the property.

501 K St., Anchorage, AK 99501. © 800/247-9070 or 907/277-9501. Fax 907/274-0333. www.voyagerhotel.com.
40 units. High season $179 (up to 3 people per room); low season $89 (up to 3 people per room). Extra person $10.
AE, DC, DISC, MC, V. No smoking. **Amenities:** Restaurant; access to nearby health club with $7.50 day pass; Wi-Fi;
coin-op laundry; dry cleaning. *In room:* A/C, TV, dataport, high-speed Internet, kitchenette, coffeemaker, hair dryer.

Finds   **Three Exceptional Downtown B&Bs**

These houses and the warm and hospitable people who live there offer some
of the most authentic and comfortable lodgings in Alaska.

G Street House, 1032 G St. (© **907/276-3284**; www.gstreethouse.com), is an
elegant home within easy walking distance of the downtown sights. The classy
rooms go for only $105 for a double with private bathroom—a bargain. The
hosts, Pam and Allan Tesche, are energetic and interesting: He's on the city
assembly and she's an expert on local history and a community volunteer. You
can book through the website.

A good place to save money is **Anchorage Downtown B&B,** 1401 W. 13th
Ave. (© **907/278-9275**; http://anchoragedowntown.com), a family home offering lodgings since 1988, well before the birth of the teen who now makes the
beds and befriends the guests. The house, behind thick greenery on a quiet residential street, has rooms ranging from a bedroom with a TV, phone, and
fridge for $89 double to a complete, two-bedroom apartment for $139.

Near the Mulcahy Park baseball stadium, a 15-minute walk to the downtown
sights, **Mahogany Manor,** 204 E. 15th Ave. (© **888/777-0346** or 907/278-1111;
www.mahoganymanor.com), feels like it's in the country, with big windows that
look out on treetops. The house was a grand mansion of the 1950s, and the old-
fashioned Alaskana atmosphere is preserved with redwood plank paneling,
indoor waterfalls, and an extraordinary collection of Alaskan art and crafts. The
rooms and property are packed with luxury amenities, including a large hot tub
and moving-water swimming unit in a solarium; summer rates range from $229
for a simple bedroom to $339 for a family-size three-bedroom suite.

INEXPENSIVE

Caribou Inn *Value*   A big, old, wood-frame house stands among office buildings, parking lots, and high-rise hotels on a corner in the very best part of downtown Anchorage. Instead of luxurious rooms you would expect on such valuable property, budget accommodations are inside—rooms decorated with as much country style as could be managed with older furniture and limited funds (for example, a flowered bedspread covering an old couch). It's clean, and the management makes an effort to cater to visitors who simply want good value for their money rather than people who can't afford to go anywhere else. You'll meet others like yourself. That's important because the rates here are so far below the market. The best room in the house, a large unit with dormers and a kitchenette, costs what you normally pay for a depressing little compartment on the edge of downtown. Add the hot breakfast served from 6am to 9am, airport transfer, and free parking pass, and you are getting an amazing deal. If you don't need polish, you can save more than $50 a night here.

501 L St., Anchorage, AK 99501. (C) **800/272-5878** or 907/272-0444. Fax 907/274-4828. www.cariboubnb.com. 14 units, 5 with shared bathroom. Summer $99 double with shared bathroom, $109 double with private bathroom; winter $49 double with shared bathroom, $59 double with private bathroom. Extra person $25. Rates include full breakfast. AE, DISC, MC, V. **Amenities:** Courtesy van. *In room:* TV w/digital cable, fridge.

The Oscar Gill House Bed & Breakfast   On the Delaney Park strip, just a few blocks from downtown, this is truly the oldest house in Anchorage—it was built in 1913, in Knik, before Anchorage was founded, and moved here on a barge a few years later. Oscar Gill was an early civic leader. The house was to be torn down in 1982 but was moved to storage by a historic preservation group; Mark and Susan Lutz saved it in 1993, transferring it to its present location and, with their own labor, restoring it authentically as a cozy bed-and-breakfast. Now it's on the National Historic Register. Appropriate antiques sit on plank floors in rooms sized in those more modest times. With the period decoration, it's like visiting your grandmother's house when it was brand new. The Lutzes are the kind of hosts who enjoy their guests. Book early, as they fill up; you can check availability and even select a room on their website.

1344 W. 10th Ave., Anchorage, AK 99501. (C)/fax **907/279-1344.** www.oscargill.com. 3 units, 2 with shared bathroom. High season $105 double with shared bathroom, $135 double with private bathroom; low season $75 double with shared bathroom, $85 double with private bathroom. Extra person $20 (except infants). Rates include full breakfast. AE, MC, V. **Amenities:** Bike loan; babysitting. *In room:* TV, Wi-Fi, hair dryer, iron.

Susitna Place *Value*   Just a few blocks from the downtown core, where a narrow residential street reaches a quiet end, a nondescript door under a car port leads into a rambling house of rooms ranging from comfortable and inexpensive to grand. It turns out the street side is really the back of the house, which sits at the top of a high bluff facing an unobstructed view of Cook Inlet and Mount Susitna beyond, a view so unlike most urban vistas it is easy to forget you are right in town. A large, gracious common room and breakfast area and an adjoining balcony command this extraordinary view, and it's enough to make you stop right there and just spend time looking. Continued remodeling has filled the house with new furniture and should be complete by 2007. The suite is quite luxurious, but the four rooms that share two bathrooms are the rarer find: Cozy and very clean, sharing this prime location, they allow travelers to save money without compromise. A good, simple room with two double beds and its own bathroom rents for $125 double. The hosts, successful journalists, are hospitable Alaskans.

727 N St., Anchorage, AK 99501. ℂ **907/274-3344.** Fax 907/272-4141. www.susitnaplace.com. 9 units, 4 with shared bathroom. High season $100–$105 double with shared bathroom, $125–$135 double with private bathroom, $155–$180 suite; low season $60–$65 double with shared bathroom, $75–$80 double with private bathroom, $90–$110 suite. Additional person $15. Rates include continental breakfast. AE, DISC, MC, V. **Amenities:** Free covered parking. *In room:* TV w/HBO.

A HOSTEL

Anchorage International Hostel–Downtown, 700 H St. (ℂ **907/276-3635;** www. anchorageinternationalhostel.org), has 95 beds and an urban feel. A coin-op laundry, kitchen, and storage are available, and they have Internet access in the lobby, a courtesy phone, and free bikes. Dorm rooms are small, with just a few bunks each. A bunk is $20. Dorms close between 10am and 5pm daily. The curfew is 1am and checkout is 10am. A homier hostel outside the downtown area is detailed below.

BEYOND DOWNTOWN

These lodging choices are spread across Anchorage, with its long, wide commercial strips. Like most residents, you need a car to stay here. On the other hand, by leaving downtown, you can sometimes find larger, newer rooms for less cost, and you avoid downtown parking problems.

EXPENSIVE

Dimond Center Hotel 𝒦𝒦 *Finds*   This hotel is unique in several ways. Owned by the Seldovia Native Association, its primary clientele is rural Alaska residents coming to the big city for shopping and entertainment. That explains the location, on the south side of town, far from downtown sites or midtown office buildings, in the parking lot between a Wal-Mart and a big shopping mall (where the large health club and pool are accessible to hotel guests). Strange as it sounds, however, the location makes sense for many visitors: Chugach State Park, the zoo, and the Seward Highway and its many attractions are closer than anywhere else you could stay. Since the owners built the hotel for themselves, the attention to comfort and detail are impressive. The common areas are stylish and decorated with Native art, and the rooms are grand: high ceilings, granite counters, attractive modern furniture, 36-inch TVs, and pillow-top beds with comforters. The bathrooms are elaborate, with large shower areas and separate soaking tubs that can connect to the bedroom by opening wooden shutters. Amenities are exhaustive: wired broadband and Wi-Fi, snacks, slippers and bathrobes, a breakfast of Belgian waffles, and so on.

700 E. Dimond Blvd., Anchorage, AK 99515. ℂ **866/770-5002** or 907/770-5000. Fax 907/770-5001. www.dimond centerhotel.com. 109 units. Summer $229–$269; winter $119–$149 (rates for up to 4 guests in a room). AE, DC, DISC, MC, V. Rates include continental breakfast. **Amenities:** Breakfast room; bar; free airport shuttle; fitness area and access to health club; coin-op laundry. *In room:* TV, high-speed Internet, Wi-Fi, microwave, fridge, coffeemaker.

Residence Inn By Marriott 𝒦   Families who can afford it should stay here (those on more of a budget should see the Parkwood Inn, listed below), and many business travelers would find it convenient, too. All units are suites with cooking facilities and most have full kitchens. They're big enough to provide family members with privacy and sanity breaks, but save money over renting adjoining rooms in an ordinary hotel and dining out for all meals. Room decoration is light and hotel-typical; common areas have an Alaska Native motif reflecting the Native corporation management of the hotel. The clapboard building has a gabled roof and stone accents, standing in a parklike enclave in the midtown commercial area, next to a high-rise office building and across the road from a large Fred Meyer grocery and department store. On-site, there's a pool and fitness area, an outdoor basketball and mini–tennis court, and a restaurant serving breakfast daily and light evening meals with beer and wine 4 days a week, included in the room rate. Get driving directions, as it's a little tricky.

1025 35th Ave., Anchorage, AK 99508. ⓒ **877/729-0197** or 907/729-0197. Fax 907/563-9636. www.residenceinn.com. 148 units. Summer $230–$344 suite; winter $129–$159 suite (rates for any number of guests). AE, DC, DISC, MC, V. Rates include full breakfast. **Amenities:** Pool; mini–tennis and basketball court; fitness room; spa; sauna; courtesy shuttle; business center; Wi-Fi; coin-op laundry; valet service; complimentary newspaper. *In room:* TV w/pay movies, broadband Internet, kitchenette or full kitchen, iron and ironing board.

MODERATE

Lake Hood Inn *Finds*   Pilot Bill Floyd built this place right next to his float plane slip (he flies a PA-12) and filled it with fascinating aviation stuff: photographs, propellers, and even rows of seats from a Russian airliner. The guestbook is an aircraft log book. On the comfortable balconies, headphones are at the ready to listen to radio traffic between the tower and the aircraft you can see taxiing on the lake in front of you. Floyd invested in commercial-quality construction, and the rooms have the feel of a solid, upscale hotel room, not a family B&B; they are decorated in cool, muted shades with Berber carpet and light flooding in through big windows. The bathrooms have large shower stalls. Beds can be configured as two twins or as one king. Two front rooms have their own balconies and cost $20 more; the two back rooms have access to a shared balcony. All four rooms are up a flight of stairs.

4702 Lake Spenard Dr., Anchorage, AK 99509. ⓒ **866/663-9322** or 907/258-9321. www.lakehoodinn.com. 4 units. $139–$159 double. Extra person 17 or over $20. Rates include free continental breakfast. MC, V. **Amenities:** Coin-op laundry; guest kitchen; fish freezing. *In room:* TV/VCR, high-speed Internet, fridge, coffeemaker, hair dryer, safe.

Parkwood Inn *Value*   Families seeking to save money will find large units similar to apartments, with full kitchens, at rates competitive with those of a basic hotel. The two-bedroom suites are big enough for a large group. They were in the process of putting in new carpet throughout when I visited in 2006, but the units are still worn around the edges and somewhat dark. The management is hospitable and works hard on the place. The location, at the intersection of two large arterials—New Seward Highway and Tudor Road—is busy and noisy, but extensive landscaping shields the inn. There's an Internet-connected computer for free guest use in the lobby and wireless Internet in some rooms.

4445 Juneau St., Anchorage, AK 99503. ⓒ **800/478-3590** or 907/563-3590. Fax 907/563-5560. www.parkwood inn.net. 48 units. High season $139–$149 double (extra person 13 or over $10), $220 suite (for any number of guests); low season $69–$79 double, $120 suite. Rates include free continental breakfast during summer. AE, DC, DISC, MC, V. **Amenities:** Internet, coin-op laundry; fish freezing. *In room:* TV, Wi-Fi (in some), kitchen.

A HOSTEL

Spenard Hostel International, 2845 W. 42nd Ave. (ⓒ **907/248-5036;** www.alaska hostel.org), is a friendly place near the airport, with free phones, inexpensive bike rental, storage, Internet access, and laundry machines. It feels more like communal housing than an impersonal hostel. There are three lounges for different activities and three kitchens. The owner has installed heat exchangers in the bedrooms to keep the air fresh. You can come and go 24 hours a day. The office is open daily 9am to 1pm and 7 to 11pm in summer, 7 to 11pm winter. Beds are $21 by cash or check, a dollar more if you use a credit card (Amex, Discover, MasterCard, or Visa).

⟮Tips⟯ Rooms near the Airport

Good, inexpensive standard motel rooms near the airport are rare to the vanishing point, although upscale rooms and B&Bs are readily available. The prize winner in my search for reasonably priced hotel rooms with consistently high quality is the **Lakeshore Motor Inn** (© 800/770-3000 or 907/248-3485; www.lakeshoremotorinn.com). The rate of $139 a night double, at peak season, includes a continental breakfast, Wi-Fi, and use of a 24-hour courtesy van. The hospitality is warm and the rooms are inviting, despite the older concrete building. If you enjoy staying with a family, **Elderberry Bed and Breakfast** (© 907/243-6968; www.elderberrybb.com) has three rooms with private bathrooms for $85 to $95 double. The hosts enjoy socializing, telling about their Alaska experiences, and orienting guests who have just arrived from the airport. I also recommend **Lake Hood Inn** (p. 219). Two good chain hotels stand near the airport, with higher rates: **Courtyard by Marriott** (© 800/314-0782 reservations or 907/245-0322; http://courtyard.com/ANCCY), with many amenities and a pool, at $179 double in summer; and the **Holiday Inn Express** (© 800/465-4329 or 907/248-8848; www.hiexpress.com), at $109 to $199 (normally nearer the high end of that range in the summer). A large, full-service hotel stands lakeside near the airport, **Millennium Alaskan Hotel Anchorage** (© 800/544-0553 or 907/243-2300; www.millenniumhotels.com). It might be a huge fishing and hunting lodge judging by the large lobby, with its warm colors and fly rods and animal mounts on display, but the rooms, on long corridors in a wooden building, are loaded with comfort and amenities. The hotel has two restaurants and offers many services. High-season rates are $239 to $285 double.

CAMPING

Anchorage is a big city, but you can find natural camping right on the urban outskirts. The municipally owned **Centennial Park** is on Boundary Road at the Muldoon Road exit from the Glenn Highway (© 907/343-6986, or 907/343-4136 off season; www.muni.org/parks/camping.cfm), just as you enter town from the north. Although it is near Muldoon's run-down commercial strip, many of the 88 sites are nicely wooded. The campground has hot showers and is suitable for tents and RVs. Sites are $20, and use of the dump station $5.

There are several RV parks within the Anchorage bowl, of which the best is the wooded and landscaped **Anchorage RV Park,** 1200 N. Muldoon Rd. (© 800/400-7275 or 907/338-7275; www.anchoragervpark.com), near Centennial Park and the Alaska Native Heritage Center. It has full services and excellent facilities, including instant phone hookups and Wi-Fi. Each of the 195 sites costs $32 to $41 per night. Reserve ahead. They don't take tenters.

The two closest state park campgrounds to Anchorage are at Bird Creek, to the south of town, and Eagle River, just to the north. The **Bird Creek Campground** is one of my favorites. It sits next to Turnagain Arm and the salmon-filled creek. A paved pathway passes by under the large spruce trees. There are 28 sites, and the fee is $15 per night. From Anchorage, drive 25 miles south on the Seward Highway to milepost 101.

The 57-site **Eagle River Campground** sits in a thickly wooded riverside spot, and it's well developed with paved roads and large sites with lots of privacy. It costs $15 a night, and sites can be reserved in advance. Book up to a year ahead at © **800/952-8624** or 907/694-7982 (www.lifetimeadventures.net). The hosts also book rafting on the Eagle River. Take the Glenn Highway 12 miles north from Anchorage and exit at Hiland Road.

3 Where to Dine
DOWNTOWN
EXPENSIVE

The Bridge ✹✹ POLYNESIAN/FUSION   The dining room was built upon a former roadway bridge over the water of Ship Creek, a short but steep downhill walk from downtown, but as I sat amid the warm colors of the sensually soothing dining room, the universe quickly narrowed to our one table and I forgot I was on a bridge. The restaurant was conceived by a partner who was born in Sri Lanka and lived years in Hawaii, and the cuisine brings new fusions of flavors to Anchorage fine dining; you can get a good steak, or a Middle Eastern lamb dish, or Alaska seafood or meat with southern Pacific influences—for example, as appetizers, a crab and mango summer roll, or tiki-grilled pork ribs, or, as a main course, citrus-marinated halibut with lemon grass and ginger. Our meals within the restaurant's first year were interesting and tasty, if not flawless. Service was excellent. Altogether, it's among the most pleasant places to dine in Anchorage.

221 W. Ship Creek Rd. © **907/677-6771.** www.thebridgesalmonbakeandgrill.com. Reservations recommended. Lunch $7.50–$14, dinner main courses $18–$30. AE, DISC, MC, V. Summer Sun–Thus 11am–9pm, Fri–Sat 11am–10pm, limited service daily 2–5pm; winter Tues 11am–9pm, Wed–Fri 11am–10pm, Sat 5–10pm, limited service daily 2–5pm.

Club Paris ✹✹ STEAK/SEAFOOD   Coming from a bright spring afternoon into midnight darkness, under a neon Eiffel Tower and past the bar, I sat down at a secretive booth for two and felt as if I should lean across the table and plot a shady 1950s oil deal with my companion. And I would probably not have been the first. In contrast to Sullivan's Steakhouse across the street, which contrives a masculine, retro feel, Club Paris is the real thing, decorated with mounted swordfish and other cocktail-era decor. The club is the essence of old Anchorage boomtown years, when the streets were dusty and an oil man needed a classy joint in which to do business. Steak, of course, is what to order, and *rare* really means "rare." It's consistently voted the best in town. Ask for the bleu cheese stuffing; the stuffed filet is worth the years it probably takes off your coronary arteries. They have a full bar.

417 W. 5th Ave. © **907/277-6332.** www.clubparisrestaurant.com. Reservations recommended. Lunch $5.75–$15; dinner $14–$44. AE, DC, DISC, MC, V. Mon–Sat 11:30am–2:30pm and 5–11pm; Sun 5–10pm.

The Marx Brothers Cafe ✹✹✹ ECLECTIC/REGIONAL   A restaurant started by three friends back when gourmet food was an exotic hobby in Anchorage is now a standard of excellence in the state. Treatments of Alaska seafood that began here as cutting-edge creative cuisine now turn up in many of the best restaurants, yet Chef Jack Amon's signature macadamia nut–encrusted halibut is nowhere done better. He still presides in the kitchen of the cottage downtown, one of the city's first houses, while maitre d' Van Hale manages the front, preparing his famous Caesar salad at tableside, a ritual that allows him to schmooze with anyone he chooses in the tiny dining rooms. His attitude mirrors the casual elegance of the entire evening, where those wearing ties are in the minority. The cuisine is creative, ranging from Asian to Italian, and always turned out flawlessly. The changing menu is not long, but the wine list is the size of a dictionary. With plenty of bottles over $1,000, it has won many awards, but the novice may find it intimidating. A meal is an experience that takes much of the evening, and most entrees are over $30. Save room for the exceptional desserts.

627 W. 3rd Ave. (℃) 907/278-2133. www.marxcafe.com. Reservations required. Main courses $18–$36. AE, DC, MC, V. Summer Tues–Sat 5:30–10pm; winter Tues–Thurs 6–9:30pm, Fri–Sat 5:30–10pm.

Orso ★★ ITALIAN/MEDITERRANEAN   This restaurant is unique in Anchorage for serving interesting food even though it is large and oriented to the downtown tourist trade. The ornate dining room is lightened with big modern paintings, and the cuisine is amped up with bold flavors and a long menu full of surprises. The mushroom ravioli, with a generous dose of smoked salmon, was rich and strongly flavored. The rice that came with my nicely seared scallops had to be passed around and started a conversation—I'm still not sure exactly what made it taste so good. The antipasto plate looked great and was generously endowed. Service is professional but not stuffy, and the food comes fast enough not to use up the entire evening. Generally, the prices are reasonable for this kind of food, but to save money, dine in the still somewhat grandiose bar.

737 W. 5th Ave. (℃) 907/222-3232. www.orsoalaska.com. Reservations recommended. Lunch $10–$15; dinner pasta or main course $12–$33. AE, DISC, MC, V. Summer Mon–Fri 11:30am–4pm and 5–11pm, Sat–Sun 5–11pm; winter Sun 5–9:30pm, Mon–Tues 11:30am–2:30pm and 5–9:30pm, Wed–Thurs 11:30am–2:30pm and 5–10pm, Fri 11:30am–2:30pm and 5–11pm, Sat 5–11pm.

Sacks Cafe ★★★ CREATIVE/ECLECTIC   This is the most fashionable restaurant in town and also one of the best. The storefront dining room, in warm Southwest colors and sharp angles, resembles a showcase for the food and diners, who can sit at tables or at the tapas bar. The cuisine defies categorization but is consistently interesting and creative, frequently with Thai influences. The menu changes, but one consistent offering was chicken with scallops, shiitake mushrooms, snow peas, udon noodles, ginger cream sauce, and black bean salsa. Vegetarians do as well as meat eaters. For lunch, the sandwiches are unforgettable, with choices such as shrimp and avocado with herb cream cheese on sourdough. Do not fail to try the tomato soup with gorgonzola. The beer and wine list is extensive and reasonably priced. They serve brunch Saturday and Sunday until 3pm.

(Finds) The Best Takeout in Town

Anchorage has great takeout food (as my family's continued survival attests). Downtown, **The Muffin Man,** at 817 W. 6th Ave. ((℃) **907/279-6836**), produces some of the best meals eaten at desks in Anchorage, including the memorably delicious smoked red salmon and cream cheese sandwich. You can eat in the sunny, tiled dining room, too. The best, most original burgers are at **Arctic Roadrunner,** with locations on Arctic Boulevard at Fireweed Lane and on Old Seward Highway at International Airport Road. Try the Kodiak Islander, which has peppers, ham, onion rings, and God knows what else on top. We get carry-out Chinese from **New Sagaya's City Market** ((℃) **907/274-6173**; www.newsagaya.com), at the corner of 13th and I streets. It's also a wonderful gourmet grocery and community meeting place, and has a good deli and Italian-style brick-oven pizza. Pack a picnic here, or eat in the enclosed or sidewalk dining areas.

328 G St. ℂ 907/274-4022. www.sackscafe.com. Reservations recommended. Lunch $5–$15; dinner main courses $18–$34. AE, MC, V. Mon–Fri 11am–2:30pm and 5–9:30pm (till 10:30pm Fri); Sat 11am–3pm, 5–10:30pm; Sunday 10:30am–3pm and 5–9:30pm.

Simon and Seafort's Saloon and Grill 🦀🦀 STEAK/SEAFOOD   Simon's, as it's known, is a jolly beef and seafood grill where voices boom off the high ceilings. On sunny summer evenings, the rooms, fitted with brass turn-of-the-20th-century saloon decor, fill with light off Cook Inlet, down below the bluff; the views are magnificent. The food is consistently good. A long list of nightly specials includes items as exotic as a tasty crab- and macadamia-stuffed halibut, but most of the cuisine is simpler. The service, too, stands out: warm and professional, and quick enough to allow time for other evening activities. Children are treated well. To enjoy the place on a budget, order a sandwich and soup for lunch in the well-stocked bar. Getting a table requires advance planning in peak season or on off-season weekends.

420 L St. ℂ 907/274-3502. Reservations recommended (make dinner reservations a couple of days in advance in summer). Lunch $9–$20; dinner main courses $18–$42. AE, MC, V. Summer Mon–Fri 11am–2:30pm and 4–10pm, Sat–Sun 4–10pm; winter Mon–Fri 11am–2:30pm and 5–10pm, Sat–Sun 5–10pm.

MODERATE

Cafe Savannah 🦀🦀 SPANISH   Right across from town square, this storefront restaurant is stylish and relaxing, and serves interesting and delightful food. The specialty is tapas, and a popular way to dine is to order many plates and share them. Selections, for $5, include items such as *hongo relleno con chorizo* (stuffed portobello mushroom caps with Spanish spicy sausage and manchego cheese) or *pinchos morunos* (grilled pork kabobs in cilantro marinade). I learned a lot eating here! The dining room has high tables and a bar decorated with colored stones and bent flatware under a hard, clear surface. Monthly art shows hang on the walls. Don't choose to dine here if you're in a rush or if you're looking for warm Alaskan hospitality; although I enjoyed the waiter's classy attitude, we didn't become buddies.

508 W. 6th Ave. ℂ 907/646-9121. All items $4–$20. MC, V. Mon–Thurs 11am–3pm and 5–10pm, Fri–Sat 11am–3pm and 5pm–midnight.

Glacier Brewhouse 🦀 GRILL/SEAFOOD/PIZZA   An eclectic and ever-changing menu is served in a large dining room with lodge decor, where the pleasant scent of the wood-fired grill hangs in the air. It's a lively place to see others and be seen. There are lots of agreeable, if trendy, touches: the glass wall showing off the brewing equipment, which produces eight or more hearty beers, and also turns out spent grain for bread that's then set out on the tables with olive oil. An advantage for travelers is the wide price range—a pizza with feta cheese, sun-dried tomatoes, pesto, and garlic is $10; crab legs are $37. The food is usually quite good. Choose this place for a boisterous meal with quick, casual service that will get you out in time to do something else with the evening. Do reserve ahead, however, as waits can be long.

737 W. 5th Ave. ℂ 907/274-BREW. www.glacierbrewhouse.com. Reservations recommended for dinner. Lunch $8–$15; dinner $9–$34. AE, DC, DISC, MC, V. Summer daily 11am–11pm; winter Mon 11am–9:30pm, Tues–Thurs 11am–10pm, Fri–Sat 11am–11pm, Sun 4–9:30pm.

Kumagoro 🦀 JAPANESE   Anchorage has several good, authentic Japanese restaurants, but this one, right on the main tourist street downtown, has the most convenient location. Among my favorite lunches anywhere is their box lunch ($15), a large sampler of many dishes, including sushi, sashimi, and other tasty things, always a little

Coffeehouses

There are coffeehouses all over the city, where people go for a cup of java and a pastry, and to meet people and engage in conversation. My favorite is **Side Street Espresso,** on G Street between 4th and 5th, a gathering place for artists, activists, and anyone who wants to trade ideas, sometimes with live acoustic music in the evening. **Cafe del Mundo,** at Northern Lights and Denali midtown, gathers an older crowd of businesspeople, yuppies, stay-at-home parents, and those looking for a comfortable meeting spot. **Kaladi Brothers,** in the shopping center on Northern Lights Boulevard between Arctic and Minnesota, is a busy place sharing space with a huge used book store and just down from the essential REI sporting goods store; it has computers with Internet access.

different, that I can't always identify. The dining room is pleasantly low key, with tables in rows, so you may have the opportunity to meet those seated next to you. The restaurant has a beer and wine license.

533 W. 4th Ave. ✆ **907/272-9905.** Lunch $7–$15; dinner main courses $14–$39. AE, DC, DISC, MC, V. Summer daily 11am–10:45pm; winter daily 11am–9:45pm.

INEXPENSIVE

Dianne's Restaurant ⒱ⓐⓛⓤⓔ SOUP/SANDWICH   This is my first choice for a quick, healthful, inexpensive lunch downtown. Located off the lobby of a tall, glass office building, Dianne's cafeteria line fills with well-dressed folk seeking the hearty freshly baked bread, soups, sandwiches, and specials turned out for the lunch hour. The atmosphere is bright and casual, and you don't waste your day eating. The restaurant does not have a liquor license.

550 W. 7th Ave., Suite 110. ✆ **907/279-7243.** Main courses $4.25–$9. AE, DISC, MC, V. Mon–Fri 7am–4pm.

Downtown Deli and Cafe DELI   When the restaurant was started by a pair of young politicians in the 1970s, the idea of a kosher deli in Anchorage that sold the Sunday *New York Times* was just this side of bizarre. As their careers rose—one became governor and the other helped create Alaska's Permanent Fund—the restaurant became a local institution and political hot spot. In 1994, President Clinton came for dinner. The restaurant that exists today, however, is less interesting than its history. The look is outdated and the food similar to what you would find in a hotel cafe. The restaurant does have convenience for tourists, who are the primary clientele: a handy location with reasonable prices (especially at dinnertime, when downtown is short on inexpensive sit-down places), and kids are treated well. They serve beer and wine.

525 W. 4th Ave. ✆ **907/276-7116.** All items $6.25–$15. AE, DC, DISC, MC, V. Summer daily 6am–10pm; winter Mon–Sat 7am–4pm, Sun 9am–4pm.

Snow City Cafe ⓕ VEGETARIAN/HOME STYLE   This is a meeting place for a young, environmentally conscious crowd, a great place for breakfast, and a handy hangout with your laptop, as they offer free Wi-Fi. The newly expanded and remodeled dining room is light and colorful and gives the restaurant a clean, modern feel, with lots of space. The food, served by a friendly staff, is laced with interesting flavors and styles of preparation, including many vegetarian dishes. For lunch, the sandwiches are filling and varied, but breakfast is the main event, a repeated winner of newspaper polls. On weekend mornings, the cafe fills with people for eggs Benedict, salmon cakes, homemade granola, and such, which are served all day. They're open Wednesday nights for an Irish music jam. Small monthly art shows begin with artist receptions every first Friday, a pattern shared with all the downtown galleries. They serve beer and wine.

1034 W. 4th Ave. ⓒ **907/272-CITY.** www.snowcitycafe.com. Breakfast and lunch $5–$10. AE, DISC, MC, V. Daily 7am–4pm (espresso counter only after 3pm on weekdays).

BEYOND DOWNTOWN
EXPENSIVE
Jens' Restaurant ⭐⭐⭐ INTERNATIONAL   Chef Jens Hansen is truly gifted. His restaurant is for the kind of diner who loves exciting food, surprises, and beautiful plates of new tastes and textures; the meals are about the food, sharing bites, and saying "Wow," and "How did he do that?" The cuisine is highly eclectic, but I won't call it experimental, despite the raw kangaroo I tried on one visit, because these dishes work far more often than any experimentalist has a right to expect. There's often only one item on the changing menu that isn't unusual or challenging: the superb pepper steak. Like everything, even that dish has a sauce, and it is complex and memorable. The wine list is exceptional but manageable and reasonably priced, and you can sip your selection while dining inexpensively on appetizers in a pleasant bar area; try the incredible spinach ravioli with Gorgonzola, for example. Desserts are sublime. The dining room is light and clean, decorated with modern art. Service is highly professional, with each formally attired waiter assigned to just a few tables, and they earn their keep as well by helping diners learn about food and wine they have probably never tried.

701 W. 36th Ave. ⓒ **907/561-5367.** www.jensrestaurant.com. Reservations recommended. Lunch $9–$25; dinner main courses $18–$37. AE, DC, DISC, MC, V. Mon–Fri 11:30am–2pm; Tues–Sat 6–10pm; wine bar serves appetizers starting at 4pm. Closed Jan.

MODERATE
Bear Tooth Grill ⭐ (Value) SOUTHWESTERN   You can't find food of this quality for prices this low anywhere else in Anchorage. Dishes such as the soy-grilled halibut are sophisticated and nicely done, but take up only a small part of a menu that goes on and on with Mexican choices, sandwiches, and other selections inexpensive enough to make the restaurant fit for an after-work impulse—most main courses are under $11. The partners who own the restaurant started in business by making beer and then opened a pizzeria to sell the beer (see the Moose's Tooth, below); next they opened a theater-pub (see "Anchorage Nightlife," later); the grill, in the same building, was the final addition. Eat tacos and wraps watching a movie or in the movie theater lobby, a loud, free-flowing setting good for kids. The grill is in a separate, calmer, and more confined dining room, best for couples and parties of four or less. The food comes more slowly, as befits the atmosphere. Tables are more comfortable than booths, but at peak times you have to take what you can get, often with a wait, so try to dine here early or late. Besides the beer, they have a full bar serving many margaritas and 20 wines by the glass.

1230 W. 27th Ave. ⓒ **907/276-4200.** Reservations not accepted. All items $6–$20. AE, DC, DISC, MC, V. Summer Sun–Thurs 4–11:30pm, Fri–Sat 4pm–midnight; winter Sun–Thurs 4–11pm, Fri–Sat 4–11:30pm.

Campobello Bistro ⭐⭐ NORTHERN ITALIAN/BISTRO   This quiet little midtown restaurant is amazingly like stepping into northern Italy, except for the Alaska seafood. Even the service has the quality of jocular professionalism I remember from Italy. The same priceless pair of waiters has developed a following for almost a decade.

Unlike most of Anchorage's best restaurants, the bistro doesn't try to reinvent the cookbook. Most of the menu consists of recognizable dishes, such as veal Marsala or Italian sausage and polenta. Meals are bold, highly flavored, and entirely satisfying. The seafood crepe is fantastic. Those seeking the bland tomatoes and cheese of a typical Italian family restaurant should go elsewhere (Sorrento's and Romano's, both on Fireweed Lane, each do that tried-and-true formula well). The wine and food are reasonably priced.

601 W. 36th, Suite 10. ✆ **907/563-2040.** Lunch $10–$13; dinner main courses $15–$25. DC, MC, V. Mon–Fri 11am–2:30pm, 5–9pm; Sat 5–9pm.

The Greek Corner ✦ GREEK/ITALIAN   When we need a relaxed place for a three-generation family meal, this place always seems to come to the top of the list. The exterior is not promising and the small, well-lit dining room is decorated with travel posters and has a homemade look, but somehow that just makes the restaurant feel more real and the warm hospitality of the service even more sincere. Sometimes it's as if you've been adopted by the wait staff, and the food comes fast. I usually order the lamb chops, which are tender and seasoned and cooked just right, and come with perfectly prepared asparagus and baby potatoes. A dozen authentic traditional Greek dishes are on the menu, mostly priced around $15, or you can order from a list of old Italian favorites such as spaghetti or lasagna. They serve pizza, too, and reasonably priced lunches—a gyro with soup or salad is $9.

302 W. Fireweed Ln. ✆ **907/276-2820.** Lunch $5.50–$10; dinner main courses $10–$20. MC, V. Mon–Fri 11am–10pm, Sat noon–10pm, Sun 4–10pm.

Noble's Diner ✦✦ *Finds* SOUTHERN/LOCAL   This unique restaurant reflects its young chef/owner's personality, life story, and hopes for the community as clearly as a painting on the wall of a museum. Rob Kinneen grew up in this depressed Mountain View neighborhood and took his first job washing dishes at a Mexican restaurant in this very building; after more restaurant jobs, he attended the Culinary Institute of America and cooked at some of the nation's most famous restaurants as well as the snootiest places in Anchorage. Finally, he and his wife, Carolyn, started the diner to contribute to a community revitalization project and to bring Rob's expert skills to comfort food with southern influences as well as local seafood and produce prepared simply to reflect its best qualities. You can order an elaborate seafood special or a toasted cheese sandwich. They want neighborhood people to be comfortable and able to afford the food, so the atmosphere is down-market—vinyl booths, linoleum, even a lunch counter—with prices to match. The result is an extremely casual dining experience with pitch-perfect food that, while not always exciting, reflects the Kinneen's goal of "straight-forward quality." The wine list is full of interesting selections and is reasonably priced; desserts are terrific.

4133 Mountain View Dr. ✆ **907/770-3811.** www.noblesdiner.com. Lunch $4–$13; dinner $4–$15. AE, MC, V. Summer Mon–Thus 11am–9:30pm, Fri–Sat 11am–10pm; winter Mon 11am–3pm, Tues–Sat 11am–9pm.

INEXPENSIVE

The Lucky Wishbone ✦ *Finds* DINER   This Anchorage institution of half a century (in high school we called it "The Bone") is where the real pioneer Alaska meets families out for a delicious, not-too-greasy fried chicken dinner and famous milkshakes (try the hot fudge) and other delights from the fountain. It is our children's favorite. One section of the counter is reserved for discussion of aviation and golf. When the beloved owners outlawed smoking years ago, it made the front page of the newspaper. You'll see few other tourists, as the location, among the car dealerships at the extreme east end of downtown, is too far to walk to from the hotels, but I ran into Alaska's powerful senior U.S. senator, Ted Stevens. They have a drive-in.

1033 E. 5th Ave. ℭ **907/272-3454.** All items $3–$9.25. MC, V. Summer Mon–Thurs 10am–10pm, Fri–Sat 10am–11pm; winter Mon–Sat 10am–10pm.

The Moose's Tooth Pub and Pizzeria ⭐⭐ (Kids PIZZA   The best pizza and beer in Anchorage undoubtedly come from this fun and friendly place. The microbrewery came first, but the pizza really is the greater accomplishment. It has a soft, light crust like Italian pizza but the oomph of American pizza. They offer many ingenious toppings, but not just to dump on: The combinations really work. The ambience is youthful, casual, and loud; the high energy means kids aren't out of place. The dining room, although handsomely rebuilt, still looks from top to bottom like a college town pizzeria. The only drawback is the restaurant's popularity, which can make for long waits at peak times.

3300 Old Seward Hwy. ℭ **907/258-2537.** www.moosestooth.net. Large pizza $13–$25. AE, DC, DISC, MC, V. Summer Sun noon–midnight, Mon–Thurs 11am–midnight, Fri–Sat 11am–1am; winter Sun noon–11pm, Mon 11am–11pm, Tues–Thurs 11am–midnight, Fri–Sat 11am–1am.

4 What to See & Do

I've arranged this section starting with a self-guided walking tour through downtown Anchorage, followed by details on the downtown museums and then attractions that are farther afield.

The best **guided tour** of the historic downtown area is by **Anchorage Historic Properties,** 645 W. 3rd Ave. (ℭ **907/274-3600**), a preservation group, offering 2-hour, 2-mile walks from June to August Monday through Friday at 1pm. Meet at the lobby of Old City Hall, 524 W. 4th Ave., next door to the Log Cabin Visitor Information Center. Tickets cost $5 for adults, $1 for children.

Motorized city tours can get you beyond downtown to see what more of the town looks like. **Anchorage Trolley Tours** (ℭ 907/276-5603) offers a 1-hour ride for $10 in a bus made up like a trolley car, taking in the downtown area, a Cook Inlet overlook near the airport, and the Lake Hood seaplane base. The operator has a fun outlook. Catch the trolley on 4th Avenue between F and G streets, across from the Alaska Public Land Information Center. For something in greater depth, **Gray Line of Alaska's** Anchorage Highlights Tour (ℭ **800/544-2206;** www.graylineofalaska.com) offers a 3-hour tour with a visit to the Ship Creek area below downtown and the Alaska Native Heritage Center. It spends an hour at the center, not as long as I like to stay. The tour costs $47 for adults, half-price ages 12 and under, including admission to the center.

Tips **Helper Bees**

The people you see downtown on bikes and on foot in bright yellow-and-black outfits are the **Anchorage Downtown Partnership Security Ambassadors,** sometimes known as the "bumblebees" for their color scheme. They are funded by a self-imposed levy on downtown property owners in part to help visitors. Stop one to ask a question or report a problem, or call ℭ **907/277-7233** (www.anchoragedowntown.org).

WALKING TOUR   DOWNTOWN ANCHORAGE

Start & Finish: 4th Avenue and F Street.
Time: 2 hours (use the shortcuts noted for a briefer tour).

Start at the **Log Cabin Visitor Information Center** at 4th Avenue and F Street. Outside is a sign that shows the distance to various cities and a 5,114-pound jade boulder put on display by Stewart's Photo Shop, an Anchorage institution that is just across the street.

Walk east, toward the mountains, to:
❶ Old City Hall (1936)

The building is on the right of 4th Avenue as you approach E Street. The lobby contains a fun and illuminating free display on city history, including dioramas of the early streetscape, old photographs, and the fire bell and fire pole that once were used in this building.

Crossing E Street, notice on the left side of 4th Avenue that all the buildings are modern—everything on that side from E Street east for several blocks collapsed in the 1964 earthquake. The street split in half, lengthwise, with the left side ending up a dozen feet lower than the right. That land was later reinforced with a gravel buttress by the U.S. Army Corps of Engineers, and the slope below forever set aside as open space because of the earthquake risk. This stretch of 4th Avenue is where the **Iditarod Trail Sled Dog Race** and the **Anchorage Fur Rendezvous World Championship Sled Dog Race** start each year in March and February, respectively.

Continue walking east. At 4th Avenue and D Street is the:
❷ Wendler Building (1915)

The old Club 25 is among the oldest buildings in Anchorage. The bronze statue of the dog commemorates the sled-dog races that start here. Across D Street is a mural that depicts a map of coastal Alaska and British Columbia, with the Iditarod Trail dimly marked.

Cross 4th Avenue to the north side to see:

❸ Ship Creek Center

The brown building on the north side of 4th calls itself a "Made in Alaska mall." It's a good place to shop for Alaska Native crafts: Among several shops is one representing the Alaska Native Heritage Center (p. 234), and Native artists sometimes carve or otherwise demonstrate their work in the indoor common area. You can sometimes catch free cultural performances here as well. On the eastern end, take in large, interesting graphics about the 1964 earthquake.

The Rusty Harpoon (p. 244) is a good craft and gift shop in the yellow building next door.

Cross back to the south side of 4th and walk a block south on D Street to see:
❹ The Culture of D Street

This 1-block street contains two of the city's most interesting cultural outlets. First on the left, at 4th and D, is **Cyrano's Off-Center Playhouse** (✆ 907/274-2599; www.cyranos.org), home of its own theater company. They really are good; the tiny theater can cause quite a stir in town and has won many awards. They also have poetry readings and the like, and you can stop in the cozy little cafe for a glass of wine or beer on performance days. Tickets are sold through **CenterTix** (✆ 907/263-ARTS; www.centertix.net). A little farther on the left, the **International Gallery of Contemporary Art** (www.igcaalaska.org) is the community's nonprofit forum for the art that is happening right now. Typically, the gallery is

Downtown Anchorage Walking Tour

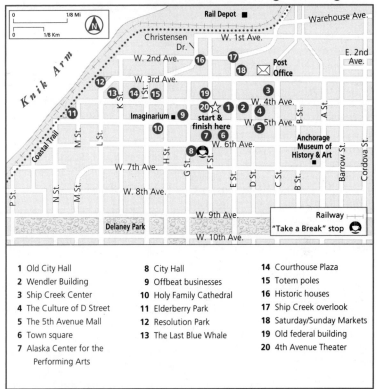

1 Old City Hall

2 Wendler Building

3 Ship Creek Center

4 The Culture of D Street

5 The 5th Avenue Mall

6 Town square

7 Alaska Center for the Performing Arts

8 City Hall

9 Offbeat businesses

10 Holy Family Cathedral

11 Elderberry Park

12 Resolution Park

13 The Last Blue Whale

14 Courthouse Plaza

15 Totem poles

16 Historic houses

17 Ship Creek overlook

18 Saturday/Sunday Markets

19 Old federal building

20 4th Avenue Theater

given over to a single artist or theme. Hours are on p. 245.

Cross 5th Avenue at the end of D Street and enter:

❺ The 5th Avenue Mall

This grand, four-story shopping center is Alaska's fanciest mall, with Nordstrom and JCPenney as its anchor stores. A large, airy food court is on the top floor. Take a look, or walk straight through to the doors on the opposite side. (Just a block east are the Anchorage Museum of History and Art and the Alaska State Troopers Museum, described below.)

Cross the mall to the doors opposite, exiting onto 6th Avenue. Turn right, walk a block, and cross E Street to:

❻ Town Square

The community raised money for improvements to the square by collecting donations of $40 each for the granite bricks, with an inscription of the contributor's choosing. There are 13,344 (bet you can't find mine). On the east side of the square, behind you, the huge whale mural was painted freehand by Wyland in 1994. He painted similar whale murals in cities all along the West Coast. The building on the northeast corner of the square is one of the city's oldest and was saved from demolition when the park was created; it contains a charming gift and candy shop owned by the mayor's wife.

On the west side of the square is the massive, highly decorated:

❼ Alaska Center for the Performing Arts

The center was completed in 1988 amid controversy about its design, among other things—it's either clever and bold or garish and busy. You decide. The lobby is usually open, and whatever your opinion of the decor, a look inside will spark a discussion. Alaskans have gotten used to it, and now we think of the building mostly as a focal point of our cultural life. Tours are held Wednesday at 1pm; a $1 donation is requested (reach the center's administrative offices at © **907/263-2900;** www.alaskapac.org). Thespians believe the building is haunted by the ghost of painter Sydney Laurence, who makes lighting mysteriously vary and elevators go up and down with no one in them. An auditorium demolished to make room for the center was named for Laurence. Check the box office for current performances in the three theaters and rehearsal hall, Alaska's premier performance venues (and see "The Performing Arts," later).

TAKE A BREAK

From the performing arts center, cross 6th Avenue at the F Street light and turn right (west) to **Humpy's** (© **907/276-2337**) a popular tavern on the south side of 6th with a huge selection of microbrews, live music, and good casual meals, including halibut tacos.

The square green office building next door to Humpy's is:

❽ City Hall

Turn left through the pedestrian walkway between Humpy's and City Hall. A large mural showing a timeline of the history of Anchorage faces the parking lot. An artistically superior mural, by Duke Russell, is on the wall in Humpy's outdoor seating area on the near side of the parking lot.

Walk west through the city hall parking lot to G Street, turn right, and proceed north to 5th Avenue. G Street between 4th and 5th avenues contains some of the downtown's best:

❾ Offbeat Businesses

First comes **Aurora Fine Arts,** an attractively cluttered arts and craft shop with plenty to see. Next are: **Darwin's Theory,** a friendly, old-fashioned bar with character that shows up in an Indigo Girls song ("Cut It Out" from the album *Shaming of the Sun*); **Suzi's Woollies** (www.suzis woollies.com), a Celtic shop carrying imported sweaters, jewelry, and CDs, and with live Irish music Saturday afternoons; **Tracy Anna Bader Design Studio,** a studio and shop of bright, graphic, wearable art; and **Side Street Espresso,** where you can get into a lively discussion on art or politics and make contact with thinking people. On the opposite side of the street, at 423 G St., the light-filled storefront of the **Alaska Glass Gallery** (www.alaska glassgallery.com) shows fanciful and dramatic glass sculptures by owner Cynthia England and by other artists from all over the United States.

Shortcut: You can cut an hour off the tour here by continuing north on G Street to 4th, then turning right, and walking 1 block to the starting point at F Street.

Backtrack to 5th and G, and then proceed west (away from the mountains) on 5th. The Imaginarium, described under "Downtown Museums," below, is on the right. Continuing west on 5th Avenue and crossing H Street, you'll see the:

❿ Holy Family Cathedral

This concrete Art Deco church is the seat of the Roman Catholic archbishop. The interior is unremarkable.

Keep going toward the water, crossing L Street and going down the hill to:

⓫ Elderberry Park

The yellow-and-brown house in the park is **The Oscar Anderson House Museum,** described under "Downtown Museums," below. Besides the good playground equipment, the park offers the easiest access point to the **Tony Knowles Coastal Trail** (see "Walking & Biking," later). The trail tunnels under the Alaska Railroad tracks from the bottom of the park.

Now hike back up the hill to L Street and turn left. At 3rd Avenue is:

⑫ Resolution Park

The bronze **Captain Cook Monument** stands on a large wooden deck, but he's gazing out to sea—the opposite of the way he was facing when he explored Cook Inlet in 1778 aboard HMS *Resolution*. Cook didn't personally come as far as Anchorage, instead sending a boat with his ship's master, William Bligh (later the Captain Bligh who inspired mutiny aboard the HMS *Bounty*). Failing to find the Northwest Passage here, Cook considered his 2 weeks in Cook Inlet a waste of time, grousing in his journal, "Nothing but a trifling point in geography has been determined." The park's informative signs, powerful mounted binoculars, and commanding vantage point make this a rewarding stop for gazing out at the water and the mountains beyond. The waters you see are ferocious and wild, with whirlpool currents and a tidal range of almost 40 vertical feet. The shore across the inlet, about 2 miles away, is virtually uninhabited.

Follow 3rd Avenue east (back toward the mountains) 1 block and turn right on K Street. On the right is:

⑬ The Last Blue Whale

Joseph Princiotti's huge 1973 bronze of combat between a whale and whalers in small boats shows the whale's point of view.

Cross K Street to walk through the:

⑭ Courthouse Plaza

The plaza frames the **Nesbett State Courthouse;** the sinuous shapes of the plaza's concrete walkways are supposed to suggest both the flow of people through the court system and a braided glacial river. The metal *Grizzly Bear and Cub*, by

Homer sculptor Mike Sirl, was installed in 2004; local and state law require projects to construct public buildings to set aside 1% of their budget for art, and this work is one result.

Cross the plaza to 4th Avenue, cross I Street, and take a look at the two:

⑮ Totem Poles

Carved of red cedar by Lee Wallace, of Ketchikan, and erected in 1997, they represent the eagle and raven moieties of the Tlingit people, intended to symbolize the balance of justice. A Tlingit creation story tells how raven stole the moon and stars and brought them to mankind; here, the moon and stars are the stars of the Alaska flag.

Walk around past the courthouse on 4th Avenue and turn left onto H Street. Follow H as it crosses 3rd Avenue and becomes Christensen Drive. Descend the hill on Christensen and turn right on 2nd Avenue, toward the mountains. Look around at the:

⑯ Historic Houses

The old wooden houses along 2nd are mostly attorneys' offices now, but once this was one of the better residential areas in town. Several houses are marked and a kiosk at 2nd and F relates some town history. If you imagine houses like this over much of downtown, you'll know what Anchorage looked like before oil.

Continue east on 2nd Avenue to E Street, where you will find:

⑰ A Ship Creek Overlook with a Monument to President Eisenhower

The bust commemorates Alaska's 1959 admission to the Union (in fact, Eisenhower was a major barrier to statehood). More interesting is the overlook. You can see the Alaska Railroad yards from here, and part of the port of Anchorage and the neighborhood of Government Hill across the Ship Creek river bottom. This is where the tent city of Knik Anchorage, later shortened to Anchorage, was set up in 1914. An informative set of signs on the overlook explains the history. The

Alaska Railroad, which helped build Anchorage, still has its headquarters in a modern brick building that stands by the creek. The nearer concrete building is the railroad's stately depot. The restored steam engine on the pedestal in front was used on construction of the Panama Canal, and then worked in the yard here as a switch engine. The creek itself is full of salmon in June and August (see "Fishing," later), and a walkway that crosses a dam just upstream from here is a good place to watch the fish and to feed ducks. But the walk down the stairs to the river bottom and back is strenuous.

Walk up the hill on E Street to 3rd Avenue. The extensively landscaped parking lot on the left becomes the:

⓲ Saturday/Sunday Markets

This street fair, held every weekend from mid-May to mid-September, draws hundreds of vendors and thousands of shoppers. You can buy everything from local vegetables to handmade crafts to tourist junk. There are food booths and music, too.

Turn right on 3rd Avenue, and then left on F Street. F Street Station, on the left, is a fun bar with an after-work crowd. Proceed to 4th Avenue, and you're back at the Log Cabin Visitor Information Center, but don't stop. Turn right on 4th Avenue. On the right side is the:

⓳ Old Federal Building

This grand, white, Depression-era structure now contains the Alaska Public Lands Information Center, with interesting displays and lots of information about the outdoors (p. 211). Don't let the security checkpoint deter you—go in and look around.

Across the street is Anchorage's most attractive historic building, the restored:

⓴ 4th Avenue Theater (1947)

The theater was built by Cap Lathrop, Alaska's first business magnate, who created it as a monument to the territory and the permanence of its new society. It flourished for decades but began losing money when one-screen downtown movie theaters became obsolete in the 1980s. A local businessman with a sentimental attachment to the building—like many residents—stepped in to save it from destruction in 1991 by converting it into a gift store and dinner theater, where anyone could look at the bas-relief murals and the blinking Big Dipper on the ceiling. In 2006, however, he declared himself done with the project. Voters defeated a bond issue to buy the building for the city. At this writing, its fate is undetermined, and whether it will be open for viewing in 2007 uncertain.

DOWNTOWN MUSEUMS

Alaska State Troopers Museum   This charming little museum has more than one way into the heart. For law enforcement people, the appeal is obvious. Others may enjoy perusing a trove of law enforcement insignia, equipment, a 1952 Hudson Hornet patrol car, photographs, and other memorabilia that all conveys the positive spirit of pioneer Alaska and the troopers' obvious pride.

245 W. 5th Ave. ⓒ **800/770-5050** or 907/279-5050. www.alaskatroopermuseum.com. Free admission. Mon–Fri 10am–4pm, Sat noon–4pm.

Anchorage Museum of History and Art 𝒜𝒜𝒜   The state's largest museum doesn't have its largest collection, but it has the room and staff to teach and to serve as a center of contemporary culture for this part of the world. Most visitors tour the large Alaska Gallery, an informative and enjoyable walk through the history and some of the anthropology of the state. In the art galleries, you can see what's happening in art in Alaska today; Alaskan art isn't all scenery and walrus ivory, but the grandeur of the state does influence almost every work. The Anchorage museum also gets the best

Big State, Big Movies

Two downtown theaters show films aimed at visitors. **The Alaska Experience Theatre** (📞 **907/272-9076;** www.alaskaexperiencetheatre.com) is on the northwest corner of Sixth Avenue and G Street, partly in a dome tent. A 40-minute Omnivision wraparound movie about Alaska costs $8 for adults, $4 for children ages 5 to 11, showing hourly. It's certainly spectacular—too much so for some people, who get motion sickness. Sit toward the center at the back. An Alaska Earthquake display that really shakes is $6 for adults and $4 for children ages 5 to 12. Combination tickets are discounted. The theater is open in summer daily from 9am to 9pm, in winter noon to 5pm. In the summer, the **Alaska Center for the Performing Arts** usually has a presentation for visitors, too. Recently they've shown *Aurora: Alaska's Great Northern Lights,* photographer Dave Parkhurst's incredible 25-year collection of auroral images (www.thealaska collection.com), set to an original musical score. Admission, at the door only, is around $10. Showings, which last 40 minutes, take place hourly all day.

touring and temporary exhibits. Depending on your interest, you could spend most of a day there. The restaurant, operated by the excellent Marx Brothers Cafe (p. 221), serves some of the best lunches to be had downtown. Call or check the website for information on films, lectures, openings, and jazz happenings staged many summer evenings, a great opportunity to meet like-minded locals. The shop is an excellent place to buy authentic Alaska Native art.

121 W. 7th Ave. 📞 907/343-4326. www.anchoragemuseum.org. Admission $6.50 adults, $6 seniors 65 and older, free for children 17 and under. May 15–Sept 15 daily 9am–6pm (Thurs to 9pm); Sept 16–May 14 Wed–Sat 10am–6pm, Sun noon–5pm.

The Imaginarium *(Kids)* Located in the mall with the Orso Restaurant and Glacier Brewhouse, mostly in the basement, this small museum is a favorite of Anchorage children under age 10, with room to play and interesting things to look at. The highlights are the excellent marine touch tanks, which are like indoor tide pools, and the display of live reptiles and amphibians. Other exhibits cover astronomy, insects, flight, and miscellaneous science topics. For families, it's a worthwhile stop; less so, if you're used to larger science museums in major cities.

737 W. 5th Ave., Suite G. 📞 907/276-3179. www.imaginarium.org. Admission $5.50 ages 13–64, $5 ages 2–12 and 65 and older. Mon–Sat 10am–6pm; Sun noon–5pm.

The Oscar Anderson House Museum This house museum, moved to a beautiful site in Elderberry Park over the water, shows how an early Swedish immigrant lived. Although far from grand, the house is quaint, surrounded by a lovely little garden, and dates from the city's founding in 1915. The 45-minute guided tour provides a good explanation of Anchorage's short history. In those small-town days, Anderson found success in the meat, coal, and aviation businesses. He died in 1974, and the house contains many of the family's original belongings, including a working 1909 player piano around which the structure was built. If you come at Christmas, don't miss the Swedish Christmas tours, the first 2 weekends in December.

420 M St. 📞 907/274-2336. Admission $3 adults, $1 children 5–12. Summer Mon–Fri noon–5pm. Closed in winter.

SIGHTS BEYOND DOWNTOWN

Alaska Aviation Heritage Museum ✻✻   Alaska's late development meant it skipped a technological step: Travel and mail went straight from dogsleds and riverboats to airplanes, without the intervening development of a significant road or rail network. One day towns were separated from the outside world by perilous journeys that could last a month; the next day, people could come and go in hours. But the peril remained. In the early days, Alaska aviators crossed vast wilderness without proper maps, landmarks, weather reports, or even formal airstrips. This museum on the shore of the Lake Hood floatplane base contains many of their planes, most of them beautifully restored (you can sometimes watch restoration work in progress), as well as artifacts from Alaska's eventful military history, films, and a flight simulator. Aviation enthusiasts shouldn't miss it. Others can get a strong feeling for that pioneering time with a little effort: Signage could be better, and the context of the planes and artifacts sometimes requires prior knowledge. In any event, it's hard to leave without a little of the bush pilot's can-do spirit sticking to you.

4721 Aircraft Dr. ✆ **907/248-5325.** www.alaskaairmuseum.com. $10 adults, $8 seniors, $6 ages 5–12. Summer daily 9am–5pm; winter Wed–Sat 9am–5pm. The museum is near the international airport; driving toward the airport on International Airport Dr., turn right toward Postmark Dr., right on Heliport Dr., and right again on Aircraft Dr.

Alaska Botanical Garden *Finds*   The garden is a pleasant place to walk and learn about native flora and some of the garden flowers and herbs that grow in Alaska. The plantings are in a few small clearings connected by gravel paths on thickly wooded grounds at the edge of a large wildland park. The quiet, shady setting of the boreal forest sets a muted tone. Gardeners will be interested in the two perennial gardens, the small rock garden, and formal herb garden. The placards on the wildflower trail will help you identify plants you see later on hikes. The Lowenfels Family Nature Trail is a 1-mile loop with a guide brochure that is pitched at an unusually thoughtful level. Along the walk is a chance to see salmon in Campbell Creek. Those without strong interest in gardening or native plants may find other attractions more deserving of limited time, however, especially considering the drive from downtown, which is 20 minutes without traffic, and possibly twice that at rush hour.

Campbell Airstrip Rd. (off Tudor Rd.). ✆ **907/770-3692.** www.alaskabg.org. Suggested donation $5 per person, $10 per family. Daily during daylight hours. Guided tours June–Aug Wed and Sat at 1pm. From downtown, drive out New Seward Hwy. (Gambell St.) to Tudor Rd., exit to the east (left), turn right off Tudor onto Campbell Airstrip Rd., and park at the Benny Benson School.

Alaska Museum of Natural History   This young museum 3 miles east of downtown has a permanent exhibit of Alaska mammals and annual exhibits that have been quite good, on dinosaurs or archeology, for example. The focus is on young people. Check what's showing when you visit.

201 North Bragaw St. ✆ **907/274-2400.** www.alaskamuseum.com. $5 adult, $3 ages 2–12. Summer daily 10am–5pm; winter Wed–Sat 10am–5pm, Sun noon–4pm.

Alaska Native Heritage Center ✻✻✻   Alaska Natives built this extraordinary center to bring their cultures to visitors. It's Alaska's best Native cultural attraction. What makes it so is not the graceful building or the professional and informative displays, but Native people themselves, who often create a personal connection with visitors and rarely come across as practiced or distant. The three main parts of the center take much of a day to absorb. First, there's a hall where storytellers, dancers, and Native athletes perform, with three 30-minute programs rotating through the day.

Next, a gallery of educational displays with a theater showing short films and a series of workshops, where artisans practice and show off traditional crafts and often teach crafts to visitors. Finally, there's a pond surrounded by five traditional Native dwellings representing each cultural group, each hosted by a member of that group. There's a snack bar and grill that serves soup, sandwiches, and other meals, and a gift shop carries inexpensive items and real Native art and crafts for sale by the center or on consignment from artisans. Getting to the center requires wheels. The center offers a free shuttle from various points around town. Call for details on where and when to catch it.

8800 Heritage Center Dr. © **800/315-6608** or 907/330-8000. www.alaskanative.net. Admission $24 adults, $21 seniors and military, $16 ages 7–16; Alaska residents $10 adult, $7 children. Summer daily 9am–5pm; winter Sat 10:30am–4:30pm. Call for additional hours and winter discounts. From the Glenn Hwy., take the North Muldoon exit.

The Alaska Zoo 🎨🎨 *Kids*   Don't expect the variety of a big-city zoo, but what the Alaska Zoo lacks in size it makes up with a charm all its own. Anchorage residents have developed personal relationships with the animals, naming many of them. That affection has made the national controversy over Maggie the African elephant an especially hot topic—animal welfare groups don't think she belongs in Alaska, and everyone from children's magazines to Jay Leno and David Letterman has weighed in. The zoo is trying to keep Maggie happy with improved indoor facilities (read the zoo's position at www.alaskazoo.org/maggienews.htm). The Alaskan animals are the zoo's best attraction. I enjoy watching Ahpun the polar bear play and swim underwater (you can check that out on a webcam, too). Gravel paths meander through the woods past large enclosures with natural flora for bears, seals and otters, musk oxen, Dall sheep, moose, caribou, waterfowl—all the animals you were supposed to see in Alaska but may have missed. (Don't get the Amur tigers, yaks, snow leopards, or Bactrian camels in your snapshots—they'll blow your story.) You can easily spend half a day here. If you don't have a car, consider using the free summer-only shuttle from downtown. It is timed to meet up with 2-hour naturalist tours that take place every day at 1pm and include some backstage stops. The tours are $20 adults, half-price for students and children ages 12 and under. A snack bar serves basic meals, and there is a gift shop.

4731 O'Malley Rd. © **907/346-3242.** www.alaskazoo.org. Admission $9 adults, $8 seniors, $5 ages 12–17, $4 ages 3–11, free under 3. MC, V. May–Aug daily 9am–6pm, till 9pm Tues and Fri Memorial Day–Labor Day; summer educational programs most Tues at 7pm, live music most Fri at 7pm; off-season daily at 10am, closing time varies depending on the time of sunset. Drive out the New Seward Hwy. to O'Malley Rd., then turn left, and go 2 miles; it's 20 min. from downtown, without traffic.

Earthquake Park   The 1964 Good Friday earthquake was the biggest ever in North America, registering at 9.2 on the Richter Scale, killing 131 people, and flattening much of the region. Downtown Anchorage and the Turnagain residential area, near the park, suffered enormous slides that turned neighborhoods into chaotic ruins. A sculpture and excellent interpretive signs commemorate and explain the event, but you can't see much through the trees that have grown up since the quake. If you are up to a walk in the woods, however, descend into the park on the paved coastal trail, and then explore the dirt paths that branch from it. Those quiet ways climb over the strange topography of hummocks and small ponds created when the ground went liquid. This also is a good access point to the Coastal Trail and a likely place to birds and moose. Early in the summer, the mosquitoes are horrendous. Continue west on the Coastal Trail or Northern Lights Boulevard to outlooks at Airport Park and Point Woronzof, within 2 miles of Earthquake Park.

West end of Northern Lights Blvd. No admission. Always open. From downtown, take L St. (it becomes Minnesota Dr.) to Northern Lights Blvd. and turn right. The park is on your right after you cross Lakeshore Dr.

Eklutna Historical Park ⟨⟩   The Native village of Eklutna has a fascinating old cemetery, still in use, in which each grave is enclosed by a highly decorated spirit house the size of a large dollhouse. These little shelters excite the imagination in a way no ordinary marker would. The unique practice evolved from the melding of Athabascan and Russian Orthodox beliefs. There are two small Russian Orthodox churches on the site, including the **St. Nicholas Orthodox Church.** Built north of here of logs sometime before 1870, it is among the oldest buildings in the Southcentral region. Guides offer a 10- to 15-minute orientation talk and then visitors walk around unguided (or skip the talk, if you want). Visitors are not allowed inside the low picket fence around the cemetery, but you can see well enough and you can enter the church. Wear mosquito repellent. If you come out this far, don't miss the Thunderbird Falls, described below under "Hiking & Mountain Biking."

About 26 miles out the Glenn Hwy. ⓒ **907/688-6026.** Admission $5 adult, $2.50 ages 10–18 and over 65, free under 10. Summer Mon–Fri 10am–6pm, Sat 10am–4pm, Sun 1–4pm. Closed winter. Take the Glenn Hwy. 26 miles to the Eklutna exit, and then go left over the overpass.

SPECTATOR SPORTS

Most big events in Anchorage happen at the **Sullivan Arena,** at 16th Avenue and Gambell Street (sometimes known as the Sully, it is named after a still living former mayor). The ticket agency is **Ticketmaster** (ⓒ 907/562-4800; www.ticketmaster.com), which also sells through local Fred Meyer grocery stores. Ticketmaster also handles events at the downtown Egan Civic and Convention Center.

BASEBALL   Anchorage has two semipro baseball teams—the **Anchorage Glacier Pilots** (ⓒ 907/274-3627; www.glacierpilots.com) and the **Anchorage Bucs** (ⓒ 907/561-2827; www.anchoragebucs.com)—with college athletes playing in a six-team Alaska league during June and July. Cool summer nights under the natural light at Mulcahy Stadium are among our family's favorite outings. You hear, smell, and feel the rhythm of the game when you sit so close in the tiny park. The quality may be uneven, but exceptional players grow up here: Among famed alumni are Mark McGwire, Rick Aguilera, Tom Seaver, Dave Winfield, Barry Bonds, Wally Joyner, and Randy Johnson. Check the *Anchorage Daily News* or the websites above for game times. Mulcahy is at 16th Avenue and A Street, a long walk or a short drive from downtown. Tickets are around $5. Dress warmly for evening games; a blanket is rarely out of order. A weekend day game is warmer, but then you won't get to see baseball played at night without lights.

BASKETBALL   The University of Alaska Anchorage basketball teams host a Division I preseason tournament, the **Carrs/Safeway Great Alaska Shootout** (ⓒ 907/786-1250; www.goseawolves.com/shootout), in late November. The noted men's tournament takes place over Thanksgiving weekend. The women's tournament is held on the days prior to Thanksgiving weekend. The Seawolves play the regular season at the Sullivan Arena and at the University Sports Center, on campus on Providence Drive.

HOCKEY   Anchorage is a hockey town. The biggest headline I've ever seen on the local newspaper is when the minor league hockey won the national ECHL championship in the spring of 2006. The team, the **Alaska Aces** (ⓒ 907/258-2237; www.alaskaaces.com), competes at the Sullivan Arena. The western division that Anchorage faces regularly includes cities such Las Vegas and San Diego. The Aces were very strong in 2005 as well. During the NHL lock-out, New Jersey Devils star Scotty Gomez, an Anchorage-raised kid, joined the Aces so he would have something to do. The season lasts from October to May. Most years, the **University of Alaska Anchorage Seawolves** (© **907/786-1250;** www.goseawolves.com) get plenty of attention all winter. They play NCAA Division I hockey, usually at the Sullivan, a notoriously noisy and raucous venue for opposing teams.

5 Getting Outside

Anchorage is unique in Alaska (and anywhere else I know) for the number of places right in and near town to hike, bike, ski, and otherwise get into the wild. I've broken the options down by activities below. In town, the city's bike trails connect through greenbelts that span the noisy, asphalt urban core with soothing creekside woods. Kincaid Park and Far North Bicentennial Park are both on the trail system within the city and encompass thousands of acres and scores of miles of trails for Nordic skiing, mountain biking, and horseback riding. The Chugach Mountains, which form the backdrop to the town, offer tundra hiking, backpacking, mountain biking, and climbs that range from easy to technical. More trails and streams, only slightly farther afield, are covered in the "Out from Anchorage" sections later in this chapter. Many cruises, tours, fishing charters, and sea-kayaking trips leave from nearby **Whittier,** easily managed as a day trip; see section 4 of chapter 7 for details.

INFORMATION The **Alaska Public Lands Information Center** (© **907/271-2737;** www.nps.gov/aplic) offers guidance for all these recreation areas and more throughout Alaska; see p. 211. For information on the bike trails, Nordic skiing parks, swimming, and other city recreation, contact **Anchorage Parks & Recreation** at © **907/343-4355** (www.muni.org/parks). Get information specific to **Chugach State Park** from the public lands center, or directly from the park at © **907/345-5014** (www.alaskastateparks.org; click on "Individual Parks"). Their *Ridgelines* newspaper is packed with useful information, including a map adequate for most day hikers. **Chugach National Forest** can be reached at © **907/743-9500** or www.fs.fed.us/r10/chugach.

The best trail guide to the entire region is *55 Ways to the Wilderness* (The Mountaineers, $17), by Helen Nienhueser and John Wolfe, Jr., available in any bookstore in the area. Two excellent trail maps are widely available: "Chugach State Park," by Imus Geographics, covers the entire park, while "Anchorage & Vicinity," by Alaska Road & Recreation Maps, covers the park's southern portion as well as the entire Anchorage bowl, and is at a finer scale than the Imus map. You can find either at sporting-goods stores or information centers.

EQUIPMENT You can rent most anything you need for outdoor activities. **Alaska Mountain Bike Source** (© **888/989-8844** or 907/245-8844; www.alaskamtnbike.com) rents, sells, and services bikes; offers information on rides and races; and operates a shuttle as far away as Denali National Park. The shuttle can drop off and pick up at different points, allowing one-way trail rides. The firm also offers free bike delivery to Anchorage hotels and B&Bs. For downtown bike rentals, see "Getting Around," p. 210.

Get advice, buy gear, and rent sea kayaks, cross-country skis, snowshoes, bear-proof containers, and mountaineering equipment at **Alaska Mountaineering and Hiking,** at 2633 Spenard Rd. (© **907/272-1811;** alaskamountaineering.com). It's a small shop where the staff takes the time to help you plan a trip. A block away, at 1200 W. Northern Lights Blvd., **REI** has a larger store (© **907/272-4565;** www.rei.com) that rents a wide range of gear, including lightweight canoes and touring kayaks with car-top carriers, camping gear, packs, tents, sleeping bags, and cross-country skis (but not bikes or ice climbing gear). It is the best-stocked place in town to buy outdoor ath-letic clothing as well. (For Arctic cold-weather gear and where to buy it, see "What to Wear" on p. 20.)

WALKING & BIKING

Anchorage has an award-winning network of paved **bike trails** spanning the city along wooded greenbelts. You rarely see a building and almost always cross roads and rail lines through tunnels and over bridges, so you're never in traffic. Here are two of the best.

TONY KNOWLES COASTAL TRAIL ✶✶✶   Leading 10 miles from the western end of 2nd Avenue along the shore to **Kincaid Park,** the coastal trail is among the best things about Anchorage. It's a unique pathway to the natural environment from the heart of downtown. I've ridden parallel to beluga whales swimming along the trail at high tide and encountered as many as six moose on a single ride. (Don't approach moose or bear or try to slip by; wait at a safe distance for them to go their own way.) The most popular entrance is at **Elderberry Park,** at the western end of 5th Avenue. **Westchester Lagoon** (a pond) is 10 blocks south of Elderberry Park. From down-town, the lagoon is a good destination for a lovely stroll and a fine place to picnic and feed the ducks, which nest on small islands.

LANIE FLEISCHER CHESTER CREEK TRAIL ✶   Starting at an intersection with the Coastal Trail at Westchester Lagoon, this trail runs about 4 miles east along the greenbelt to **Goose Lake,** where you can swim or paddle a rented boat in a cool woodland pond at the end of a hot bike ride and buy ice cream or other snacks from a little cafe—still, improbably enough, in the middle of the city. South from the lake, a wooded trail leads partway through the university campus. The paved bike trails, including the Fleischer, stay well back in the trees, so you rarely see a building, and tunnels and bridges span all road and railroad crossings, so you're never in traffic.

HIKING & MOUNTAIN BIKING

Besides these hikes and bikes in Anchorage proper, more excellent, nearby options are along Turnagain Arm and in Girdwood, covered in sections 8 and 9 of this chapter.

KINCAID PARK ✶✶   Covered in more detail below, Kincaid Park is an idyllic summer setting for mountain biking and day hikes. Moose sightings are a common daily occurrence on wide dirt trails that snake for about 40 miles through the birch and white spruce of the park's hilly 1,500 acres of boreal forest, often with views of the sea and mountains beyond, including McKinley. Trails open to bikes around June 1, or as soon as they dry, and a mountain bike race series runs through the summer. On the busiest summer day, however, there is plenty of room for relaxed, solitary ram-bling or cycling. Within the park, wooded Little Campbell Lake is a picturesque spot for family canoeing and fishing for stocked trout; there is no lifeguard. There's also an 18-hole Frisbee golf course. *Note:* The park gates are locked at 10pm, so get your car out before then or park in one of the lots outside the gates.

FAR NORTH BICENTENNIAL PARK ✶   The 4,000-acre park and associated Bureau of Land Management Campbell Tract, on the east side of town, is a unique patch of urban wilderness, a habitat for bears, moose, and spawning salmon. People use it for dog mushing and skiing in winter, and for exceptional mountain biking and day hiking in summer. The Alaska Botanical Garden, listed above, and the Hilltop Ski Area, later, are both within the park's boundaries. A good place to start a hike or ride through the woods is the **Campbell Creek Science Center** (© 907/267-1247; www. blm.gov/ak/sciencecenter), an educational facility operated by the BLM. Staff are often on hand to answer questions, and you can consult books and maps and look at an aquarium of native fish. To get to the science center from downtown, take Gambell Street (it becomes New Seward Hwy.) south to Dowling Road, go east (toward the mountains), turn right on Lake Otis Road, turn left on 68th Avenue, and follow 68th to its end. The unpaved entrance route is just across Abbott Road.

FLATTOP MOUNTAIN & THE GLEN ALPS TRAILHEAD 🎖🎖🎖   There are many ways to reach the alpine tundra, intoxicating fresh air, and cinematic views in the Chugach Mountains behind Anchorage, but the easiest and best developed portal is the Chugach State Park Glen Alps Trailhead. Even those who aren't up to hiking should go for the drive and a walk on a short, paved loop with incredible views and interpretive signs. If you are ready for a hike, you can start at the trail head for trips of up to several days, following the network of trails or taking off across dry, alpine tundra by yourself, but usually within cellphone range. Camping is permitted anywhere off the trails.

Flattop Mountain is the most popular hike from Glen Alps and a great family climb, if a bit crowded on weekends. It's a steep afternoon hike, easy for fit adults and doable by school-age children. There's a bit of a scramble at the top, easiest if you stick to the painted markers on the rocks. Dress warmly and don't go in the rain, when slick rocks at the top could cause a fall.

For a longer or less steep hike or a mountain-biking trip, follow the broad gravel trail that leads up the valley from the Glen Alps Trailhead to several other great routes. Trails lead all the way over the mountains to Indian or Bird Creek, on Turnagain Arm, up some of the mountains along the way or to round alpine lakes in high, rocky valleys. You're always above the tree line, so you don't need to follow a trail if you have a good map. This is wonderful backpacking country.

To get to the trail head, take New Seward Highway to O'Malley Road, head east toward the mountains, then turn right on Hillside Drive, and left onto Upper Huffman Road. Finally, turn right on the narrow, twisting Toilsome Hill Drive. Don't forget to bring cash or a check for the self-service day-use fee of $5 (not required if you are going only to the overlook and park in the designated spaces).

EAGLE RIVER VALLEY 🎖🎖   The **Eagle River Nature Center,** at the end of Eagle River Road, 12 miles up Eagle River Valley from the Glenn Highway exit (© 907/694-2108; www.ernc.org), resembles a public wilderness lodge, with hands-on nature displays about the area and daily nature walks in the summer and weekends year-round (2pm weekends, call for other times). Operated by a nonprofit concessionaire for Chugach State Park, it's open June through August Sunday through Thursday from 10am to 5pm, Friday and Saturday from 10am to 7pm; May and September from 10am to 5pm except Monday; October through April Friday through Sunday from 10am to 5pm. There's a $5 parking fee.

The .75-mile **Rodak Nature Trail,** with interpretive signs, leads to viewing platforms over a beaver pond. The **Albert Loop Trail** is a 3-mile route; a geology guide from the center matches with numbered posts on the way. Both trails have good bird

Fun Fact **Anchorage's Water Source**

The glacial melt water from Eklutna Lake is where Anchorage gets most of its city water. You pass the water plant on the way up the road to the campground and trail head. A tap at the same plant fills tanker trucks with water that is bottled and sold in stores as "glacier water."

and wildlife watching. The 25-mile **Crow Pass Trail,** a portion of the historic Iditarod Trail, continues up the valley into the mountains along the river. You can make a day-hike loop of 6 miles or less by returning on the **Dew Mound Trail.** Continuing, the Crow Pass Trail eventually surmounts the Chugach in alpine terrain and passes near Raven Glacier before descending into Girdwood (p. 251). There are campsites with fire rings along the way, and a mile up the trail the center rents out a public-use cabin for $65 a night. A yurt on the Crow Pass Trail and another on the Albert Loop rent for the same price. Reserve well ahead for weekends. Availability is shown on the website.

THUNDERBIRD FALLS & EKLUTNA LAKE 𝒻𝒻   The hike to Thunderbird Falls is an easy 1-mile forest walk with a good reward at the end; you can see the falls without the steep final descent to their foot. Take the Glenn Highway north to the Thunderbird Falls exit, 25 miles from Anchorage. Continuing 10 miles up the Eklutna Lake Road, you come to an appealing state parks campground ($10 a night, $5 day-use fee) and the glacial lake for canoeing, hiking, and exceptional mountain biking. The Lakeside Trail leads 14 miles to Eklutna Glacier; you can camp on the way, stay at the state park's Yuditna Creek Cabin at 3 miles, or stay in the communal Serenity Falls hut at 13 miles. Advance reservations are required for the cabin or hut. See "State Parks Cabin Reservations," p. 262. For the hut, you can reserve in person or by fax only. Rental bikes, kayaks, and other equipment, and guided kayak tours, are offered by **Lifetime Adventures,** with a booth at the trail head of the Lakeside Trail (② **907/746-4644;** www.lifetimeadventures.net). For $75 you can kayak 8 miles to the other end of the lake and pick up a bike there to ride back.

BIRD-WATCHING

The Anchorage bowl contains varied bird habitat that is easily accessed and close at hand: lakes, streams, lagoons, freshwater and salt marshes, seashore, woodlands, and so on. Visiting birders can see species they don't encounter at home (Pacific loons, Hudsonian godwits, boreal chickadees) and familiar birds in breeding plumage unique to these northern latitudes (a red-necked grebe that actually does have a red neck, for example). Local birders have recorded more than 225 species in the city. Bird self-guided with the help of a rental car or at least a bike. Potter Marsh is a superb freshwater birding area (see section 8, later in this chapter). Salt marshes lie along the Tony Knowles Coastal Trail near Kincaid Park (see above). Right downtown, Ship Creek provides a river habitat. You can join field trips and network with local birders through the **Anchorage Audubon Society** (www.anchorageaudubon.org). The site contains an updated log of unusual sightings, which you can also check on a recorded hotline (② **907/338-BIRD**).

A terrific booklet, *Anchorage Wildlife Viewing Hot Spots,* published by the Alaska Department of Fish and Game, is sold for $6 at the Alaska Public Land Information Center. It has more places to go than I can include here, detailed directions, and helpful information. Learn more about wildlife viewing around Alaska at www.wildlifeviewing.alaska.gov.

FISHING

There are hatchery salmon in several of Anchorage's streams, and stocked trout, salmon, or char in 28 lakes, so you need not leave town to catch a fish. The **Alaska Department of Fish and Game,** 333 Raspberry Rd., Anchorage, AK 99518-1599 (© **907/267-2218;** www.alaska.gov/adfg, click on "Sport Fisheries," then navigate by using the maps), publishes informative booklets on the Web and on paper and an online fishing report updated weekly in season. There's also a recorded information line (© **907/267-2503**) with what's hot and lots of other advice. See chapter 2 for general guidance and license information, and information for planning a fishing vacation, and see chapter 7 for the famous fishing opportunities on the Kenai Peninsula.

ROADSIDE FISHING   Although the setting (under a highway bridge in an industrial area) might not be the wilderness experience you've dreamed about, the 40-pound king salmon you pull from **Ship Creek** may make up for it. From downtown, just walk down the hill to the railroad yard. A couple of shacks sell and rent gear in the summer. Fishing for kings is best in June and for silvers in August and September. Fish only on the rising tide, when the fish come into the creek. Fishing near the end of the rising tide will mean crossing less mud, but one successful angler I know insists it's the start of the tide that's best. Either way, you'll need rubber boots, preferably neoprene chest waders, for the muddy banks, but don't go too far out, as the mud flats are dangerous and several times every summer the fire department has to rescue stuck fishermen.

Campbell Creek, a more natural urban stream, is stocked with silver salmon that make good fishing in August and September, and rainbow trout and Dolly Varden char are in the creek year round. The creek runs along a greenbelt across the city through residential and industrial neighborhoods; the adjacent bike trail is a good access route. You can join the trail on Dimond Boulevard east of Jewel Lake Road, or where C Street crosses the creek just north of Dimond, among other places; or ask for directions and tips at the Public Land Information Center.

Bird Creek, 25 miles south of Anchorage on the Seward Highway (see "Out from Anchorage: Turnagain Arm & Portage Glacier" later in this chapter), is known for hot silver salmon fishing in the late summer and fall. Pinks run from late June to early August during even-numbered years. Other creeks along the Arm have similar but smaller runs.

FLY-IN FISHING ⚓⚓⚓   Serious anglers will use Anchorage as a base from which to fly to a remote lake or river with more fish and fewer people. Such a flight can be an unforgettable experience for those who are less than enthusiastic about fishing, too. The plane lifts off from Anchorage's Lake Hood floatplane base and within half an hour smoothly lands on a lake or river, often all alone. You climb out and watch as the plane lifts off and disappears, leaving behind the kind of silence unique to true wilderness. It's on these trips that avid anglers are made—or spoiled. I've heard people complain of how sore their arms got from pulling in too many salmon.

Several companies offer fly-in trips; among the best established is **Rust's Flying Service** (© **800/544-2299** or 907/243-1595; www.flyrusts.com). They can take you out guided or on your own, for the day or for a longer stay in a cabin or lodge. If you fly to a lake, they'll provide a boat. They can't make fish appear if none are running, but they will try to take you to the hot spots. You can bring your own gear, or they can provide it. Prices for an unguided day trip start at around $220 per person, with a two-person minimum; guided, $399.

OTHER SUMMER ACTIVITIES

FLIGHTSEEING   Small planes are the blood cells of Alaska's circulatory system, and Anchorage its heart. There are several busy airports in Anchorage, and Lake Hood is the world's busiest floatplane base. More than two dozen operators want to take you on a flightseeing tour. If you will travel to Talkeetna, Denali National Park, Juneau, Glacier Bay National Park, or Ketchikan, it might be wise to save your flightseeing splurge for those extraordinary places. Likewise, for bear-viewing flights, Katmai National Park, Homer, Kodiak, Juneau and Wrangell are closer to the action. (All those places are covered in this guide with the details for flights; check the table of contents or index.) On the other hand, if time is short, you can see some very impressive scenery and even, for a price, get to bears from Anchorage. Rust's Flying Service (see "Fly-In Fishing," above) is a reliable operator and can get you in the air for as little as $89. A flight to Mount McKinley is $269 and takes 3 hours; for another $100, you can land on the mountain (well worth the added cost). A bear-viewing tour from Anchorage is in the $460 to $600 per person range. All these prices may change depending on fuel prices.

RAFTING   There are several white-water rivers within a 90-minute drive of Anchorage. **Nova Raft and Adventure Tours** (© 800/746-5753 or 907/745-5753; http:// novaalaska.com) has more than 30 years of experience offering trips all over the state and five different half-day floats in the Anchorage area. Various rafting trips are available, ranging from the relatively easygoing Matanuska and Kings rivers to the Class IV and V white water of Six-mile Creek, which begins with a required instructional swim and includes fun optional swims. That wild white water is about an hour south of Anchorage on the Seward Highway. White-water rafting always entails risk, but Nova's schedule allows you to calibrate how wild you want to get. Call to reserve and let them guide you as to the float that fits you best. The company also offers add-ons for self-paddling, helicopter flightseeing, or glacier hiking. The half-day trips range in price from $70 to $250. Children 5 to 11 can go on the calmer Matanuska River float for $35. Other trips are suitable only for older children and adults. You'll need your own transportation to the river and may need to bring your own lunch. **Chugach Outdoor Center** (© 866/277-RAFT or 907/277-RAFT; www.chugachoutdoorcenter.com) also offers several rafting options south of Anchorage. The company has two daily choices on Six-mile Creek, floats in Turnagain Pass and in Seward's Resurrection River, and sea kayaking on Kenai Lake.

If you want to go rafting without traveling to the Matanuska River or Six-mile Creek, you can save time and money by taking a shorter, somewhat less dramatic ride closer to town on the Eagle River, which runs past the Anchorage suburb of the same name. A whitewater ride is as little as $35 with **Lifetime Adventures** (© 907/746-4644; www.lifetimeadventures.net), and they have longer floats that also include more smooth water. The rides go several times a day every day of the summer.

SEA KAYAKING   Except at Eklutna Lake (see above), kayaking day trips from Anchorage go through Whittier, on Prince William Sound (see section 4 of chapter 7 for complete details).

SWIMMING   I'm betting that most visitors from warmer climes won't be interested in chilly lake swimming in Anchorage (the best spot is Goose Lake, off Northern Lights Boulevard east of Lake Otis Road). If you have children and need to burn off some energy, however, you won't find a better spot than an indoor water park called **H2Oasis** (© **888/H2OASIS** or 907/522-4420; www.h2oasiswaterpark.com), near the intersection of O'Malley Road and the New Seward Highway. A big wave pool and a 500-foot "watercoaster" are the top attractions. Adults should bring earplugs, as the noise is unbearable, and a full wallet, as admission is $22 for ages 13 and older, $17 ages 3 to 12, free under age 3.

WINTER ACTIVITIES

The best downhill skiing and snowmobile tours are covered in the Girdwood section, on p. 251.

ICE SKATING   **Westchester Lagoon,** just 10 blocks from downtown (see "Walking & Biking," above), is a skating paradise in the winter. When the ice gets thick enough, usually by mid-December, the city clears a large rink and over a mile of wide paths that wind across the pond, mopping the ice regularly for a smooth surface. Skaters gather around burn barrels, well stocked with firewood, to socialize and warm their hands, and on weekends vendors often sell hot chocolate and coffee. Ice skates are for rent for $10 a day at **Champions Choice,** a hockey shop in the University Center Mall at Old Seward Highway and 36th Avenue (© **907/563-3503**).

SKIING   **Kincaid Park** is one of the best **cross-country skiing** areas in the country, with the first World Cup–certified trails in the U.S. About 65km of trails are geared to every ability level, but mostly intermediate and expert. Besides the superb trails, it's a beautiful place to ski, through rolling hills of open birch and spruce, with views of the mountains and ocean. Most trails are expertly groomed for skating and classical techniques, with two loops reserved for classical only. Sixteen kilometers are lighted, an important feature on short winter days. The **Kincaid Park Outdoor Center** (© **907/343-6397**) is open daily from 10am to 9:45pm, shorter hours on holidays. The gate closes at 10pm, so park at one of the lots outside it if you will be skiing later. Skiing usually lasts well into March and sometimes into April. Big races come in late February and early March (see "Only-in-Alaska Events," in chapter 2). **Far North Bicentennial Park** also has some excellent trails—32km total, 7km lighted—and a slightly longer season because of a hillside location. Start at Hilltop Ski Area. Many other parks and the bike trails have lengthy skiing routes, too, some lighted. See "Equipment," on p. 237 for information on where to rent skis.

Anchorage has several **downhill ski areas.** The best, **Alyeska Resort,** is described on p. 254. **Hilltop Ski Area,** in Bicentennial Park in town, is a great place to learn to ski, with one long beginner slope, at 7015 Abbott Rd. (© **907/346-2167**; www.hilltopskiarea.org). One-day lift tickets are $22 to $26, and ski package rentals $20 to $26 a day.

Anchorage also is a great starting point for **backcountry skiing.** Nonexperts should go with a guide (you can find one through Alyeska Resort). Experts can get ideas from some of the folks mentioned under "Equipment," p. 237. The key safety consideration is, of course, avalanche awareness and preparation. I've described that on p. 47, but if you are turning to this book to learn how, you are not ready to go without a guide. An avalanche hotline is available for the Chugach National Forest near Anchorage (© **907/754-2369**; www.fs.fed.us/r10/chugach/glacier/snow.html).

6 Shopping

Some of the most interesting shops are mentioned earlier, in the walking tour of downtown, where most galleries and gift shops are located.

NATIVE ARTS & CRAFTS   Several shops in Anchorage carry Native Alaskan arts and crafts. Before making major purchases, know what you're buying (see "Native Art: Finding the Real Thing," in chapter 2).

Nowhere else will you find another business like the **Oomingmak Musk Ox Producers' Co-operative** (© 888/360-9665 outside Alaska or 907/272-9225; www.qiviut.com), located in the house with the musk ox on the side at 6th Avenue and H Street. Owned by 250 Alaska Native women living in villages across the state, the co-op sells only scarves and other items they knit of *qiviut* (*ki*-vee-ute), the light, warm, silky underhair of the musk ox, which is collected from shedding animals. Each village has its own knitting pattern. They're expensive—adult caps are $130 to $180—but the quality is extraordinary. The website contains the women's fascinating correspondence and links to two of the rural knitters' own pages.

As an aside, if you are driving north from Anchorage, you may also want to stop at the **Musk Ox Farm** (© 907/745-4151; www.muskoxfarm.org), just north of Palmer on the Glenn Highway, where you can see the strange-looking creatures close up (summer daily 9am–7pm; admission $9 adults, $7 seniors, and $6 ages 5–12). Musk oxen also are at the Alaska Zoo (covered earlier in this chapter) and are easy to see in the wild near Nome (see section 6 in chapter 10).

Anchorage has several small shops and local secret places to find authentic Native artwork.

The **Yankee Whaler,** in the lobby of the Hotel Captain Cook, at 5th Avenue and I Street, is a small but well-regarded shop carrying Native arts. In a bright yellow building, **The Rusty Harpoon,** at 411 W. 4th Ave., has authentic Native items, Alaskan jewelry, less expensive crafts, and reliable, longtime proprietors who only buy direct from Native artists they know. Locals shop here. Next door to the yellow building to the east on 4th is a deep brown one, Ship Creek Center, which has been converted to a collection of Native-oriented shops, including one representing the Alaska Native Heritage Center. Artists sometimes work in the central common area. At the **Anchorage Museum of History and Art** at 7th and A streets (p. 232), check out the gift shop for a tastefully selected and beautifully displayed array of Alaska Native art.

If you can get beyond the downtown area, you can shop at the best place for Native crafts in Anchorage (and maybe all of Alaska), the **Hospital Auxiliary Craft Shop** in the Alaska Native Medical Center, off Tudor east of Bragaw (© 907/729-1122), where everything is made by those eligible to use the hospital. The work you find here is all authentic and entirely traditional, and it's possible to find artistic masterpieces. The shop is open Monday through Friday from 10am to 2pm, and the first and third Saturday of each month from 11am to 2pm. They don't accept credit cards. There's exceptional Native art to see on the walls of the hospital, too.

FURS   If you're in the market for a fur, Anchorage has a wide selection and no sales tax. **David Green Master Furrier,** at 130 W. 4th Ave. (www.davidgreenfurs.com), is an Anchorage institution. Others are nearby.

GIFTS   There are lots of places to buy both mass-produced and inexpensive handmade crafts other than Alaska Native items. If you can be in town on a weekend during the summer, be sure to visit the **Saturday/Sunday Market** street fair, in the parking lot at 3rd Avenue and E Street, with food, music, and hundreds of miscellaneous crafts booths. You won't have any trouble finding gift shops on 4th. Our favorite is the relatively classy **Cabin Fever,** at 650 W. 4th. The **Kobuk Coffee Company,** at 5th Avenue and E Street, next to the town square, occupies one of Anchorage's earliest commercial buildings; it's a cozy candy, coffee, and collectibles shop, with a tiny bakery and eatery in the back. Midtown, on International Airport Road between the Old and New Seward highways, **Alaska Wild Berry Products** is a fun store to visit. There's a chocolate waterfall and a big window where you can watch the candy factory at work. The owners have turned the grounds into a visitor complex, with buses regularly stopping.

FINE ART Downtown has several galleries. Openings are coordinated to happen on the first Friday of each month, allowing for an evening of free party hopping and art shopping. The **International Gallery of Contemporary Art,** 427 D St., is a nonprofit space dedicated to artists. Come here for an in-depth look at just a few artists' work and to meet people who really care about art. Since it is run on contributions by volunteers, hours are short and changeable; currently: Wednesday through Sunday noon to 4pm, Tuesday 5:30 to 8:30pm, closed Monday. They're also open for first Friday, 6 to 8pm.

Artique, at 314 G St., is Anchorage's oldest gallery and has a large selection. Half of the gallery is given over to big oils and other gorgeous originals; the other half is chock-full of prints, less-expensive ceramics, and some mass-produced and/or corny stuff. At 5th and G, **Aurora Fine Arts** carries pottery, prints, and gifts. Directly across G is a gallery showing only glass sculpture.

7 Anchorage Nightlife

THE PERFORMING ARTS

WHAT'S PLAYING The primary arts season begins in the fall and ends in the spring, but in the summer you can catch traveling performers, music festivals, and live music at the nightclubs and coffeehouses. To find out what's happening, pick up the free weekly *Anchorage Press,* which is given away in racks all over town. Their extensive event and music scene calendar is online, too, at www.anchoragepress.com. Friday's edition of the *Anchorage Daily News* has a section called "Play" that includes reviews and listing information in grid format. See "Special Events," earlier in this chapter, for some major happenings.

BUYING TICKETS **Ticketmaster** (② 907/562-4800; www.ticketmaster.com) handles the Sullivan Arena and Egan Civic and Convention Center, and sells tickets at Fred Meyer grocery stores. The Alaska Center for Performing Arts, at 631 W. 6th Ave. (www.alaskapac.org), operates its own ticket agency, **CenterTix** (② 907/263-ARTS; www.centertix.net). The call center and box office in the center are open Monday through Friday 9am to 5pm, Saturday noon to 5pm, and evenings prior to events.

PRESENTERS The **Anchorage Concert Association** (② 907/272-1471; www.anchorageconcerts.org) offers a fall-through-spring schedule of classical music, theater, dance, and other performing arts. **Whistling Swan Productions** (www.whistlingswan.net) promotes folk and acoustic alternative performers in intimate venues. The **Anchorage Symphony** (② 907/274-8668; www.anchoragesymphony.org) performs during the winter season. Anchorage also has lots of community theater and opera, and limited professional theater, including the experimental **Out North Contemporary Art House** (© **907/279-3800;** www.outnorth.org), which produces local shows and imports avant-garde performers. Downtown, **Cyrano's Off Center Playhouse** (© **907/274-2599;** www.cyranos.org), at 4th Avenue and D Street, is a tiny theater with its own semiprofessional repertory company.

NIGHTCLUBS

Blues Central/Chef's Inn, 825 W. Northern Lights Blvd. (© **907/272-1341**), is dedicated to showcasing the best blues performers available, virtually every night. Major names come through on a regular basis. Shows start at 9:30pm. They're also known for their beef.

The most famous bar in Anchorage, with the slogan, "We cheat the other guy and pass the savings on to you," is the huge **Chilkoot Charlie's,** at Spenard Road and Fireweed Lane (© **907/272-1010;** www.koots.com). It has two stages, three dance floors, and 10 bars with different themes. The place is huge and full of entertainment, like an adult Disneyland—order vodka from a Russian-themed bar with an ice countertop—but I find it claustrophobic when crowded, with low ceilings and a dark, roadhouse atmosphere. It's open every day of the year until after 2am. If you do go there late, avoid conflict and use caution when leaving, as it can be a rough crowd and neighborhood.

THE MOVIES

A movie at the **Bear Tooth TheatrePub,** at 1230 W. 27th Ave. (© **907/276-4200;** www.beartooththeatre.net), is a chance to sit back with a big glass of craft-brewed beer and a plate of nachos or a full dinner—it feels a lot like watching at home except for the big screen and the other people around you in the dark. (Well, our home is usually a bit cleaner, but our cooking isn't as good.) The films tend to be independent or second run, either campy or deep. The dining choices include gourmet tacos, pizzas, and other hand-held selections. Everything is quite good. They also put on concerts monthly: check the website. And now the fine print. Even bad movies sell out and there's often a crush. You must arrive quite early to get your ticket and seat, order your food and beer, and finish waiting in various lines before the movie starts. The staff brings the meal to you in the theater.

There are several multiplexes in Anchorage playing all the current Hollywood output; check the sources at the beginning of this section for listings and reviews. The closest modern theater to the downtown area is the **Century 16,** 301 E. 36th Ave. (© **907/929-3456;** www.centurytheatres.com).

8 Out from Anchorage: Turnagain Arm & Portage Glacier

One of the world's great drives starts in Anchorage and leads roughly 50 miles south on the Seward Highway to Portage Glacier. It's the trip, not the destination, that makes it worthwhile. The two-lane highway along Turnagain Arm, chipped from the foot of the rocky Chugach Mountains, provides a platform to see a magnificent, ever-changing, mostly untouched landscape full of wildlife. I've listed the sights in the style of a highway log, for there are interesting stops all the way along the road. It will take at least half a day round-trip, and there's plenty to do for an all-day excursion. Use your headlights for safety even in daylight, and be patient if you get stuck behind a summertime line of cars—if you pass, you'll just come up behind another line ahead. Mileage markers count down from Anchorage. Continue with this highway log on to the Kenai Peninsula and Seward in chapter 7, starting at p. 262. Car rental is covered in "Getting Around," earlier in this chapter. Many bus tours follow the route and visit Portage Glacier (see "Getting There: By Bus" under "Essentials," earlier). **Gray Line of Alaska** (© 800/544-2206 or 907/277-5581; www.graylineofalaska.com) offers a 7-hour trip that includes a stop in Girdwood and a boat ride on Portage Lake for $67 adults, $34 ages 2 through 12, twice daily in summer.

You can also see this incredible scenery—and more—from a train, although, of course, without stopping along the way for hikes or wildlife viewing. The **Alaska Railroad** (© 800/544-0552 or 907/265-2494; www.alaskarailroad.com) operates summer trains to Whittier and Seward that trace Turnagain Arm on the way, as well as a daytrip tour to the glaciated interior of the Kenai Peninsula, where no road extends. You can join that tour, called the "Glacier Discovery Train to Grandview," in Anchorage, Girdwood, Whittier, or Portage; if starting from Anchorage, the return from Portage is by bus. The tour is $95 adults from Anchorage or Girdwood, $75 from Portage or Whittier, and roughly half-price for children. It takes all day. They have a white-water rafting option, too.

POTTER MARSH (Mile 117)   Heading south from Anchorage, the Seward Highway descends a bluff to cross a broad marsh formed by water impounded behind the tracks of the Alaska Railroad. The marsh has a boardwalk from which you can watch a huge variety of birds. Salad-green grasses grow from sparkling, pond-green water.

POTTER SECTION HOUSE (Mile 115)   Located at the south end of Potter Marsh, the section house was an early maintenance station for the Alaska Railroad. Today it contains the offices of Chugach State Park, open during normal business hours, and, outside, a few old train cars and interpretive displays. Just across the road is the trail head for the **Turnagain Arm Trail.** It's a mostly level path running down the arm well above the highway with great views breaking now and then through the trees. Hike as far as you like and then backtrack to your car; or, if you can arrange a one-way walk with a ride back from the other end, continue 4 miles to the McHugh Creek picnic area and trail head, or 9 miles to Windy Corner.

McHUGH CREEK (Mile 111)   Four miles south of Potter is an excellent state park picnic area and a challenging day hike with a 3,000-foot elevation gain to Rabbit Lake, which sits in a tundra mountain bowl, or to the top of 4,301-foot McHugh Peak. You don't have to climb all the way; there are spectacular views within an hour of the road. From this point onward, most of the stops are on the right or ocean side of the road: Plan your stops on the outbound trip, not on the return, when you would have to make left turns across traffic.

BELUGA POINT (Mile 110)   The state highway department probably didn't need to put up scenic overlook signs on this pull-out, 1½ miles south of McHugh Creek—you would have figured it out on your own. The terrain is simply awesome, as the highway traces the edge of Turnagain Arm, below the towering cliffs of the Chugach Mountains. If the tide and salmon runs are right, you may see beluga whales, which chase the fish toward fresh water. Sometimes they overextend and strand themselves by the dozens in the receding tide, farther along, but they usually aren't harmed. The pull-out has spotting scopes to improve the viewing. The further right-side pull-outs over the next few miles have interpretive signs about the 1895 gold rush in this area and other topics.

Tidal Wave

Tides in Turnagain Arm rise and fall over a greater range than anywhere else in the United States, with a difference between an extreme high and low of more than 41 feet. When the tide is rising, the water can grow deeper by as much as 7 feet an hour, or a foot of water every 8½ minutes. If your foot gets stuck in the mud, it takes less than an hour to drown. (Yes, that has really happened.) Amazing as that speed is, the tide here can go even faster. A breathtaking wall of water up to 6 feet tall called a bore tide can roar up Turnagain Arm twice a day. To see the ocean do such a thing is so unfamiliar it looks almost like science fiction, as the wide arc of foam rushes ahead of a noticeably deeper sea. You can (theoretically) predict the bore tide. Get a tide-table book or look up them up on the Web (start at **www.tidesandcurrents.noaa.gov** and pull down "Products"). Note the size of the tidal range for the day you are visiting: The bore tide will be most noticeable during periods of large tides. (The magnitude of tides varies on the lunar cycle.) Find the time of low tide in Anchorage. Now add the following intervals to the time of the Anchorage low for a prediction of when the bore tide will pass each of these spots on the highway:

- Beluga Point (Mile 110): 1 hour 15 minutes
- Bird Point (Mile 96): 2 hours 15 minutes
- Twentymile River (Mile 80): 4 hours

The best viewing is Beluga Point to Bird Point; at the latter wayside, a set of signs explains the tides.

WINDY POINT (Mile 106)   Be on the lookout on the mountain side of the road for Dall sheep picking their way along the cliffs. It's a unique spot, for the sheep get much closer to people here than is usual in the wild; apparently, they believe they're safe. Windy Point is the prime spot, but you also have a good chance of seeing sheep virtually anywhere along this stretch of road. If cars are stopped, that's probably why; get well off the road and pay attention to traffic, which will still be passing at high speeds.

You may also see windsurfers in the gray, silty waters of the Arm. They're crazy. The water is a mixture of glacial runoff and the near-freezing ocean. Besides, the movement of water that creates the huge tides causes river-like currents, with standing waves like rapids.

INDIAN VALLEY (Mile 104)   Up the road by the Turnagain House restaurant is the **Indian Valley** trail head, a gold rush–era trail that ultimately leads 24 miles to the other side of the mountains. The path, while often muddy, rises less steeply than other trails along the Arm.

BIRD RIDGE TRAIL (Mile 102)   This is a lung-busting climb of 3,000 vertical feet in a little over a mile. It starts with an easy, accessible trail, and then rises steeply to views that start at impressive and get more amazing as you climb. With the southern exposure, it's dry early in the year.

BIRD CREEK (Mile 101)   The excellent state campground on the right side of the highway, over the water, is described on p. 220, and the productive salmon fishing in the creek is described on p. 241. If you stop, use the lot on the left side of the road before you reach the creek. There is also a short trail, interpretive signs, an overlook, and a platform that makes fishing easier for people with disabilities. Pink salmon run from late June to mid-August, silver salmon mostly in August. A scenic bike trail starts here and runs 10 miles to Girdwood, much of it on an older highway alignment.

BIRD POINT (Mile 96)   The remarkable wayside here is not to be missed. A paved pathway rises up to a bedrock outcropping with a simply wonderful view—all the severity of the Turnagain Arm, but framed by the soft green of a freshwater wetland with a beaver lodge. Take a look at the fascinating interpretive signs on many subjects.

THE FLATS (Miles 96–90)   At Bird Point, the highway descends from the mountainside to the mud flats. Several pull-outs on the right side of the highway have interpretive signs. At high tide, water comes right up to the road. At low tide, the whole Arm narrows to a thin, winding channel through the mud. The Arm is not practically navigable, and navigational charts are not even available. Few have ever tried to navigate it other than gold prospectors in rowboats a century ago or today's occasional death-defying canoeist or kayaker. The first to try was Capt. James Cook, in 1778, as he was searching for the Northwest Passage on his final, fatal voyage of discovery (he was killed by Hawaiians later that year). He named this branch of Cook Inlet Turnagain Arm because the strength of the currents and shoals forced the boat he sent to keep turning around.

TURNOFF TO GIRDWOOD (Mile 90)   The attractions of Girdwood, covered below, are worth a visit, but the shopping center here at the intersection is not chief among them. Stop for a simple meal or a restroom break (the convenience store has large public restrooms), or to fill your gas tank for the last time for many a mile.

TWENTYMILE RIVER (Mile 80)   Three species of salmon and a small smelt, the eulachon, known locally as the hooligan, spawn in this river. In the spring you can see Native people dip-netting the hooligan. There is good bird-watching here and from turnouts farther on, but venturing out on Turnagain Arm's tidal mud carries the real risk of getting stuck in quicksand-like mud and drowning in the tide. Don't do it.

OLD PORTAGE (Mile 80)   All along the flats at the head of Turnagain Arm are large marshes full of what looks like standing driftwood. These are trees killed by salt water that flowed in when the 1964 quake lowered the land as much as 10 feet. On the right, ¾ mile past the Twentymile River and across from the rail depot, a few ruins of the abandoned town of Portage are still visible, more than 40 years after the great earthquake.

ALASKA WILDLIFE CONSERVATION CENTER (Mile 79)   Originally conceived as a tourist attraction, the center has become a nonprofit organization giving homes to injured and orphaned deer, moose, owls, elk, bison, musk ox, bear, fox, and caribou (✆ **907/783-2025**; www.alaskawildlife.org). Visitors can drive a short course on the 140-acre compound to see the animals in fenced enclosures as large as 18 acres—at times, some animals are not visible among the natural vegetation. You can usually get closer to the animals at the Alaska Zoo and see a larger variety (p. 235), but these large enclosures are more natural. A big, log gift shop and outdoor snack bar are at the end of the tour. Admission is $7.50 for adults and $5 for military, seniors,

Gone but Not Forgotten

The **Begich-Boggs Visitor Center** at Portage Glacier is named for Hale Boggs, who was U.S. House majority leader, and Rep. Nick Begich, then Alaska's lone congressman, who disappeared together in a small plane during Begich's 1972 reelection bid. The most likely theory is that the wings iced up in Portage Pass, causing a crash into Prince William Sound just beyond the mountains. No trace was ever found—as with many other Alaskan planes that have simply flown off into oblivion. Begich was reelected anyway. His opponent, Republican Don Young, later won a special election and continues to serve as Alaska's only congressman. Boggs' wife, Lindy, went on to serve out his term and eight more. Boggs' daughter, Cokie Roberts, is the famous broadcast journalist. Begich's son, Mark, is mayor of Anchorage.

and children 4 to 12, with a maximum of $25 per vehicle. In summer, it's open daily from 8am to 8pm (last vehicle in at 7:30 pm); in winter, daily from 10am to 5pm.

PORTAGE GLACIER (Take the 5½-mile spur road at Mile 78.)   The named attraction has largely melted, receding out of sight of the visitor center. (The glacier you *can* see is Burns.) When the center was built in 1985, it was predicted that Portage Glacier would keep floating on its 800-foot-deep lake until 2020. Instead, it withdrew to the far edge of the lake in 1995. Today the exhibits in the lakeside **Begich–Boggs Visitor Center** focus on the Chugach National Forest as a whole, rather than just the glacier, and they're worth an hour or two to become oriented to the area's nature, history, and lifestyles. Children and adults find much to hold their interest here. To see Portage Glacier itself, take the road toward Whittier that branches to the left just before the visitor center and stop at a pullout beyond the first (toll-free) tunnel, or take the boat mentioned below.

Several short trails start near the center. Rangers lead nature walks on the .25-mile, paved Moraine Trail. Another trail leads less than a mile to Byron Glacier, in case you're interested in getting up close to some ice. Always dress warmly, as cold winds are the rule in this funnel-like valley.

A **day boat** operated by **Gray Line of Alaska** (© **800/478-6388,** 907/277-5581 for reservations, or 907/783-2983 at the lake; www.graylineofalaska.com) traverses the lake right up to Portage Glacier on hour-long tours, ice conditions permitting. It costs $29 adults, $15 ages 2 to 12, and goes five times daily in summer every 90 minutes, starting at 10:30am. If this is your only chance to see a glacier in Alaska, it's a good choice, but if your itinerary includes any of the great glaciers in Prince William Sound, Kenai Fjords National Park, or the like, you won't be as impressed by Portage.

Sandwiches and other simple meals are sold at a cafeteria near the visitor center called the **Portage Glacier Lodge** (© **907/783-3117**).

There are no lodgings in Portage, but two **Forest Service campgrounds** are on the road to the visitor center, with 72 sites between them (more details are in the Chugach National Forest section in chapter 7). At the Williwaw Campground, there's also a place to watch red salmon spawning in mid-August, but no fishing.

9 Out from Anchorage: Girdwood & Mount Alyeska

Girdwood, 37 miles south of Anchorage, is proof that a charming little town can coexist with a major ski resort, as long as the resort goes undiscovered by the world's skiers. Girdwood still has a sleepy, offbeat character. Retired hippies, ski bums, a U.S. senator, and a few old-timers live in the houses and cabins among the big spruce trees in the valley below the Mount Alyeska lifts. They all expected a development explosion to follow the construction of an international resort here a number of years ago, but it hasn't happened. That may not be good news for the Japanese investors in the resort, but it is for skiers and other visitors who discover this paradise. They find varied, uncrowded skiing through long winters, superb accommodations, and an authentically funky community.

The primary summer attractions are the hiking trails, the tram to the top of Mount Alyeska, and the Crow Creek Mine, described below. In winter, it's skiing. Mount Alyeska doesn't have the size of the famous resorts in the Rockies, but it's more than large and steep enough. Better still, there's plenty of room, half the mountain is above the tree line, and the snow lasts a long time. Olympian Tommy Moe trained here and the Alpine national championships raced down these slopes in 2004. Skiers used to tamer, busier slopes rave about the skiing here, with long, challenging downhills, few lift lines, and stunning views of the Chugach Mountains and glistening Turnagain Arm below.

ESSENTIALS A **rental car** is the most practical means for getting to Girdwood. If you will only ski, however, you may be able to take a shuttle; call the resort before you come, as these arrangements change frequently. The **Girdwood Chamber of Commerce** maintains a website at **www.girdwoodalaska.com**. For more guidance, check the Anchorage visitor information listed in section 1 of this chapter.

EXPLORING GIRDWOOD

Crow Creek Mine ⋆ This mine, opened in 1898, is still operated in a small way by the Toohey family, but mostly they use the paths and eight small original buildings as a charming tourist attraction. You can see the frontier lifestyle and watch rabbits and ducks wandering around. A bag of dirt, guaranteed to have some gold in it, is provided for gold panning, and you can dig and pan to get more if you have the patience for it. Crow Creek Road, off the Alyeska Highway, can be quite rough and muddy in the spring. Camping is $5 a night, with portable toilets.

Crow Creek Rd. (off the Alyeska Hwy.), Girdwood, AK 99587. ✆ 907/278-8060. $3 adults, free for children. Gold panning $5 adults, $4 children 11 and under. May 15–Sept 15 daily 9am–6pm.

Mt. Alyeska Tram ⋆ The tram isn't cheap, but I think it's worth it for anyone who otherwise might not make it to high alpine tundra during an Alaska trip. (In winter, ride on your lift ticket; in summer, ride free with a meal at the Seven Glaciers Restaurant at the top, p. 254.) The tram takes 7 minutes in summer to get to the 2,300-foot level, where it stops at a station containing both the Seven Glaciers Restaurant and an attractive but overpriced cafeteria. Whether or not you eat here, the tram presents an opportunity for everyone, no matter how young, old, or infirm, to experience the pure light, limitless views, and crystalline quiet of an Alaskan mountaintop. Take the opportunity to walk around and enjoy it. Dress very warmly.

At the Alyeska Prince Hotel (see below). $16 adults ($14 Alaska residents), $15 ages 55 and older, $12 ages 8–17, $7 ages 7 and under. Summer daily 10am–9:30pm; winter when lifts operate (call to check, as hours vary).

ACTIVITIES

Here I have covered activities right in Girdwood. In nearby Whittier (p. 270), you can go ocean fishing or sea kayaking, or take a glacier and wildlife cruise. The Turnagain Arm and Portage area (p. 246) offers sightseeing along Turnagain Arm, hiking, and other summer activities.

SKIING   Mount Alyeska, at 3,939 feet, has 1,000 acres of skiing, beginning from a base elevation of only 250 feet and rising 2,500 feet. The normal season is from early November to April, and it's an exceptional year when there isn't plenty of snow all winter (although the warming climate has brought some poor ski seasons). Skiing on the upper mountain usually lasts through Memorial Day weekend (not for beginners). The average snowfall is 721 inches, or 61 feet. Because it's near the water, the weather is rarely very cold. Light is more of an issue, with short days in midwinter. There are 27 lighted trails covering 2,000 vertical feet on Friday and Saturday evenings from mid-December to mid-March, but the best Alaska skiing is when the days get longer and warmer in the spring.

Alyeska has 10 lifts, including the tram. Two chairs serve beginners, with a vertical drop of around 300 feet. The other 89% of the mountain is geared to intermediate to expert skiers. The biggest drawback for less experienced skiers is a lack of runs in the low-to-intermediate ability range. After graduating from the primary beginners' lift, Chair 3, skiers must jump to significantly more challenging slopes. That explains the long lines in busy periods on Chair 3 (it is the only lift on the mountain with real lines). More confident skiers like the mountain best. Most of it is steep, and the expert slopes are extreme. Helicopter skiing goes right from the resort's hotel as well.

For children and nonskiers, the Kraft Glacier Tubing Park was added in 2005, and it has been hugely popular. Riders go uphill on a lift that is designed to carry passengers and inner tubes, and then slide down a long, bouncy run. Tickets are for 90-minute sessions during the day and cost $15 adults and $10 ages 6 to 13. Children must be at least 42 inches tall.

An all-day lift ticket costs $52 for adults ($45 for Alaska residents, $41 for hotel guests), $34 for ages 14 to 17 or 60 to 69, $26 for ages 8 to 13, and $10 for ages 7 and under or over 70. Discounts apply for families. Private and group instruction are available, and you can save a lot by buying your lessons, lift ticket, and equipment rental at the same time. The day lodge rents basic gear and the hotel rents high-performance gear. A basic rental package costs $27 a day for adults, $18 for ages 13 and under or over 60; high performance $32 and $21, respectively. There are groomed **cross-country trails** as well, and gear for rent, but the best Nordic skiing is in Anchorage.

Tips Ski Conditions

The rainforest of Girdwood and the dry Anchorage bowl often have different weather, despite being within the same municipality. Before heading down the road for a day of skiing, check out the conditions. Call © **907/SKI-SNOW** for snow, weather, and visibility conditions, or check that information online at www.alyeskaresort.com. For visibility from below, check out the cam at www.chairfive.com.

A center operated by **Challenge Alaska** (© **907/783-2925** or 907/344-7399; www.challengealaska.org) allows skiers with disabilities to use the mountain, skiing down to the lift to start and back to the center at day's end. It's called the Keil Center for Adaptive Sports and Therapeutic Recreation. They also rent the latest adaptive ski equipment.

A utilitarian **day lodge** with snack and rental counters is located at the front of the mountain, as is the **Sitzmark Bar,** a more comfortable place for a meal (burgers are around $8). The Alyeska Prince Hotel (p. 254) is on the other side of the mountain, connected to the front by the tram to the top and beginner-level chair 7 (you can ski right from the door). It makes a quieter and more genteel starting point for day-trippers as well as guests, as it has its own day lockers and an equipment-rental counter with higher-quality equipment (and higher rates) than the day lodge. There are several dining choices here and at the top of the tram (see "Where to Stay," below).

HIKING   There are a couple of great Chugach National Forest trails starting in Girdwood.

Among the best trails in the region for a family hike is the **Winner Creek Trail,** which begins behind the Alyeska Prince Hotel and leads to a roaring gorge where Winner Creek and Glacier Creek meet; a hand-operated tram crosses the water. The trail is essentially level and a good length for an afternoon: The round-trip to the gorge is about 4.5 miles. People with mobility problems may not make it that far but can still enjoy the first .65 miles of the trail, which are built up with wide boardwalks and gravel nearly to the point of wheelchair accessibility. Beyond that part, the trail has roots and muddy spots but is still well maintained. A winter ski trail takes a separate route through a series of meadows to the same destination.

The **Crow Pass Trail** is more ambitious. The route rises into the mountains and continues all the way over to Eagle River, after a 26-mile hike that can take a couple of days. But with less expenditure of time, you can make a strenuous day hike of it going just up to the pass, where you can see the glaciers, wildflower meadows, and old mining equipment. The Forest Service's A-frame Crow Pass public-use cabin makes an excellent destination for an overnight from Girdwood; it lies on a lake at 3,500-feet elevation, half a mile from the pass. The trail head is up Crow Creek Road, off the Alyeska Highway. For more information on the national forest and cabin reservations, see section 3 of chapter 7.

SNOWMOBILING   **Glacier City Snowmobile Tours** (© **877/783-5566** or 907/783-5566; www.snowtours.net) operates out of the Great Alaskan Tourist Trap gift shop in the shopping center on the Seward Highway. Guides suit up clients—most of whom have never been on a snowmobile—and drive them to a promising site, determined according to snow conditions. At best, the winter tours make it all the way to Spencer Glacier. Groups are no larger than six and the attitude is casual: After a brief introduction, you are driving your own machine, using your own judgment. The entire outing lasts as long as 6 hours, with 3½ hours of riding. The cost is $220 per person. The same outfit offers summertime snowmobiling. For $389 each, a helicopter carries clients to the Eagle Glacier for more than 2 hours of riding on the snow field.

WHERE TO STAY

Besides the resort hotel, there are plenty of condos and B&Bs in town. **Alyeska Accommodations,** on Olympic Mountain Loop (© **888/783-2001** or 907/783-2000; www.alyeskaaccommodations.com), offers rooms, condos, cabins, and luxurious houses.

Alyeska Prince Hotel ⭐⭐⭐ The Alyeska Resort's hotel is among Alaska's best. The beauty of the building alone separates it from the competition, as does its location in an unspoiled mountain valley among huge spruce trees. Studded with dormers and turrets, it impresses on first sight. Inside, sumptuous cherrywood and rich colors unite the welcoming common rooms and elegant guest rooms. Although not large, rooms have every convenience. The saltwater swimming pool is magnificent, with a cathedral ceiling and windows by the spa overlooking the mountain. The location and activities alone make the hotel worth visiting. A few days spent here skiing and swimming make the rest of life seem too drab. Now for the bad news. On weekends and school holidays in the winter, the hotel is overrun by partying families from Anchorage who overtax the facilities and destroy the peaceful ambience. Children run wild, the pool becomes impossibly crowded, and service deteriorates to an unacceptable level. If coming for a skiing vacation, avoid these times.

Four restaurants vie for attention. **The Seven Glaciers,** 2,300 feet above the lobby by tram on Mount Alyeska, serves trendy and beautifully presented dinners in a sumptuous dining room floating above the clouds. Service is warm and highly professional. Meals are expensive, especially since the small servings make it desirable to order several courses. The restaurant opens only on the weekends in the winter. A mountaintop cafeteria is right next door (great views, limited choices). At the base level, the Japanese cuisine at the **Katsura Teppanyaki** has developed a good reputation. The **Pond Cafe** is good when not jammed on the weekends and has a nice view.

1000 Arlberg Ave. (P.O. Box 249), Girdwood, AK 99587. © 800/880-3880 or 907/754-1111. Fax 907/754-2200. www.alyeskaresort.com. 307 units. Summer and Christmas $275–$360 double, $420–$1,700 suite; winter $145–$240 double, $260–$1,400 suite. Extra adult $25; children stay free in parent's room. AE, DC, MC, V. **Amenities:** 4 restaurants; 2 bars; indoor pool; health club; spa; bike rental; children's programs; concierge; tour desk; business center; shopping arcade; limited room service; massage; babysitting. *In room:* TV w/pay movies, dataport, Wi-Fi (floors 2–3), fridge, coffeemaker, hair dryer, iron, safe.

WHERE TO DINE

Also see directly above for restaurant options at the Alyeska Prince Hotel.

Chair 5 Restaurant ⭐ *Kids* SEAFOOD/BURGERS/PIZZA This is where Girdwood locals meet their friends and take their families for dinner, and it's also one of our favorites after skiing. One afternoon, Bob Dylan music accompanied a friendly game of pool while men with ponytails and beards sipped microbrews. Another evening, a guy in the entryway entertained the children with magic tricks and the waitress asked them to draw pictures to enter into a contest. The menu offers choices pleasing to each family member, including pizza, burgers, fresh fish, and steaks.

5 Lindblad Ave., in the New Girdwood Town Square. © 907/783-2500. www.chairfive.com. Lunch $9–$10; dinner $16–$24; large pizza $18–$21. AE, DC, DISC, MC, V. Daily 11am–11pm (bar open till 2am).

Double Musky Inn ⭐⭐⭐ CAJUN The ski-bum-casual atmosphere and rambling, cluttered dining room among the trees match the wonderful Cajun and New Orleans food in a way that couldn't have been contrived—it's at once too improbable and too authentic. Service is relaxed to a fault, and food takes a long time to arrive, but when it does, every dish is flawless. I love the jambalaya, and the steaks are famous (by which I mean really famous—Food Network chose this as one of the 10 best restaurants in America). On my most recent visit, with two couples, each item on our plates from appetizers through dessert became a topic of conversation; since I love talking about the food over dinner, I love this place. The Double Musky isn't to everyone's taste, however; your senses can feel raw after the extreme noise, highly spiced food, and crowds, and parking can be difficult. Loud groups will enjoy it more than couples, and families don't really fit. Since the restaurant doesn't take reservations, here's an important tip: Grab seats in the bar and dive into your meal there with appetizers and drinks rather than simply waiting.

Mile 3, Crow Creek Rd., Girdwood. ℂ 907/783-2822. No reservations. www.doublemuskyinn.com. Main courses $18–$37. AE, DC, DISC, MC, V. Tues–Thurs 5–10pm; Fri–Sun 4:30–10pm. Closed Nov.

10 Out from Anchorage: The Matanuska & Susitna Valleys

On a longer visit to Anchorage, you may want to spend a day or two in the suburbs to the north, known as the Mat-Su Valley. Reached by the Glenn Highway about 40 miles from Anchorage, the area is both a bedroom community for the city and a former frontier farming region with its own quirky identity. If you are driving anywhere north from the city, you will pass through this area, and there are some interesting places to stop if you have the time. In this summary, I've covered a few highlights in the central area (the whole thing is the size of West Virginia). Some of the best attractions are covered in other parts of the book. **The Alaska State Fair,** held before Labor Day, is covered under "Special Events," near the beginning of this chapter. **The Musk Ox Farm** is under "Shopping," earlier in this chapter. Funky Talkeetna, a gateway to Denali National Park, is in chapter 8. The Matanuska Glacier area (on the Glenn Highway), with its great canyon views and late-season cross-country skiing and snowmobiling, is in chapter 9. You can learn more about visitor attractions, lodging, and the area's greatest strengths—its hiking, fishing, and skiing—from the **Mat-Su Visitors Center,** 7744 E. Visitors View Court, Palmer, AK 99645 (ℂ 907/746-5000; www.alaskavisit.com). To find the center, take the Trunk Road exit from the Parks Highway near the intersection with the Glenn Highway.

THROUGH HATCHER PASS

If you're headed north to Denali National Park or Fairbanks, the winding road through Hatcher Pass to Willow makes a glorious alpine detour around the least attractive part of your drive. Past the mine and skiing area, the road is unpaved and open only in summer and is not suitable for large RVs. Just after the Parks Highway branches from the Glenn Highway, exit to the right on the Trunk Road and keep going north on Fishhook Road, which becomes Hatcher Pass Road. From the Glenn Highway near Palmer, take Palmer Fishhook just north of town.

Even if you're not headed north, a trip to Hatcher Pass combines one of the area's most beautiful drives, access to great hiking and Nordic skiing, and interesting old buildings to look at. The **Independence Mine State Historical Park** 𝒜𝒜 (ℂ 907/745-2827 or 907/745-3975; www.alaskastateparks.org, click on "Individual Parks") takes in the remains of a hard-rock gold mine operation that closed down in 1951. Some buildings have been restored, including an assay office that's a museum and the manager's house that's a welcoming visitor center, while a big old mill, towering on the hillside, sags and leans as a picturesque ruin. A visit is interesting even if you don't go inside, using the interpretive panels and map on a self-guided tour. The paved trails are easily navigable by anyone. The setting, in a bowl of rock and alpine tundra, is spectacular. The day-use fee is $5 per vehicle. A guided tour is an additional $5 per person and leaves at 1:30pm and 3:30pm weekdays, plus 4:30pm weekends. Tours depend on staffing and may be increased or decreased from these hours. The visitor center is open from 10am to 7pm daily in the summer, closed off-season.

Leave some time for a summer ramble in the heather if you visit the mine. In the winter, the Nordic or telemark skiing is exceptional, with a few kilometers of groomed trail and miles of open country to explore. (See the Hatcher Pass Lodge, below, for more details.) There are four hiking trails and two mountain-biking routes in the area—ask at the visitor center. The **Gold Cord Trail** is one of the shorter choices. The **Reed Lakes Trail** is spectacular for its mountain scenery and waterfalls; starting from the Archangel Road, it gains 3,000 feet over 4.5 miles to Upper Reed Lake. Another challenging hike is the 8-mile **Gold Mint Trail,** which starts across the road from the Motherlode Lodge on Hatcher Pass Road and ends at the Mint Glacier, where you have to turn around to hike back.

ON THE PARKS HIGHWAY

The Museum of Alaska Transportation and Industry ⚔, off the Parks Highway at Mile 47, west of Wasilla (✆ **907/376-1211;** www.museumofalaska.org), is a paradise for gearheads and tinkerers. The volunteers have gathered every conceivable machine and conveyance—13 fire trucks, 7 locomotives, and 2 steam cranes, for example—and fixed up to running order as many as they can. An indoor museum displays their finished masterpieces, while the 20 acres outside are crammed with future projects—trains, aircraft, tractors, fishing boats, and mining equipment—all grist for memories and imagination. It's open May 1 to September 30 daily from 9am to 6pm, winter Saturday from 10am to 5pm, or by appointment. Admission is $8 for adults, $5 for students and seniors, $18 for families.

WHERE TO STAY & DINE

Three good places to eat in the Valley are at the accommodations I have described below. In addition, there are unlimited fast food spots and roadhouse burger places. Here is a stop to plan on in Wasilla on your way to Denali or back to Anchorage: The **Valley Bistro,** at 405 E. Herning Ave., is a memorable cafe near the intersection of the Parks Highway and Main St. in Wasilla (✆ **907/357-5633**), which occupies the town's primary historic building, the old Tecland's country store. The dining room is pleasing, with antiques, wood floors, and high ceilings. The menu includes quiche, soups, and specials. It is open Monday through Saturday 7am to 8pm and Sunday 10am to 4pm.

HATCHER PASS

Hatcher Pass Lodge ⚔ *Finds*   A charming family presides at this tiny mountain lodge in the treeless alpine bowl that also contains the Independence Mine State Historic Park, 3,000 feet above the sea, which glistens in the grand vista down below. Out on the open snowfield in winter, or the heather in summer, the nine cabins and A-frame lodge seem far more remote than they really are, just 90 minutes from Anchorage. There is a phone in the main lodge for emergencies but no TV. Our family went for a glorious Nordic skiing vacation there, and the 12 of us, ages 2 through 75, all had a great time. A place with nothing to divert you but snow, a warm cabin, and good meals brings a family closer. The cabins are clean and nicely set up, with no rustic edge except chemical toilets and the lack of running water. The rates reflect the off-grid remoteness, not exceptional luxury. Guests go to the main lodge for showers, meals, and drinks; the family produces surprisingly professional meals there. Stay in summer for a taste of the real Alaska with doorstep access to wonderful alpine hiking.

P.O. Box 763, Palmer, AK 99645. ✆ **907/745-5897.** www.hatcherpasslodge.com. 9 cabins, 3 lodge rooms. $157 cabin for 2; lodge rooms $95 double. Extra person $15. AE, DC, DISC, MC, V. **Amenities:** Restaurant; bar; sauna. *In room:* No phone.

WASILLA

Best Western Lake Lucille Inn ✦ This well-run, attractive lakeside hotel in Wasilla has the best standard rooms in the valley. They're large and well appointed, and those facing the lake have balconies and a grand, peaceful view. The hotel helps with activities and offers discounts on some. Flightseeing trips take off from the dock below the lawn. The **restaurant** is one of the best in the area, with a light, quiet dining room looking out on the water. It's open for three meals a day. The dinner menu of beef and seafood ranges from $15 to $38. The property is nonsmoking except in the lounge.

1300 W. Lake Lucille Dr., Wasilla, AK 99654. ✆ **800/528-1234** or 907/373-1776. Fax 907/376-6199. www.bestwestern lakelucilleinn.com. 54 units. High season $169 double, $229 suite; low season $89 double, $175 suite. Extra person $10. AE, DC, DISC, MC, V. **Amenities:** Restaurant; exercise room; Jacuzzi; sauna; coin-op laundry. *In room:* TV, free high-speed Internet, Wi-Fi, coffeemaker, hair dryer, iron.

PALMER

Colony Inn ✦ *Finds* This classic country inn occupies a restored teacher's dormitory from the New Deal Colony Project, right in the middle of Palmer. The rooms are attractively old-fashioned, although a little worn in spots, with rockers and comforters but also Jacuzzi bathtubs and big TVs with VCRs. A large sitting room and a dining room downstairs are decorated with historic photographs that help tell the building's story. Meals are served here during the summer at the **Inn Cafe** (✆ **907/746-6118**): lunch Monday through Friday, dinner Friday night with live jazz, and a popular Sunday brunch. Guests check in at the comparatively down-scale Valley Hotel, at 606 S. Alaska St., and there often is no innkeeper on-site to let you in or help with problems.

325 E. Elmwood, Palmer, AK 99645. ✆ **907/745-3330.** Fax 907/746-3330. 12 units. $110 double; $196 suite. AE, DISC, MC, V. **Amenities:** Restaurant; laundry machines. *In room:* TV/VCR, dataport, fridge.

7

The Kenai Peninsula & Prince William Sound

The Gulf of Alaska arcs at its northern edge, forming the rounded northern shore of the Pacific Ocean, a zone of great collisions. This is where the earth's tectonic plates collide, spewing forth froths of hot lava from dozens of volcanoes and fracturing and folding the earth with titanic earthquakes. Here the ocean's wildest weather hits mountains jutting miles high from the sea, growing immense prehistoric ice sheets and glaciers that carve the rock into long, deep, intricate fjords. The sea proffers prodigious biological wealth on these shores, including the salmon it unleashes into the rivers in furious swarms of life that climb over the mountains and into the Interior to spawn. Nature seems giant and superabundant along this magnificent arc of land and water.

Geography endowed this one stretch of coast with several of the world's great natural places. On the east, near Cordova, the **Copper River**'s immense, entirely unspoiled delta is the largest contiguous wetlands in the Western Hemisphere. On a day trip, you're immediately alone with flocks of rare, graceful waterfowl that congregate on shallow ponds surrounded by miles of waving grass. **Prince William Sound** is a vast protected sea of wooded mountains and mammoth glaciers. This is our family's favorite place on earth, where we go each summer to camp among the otters and eagles on tiny islands out of contact with the rest of mankind. **Kenai Fjords National Park** takes in bays off the open ocean where

the mountains soar a mile straight up from the water. Boats travel here among humpback, gray, and orca whales; spot otters, seals, and sea lions; and visit swarming colonies of puffins and other seabirds. The **Kenai River** harbors the world's biggest salmon, on the western side of the Kenai Peninsula; and on its southern tip, **Kachemak Bay** is like a miniature Prince William Sound, but with people. The bay's shores are dotted by tiny towns with lodges, art galleries on pilings, and some of Alaska's best restaurants.

The whole region is exceptionally accessible, by Alaska standards. The Kenai (*keen*-eye) Peninsula, in particular, is easy to get to without the expense and exhausting travel that can make much of the state difficult. Most of what you're looking for in Alaska lies along a few hundred miles of blacktop, within reach of a rental car and perhaps a tour boat ticket: glaciers, whales, legendary sportfishing, spectacular hiking trails, interesting little fishing towns, bears, moose, and high mountains.

People from Anchorage go to the peninsula for the weekend to fish, hike, dig clams, paddle kayaks, and so on, and certain places can get crowded. There's a special phrase for what happens when the red salmon are running in July on the Kenai and Russian rivers: *combat fishing*. At hot times in certain places, anglers stand elbow to elbow on the bank, each casting into his or her own yard-wide slice of river, and still catch plenty of hefty salmon. The peninsula also exerts a powerful magnetic force on RVs, those road-whales that you find at the head of lines of cars on the two-lane highways. During the summer, the fishing rivers, creeks, and beaches on the west side of the peninsula and the end of the Homer Spit can become sheet-metal cities of hundreds of Winnebagos and Airstreams parked side by side. Often some local entrepreneur will be selling doughnuts or newspapers door-to-door.

Yet the decision is yours as to whether you spend time in the company of tourists. If the roadside fishing is hairy, hiking a little farther down the bank usually means you can be by yourself. In this chapter, I'll describe some towns of unspoiled charm, where you can kayak virtually from your room. Being alone is easy. You can paddle among otters in Resurrection Bay; tramp over the heather in Turnagain Pass; hike, bike, or ski one of the many maintained trails in Chugach National Forest. And when you're ready to come back to the comforts of civilization, you'll find that some of the state's best restaurants and most interesting lodgings are here, too.

1 Exploring the Kenai Peninsula & Prince William Sound

THE TOWNS

Kenai, on Cook Inlet on the west side of the Kenai Peninsula, is the largest town in the region. Ten miles up the Kenai River, **Soldotna** is Kenai's twin, and together they form a unit with about a fourth of the Kenai Peninsula's population of 50,000. They're also the least interesting of the peninsula's communities. **Homer,** at the southern end of the peninsula, has wonderful art and character and lots of ways to get out on the water. **Seward,** on the east side, is smaller and quieter, a charming gateway to Kenai Fjords National Park.

There are three towns on Prince William Sound. **Valdez** is an oil town at the southern terminus of the trans-Alaska pipeline where tankers are loaded. **Cordova** is more attractive, a historic community on the eastern side of the Sound, with outdoor activities close at hand. **Whittier** is a grim former military outpost, but a convenient gateway to the protected fjords and glaciers of the western Sound.

GETTING THERE & GETTING AROUND

BY CAR   Highways connect all the region's large towns, except Cordova, which is reached only by air or water. Like all of Alaska's main highways, these are paved two-lane roads. The Seward Highway runs south from Anchorage to the Kenai Peninsula. That route is described below. A road built in a railway tunnel connects Whittier, on Prince William Sound, to the Seward Highway. The Glenn and Richardson highways reach from Anchorage to Valdez through Alaska's Interior. Stops along that route are described in chapter 9, and all of Alaska's highways are summarized on p. 404.

BY FERRY   The ferry system connects Whittier with Valdez and Cordova via the fast ferry *Chenega,* launched in 2005. Driving from Anchorage to Whittier, taking the ferry to Valdez, and then driving back to Anchorage (or north to Fairbanks) makes a great loop. The Chugach National Forest usually has rangers on board offering programs and interpretation. The ferry *Tustumena* (the *"Tusty"*) connects Homer to Kodiak Island and the Aleutian Archipelago (covered in chapter 10), and also runs from Homer to Seldovia. The schedule is not convenient for Seldovia, however; for that trip, it's easier to take one of the private passenger ferries that serve the towns and remote sites around Kachemak Bay from Homer. A U.S. Fish and Wildlife Service ranger offers programs on the *Tusty.* For more on the ferry system, see section 1 of chapter 5, call © **800/642-0066,** or visit www.ferryalaska.com.

BY AIR   Commuter aircraft connect Anchorage to Kenai, Homer, Valdez, and Cordova. You can also fly between Anchorage and Cordova on an Alaska Airlines jet once a day in each direction (the northbound originates in Seattle). Scheduled and air-taxi services use these smaller towns as bases for the villages, carrying passengers, mail, and cargo, and flying to remote lodges and cabins for fishing or other outdoor activities. Valdez, Cordova, and Anchorage operators serve the Prince William Sound region. Kenai and Anchorage companies cover Cook Inlet and remote public lands such as Lake Clark National Park. Homer is the base for villages around Kachemak Bay and lower Cook Inlet bear-viewing sites.

BY TRAIN   The **Alaska Railroad** (© **800/544-0552** or 907/265-2494; www.alaska railroad.com) runs from Anchorage south to Seward or Whittier and back daily in the summer.

VISITOR INFORMATION

For information on the peninsula as a whole, contact the **Kenai Peninsula Tourism Marketing Council,** 35477 Kenai Spur Hwy., Suite 205, Soldotna, AK 99669 (© **800/535-3524** or 907/262-5229; www.kenaipeninsula.org), which distributes a vacation planner with information on businesses and trip planning in the area (order through the website). The staff will answer inquiries during normal business hours.

GETTING OUTSIDE

The towns of the region are like beads strung along the laces of the highways; everything else is wilderness. You can find all the activities and isolation you seek here, yet the presence of the towns means that comfort is closer at hand than in other parts of Alaska.

Chugach National Forest takes in all of Prince William Sound and most of the eastern Kenai Peninsula. At 5.3 million acres, it's more than double the size of Yellowstone National Park. Anywhere else but Alaska it would be a national park, and one of the largest and most spectacular, with some of the best sea kayaking, hiking, backpacking, wildlife watching, and scenery anywhere. General information, camping, and ideas on remote areas in the Chugach are covered in section 3, while details about National Forest areas near towns are in the appropriate town sections.

Kenai Fjords National Park (section 6), protecting the outer edge and ice cap of the Kenai Peninsula's southern side, is incomparable in its remoteness, stark beauty, and abundance of marine wildlife. Access is though Seward (section 5).

On the peninsula's western side, **Kenai National Wildlife Refuge** (section 9) has Alaska's most accessible wilderness lake and river canoeing, as well as extraordinary fishing, with access from roads near Soldotna (section 8).

Kachemak Bay State Park offers good sea-kayaking waters and wilderness hiking not connected to any road. The **Alaska Maritime National Wildlife Refuge** protects the wildlife habitat of remote islands and seashores around the state. Both are covered in section 10 of this chapter, on Homer.

VISITOR INFORMATION   The region's best and most central place to get outdoor information is the **Alaska Public Lands Information Center,** 605 W. 4th Ave., Suite 105, Anchorage, AK 99501 (© **866/869-6887,** 907/271-2737, or 907/271-2738 TTY; www.nps.gov/aplic). You'll be able to ask guidance of residents who have spent

The Kenai Peninsula & Prince William Sound

Tips State Parks Cabin Reservations

Alaska's state parks rent remote public cabins, such as the famous Forest Service cabins (see section 3), but they're usually newer, larger, and easier to get to. Most are in Southcentral Alaska—in this chapter, they're mentioned near Homer, Seward, and Valdez. Like the Forest Service cabins, it takes a hike, boat ride, or air taxi to get to the cabins, and you need cabin equipment, such as a cookstove and sleeping bags, but once there you can experience the real Alaska all by yourself.

Some of these cabins book up the minute they become available and, since Alaska residents get a jump on the reservation system, visitors are unlikely to be able to use the most popular cabins at peak periods. But if you can be flexible about where you go, or if you can travel out of the peak season, you can probably find a cabin. Alaska residents can reserve 7 months ahead, nonresidents 6 months ahead; however, reservations do not initially open on weekends or holidays, only at 10am Alaska time on the following business day. Once a date opens on the system, it stays open 24 hours a day until someone takes it.

The easiest way to reserve is by using the online system with a MasterCard or Visa, but you can also reserve in person, by mail, or by fax (you can ask questions by phone but not apply). The staff is friendly and will guide you around the system, and help you find a cabin where you can get a permit, even if it's not your first choice. The main information and reservations desk is the **Department of Natural Resources Public Information Center—Anchorage,** 550 W. 7th Ave., Suite 1260, Anchorage, AK 99501-3557 (© **907/269-8400,** or 907/269-8411 TTY; fax 907/269-8901; www.alaskastateparks.org). The website is the best source of information about the cabins, with a picture and description of each and a real-time availability calendar. The center is open Monday through Friday 10am to 5pm. Cabins rent for $25 to $75 a night, with fees highest for popular cabins at peak periods.

---

time in the places you'll be visiting, and there are exhibits on the wildlife and outdoor opportunities in the region—even maps showing where to find various species of fish. Land agencies present information on the whole state. Pick up books and maps here and buy tickets for the ferries. Summer hours are daily from 9am to 5pm, winter Monday through Friday from 10am to 5pm. Visitor centers for particular areas are covered in the appropriate sections.

2 The Seward Highway: A Road Guide

The Kenai Peninsula's lifeline is the road down from Anchorage, a 127-mile drive to Seward on a good two-lane highway, most of it through public land without development or services. Highway 1, commonly known as the Seward Highway, is more than scenic—it's really a wonderful attraction in itself, designated a National Scenic Byway and an All-American Road. A detailed booklet about the highway with maps and mile-by-mile descriptions, *The Seward Highway: Alaska's All-American Road,* is distributed by the public land information center in Anchorage (p. 211). There are excellent campgrounds and hiking trails all along the way in the Chugach National Forest, which I've covered in section 3 of this chapter.

The mileposts start in Seward. Here we count backward, since you'll likely start from Anchorage.

MILES 127–179   The highway begins at the south end of Anchorage, the only way out of town in that direction, and runs along Turnagain Arm 48 miles to the Portage Glacier. I've written about that spectacular portion of the drive in chapter 6 under section 8, "Out from Anchorage: Turnagain Arm & Portage Glacier."

MILES 79–75   Beyond the Portage Glacier turnoff, the road traverses the salt marshes to the south side of the Arm. These wetlands are good bird-watching grounds. The dead trees on the flats are left over from before the 1964 earthquake. The area was inundated in the quake, when the entire region shifted—including the Kenai Peninsula and Prince William Sound—lowering this area 12 feet and raising areas to the east as much as 30 feet. Everything moved laterally, too. Besides being the second-strongest earthquake ever recorded, the '64 quake moved more land than any other. People who were here tell of their surprise when the tide came far higher than they had ever seen it before in the days after the earthquake, until finally they realized that the land itself had sunk. Large parts of Homer, Hope, and Seldovia disappeared under the waves at high tide. Seward, Whittier, Valdez, and Kodiak were swept by destructive tsunami waves.

MILES 75–68   The highway steeply climbs through the spruce forest to the fresh, towering alpine terrain of the 1,000-foot-elevation **Turnagain Pass.** The vistas here are stupendous year-round.

MILE 68   If you find the meadow and tundra hard to resist for a walk, go ahead. Park at the pull-out with the toilets on the right side at the pass summit and follow the path, or just amble off into the wildflowers (assuming the ground is dry when you're there). In the winter and spring, this is a backcountry skiing and snowmobiling paradise. Skiers go on the left (east) side of the road and snowmobilers on the right. Always check with the Chugach National Forest (see section 3, below) for avalanche conditions first. An avalanche near here killed five riders in spring 1999.

MILES 68–57   The pass forms a divide; crossing it, Granite Creek flows down toward the south. The road follows, falling back below the tree line of stunted spruce and then popping back up into sweeping views. Arcing to the northwest after the Granite Creek Campground, the highway follows another north-flowing river, Sixmile Creek.

MILE 57 & HOPE HIGHWAY   The Hope Highway divides off to the north and west along Sixmile Creek while the Seward Highway continues south. Rafting companies based in Anchorage use this wild stretch of water for some of their most challenging rides (see chapter 6).

A Side Trip to Hope   If you want a break, you'll find **Hope** at the end of the 17-mile Hope Highway. It's a charming gold rush–era village and the starting point for some great hikes (see the Resurrection Pass Trail, p. 266, and Porcupine campground, p. 269). A few white frame buildings remain from the days when Hope was a gold-mining boomtown after a strike in 1894. Before the 1964 earthquake, the rest of the town used to stand where the creek gives way to a tidal meadow. Wandering the gravel roads, you'll find more quaint spots. Today, Hope's year-round population is about 150. For information, contact the **Hope-Sunrise Community Library** (© **907/782-3121**), which is open daily in summer from 11am to 4pm, when volunteer manpower allows. You can also find Hope information online at www.advenalaska.com/hope.

Why All the Dead Trees?

Whole mountainsides on the Kenai Peninsula and in Anchorage lack large trees or have huge groups of dead, weathered, or downed trees. The spruce bark beetle is to blame. Although a natural part of the forest system, the beetles' population exploded in the last 2 decades and swept across Southcentral Alaska, wiping out 4 million acres of white and Sitka spruce, the biggest single insect kill of trees ever in North America. The beetles bore under the outer bark layer to eat the trees' phloem, the soft inner bark that carries food manufactured in the needles down to the roots. The beetles reproduce in the tree, sending the next generation in flight in May and June in search of more victims. The blight stopped spreading only when susceptible trees were dead.

Scientists believe global climate change allowed short, spotty beetle outbreaks to become a long, wide plague. Cool, damp springs can stop beetles in a year or two, but since 1987 the state has had a solid string of exceptionally warm, dry seasons. Ecologists also have noticed shrinking ponds, a rising tree line, and many other indicators of a changing climate on the Kenai Peninsula. In places, the ecological makeup in the forest appears to be transformed, but it will be decades before we learn if natural succession leads back to a new spruce forest, or if large tracts become grassy, parklike areas. In the meantime, be careful with fire. (You can learn more on my website at www.wohlforth.net/SpruceBarkBeetles.htm.)

The **Hope and Sunrise Historical and Mining Museum** (© 907/782-3740) is a one-room log cabin displaying historic objects and photographs, a barn, blacksmith's shop, miner's bunkhouse, and old-time school. Volunteers keep the museum open Memorial Day to Labor Day daily noon to 4pm. One of the best places to eat in town is the **Discovery Café** (© 907/782-3274), the community's hub and a place to get a generous burger and meet the beloved proprietor. The cafe burned to the ground in 1999 and was rebuilt almost entirely by volunteer labor, reopening in the summer of 2001.

MILES 57–46 The Seward Highway climbs steeply from the Hope Highway intersection, up the canyon of Canyon Creek, before leveling out above the tree line at about 1,400 feet elevation. Next comes a series of alpine lakes in a narrow mountain valley.

MILE 46 Upper Summit Lake lies smooth and reflective in a steep alpine valley. On the far side is the Tenderfoot Creek Campground, a calming spot warmed by sun off the water (p. 269). On the near side is a traditional highway stopping place without neighbors for miles in any direction, the **Summit Lake Lodge**, at Mile 45.5 (© 907/244-2031). The main building is a traditional log roadhouse that's been updated to house a modern restaurant. Meals can take some time, so eat here only if you're not in a rush. Even if you don't want dinner, however, the location can't be beat for a driving break. You can enjoy ice cream from the counter in the log gift shop while you stroll near the lake. The lodge rents six motel rooms with private bathrooms, but without TVs or phones.

MILES 46–37 The highway continues through similar mountain terrain before descending into the trees again and branching at **Tern Lake.** This is a stirringly beautiful spot year-round, and a good place to get out and taste the fresh mountain air and watch for moose, waterfowl, and other birds. There's a picnic area. To the right at the intersection, the Sterling Highway leads to Cooper Landing, Soldotna, Kenai, and Homer.

MILE 32   Moose Creek has a viewing platform to watch thousands of spawning salmon in season; half a mile on, the Trail Lake Fish Hatchery sits on the edge of Upper Trail Lake. This is the first of a string of sparkling mountain lakes that the road will follow for the next 15 miles.

MILE 30   The community of Moose Pass, with a population of about 200, sits on the shore of Upper Trail Lake.

MILE 18–0   Down among the big spruces of the coastal forest, the highway comes to Seward.

3 Chugach National Forest: Do-It-Yourself Wilderness

I've lived near the Chugach National Forest all my life, but it wasn't until well into adulthood that I had seen all its parts and appreciated its vastness and variety. Still, I doubt I'll ever really know this seemingly infinite land. **Prince William Sound,** just one of the National Forest's three parts, has 3,500 miles of shoreline among its folded islands and deeply penetrating fjords and passages. It would take a lifetime to really know all those cove beaches, climb all the island mountains, and explore to the head of every narrow bay under big rainforest trees. The **Copper River Delta** is another world entirely. Unlike the musty secrets of the Sound's obscure passages, the delta opens to the sky like a heavenly plain of wind and light, its waving green colors splashed by the airiest brushstrokes. It's another huge area: Just driving across the delta and back from Cordova takes most of a day. Finally, there's the western part of the national forest, on the **Kenai Peninsula.** This is largely an alpine realm. The mountains are steep, their timber quickly giving way to rock, tundra, and wildflowers up above. It's got remote, unclimbed peaks, but also many miles of family hiking trails, accessible fishing streams, and superb campgrounds. This is where you go in Alaska for multiday trail hikes.

The Chugach is managed primarily for recreation and conservation. Logging in Prince William Sound was essentially stopped by the *Exxon Valdez* oil spill, when conservationists recognized the need to prevent further environmental damage to support recovery from the disaster. When Exxon was forced to pay $1 billion to a recovery fund, government trustees spent much of the money to buy back timber rights in the Sound and beyond to protect the trees. They bought 1,419 miles of coastline and almost as much land as is in all of Yosemite National Park. Still, that was only a sixth of the area the Chugach already encompassed.

ESSENTIALS

GETTING THERE & GETTING AROUND   There are many ways to the Chugach National Forest. For Prince William Sound, use Whittier, Valdez, or Cordova as gateways; for the Copper River Delta, go through Cordova. Trails and campgrounds on the Kenai Peninsula generally meet the Seward or Sterling highways, or spur roads from the highways. The individual town listings later in this chapter provide details on how to get there and into that part of the national forest. Section 2, above, describes the Seward Highway.

VISITOR INFORMATION   The most central place for information on the national forest is the Alaska Public Lands Information Center in Anchorage (p. 211). For general forest inquiries, you can also contact the **forest headquarters,** 3301 C St., Suite 300, Anchorage, AK 99503 (© **907/743-9500;** www.fs.fed.us/r10/chugach). The national forest also has three ranger district offices, where you can get up-to-date local information and personal advice: **Glacier Ranger District,** on Monarch Mine Road, near the Seward Highway off Alyeska Road, in Girdwood (© **907/783-3242**); **Seward Ranger District,** 4th Avenue and Jefferson Street, in Seward (© **907/224-3374**); and **Cordova Ranger District,** 2nd and Browning streets, in Cordova (© **907/424-7661**). You can't reserve campground sites and remote cabins through these local offices—for that you must use the national system listed below under "Where to Stay"—but you can call them with questions.

GETTING OUTSIDE
HIKING, MOUNTAIN BIKING & BACKPACKING

Alaska's best long trails lead through the mountain passes of Chugach National Forest, including historic gold-rush trails and portions of the original Iditarod trail (the race doesn't use these southern portions). The Forest Service maintains **public cabins** on many of these trails and in other remote spots reachable only with a boat or small plane. If the nights you need are available, you can use the cabins instead of a tent on a backpacking trip. Or make a cabin your destination and spend a few days there hiking or fishing. I've covered trails near Cordova in section 12 of this chapter, and some shorter hikes are mentioned below with the campgrounds under "Where to Stay." In addition, the superb Winner Creek Trail and Crow Pass Trail, from Gridwood, are described on p. 253. Two excellent trail guides cover the peninsula. *55 Ways to the Wilderness,* by Helen Nienhueser and John Wolfe (The Mountaineers, $17), is the most complete, with detailed coverage in readable prose. The newer *Kenai Trails* (Alaska Natural History Association, $8) includes an extremely detailed topographic map along with each trail description. **Trails Illustrated** publishes excellent plastic maps of the region (© **800/962-1643;** http://maps.nationalgeographic.com/trails).

CARTER LAKE TRAIL   An excellent day hike starts from Mile 33 of the Seward Highway, a few miles east of Tern Lake (p. 265), rising about 1,000 feet over 2 miles to alpine views and Carter Lake, which is stocked with rainbow trout. Continuing another 1.3 miles brings you to the east end of Crescent Lake.

RESURRECTION PASS TRAIL   This gold-rush trail begins 4 miles above the town of Hope (mentioned above in the preceding section on the Seward Hwy.) and runs over the top of the Kenai Peninsula to Cooper Landing (covered in section 7 of this chapter). It's a beautiful, remote, yet well-used trail for hiking, mountain biking, Nordic skiing, or snowshoeing; it rises through forest, crosses the alpine pass, and then descends again to a highway trail head where you'll need to have transportation waiting. The 39-mile trail has eight public-use cabins, available for $35 to $45 a night. (See "Where to Stay," below, for reservation information.) The cabins are well spaced to cover the trail in an easy 5 days, and those on lakes have boats for fishing. Cabins book up well ahead winter and summer, but there are lots of good camping spots, too. The **Devil's Pass and Summit Lake trails** cut off from the Resurrection to the Seward Highway south of Summit Lake, shortening the route. The difficulty of doing the whole trail, by any of the entrances, is that you need either two cars or someone willing to drive you back to your starting point.

RUSSIAN LAKES TRAIL   This trail begins in Cooper Landing (covered in section 7 of this chapter), near the end of the Resurrection Pass Trail, and leads to three remote cabins and a series of lakes. There's excellent fishing and wildlife viewing (bears are common). It's less than 3 miles with little elevation gain to Lower Russian Lake and the cabin there, or you can make a backpacking trip over the entire 21 miles.

JOHNSON PASS TRAIL   The 23-mile trail climbs to a pair of lakes above the tree line at the 1,450-foot Johnson Creek Summit, tracing impressively narrow mountain valleys. The route, part of the Iditarod National Historic Trail, leads from near the Trail Lake Fish Hatchery, at Mile 32 of the Seward Highway, to near the Granite Creek Campground, on the highway at Mile 63. Plan to do the trail as an overnight and have transportation ready at each end.

LOST LAKE TRAIL & PRIMROSE TRAIL   With their fields of alpine wildflowers and small lakes, these connected trails offer one of the most beautiful hikes in the area. Snow lasts until late in the season up at the top. The upper, northern trail head is at the 10-site Primrose Campground, on vast Kenai Lake, 17 miles from Seward off the Seward Highway on Primrose Road. The trail rises through hemlock past a waterfall about 2 miles up (look for the spur to the right when you hear water), past an old mining cabin, and then through ever-smaller trees and above the tree line. A Forest Service cabin is on a 2-mile spur about 11 miles along the 16-mile route. Strong hikers can do the whole trail in a long day, but it makes more sense to hike in and out on the upper end, or to spend the night along the way. The lower Lost Lake trail head is in a subdivision near Seward; ask for directions at one of the visitor centers.

FISHING

The national forest contains some of the most famous, and crowded, fishing banks in Alaska, including the **Russian River,** near Cooper Landing, with its incredible run of red salmon in July and good fishing lasting into September. Easiest access is at the Russian River Campground, just west of the village. There are plenty of other roadside salmon streams and remote fishing rivers and lakes in the national forest where you can lose sight of other anglers. Some remote lakes have Forest Service cabins for rent on their shores, with rowboats. The Forest Service publishes information on these opportunities. See chapter 2 for other information sources.

SEA KAYAKING & BOATING

A variety of Prince William Sound tour boats are listed in the Whittier, Valdez, and Cordova sections of this chapter. Whittier offers the greatest number of boats and the most impressive scenery, with big glaciers that come right to the water.

   All three communities also have operators offering sea-kayak rentals and guided outings of various lengths. The best sea kayaking is near Cordova or east of Whittier. The long fjords reached from Whittier feature calving glaciers, narrow passages, and Forest Service cabins, but to get out there, you need a boat ride first—the waters right around Whittier aren't as interesting—and that is expensive. The local sea-kayaking operators can help you arrange drop-off service. Cordova has more interesting waters right near town, so you can paddle from the boat harbor. Those who haven't done much sea kayaking should consider only a guided trip; if it's your first time, start with a guided day trip rather than an overnight.

   Renting a skiff or chartering a small boat is a great alternative for those who aren't up to paddling but don't want to ride a big tour boat. Boat-rental operators in all three towns' harbors offer skiffs with fishing gear, and small-boat natural history tours go from Whittier. Exploring the Sound in a small boat is our family's favorite activity.

WHERE TO STAY
REMOTE CABINS

There is no more authentic Alaska accommodation than a pioneer cabin with a wood-stove—a place to give you a better feel for the soul of a wild place. Chugach National Forest maintains more than 40 remote recreation cabins for rent to the public. This is simple shelter: Cabins don't have electricity or plumbing; you bring your own sleeping bags, cooking equipment, and other gear; and the cabin is only as clean as the last user left it. But no other room you can rent has a better location or greater privacy. Some cabins are along hiking and skiing trails, others on shores where boats and kayaks can pull up, and others on remote fishing lakes accessible only by floatplane. You can stay up to a week in most, with a summer limit of 3 days in the Resurrection Trail cabins.

The Forest Service prints a free listing of the cabins, with short descriptions of each. You will also need a trail guide and detailed map (see "Getting Outside," above). Cabins rent for $35 or $45 a night, with most priced at $45 a night. Typically, the price of the cabin itself is not your major expense: You'll need a way to get there, either by plane, by boat, or by having a vehicle to drive to a trail head and then hiking. If you're flying, contact flight services in the nearest town (listed in the sections later in this chapter) to find out the cost *before* you book the cabin. Flight time is several hundred dollars an hour. You can rent the camping equipment you'll need at the businesses listed in the Anchorage chapter on p. 237, but you should talk to a ranger first to get details about access and what to take. And start planning early. For summer dates, many cabins book up the second they become available on the reservation system, 6 months prior. This is not an exaggeration.

The National Recreation Reservation Service (NRRS), operated by **Reserve America,** a company in upstate New York, handles the reservation system. Use them to book a cabin, but contact the ranger stations first (p. 266) to choose a cabin that is right for you and to find out what to expect. The easiest way to reserve a cabin is online at **www.reserveusa.com** because the interactive maps and availability calendars allow you to shop for open days at various cabins. To reserve by phone, call ✆ **877/444-6777,** 877/833-6777 TTY, or 518/885-3639 from overseas. The phone lines are open April 1 through Labor Day Monday through Friday from 8am to midnight EST, Saturday and Sunday 8am to 9pm; in winter Monday through Friday 10am to 7pm, Saturday and Sunday 10am to 5pm. The website takes reservations only during those hours as well. They accept American Express, Discover, MasterCard, and Visa, or you can reserve on the phone and then pay by certified check or money order. Campsites can be reserved starting 240 days ahead, cabins 180 days ahead.

CAMPGROUNDS

Forest Service campgrounds mostly have pit toilets and water from hand pumps, and roads usually are not paved. But some of these places are truly spectacular. I've listed them in order of distance from Anchorage, counting in reverse direction on the Seward Highway mileposts. For information on campgrounds below Mile 60, call the Seward Ranger District; for the others, call the Glacier Ranger District, in Girdwood (p. 266 for phone numbers). Sites in a few of the following campgrounds, as noted, take reservations through the national system explained above. RVs and cars can access and park at all of the campgrounds, but Williwaw is the only campground intended primarily for RVs.

Williwaw & Black Bear   These two campgrounds are next to each other near Portage Glacier, along a creek where you can watch spawning red salmon in mid-August (no fishing is allowed). Williwaw is one of the better-developed campgrounds in the national forest, with paved roads and pumped water, and is intended primarily for RVs.

Mile 4, Portage Glacier Rd. (turn at Mile 78.9 Seward Hwy.). Williwaw: 60 sites. Reservations accepted with additional fee. $10 per night. Black Bear: 12 sites. $9 per night.

Bertha Creek   This one's in the high country.

Mile 65.5, Seward Hwy. 12 sites. $10 per night.

Granite Creek   Near the Johnson Pass trail head.

Mile 63, Seward Hwy. 19 sites. $10 per night.

Porcupine   This campground near the gold-rush village of Hope is among the most beautiful in the Chugach National Forest. The sites are on a mountainside overlooking Turnagain Arm, five with sweeping ocean views. The thick trees make for privacy, but also mosquitoes. Bring repellent. Two good day hikes leave from the campground: The level 5-mile trail to **Gull Rock** makes a good family ramble, and with some effort you can scramble down to remote beaches along the way, where we've enjoyed a picnic. The **Hope Point Trail** is a stiff climb that rises 3,600 feet to expansive views.

At the end of the Hope Hwy. 24 sites. $10 per night.

Tenderfoot Creek   This pleasant campground lies across Summit Lake from the Seward Highway as it passes through a narrow mountain valley above the tree line. Campsites look out on the water from a peaceful, sunny hillside. The nearby Summit Lake Lodge, described on p. 264, offers meals and is the only business on the Seward Highway for many a mile.

Mile 46, Seward Hwy. 27 sites. $10 per night.

Ptarmigan Creek & Trail River   Near the tiny towns of Moose Pass and Crown Point, the Ptarmigan Creek campground is at the trail head for the trail to Ptarmigan Lake, 4 miles away with only 500 feet in elevation gain—a good place for a picnic or fishing for Dolly Varden char and rainbow trout. Trail River campground is a mile away and on the other side of the highway.

Mile 23, Seward Hwy. 16 and 63 sites, respectively. Reservations accepted, with additional fee. $10 per night.

Primrose   Another favorite, this lovely campground lies on the edge of Kenai Lake and at the base of the Primrose Trail to Lost Lake, one of the area's most beautiful (see "Getting Outside," above). This campground is the closest to Seward that has a sense of natural isolation.

Mile 17, Seward Hwy. 10 sites. $10 per night.

Russian River   This large, well-developed campground mainly serves fishermen pursuing red salmon on the river. When the fishing is good, the campground overflows and can be noisy. Overnight parking is $6. Reserve ahead.

Mile 52, Sterling Hwy., just west of Cooper Landing. Reservations accepted with additional fee. 84 sites. 3-day limit. Flush toilets. $13 per night.

Cooper Creek The campground has two halves bisected by the highway right in Cooper Landing. Ten sites are on the Kenai River, and the balance across the road and somewhat better screened and separated.

Mile 50.7, Sterling Hwy. Reservations accepted. 26 sites. $10 per night.

Quartz Creek Thickly wooded sites stand well separated a bit off the highway, many right on Kenai Lake and others with good mountain views. There is a boat ramp in the campground and a lodge nearby.

Quartz Creek Rd., at Mile 45 Sterling Hwy. 45 sites. Reservations accepted. Flush toilets, boat launch. $13 per night.

Crescent Creek This campground is quieter and more secluded than others near Cooper Landing, at the Crescent Lake trail head. The 6.5-mile trail leads to the Crescent Lake Forest Service Cabin, where renters have a boat for grayling fishing.

Mile 3 Quartz Creek Rd., at Mile 45 Sterling Hwy. 9 sites. $10 per night.

4 Whittier: Dock on the Sound

Whittier is Anchorage's portal to Prince William Sound. Although Anchorage itself is on Upper Cook Inlet, that muddy, fast-moving water is little used for recreational boating. Whittier, on the other hand, stands on the edge of a long fjord in the northwest corner of the Sound, whose clear waters are full of salmon, orcas, and otters, and bounded by rocky shores, rainforests, and glaciers. In the past, getting to Whittier meant riding through a mountain by train. Now the railway tunnel is paved, which has created North America's longest highway tunnel and, in theory, puts Whittier only an hour away from the city. But only in theory because the tunnel is also among the most inconvenient to use in North America. It has only one lane, and that lane must be shared by traffic and trains in both directions, and in between trips the tunnel often must be aired out. A wait is almost assured.

Whittier certainly has major advantages for visitors seeking to get out on the water. The water is calmer here than on excursions to Kenai Fjords National Park, so seasickness is rare, and the glaciers are even more numerous. One company's selling point is a "26-glacier cruise," all done in a day trip from Anchorage by rail and large tour boat (see below). Prince William Sound boats also see otters and sometimes whales; Kenai Fjords tours, on the other hand, more often see whales and see more birds. Sea kayakers also have great places to go from Whittier. Almost all of Prince William Sound is in Chugach National Forest, with its public-use cabins in lovely, remote spots on the shores (see the previous section).

There's little other reason to go to Whittier, unless you're on a quest to find the oddest towns in America. Most of the roughly 180 townspeople live in a single 14-story concrete building with dark, narrow hallways. The grocery store is on the first floor and the medical clinic on the third. The rest of the people live in one other building. **The Begich Towers,** as the dominant structure is called, was built during the 1940s, when Whittier's strategic location on the Alaska Railroad and at the head of a deep Prince William Sound fjord made it a key port in the defense of Alaska. Today, with its barren gravel ground and ramshackle warehouses and boat sheds, the town maintains a stark military-industrial character. The pass above the town is a funnel for frequent whipping winds, it always seems to rain, and the glaciers above the town keep it cool even in summer. As one young town ambassador told me once when I was on a visit, "You're thinking, 'Thank God I don't live here,' right?" The official boosters look more on the bright side: Having everyone live in one building saves on snow removal in a place that gets an average of 20 feet per winter. Kids don't even have to go outside to get to school—a tunnel leads from the tower to the school.

ESSENTIALS

GETTING THERE By Car Take the Seward Highway to the Portage Glacier Road, at Mile 78.9 (48 miles from Anchorage). The road through the 2¾-mile-long World War II rail tunnel to Whittier is only one lane and also

> **Tips Be Prepared**
>
> Whittier lacks a bank, large stores, or downtown businesses. Bring what you need.

accommodates trains, so you'll have to wait your turn. Get the schedule through the tunnel's website (go to www.tunnel.alaska.gov), through its phone recording (© **877/ 611-2586** or 907/566-2244), or by tuning to 1610AM in Portage or 530AM in Whittier. Checking the schedule helps you avoid a wait of an hour or more if you miss the opening, but you can also wait if you arrive just on time at peak hours, when there may be too many vehicles in line to get through during one open period. Typically, the crowding comes in the summer around 6 to 7pm Friday through Sunday. The tunnel closes altogether at night. In summer, the first opening from Whittier is at 5:30am and the last to Whittier is at 11:15pm. Winter hours are shorter and change-able, so check ahead. The toll is $12 for cars; $20 for RVs, cars with trailers, or large vans. It is charged only going toward Whittier. Special permits are required for really huge vehicles (over 14 ft. high or 10 ft. wide). Parking in Whittier is $10 a day. As I mentioned in the introduction, Whittier really isn't worth the trouble unless you are going out on the water.

By Train If you plan to take a day trip on the Sound from a base in Anchorage (or Girdwood)—the way most people use Whittier—you can leave the car behind and take the train. The large tour operators will book it for you when you buy your boat ticket. The **Alaska Railroad** (© **800/544-0552** or 907/265-2494; www.alaskarailroad.com) runs a daily train timed to match the schedules of Prince William Sound tour boats. Unless you have planned an activity or tour on the water, however, you'll find the 6-hour stay in Whittier is too long to just hang around. The round-trip fare is $68, one-way $55, half-price ages 2 to 11. The train ride is scenic and fun, but a rental car will take about half as long and save money if there is more than one of you along.

By Bus Boat tour operators have buses that can save time and money over the train. Reserve when you buy your boat cruise ticket.

By Ferry Ferries of the **Alaska Marine Highway System** (© **800/642-0066,** or 800/764-3779 TTY; www.ferryalaska.com) connect Whittier, Valdez, and Cordova. The new fast ferry *Chenega* has dramatically cut travel times and increased sailings in the summer. However, the boat has been something of a political football, moved around the state by the state government, so don't plan too much around it without calling to verify the schedule. The fare from Whittier to either Valdez or Cordova is $86 for an adult, half-price ages 5 to 11, free under 5. A 15-foot car costs $102 to take along. The Whittier-Valdez run creates the opportunity for a wonderful loop tour of a couple days or more: Drive Anchorage to Whittier, take the ferry to Valdez, then return to Anchorage via the Glenn Highway or continue up the Richardson Highway to Fairbanks, and drive back to Anchorage on the Parks Highway. See chapter 3 for a complete loop itinerary.

Whittier is the system's main port connecting Southeast and Southcentral Alaska via the oceangoing ferry *Kennicott*. The ship's route spans the state, from Prince Rupert, British Columbia, to Juneau, across the Gulf of Alaska to Whittier, around the Kenai Peninsula to Homer, and out to Kodiak. The entire loop takes 2 weeks. The fare for the 2-day voyage between Whittier and Juneau is $114 for adults, $468 for a 15-foot vehicle, and $183 to $343 for a cabin. See section 1 in chapter 5 for information about the system.

VISITOR INFORMATION   There is no visitor center, but you can contact the **city offices** at ℂ **907/472-2327** or the **chamber of commerce** at ℂ **907/472-2493.** The chamber of commerce maintains a website with a business directory and links at **www.whittieralaska.com**. The people at the harbormaster's office are helpful and maintain public toilets and showers; it's the two-story building at the harbor (ℂ **907/472-2327**).

GETTING OUT ON THE SOUND

Whittier is the entrance to western Prince William Sound, at the end of one of many long, deep fjords where marine mammals and eagles are common. Glaciers at the heads of many of the fjords dump ice in the water for the tour boats that cruise from Whittier.

LARGE TOUR BOATS

Several companies with offices in Anchorage compete for your business for day-trip tours to the Sound's western glaciers. Besides having incredible scenery, the water is calm, making seasickness unlikely—for the queasy, this is a much better choice than Kenai Fjords National Park. Each operator times departures to coordinate with the daily Alaska Railroad train from Anchorage, described above, which means they have up to 6 hours for the trip. Some try to see as much as possible, while others take it slower to savor the scenery and wildlife sightings. Between the train and boat fare, expect to spend $190 per person for this day's outing, leaving Anchorage at 10am and returning at 9:30pm. You can save $10 to $15 a person and up to 3 hours by taking a bus the tour boat arranges instead of the train. If you have two or more people, you can save by renting a car and driving. You will be able to buy meals on board or one will be provided.

Phillips' Cruises and Tours   The 26-glacier cruise travels the Sound on a fast three-deck catamaran, covering many miles of scenery and counting the glaciers as they go. The boat ride is 4½ hours, so if you use their bus you cut the total time from Anchorage to under 8½ hours. The boat has a snack bar, and a hearty snack is provided with the fare. They knock $20 off in May and September.

519 W. 4th Ave., Anchorage, AK 99501. ℂ **800/544-0529** or 907/276-8023. www.26glaciers.com. 4½-hour cruise $129 adults, $69 children under 12.

Major Marine Tours   This company operates a smaller, 149-passenger vessel at a slower pace than Phillips—they hit a mere 10 glaciers but spend more time waiting for them to calve. Another important feature: The tour is narrated by a Chugach National Forest ranger, not the company. The route goes up Blackstone Bay. The boat is comfortable, with reserved table seating. They also put more emphasis on their food, which costs extra; the salmon and prime rib buffet is $15 for adults, $7 for children. It's quite good. Time on the water is 5 hours.

411 W. 4th Ave., Anchorage, AK 99501. ℂ **800/764-7300** or 907/274-7300. www.majormarine.com. $99 adults, $49 children ages 11 and under.

SMALL BOAT TOURS

Instead of getting on a giant tour boat with a crowd of people, you can go on a small boat with a local whom you'll get to know as he shows off favorite places and lands on beaches to picnic and walk. If you see a whale or other point of interest, you stay as long or as short a time as you like. What you give up is the comfort of a large, tour-bus-like vessel, you pay more, and most small boats have a four-person minimum.

Sound Eco Adventures   Gerry Sanger is a retired wildlife biologist who spent years researching the waterfowl and ecology of Prince William Sound. Now he carries up to six passengers at a time on whale, wildlife, and glacier tours from his 30-foot aluminum boat, which has a landing-craft-like ramp perfect for pulling up on gravel beaches, and suitable for wheelchairs. Finding whales in the Sound takes skill and requires covering a lot of water; Gerry's success rate is better than 90% since 1999, and he has gone years without missing once. His shorter, 5-hour tours usually do not encounter whales. Prices listed are examples; you can customize and arrange discounts in certain circumstances. Fares include lunch and snacks.

P.O. Box 707, Whittier, AK 99693. ℂ **888/471-2312** or 907/472-2312. www.soundecoadventure.com. 10-hr. whale and wildlife cruise $210–$235 per person; 8-hr. $180; 5-hr. sightseeing $160; or charter the whole boat for $125–150/hr.

Honey Charters   A family runs three sturdy aluminum boats built for these waters, specializing in personal tours, water transportation, and kayaker drop-offs. They operate with a minimum of four passengers; by paying the four-person minimum, you can have a boat to yourself. For larger groups, their *Qayaq Spirit* carries up to 30 passengers for kayaking or sightseeing cruises. Bring your own food.

On the Whittier waterfront (P.O. Box 708), Whittier, AK 99693. ℂ **888/477-2493** or 907/472-2493. www.honey charters.com. 3-hr. cruise $99 per person; 6-hr. $149 per person.

FISHING

About 30 charter fishing boats operate out of Whittier, the closest saltwater fishing to Anchorage, mostly targeting halibut but also getting salmon at certain times. The **Whittier Harbormaster** can give you a list of operators (ℂ **907/472-2327,** ext. 110 or 115). **Bread N Butter Charters** (ℂ **888/472-2396** or 907/472-2396; www.bread nbuttercharters.com) has been around for many years. They charge $245 per person for a day of halibut fishing and have an office on the waterfront. Honey Charters,

---

Finds The Sound by Yacht

I came across the *Discovery* one evening in a secret little cove in the remote southwestern corner of Prince William Sound's Knight Island. Briefly pulled from my rough camping existence, I suddenly found myself sitting on a soft couch in a sumptuous mahogany lounge, eating a delicious chocolate desert, and sipping wine. The *Discovery* is a classic old wooden vessel, and accommodations are nautical and yacht-like, not as fancy even as a small cruise ship. But it's comfortable, groups are only about a dozen per trip, and the owner and skipper knows the Sound well, taking passengers to its most intimate and beautiful spots—places like that cove that hardly anyone knows about. It's like a first-class wilderness lodge afloat. Six-day voyages are around $3,600 per person, double occupancy. Contact **Discovery Voyages** at ℂ **800/324-7602;** www.discoveryvoyages.com.

listed above under "Small Boat Tours," has a similar service. You can also rent your own boat for fishing, camping, or even sleeping on board, from **Whittier Boat & Tackle Rentals** (© **866/667-2628** or 907/632-1188; www.whittierboatrentals.com). The company carries quality equipment, including boats suitable for an extended trip. Full-day rentals range from $300 to $725.

SEA KAYAKING

Whittier is a popular starting point for kayak trips to beautiful and protected western Prince William Sound. Day trips for beginners paddle along the shore near Whittier, often visiting a bird rookery, or take a boat 5 miles from the harbor to Shotgun Cove and paddle back. Longer multiday trips go by boat to even more interesting waters where you can visit glaciated fjords and paddle narrow passages.

Several businesses compete in Whittier. **Alaska Sea-Kayakers** (© **877/472-2534** or 907/472-2534; www.alaskaseakayakers.com) offers 3- and 5-hour day trips for $79 to $175; paddles at Blackstone Glacier that begin and end with a charter boat ride for $300; and extended trips. Guides are well trained and they occasionally offer weekend instructional clinics (check the website for times). Offices are at each end of Whittier Harbor. They rent to experienced paddlers, too. The **Prince William Sound Kayak Center** (© **877/472-2452** or 907/472-2452; www.pwskayakcenter.com) offers guided half-day trips starting at $55, as well as full days and other options, and rents kayaks. They've been in business since 1981.

Most self-guided kayakers charter a boat to drop them off among the islands beyond the long, deep fjord in which Whittier is located. Honey Charters, listed above under "Small Boat Tours," offers a drop-off service. There are six Forest Service cabins in this idyllic area, which must be reserved 6 months ahead. Flat sites suitable for a tent are not plentiful on these rocky shores, which dropped in the 1964 earthquake, so do some research with the Forest Service or Alaska Public Lands Information Center in Anchorage before you go (the tent platforms at Surprise Cove State Marine Park make an excellent remote base camp). For information and cabin reservations, see section 3, "Chugach National Forest: Do-It-Yourself Wilderness."

WHERE TO STAY & DINE

Most meals served in Whittier are for people grabbing a sandwich while waiting for a boat or otherwise passing through. Several such restaurants are in the triangle at the east end of the harbor, where you can conveniently check them all out before making a choice. As I mentioned previously, the purpose of going to Whittier, to get out on Prince William Sound, probably won't require you to find overnight accommodation. If you do need to stay, however, there are two excellent choices.

Inn at Whittier   𝒢𝒢   This is an exquisite Arts and Crafts–style building with authentic post-and-beam construction using enormous cedar timbers and natural rock, yet it stands at the harbor mouth, where all around is gravel, marine junk, and the cheapest, low-slung plywood buildings. When this improbable venture ran into financial trouble in 2006, it didn't come as a great surprise. At this writing, the inn was attempting rebirth with a time-share financial model. While the craftsmanship of the building and rooms may justify the rates, the attractions of Whittier do not. The restaurant has been good, and the dining room is gorgeous.

Harbor Loop Road (P.O. Box 609), Whittier, AK 99693. © **866-472-5757** or 907/472-7000. www.innatwhittier.com. 25 units. High season $249–$299 double, $399–$599 suite; low season $99–$169 double, $199–$399 suite. $10 each additional person. AE, MC, V. **Amenities:** Restaurant. *In room:* Satellite TV, Wi-Fi, coffeemaker.

June's Whittier Bed and Breakfast Condo Suites ⚲   Nine of these condo units are in the top two floors of the Begich Towers, the concrete building that dominates Whittier, allowing guests to live as Whittier people do, with narrow corridors and a funky elevator leading to rooms with breathtaking views and hummingbirds feeding at the high-rise windows (one unit is on the first floor). Rather than a traditional B&B, you are essentially renting an equipped apartment for the night. All units have full kitchens, and some have stereos and big living rooms that are the equivalent of a nice family home. Housekeeping is first rate. The friendly hostess, June Miller, and her husband, Ken, also have a fishing charter and sightseeing business, Bread N Butter Charters, listed above; you check in at their harborside office.

P.O. Box 715, Whittier, AK 99693. © **888/472-2396** or 907/472-2396. Fax 907/472-2503. www.breadnbuttercharters.com. 10 units. $125–$450 double. Extra person 6 and over $15. AE, MC, V. **Amenities:** Harbor shuttle; coin-op laundry. *In room:* TV/DVD, high-speed Internet, kitchen.

5 Seward: Gateway to Resurrection Bay & Kenai Fjords

Located by the broad fjord of Resurrection Bay, Seward's main reason to exist has always been its ocean dock. The agreeable little town started life as a place to fish and to get off boats arriving in Alaska; it then continued as a place for Alaskans and visitors to get *on* boats and see the bay and Kenai Fjords National Park (described in section 6 of this chapter). With the growth of the cruise industry, Seward again is a place to get off the boat. Most cruises that cross the Gulf of Alaska start or end here, with their passengers taking a bus to or from the airport in Anchorage. The minority of them who spend any time in town finds a mountainside grid of streets lined with old wood-frame houses, the sort of place where pedestrians casually wander across the road, hardly glancing for cars, for there likely won't be any, or, if there are, they'll be ready to stop. Increasing tourism has brought more traffic and development, but the growth mostly has been of a quality that hasn't damaged the town's character. Seward isn't spoiled yet.

Seward's history is among the oldest in Alaska. The great Russian governor Alexander Baranof stopped here in 1793, named Resurrection Bay, and built a ship, which later sank, probably because Baranof's workers didn't have proper materials. Gold prospectors blazed trails from here to finds on Turnagain Arm starting in 1891, and in 1907 the army linked those trails with others all the way to Nome, finishing the Iditarod Trail. Today that route is discontinued south of Anchorage, but you can follow it through Seward and hike a portion of it on the Johnson Pass Trail north of town (p. 267). More relevant for current visitors and the local economy, the federal government took over a failed railroad-building effort in 1915, finishing the line to Fairbanks in 1923. Until the age of jet travel, most people coming to the main part of Alaska arrived by steamer in Seward and then traveled north by rail. The train ride to Anchorage, daily during the summer, is still supremely beautiful.

Seward's in-town highlight is the Alaska SeaLife Center, a research aquarium that's open to the public. Combined with Seward's excellent ocean fishing, the national park, the wonderful hiking trails, and the unique and attractive town itself, the center helps make Seward well worth a 2-day visit.

ESSENTIALS

GETTING THERE   By Car   See section 2 of this chapter, on the Seward Highway, for how to make the spectacular 127-mile drive down from Anchorage. All major car-rental agencies are represented in Anchorage.

Seward

Information (i)
Post Office ⊠
Railway |—|
Whale-watching 🐋

To Anchorage ↗

New Airport Blvd.

Seward Airport ✈

Seward Hwy

Old Seward Hwy

1st. St.

Bear Dr.

Resurrection Blvd.

Old Airport Blvd.

Fresh Water Lagoon

(i) Cruise Ship & State Ferry Dock

Small Boat Harbor

Harbormaster

Kenai Fjords National Park Headquarters and Visitor Center

Van Buren St.
D St.
C St.
B St.
A St.
Monroe St.
Madison St.
Jefferson St.
Adams St.
Washington St.

1st Ave.
2nd Ave.
3rd Ave.
4th Ave.
5th Ave.
6th Ave.

Ballaine Blvd.

Two Lakes Trail

Mt. Marathon Trail

Lowell St.

Railway

Iditarod Trailhead Park

To Lowell Point ↓

Resurrection Bay

0   1/4 Mi
0   1/4 Km
N

ACCOMMODATIONS ■
Ballaine House
  Bed and Breakfast **7**
The Breeze Inn **4**
Harborview Inn **6**
Holiday Inn Express Seward **2**
Hotel Edgewater **12**
Moby Dick Hostel **7**
Murphy's Motel **5**
Seward Windsong Lodge **1**
Van Gilder Hotel **11**

DINING ◆
Apollo Restaurant **8**
Ray's Waterfront **3**
Ranting Raven **13**
Resurrection Roadhouse **1**

ATTRACTIONS ●
Alaska SeaLife Center **14**
Exit Glacier **1**
Seward Museum **9**
St. Peter's Episcopal
  Church **10**

Alaska

Fairbanks ○

Anchorage ○ Cordova Skagway
  Kenai ○ ○ ○ Juneau
    Seward Sitka ○
      Ketchikan ○

By Bus   The **Seward Bus Line** (© **907/224-3608** in Seward or 907/563-0800 in Anchorage) makes a round trip from Seward to Anchorage and back daily, year-round (except Sun Oct–Apr); the fare is $45 one-way, $85 round-trip. They'll pick up and drop off passengers anywhere en route and, for an extra $5, take you to the airport. They share a ticket office with Homer Stage Line in Anchorage at 3333 Fairbanks St. **The Park Connection Motorcoach Service** (© **800/266-8625** or 907/245-0200; www.alaskatravel.com/bus-lines) connects Seward with Anchorage and Denali National Park twice daily in summer in each direction with big, comfortable coaches. The fare is $54 between Seward and Anchorage, $130 between Seward and Denali, half off under age 12. Passengers between Seward and Anchorage get a pass to the Anchorage Museum of History and Art.

By Train   The train ride between Anchorage and Seward is one of miraculous beauty. The **Alaska Railroad** (© **800/544-0552** or 907/265-2494; www.alaskarailroad.com) offers passenger service from Anchorage and back daily in summer. The route is even prettier than the highway, passing close by glaciers and following a ledge halfway up the narrow, vertical Placer River gorge, where it ducks into tunnels and pops out at bends in the river. The landscape looks just as it did when the first person beheld it. The railroad's young guides are well trained. The fare is $62 one-way, $103 round-trip; children ages 2 to 11 half-price. A rental car will almost always be cheaper, but the train ride is unforgettable. The railroad also offers packages with lodging and activities in Seward. Don't try to do it in 1 day from Anchorage—the 16-hour marathon is too much.

GETTING AROUND   You can easily cover downtown Seward on foot, although a little help is handy to get back and forth from the boat harbor. If it's not raining, a bike may be the best way. **Seward Bike Shop** (℗ **907/224-2448**), in a railcar near the depot at the harbor, rents high-performance mountain bikes and models good for just getting around town, plus accessory equipment. A cruiser is $12 half-day, $19 full day, a mountain bike $18 and $30. **PJ's Taxi** (℗ **907/224-5555**) is one of the cab companies in Seward.

VISITOR INFORMATION   The **Seward Chamber of Commerce,** P.O. Box 749, Seward, AK 99664 (℗ **907/224-8051;** www.sewardak.org), has two visitor centers. The one on the right side of the Seward Highway as you enter town is open year-round (summer daily 8am–6pm; winter Mon–Fri 9am–5pm). A summer-only infor-mation kiosk is on the cruise-ship dock. The chamber can give business information and last-minute help in finding a room. In addition to these town information sources, the **Kenai Fjords National Park Visitor Center** is covered in section 6, later in this chapter. For contacts for the Chugach National Forest, see section 3.

SPECIAL EVENTS   The **Fourth of July** is the biggest day of the year in Seward, when the whole town explodes with visitors, primarily from Anchorage. Besides the parade and many small-town festivities, the main attraction is the **Mount Marathon Race,** run every year since it started as a bar bet in 1915. The racers go from the mid-dle of town straight up rocky Mount Marathon to its 3,022-foot peak, and then tum-ble down again, arriving muddy and bloody at the finish line in town. Strong binoculars allow you to see the whole thing from town, including the pratfalls of the runners on their way down.

The **Silver Salmon Derby** starts the second Saturday of August, although the peak of silver season comes later. The chamber of commerce visitor centers can provide tickets and rules.

FAST FACTS: Seward

Bank **Wells Fargo** is at 908 3rd Ave., with an ATM.

Hospital **Providence Seward Medical Center** is at 417 1st Ave. (℗ **907/224-5205**).

Internet Access Free at the **Seward Public Library,** 5th and Adams.

Police For nonemergency situations, call the **Seward Police Department** (℗ **907/224-3338**) or, outside the city limits, the **Alaska State Troopers** (℗ **907/ 224-3346**).

Post Office It's at 5th Avenue and Madison Street.

Taxes **Sales tax** is 5%. The **room tax** totals 9%.

GETTING OUTSIDE

Here I've described things to do out of Seward other than visiting the national park, which includes the fjords and Exit Glacier. See section 6, "Kenai Fjords National Park," later in this chapter, for that information.

BOATING & SEA KAYAKING

Miller's Landing, at Lowell Point, 3 miles south of town ((*C*) **866/541-5739** or 907/224-5739; www.millerslandingak.com) is a good place to know about if you intend to spend any time outdoors around Seward, especially if you like to do things on your own. They have a campground and cabins (described later), a boat launch with skiffs, sea kayaks for rent, kayaking lessons, and fishing charters with experienced skippers. Skiffs rent for $80 for 4 hours; kayaks are $42 a day single, $52 double (they offer reasonably priced guided outings, too). Fishermen hang around the shop trading lies and advice (5¢, with a money-back guarantee). The staff will teach you how to fish for salmon and send you out on your own or on a guided charter. The water-taxi operation, a landing craft with a bow ramp, charges flat rates to take travelers to remote beaches and public cabins around the bay or to the national park—great for sea kayakers or those who just want to get off on their own ($35 one-way per person to Caines Head, $275 per person round-trip to the park service cabin in Aialik Bay.) They offer many other services, too, including booking full Seward visits.

For guided sea kayaking, **Sunny Cove Sea Kayaking** ((*C*) **800/770-9119** for reservations, or 907/224-8810; www.sunnycove.com) offers day trips suitable for beginners as part of the Kenai Fjords Tours trips to its Fox Island lodge, and day trips and multiday trips into the fjords themselves (see the Kenai Fjords National Park section later in this chapter). They've earned a good reputation. On a budget, you can take one of their tours right from Seward. They launch from Lowell Point, following the shore toward Caines Head State Recreation Area, where you can see sea otters, seabirds, intertidal creatures, and the salmon in Tonsina Creek. Three-hour paddles are $59; 8-hour trips are $125. A trip to Fox Island is more expensive but comes with a fjords boat tour and salmon bake, so the cost of the kayaking comes out roughly the same.

FISHING

Seward is renowned for its saltwater silver salmon fishing. The silvers start showing up in the bay in mid-July and last through September. You can catch the fish from shore, from Lowell Point south of town, or even near the boat harbor, but your chances of success are far greater from a boat. I prefer small six-passenger boats because you can get to know the skipper better and can learn more about fishing. If your party has the whole boat, you can control where it goes, perhaps adding whale-watching or sightseeing to the day. Larger boats add more comfort and stability in the waves. The going rate for a guided charter, with everything provided, is around $175 per person, or $245 to go for salmon and halibut on the same day. Andrew Mezirow, a marine biologist and maritime instructor, operates two boats, including a 12-passenger vessel and a 6-passenger boat custom-built for fishing salmon in Resurrection Bay year round. Besides day fishing, he takes guests on multiday fishing expeditions to extremely remote and beautiful places. His business is **Crackerjack Sportfishing Charters** ((*C*) **877/224-2606** or 907/224-2606; www.crackerjackcharters.com). The office is on the boardwalk at the top of the harbor ramps.

There are many other fishing charter companies, mostly booked through central charter agencies, which makes life simpler for visitors. **The Fish House** is the largest charter fishing agency in Seward, located at the Small Boat Harbor. The store also sells and rents ocean-fishing and spin-casting gear, and carries some fly-fishing supplies. For charters, reserve ahead at P.O. Box 1209, Seward, AK 99664 (© **800/257-7760** or 907/224-3674; www.thefishhouse.net). If you want a small boat, ask to be put on a "six pack," as vessels licensed for six or fewer passengers are known. See "Boating & Sea Kayaking," above, for details on the less expensive option of renting your own skiff and fishing without a guide, and for another charter booking agency, Miller's Landing.

HIKING

There are several excellent hiking trails near Seward. You can get a complete list and directions at the Kenai Fjords National Park Visitor Center (p. 285).

The **Mount Marathon Trail** is a tough hike right to the top of a 3,022-foot mountain. The route of the famous Mount Marathon footrace is the most strenuous choice, basically going straight up from the end of Jefferson Street; the hikers' route starts at the corner of 1st Avenue and Monroe Street. Either trail rises steeply to the top of the rocky pinnacle and the incredible views there. Allow all day, unless you're a racer; in that case, expect to do it in under 45 minutes.

The **Caines Head State Recreation Area** (www.alaskastateparks.org, click on "Individual Parks") has a 7-mile coastal trail south of town. Parts of the trail are accessible only at low tide, so it's best done either as an overnight or with someone picking you up or dropping you off in a boat beyond the beach portion—the Miller's Landing water taxi (see p. 278) offers this service for $35 per person one-way. The trail has some gorgeous views, rocky shores, and a fascinating destination at the end, a towering promontory with the concrete remains of Fort McGilvray, a World War II defensive emplacement. Take flashlights and you can poke around in the spooky, pitch-dark underground corridors and rooms and imagine what each was used for (going in without lights would be foolhardy). We've rarely enjoyed a hike more. Three campsites are at Tonsina Point, about 2 miles in, and a state park public-use cabin is 2 miles farther (see "Where to Stay," below, and "State Parks Cabin Reservations," p. 262). At North Beach, 4½ miles from the trail head, are two camping shelters, a ranger station, and the trails to the fort and South Beach. For an easy 2-mile hike to Fort McGilvray, start with a boat ride to North Beach. The main trail head is south of town on Lowell Point Road; pull off in the lot right after the sewage plant, then cross the road through the gate, and follow the dirt road a bit until it becomes the actual trail. Stop at the Kenai Fjords National Park Visitor Center for tide conditions and advice.

DOG MUSHING

When Mitch Seavey won the Iditarod Trail Sled Dog Race in 2004, many agreed it couldn't have happened to a nicer guy. He had made a lot of friends over the years offering rides with his dogs. It's a family business, including the four boys (one is a Junior Iditarod champ), making use of their kennel on Old Exit Glacier Road off Herman Leirer Road. They offer summer rides in Seward and in winter in Sterling (near Soldotna). The summer ride uses a wheeled sled and a full, 12-dog team—not the real thing (no snow), but you'll get a feeling for the dogs' power and intelligence. The 90-minute tour costs $49 for adults, $24 for children 11 and under. Husky puppies are available for cuddling, too. They call their company **IdidaRide** (© **800/478-3139** or 907/224-8607; www.ididaride.com).

Those with eight times as much to spend should consider mushing on snow at the height of summer by joining a helicopter tour to Godwin Glacier from the Seward Airport with **Godwin Glacier Dog Sled Tours** (© **888/989-8239** or 907/224-8239; www.alaskadogsled.com). A chopper lands at a camp of 100 dogs, where guests take a ride in the dog sled (the company also offers glacier hikes and overnight camping on the ice). They charge $413 adults, $365 children 12 and under.

EXPLORING THE TOWN

Besides the Alaska SeaLife Center (see below), most of Seward's in-town attractions are of the modest, small-town variety. The **Iditarod Trailhead,** on the water just east of the SeaLife Center, is where pioneers entered Alaska. The broken concrete and twisted metal you see on the beach walking north are the last ruins of the Seward waterfront, which was destroyed by a tsunami wave in the 1964 earthquake. Sometimes you can see sea otters swimming just offshore. During silver salmon season, in August and September, it's possible to catch them by casting from shore here, although your chances are far better from a boat (see "Fishing," above).

The **Seward Museum,** at 3rd and Jefferson (© **907/224-3902**), is a charming grandma's attic of a place, with clippings, memorabilia, and curiosities recalling the history of the town and of the Iditarod Trail, painter Rockwell Kent, and the ways of the past. Admission is $3 for adults, 50¢ under age 18. It's open during the summer daily from 9am to 5pm, in winter usually weekends noon to 4pm (call ahead). Evening slide programs takes place during the summer months.

The steep-roofed **St. Peter's Episcopal Church** is a delightful little chapel under the mountains at 1st Avenue and Adams Street. Go inside to see the mural in the front of the church, which shows what the Resurrection would have looked like if it had happened in front of Seward locals in the 1930s.

Alaska SeaLife Center 🎣🎣🎣   The center is a serious research institution and a fascinating aquarium of creatures from the nearby Alaska waters. You may have seen puffins diving into the water from a tour boat; here you can see what they look like flying *under* the water. Seabirds, harbor seals, octopus, and sea lions reside in three spectacular exhibits that you can see from above or below—you can get within a few feet of the birds without glass. There are smaller tanks with fish, crab, and other creatures; a touch tank where you can handle starfish and other tide-pool animals; and exhibits on changes in the Bering Sea and on jellyfish. Another exhibit updates the status of *Exxon Valdez* spill damage to birds and marine mammals; Exxon settlement money made the center possible. The center is not as large as a big-city aquarium, however, and you're not likely to spend more than a couple of hours here unless you sign up for one of the special programs for adults and children that happen all day: Go behind the scenes and see puffins or octopus up close and learn about the center's work. To make the most of the admission price, call ahead so you can catch a program that interests you.

301 Railway Ave. (P.O. Box 1329), Seward, AK 99664. © 800/224-2525 or 907/224-6300. www.alaskasealife.org. $15 adults, $12 children 7–12, free for children 6 and under. Apr 15–Sept 15 daily 8am–7pm; Sept 16–Apr 14 daily 10am–5pm.

WHERE TO STAY

Alaska's Point of View Reservation Service (© **907/224-2323;** www.alaskasview. com) is a Seward lodging and tour-booking agency. The website has an impressive search function for B&Bs, cabins, hotel rooms, and all other lodgings.

You can get a list of B&Bs from the chamber of commerce visitor center (see p. 277).

Seward has several hotels beyond those I can list here; in fact, I'm not aware of a bad hotel in Seward. The newest addition is the **Holiday Inn Express Seward Harbor** (✆ **888/465-4329** or 907/224-2550; www.hieseward.com), standing right on the small-boat harbor wall and a few steps from the railroad depot. The hotel has excellent amenities, including a pool and broadband Internet, and superb views. Summer rates are $169 to $269 double. At the other end of town from the Holiday Inn, the **Hotel Edgewater,** 200 5th Ave. (✆ **888/793-6800;** www.hoteledgewater.com), stands right across the street from the ocean and the SeaLife Center and has similar rooms and rates, with excellent views and a large lobby atrium. **Murphy's Motel** (✆ **800/686-8191** or 907/224-8090; www.murphysmotel.com), near the boat harbor, has very good rooms with views in a new building and budget rooms in an older building.

Ballaine House Bed and Breakfast *Finds*   This 1905 house near downtown is a classic B&B, with wooden floors, a large living room, and tall, double-hung windows. It's decorated with antiques and handmade quilts, and is on the National Register of Historic Places and the town walking tour. It's a social place with service that is accommodating and fun, and the hostess offers raincoats, binoculars, and other gear for outings; cooks breakfast to order; and even does laundry. The B&B can also book your activities and boats in Seward and some other towns, giving you the booking commission, which can save as much as 20%. The rooms are not large, suitable for only one or two people, and all bathrooms are shared. The B&B does not take children under 8.

437 3rd Ave. (P.O. Box 2051), Seward, AK 99664-2051. ✆ **907/224-2362.** www.superpage.com/ballaine. 5 units, all with shared bathroom. $92 double. Rates include full breakfast cooked to order. No credit cards. No children under 8. **Amenities:** Tour booking; laundry service; shared Internet access. *In room:* TV/VCR.

The Breeze Inn *✦*   Located right at the busy boat harbor, this large, three-story, motel-style building offers good standard accommodations with the most convenient location in town for a fishing or Kenai Fjords boat trip. Rooms are frequently renovated. An annex building has excellent upscale rooms, some overlooking the harbor.

1306 Seward Hwy. (P.O. Box 2147), Seward, AK 99664-2147. ✆ **888/224-5237** or 907/224-5237. Fax 907/224-7024. www.breezeinn.com. 100 units. Summer $139–$199 double; winter $49 double. Extra person $10. AE, DC, DISC, MC, V. **Amenities:** Restaurant; bar; courtesy van; guest laundry. *In room:* A/C, TV, dataport, Wi-Fi, fridge, coffeemaker, hair dryer, iron.

Harborview Inn *✦✦*   The inn grew from Jerry and Jolene King's bed-and-breakfast operation and still shows the taste and attention to detail that made it such a success. The rooms are among the most attractive in town, with lots of light, Mission-style furniture, and Tlingit art based on Jolene's tribal crest. The rates are not out of line by Seward high standards, and the location, midway between the small-boat harbor and downtown, puts both within long walking distance. Families and large groups especially should consider a stay. The inn has a four-bedroom family suite with the features and size of a house—it's 2,500 square feet—renting for $199 double plus $10 for each additional person. Two two-bedroom apartments on the beach along Ballaine Avenue are perfect for families as well and rent for $189 a night for four. There are other suites, too.

804 3rd Ave. (P.O. Box 1305), Seward, AK 99664. ✆ **888/324-3217** or 907/224-3217. Fax 907/224-3218. www.sewardhotel.com. 35 units, 4 apts. High season $144 double, $159–$259 apartment; low season $59 double, $69–$219 apartment. Extra person $10. AE, DISC, MC, V. *In room:* TV, Wi-Fi, coffeemaker, hair dryer.

Seward Windsong Lodge 🏔🏔 This hotel is the only one at Kenai Fjords National Park with a national park atmosphere. The big lobby, with its high ceiling, huge wood beams, fireplace, and cedar shingles, could be at Yellowstone. Moreover, the posh, solidly finished quality of the place puts it in first place among Seward's hotels. The location is out of town, among spruce trees on the broad valley of the Resurrection River, and the collection of buildings goes on and on. Rooms are in separate lodges with entry from exterior porches. They have a crisp feel, all with two queen beds and rustic-style furniture and good amenities. The hotel restaurant, the Resurrection Roadhouse, is reviewed below, under "Where to Dine."

½ mile, Herman Leirer Rd. (also known as Exit Glacier Rd.). (Mailing address: 2525 C St., Suite 405, Anchorage, AK 99503) ℂ 888/959-9590 or 907/265-4501 in Anchorage, or 907/224-7116 in Seward. www.sewardwindsong.com. 108 units. High season $209–$259 double; low season $129–$179 double. Extra person 12 and over $15. AE, DISC, MC, V. Closed Oct–Apr. **Amenities:** Restaurant; tour desk; courtesy van. *In room:* TV/VCR, coffeemaker.

Van Gilder Hotel 🏔 This historic building was restored and decorated with the wallpaper of a century ago, Victorian reproductions, and other authentic period details. Even the tiny bathrooms, mostly with shower stalls, not tubs, are tiled in the appropriate style and immaculately clean, and three rooms share bathrooms. The rooms tend to be small and oddly shaped, as you would expect, but all have queen-size beds and some also have a fold-down Murphy bed for a third person. In Seward's high-priced lodging market, these rooms are a great value for a party of three. Perhaps best is the warm, professional management: They thought of including a community kitchen on the main floor where guests can stop for a free hot drink at any time or even cook their own meals. The location, right downtown, is prime.

308 Adams St. (P.O. Box 609), Seward, AK 99664. ℂ 800/204-6835 or 907/224-3079. Fax 907/224-3689. www.van gilderhotel.com. 24 units. High season $109 double with shared bathroom, $149–$169 double with private bathroom, $199 suite; low season $59 double with shared bathroom, $69–$79 double with private bathroom, $129 suite. Extra person $10. AE, DC, DISC, MC, V. *In room:* TV.

A HOSTEL, CAMPING & CABINS

A friendly family runs the **Moby Dick Hostel,** at 432 3rd Ave. (ℂ **907/224-7072;** www.mobydickhostel.com). They charge $17 for a bunk, $50 for private hostel rooms, and $60 to $65 for rooms with kitchenettes.

The best campgrounds near Seward are those in Chugach National Forest, described earlier in section 3. The only campground in Kenai Fjords National Park is near Seward, the **Exit Glacier Campground** at Mile 8.5 of Herman Leirer Road (aka Exit Glacier Rd.). The campground is on willow-covered, gravel ground that plants haven't yet reclaimed from the retreating ice. Sites are far apart and almost completely private but lack any amenities—no picnic tables, fire grates, or anything. Use the food lockers and central cooking to keep bears away. Snow lingers into early June; later in the summer, the campground often fills by early evening. There is no fee for the 12 sites, and reservations are not taken. It's open for tents only and has pit toilets and hand-pump water.

In the town of Seward itself, the seaside Waterfront Park on Ballaine Boulevard is acceptable for RV camping, but the tent sites are too noisy and exposed for my liking. Seward has tried to crack down on drinking and rowdiness in its campgrounds with partial success. The fee is $8 for tents, $12 for RVs, plus $25 for a site with utilities, and showers are $2. It's operated by the city parks and recreation department (ℂ **907/ 224-4055;** www.sprd.cityofseward.net). A quieter town campground is **Forest Acres**

Park, among the spruce trees at Hemlock and Sealion Boulevard, just off Seward Highway near the Army Recreation Center. Fees are the same. Neither campground accepts reservations. RVs are welcome, but there are no hookups.

More appealing is **Miller's Landing,** a homestead on Lowell Point Road south of town (© **866/541-5739** or 907/224-5739; www.millerslandingak.com). Sites are along the beach or among large spruce trees. Electric hookups are $28 to $30 a night, tent sites are $23, rustic sleeping-bag cabins start at $45, and cabins with kitchens and bathrooms, ranging in size up to large enough to sleep 10, run $79 to $299. As rustic as the place seems, it has Wi-Fi and public-access computers around the wood stove in the store. There's lots to do here; see "Boating & Sea Kayaking," earlier.

The Alaska Division of Parks maintains two cabins for rent in the **Caines Head State Recreation Area,** south of town, and two in **Thumb Cove State Marine Park,** across the bay from Caines Head (see "State Parks Cabin Reservations," in section 1 of this chapter). These cabins are in high demand and difficult to reserve, but there are good areas for camping in both parks. It's possible to hike to the Caines Head cabins (see "Hiking," above), but to get to Thumb Cove you need a boat. Water taxi service is offered for $55 per person round-trip by Miller's Landing (see "Boating & Sea Kayaking," earlier). The Thumb Cove cabins lie in an impossibly steep bowl of mountains, a grand and lovely setting that, along with the excellent salmon fishing nearby, explains their popularity. Camping is permitted along the same beach without a permit, with plenty of space and an outhouse for campers' use. Cabins in Chugach National Forest and Kenai Fjords National Park are mentioned in those sections.

WHERE TO DINE

There are various places at the harbor to grab a sandwich or other quick meal on the way out to sea; they change too frequently for me to include here. Downtown, the **Ranting Raven,** at 228 4th Ave. (© **907/224-2228**), is a great little gift and coffee shop serving pastries, sandwiches, and soup, open April through Christmas.

Apollo Restaurant ✿ (Kids) MEDITERRANEAN/SEAFOOD   This is a surprisingly good small-town restaurant. Seward families come back for a menu that includes Greek and southern Italian cuisine, steaks, seafood, pizza, and much more. They'll even cook your own day's catch. But the food is far more sophisticated and expertly turned out than you expect in such a place, especially the seafood dishes, and the service is fast, skilled, and flexible, great for families with children. The dining room, with many booths, takes the Greek theme as far as it will go—I especially enjoyed the miniature Doric columns. They serve beer and wine.

229 4th Ave. © **907/224-3092.** www.apollorestaurantak.com. Main courses $10–$24. AE, MC, V. Daily 11am–11pm.

Ray's Waterfront ✿ STEAK/SEAFOOD   The lively, noisy dining room looks out from big windows across the small-boat harbor, with tables on terraces so everyone can see. The atmosphere is fun and the consistently good food is just right after a day on the water. While not perfect, it's more nuanced than the typical harborside place; the seafood chowder is great. Most important, they don't overcook the fresh local fish—and that's really all you can ask. On a busy summer weekend, however, the place can be overrun, with long waits and harried servers. They have a full bar.

At the small-boat harbor. © **907/224-5606.** Lunch $8–$15; dinner main courses $15–$30. AE, DISC, MC, V. 18% gratuity added for parties of 6 or more. Daily 11am–11pm. Closed Oct to mid-Mar.

Resurrection Roadhouse ⋒ ALASKAN SPECIALTIES/PIZZA   This place sometimes sees an annual shift in quality typical of seasonal restaurants, but I've had wonderful food here. The menu includes fish, venison, and ribs smoked in-house. They
also serve hand-thrown gourmet pizzas. The view of the mountains is great and there's
plenty of space. It's a relaxing alternative to noisy Ray's. The bar's collection of Alaska
craft brews on tap is exhaustive. Do call ahead, as they fill at dinner time.

²⁄₃ mile, Herman Leirer Rd. (also known as Exit Glacier Rd.). ⓒ 907/224-7116. Dinner reservations recommended.
Lunch $9–$13; dinner main courses $9–$24. AE, DISC, MC, V. Daily 6am–2pm and 5–10pm. Closed mid-Sept to May.

6 Kenai Fjords National Park

Kenai Fjords is all about remote rocks, mountains, ice that meets the ocean, and the
animals that live there. The park comprises 670,000 acres of the south coast and interior landmass of the Kenai Peninsula. The shore here is exposed to the Gulf of Alaska,
whose wild, recurrent storms beat against the mountainous shore unbuffered by any
landmass from the vast expanse of the Pacific to the south. Wildlife thrives, but
humans have never made a mark.

The geological events that formed this landscape are vast and ongoing. The steep
coastal mountains amount to a dent in the earth's crust where the northward-moving
Pacific tectonic plate collides and adds land to the southern edge of Alaska. As the
Pacific plate pushes under Alaska, it slams islands onto the Alaska coast and then pulls
them under into the molten layer down below. These mountains are shrinking meas-
urably as the earth swallows them up. The 1964 earthquake dropped them by 6 to 8
feet. As your boat passes the park's small, sharp, bedrock islands, now populated by
seabirds and marine mammals, you are seeing the tips of ancient peaks that once stood
far above the shore like today's coastal mountains.

The park's history has barely started. The fjords became a park only in 1980. In
1976, when the National Park Service explored more than 650 miles of coastline,
including the park area, they didn't find a single human being. The same was true
when geologists came in 1909. British explorer Capt. James Cook made the first maps
of the fjords area in 1778, but the coast was too rugged and rocky for him to land. We
don't know much about Native Americans who lived in the fjords. Scientists have
found some areas where people lived, or at least had camps, but no one knows exactly
who they were or what they were doing here. The earth, through earthquakes or glacial action, has erased most remains. Anthropologists call these people *Unegkurmiut*
and believe they were Alutiiq, Eskimos who lived on the Pacific coast, closely related
to the Chugach people of Prince William Sound and the Koniag from Kodiak Island
to the south. Those groups are still around; scientists are studying the Unegkurmiut
and what happened to them from the little evidence they can find on the fjord's
beaches.

The Natives probably never ventured inland over the impossibly rugged interior of
the Kenai Peninsula, leaving its heart to be discovered in 1968, when the first mountain climbers crossed the Harding Ice Field, which covers most of the national park.
Exit Glacier and all the glaciers of Kenai Fjords flow from this ice age leftover, which
may be a mile thick. The ice field lies in a high bowl of mountains that jut straight
out of the ocean to heights of 3,000 to 5,000 feet. When moisture-laden ocean clouds
hit those mountains, they drop lots of rain and snow—up on the ice field 40 to 80
feet of snow fall each winter, with a water equivalent of 17 feet. Summer weather isn't

warm enough to melt the snow at that elevation, so it packs down ever deeper until it turns into the hard, heavy ice of glaciers and flows downward to the sea.

The area's history finally got an ugly start in 1989, when the tanker *Exxon Valdez* crashed into a rock about 150 miles northeast of the park in Prince William Sound and spilled about 11 million gallons of oil. Exxon did a poor job of catching the oil before it spread, and by the end of the summer, the sticky, brownish-black muck had soiled beaches in the western Sound, across the fjords, and all the way to Kodiak Island and the Alaska Peninsula. More than 1,000 miles of shoreline were oiled to some degree, 30 miles in the park. Hundreds of sea otters and hundreds of thousands of seabirds were killed in the Sound and on the islands near the fjords. Nature scrubbed the oil off the rocks again, and you will see no evidence of it in the park today; but government scientists say many of the affected species of birds and animals haven't come back completely. Nonetheless, you'll still see more wildlife on a boat ride here than anywhere else I know.

Most of the park is remote and difficult to reach. A large vessel, such as a tour boat operating out of Seward, is the only practical way for most people to see the marine portion of the park. That's not cheap or quick, and there are better destinations for people subject to seasickness. The inland portion is accessible only at Exit Glacier, near Seward.

ESSENTIALS

GETTING THERE   Seward is the threshold to the park. Exit Glacier is 13 miles from the town by road, the Kenai Fjords National Park Visitor Center is at the Seward small-boat harbor, and the tour boats that visit the park leave from Seward.

Some visitors try to see the park in a day, coming from Anchorage by train or road, touring the park by boat and then returning that evening. I do not recommend this. To really get to the park, you need to be on an all-day boat trip—most half-day trips barely leave Resurrection Bay and hardly see the park proper. More important, a lot of visitors riding the train back to Anchorage after a 16-hour marathon to Kenai Fjords are so tired they can't keep their eyes open for the extraordinary scenery passing by. A better plan is to spend at least 1 night in Seward and take in the full Kenai Fjords boat trip and Exit Glacier.

VISITOR INFORMATION   At the **Kenai Fjords National Park Information Center,** Seward Small Boat Harbor (P.O. Box 1727), Seward, AK 99664 (© **907/ 224-7500;** www.nps.gov/kefj), you will find rangers to answer questions about the park and provide information on the all-important tour boats, and a small but handy bookstore. Call or drop by here for advice on public-use cabins for rent in the fjords, guidance on a sea-kayaking expedition there, or information on hikes and trail conditions. They're open Memorial Day through Labor Day daily 9am to 7pm. Hours in May and September will be shorter but had not been determined by press time. The center is closed October through April.

ACCOMMODATIONS & CAMPING   There are no hotels in the park; it's best to base yourself in Seward (see my recommendations earlier in this chapter). The **Exit Glacier Campground,** the only campground in the park, also is listed on p. 282. In the heart of the park, you can camp anywhere if you observe correct backcountry precautions. A free park service map shows the location of food lockers and hanging cables to keep your stuff away from bears in the kayaking waters of Aialik Bay and Northwestern Fjord. The Park Service gives voluntary permits to record your itinerary and an emergency contact phone number in case you don't return. Send away for a packet of information from the park. They also rent out three **public-use cabins** in the fjords, reachable only by boat or floatplane. Contact the Alaska Public Lands Information Center in Anchorage (p. 211) for a $50-a-day cabin permit, open for reservations starting January 2 each year.

SEEING THE PARK
SIGHTSEEING & WILDLIFE CRUISES

Kenai Fjords is essentially a marine park. On a boat tour, you'll see its mountains, glaciers, and wildlife. On any of the tours, you're sure to see sea otters and sea lions, and you have a good chance, depending on the season, conditions, and luck, of seeing humpback whales, orcas, mountain goats, and black bears. I saw all those on one trip to Aialik Bay. Gray whales come in the early spring and huge fin whales show sometimes, too, but are hard to see. Bird-watchers may see bald eagles, puffins (both tufted and horned), murrelets (marbled and Kittletz's), cormorants (red faced, pelagic, and double-crested), murres (common and thick billed), auklets (rhinoceros and parakeet), and various other sea ducks, alcids, and gulls.

The farther you go into the park, the more you'll see. If you really want to see Kenai Fjords National Park and glaciers that drop ice into the water, the boat has to go at least into Aialik Bay to Holgate Glacier. Northwestern Glacier is even deeper in the park. Half-day Resurrection Bay cruises offer plenty of impressive scenery but pass only one large glacier, and that at a distance. They have less chance of seeing whales and also see fewer species of birds. The longest trips into the heart of the park proper encounter the greatest variety and number of birds and animals. If you're lucky with the weather, you can make it to the exposed Chiswell Islands, which have some of the greatest bird rookeries in Alaska, supporting more than 50,000 seabirds of 18 species. I've seen clouds of puffins swarm here. The day-long trips also allow you more time to linger and really see the behavior of the wildlife. Whatever your choice, binoculars are a necessity, but if you didn't bring your own, you can often rent them on board.

Prices are around $150 to go to Northwestern Glacier in Northwestern Fjord off Harris Bay, a 10-hour trip; $130 to go to Holgate Glacier in Holgate Arm off Aialik Bay, which takes 6 to 8 hours (the most common destination); and $60 to $80 for a 3- to 4-hour Resurrection Bay tour, which doesn't go to the national park at all. Children's prices are around half off. I have seen misleading publicity material from the tour operators, so ask exactly where the boat goes or get a map of the route. They sometimes brag about going to Bear Glacier, but that's a let-down because boats can't get close to it. You have to go at least to Holgate Glacier for a noteworthy glacier encounter.

The season begins in April with tours to see the gray whale migration, mostly within Resurrection Bay. That's done by mid-May, when the regular schedule of tours begins, which lasts into September.

Fares with each operator differ little, although you can sometimes get early season or Web specials; instead, shop for the destination, length of trip, food service, interpretation, and size or intimacy of the boat. Ask about the seating arrangement. How many passengers will be on board and how many crew members to answer questions? Is lunch provided, and what does it consist of? Another important point of comparison is whether you have a ranger doing the commentary or the captain—some of these captains don't know when to shut up, and they can give inaccurate information.

Tips It's Not Easy Being Green

A critical factor in choosing your boat tour is your susceptibility to **seasickness.** To reach the heart of the park, vessels must venture into the unprotected waters of the North Pacific. Large, rolling waves are inevitable on the passage from Resurrection Bay to the fjords themselves, although once you're in the fjords, the water is calm. On a rough day, most boats will turn back for the comfort of the passengers and change the full-day trip into a Resurrection Bay cruise, refunding the difference in fare. Of course, they'd rather not do that, and the decision often isn't made until the vessel is out there and some people are sick. This happened on our last trip. About 80% of the passengers were already vomiting when the boat turned around. (Even for those who don't lose it, being around that much puke isn't fun.) If you get seasick easily, my advice is to stick to the Resurrection Bay cruise or take a boat tour in protected Prince William Sound out of Whittier (see section 4 in this chapter), where the water is smooth. We always take Dramamine or Bonine at least 30 minutes before leaving the dock for the fjords, and it works. If you wait until the boat is moving, the drug probably won't help you. These drugs can make you sleepy, but it's worth it unless you have an iron stomach and know you won't get sick. In any event, ask about the tour company's policy on turning back and refunds.

Try to schedule loosely so that if the weather is bad on the day you choose for your boat trip, you can wait and go the next day. If the weather's bad, you'll be uncomfortable and the animals and birds won't be as evident, or the boat may not go out of the bay at all. If you pay up front to hold a reservation on a boat—probably a good idea in the busy season—find out the company's refund and rescheduling policy.

Most operators offer packages with the Alaska Railroad and the SeaLife Center, or even with a local hotel, which may save money, but make sure you have enough time to do everything you want to do in Seward. All have offices at the Small Boat Harbor in Seward. Here are two of the best.

Kenai Fjords Tours   This is the dominant tour operator, with the most daily sailings and choices of destination. The main part of the operation uses 90- to 150-passenger vessels, many of which have forward-facing seats, like an airplane's. They're professionally staffed. The whole operation runs remarkably smoothly and we found the crew extremely attentive. When the ships are crowded, however, the experience becomes more impersonal. On most tours, the captain or an employee provides the commentary, but interpretive park rangers join selected tours—I recommend choosing one of those boats. The same company also owns **Mariah Tours,** which operates more intimate 16-passenger vessels. Their trips are more spontaneous and go farther; the downside is that the smaller boats are less stable in the waves.

Most of the large Kenai Fjords vessels call on a lodge the company owns on Fox Island, in Resurrection Bay. It sits on the long cobble beach of Sunny Cove, where painter Rockwell Kent lived in seclusion with his son in 1918 and 1919 and produced the art that made him famous, as well as his classic book *Wilderness: A Journal of Quiet Adventure in Alaska* (Wesleyan University Press). It is an inspiring spot. The lodge itself stands on a narrow strip of land between the beach and a pond, which visitors overlook from large wooden decks. Boats stop for a lunch of grilled salmon. Big, touristy salmon bakes tend to overcook the food, and we found no exception here, but it was a pleasant meal nonetheless. Some passengers spend the night at the lodge. An overnight package on the island costs $329 per person, with the day cruise and meals included. Half-day sea-kayaking paddles from the island are offered for day-trippers or overnight guests: $79 to $89 per person as an add-on for overnighters; or $149 to $169, including a Resurrection Bay tour boat ride, for day-trippers.

At the Seward small-boat harbor. © **800/478-8068,** 907/224-8068 in Seward, or 907/276-6249 in Anchorage. www.kenaifjords.com.

Major Marine Tours   This company pioneered first-class onboard dining and commentary by park rangers, who go on every trip—a decisive advantage, in my judgment. Their boats are slower than some of the competitors', so they don't make the long trip to Northwest Glacier; they either head into Aialik Bay to see Holgate Glacier or tour Resurrection Bay around Seward. Instead of bringing sandwiches or stopping for a meal, they serve a buffet of salmon and prime rib on board for $15 per person, $7 for children. The food is surprisingly good. I also like their table-seating arrangement with forward-facing seats. Your seat is assigned, so there's no need to rush aboard or try to stake out your spot.

411 W. 4th Ave., Anchorage. © **800/764-7300** or 907/274-7300, or 907/224-8030 in Seward. www.majormarine.com.

SEA KAYAKING

The fjords are calm yet rugged, intricate, and full of wildlife and soaring vistas. It's hard to imagine a better place for a sea-kayaking expedition. They also are extremely remote and very rainy, however, so a trip there is a poor choice for your very first outing. Experienced cold-water paddlers can rent kayaks and explore on their own, using the park service cabins for shelter (see above under "Accommodations & Camping"). I've listed an agency that rents kayaks and offers water taxis under "Boating & Sea Kayaking" in the Seward section on p. 278. **Sunny Cove Sea Kayaking** offers a kayaking day trip to Aialik Bay. They take you out on a small charter boat for a wildlife tour and then you launch and paddle in front of the glacier while the boat stands by. The price for the day trip is $375; expensive, but it is the best of the best. For a visit with time to get more of a feel for the place, spend a couple of days. Sunny Cove's 2-day, 3-night glacier trip costs $879.

EXIT GLACIER

When I visited Italy years ago, I got to the point where I thought I'd scream if I saw another painting of the Madonna. If your trip to Alaska is long, you may start to feel the same way about glaciers. But, although relatively small, Exit Glacier really is unique, and my family still enjoys visits there even as jaded lifelong Alaskans. (And I've probably seen even more glaciers than Madonnas.)

You can walk close to Exit Glacier, see its brittle texture, and feel the cold, dense spires of looming ice. Cold air breathes down on you like air from an open freezer door. Approaching the glacier, you can see the pattern of vegetation reclaiming the land that the melting ice has uncovered, a process well explained by interpretive signs and a nature trail. The National Park Service opened a new nature center here in 2004, adding to the comfort and educational content of a visit (the building is also interesting technically, as it is powered by a hydrogen fuel cell). You can easily spend a couple of hours on a casual, pleasant visit to the glacier (longer if you do a hike).

A safety note: Big chunks fall off the glacier ever more frequently as Alaska's climate warms. Stay behind the signs or you stand a good chance of being crushed.

The easiest way to get to the glacier is to drive. The clearly marked 9-mile road splits from the Seward Highway about 3½ miles north of town. In winter, the road is closed to vehicles. If you don't have a car, a shuttle may be available; check with the park visitor center (p. 285) to see who is currently offering service. Entrance to the park is currently free.

Following the road along the broad bed of the wandering Resurrection River, you'll see in reverse order the succession of vegetation, from mature Sitka spruce and cotton-wood trees down to smaller alders and shrubs. It takes time for nature to replace the soil on sterile ground left behind by a receding glacier. As you get closer, watch for signs with dates starting a couple of centuries in the past; they mark the retreat of the glacier through time.

The Exit Glacier Nature Center is open Memorial Day weekend through Labor Day daily 9am to 8pm. Ranger-led nature walks start daily at 10am, 2pm, and 4pm on the short trail to the glacier. It's easy to find your way to the glacier and back on a variety of short trails.

One of the glacier's striking features is a high berm of gravel that fits around its leading edge like a necklace. This is a moraine, the glacier's refuse pile. The glacier gouges out the mountains with its immense, moving weight as new ice flows down from the ice field above and melts here. It carries along the rock and gravel torn from the mountain like a conveyor belt. This moraine is where the conveyor belt ends and the melting ice leaves the debris behind in a big pile. Probably without knowing it, you've seen hundreds of moraines all over North America, where the glaciers of the last ice age piled debris into hills, but this is the most obvious moraine I've ever seen, and it helps you understand how they work.

An all-day hike, 8 miles round-trip, climbs along the right side of the glacier to the Harding Ice Field—the glacier gets its name for being an exit from that massive sheet. It's a challenging walk with a 3,000-foot elevation gain, but it's the easiest access I'm aware of to visit an ice field on foot. The upper trail isn't free of snow until late June or early July. The ice field itself is cold and dangerous, and there's an emergency shelter maintained by the park service. Don't trek out on the ice unless you have glacier-climbing experience. The park service leads hikes up the trail Saturday in July and August, leaving at 9am from the nature center.

The Resurrection River Trail, in Chugach National Forest, begins from the road just short of the last bridge into the Exit Glacier area. It's a pleasant day hike, with lots of wildflowers in the fall, or the start of a long hike deep into the mountains.

7 Cooper Landing: Road Meets River

The little roadside community of Cooper Landing, in a wooded mountain valley along Kenai Lake and the Kenai River, begins about 8 miles west of Tern Lake, where the Sterling Highway splits from the Seward Highway and continues sporadically along the highway for about 7 miles. (The Sterling runs generally west until Soldotna, where it heads south again.) The frothing upper **Kenai River** is the community's lifeline, each summer bringing the salmon that, in turn, draw visitors, who fill hotels, restaurants, and the date books of fishing guides. The **Russian River** meets the Kenai at the western edge of the community, where a mad fishing frenzy for the July red salmon season occurs. A ferry takes anglers across the river from the highway. For information on how to fish the Kenai, see "Fishing" in section 8 of this chapter on Kenai/Soldotna; there's additional information in chapter 2.

If you're not an angler, there's not much here—a couple of operators do rafting trips and some trails start here. Cooper Landing is the starting or ending point for back-packing trips in the Chugach National Forest, described in section 3 of this chapter. Look there also for descriptions of several campgrounds for tents or RVs (there are also RV hookups at the Kenai Princess Lodge, reviewed below).

Cooper Landing has a post office, service stations, and small stores selling fishing gear and essentials, but it's not a real center of commerce. For banking or anything else not directly related to catching a salmon, you'll have to drive to Sterling, 30 miles away to the west, or Soldotna, 14 miles beyond that.

VISITOR INFORMATON   A visitor information booth is at the day-use area and boat ramp, known as the landing, on the right side of the highway just after it crosses the source of the Kenai River at Kenai Lake. The area is a good place to stop anyway, with a pleasant boardwalk trail to stretch your legs (a $5 day-use fee applies) and a tackle shop and booking service nearby. The information booth is operated by the **Cooper Landing Chamber of Commerce** (© **907/595-8888;** www.cooperlanding chamber.com) and is open May 15 to September 15.

FISHING LODGES

The three lodges below can take care of everything, so you can set up your fishing and other activities with a single phone call. If what you need is a simple room that is clean, comfortable, and inexpensive, try **The Hutch Bed and Breakfast,** Mile 48.5, Sterling Highway (© **907/595-1270;** www.arctic.net/~hutch). In nice weather, you can sit at the fire pit and watch the bunny rabbits hop by.

Gwin's Lodge   This is the town's old original log roadhouse, dating from the 1940s. Standing just a mile east of the Resurrection trail head and the Russian River Camp-ground, Gwin's is convenient and has loads of character. The owner, a dynamic for-mer F-15 fighter pilot, keeps it open 24 hours a day all summer long as the nerve center for the 24-hour fishing on the Russian River. It includes a liquor store and a large store selling tackle, snacks, and clothing, and freezing anglers' fish. You can also book fishing, rafting, flightseeing, and other many activities. The lodgings range from old-fashioned cabins to modern trailer-size units called "chalets" with kitchenettes, mock log exteriors, and sleeping lofts with tiny dormers. All have shower stalls, not tubs. The least expensive cabins are old log structures and not as plush. All are quite clean, with a woodsy cabin smell.

Over 50 years, the **restaurant** has welcomed many a tired angler or backpacker for a hearty meal, including me; after a long day outdoors, it's hard to be objective about food, but the chowder has won awards. Choices in the seven-table dining room range broadly: burgers, quiche, steak, pies, and seafood. Meals are hearty and good, well above the greasy-spoon tradition of such places. The restaurant, bar, and espresso stand are open around the clock in summer, and the "gourmet to go" shop sells the restaurant's fare for takeout.

14865 (Mile 52) Sterling Hwy., Cooper Landing, AK 99572. © **907/595-1266.** www.gwinslodge.com. 15 cabins. High season $115–$184 double; low season $79–$99 double. Extra person age 3 or older $15. DISC, MC, V. **Ameni-ties:** Restaurant; bar; fishing rentals; activity desk. *In room:* Wi-Fi, coffeemaker.

Kenai Princess Lodge ☆☆☆   This is one of the best in the region. Each room in the red-roofed buildings feels like a remote cabin, with balconies overlooking the wooded valley, woodstoves stocked with firewood, and many unique details; yet they're luxurious hotel rooms at a resort with a spa and fine restaurant. There are three classes of rooms with a $30 price difference between each. The middle, premium class, is halfway up the hill, with rooms separated by a divider into two parts, like a real cabin. At the top level, the deluxe rooms, highest on the hill, have more of a clean, elegant feel. Bathrooms are surprisingly small in all the rooms. Currently closed off season, most rooms fill in the summer with Princess cruise-ship passengers. The cycle of the ships determines whether rooms are open for independent travelers. The lodge books guided fishing, horseback riding, tours, and other activities, and there are hiking trails nearby. An attractive 35-space RV park with full hookups is on-site, with access to the facilities.

The Eagle's Crest restaurant has a varied and sophisticated menu, with good use of Alaskan seafood, and a light dining room that follows the hotel's generally rustic theme. Dinner main courses are $20 to $30; the lunch menu has the expected items, plus choices such as calamari and some unusual salads, generally under $10. Even if you have no reason to stay in Cooper Landing, consider planning your drive to include a meal here that will be several steps up from highway fare and enjoy the relaxing ambience of the lodge.

Up Bean Creek Rd. above Cooper Landing (P.O. Box 676, Cooper Landing, AK 99572). ☎ **800/426-0500** or 907/595-1425. Fax 907/595-1424. www.princesslodges.com. 86 units. High season $239–$299 double; low season $159–$189 double. RV sites $30. AE, DC, DISC, MC, V. Closed Oct–Apr. **Amenities:** Restaurant; bar; exercise room; Jacuzzi; tour desk; coin-op laundry. *In room:* TV, dataport, coffeemaker.

Kenai River Sportfishing Lodge/Kenai Riverside Lodge ☆☆   The compound lies between the highway and the river, but down among the trees it feels like a remote lodge. I'd call the cabins faux rustic—I've never seen real Bush cabins with smooth walls, wainscoting, bright rag rugs, and private bathrooms, but these trim places still feel like the outdoorsy real thing, with no TVs or phones. The location is the real advantage: Kenai River fishing frontage. Whitewater-rafting rides and fishing floats

---

Floating the Kenai River

The Kenai is more famous for fishing than rafting, but the area is beautiful and the Kenai Canyon, below Cooper Landing and above Skilak Lake, has frothy water between vertical canyon walls. **Alaska Wildland Adventures,** at the Kenai Riverside Lodge (☎ **800/478-4100** or 907/783-2928), is the most established operator and has a great reputation. They offer a 7-hour float through the canyon for $125 adults, $95 children ages 7 to 11; and a placid 2-hour float down the upper Kenai for $49 adults, $29 children ages 5 to 11; children younger than the age ranges for the prices are not permitted. Their guided fishing is $210 to $225 for a full day, including lunch and gear.

Alaska Rivers Co., Mile 50, Cooper Landing (☎ **907/595-1226**; www.alaska riverscompany.com), has more than 25 years of experience. They offer scenic rafting ($49 adults, children ages 12 and under half-price, all ages welcome), canyon floats ($108), and guided fishing ($95 half-day, $170 all day). They rent cabins, too.

leave right from the riverfront. The lodge also possesses a scarce resource in its coveted guide permits for the hot fishing river section that runs through the Kenai National Wildlife Refuge.

Everything is covered by one price: transportation from Anchorage, meals in a central lodge building, guided salmon fishing or fly-fishing for rainbow trout in drift or power boats, and, on longer visits, halibut fishing (done from boats in salt water). You provide your own booze and fishing license, and pay the tip. Many visitors come as part of a "safari" package that takes them to various outdoor activities and sites, such as the Alaska Wildland Adventures safari that's described in chapter 2 on p. 40.

Alaska Wildland Adventures, Mile 50.1 Sterling Hwy. (P.O. Box 389, Girdwood, AK 99587-0389). © **800/478-4100** or 907/783-2928. www.alaskasportfish.com. 16 cabins. 3-day, 4-night inclusive package $1,895. MC, V. **Amenities:** Restaurant (family style); sauna; river equipment included. *In room:* No phone.

8 Kenai/Soldotna & Sterling: Giant Salmon

These quintessential western U.S. towns, dominated by shopping malls and fast-food franchises facing broad highways, have a single claim to fame, but it's a pretty good claim: The largest sport-caught king salmon in the world, almost 100 pounds, came from the Kenai River. The Kenai's kings run so large there's a different trophy class for the river—everywhere else in the state, the Alaska Department of Fish and Game will certify a 50-pounder as a trophy, but on the Kenai it has to be at least 75 pounds. That's because kings in the 60-pound class—with enough wild muscle to fight ferociously for hours—are just too common here. Anglers prepared to pay for a charter will be in their element on the river when the fish are running hot. Catching a big king is not easy or quick, however, and success rates vary greatly year to year and week to week.

Those not interested in fishing will find, at most, a day's sightseeing in these towns. Instead, use the towns as a base for the outdoors. Kenai has a strangely beautiful ocean beach and the Kenai River mouth, with exceptional bird-watching during migrations. Beyond the towns, you'll find a wealth of outdoor activities, primarily in the lake-dotted **Kenai National Wildlife Refuge,** which has its headquarters in Soldotna. The refuge is covered in the next section.

Kenai came into being with the arrival of the Russians at the mouth of the Kenai River more than 200 years ago, but it came into its own only with the discovery of oil on the peninsula in 1957. Today its economy relies on oil, commercial fishing, and, to a smaller extent, tourism. Soldotna, a smaller, newer, and less attractive town, is the borough seat and the primary destination for anglers. Sterling is just a wide place in the road—incredibly wide, as a matter of fact (no one is quite able to explain why such a small town needs such a big road).

ESSENTIALS

GETTING THERE From Anchorage, the drive on the Seward and Sterling highways to Soldotna is 147 miles. Allow 3 hours, without stops: In summer, traffic will slow you down; in winter, speeds are limited by ice and the fear of hitting moose. Kenai is 11 miles from Soldotna on the Kenai Spur Highway, the first major right as you enter Soldotna from the north on the Sterling Highway. The **Homer Stage Line** (© **907/235-2252** or 907/399-1847; www.homerstageline.com) connects Anchorage, Homer, Seward, and points between with van service. In summer they run to Homer daily from Anchorage and Seward, less frequently in winter. The fare from

Anchorage to Soldotna is $50 one-way, $90 round-trip. The pick-up point in Soldotna is the Thompson's Corner gift store at 44224 Sterling Hwy. The Anchorage ticket office is at 3335 Fairbanks St. (© **907/868-3914**). Kenai receives very frequent flights from Anchorage from **Era Aviation** (© **800/866-8394;** www.flyera.com). Use a credit card, as the airline has had financial problems.

GETTING AROUND   The area is so spread out that walking most places really isn't possible, and there's no public transportation. Everyone drives. Four car-rental companies operate at the Kenai airport: **Hertz, Avis, Budget,** and **Payless.** If you plan only to fish, however, you may not need a car, instead getting rides from your guide, your host, or a taxicab. Ask about transportation options when you reserve your rooms. There are several cab companies; try **Alaska Cab** (© **907/283-6000** in Kenai or **907/262-1555** in Soldotna).

VISITOR INFORMATION   The **Soldotna Visitor Information Center,** 44790 Sterling Hwy., Soldotna, AK 99669 (© **907/262-9814** or 907/262-1337; www. soldotnachamber.com), is located on the south side of town; drive through the commercial strip and turn right after the Kenai River Bridge. It's open daily in summer from 9am to 7pm; in winter, Monday through Friday from 9am to 5pm. Aside from the usual brochures and free maps, they maintain notebooks full of comparative information about lodgings, camping, and other services, and will help you find a room or charter. Anglers should stop in to see the world-record 97-pound King salmon and a 20-pound rainbow trout.

In Kenai, the **Kenai Visitors and Cultural Center** at 11471 Kenai Spur Hwy., Kenai, AK 99611 (© **907/283-1991;** www.visitkenai.com), is an attraction in itself. A museum does a good job of using artifacts to explain the cultures that passed through the Kenai: the Natives, the Russians who settled in 1791, and the later pioneers and oil workers. Look for the "King of Snags," an immense conglomeration of lost fishing lures, rods, and sticks from the bottom of the river. Temporary art exhibitions are mounted, too (see "Special Events," below). To get there, follow the Spur Highway past Main Street and look for the large, landscaped building on your left. In summer, admission to the museum portion is $3, free for students through high school; off season, admission is free. They are open summer Monday through Friday from 9am to 7pm, Saturday and Sunday from 10am to 6pm; and off season Monday through Friday from 9am to 5pm and Saturday 11am to 4pm.

SPECIAL EVENTS   Kenai Visitors and Cultural Center (see above) hosts invitational art shows each summer. Works usually cross media and include contemporary art and traditional Alaska Native work. Admission is $3 adults, free for minors. **The Kenai River Festival** (© **907/260-5449**), over the second weekend of June, has food, music, crafts, and games.

In Soldotna, the **Tustumena 200 Sled Dog Race** (© **907/262-3270**), held in late January, helps kick off the mushing season. **Progress Days** (© **907/262-9814**), in late July, offers a parade, rodeo, car shows, and other festival events commemorating the completion of a gas pipeline in 1960—that's the area in a nutshell.

In Ninilchik, the **Kenai Peninsula State Fair** (© **907/567-3670**), south at Mile 136 on the Sterling Highway, is the third weekend in August (Aug 17–19, 2007), with rodeo, music, crafts, games, agricultural and crafts exhibits, and other country attractions, plus a few kids' rides. One-day admission is $7 adults, $5 ages 6 to 12 and seniors.

FAST FACTS: Kenai & Soldotna

Banks You will find them on the Kenai Spur Highway in the middle of town and in Soldotna, on the Sterling Highway commercial strip. In addition, ATMs are in grocery stores all over the area.

Hospital **Central Peninsula General** is in Soldotna at 250 Hospital Place (© **907/ 262-4404**); from the Sterling Highway, take Binkley Street to Marydale Avenue.

Internet Access Connect to the Web for free at the **Kenai public library,** 163 Main St. Loop (© **907/283-4378**), or at the **Soldotna public library,** 235 Binkley St. (© **907/262-4227**).

Police For nonemergencies in Kenai, call the Kenai Police Department (© **907/ 283-7879**); in Soldotna, call the Soldotna Police Department (© **907/262-4455**); outside city limits, call the Alaska State Troopers (© **907/262-4453**).

Post Office In Kenai, it is at 140 Bidarka St, just off Main Street Loop.; in Soldotna, 175 N. Binkley St. (take East Park Avenue from the Kenai Spur Highway).

Taxes There's a 5% **sales tax** in Kenai and Soldotna, and 2% outside city limits.

FISHING

Fishing the Kenai River is the whole point of coming to the area for most visitors. Check at the Soldotna Visitor Information Center (p. 293) for information and regulation booklets. Or contact the **Alaska Department of Fish and Game,** 43961 Kalifornsky Beach Rd., Suite B, Soldotna, AK 99669 (© **907/262-9368** or 907/262-2737, for a recorded fishing report; www.alaska.gov/adfg). Serious anglers shouldn't miss that website, which includes daily sonar counts of salmon in the river and information on biology and fishing techniques; navigate through "Sport Fisheries" and click on the Southcentral region on the map. Licenses are for sale on the site and in virtually any sporting-goods store. Also read "A Salmon Primer" and "Fishing" in chapter 2. There are more than two dozen public access points over the 80 miles of the Kenai River. A **guide brochure** with a map is available from the state **Division of Parks,** P.O. Box 1247, Soldotna, AK 99669-1247 (© **907/262-5581;** www.alaska stateparks.org); you also can pick up a copy at one of the visitor centers.

For anglers interested in less competition and more of a wilderness experience, Kenai is a gateway for vast wild lands accessible by air on the west side of Cook Inlet. There you may be able to fish a stream packed with salmon but few other anglers. Among others, **High Adventure Air** (© **907/262-5237;** www.highadventureair.com) offers guided day trips for $250 to $350 per person.

KINGS King salmon, the monsters of the river, come in two runs. The early run comes from mid-May to the end of June, peaking in mid-June. On average less plentiful and smaller, in the 20- to 40-pound range, the run did also produce the sport-caught world's record (97 pounds, 4 ounces). The second run comes during the month of July and includes more of the massive fish. Most people fish kings from a boat, fishing certain holes. Boats hold stationary or back slowly down the river, or fishermen drift down river. Your chances from the bank are low; on average, with or without a boat, it takes 29 hours of fishing time to land a king (you'll likely get at least a dozen strikes for every fish that makes it into the boat). With a guide, the average time to land a fish is cut in half, but that still means that if you fish for only 1 day, chances are good that you'll get skunked. A boat of three anglers on a half-day guided charter has roughly a 50% chance of landing a king among them.

A guided charter averages $150 to $170 for a 6½-hour day trip, $250 to $265 full day. There are dozens of guides. Contact the visitor center in Kenai or Soldotna (see p. 293) to get in touch with a guide; also, many hotels and lodges have their own. It's possible to rent a boat, but this is advisable only if you are experienced in boats and stay out of the hazardous, faster-flowing parts of the river. The **Sports Den,** at 44176 Sterling Hwy. in Soldotna (✆ **907/262-7491;** www.alaskasportsden.com), is one charter operator, with river and ocean trips for salmon or halibut, fly-in fishing, and hunting, and they also offer lodging packages with large units. I've found them friendly and helpful over the years.

REDS   The area really goes crazy when the red (or sockeye) salmon join the kings in the river, from mid-July to early August. You can fish reds from the bank or from a boat. Reds are plankton eaters; some say they won't strike a lure, some say they do. In the most popular fishing areas, near the confluence of the Russian River or Moose River with the Kenai, regulations allow only the use of flies. Most people around here cast the flies with spinning gear, weighting the line 18 inches from the fly so it bounces along the bottom. Cast upstream from shore and allow the fly to drift down, keeping near the bank. While waiting for a strike, debate whether the fish really attack the flies or whether they get caught when they instinctively move their mouths in an eating motion, which they do in quick-moving water.

SILVERS   Silvers first arrive in late July, peaking during August, but continue to be in the river through September and even in October. They're easiest to catch anchored in a boat, but you can also do well from shore. Lures work well, as does a bait of salmon eggs.

OTHER SPECIES   Trophy-size rainbow trout and Dolly Varden char also come out of the river. Anglers using light tackle may also enjoy catching pink salmon, which are plentiful in the Kenai during even-numbered years, arriving in late July and lasting until mid-September. Use spinning gear and lures. Most Alaskans turn up their noses at this easy-to-catch 4-pound fish; just smile and keep hauling them in. Fresh, bright pinks taste great over a campfire.

EXPLORING THE TOWNS

Kenai's historic sites, beach walking, and bird-watching can occupy you for much of a day. Start at the visitor and cultural center mentioned above and get a copy of the *Old Town Kenai Walking Map;* follow the numbered markers. Not many of the simple, weathered buildings remain from Kenai's life before oil, but those that do are interesting and lie only a few blocks down Main Street from the center, along the Cook Inlet and Kenai River bluff.

The **Holy Assumption of the Virgin Mary Russian Orthodox Church** is the area's most significant building. The parish was founded in 1845 and the present church was built in 1895. It's a quaint, onion-domed church, brightly kept but with old icons. A donation is requested. Several nearby buildings are interesting for their interlocking log construction and weathered exteriors.

The bluff nearby provides an overlook for the broad, sandy ocean beach. A dirt path runs down from Alaska Avenue between the apartment building and the houses that contain professional offices (please don't park near here, as an excess of tourists' cars has caused a problem for the apartment building). To drive down, return to the Kenai Spur Highway, turn to the northwest (left), and then turn left on South Spruce Street. There's a big parking lot with a $10 fee, which seems strange on the deserted beach until dipnetting season begins—then you will understand why. At a certain point in the summer salmon run, Alaska residents can fish from this beach by scooping up passing fish with long-handled dipnets. That's also when you can see white beluga whales chasing salmon upriver, sometimes in great numbers. If you just want to watch, the viewpoint from the top of the bluff at Erik Hansen Scout Park, at Cook and Mission avenues, is a prime spot. However, the beach also is a lovely place for a walk. It's easy to imagine the Russians' first arrival. On a calm day, the beach sand, the mud flats, and the Inlet's gray, glacial water seem to meld together into one vast shimmering plain. The water is far too cold for swimming.

The mouth of the river and the wetlands of its delta make for fine **bird-watching,** especially during spring and fall migrations. One of the best places to get to the tidal Kenai River Flats is along Bridge Access Road, which branches from the Spur Highway. The state of Alaska has developed viewing areas at each end of the bridge.

A family looking for something to do while one parent is off fishing may enjoy the magnificent **North Peninsula Recreation Area Nikiski Pool** (© 907/776-8472), 10 miles north of Kenai on the Kenai Spur Road. The facility occupies a large dome and has a 136-foot water slide, mushroom fountains of water, and a raised hot tub from which parents can watch their children play in the pool below. The water slide is open Tuesday through Sunday from 1 to 5pm and from 6 to 9pm in the summer (lap swimming opens those days at 7am); the winter hours are complicated, so call for details. Pool admission is $3, or $6 to use the slide and pool. Weekends can be crowded.

WHERE TO STAY

Rates at many hotels are on seasonal schedules with three, four, or even more levels linked to the salmon runs. I've listed the highest and lowest. One unique lodging choice, worth an exploratory visit even if you don't stay there, is the **Historic Kenai Landing** (© 907/335-2500; www.kenailanding.com), where a complex of cannery buildings dating from 1912 has been remodeled into simple rooms, a restaurant, and shops. The location is scenic but out of the way, on the opposite side of the river mouth from Kenai: after crossing the bridge, turn right on Kalifornsky Beach Road and right again on Cannery Road.

Aspen Hotel Soldotna 🌟🌟   This small chain of hotels was built in recent years by Alaska businesspeople who found a niche in certain towns for accommodations with high-end amenities in an up-to-date corporate style. In Soldotna, they produced the best rooms in town in a building with high ceilings and a solid feeling of quality, if not much personality. It has the only hotel swimming pool on the whole Kenai Peninsula (small, but with a large spa beside it). Room choices include family suites with bunkbeds, providing privacy between parents and kids, and PlayStation video games. Suites with cooking facilities are available, too. All rooms are decked out with lots of amenities, including DVD players and speaker phones. The hotel is behind Arby's on the commercial strip, but the view out the back is of a settling pond and the river.

326 Binkley Circle, Soldotna, AK 99669. © 888/308-7848 or 907/260-7736. Fax 907/260-7786. www.aspenhotels ak.com. 63 units. High season $169–$179 double, $199 suite; low season $99 double, $119 suite. $10 extra person over age 18. Rates include continental breakfast. AE, DC, DISC, MC, V. **Amenities:** Pool; exercise room; spa, business center w/computers; guest laundry room. *In room:* TV/DVD, Wi-Fi, microwave, fridge, coffeemaker, hair dryer, iron.

Daniels Lake Lodge Bed and Breakfast ✿ *Finds*   Located on peaceful and sparsely built Daniels Lake, this lovely, relaxing place has a boat and canoe you can rent for trout fishing right out the back door, among the resident ducks. Rooms are comfortable and thoughtfully decorated, with access to a shared kitchen, and the cabins, with kitchens, are remarkable—just right for these 9 acres of woods, with choices for couples or big groups. The gregarious hosts, Jim and Karen Burris, share their Christian faith with guests and, along with their dog and rabbits, eagerly make friends. It's not a 1-night stopover, but a place to stay for a couple of days of relaxation, closer to the Nikiski Pool and the outlet of the Swanson River Canoe route of the Kenai National Wildlife Refuge than to any town. Smoking is not allowed indoors.

21 miles north of Kenai (P.O. Box 1444), Kenai, AK 99611. ⓒ 800/774-5578 or 907/776-5578. www.danielslake lodge.com. 4 units, 4 cabins. High season $95–$130 double, $150–$280 cabin; low season $50–$120 any unit. High season extra adult or teen $20, extra child 11 and under $10, 2-night minimum in cabin; low season extra person $15. AE, DISC, MC, V. Deposits by check only. **Amenities:** Outdoor hot tub; high-speed Internet; boat or canoe rental. *In room:* TV.

Great Alaska Adventure Lodge ✿✿   For anglers, it's the location that counts, and for that this lodge is hard to top, with a third of a mile of river frontage where the Moose and Kenai rivers converge, a hot fishing spot since time immemorial, as an ancient Native site attests. In the evening, the lodge keeps a guide and campfire on the beach so you can keep casting in the midnight sun. The newly remodeled lodge rooms overlooking the river are spacious and have gas fireplaces and private bathrooms. Unfortunately, the site suffers from vehicle noise from the adjacent Sterling Highway. The lodge offers a wide variety of guided fishing activities, including fly-fishing and halibut outings. For guests interested in seeing wildlife and the glorious wilderness of the Kenai National Wildlife Refuge, the lodge offers trips to cushy backcountry tent camps. They also arrange day trips and overnights to a camp across Cook Inlet to watch resident brown bear engaging in natural behavior. Check the lodge's website for information on the many tours and wilderness safaris that they offer, as well as rates, which are too complicated to itemize here.

Moose River, 33881 Sterling Hwy., Sterling, AK 99672 (in winter, P.O. Box 2670, Poulsbo, WA 98370). ⓒ 800/544-2261 or 907/262-4515. Fax 907/262-8797 in summer, 360/697-7850 in winter. www.greatalaska.com. 25 units. Rates from $175–$345 for a day trip without lodging; packages of 2–10 days $995–$4,995. Rates include all meals, guide service, transfers, and travel from Anchorage. AE, MC, V. Closed Oct to mid-May. **Amenities:** On-site guiding and fishing. *In room:* Gas fireplace, no phone.

Harborside Cottages Bed and Breakfast ✿   On a grassy compound at the top of the bluff over the mouth of the Kenai River in Old Town, these little white cottages make the most of a perfect site. The view and quiet can keep you in a peaceful reverie all day. Inside, the cottages are as immaculate as if brand new, each with its own light country decoration. They have either king-size beds or pairs of twin beds. There are no tubs, just shower stalls. The hostess stocks a self-serve breakfast the night before. Outside is a patio with a picnic table and gas barbecue. Nice as the place is, however, the summer rates are a bit high.

13 Riverview Dr. (P.O. Box 942), Kenai, AK 99611. ⓒ 888/283-6162 or 907/283-6162. www.harborsidecottages. com. 5 cottages. High season $175 double; low season $135 double. Rates include continental breakfast. AE, DISC, MC, V. Closed winter. *In room:* TV, microwave, fridge, coffeemaker, iron.

Log Cabin Inn ✿   Ted and Carol Titus built this log house specifically to be a B&B, but with its huge common room—with a fireplace and towering cathedral ceiling—it feels more like a wilderness lodge. Located off Kalifornsky Beach Road a little south of the bridge in Kenai, the house stands over an active beaver pond with a deck and lots of windows to watch the beavers. The upstairs rooms, which cost $10 more, are well worth it—they're large and airy. A room on the main floor has French doors to a deck over the pond. Several other rooms, in the half-basement, are cute but smaller, with country decoration. If you like to stay up late or rise early, the strict 10pm to 7am quiet hours in the house could make the cabins an attractive choice. They are large and comfortable, but authentic, with plank floors, rag rugs, and rough-cut wood walls. Carol serves a full breakfast.

49860 Eider Rd. P.O. Box 2886, Kenai, AK 99611. ℂ/fax **907/283-3653.** www.acsalaska.net/~ted.titus. 9 units, 3 cabins. High season $100–$110 double; low season $80–$100 double. Extra adult $25; extra child 11 and under $10. Rates include full breakfast. AE, DISC, MC, V. **Amenities:** Jacuzzi. *In room:* No phone.

CAMPING

Soldotna's appealing **Centennial Park Campground** extends along a long section of the Kenai River bluff among thick spruce and birch trees with ramps down to fishing spots on the river. Although natural in its setting, it has a coffee stand and newspaper vending machine, and is next door to the visitor center and close to stores. Turn right on Kalifornsky Beach Road just after the bridge on the Sterling Highway. Camping fees are $11 a night and day use is $5, payable at a manned entrance booth. The park is open May 1 to October 1. There's a dump station, usable for a $10 fee. **Swiftwater Park** is a similar city-operated riverside campground near the Fred Meyer grocery store and Taco Bell as you enter town from the north. For a quieter, oceanfront public campground, see the Captain Cook State Recreation Area, p. 301.

RV parks are scattered about. The one with the best location is Beluga Lookout **Lodge and RV Park,** 929 Mission Ave. (ℂ **907/283-5999;** belugarv@ptialaska.net). It's in Kenai's Old Town, at bluff's edge over the inlet and the river's mouth. Full hookups are $20 to $50 a night. They offer bike rentals and charters for salmon and halibut fishing and bear or beluga watching.

WHERE TO DINE

Franchise fast-food and burger-steak-seafood places dominate in Kenai and Soldotna. **Paradisos,** at Main Street and Kenai Spur Highway in Kenai (ℂ **907/283-2222**), is an excellent family restaurant serving Italian and Mexican food and the specialty, Greek. In business here since 1971, they've got the formula right: big portions of familiar food, reasonable prices, and an ambience suitable for taking grandma out for a special evening. **Louie's,** in the Uptown Motel at 47 Spur View Dr. (ℂ **907/283-3660**), serves good, solid food in a dining room and bar room that call to mind the den of a maniacal sportsman—if the animal mounts came to life, you'd be crushed in a stampede.

Charlotte's Bakery, Café, Espresso ✸ SANDWICHES   Rich-textured bread from the bakery anchors the sandwiches, and lettuce from a nearby garden completes the large, filling salads, but the motherly owner doesn't make a point of that—hers is not a trendy or gimmicky place. Locals fill the big wooden chairs in the bright dining room because the food is wonderfully flavored, the service sweetly attentive, and the prices reasonable. The cafe serves beer and wine.

115 S. Willow, Kenai. ℂ **907/283-2777.** www.charlottesrestaurant.net. All items $5–$11. MC, V. Mon–Fri 7am–4pm.

Mykel's ⭐⭐⭐STEAK/SEAFOOD   This is a traditional fine-dining restaurant for a date or an especially relaxing evening. Located in the Soldotna Inn, near the intersection of the Sterling and Kenai Spur highways, the dining room, with high-backed booths and Formica-topped tables, is well kept but dated and not up to the style of the food. That's the only demerit I can give. The cuisine is exceptional and the service professional and more than friendly. Nothing else in the area even plays in the same league, and Mykel's is only a half-step below Alaska's best. The dinner menu contains many familiar beef and chicken dishes done just right. When they "borrowed" the pepper steak created by Jens Hansen at his restaurant in Anchorage, they admitted it on the menu—classy. In addition, the restaurant offers various ways of having local seafood in creative ways. The nightly specials, with wine pairings, run to a full page. Servings are large, even for the exceptional desserts, so don't order extra courses. The lounge has 18 wines by the glass and many microbrews. At lunchtime there are lots of salads to choose from besides the expected sandwiches.

35041 Kenai Spur Hwy., Soldotna. ☎ 907/262-4305. www.mykels.com. Reservations recommended. Lunch $8–$13; dinner $18–$28. V. High season daily 11am–10pm; low season Tues–Thurs and Sun 11am–9pm, Fri–Sat 11am–10pm.

Sal's Klondike Diner DINER   It certainly looks corny and touristy from the outside, but Sal's turns out to be a classic Western highway diner, with big portions, fast service, and nothing fancy that doesn't have to be. Our sandwiches, burgers, and halibut fish and chips were just what we wanted for a quick lunch, and our coffee cups stayed full. The children's menu is good and cheap.

44619 Sterling Hwy., Soldotna. ☎ 907/262-2220. Lunch $4.50–$9; dinner main courses $7–$18. AE, MC, V. Daily 24 hr.

Suzie's Place ⭐ DOWN HOME   If you are traveling the Sterling Highway and want a pleasant and filling lunch or dinner, you'll do no better than this local favorite on the east side of the road in the town of Sterling itself. Cheerful, efficient servers bring big plates of comfort food and hearty sandwiches. The dining room, heavily decorated in burly country style, has only seven tables and a small lunch counter, and no room for waiting. Busy winter and summer, it is kept bright and immaculate.

Mile 87.2 Sterling Hwy., Sterling. ☎ 907/260-5751. All items $7–$25. MC, V. Daily 11am–8pm.

9 Kenai National Wildlife Refuge

Floating through the Kenai National Wildlife Refuge in a canoe narrows the world into a circle of green water, spruce, and birch. You can paddle and hike for days without encountering more than a few other people, your only expense the cost of your canoe and the vehicle that carried you to the trail head. Out there with my older son, I once noticed that, other than his voice, the only sounds I had heard in 2 days were the gurgling of the water and the wind shushing in the birch leaves. You rely on yourself, but your greatest tests are not overly taxing. Trail a line behind the canoe, and, when you catch a rainbow trout, land it and make a fire to cook it. Launch your body into the clear, frigid water to rinse off the sweat on a warm day. Float slowly, watching eagles circle the treetops and puffy clouds drift like ships past your little world.

Most of the western half of the Kenai Peninsula lies within the 2 million acres of the refuge—it's almost as large as Yellowstone National Park—and much of that land is impossibly remote and truly dedicated to the wildlife. The Kenai River flows through part of the refuge, but the refuge is just a name to the anglers who pursue its salmon. (Information about fishing and rafting the river is covered earlier, in the Kenai/Soldotna and Cooper Landing sections.) Canoeists will be more interested in the lowlands on the west side, west of the Sterling Highway and north of Kenai and Soldotna. The lakes there are as numerous as the speckles on a trout's back, or at least that's how they appear from the air. From the ground, the region is a maze of lakes connected by trails—more than 70 lakes you can reach on canoe routes stretching more than 150 miles. It's the easiest way to real Alaska wilderness I know.

ESSENTIALS

GETTING THERE The refuge surrounds much of the land from Cooper Landing at the north to Homer at the south and Cook Inlet to the west. The Sterling Highway and roads that branch from it are the main ways to the lakes, trails, and rivers, and there is no practical way there without a vehicle.

VISITOR INFORMATION Stop in at the **Kenai National Wildlife Refuge Visitor Center,** Ski Hill Road (P.O. Box 2139), Soldotna, AK 99669 (© **907/262-7021;** http://kenai.fws.gov), for guidance before plunging into the wilderness. The U.S. Fish and Wildlife Service, which manages the refuge, exhibits natural history displays here, shows a film each hour in the afternoon in the summer, and maintains a 3-mile nature trail. The staff offers advice and sells books and maps that you'll definitely need for a successful backcountry trip. To find the center, turn left just south of the Kenai River Bridge, taking a right turn in front of the building-supply store uphill on the unpaved road. It's open June through August Monday through Friday from 8am to 5pm, Saturday and Sunday from 9am to 5pm; October through May, Monday through Friday from 8am to 4:30pm, Saturday and Sunday from 10am to 5pm. The website also contains detailed trip-planning information for the canoe routes.

GETTING OUTSIDE
CANOEING

Once known as the Kenai National Moose Range, the refuge's brushy wetlands are paradise for moose, rich in their favorite foods of willow and birch shoots and pond weeds. Moose like to dine while wading. Waterfowl and other birds, beavers, muskrats, and other aquatic animals are common on the lakes. People also must be partly aquatic to explore the lakes, paddling canoes across their surfaces, pushing through lily pad passages between lakes, and frequently hiking in rubber boots between lakes while carrying the canoe and camping gear.

There are two main canoe routes, both reached from Swanson River and Swan Lake roads, north of the Sterling Highway from the town of Sterling. The **Swan Lake Canoe Route** is a 60-mile network of 30 connected lakes. It meets Swan Lake Road twice, allowing a loop of several days, and in between, adventurers can penetrate many lakes deep into the wilderness, visiting remote lakes they'll have all to themselves. It's also possible to canoe through to the Moose River and ride its current 17 miles over a long day back to the Sterling Highway.

Getting anywhere requires frequent portages of a quarter-mile or so, and more ambitious routes have mile-long portages. You can skip all the portaging, however, by floating 2 days down the **Swanson River** to its mouth, at the Captain Cook State Recreation Area (see below), joining the river at a landing at Mile 17.5 of Swanson River Road. The water is slow and easy all the way.

The most challenging of the routes is the **Swanson River Canoe Route,** which connects to the river's headwaters through a series of lakes and longer portages. The route covers 80 miles, including 40 lakes and the river float. Both routes have many dozens of remote campsites—just lakeside areas of cleared ground with fire rings—and most of the portages are well marked and maintained with wooden planking over the wet areas.

You can rent canoes and everything else you need for a wilderness trip on the refuge canoe routes near the intersection of Swanson River Road and the Sterling Highway in Sterling, where the Finch family operates **Alaska Canoe & Campground (*C* 907/ 262-2331;** www.alaskacanoetrips.com). Coleman canoes rent for $40 for 24 hours and lighter fiberglass canoes for a little more. They offer a shuttle service to carry canoeists from one entrance to another so you don't have to double back on your trip, and they can give valuable expert advice. And they rent a lot of other outdoor stuff: kayaks, mountain bikes, rafts, and so on. Call ahead to check on equipment and to reserve yours. Their campground is fully equipped, too, a good base where you can return for showers and laundry.

The Finches' business also offers guided trips, but you don't need a guide if you know how to canoe and are prepared for wilderness. If that's your approach, among your most important tools will be the book *The Kenai Canoe Trails,* by Daniel L. Quick (Northlite Publishing, $19). This extraordinary guide contains superdetailed maps and directions, and advice on how to plan your trip and fish and camp on your way—I've never seen a trail guide like it. I haven't provided detailed driving instructions because you'll need detailed maps to go at all. **Trails Illustrated** produces a good detailed map of the whole area, printed on plastic (see "Fast Facts: Alaska," in chapter 2 for details). A serviceable free map is distributed by the refuge visitor center.

There's much more to do in the refuge too, including several upland hiking trails. The refuge visitor center provides guidance and maps.

CAMPING

For car camping away in a wild, oceanfront setting, remote from the region's fishing mayhem, try the **Captain Cook State Recreation Area.** The lovely and underused 3,460-acre area faces Cook Inlet 25 miles north of Kenai on North Kenai Road at the mouth of the Swanson River. There are lots of attractive sites among large birches, trails, beach walking, a canoe landing at the end of the Swanson River Canoe Route, and lake swimming. The State Parks camping fee is $10. **Daniels Lake Lodge,** listed earlier in section 8 (on Kenai/Soldotna) of this chapter, is nearby.

There are many campgrounds within the refuge, too, some of them lovely, quiet spots on the edge of uninhabited lakes, such as the small **Rainbow Lake** and **Dolly Varden Lake campgrounds,** on Swanson River Road near the start of the canoe routes, and the **Watson Lake** and **Kelly-Peterson Lake campgrounds** on the Sterling Highway between Sterling and Cooper Landing. Get a complete listing from the visitor center. Only two campgrounds have fees: **Hidden Lake** and **Upper Skilak Lake,** which are closer to Cooper Landing, charge $10.

10 Homer & Kachemak Bay: Cosmic Hamlet by the Sea

Homer's leading mystic, the late Brother Asaiah Bates, always maintained that a confluence of metaphysical forces causes a focus of powerful creative energy on this little seaside town. It's hard to argue. Homer is full of creative people: artists, eccentrics, and those who simply contribute to a quirky community in a beautiful place. Indeed, Brother Asaiah may have been the quintessential Homeroid, although perhaps an extreme example, with his gray ponytail, extraordinary openness and generosity, and flowery rhetoric about "the cosmic wheel of life." Homer is full of outspoken, unusual, and even odd individualists—people who make living in the town almost an act of belief. I can say this because I'm a former Homeroid myself.

The geography of Homer—physical as well as metaphysical—has gathered certain people here the way currents gather driftwood on the town's pebble beaches. Homer is at the end of the road; the nation's paved highway system comes to an abrupt conclusion at the tip of the Homer Spit, almost 5 miles out in the middle of Kachemak Bay, and believers of one kind or another have washed up here for decades. There were the "barefooters," a communal group that eschewed shoes, even in the Alaska winter (Brother Asaiah came with them in the early 1950s). There are the Russian Old Believers, who organize their strictly traditional communities around their objection to Russian Orthodox church reforms made by Peter the Great. There are the former hippies who have become successful commercial fishermen after flocking here in the late 1960s to camp as "spit rats" on the Homer Spit beach. And there are even the current migrants—artists and retired people, fundamentalist preachers and New Age healers, wealthy North Slope oil workers and land-poor settlers with no visible means of support—all people who live here simply because they choose to.

The choice is understandable. Homer lies on the north side of Kachemak Bay, a branch of lower Cook Inlet of extraordinary biological productivity. The halibut fishing, especially, is exceptional. The town has a breathtaking setting on Homer Spit and on a wildflower-covered bench high above the bay. The outdoors, especially on the water and across the bay, contains wonderful opportunities. And the arts community has developed into an attraction of its own. There are several exceptional galleries and the Pratt Museum, which has a national reputation.

You'll be disappointed, however, if you expect a charming little fishing town. Poor community planning has created a town that doesn't live up to its setting—indeed, highway sprawl is in the process of ruining some of it. Homer Spit in summer is a traffic-choked jumble of cheap tourist development and RVs.

Homer began to take its modern form after two events: In the 1950s, the Sterling Highway connected it to the rest of the world, and in 1964 the Good Friday earthquake sank the spit, narrowing a much larger piece of land with a small forest into the tendril that now barely stands above the water. If not for constant reinforcement by the federal government, the spit long since would have become an island, and Homer would hardly exist. As long as it survives, however, the town makes the most of that unique finger into the sea. Whether or not it is a cosmic focal point, it certainly is an exceptional launching point to one of the world's great marine recreation areas.

ESSENTIALS

GETTING THERE   By Car   At about 235 miles, Homer is roughly 4½ hours from Anchorage by car, if you don't stop at any of the interesting or beautiful places along the way. It's a scenic drive. If you take a rental car, drive it both ways, as the drop-off fees from Anchorage to Homer are high.

By Bus   Homer Stage Line (© **907/235-2252** or 907/399-1847; www.homerstage line.com) runs to Anchorage and Seward and back daily during the summer, less frequently the rest of the year. The Anchorage-Homer fare is $60 one-way, $110 round-trip. Tickets are for sale at **Quicky Mart**, 1242 Ocean Dr., in Homer (© **907/235-2252**). In Anchorage, the ticket office is at 3335 Fairbanks St. (© **907/868-3914**).

ACCOMMODATIONS ■
Driftwood Inn **5**
Heritage RV Park **18**
Homer Hostel **7**
Hornaday Campground **1**
Land's End Resort **23**
Magic Canyon Ranch
    Bed and Breakfast **15**
Ocean Shores Motel **2**
Oceanview RV Park **3**
Old Town
    Bed and Breakfast **6**
Pioneer Inn **8**

The Sea Lion Cove **17**
Seaside Farm **15**
DINING ◆
Boardwalk Fish and Chips **20**
Café Cups **9**
Chart Room **23**
Cosmic Kitchen **13**
Duncan House Diner **11**
Fat Olive's **4**
Fresh Sourdough Express
    Bakery and Cafe **16**
The Homestead **15**
Panarelli's Cafe & Deli **6**

ATTRACTIONS ●
Art Shop Gallery **8**
Bunnell Street Gallery **6**
Coal Point Trading Co. **21**
Fireweed Gallery **12**
Islands and Oceans
    Visitor Center **14**
Pier One Theatre **19**
Pratt Museum **10**
Ptarmigan Arts **12**
Salty Dawg Saloon **22**
Sea Lion Gallery **17**

By Air **Era Aviation** (© **800/866-8394;** www.flyera.com) serves Homer from Anchorage several times a day. Small air-taxi operators use Homer as a hub for outlying villages and the outdoors.

By Ferry The **Alaska Marine Highway System** (© **800/642-0066;** www.ferry alaska.com) connects Homer to Seldovia, Kodiak, and points west along the Alaska Peninsula and Aleutian Archipelago, with the ferry *Tustumena*. The *Kennicott* also goes to Kodiak, and to the east rounds the Kenai Peninsula to Whittier and thence across the Gulf of Alaska to Southeast Alaska and British Columbia (see "Getting There" in section 4, on Whittier). The run to Kodiak takes 9½ hours and costs $72 for an adult walk-on passenger (children 5–11 half off). It's a long trip, but a memorable one.

VISITOR INFORMATION   The **Homer Chamber of Commerce Visitor Information Center,** 201 Sterling Hwy. (P.O. Box 541), Homer, AK 99603 (© **907/235-7740;** www.homeralaska.org), is on the right as you enter town. In summer, staff is on hand Monday through Friday from 9am to 7pm, Saturday and Sunday 10am to 6pm. Besides answering questions and handing out brochures on local businesses and public lands, they sell tickets for the halibut derby (p. 305). Winter hours are Monday through Friday from 9am to 5pm.

The **Islands and Oceans Visitor Center,** 95 Sterling Hwy., Homer, AK 99603 (© **907/235-6961;** www.islandsandocean.org), is more than a visitor center; it's one of Homer's best attractions—a sort of museum of the outdoors for the Alaska Maritime National Wildlife Refuge and the Kachemak Bay Research Reserve, the co-sponsoring organizations. Everyone coming to Homer should stop in to see the building, an architectural gem that perfectly reflects the rocky shores that the refuge and reserve take in, and to experience exhibits that use technology and a deft sense of theater to re-create those remote places in thought and feel. A film about the work of the brave scientists who work in the fierce wilderness of the refuge's outer reaches, in the Aleutian Islands, shows frequently in the auditorium. The center is also the best place to stop for information if you plan to go outdoors anywhere in the area. An easy nature trail descends to the salt marsh below the center. Admission is free. The center is open summer daily 9am to 6pm; check the website or call for winter hours.

The refuge itself consists of islands off Alaska from the Arctic to near British Columbia that include some of the world's most prolific bird and marine mammal habitat. The U.S. Fish and Wildlife Service manages these lands for the benefit of the animals and people rarely set foot on their shores, but rangers in Homer offer bird and guided tide pool treks frequently in the summer and give programs at the center. Call for times, and see more on tide pooling below. In addition, birders can call the **Kachemak Bay Bird Alert Information Line** (© **907/235-7337**) to find out about recent sightings and upcoming birder events, and to leave news of your own observations, in season.

The **Kachemak Bay State Park District Office,** Mile 168.5 on the Sterling Hwy., 4 miles from town (© **907/235-7024;** www.alaskastateparks.org), can help answer questions about planning a trip to the trails and beaches across Kachemak Bay from Homer and give advice on renting remote cabins (although you make the reservation through the Anchorage office—see "State Parks Cabin Reservations," in section 1 of this chapter). Depending on staffing, the office should be open Monday through Friday from 9am to 5pm.

GETTING AROUND   The best way to get to and around Homer is by car. If you didn't bring one, you can rent a car at the airport from **Hertz** (© **800/654-3131** or 907/235-0734; www.hertz.com) or one of three local firms. Taxis are available from **CHUX Cab** (© **907/235-CHUX**), among others. For strong riders, a bike is a good way around town. You do have to dodge traffic in places downtown, but a paved trail parallels the road for the 5 miles of the spit, and another runs 5 miles east of town.

Some excellent mountain-biking routes are mentioned below. **Homer Saw and Cycle,** 1532 Ocean Dr. (© **907/235-8406;** www.homersaw.com), rents mountain bikes, street bikes, kid's bikes, and trailers. Bike rentals start at $25 a day and come with helmets and locks. The shop keeps track of trail conditions and is a good source of advice. It is open Monday through Friday from 9am to 5:30pm, Saturday from 11am to 5pm. They rent as well from Land's End Resort at the end of the spit, open every day. It's wise to reserve bikes a day or two ahead, especially if an outing depends on getting one.

SPECIAL EVENTS   Homer's **Winter Carnival** (© 907/235-7740), in mid-February, is a big community event, a small-town celebration with a beer-making contest, parade, and snow-sculpture competition, among other highlights.

The **Kachemak Bay Shorebird Festival** (© **907/235-7740;** http://homeralaska. org/shorebird.htm), held in early May, includes guided bird-watching hikes and boat excursions, natural history workshops, art shows and performances, and other events. It's organized by Alaska Maritime National Wildlife Refuge and the Homer Chamber of Commerce to mark the return of the annual migration. **The Kachemak Bay Wooden Boat Festival,** which takes place at the same time as the Shorebird Festival, displays handmade boats from around the region and presents workshops and films. **Kachemak Kayak Fest** (© 907/235-7740; www.kachemakkayakfest.com) is a 4-day schedule of events, instruction, and paddles in late May.

Concert on the Lawn, held the last weekend in July by KBBI public radio (© **907/ 235-7721**), is a 2-day outdoor music, craft, and food festival that brings together the whole town.

The **Jackpot Halibut Derby** (© 907/235-7740; www.homerhalibutderby.com), lasting the whole summer, has a top prize that has reached over $50,000 for the biggest fish of the summer, and smaller monthly prizes and tagged fish prizes. Grand-prize fish are usually 300 pounds or more. Of course, you must buy your $10 ticket before you fish.

FAST FACTS: Homer

Bank Three banks with ATMs, including **Wells Fargo,** are on the Sterling Highway near Heath Street.

Hospital **South Peninsula Hospital** is at the top of Bartlett Street, off Pioneer Avenue (© **907/235-8101**).

Internet Access **Tech Connect Computer Sales and Services,** 432 E. Pioneer Ave. (© **907/235-5248**), offers broadband access for $5 an hour on their computers or Wi-Fi on yours.

Police For nonemergencies within the city limits, call the **Homer Police Department** (© **907/235-3150**); outside the city, phone the **Alaska State Troopers** (© **907/235-8239**). The police station is across Pioneer Avenue from the intersection with Heath Street.

Post Office It's on the Sterling Highway at Heath Street.

Taxes **Sales tax** in Homer is 6.5%. Outside the city, you pay 2%.

EXPLORING THE TOWN

The best activities are on the beaches, in the hilltop meadows, and on Kachemak Bay, and the best man-made attractions all somehow relate to that setting. The art inspired by Homer's environment shows in more than a dozen galleries and studios in town, not including those across the bay in Halibut Cove (discussed later). New shows open all over town on the first Friday of the month, when restaurants hold special evenings and the entire community comes out for an evening of gallery hopping.

A widely distributed brochure lists most of the galleries in town, with a map. Most are close together on Pioneer Avenue. You'll mostly find photography, prints, pottery, fabric, woodwork, and other crafts, since these are small businesses owned by local people trying to make a living. But there is some expensive fine art, too. Among my favorite galleries are **Ptarmigan Arts,** at 471 E. Pioneer Ave. (© **907/235-5345**), an artists' co-op showing a cross-section of what the area offers; the **Fireweed Gallery** (© **907/235-3411;** www.fireweedgallery.com), next door to Ptarmigan, with true fine art in an elegant, airy space; and the large, friendly, and well-stocked **Art Shop Gallery** (© **907/235-7076;** www.artshopgallery.com), in the two-story, octagonal building at 202 W. Pioneer Ave.

There are galleries on Homer Spit, too, among all the ticky-tacky gift shops, food stands, and fishing charters' offices. My favorite there is Gary Lyon's **Sea Lion Gallery,** on the Central Charters Boardwalk at 4241 Homer Spit Rd. (© **907/235-3400;** www.sealiongallery.com). Lyon's work captures Alaska wildlife in spectacular detail but also transforms his subjects with a distinctively dreamy vision. His gallery is a tiny jewel box of valuable works.

Bunnell Street Gallery ★★ This nonprofit gallery, located in a perfect space in an old hardware store near Bishop's Beach at the lower end of Main Street, is my favorite in Alaska. Unlike most other Alaska galleries, which double as tourist gift shops, Bunnell was made by and for artists, and the experience is noncommercial and often challenging. You may be tempted to become a member of the nonprofit corporation that runs it, for membership comes with a one-of-a-kind plate made by one of the artists. As with all Homer art, the themes of the work tend to be fishy, and the medium and style can be anything. The gallery also mounts invitational or juried art shows from beyond the community and also puts on folk and classical music concerts, poetry readings, and films.

106 W. Bunnell Ave. © **907/235-2662**. www.bunnellstreetgallery.org. Summer daily 10am–6pm; winter Tues–Sat 10am–6pm.

Norman Lowell Studio & Gallery ★ (Finds) Lowell built his own huge gallery on his homestead to show his life's work. The immense oils of Alaska landscapes, which are not for sale, hang in a building that counts as one of Alaska's larger art museums. Although Lowell's work is traditionally representational, many of the paintings carry raw emotions capable of reaching the most cynical viewer. Admission is free, and Lowell and his wife, Libby, usually host guests who walk through. Their old-time Alaskan hospitality is a delight. At the end of the exhibit, a large gift shop sells nothing but Lowell's work; paintings range from $750 to $30,000, and prints start at $100. They don't take credit cards. Take a moment to wander the grounds, too, as it's an opportunity to see a real wilderness homestead that has survived largely unchanged from the early days.

Late March Is Perfect

On a recent spring-break trip to Homer in late March, I enjoyed spectacular cross-country skiing on deep snow on lengthy trails leading to lofty Diamond Ridge, and from there I could see a fleet of hundreds of small boats returning across the bay from salmon fishing. We'd spent time viewing the galleries, eating in fantastic restaurants, and staying in a luxurious waterfront room for an amazing bargain price. A smart visitor touring Alaska could combine skiing and fishing in Homer with other March highlights, including the Iditarod Trail Sled Dog Race in Anchorage and the World Ice Art Championships in Fairbanks (see "Alaska Calendar of Events," p. 21). Homer even has a B&B where you can ski the trails from your room, **Alaska Ridgetop Inn** (© **888/357-4343**; www.alaska ridgetopinn.com). The owner is one of the volunteer ski trail groomers.

Norman Lowell Dr. © **907/235-7344**. Free admission. May Mon–Sat 9am–5pm, Sun 1–5pm; June–Aug Mon–Sat 9am–7pm, Sun 1–5pm; Sept Mon–Sat 10am–5pm. Closed Oct–Apr. Turn from Sterling Hwy. at Mile 160.9 (4½ miles from Anchor Point, about 12 miles from Homer).

Pratt Museum 🎦🎦🎦   The Homer Society of Natural History's museum is as good as any you'll find in a town of this size, and it has achieved a well-deserved national reputation. The Pratt displays art and explains local history, too, but it is strongest in natural history. It helped pioneer technology that allows viewing of wildlife through live remote-control cameras without disturbing the animals. Visitors at the museum can watch puffins and other birds on Gull Island, and operate the camera's controls. There is a saltwater aquarium housing local marine life, and if you're curious about all the fishing boats down in the harbor, you can find out about the different types of gear as well as the fish they catch. In the small botanical garden outside, you can learn to identify all the local wildflowers, and a forest trail teaches about the area's ecology. There's much more to see, too, including a good gift shop.

3779 Bartlett St. (at Pioneer Ave.). © **907/235-8635**. www.prattmuseum.org. Admission $6 adults, $5.50 seniors, $3 children ages 6–18, $20 family rate. High season daily 10am–6pm; low season Tues–Sun noon–5pm. Closed Jan.

GETTING OUTSIDE

The best **map of the Kachemak Bay area** is produced by Alaska Road and Recreation Maps. Available all over town, it costs around $5.

ON THE HOMER SIDE OF KACHEMAK BAY

TIDE POOLING   Exploring Kachemak Bay's tide pools is the best way to really get to know the sea and meet the strange and wonderful animals that live in it, and it doesn't cost anything but the price of a pair of rubber boots. First, check a tide book, available for free in virtually any local store, or ask a local to check one for you. You need a low tide of −2 or lower, meaning that low water will be at least 2 feet below the normal low, some 25 feet below the high. Extra-low tides expose more of the lower intertidal zone that contains the most interesting creatures. At a −5 tide, you could find octopus and other oddities. Also, the lower the tide, the more time you'll have to look. Keep track of the time: The tide will come in faster than you imagine, and you could get stranded and drown in the cold water.

The best place to go tide pooling right in town is reached from Bishop's Beach Park, near the lower end of Main Street. Walk west on the beach toward the opening of the bay to Cook Inlet. It's at least a half-hour brisk walk to the Coal Point area, where the sand and boulders end. This is where you'll find pools of water left behind by the receding tide, many full of life. Explore patiently and gently—look at the animals and touch them, but always put them back as they were and try not to crush them underfoot. Marine invertebrate identification keys and many other field guides are sold at the Islands and Ocean Visitor Center, above under "Visitor Information," where rangers happily give advice. They also offer ranger-guided tide pool beach walks. If you want to keep going beyond Coal Point, there's usually a sea otter raft offshore about 3 miles down the beach. Just continue walking, keeping your eyes on the water. As always with watching wildlife, binoculars will improve the experience.

HIKING AND NATURE WALKS   The **Wynn Nature Center,** operated by the nonprofit **Center for Alaskan Coastal Studies** (© 907-235-6667; www.akcoastal studies.org), offers a chance to learn about the ecology of the area and see its birds and wildflowers on an easy walk or hike while taking in sweeping ocean views. The center encompasses 140 acres of spruce forest and wildflower meadow off Skyline Drive, with an 800-foot boardwalk accessible to people with disabilities. This is a lovely area, and the center has done a fine job of adding an educational component without diminishing it—including a log cabin where you can meet a host and ask questions. The center is open daily from 10am to 6pm mid-June through Labor Day, with guided walks twice a day. You can also hike on your own with a printed guide. Fees for adults are $5, seniors $4, ages 18 and under $3. Call about interesting weekly programs as well.

   More ambitious hikes explore more of the bench of land above Homer or the mountains across the bay at Kachemak Bay State Park (see below). The 7-mile **Homestead Trail** is an old wagon road used by Homer's early settlers. The largely informal trail is lovely and peaceful, tunneling through alders, crossing fields of wildflowers, and passing old homestead cabins. From a hilltop meadow, you can see all the way to the inlet and the volcanoes beyond. The eastern trail head is at the reservoir on Skyline Drive—drive up West Hill Road from the Sterling Highway, turn right, and follow Skyline to the fourth left. The western trail head is on Rogers Loop, which branches from the Sterling Highway just before it crests the last big hill before entering Homer. (That's also the place to join Homer's outstanding cross-country ski trails.) A map and guide produced by the Kachemak Heritage Land Trust is available at the visitor center.

DRIVING OR MOUNTAIN BIKING   Several gravel roads around Homer make for exquisite drives or bike rides. Mountain bikers can use the Homestead Trail, too (it is described under "Hiking"). A lovely drive leads out **East End Road,** through seaside pastures, a forest, and the village of Fritz Creek; it then follows the bluff line through meadows toward the head of the bay. When the road gets too rough, explore onward on a mountain bike. **Skyline Drive** has extraordinary views of high canyons and Kachemak Bay; drive up East Hill Road just east of Homer. **Homer Saw and Cycle,** the bike shop listed above, under "Getting Around," can give you many more ideas. The great mountain biking across the bay is described below.

HORSEBACK RIDING   Ranchers have worked around Kachemak Bay for decades. Drive east of town on East End Road to see pastures overlooking spectacular marine and mountain views. Go beyond the road, and you're in some of Alaska's most beautiful untamed country. Mark Marette guides trail rides to the head of Kachemak Bay, leading every group himself, as he has since 1986. Guests used to typical, boring tourist horseback riding come back thrilled at how adventurous their ride has been. Marette's business is **Trails End Horse Adventures** (© **907/235-6393**), 11.2 miles out East End. He charges $20 per hour, or $75 for a 4-hour trip. He takes all ages and raw beginners.

ON & ACROSS KACHEMAK BAY

Along the south side of the Kachemak Bay, glaciers, fjords, and little wooded islands are arrayed like a smorgasbord before Homer. A quick boat ride puts you there for sea kayaking, mountain biking on unconnected dirt roads, hiking in the mountains, or eating sushi in a top-flight restaurant on pilings. Or gallery hopping, or resting at a remote lodge, or studying at a nature center, or walking the streets of a forgotten fishing village. The far side of the bay has no road link to import the mundane, mass-produced world, but it does have people, and they make the landscape even richer and more enchanting than it would be alone. And underneath the water, there's a wealth of halibut and salmon.

PLANNING AN OUTING   **Central Charters,** 4241 Homer Spit Rd., Homer, AK 99603 (© **800/478-7847** or 907/235-7847; fax 907/235-2895; www.centralcharter. com), is a long-established booking agent that represents businesses for many of the most popular activities, including halibut fishing, water taxis, boat tours to Seldovia and Halibut Cove, and even local theater. They have a ticket office on the right side of the spit as you drive out.

TRANSPORTATION ACROSS THE WATER   Many water taxis operate from Homer to wilderness cabins, kayaking waters, hiking trails, and mountain-biking roads accessible from the Jakolof Bay Dock, Seldovia, Halibut Cove, Kachemak Bay State Park, and other remote points. Rates vary little; it's around $60 per person to get to Kachemak Bay State Park, plus a $4 park fee, for example. Water taxis can be booked through Central Charters, mentioned above. **Mako's Water Taxi** (© **907/235-9055;** www.makoswatertaxi.com) has experience and a good reputation. Mako Haggerty also rents sea kayaks and drops them off; with his advice, you can plan a one-way paddle, with the water taxi providing a lift at each end. Karl Stolzfus's **Bay Excursions Water Taxi and Tours** (© **907/235-7525;** www.bayexcursions.com) offers transportation across the bay but also specializes in small-group tours—he takes no more than 12 at a time—for serious bird-watching or, on other days, to encounter sea otters as well as see the bird rookeries. Stoltzfus rents kayaks, too.

KACHEMAK BAY STATE PARK   The park comprises much of the land across the water that makes all those views from Homer so spectacular. For around $60, you can be dropped off there after breakfast, walk the beach, hike in those woods, climb the mountains, and then meet your boat in time to be back in Homer for dinner and the first other people you've seen all day. This is heaven, as far as I'm concerned.

The park's main office is at the ranger station listed on p. 304. Its center, however, is across Kachemak Bay at the summer-only **ranger station** in Halibut Cove Lagoon, where there's a dock and mooring buoys for public use, three public rental cabins over the water, a campsite, and excellent king salmon fishing in mid-June.

The park has about 80 miles of trails, mostly linking at the ranger station; a free trail guide is available there, but you're well advised to get a good map before you leave Homer. The trails generally start at tidewater amid a lush, mossy forest and rise into the craggy mountains—up sharp peaks to a glacier, or, if you don't want to climb, over the hills to the next secluded beach. Bring mosquito repellent and review bear-avoidance skills (see "Outdoor Health & Safety," in chapter 2). You can hike to a public-rental cabin on secluded China Poot Lake less than 3 miles from the Halibut Cove dock. The park's fifth cabin is on Tutka Bay, off the Halibut Cove trail network. You can also use one of these places as a base for self-guided sea kayaking. Cabin permits are $65 a night and usually must be reserved 6 months in advance (see "State Parks Cabin Reservations," in section 1 of this chapter).

SELDOVIA   This historic fishing village is like Homer without all the cars and people: just a lot of quiet, the lovely ocean waters, and some nice places to stay. It belongs in this outdoor section only because there's nothing at all to do there other than bike, paddle, or fish (you can do nothing there very well, too).

The trip across Kachemak Bay to Seldovia is one of the best parts of going there. For most people, the **Rainbow Tours** (ⓒ **907/235-7272**; www.rainbowtours.net) daily round-trip is the practical alternative. They leave Homer Harbor at 9am and return from Seldovia Harbor at 5pm. After subtracting the time on the boat, you have 6 hours free in the village—plenty of time for lunch, a bike ride, a kayak tour, or seeing the town. While visitors are in Seldovia, the boat continues on for whale-watching (see "Whale-Watching," below). Round-trip fares to Seldovia are $35 adults, $30 seniors, $25 children 12 and under; one-way $20 for everyone.

Go sea kayaking in Seldovia with **Kayak'atak** (ⓒ **907/234-7425**; www.alaska. net/~kayaks). The couple doing the tours, longtime Seldovia residents, takes pride in showing off the wildlife and beauty of this little-used area. They charge $120 for a 5-hour tour including lunch, or $80 for a 3-hour tour without lunch. They also rent kayaks and offer overnight trips. For a less taxing look at Seldovia Bay, take their evening skiff tour for $35 per person (with 2–4 passengers).

King salmon are stocked in Seldovia Slough, which passes right through the town. The run peaks in mid-June, and you can fish from shore. Seldovia also has an edge for halibut anglers because you start out an hour closer to the **halibut** grounds than anglers at Homer, potentially giving you more time to actually fish. You can find a charter through the Seldovia Chamber of Commerce (ⓒ **907/234-7803**; www. seldovia.com).

JAKOLOF BAY   A state-maintained dock opens an area of gentle shorelines and abandoned roads to visitors who seek the wilderness without paying to stay at a wilderness lodge. West of Kachemak Bay State Park and east of Seldovia, the lands have roads, but the roads aren't connected to anything and are used as much by mountain bikers as by anyone else. You can take a water taxi straight to the Jakolof dock. Lodgings are nearby at Across the Bay Tent and Breakfast, listed under "Lodgings across the Bay" in the "Where to Stay" section later in this chapter. There's plenty to do in the area. The waters of Jakolof, Little Jakolof, Kasitsna, and Little Tutka bays, and the tiny Herring Islands, are appealing and protected for sea kayaking. Supreme mountain-biking trails lead along the shore and right across the peninsula through forest and meadows for berry picking. The Red Mountain and Rocky River roads are prime routes, different each year depending on washouts and intermittent maintenance—that's part of the adventure. A maintained 10-mile road west leads to the charming village of Seldovia, described above.

GULL ISLAND   The island is a rock across the bay from Homer Spit that is a busy bird colony in the summer. It's easy to get to and boats can edge close, as the water is deep all around. You can usually see tufted and horned puffins, black-legged

A Day Trip to Halibut Cove

The artists' colony of Halibut Cove sits on either side of a narrow, peaceful channel between a small island and the mainland; the water in this channel is the road. Boardwalks connect the buildings, and stairs reach down to the water from houses perched on pilings over the shore. The post office and espresso stand float on docks. Visitors arrive each afternoon to walk the boardwalks, visit the galleries, and eat at the restaurant, the **Saltry.** That's a place to sit back on the deck and sip microbrews and eat fresh-baked bread, mussels, sushi, and locally grown salads, followed by fresh fish grilled over charcoal.

The classic wooden boat *Danny J* (book through Central Charters at ✆ **800/478-7847** or 907/235-7847; www.centralcharter.com) leaves Homer daily in the summer at noon, brings back day-trippers, takes guests to the Saltry at 5pm, and brings back the diners later in the evening. The noon trip includes bird-watching at Gull Island. Seating is mostly outdoors, and I wouldn't take the trip in the rain. You also take the *Danny J* if you're spending the night in Halibut Cove. The noon trip is $47 for adults, $40 seniors, $25 children 12 and under; the dinner trip is $25 for everyone, regardless of age, but to go you must have a dinner reservation at the Saltry (also made at Central Charters). On the noon trip only, they sometimes take more passengers than *Danny J* can carry, putting the overflow aboard the steel *Storm Bird.* Reservations and fares are identical to those of the *Danny J.*

On the afternoon trip, you can bring lunch or eat at the Saltry, described above, and then explore the **boardwalk** that runs from the restaurant along Ismailof Island past the galleries, boat shops, and houses. There's also a barnyard, perched on a patch of ground along the boardwalk, where kids, who already will be in heaven, can look at rabbits, pigs, chickens, ponies, and other animals. The summer-only **Halibut Cove's Experience Fine Art Gallery** (✆ 907/296-2215) is the first building past the farm on the boardwalk, on pilings above the water. The airy room contains works by Halibut Cove artists only. Farther on, Diana Tillion, who, with her husband, Clem, pioneered the community, opens her **Cove Gallery** (✆ 907/269-2207) and studio to guests year-round. Since the 1950s, she has worked in many media but is best known for her sepia paintings made with octopus ink, which is painstakingly extracted with a hypodermic needle. Trails branch from the boardwalk across the island to broad views of the bay or to the quiet opposite end of the island.

Exceptionally appealing overnight accommodations at Halibut Cove are covered under "Lodgings Across the Bay," p. 317.

kittiwakes, common murres, red-faced and pelagic cormorants, pigeon guillemots, and glaucous-winged gulls. Tour boats to Halibut Cove or Seldovia may cruise by the island, and if you are taking a water taxi to Halibut Cove Lagoon, ask to take a look on your way.

ACTIVITIES

FISHING   Homer is known for **halibut,** those huge, flat-bottom fish, and the harbor is full of charter boats that will take you out for the day for around $225 per person in the high season. Every day, a few people catch fish that are larger than they are, and halibut over 50 pounds are common. Getting out to where the fish are plentiful requires an early start and a long ride to unprotected waters. People who get seasick easily shouldn't go, as the boat wallows on the waves during fishing. (Take Dramamine *before* you set out; if you wait, it probably won't do any good.) Using gear and lines that look strong enough to pick up the boat, you jig the bait (chunks of herring or cod) up and down on the bottom. Halibut aren't wily or acrobatic, and fighting one can be like pulling up a sunken Buick. One good full-day operator is **Silver Fox Charters** (© **800/478-8792** or 907/235-8792; www.silverfoxcharters.com). Half-day charters have less chance of getting way out to the biggest fish but cost a lot less. **Rainbow Tours** (© **907/235-7272;** www.rainbowtours.net) operates a big boat for the shorter outings, charging $95 adults, $85 seniors, and $75 ages 12 and under. This choice makes good sense if you are not a fishing fanatic or are taking kids along, as a full day of halibut fishing is exhausting and can be tedious. Other charter boats can

---

Tips   **Getting Your Fish Home**

A typical angler comes back from a halibut charter with around 60 pounds of fish that, when cleaned, will yield 30 pounds of filets. A large serving is less than a pound of halibut. Eat as much fresh as you can, as it will never be better, but be prepared for how you will deal with the rest of your bounty. The typical 30 pounds is worth more than $250 in the grocery store (it's illegal to sell sport-caught fish). If it is properly and quickly frozen, it will retain much of its quality well into the winter; if not, you waste this superb food. If you're lucky enough to catch that much salmon, the problem is even more immediate, as salmon is more sensitive to proper handling. Most fishing towns have a sport processor who can vacuum-pack and flash-freeze your catch for around $1 a pound. The best way to get it home is as checked baggage; the processor can provide sturdy fish boxes and cold packs. If you aren't leaving right away, processors will hold the fish, and many hotels have freezer facilities. If you have to ship it, use an overnight service (expensive) and make sure someone is there to put it in the freezer on the other end. Above all, keep the fish *hard frozen;* thawing and refreezing diminishes the quality off any fish and can turn salmon into mush (if your fish thaws, call the processor for advice on how to proceed). Consider having some of your salmon smoked, if possible, making it a ready-to-eat delicacy very welcome as a homecoming gift. Halibut can be smoked, too, but because of its low fat content and delicate flavor and texture, it doesn't smoke as well as salmon. In Homer, **Coal Point Trading Co.,** 4306 Homer Spit (© **907/235-3877;** www.welovefish.com), will process, pack, and ship your catch as ordered. Ask your charter captain—if you don't want to, you don't ever have to touch your fish until you're ready to eat it back home.

be booked through Central Charters, listed above under "Planning an Outing," or you can find one through the **Homer Charter Association** (© **907/235-2282;** www. homercharterassociation.com). The website has links to many operators.

   Salmon use Cook Inlet year-round, not only when they're returning to the streams to spawn, and Homer anglers pursue them with trolling gear even in the dead of winter. The town has a Winter King Salmon Tournament in March (check with the chamber of commerce). Most people, however, fish salmon in summer. Although without as many great road-accessible, streamside fishing spots as found further north, the bay does have some good salmon fishing. A small inlet called the Nick Dudiak Fishing Lagoon on the Spit is stocked with king and silver salmon by the Alaska Department of Fish and Game. Kings return to the lagoon from late May to the end of June. Silvers arrive in mid- to late July, peaking in early August and finishing by midmonth. These salmon have nowhere to spawn, so all must be caught (some anglers scorn such "fish-in-a-barrel" fishing). At the end of the runs, Fish and Game announces that snagging is permitted, which is something like mugging salmon and can be a lot of fun, if not something you'll brag about later at the Rod and Gun Club. For salmon fishing in a more natural setting, head across the bay to Halibut Cove Lagoon (see Kachemak Bay State Park, above) or Seldovia, or drive back up the Sterling Highway to the Anchor River, a famous steelhead trout stream (catch-and-release only) also good for salmon, rainbow trout, and Dolly Varden char. Several popular fishing streams cross the Sterling Highway between Homer and Soldotna. The **Alaska Department of Fish and Game** maintains a fishing hotline at © **907/235-6930.** They're located at 3298 Douglas Place (© **907/235-8191**).

NATURAL HISTORY TOURS   The nonprofit **Center for Alaskan Coastal Studies** (© **907/235-6667;** www.akcoastalstudies.org) is dedicated to educating the public about the shore, interpreting Kachemak Bay for visitors on daily explorations of the Peterson Bay and China Poot Bay area, across the water from Homer. At low tide they lead guests on a fascinating guided tide-pool walk. The center also has access to lovely woodlands where nature walks cover forests ecology and geology and visit an archaeological site. Saltwater tanks at the lodge contain creatures from the intertidal zone and microscopes to inspect your finds. It's a relaxed and truly Alaskan outing. You can add on sea kayaking or an overnight stay. Make reservations by calling the center at the number above, or by e-mail at info@akcoastalstudies.org. The all-day tour is $100 adults, $63 under age 12, and operates daily Memorial Day to Labor Day. Pack your own lunch or buy a light lunch there; bring footwear suitable for hiking and potentially wet beach walks, and warm clothing for the boat ride.

SEA KAYAKING   Silence fell as the boat pulled away from the beach, leaving us behind with the kayaks and our guide. For the rest of the day, my son and I absorbed the water-reflected sunlight and glided past fancifully shaped rocks and resident sea otters around Yukon Island. We explored beaches, picnicked, raced, and discovered tiny bays too small for any other craft. At the end of the day, we had a new friend in our quietly cheerful guide, Alison O'Hara, and discovered that she'd imperceptibly taught us a lot about sea kayaking. O'Hara runs **True North Kayak Adventures** (© **907/235-0708;** www.truenorthkayak.com). Her 8-hour beginner day trips cost $135, including lunch and passage across the bay. Most kayaking day trips in Alaska towns barely get out of the small boat harbor. This trip doesn't feel so tame—it's more like a miniexpedition. They also offer more challenging overnight and multiday trips to remote waters in the area, and a $245 package that includes the day tour, a night in the attractive Hesketh Island Cabins, and a second day of hiking.

Various others offer Kachemak Bay kayak trips. You can choose through Central Charters (p. 309). The protected waters, tiny islands, and remote settlements are fascinating paddling no matter who you go with or, for experienced paddlers, if you go on your own. Kayakers can take a water taxi across and explore at will, camping or staying in cabins over much of the bay. Check with Kachemak Bay State Park for guidance. **Mako's Water Taxi** (© **907/235-9055;** www.makoswatertaxi.com) offers rides and rents and delivers kayaks. True North Kayak (see the previous paragraph) also rents to experienced paddlers and rents camping gear. For kayaks, expect to pay $65 a day for a double, $45 single.

FLIGHTSEEING & BEAR VIEWING   One gets used to thinking of the mountains across Kachemak Bay from Homer as the far side of a magnificent stage set, so it's somewhat mind-blowing to fly beyond that first line of mountains and see how they are just the beginning of a much more complex topography of peaks, glaciers, chasms, and ice fields. The best person to show you that wild country is Bill de Creeft. His **Kachemak Bay Flying Service** (© **907/235-8924;** www.alaskaseaplanes.com) offers spectacular scenic flights starting at $150 per person. Having flown out of Homer since 1967, de Creeft is experienced enough to qualify as a pioneer aviator, but the real old-timer is his favorite plane, a restored 1929 Travel Air S-6000-B, one of only six remaining examples of the executive aircraft, with mahogany trim and wicker seats, which he has been flying and caring for since 1969. Jim Reardon wrote a book about this relationship of man and plane (see the website). The tours begin with the thrill of a water takeoff from Beluga Lake in this unique aircraft.

Homer has several good air taxis providing access to the very remote areas of the southern Kenai Peninsula and lower Cook Inlet that you can't easily reach by boat. You can also use their scheduled service to explore, flying to Seldovia or even one of the two Alaska Native villages across the bay. If your main objective is to see bears, however, the best guides are at **Emerald Air Service** (© **907/235-6993;** www.emeraldairservice. com). Ken and Chris Day specialize in all-day bear-viewing flight expeditions. Unlike some air services I've flown with, whose pilots may not know much about bears and land only briefly, the Days make a point of teaching about bears and their habitat in extended visits. They helped the National Wildlife Federation film an IMAX movie called *Bears* and starred in it along with the title characters. Trips include a flight by float planes on fresh or salt water and then a naturalist-guided hike to see the wildlife. The couple pride themselves on their care for the environment. The trips cost $540 per person.

WHALE-WATCHING   Whales can't be counted on to come into Kachemak Bay, but a long-established tour boat operator, **Rainbow Tours** (© **907/235-7272;** www. rainbowtours.net), takes visitors beyond the bay to where whales turn up reliably in the waters at the entrance of Cook Inlet and in the Barren Islands. That's a long ride and the seas can be large, so these trips are not a good idea for those who get seasick, but the trip is a good chance to see humpback and orca whales and sometimes minke and fin whales. The trip takes all day, from 9am to 6pm, and includes lunch on board a comfortable 100-passenger vessel, the *Rainbow Connection,* which also serves the town of Seldovia as a passenger ferry. The fare is $125 adults, $110 seniors, and $85 children 12 and under.

WHERE TO STAY

Homer has many good B&Bs. The Homer Chamber of Commerce (www.homeralaska. org) has links to a prodigious number of them. In addition to the places I've listed in detail, **The Sea Lion Cove,** above the Sea Lion Gallery on Homer Spit (© **907/235-3400** in summer or 907/235-8767 in winter; www.sealiongallery.com/cove), has two comfortable rooms with kitchens and a deck right over the beach where you can hear the waves roll in at night.

Up the hill outside of town, **A Memorable Experience Bed and Breakfast** (© **800/720-9275,** ext. 7374 or 907/235-7374; www.amemorableexperience.com) offers huge rooms and a large cottage with spectacular views and an expansive garden setting. The owners know how to do things right. They also run the Fresh Sourdough Express restaurant and, besides a great breakfast, offer guests a voucher for goodies there.

If you just want good, simple lodgings downtown, you'll find an extraordinary value at the clean and friendly **Pioneer Inn,** 244 W. Pioneer Ave. (© **800/782-9655** or 907/235-5670; www.xyz.net/~abc), which offers big apartment-style units for $99 in summer ($109 in July) with up to four people in the room. Rooms with two twins or a queen bed are $79 to $89 in summer. They also have a house that sleeps up to nine for $250 a night.

Driftwood Inn *Value* The historic building a block from Bishop's Beach and across from the Bunnell Gallery resembles a lodge or B&B with its large fireplace of beach rock, the hot coffeepot and inexpensive self-serve breakfast in the lobby, and a friendly attitude. There are two parts to the inn. The old section has a cozy feel that's somehow enhanced by sloping floors and old fixtures. Its rooms are like Pullman compartments in size and configuration, but they are cute and clean and have some real style. And they're inexpensive. Nine bedrooms share two bathrooms. A new section has larger rooms, all with king-size beds. The walls are thin, so there's a no-noise policy during evening hours. There's also an appealing 22-site RV park. The inn offers a fish-cleaning station, freezing facility, and year-round fishing charters.

135 W. Bunnell Ave., Homer, AK 99603. © 800-478-8019 or phone/fax 907/235-8019. www.thedriftwoodinn.com. 27 units, 11 with shared bathroom. High season $65–$175 double; low season $45–$99 double. RV sites $29–$35, full hookup. Extra person $10. DISC, MC, V. No smoking. **Amenities:** Coin-op laundry. *In room:* TV.

Land's End Resort *★★★* Traditionally *the* place to stay in Homer, Land's End would be popular no matter what it was like inside because of its location at the tip of Homer Spit, the best spot in Homer and possibly the best spot for a hotel in all of Alaska. It's composed of a line of weathered buildings that fittingly straggle along the beach crest like driftwood logs. Inside, the local owners keep high standards and make constant improvements. Rooms and public areas are decorated with town history and old photographs, nautical memorabilia, and bold colors. Rooms range from cute ship-like compartments with fold-down Murphy beds to big two-story suites. Newly built two-room suites sleep five comfortably, with a small private balcony in the parent's room. Resort attractions include a spa in a calming space with a professional massage staff, called the Raven's Nest; a tiny moving-water lap pool; bike rentals; and an activities desk. The hotel is near the boat harbor, and some people fish right from the beach in front. The front desk also rents a series of privately owned townhouse condos next door; for groups or couples on extended visits, these are the best accommodations in the region, with stylish furniture, lots of space and light, and a beachfront location second to none. The condos rent for $300 to $425 a night.

The **Chart Room restaurant** makes good use of its wonderful location, looking out over the beach and bay from big windows. There's a casual, relaxing atmosphere in the long, wood-trimmed dining room. The deck outside has glass wind shields, making it a warm, satisfying place to sit over coffee on a sunny day. You can watch otters, eagles, and fishing boats while you eat. The selection of main courses, priced $16 to $38, is fairly typical of a seaside fine dining restaurant, and the food is good, if not memorable. The appetizer menu, however, is much more extensive and interesting, and the appetizer portions are easily large enough to make a full meal.

4786 Homer Spit Rd., Homer, AK 99603. © **800/478-0400** or 907/235-0400. Fax 907/235-0420. www.lands-end-resort.com. 95 units. High season $125–$225 double; low season $69–$99 double. Extra person $10. AE, DC, DISC, MC, V. **Amenities:** Restaurant; bar; indoor lap pool; exercise room; spa; outdoor Jacuzzi; sauna; tour desk. *In room:* TV, coffeemaker.

Magic Canyon Ranch Bed and Breakfast At the top of a canyon road off East End Road, the Webb family shares its charming home, 74 unspoiled acres, a tree house, and sweeping views with guests, a cat, and a herd of retired llamas. The air is mountain clear and quiet between the high canyon walls—you start to relax as soon as you get out of the car. The Webbs serve sherry in the evening and a full breakfast in the morning. The four rooms, some nestled cozily under the eaves, are decorated in country and Victorian style, with lots of nice details and some family antiques. The house isn't historic, by any means, but it feels like it is. A note for those with allergies: The family has a cat.

40015 Waterman Rd., Homer, AK 99603. ©/fax **907/235-6077.** www.magiccanyonranch.com. 4 units, 2 with shared bathroom. High season $100–$115 double; low season $70–$85 double. Extra adult $25; extra child 12 and under $20. Rates include full breakfast. MC, V. Closed winter. **Amenities:** Hiking; wildlife viewing. *In room:* No phone.

Ocean Shores Motel Buildings on a grassy compound have a commanding view of Kachemak Bay, with a path leading down to Bishop's Beach, yet the location is right off the Sterling Highway as you enter town, within walking distance of downtown Homer. Rooms are fresh and bright, most with private balconies, refrigerators, and microwaves; four have full kitchens (one rents for only $109). The less expensive rooms lack the views and are older, but are still modern and have cute touches. The place is decorated with photographs and art collected over a family's five generations in Alaska. Smoking is not allowed.

451 Sterling Hwy. no. 1, Homer, AK 99603 © **800/770-7775** or 907/235-7775. Fax 907/235-8639. www.oceanshores alaska.com. 38 units. High season $99–$159 double; low season $59–$75 double. Extra person $5. AE, DISC, MC, V. *In room:* TV, dataport, kitchen (in some), fridge, microwave .

Old Town Bed and Breakfast *Finds* These rooms combine the artiness of the excellent Bunnell Street Gallery downstairs (see "Exploring the Town," earlier) and the funky, historic feel of the old trading post/hardware store that the building used to house. The wood floors undulate with age and settling, their imperfections picked out by light from tall, double-hung windows that look out at Bishop's Beach. The antiques—handmade quilts and wonderful original art—fit in as if they have always been there, yet the rooms are comfortable, fresh, and clean. The B&B has no TVs or in-room phones. The rates include a hot breakfast from 8 to 10am in the parlor and afternoon tea. This is not a good choice for people who have any trouble with stairs.

106–D W. Bunnell, Homer, AK 99603. © **907/235-7558.** Fax 907/235-9427. www.oldtownbedandbreakfast.com. 3 units, 2 with shared bathroom. High season $89 double with shared bathroom, $108 double with private bathroom; low season $56 double with shared bathroom, $70 double with private bathroom. Extra person $15. Rates include full breakfast and tax. MC, V. **Amenities:** Afternoon tea. *In room:* No phone.

Seaside Farm *(Finds* Mairiis Kilcher's farm is populated by Morgan horses, cows, chickens, latter-day hippies, and international backpackers, many of whom do chores in exchange for lodging (when chores are needed): 2 hours of work equals a night in the hostel bunks, and 1 hour earns a campsite in the pasture above the bay. Campers have use of an outdoor cooking and washing area, fire pit and barbecue, and autumn raspberry picking. Some of the quaint, unpolished cabins sit in lovely, quiet places; two are right on the water. The farm, its meadows dotted with cottonwood trees, slopes spectacularly to Kachemak Bay. Homer's pioneering and beloved Kilcher family spawned the singer Jewel (rarely seen hereabouts any longer).

40904 Seaside Farm Rd. (5 miles from downtown off East End Rd.), Homer, AK 99603. *(* **907/235-7850.** www.xyz.net/~seaside. 4 units, 4 cabins, 12 hostel beds (co-dorms). $55–$75 cabin for 2; $50–$75 private room with shared bathroom; $15 per person hostel bunk; $10 campsite. Extra adult or teen in room or cabin $15, free under age 12. MC, V. Dogs allowed only with prior approval. *In room:* No phone.

CAMPING & HOSTELS

The most popular place to camp in Homer is out on the spit, amid the sand and pebbles. It can be windy and crowded, but waking up on a bright, pebbled beach makes up for much. The city charges $8 for tents, $15 for RVs, payable at a small log cabin on the spit across the road from the fishing hole (RVers should read the next paragraph for another option on the spit). The city also operates the more protected **Hornaday Campground** near the hospital: From Pioneer Avenue, take Bartlett Street uphill; turn left on Fairview and right on Campground Road. For information, call **Homer Public Works** at *(* **907/235-3170** (http://publicworks.ci.homer.ak.us and click "Parks and Recreation").

If RV hookups are a priority, you can still stay on the Homer Spit—for a price. **Heritage RV Park** is on the spit right next to the fishing hole (*(* **800/380-7787** or 907/235-7787; http://alaskaheritagervpark.com) and has all the usual amenities. Sites with full hookups, including telephone with voice mail and satellite TV, go for $65 a night. There are plenty of places to go off the spit and get RV hookups more affordably, including the Driftwood Inn, above. **Oceanview RV Park,** 455 Sterling Hwy. (*(* **907/235-3951;** www.oceanview-rv.com), has 100 spaces near the downtown area overlooking the water with a trail to the beach. Rates are $35 a night for full hookups, including cable TV, Wi-Fi, laundry, and showers. Campers also get halibut charter discounts.

Tent campers will find a natural, pastoral setting at Seaside Farm, mentioned above, which also has hostel beds. More conveniently located hostel rooms are at **Homer Hostel,** 304 W. Pioneer Ave. (*(* **907/235-1463;** www.homerhostel.com), charging $23 a night for beds in gender-separated or co-ed dorms with 4 to 6 bunks each, or $50 for private rooms (tax included). It's a nice old house with a shared full kitchen, but common areas are small. They also rent bikes and fishing rods and have a grill on the porch guests can use.

LODGINGS ACROSS THE BAY

These places to stay all are based across Kachemak Bay from Homer, each in its own remote cove, bay, or village, and each in its own market niche, from family lodgings to luxurious accommodations. It's wise to reserve rooms at any of these places months in advance (the preceding winter isn't too soon). I regret I can't include many more that are also deserving—and there are many—but you can find a score of them listed with links at www.homeralaska.org (click "Where to Stay," then "Across Kachemak Bay"). Here are some other standouts to consider: **Sadie Cove Wilderness Lodge** (𝒸 **888/283-7234** or 907/235-2350; www.sadiecove.com), a *Swiss Family Robinson* collection of weathered wood cabins and boats housing just a few guests on the side of a steep fjord where the personable hosts offer great food, remoteness, and a fascinating glimpse of their rough-hewn, environmentally sustainable lifestyle; the **Otter Cove Resort** (𝒸 **800/426-6212** or 907/235-7770; www.ottercoveresort.com), with a collection of attractive, affordable cabins and a shower house, where guests can cook their own meals or dine in a well-made restaurant, and access to excellent hiking and sea kayaking (see "Dining across the Bay," below); **A Stillpoint In Halibut Cove,** home of the Alaska Center for Creative Renewal (𝒸 **907/296-2283;** www.centerfor creativerenewal.com), which offers an individual wilderness lodge experience as well as retreats and art workshops for groups—it's an astonishing work of art itself, full of exquisite stone, dramatic spaces, and even an indoor creek and waterfall—making a good site for a vacation or, as they say, "to provide an optimal nurturing atmosphere to inspire personal discoveries"; and, in Seldovia, **Alaska Dancing Eagles B&B and Cabin Rental** (𝒸 **907/234-7627** in summer or 907/332-0041 in winter; www. dancingeagles.com) a picturesque and relaxing house on the town's historic boardwalk overlooking calm water and usually a sea otter.

Across the Bay Tent and Breakfast 𝒜 Tony and Mary Jane Lastufka created this unique place, a spot where you don't have to be rich to stay for a few days in a backwoods paradise, beachcombing by day and feasting on Tony's grilled seafood in the evening. It looks like a summer camp, with large canvas tents on wooden platforms that stand off by themselves on a steep hillside among towering spruce trees. There's a central house for relaxation, evening games, or conversation, an organic garden to produce the food, two outhouses with stained-glass windows, a bathroom with plumbing, and a forest volleyball court. The beachfront faces placid Kasitsna Bay—that's where water taxis drop off visitors and where guided sea-kayaking excursions depart ($85 half-day, $110 full day per person). Up the stairs to the road, mountain bikes are for rent ($15 half-day, $25 full day) to explore the area's network of abandoned logging roads or to pedal to Seldovia. The tents have beds, but you sleep in your own bag. You can save further by cooking your own meals.

On Kasitsna Bay (P.O. Box 81), Seldovia, AK 99663. 𝒸 **907/235-3633.** (Winter P.O. Box 112054, Anchorage, AK 99511; 𝒸 **907/345-2571.**) www.tentandbreakfastalaska.com. 6 tents. $75 per person with breakfast; $110 per person with all meals. Half-price for children 6–11, free for children 5 and under. MC, V. Closed mid-Sept to Memorial Day. **Amenities:** Sauna; bike rentals; volleyball; barbecue. *In room:* No phone.

Kachemak Bay Wilderness Lodge 𝒜𝒜𝒜 I can think of no more idyllic way to become acquainted with Alaska's marine wilderness than by staying at this intimate lodge, run for more than 25 years by hospitable and generous Mike and Diane McBride. I only wish it were affordable for more people because it's a place of unforgettable experiences. The site, on China Poot Bay, is uniquely perfect: on an isthmus, arrayed among big trees, beach grass, and interesting topography, a peaceful and lovely setting with excellent tide pooling, kayaking, and good hiking trails nearby. Environmentally conscious guides, who have included noted experts on the science and history of the area, lead just a few guests at a time for sea kayaking, hiking, wildlife watching, and learning about nature; guests set the agenda, and everything is included. The manmade part of the lodge is extraordinary, too. Instead of trying to pack glossy luxuries into their cabins and main lodge, the McBride's have retained the rough texture of a remote Alaskan camp while subtly enhancing it: One cabin has linoleum floors and well-used furniture, but also fine rugs, a hidden Ethernet connection, and a wine and brandy list to order from. Each unit has a history to tell. The McBrides' meals are legendary, and guests can join yoga classes, use the private 1930-vintage sauna or hot tub, or learn about natural history in evening slide shows. With a 3-day add-on, a lucky few can visit the remote Loonsong Mountain Camp, where Mike and Diane personally guide and cook for just two couples or one family of four at a time in a lodge on its own mountain lake reached by float plane.

China Poot Bay (P.O. Box 956), Homer, AK 99603. © **907/235-8910.** Fax 907/235-8911. www.alaskawilderness lodge.com. 5 cabins. $2,800 per person for a 5-day stay; $1,800 Loonsong 3-day add-on. Rates all-inclusive, Mon–Fri package only. No credit cards; checks accepted. Closed Oct 15–May 1. **Amenities:** Hot tub and sauna; boating, kayaking, and all guiding included. *In room:* No phone.

Quiet Place Lodge ★★★   A series of beautifully finished cabins and lodge buildings perch on the edge of the narrow waterway that is the main street of the artists' colony of Halibut Cove (p. 311), putting a few guests in the heart of this fascinating community in complete, relaxed comfort. You can walk down to the floating dock whenever you like and get aboard your own hand-built wooden row boat or sea kayak to explore the village or paddle across the water for a spot of sushi at the Saltry Restaurant or an espresso from a stand on a floating dock. The lodge itself serves all meals, included in the package prices. The required 2- or 4-day packages also include guided fishing and sea kayaking. A wonderful family created this place and for years has treated guests as friends; their openness and authentic hospitality are among the lodge's best assets.

Halibut Cove (64362 Bridger Rd, Homer, AK 99603). © **907/235-1800.** www.quietplace.com. 3 cabins. $500 per person per day, all meals and limited guiding included; 2- or 4-day package only. MC, V. Closed Sept–May. **Amenities:** Sauna; row boats; sea kayaks; guided fishing. *In room:* No phone.

Tutka Bay Wilderness Lodge ★★★   Jon and Nelda Osgood's personalities are reflected in the amazing place they've built—open and enthusiastic, perfectionist and safety conscious, clean-cut but truly Alaskan. On pilings and on a narrow, grassy isthmus by the green water of the Tutka Bay fjord, they've put together what amounts to an upscale hotel in the wilderness, with cabins connected by long boardwalks, a deck large enough for a helicopter to land on, and a kitchen capable of producing gourmet meals. It's quite a feat—the water system alone is a wonder. There's plenty to do: guided tide-pool and forest walks, bird-watching, hiking, berry picking, rowing, fishing from the dock, and other activities around the lodge; you can pay extra for guided fishing or kayaking, bear-viewing flights, and other outdoor experiences that go farther afield.

Tutka Bay (P.O. Box 960, Homer, AK 99603). © **800/606-3909** or 907/235-3905. www.tutkabaylodge.com. 6 cabins. $390–$450 per person per night. Rates include all meals. 2-night minimum stay. MC, V. Closed Oct–Apr. **Amenities:** Sauna; hot tub; high-speed Internet access. *In room:* TV/VCR, stocked fridge, coffeemaker, hair dryer.

WHERE TO DINE

Besides those places listed here, don't miss the **Chart Room** at Land's End, described under "Where to Stay," earlier.

Our current favorite in Homer for a quick, casual meal is **Cosmic Kitchen** (© **907/ 235-6355**), a cheerful place on Pioneer Avenue producing Mexican lunches and breakfasts, especially large burritos stuffed with fresh, high-quality ingredients along with rice and other side items in disposable baskets. An enormous meal comes in at under $8 per person. Limited indoor seating is supplemented by a pleasant deck out front protected from the wind by glass, but during peak hours the place is jammed and taking away your meal would be advisable.

Dining across the Bay

In a lovely dining room and bar with vaulted ceilings, wood and tile floors, and extraordinary wilderness views of Eldridge Passage, you can order draft beer or a delicious halibut or steak dinner or simpler meals. But you can't get there without a boat. That turns out to be okay because the ride to **Otter Cove Resort** (℆ 800/426-6212 or 907/235-7770; www.ottercoveresort.com) is one of the best parts of dining there. The owner, Homer Ocean Charters, carries passengers across for only $20 in the evening; at lunch time, the price is $55, but the meal is included in the price (and you still get to order from a menu). It's the cheapest way to get out on the water. They offer inexpensive cabins, too (p. 318). For another dining option across the bay, see "A Day Trip to Halibut Cove," p. 311.

For good local halibut and cod, burgers, chicken, and milkshakes in an attractive beachfront dining room, try **Boardwalk Fish and Chips** (℆ 907/235-7749), on the boardwalk across from the harbormaster's office on the spit. It's relaxed fast food, but the place is clean and grown-up and serves local beer. **Duncan House Diner** (℆ 907/235-5344), downtown at 125 E. Pioneer Ave., is a good traditional place, popular with coffee-sipping locals (but smoke-free). You can eat at a counter or in booths. It is open summer daily 6am to 3pm, winter 7am to 2pm. **Panarelli's Cafe & Deli,** next to the Bunnell Gallery at 106 W. Bunnell St. (℆ 907/235-1555), produces tasty sandwiches to eat in a tiny dining room, on the porch, to take away, or as sack lunches to take fishing. It is open in summer Monday through Saturday 10am to 7pm, winter 11am to 6pm. The cafe doesn't take credit cards.

Café Cups 𝒜𝒜𝒜 SEAFOOD/SANDWICHES   The facade of the yellow house on Pioneer Avenue is unmistakable, with its elaborate bas-relief sculpture. The small dining room is a work of art, too, a masterpiece of wood, light, and space. Jennifer Olsen seats guests, and her husband, David, is the chef. As the owners, they've combined a love for good food with practicality in a small town. The menu comes in two parts. The regular daily menu is mostly mainstream—aimed at local diners looking for something familiar—but they also have an extensive daily menu of orally described specials, usually including many of interesting choices based on local seafood. Do not make a choice before considering these, which are the heart of the experience. David has a terrific sense of the texture of food—the lamb chops I had on my last visit were a sensual delight, crisply seared on the outside, tender and juicy inside, on rich mashed potatoes. Portions are large. They serve beer and wine.

162 W. Pioneer Ave. ℆ 907/235-8330. Reservations recommended. Lunch $6–$10; dinner main courses $16–$23. MC, V. High season Mon–Sat 11am–10pm; low season Mon–Sat 11am–9pm.

Fat Olives 𝒜𝒜𝒜 NORTHERN ITALIAN   Built with great style in a former school bus garage on the Sterling Highway near the visitor center, the restaurant is a wonder of warm Mediterranean colors, shiny metal, and primitive art—not the sort of place you expect to find in a small town in Alaska. The cuisine brings further surprises: bold flavors and textures, a little Tuscany, and plenty of Homer, too, including local seafood. The centerpiece is a wood-fired Italian brick oven that produces gourmet pizzas, sandwiches, and other delights. They serve local beers on tap and 30 wines by the glass. With all that said, you wouldn't expect it was a place to take kids, but when we showed up tired and hungry with our tribe one night, they rushed to find us a table

and got us fed quickly and well, and with a bill that was reasonable. The restaurant
has a takeout counter.

276 Olson Lane. ⓒ **907/235-8488.** Reservations not accepted. Lunch $7–$12, dinner main courses $16–$26. MC,
V. Daily 11am–10pm.

Fresh Sourdough Express Bakery and Restaurant ⓡ ⓚⁱᵈˢ BAKERY/CAFE

Ebullient Donna and Kevin Maltz's organic eatery is quintessential Homer, starting
with its motto: "Food for people and the planet." But there's no New Age dogma here.
The Sourdough Express is fun and tasty, even as it grinds its own grain and recycles
everything in sight. An inexpensive lunch menu features an array of vegetarian choices
as well as hearty sandwiches. The evening menu includes many specials; elaborate
dishes, including huge portions of local seafood with rich sauces; and, perhaps more
remarkably, simple, solid choices too for those who don't want to spend a lot. All-you-
can-eat crab is served from 3 to 6pm. Families will enjoy the relaxed atmosphere and
the big sandbox and an old van out front where kids can play while you wait for your
meal. Stop by on the way to a day on the water for a hearty breakfast or to pick up
the brown-bag lunch you will need for a charter fishing trip. Don't miss dessert from
the made-from-scratch bakery.

1316 Ocean Dr. ⓒ **907/235-7571.** www.freshsourdoughexpress.com. Breakfast $4–$8, lunch $5.50–$10; dinner
main courses $7.50–$20. MC, V. High season daily 7am–9pm; low season daily 8am–3pm.

The Homestead ⓡⓡⓡ STEAK/SEAFOOD   The ambience is that of an old-fash-

ioned Alaska roadhouse, in a large log building decorated with contemporary art and
lots of summer light. The food is wonderfully satisfying. The seafood is done simply
but right, often just grilled to a turn, which is a good call with this wonderful Alaskan
fresh fish. The salads and the side dishes let the chef show more sophistication, and
we've always been impressed. The seafood portions are generous, and if you want a big
piece of rare prime rib, go no further. After a day outdoors, it's a warm, exuberant place
for dinner, but with polished edges: white table linens, and with intimate but professional service. We chose the restaurant for our 20th anniversary, and we couldn't have
been happier. The wine list is well selected but not intimidating, and mostly in the $22
to $28 range. They also have a full bar with local beers on tap.

Mile 8.2, East End Rd. ⓒ **907/235-8723.** Reservations recommended. Main courses $21–$39. AE, MC, V. Jun–Aug
daily 5–10pm; March–May and Sept–Dec Wed–Sat 5–9pm. Closed Jan–Feb.

HOMER NIGHTLIFE

The **Pier One Theatre** (ⓒ **907/235-7333;** www.pieronetheatre.org) is a strong community theater group housed in a small corrugated-metal building on the spit,
between the fishing hole and the small-boat harbor. Instead of the ubiquitous gold-
rush melodrama and Robert Service readings, Pier One often presents serious drama,
musicals, and comedy—not just schlock. They also produce dance, classical music,
and youth theater events during the summer. There's generally something playing
Thursday through Sunday nights in the summer. Check the *Homer News* or the website for current listings. They strongly recommend making reservations by phone; they
can be changed or canceled, if necessary. Tickets may also be available at the door.

   The landmark **Salty Dawg Saloon** is a small log cabin on the spit with a lighthouse
on top. It's the place to swap fish stories after a day on the water. Wherever you go to
hoist a beer, order a draft from the **Homer Brewing Company** (Red Knot Ale is my
favorite).

Hermits on the Homestead

Late in October, the ground was frozen, the swamp grasses stiff and painted with frost. This was the one time of year when, with a four-wheel-drive truck, you could drive into Ben's cabin. It stood amid his hundreds of acres of swampy ground, the only spot where trees could get out of the dampness and grow. The heavy, lovingly peeled logs of the house lay horizontally amid big birch and white spruce trees. Ben had dragged these huge tree trunks from far afield, by himself, when he started his homestead nearly 40 years earlier, so he could keep living trees near his house.

I'm not using his real name. Ben was a private guy. He generously invited us in, offered coffee from the percolator on the soapstone woodstove, but it was clear that he wasn't quite sure he remembered how to talk to people—where to look, for example—and he kept mumbling and looking at my feet or the sky. He showed us around the house: the huge rocks he'd dragged in to build a foundation, the cellar where he stored his food, the collection of moose racks. Food tended to walk by each fall—he never had to go far to get his moose, and one of the biggest he shot right on the doorstep. Everything about his home was exactly how he wanted it, the product of immense effort with his own hands. I could see plainly how he'd spent his days all these years. But I could only imagine what his nights must have been like, all alone out here—the piles of *Reader's Digest* and *National Geographic* magazines, the insistent silence.

I finally asked Ben why he'd spent his whole adult life on this homestead, so far from other people. Why not move to town, where life is easier and there's someone to talk to? Well, he said, he did work construction in the summer for cash. But I knew that was an evasion. How, I asked, did he first end up out here, in the middle of nowhere, in a huge swamp? What made him want to be off by himself when he first came out here, so long ago? Pause—check the shoes, check the sky—well, he said, it seems there was a woman. She chose the other guy.

Years ago, *U.S. News & World Report* did an article about a homesteader on the Kenai Peninsula who was a Vietnam veteran—just one of the many mad hermits from the war who had hidden in the Alaska woods. The subject of the story, a well-respected member of his little homesteading community, resented the characterization, and the magazine later paid him to settle his libel suit and printed a retraction. Everyone in the area knew the article was a bunch of baloney; Alaska homesteaders are as varied as people in the city. They aren't all crazed veterans any more than they're all victims of unrequited love, although those make the best stories. What they do have in common is a willingness to invest hard physical labor every day into things the rest of us obtain effortlessly by turning a thermostat or a faucet handle.

Alaska's homesteaders came in waves. There were the prospectors from the gold rush who stayed. Then, after World War II, GIs with families looking for new opportunities came north. The counterculture movement of the 1960s brought yet another group. Federal homesteading laws written to open the Great Plains to agriculture in the 19th century made getting land difficult and required Alaska homesteaders to do a lot of anachronistic, absurd work, such as clearing large tracts for farming that could never occur. The homesteaders had to survey the land, live on it, clear much of it, and then answer any challenges about their accomplishments at a hearing. If they passed the test, they received a patent to up to 160 acres.

The laws allowing homesteading on federal lands in Alaska were all repealed by 1986, but the state government still sometimes provides land to its citizens under laws that allow homesteading, lotteries, and sale of remote land. The parcels are very remote and smaller than the old federal homesteads, and the rules still don't make it easy.

Homesteading isn't like camping. Outdoor skills won't help unless you also know how to repair engines below zero, build houses without power tools, carry all your own water and firewood, and live poor, largely without an income or any of the things money can buy. You have to be willing to bathe rarely, be cold in winter, be eaten alive by mosquitoes in summer, and end up with land that isn't really worth anything.

Many successful homesteading experiences end with raising children. When children get to a certain age, they need to go to school and be around other children. The families often expect to go back to the homestead someday, but somehow they rarely do. Areas that were thriving little communities of neighbors in the 1950s or 1960s are deserted now, perhaps with one hermit left—like my friend Ben. Only about 160,000 acres of Alaska today—out of a total landmass of 365 million acres—show any signs of human habitation. Less than 1% is in individual ownership.

My favorite story is of Rose and her lover. They lived in the same area in Northern California where my wife Barbara's parents grew up. Everyone in town knew the story of the red-headed beauty who had an affair with an older man. Rose's parents refused to let her marry him and decreed that the couple couldn't see each other anymore. She entered a convent, and he disappeared, never to be seen in the town again. Many years later, after moving to Alaska, Barbara's parents were boating in Kachemak Bay when they got caught by bad weather on the opposite side of the bay from Homer. On their own in an open boat and looking for shelter, they found a cabin on a remote beach of an otherwise uninhabited island. They were taken in and befriended by the hermit who'd homesteaded there for years. After warming up with coffee, they got to talking about where they'd come from and how they'd ended up in Alaska. When it came time for their host to tell his story, it was about a beautiful young woman he'd loved, named Rose.

11 Valdez

Big events have shaped Valdez (val-*deez*). The deepwater port, at the head of a long, dramatic fjord, first developed with the 1898 Klondike gold rush and an ill-fated attempt to establish an alternative route to the gold fields from here. Later, the port and the Richardson Highway, which connected Valdez to the rest of the state, served a key role in supplying materials during World War II. On Good Friday, March 27, 1964, all of that was erased when North America's greatest recorded earthquake occurred under Miners Lake, west of town off a northern fjord of Prince William Sound. It set off an underwater landslide that caused a huge wave to sweep over the waterfront and kill 32 people. The U.S. Army Corps of Engineers moved the town, rebuilding a drab replacement in a safer location that slowly filled with nondescript modern buildings.

The construction of the trans-Alaska pipeline, completed in 1977, brought a new economic boom to Valdez and enduring economic prosperity as tankers came to fill with the oil. Then, on March 24, 1989, on Good Friday 25 years after the earthquake, the tanker *Exxon Valdez*, on its way south, hit the clearly marked Bligh Reef, causing the largest and most environmentally costly oil spill ever in North America. The spill cleanup added another economic boom. More than 17 years later, some wildlife populations have recovered and some have not, although visible signs of the spill are difficult to find.

Today, Valdez is a middle-American town, driven by industry but turning to the vast resources of Prince William Sound for outdoor recreation. In town you can tour two small museums and take a hike or a river float. The town has made major strides in improving its appearance, especially on the waterfront, but it isn't the sort of historic or charming fishing village that justifies a trip all by itself. Instead, come for the setting—the wildlife, fishing, and sightseeing in the Sound, and the spectacular drive down the Richardson Highway.

Because Valdez lies at the end of a funnel of steep mountains that catches moisture off the ocean, the weather tends to be overcast and rainy in summer and extremely snowy in winter.

ESSENTIALS

GETTING THERE   By Car   The **Richardson Highway** (section 7 in chapter 9) dramatically crosses Thompson Pass and descends into the narrow valley where Valdez lies. Try to do the trip in daylight, in clear weather, and stop at the Worthington Glacier. This is the only road to Valdez. The drive from Anchorage is 6 hours without stops.

By Ferry   The **Alaska Marine Highway System** (© **800/642-0066** or 907/835-4436; www.ferryalaska.com) connects Valdez, Whittier, and Cordova by ferry. One time-tested way to see the Sound is to put your vehicle on the ferry in Whittier for the run to Valdez and then drive north on the Richardson Highway. A new fast ferry, the *Chenega*, cuts travel time from Anchorage to Valdez to less than driving (about 90 min. by car from Anchorage to Whittier and 4 hr. by ferry from Whittier to Valdez). The current fare is $102 for a car up to 15 feet long and $86 for an adult passenger (children 5–11 half-price).

By Air   Era Aviation (© **800/866-8394;** www.flyera.com) flies several times a day each way between Anchorage and Valdez.

GETTING AROUND   The main part of the town and boat harbor are compact enough to walk, but you will need wheels for the airport, the attractions on Dayville

Valdez

To Airport, Solomon Gulch Hatchery, The Maxine & Jesse Whitney Museum, and Valdez Glacier Campground

Valdez Bay

Community College

Pioneer Dr.

City Hall

Public Boat Lauch

Small Boat Harbor

Ferry Terminal

Port Valdez

Robe River Dr.
Hanagite St.
Oumalik
Nabesna
Mendeltna
Lowe St.
Klutina
Jago
Iditarod
Pioneer Dr.
Gulkana
Foraker
Eklutna
Dadina
Chena
Bremner
Tatitlek Ave.
Chenega Ave.
Fairbanks Dr.
Meals Ave.
Hazelet Ave.
Egan Dr.
Galena Dr.
Clifton Ave.
Fidalgo Dr.
Ferry Way
Richardson Highway
Chitina Dr.
South Harbor Dr.
North Harbor Dr.
Kobuk Dr.
South Harbor Dr.

Information (i)
Post Office ✉

ACCOMMODATIONS ■
Aspen Hotel Valdez **1**
Best Western Valdez
   Harbor Inn **6**
Blueberry Mary's
   Bed and Breakfast **3**
Keystone Hotel **4**
Sea Otter RV Park **8**
Wild Roses by the Sea
   B&B Retreat **3**

DINING ◆
Alaska's Bistro **7**
Fu Kung Chinese Restaurant **5**

ATTRACTIONS ●
The Valdez Museum
   and Historical Archive **2**

Alaska
Fairbanks
Anchorage **Valdez** Juneau
Kenai Cordova
Sitka
Ketchikan

Road, and most of the hiking trails. Rental cars are available at the airport from **Valdez-U-Drive** (© **907/835-4402;** www.valdezudrive.com). Taxis are available from **Valdez Yellow Cab** (© **907/835-2500**).

VISITOR INFORMATION   The Valdez Convention and Visitors Bureau maintains a **Visitor Information Center** at 200 Fairbanks Dr., a block off Egan Drive (P.O. Box 1603), Valdez, AK 99686 (© **907/835-4636;** www.valdezalaska.org). Pick up the free town map and useful *Vacation Planner.* They're open in summer daily 8am to 7pm and winter Monday through Friday 8am to 5pm.

SPECIAL EVENTS   The town has two **summer fishing derbies.** The **Halibut Derby** runs all summer and the **Silver Salmon Derby** is the entire month of August. Derby tickets are available all over town.

The **Last Frontier Theater Conference** (© 907/834-1614; www.pwscc.edu) brings playwrights, directors, and actors from all over the U.S. for seminars and performances June 23 to 30, 2007. Performances are staged every night over the 8-day event, and workshops and readings last all day. Those interested in literature and theater will find it worth arranging a trip around the event.

FAST FACTS: Valdez

Banks Two **banks** are on Egan Drive, both with ATMs.

Hospital **Providence Valdez Medical Center** (© 907/835-2249) is at 911 Meals Ave.

Internet Access You can go online free at **Valdez Consortium Library** (© 907/835-4632), at 260 Fairbanks St., but you may need to call ahead to reserve a time.

Police For nonemergencies, phone the **Valdez Police Department** at © 907/835-4560, at 212 Chenega Ave.

Post Office Located on Galena Drive and Tatitlek Street, it's 1 block back from Egan Drive.

Taxes Valdez has no sales tax but does charge a 6% **bed tax**.

GETTING OUTSIDE
SIGHTSEEING & WILDLIFE TOURS

For most visitors, a day-long ride on a tour boat into the Sound is likely to be the most memorable part of a visit to Valdez. The main tour boat company in town is **Stan Stephens Glacier and Wildlife Cruises** (© 866/867-1297 or 907/835-4731; www.stanstephenscruises.com). The office is on the dock at the end of the small-boat harbor near the Best Western Valdez Harbor Inn. Stephens has been showing off the Sound and defending it from pollution for decades. After passing through the long fjord of Port Valdez, boats enter an ice-choked bay in front of **Columbia Glacier** on a 6-hour tour that often encounters birds, seals, sea otters, and sea lions, and sometimes whales, for $90 adults. A light lunch is served. Going on to Meares Glacier, farther west, adds 3 hours to the round-trip but brings you to a glacier you can get a better look at and that may drop ice into the water. That cruise is $130 and includes a hot lunch and a snack. Prices are half for children 2 to 11 on either trip.

SEA KAYAKING & SAILING

Raven Charters, Slip C-25, Valdez Boat Harbor (© 907/835-5863; www.alaska.net/~ravenchr), is run by a family who shares its home on a 50-foot boat with clients to sail and explore the Sound. The wind tends to be light and changeable, but a sailboat makes a comfortable base for discovering interesting, isolated places. All-inclusive prices for the whole boat start at $850 per night for up to four passengers, or $700 for a day charter, with discounts for longer trips.

Right around Valdez, short sea-kayaking day trips to see wildlife on the **Duck Flats** may be just what you want for a first try at the sport, but that area is hardly wilderness, as it's also reached by road and is within sight of the oil facilities. Day trips to Shoup or Columbia glaciers get you into more of the beautiful, remote country that makes Prince William Sound so exceptional. **Pangaea Adventures** (*©* **800/660-9637** or 907/835-8442; www.alaskasummer.com) offers guided sea kayaking from Valdez, or rentals for experienced paddlers (for whom the Sound is a paradise). They also offer multiday guided camping trips deeper into the Sound or, for those who prefer a bed, lodge and "mother ship" expeditions, wherein clients paddle by day and stay on board or in a lodge at night. Pangaea offers many other services as well: water taxi and kayak drop-off, ice climbing and glacier hiking, river rafting, and even trips that combine these activities in the Sound and Wrangell–St. Elias National park. Check out the website.

FISHING & BOATING

The ocean waters around Valdez are rich in salmon and halibut. It's possible to fish for salmon from shore. Popular spots include Dayville Road west of the fish hatchery, the city dock near the ferry dock in town, and even the harbor floats. Except at the hatchery, you're hoping a fish swims by your lure or bait at the right moment: There isn't a fresh water destination to concentrate the fish. Chances and the fishing experience are improved if you get out on the water. Many small fishing charter boats are available in the boat harbor, or you can rent your own boat and gear; book either through **Fish Central** (*©* **888/835-5002** or 907/835-5002; www.fishcentral.net). They can also take care of processing and freezing your catch for shipment.

HIKING & MOUNTAIN BIKING

Valdez has a broad selection of good day hikes and an overnight. The visitor center can advise you on choices beyond those I list here. In addition, you can join guided hiking and glacier activities with Pangaea Adventures (see "Sea Kayaking and Sailing," above).

The easiest hike is a pleasant forest and shore walk to **Dock Point,** starting at the east side of the boat harbor, at the end of North Harbor Drive. It's a peaceful, natural walk close to town, with boardwalks and overlooks and berries along the way in season.

For a longer hike and perhaps an overnight, the **Shoup Glacier Trail** runs 12 miles west from town along the shore of Port Valdez to a lagoon in front of the glacier's face. The going is generally flat and there are many places to get down to the beach, with wild iris and many other flowers. Cool yourself in a waterfall. Camping is unrestricted, but be sure to bring mosquito repellent and review bear-avoidance techniques (see "Outdoor Health & Safety," p. 47). If you plan to go all the way, consider reserving one of the three state parks cabins near the glacier (see "State Parks Cabin Reservations," in section 1 of this chapter). Or you can get a lift one way from a water taxi, such as the service offered by Pangaea Adventures. The trail starts at the end of West Egan Drive.

RAFTING

Keystone Raft and Kayak Adventures (*©* **907/835-2606;** www.alaskawhitewater.com) takes five trips a day 4½ miles down the amazing Keystone Canyon, a virtual corridor of rock with a floor of frothing water, past the crashing tumult of the 900-foot Bridal Veil Falls. The whitewater is rated Class III, meaning it is not too wild for most people, but rafting is not without risk—serious mishaps can sometimes occur. They charge $40 per person. The company also has numerous longer trips, ranging from a day to 10 days, on many of the region's rivers.

HELI-SKIING

Valdez is a magnet for backcountry alpine and extreme skiing and snowboarding, thanks to its prodigious snow and limitless steep mountains. A bunch of guide companies offer these trips, operating by helicopter from mid-February to mid-May. One established operator is **Valdez Heli-Ski Guides** (© **907/835-4528;** www.valdezheli skiguides.com). Expect to pay around $750 a day.

EXPLORING THE TOWN

The community college's **Maxine & Jesse Whitney Museum,** at the airport (© **907/ 834-1614;** www.pwscc.edu), contains a large collection of Alaska Native arts and crafts and animal mounts accumulated by the couple over 50 years. It is open from May to mid-September daily from 9am to 6pm; admission is $5.

The Valdez Museum and Historical Archive ✸✸   The museum contains an exceptional history display that follows the story of the area from early white exploration through the oil spill. Among the most popular exhibits are the shiny old fire engines, dating back to 1886, and the annual summer show of local quilting and fiber crafts. The "Remembering Old Valdez" exhibit, in an annex, contains a remarkable ¹⁄₂₀-scale model of how Valdez looked at its old site, before the 1964 earthquake forced the town to move. Using photographs, records, and old-timers' memories, they have brought that lost city back to life in 400 miniature buildings. The annex is at 436 S. Hazelet Ave. Admission covers both buildings.

217 Egan Dr. © **907/835-2764.** www.valdezmuseum.org. $5 adults, $4.50 over age 65, $4 ages 14–17, free for children under 14. Memorial Day–Labor Day both buildings daily 9am–6pm; low season main building Mon–Fri 1–5pm, Sat noon–4pm, annex by appointment.

WHERE TO STAY

Aspen Hotel Valdez ✸✸   Stay here for standard rooms at the quality level you would find in a corporate travel hotel. The home-grown Aspen chain took an old building, gutted and remodeled it, and then added rooms and major amenities, including the town's only hotel swimming pool. The Aspen has wide halls and spacious rooms decorated in burgundy, hunter green, and dark wood, with lots of extras, large TVs, and mirrors. A continental breakfast is included in the rate. Ask about discounts you may qualify for.

100 Meals Ave., Valdez, AK 99686. © **800/478-4445** or 907/835-4445. Fax 907/835-2437. www.aspenhotelsak. com. 104 units. High season $129–$149 double; low season $99 double. Rates include continental breakfast. AE, DISC, DC, MC, V. **Amenities:** Indoor pool; exercise room; spa; business center (computer, printer, copier, dataport); coin-op laundry. *In room:* TV/VCR, Wi-Fi, fridge, microwave, coffeemaker, hair dryer, iron.

Best Western Valdez Harbor Inn ✸   This up-to-date hotel commands the best location in town, right on the harbor near the tour boats, although few rooms have views. The rooms are well equipped, set up to make snacks or breakfast and with DVD players connected to the big TVs to play movies rented from the front desk. You can get a massage or a haircut onsite, and dine in a good restaurant, Alaska Bistro, described below. Wireless Internet is available throughout; business-class rooms have wired DSL connections and king-size beds.

100 N. Harbor Dr. (P.O. Box 468), Valdez, AK 99686. © **888/222-3440** or 907/835-3434. Fax 907/835-2308. www. valdezharborinn.com. 88 units. High season $139–$149 double; low season $69–$79. Additional person age 12 and older $15. AE, DISC, MC, V. **Amenities:** Restaurant; exercise room; limited room service; coin-op laundry. *In room:* A/C, TV/DVD, Wi-Fi, fridge, microwave, coffeemaker, hairdryer, iron.

Blueberry Mary's Bed and Breakfast *⊀* *(Value)*   A lucky few get to sleep under Mary Mehlberg's handmade quilts on her feather beds, gaze at the ocean views, bake in the sauna, and breakfast on her blueberry waffles made from wild berries that grow just outside the house. She only takes parties of two or less and sometimes closes for breaks. Those who do stay here get a terrific deal on immaculate, handcrafted rooms at a prime location.

810 Blueberry Hill Rd., off W. Egan Dr. (P.O. Box 1244), Valdez, AK 99686. ℂ 907/835-5015. http://home.gci.net/~ blueberrymary. 2 units. $90–$100 double. Rates include full breakfast. No credit cards. Closed Sept 15–June 1. **Amenities:** Sauna. *In room:* TV/VCR, fridge, microwave, coffeemaker, hair dryer, iron.

Keystone Hotel *(Value)*   This basic budget hotel, made of modular units, was built by Exxon to serve as its offices for the oil-spill cleanup operation but wasn't completed until late summer 1989, so the company occupied it for only about a month. It stood vacant for 5 years before a new owner remodeled it into a hotel, with small rooms that mostly have two twin beds or one double bed, though some have two doubles. Select a room when you check in, as they vary in decor.

401 W. Egan Dr. (P.O. Box 2148), Valdez, AK 99686. ℂ **888/835-0665** or 907/835-3851. Fax 907/835-5322. www. keystonehotel.com. 98 units. $95 double. Extra person 13 and over $10. Rates include continental breakfast. AE, MC, V. Closed in winter. **Amenities:** Coin-op laundry. *In room:* TV.

Wild Roses by the Sea B&B Retreat *⊀⊀*   Light pours from bay windows that overlook the water and surrounding woods into large, elegantly appointed rooms with high ceilings, decorated with Asian and contemporary art, and finished in light colors, wood floors, and Berber-style carpets. Best of all is the spacious and private "Ocean View Guesthouse," a downstairs suite with a kitchen and living room. The hostess, Rose Fong, prepares elaborate breakfasts in the summer and feeds guests snacks and beverages all day. The location is half a mile from the Shoup Glacier Trail (see above) and less than a mile from a state park beach.

629 Fiddlehead Lane (P.O. Box 3396), Valdez, AK 99686. ℂ **907/835-2930.** Fax 907/835-4966. www.alaskabythe seabnb.com. 3 units. Summer $128–$165 double, including full breakfast; winter $89 double, including continental breakfast. Extra adult $20, child $15. MC, V. *In room:* TV, dataport, hair dryer, iron.

CAMPING

The **Sea Otter RV Park,** P.O. Box 947, Valdez, AK 99686 (ℂ **907/835-2787**), sits on the outside of the boat harbor breakwater, a mosquito-free spot with views and beachfront where you can fish for salmon or watch the harbor otters. The RV park has a laundry and other facilities, and charges $27 for full hookups. The town's **Valdez Glacier Campground** (ℂ **907/835-2282;** www.valdezcampgrounds.com), near the airport, has 106 sites with tables and fire pits well screened by alder and cottonwood trees—but the trees also make it a mosquito haven. The campground has pit toilets; water comes from a big container. The fee is $12 per night. To get there, take the Richardson Highway to Airport Road.

The best campground in the area is the state's **Blueberry Lake Campground,** 24 miles out of town on the Richardson Highway, just below Thompson Pass. The campground is above the tree line, with mountaintop views and access to limitless alpine hiking. It can be windy and cold. The small lake is stocked with trout. Fifteen well-screened sites are $12 on a self-serve system. There are pit toilets. RVs are welcome, but there are no hookups.

WHERE TO DINE

Alaska's Bistro ☞ MEDITERRANEAN/PIZZA A harborside dining room with big windows creates a proper setting for a restaurant with fine-dining aspirations. The food includes lots of local seafood prepared in Northern Italian and similar styles; the chicken, pork, and beef also get more than the typical small-town treatment, although you can also get a simple grilled steak. The pizza is European, too, with toppings such as pesto, sun-dried tomatoes, and feta cheese. It's obviously the work of a single mind: The chef even contributes the paintings on the walls as well as his special paella. They have a full bar.

102 N. Harbor Dr. ℂ **907/835-5688.** Reservations recommended. Lunch $9–$15, dinner main courses $10–$30. AE, MC, V. Daily 6–10:30am, 11:30am–2:30pm, 5–10pm.

Fu Kung Chinese Restaurant ☞ CHINESE This long-established family restaurant near the harbor serves some of the best meals in town; in Valdez, that's not a huge claim to fame, but this place is good. The interior is clean and pleasant, with a fish tank, warm colors, and plenty of room. The food is plentiful and tasty, especially the gingery bean curd with vegetables, the hot-and-sour soup, and the kung pao chicken. They feature local seafood in Chinese dishes and serve some Thai and sushi selections, too. Service is fast and attentive. In winter, they often close earlier than the hours listed below.

207 Kobuk Dr. (1 block from the boat harbor). ℂ **907/835-5255.** Lunch $6.75–$8.75; dinner main courses $11–$16. MC, V. Daily 11am–11pm.

12 Cordova: Hidden Treasure

The first time I ever went to Cordova, my companion and I arrived at the Mudhole Smith Airport in a small plane and happened upon an old guy with a pickup truck who offered to let us ride in back with some boards the 10 miles to town. The highway led out onto a broad wetland plain—the largest contiguous wetland in the Western Hemisphere, as it happens. Our guide's voice, studded with profanity, boomed through the back window as he told us proudly about the diversity of the wildlife to be found out there. Then, absolutely bursting with enthusiasm, he leaned on the horn and bellowed, "Look at them f—ing swans!" We looked; trumpeters paddling in the marsh looked back. He would have invited them along to the bar, too, if he'd known how.

Every time I've been to Cordova since, I've been taken under the wings of new friends. Although they usually don't express themselves the same way that first gentleman did, they are just as enthusiastic to show off the amazing natural riches of their little kingdom. Tourists are still something of a novelty here, for Cordova isn't just off the beaten track—it's not on the track at all. There's no road to the rest of the world, and the town is an afterthought on the ferry system. Boosters call their town "Alaska's Hidden Treasure." For once, they're right.

Our family has had some of our happiest times in Cordova, visiting the Childs Glacier and seeing the swans and geese on the delta; hiking into the mountains behind town; boating on the Sound to meet the sea otters, sea lions, eagles, and spawning salmon; hiking and canoeing at a remote lake cabin—and meeting no other people at all. In town, we made new friends whenever we turned around and received hearty greetings from old friends from previous visits. Leaving on the ferry for Valdez, I've watched Cordova shrinking behind us with a wistful hope that it would never change.

So far, I've gotten my wish. You can feel a bit like an anthropologist discovering a tribe lost to time, for Cordova has the qualities small towns are supposed to have had

Cordova

↑ To Ferry Terminal

U.S. Coast Guard

Seafood Lane

Breakwater Ave.

Ocean Dock Rd.

Sixth St.

Small Boat Harbor

Railroad Ave.

Council Ave.

Third St.

Fourth St.

Browning Ave.

City Hall

First St.

■ Pool

Adams Ave.

Second St.

Fifth St.

Sixth St.

Seventh St.

Eighth St.

Ninth St.

Lake Ave.

Lefever St.

Alaska

Tidal Flat

Fairbanks ○

Anchorage ○ Valdez

Kenai ○ Cordova ○ Juneau

Sitka ○

Ketchikan

Odiak Slough

■ **Hospital**

Chase Ave.

Copper River Highway

To Airport and Copper River Delta

Information ⓘ

Post Office ✉

ACCOMMODATIONS ■
The Northern Nights Inn **4**
Orca Adventure Lodge **2**
Prince William Motel **5**
Reluctant Fisherman Hotel **8**

DINING ◆
Ambrosia **3**
Baja Taco **9**
Killer Whale Cafe **6**

ATTRACTIONS ●
Cordova Historical Museum **7**
Ilanka Cultural Center **10**
Tripod Mountain Trail Head **1**

but lost long ago in America. Walking down 1st Street, you pass an old-fashioned independent grocery store and drug store, the fishermen's union hall, and Steen's gift shop, run by the same family since 1909—no chains or franchises. My children thought the street looked like a movie set on our most recent visit. The best part of their week was the novel freedom to roam and shop on their own. It was clearly safe. People leave their keys in the car and their doors unlocked at night. When a friend of mine bought one of the quaint, moss-roofed hillside houses years ago, he didn't receive a key—the simple reason was that the front door didn't have a lock.

Cordova owes much of its uniqueness to a rich history and remote location. Its biggest political controversy—simmering for almost 70 years—concerns whether to build a road to the outside world. The town's heyday was in 1911 when the Copper River and Northwestern Railroad opened, carrying copper ore down from the mine at Kennecott; it hit a low when the mine closed in 1938. Since then, boosters have been trying to get a road built on the old rail line, north along the Copper River to Chitina (that fascinating area is covered in chapter 9, under "Wrangell–St. Elias National Park & Kennecott"). The road builders have made it only about 50 miles out of town so far. From Cordova, the **Copper River Highway** provides access to the best bird-watching and, in my judgment, the most impressive glacier in Alaska, as well as trails and magnificent vistas and areas to see wildlife. In town, the small-boat harbor is a doorway to Prince William Sound.

ESSENTIALS

GETTING THERE   By Ferry   Cordova is served by ferry from Valdez and Whittier by the **Alaska Marine Highway System** (𝒞 **800/642-0066** or 907/424-7333 local dock; www.ferryalaska.com). It's a spectacular ride, with a good chance of seeing wildlife. The new, fast ferry *Chenega* promises to alleviate some of Cordova's remoteness with a faster, more convenient schedule. The passenger fare from Valdez is $48, from Whittier $86; children 5 to 11 pay half. Taking a vehicle under 15 feet one-way from Valdez to Cordova is $91, Whittier $102. You can also rent a car in Cordova. See section 1 of chapter 5 for information about the ferry system.

By Air   Alaska Airlines (𝒞 **800/426-0333;** www.alaskaair.com) flies daily each direction, from Anchorage to the west and Yakutat, Juneau, and Seattle to the southeast, with more flights Anchorage operated by **Era Aviation** (𝒞 **800/866-8394;** www. flyera.com).

GETTING AROUND   You can easily walk around downtown Cordova, but that's not where the most interesting sights are. To get out on the Copper River Highway, you'll need a car, a bus, or, if you're vigorous, a bike. Cars are for rent from **Chinook Auto Rentals** (𝒞 **877/424-5279** or 907/424-5279), at Northern Nights Inn (p. 337). Taxis are available from **Cordova Taxi** (𝒞 **907/424-5151**). Water taxi and rental of bikes, kayaks, skiffs, canoes, and fishing and camping gear are available at **Cordova Coastal Outfitters,** south of the boat harbor near the Alaska Commercial grocery store (𝒞 **800/357-5145** or 907/424-7424; www.cordovacoastal.com). They also offer drop-off and pick-up service on the Copper River Highway, allowing visitors to go for a canoeing or cabin trip without renting a car. They're described in full below. To get to remote cabins and fly-in fishing, try **Cordova Air** (𝒞 **907/424-3289**) or **Copper River Air Taxi** (𝒞 **907/424-5371**), both based on Eyak Lake, just north of town.

VISITOR INFORMATION   The **Cordova Chamber of Commerce Visitor Center** (𝒞 **907/424-7260;** www.cordovachamber.com) is at 404 1st St., north of Council Avenue (P.O. Box 99, Cordova, AK 99574). They're open Monday through Friday 10am to 4pm, with occasional Saturday hours. Besides the usual information, the center has a 60-minute recorded walking tour that you can listen to as it guides you around town.

The **Cordova Ranger District** of the Chugach National Forest, upstairs in the old white courthouse at 2nd Street and Browning (P.O. Box 280), Cordova, AK 99574 (𝒞 **907/424-7661;** www.fs.fed.us/r10/chugach), has displays and provides maps and guide information that's indispensable for planning outdoor activities. The staff will sit down and help you figure out what you want to do.

SPECIAL EVENTS   The **Cordova Ice Worm Festival** is a winter carnival the first full weekend in February, culminating in the appearance of the big ice worm—or, to be precise, ice centipede—in a parade. **The Copper River Delta Shorebird Festival** revolves around the coming of dizzying swarms of millions of shorebirds that use the delta and beaches near the town as a migratory stopover in early May. The whole community gets involved to host bird-watchers and put on a full schedule of educational and outdoor activities that lasts 3 days. **Wild Copper River Salmon Days,** over a weekend in mid-July, includes the Alaska Salmon Runs (a marathon and other, shorter races), a music festival, and a dinner. For details on any of these happenings, contact the Cordova Chamber of Commerce or check their website, listed above under "Visitor Information."

FAST FACTS: Cordova

Banks There are two banks on 1st Street, with **ATMs.**

Hospital **Cordova Community Medical Center** and **Ilanka Community Health Center** are located together on Chase Street (② **907/424-8000**), off the Copper River Highway near the slough.

Internet Access Find it at the **Cordova Public Library** (② **907/424-6667**) and at **Orca Book and Sound** (② **907/424-5305**), both on 1st Street.

Police For nonemergencies, call ② **907/424-6100.**

Post Office It's at Railroad Avenue and Council.

Taxes Sales **tax** is 6%; **rooms and car rentals** carry an additional 6%.

EXPLORING THE TOWN & HIKING NEAR TOWN

ATTRACTIONS   Cordova mostly is for outdoor activities (covered below), but save some time to wander around town, make discoveries, and meet people, possibly with the help of the **historic walking tour booklet** produced by the historical society, available from the chamber of commerce.

The **Cordova Historical Museum,** at 622 1st St. (② **907/424-6665;** www.cordova museum.org), mostly in one room, does a good job of presenting some valuable artifacts reflecting Cordova's eventful past, a collection of classic Alaskan art, and some odd and fascinating stuff. There's a historic lighthouse lens, a Linotype machine, the interior of a fishing boat, a parka made of bear gut, basketry, and photographs of fishing and historic scenes. Our entire family enjoyed it. The museum is open summer Monday through Saturday from 10am to 6pm, Sunday from 2 to 4pm; winter Tuesday through Friday from 10 to 5pm, Saturday from 1 to 5pm. Recommended donation is $1.

Cordova is a center for the Eyak, a small but linguistically and ethnographically distinct people. Make a point of stopping in at the Native Village of Eyak's **Ilanka Cultural Center,** at 110 Nicholoff Way (across from the Fishermen's Memorial at the small-boat harbor; ② **907/424-7903**). Although small, the center is new and growing, and we experienced a warm link with the Eyak people we met. The collection includes Eyak, Alutiiq, Tlingit, and Ahtna artifacts, photographs, and oral histories. There is also a fully reconstructed orca whale skeleton. The gallery sells art, books, and other items made in Alaska, especially by Alaska Natives. Artists sometimes offer classes and demonstrations. Hours are summer Tuesday through Saturday 10am to 5pm. Admission is free, but donations are encouraged.

HIKING   Cordova has more good hiking trails per capita than any place I know. The Cordova Ranger Station can provide you with a free trail-guide booklet with lots of ideas and maps. There are three hikes close to town and more on the Copper River Delta, covered below in the section on the Delta, and at Hartney Bay (ask at the ranger station).

The **Tripod Mountain Trail** begins right from town and climbs 1,255 feet over less than a mile up the first mountain back from the shore, a half-day hike with views that present the Sound and Cordova like a map below you. The trail begins at the foot of the town ski lift, on Sixth Street—take Browning up the hill.

Partway up Tripod Mountain, near the middle drop-off of the ski lift, a 1-mile trail links to the **Crater Lake Trail,** which eventually joins the **Power Creek Trail** on a loop of 12 miles. An easier start for that route is the Power Creek Road—drive it along the north side of Eyak Lake to the end, 7 miles from town. The creek has spawning red salmon in July and attracts a lot of bears; watch, but don't get out of your car if you come upon one. The trail follows the creek through dramatic scenery 4.25 miles to the Power Creek Forest Service cabin, with a great view (reserve through the system described on p. 268).

THE COPPER RIVER DELTA

The delta and its star attraction, the **Childs Glacier,** make an unforgettable day trip by car or tour bus from Cordova, but if you have a couple of days, you can do much more. The backwaters, sloughs, and ponds beg to be explored by canoe. Bird-watchers will especially enjoy paddling here and visiting the boardwalks and blinds set up by the Forest Service. You can raft the rivers. There are excellent hiking trails and mountain-biking routes branching from the road, and Forest Service cabins to stay in. And the river itself has many miles of deserted sandy beaches for long walks or sand castles on a sunny day.

The delta seems to go on forever, a vast patchwork of marsh, pond, small hills of trees, and the huge, implacable gray river itself. The glacial silt it carries away—some 2 million tons a day—has built this 700,000-acre wetland. A well-maintained gravel road leads across it, all in Chugach National Forest, and the rangers have done a good job of providing ways and places to enjoy and learn about the area. The road itself is the old bed of the Copper River and Northwestern Railroad. It leads 48 miles to the **Million Dollar Bridge.** Built by Michael Heney, a magician of a 19th-century railroad builder who also constructed the White Pass and Yukon Route in Skagway, the 200-mile Copper River line was an engineering triumph that brought the mind-boggling wealth of the Kennecott Copper Corporation to ships in Cordova (read more about the mine in section 8 in chapter 9). The bridge over the Copper River was built in a race against time between two surging glaciers in 30-foot-deep, fast-flowing glacial water, in winter. It stood for 56 years until the 1964 earthquake knocked down one end of one of the spans, driving it into the riverbed. In 2004, your highway dollars repaired that span, and once again you can drive to the other side, where only a neglected road soon peters out into a rough trail.

GETTING THERE
BY CAR   Driving gives you the most freedom. The road is gravel, but it's wide and level. Beyond the Million Dollar Bridge, however, it's a rough four-wheel-drive track at best, and if you get stuck, you'll be there for a long time. Check at the Forest Service Cordova Ranger Station for the latest news about the road and pick up their road guide.

BY BIKE   Mountain-biking the highway is the adventurous way to travel, camping or staying in a Forest Service cabin on the way. The drawbacks are the distances, the delta's strong winds, and a lot of road dust. Of course, you don't have to ride all the way to see lots of birds and wildlife, and there are good mountain-biking routes on the delta away from the road. The 3-mile **Saddlebag Glacier Trail,** at Mile 25 of the Copper River Highway, leads to a stunning vista of a glacial lake surrounded by rocky peaks. Bikes are for rent from Cordova Coastal Outfitters (see "Out on Prince William Sound," below) for $18 a day.

ALONG THE ROAD

Keep your eyes scanning the wetlands and mountains around you as you drive out the road. The **wildlife** you may see along the way includes black and brown bears, wolf, coyote, moose, and mountain goats. The entire world population of dusky Canada geese nests on the delta, and you're likely to see eagles and trumpeter swans without really looking. The ranger station provides a wildlife-viewing guide and several places to stop along the way designed for bird-watching. The first is a platform with interpretive signs as you leave town, an introduction to the delta; this stretch of the road is fine for bird-watching.

Don't skip the **Alaganik Slough Boardwalk.** Take the 3¼-mile spur road to the right 17 miles out the Copper River Highway; it's marked. The sky here is big and certain, while the land is ambivalent—it doesn't know if it wants to be waving grass of green and gold or shallow, shimmering ponds and tendrils of water. The road leads to the start of the 1,000-foot boardwalk with a blind and to a riverside path. Water reflects the sun and the colors of the marsh. We were speechless one evening at sunset, even in the complete absence of birds. Often in the summer you can see breeding trumpeter swans, ducks, and grebes, and in the spring and fall migrating waterfowl and shorebirds make appearances. The path is on the left just before you arrive at the boardwalk and picnic area; the 1-mile Fisherman's Trail is a meandering route among water and brush.

You can stop at any of the bridges crossing the Copper River for a romp in the sand. The river beaches of fine sand extend practically forever.

The highway ends with the area's best attraction, the advancing **Childs Glacier.** This is the most amazing glacier I've ever seen and no one seems to know about it outside Cordova. The advancing wall of ice, 300 feet tall, comes right down to the quarter-mile-wide river, battling the flowing water for control of the land here. The glacier tries to divert the river while the river tries to cuts the glacier like a knife, eroding the base and bringing down huge ice chunks. As you sit on the bank, the glacier on the opposite side is too large to see—it completely fills your field of vision, creating an eerie and hypnotic sense of scale. On a warm summer day, you can feel the glacier's thunder as the ice shifts and see pieces fall off. A chunk the size of a car barely registers, but when an office building–size hunk falls, there's a roar and gray breakers radiate out across the river. Falling glacier pieces have made waves large enough to uproot trees here, not to mention hurl a few fish around—at the Forest Service viewing and picnic area across the river, salmon have been found high up in the trees and boulders in odd places. Several years ago, such a wave injured some visitors, and now the Forest Service warns that anyone who can't run fast should stay in the observation tower. A construction project likely will be in progress here in 2007, adding more camp sites and picnic facilities, wells, toilets, and so on. A path leads less than a mile to the **Million Dollar Bridge,** or drive by on your way out.

ACTIVITIES

CANOEING   The delta's canoe routes are little used, leading to remote places where birds and aquatic animals rule. You can launch on Alaganik Slough at a picnic area at

Mile 22 on the Copper River Highway, paddling placid waters into stunningly beautiful marsh lands, perhaps headed for the Tiedeman Forest Service Cabin for a few days. Taking the "Wrong Way" route that starts a couple of miles up the road, you can float several miles of challenging water down to McKinley Lake, stay at the Forest Service cabin, and then float downstream again to the slough launch, back at the road. It's ideal overnight, or you could do it in a day or, as we did, spend an extra day and night at the cabin. The couple who run **Cordova Coastal Outfitters** (see below, under "Out on Prince William Sound") rents canoes for $35 a day, offers drop-off, and will help you decide what route to take. You can ride out on one of their bicycles and pick up the canoe already at the launch site. They rent camping gear, too. Make sure to get their advice on current conditions before setting out on the water.

FISHING   Anglers can fish the delta's lakes and streams for all species of Pacific salmon except kings (which you can fish in salt water), as well as Dolly Varden char and rainbow and cutthroat trout. The Cordova Ranger Station can offer guidance, or contact the Cordova office of the **Alaska Department of Fish and Game** (© **907/424-3213;** www.alaska.gov/adfg, click "Sport Fisheries," then the Southcentral region, and then "Prince William Sound Area"). See "Fishing" in chapter 2 for general guidance.

HIKING   The Forest Service maintains several trails on the delta. The **Alaganik Slough Boardwalk** and **Saddlebag Glacier Trail** are mentioned on p. 335. The Copper River beaches make for sublime off-trail hikes. The **Haystack Trail,** starting on the right just past the 19-mile marker on the highway, climbs through mossy rainforest from the delta's floor onto an odd little hill. The glaciers that once covered the delta spared this bedrock outcropping. The trail is steep in places but only three-quarters of a mile in length, and it leads to an overlook.

The **McKinley Lake Trail,** at Mile 21.6 on the highway, leads 2.5 miles through rainforest vegetation to a lake-bearing trout (although we got no bites) and a little farther to the overgrown ruins of a gold mine. You can also get there by canoe (see "Canoeing," above). There are two Forest Service cabins on the trail, the small McKinley Trail Cabin, near the highway, and the McKinley Lake Cabin, beautifully situated among big trees above the lake. Each costs $35 a night and can be reserved through the national system described in section 3 of this chapter, on the Chugach National Forest.

You can also join a guided nature hike or guided glacier trek with Alaska River Expeditions (see "Rafting," directly below).

RAFTING   The immense quantity of water draining the Wrangell–St. Elias Mountains through the Copper River Delta, and the Copper River Highway that provides river access, make this a perfect venue for rafting. **Alaska River Expeditions** (© **800/776-1864** or 907/424-7238; www.alaskarafters.com) is well regarded by locals. Their diverse territory means they can offer quite a range of trips, from easy floating to white water, or even rafting right in front of the Childs Glacier. Trips range in duration from half- to multiday. A 4½-hour trip is $85 adults, $65 ages 6 to 12; all day, with flightseeing, $275. They guide nature hikes, glacier treks, and mountain biking, too.

OUT ON PRINCE WILLIAM SOUND

The waters of Prince William Sound around Cordova, although lacking the tidewater glaciers found in the western Sound, are protected and rich in marine life. Sea otters don't receive a second glance from locals, congregating in rafts of many dozens or even hundreds. Sea lions can be found predictably, too, and orcas and humpback whales are not out of the ordinary. Bird-watchers can expect harlequin ducks and many other marine birds.

Cordova Coastal Outfitters is a good place to start for any outdoor activities (© **800/357-5145** or 907/424-7424; www.cordovacoastal.com). Andy Craig and Seawan Gehlbach know the equipment, the skills, and the area, and they convey that knowledge with casual enthusiasm. Their office is south of the boat harbor, between the Alaska Commercial grocery store and Baja Taco. They guide sea kayaking, rent kayaks, and offer water taxi drop-off for kayakers. The **guided sea-kayaking trip** for beginners lasts 4 hours and costs $75, concentrating on wildlife sightings; a 7-hour guided trip is $125, including lunch. An advantage of planning your kayaking here is that there is plenty to see near the harbor and not much boat traffic. If your group isn't up to kayaking, consider renting a motorboat. You won't believe the sense of freedom you feel clearing the harbor breakwater to explore Orca Inlet and the bays of Hawkins Island, on the far side. Boats rent for $150 a day, fishing gear extra.

Several vessels are available for fishing charters or day trips to see whales and other wildlife. The chamber of commerce (see p. 332) has links to other charter operators on its website, or call them for a referral.

WHERE TO STAY

The Northern Nights Inn ☆ ⟨Value⟩   Our family spent a week here last summer, and the visit was supremely relaxing and pleasant, because of both the wonderful hospitality and a big apartment-style room that fit our six perfectly. Cordova is so safe, the kids were able to walk out the front door and explore on their own—they couldn't believe it. Each room has been lovingly renovated, with antiques, reproductions, and quilts. They're generally spacious, some have views, and all are loaded with amenities— an almost unreal value. All but one has a full kitchen, and breakfast supplies are provided. The inn is Becky Chapek and Bill Myers's historic 1906 house, a couple of blocks above the town's main street. Becky loves to talk and share her enthusiasm for Cordova, and you couldn't start with a better person for helping you figure out what you want to do.

500 3rd St. (P.O. Box 1564), Cordova, AK 99547. © **907/424-5356.** Fax 907/424-3291. www.northernnightsinn.com. 5 units. $75–$95 double. Extra adult $10; children stay free in parent's room. AE, DISC, MC, V. **Amenities:** Free bike loan; car rental; babysitting; free laundry machines; fish freezing. *In room:* TV/VCR and HBO, Wi-Fi, fridge, microwave, coffeemaker, hair dryer, iron.

Orca Adventure Lodge ☆   A picturesque old cannery north of town was renovated into simple guest rooms with private bathrooms (no phones or TVs, however) while retaining the exterior and muscular ambience that made it attractive in the first place. But it's the location and the things you can do here that make the place: on a gravel beach with a dock where sea kayaks, fishing boats, and float planes pick up guests, and where thousands of pink salmon spawn in a small creek. In the late winter, helicopters land on the grounds to carry guests to ski in the vast and trackless Chugach Mountains. Guests can use the place as a hotel, paying the regular nightly rates listed below, or come with a package, which includes all meals and outdoor equipment, such as kayaks, bikes, and fishing poles (guiding is extra), for $145 per person per day.

2500 Orca Rd. (P.O. Box 2105), Cordova, AK 99574. © **866/424-ORCA** or 907-424-7249. www.orcaadventurelodge. com. 34 units. Summer $140 double, $175 suite; winter $95 double, $110 suite. **Amenities:** Restaurant; watersports equipment/rentals; bike rentals. *In room:* No phone.

Prince William Motel   This is a clean, comfortable motel. The lower rooms look out onto an air shaft, but that may be an advantage if you're trying to get to sleep when it's still light out. Eight rooms have kitchenettes, with a $20 premium. Not a good choice if you have trouble with stairs. For anglers, the motel provides barbecues and freezer space.

2nd St. and Council (P.O. Box 908), Cordova, AK 99574. © **907/424-3201.** Fax 907/424-2260. 16 units. $110–$130 double. Extra adult $10. Children 11 and under stay free in parent's room. AE, MC, V. **Amenities:** Coin-op laundry; fish freezing; barbecue. *In room:* TV, kitchenette (in some), fridge, microwave, coffeemaker.

Reluctant Fisherman Hotel 🐟🐟   Once among Alaska's best, this hotel fell on hard times and closed—a blow like the loss of a vital organ for the town—but a commercial fishing family with three generations of history in Cordova took over and poured money and effort into reviving the place. The sale of Greg and Sylvia Lange's fishing assets became a new roof, snow-white comforters in all the rooms, a new deck with a teak railing, a renovated kitchen, and even four new furnaces. The location certainly justifies the effort, overlooking the boat harbor at the heart of the town, as does the comfortable yet historic feel of the property. The rooms have the look of an upscale hotel, with great views on the water side. A bar and cafe serves casual lunches and dinners every day, and a continental breakfast is provided to guests in the lobby.

407 Railroad Ave. (P.O. Box 150), Cordova, AK 99574. © **877/770-3272** or 907/424-3272. Fax 907/424-7465. www.reluctantfisherman.com. 40 units. High season $90–$140 double, $200 suite; low season $75–$110 double, $150 suite. Additional adult in room $10; children 17 and under free. Rates include continent breakfast. AE, MC, V. **Amenities:** Restaurant; bar; airport shuttle ($10); Internet; laundry; fish cleaning/freezing. *In room:* TV w/HBO, Wi-Fi.

WHERE TO DINE

Some of Cordova's best meals, for lunch or dinner, come from **Baja Taco** (© **907/424-5599**), near the south end of the boat harbor. The kitchen and espresso machine are in an old bus, with a window for ordering, and there are comfortable indoor and outdoor seating areas for diners, with free Wi-Fi. The salmon tacos are exceptional, and all the meals are tasty and generous. The proprietor, who lives in Baja in the winter, operates here May through September.

Ambrosia, at 410 1st St. (© **907/424-7175**), is a solid, well-run family restaurant in a light storefront with an extensive menu, including pizza. It's the kind of place that stays in business in a small town: The food is reliable, the portions large, and the service friendly and helpful. My children became addicted to the gooey fettuccine Alfredo with chicken and are still experiencing withdrawal symptoms. The restaurant serves beer and wine. Prices range from $10 to $21. Hours are Monday through Saturday 4 to 10pm.

The primary small town eat-and-meet place is the vegetarian-friendly **Killer Whale Cafe** (© **907/424-7733**), on First. All-day breakfast includes a selection of omelets and other ways of having eggs, and for lunch there are sandwiches in the $8 to $11 range, including salmon and halibut, burgers, and the like. Besides the expected, the cafe serves salmon cakes, smoothies, and espresso. Hours are Monday through Saturday 7am to 3pm, Sunday breakfast only 8am to 1pm. They take Visa and MasterCard.

The Denali National Park Region

Denali (Den-*al*-ee) stands alone among the national parks: It gives regular people easy access to real wilderness, with sweeping tundra vistas, abundant wildlife, and North America's tallest mountain. Other wilderness areas in Alaska may have equally inspiring scenery and even more animals, but Denali is unique because of its accessibility to visitors—and because that accessibility hasn't spoiled the natural experience, as it has at so many other parks.

It's a sad truth that even the largest national parks in the Lower 48 are too small to comprise complete ecosystems. The dream of leaving nature undisturbed is essentially lost in those places, and only through human intervention do the natural systems within the parks stay as close to their primeval state as they do (this is demonstrated by the efforts of Yellowstone rangers to drive bison back within park boundaries so they won't come to harm outside). Millions of cars driving through the parks further interfere with nature. At Rocky Mountain National Park, there's a crossing guard for bighorn sheep. Yosemite Valley and Grand Canyon Village can be choked with cars in summer, yet attempts to get rid of the cars have so far been thwarted.

On the other end of the spectrum, Alaska has many parks with immense, intact ecosystems that have remained unchanged, still existing as they did before the first white contact. More than two-thirds of America's national park acreage is in Alaska, taking in inconceivably huge swaths of land without roads, buildings, or landing strips. They're natural, all right, but almost no one goes there. Some of these parks receive a few hundred visitors a year—only the indigenous people of the surrounding villages and the hardiest and wealthiest outdoors people. Just chartering a plane to get to some of these places can cost as much as most people spend on their entire vacations. With so many people on the earth, wilderness survives only when it's rationed somehow. In most of Alaska, the rationing system is simply the expense and difficulty of getting to the wilds.

At Denali, on the other hand, you can see the heart of the park for little more than it would cost for you to visit Yellowstone. And when you get there, it's a pristine natural environment where truly wild animals live in a nearly complete ecosystem without much human interference. A single National Park Service decision makes this possible: The only road through the park is closed to the public. This means that to get into the park, you must ride a bus over a dusty gravel road hour after hour, but it also means that the animals are still there to watch and their behavior remains essentially normal. From the window of the bus, you're likely to see grizzly bears doing what they would be doing even if you weren't there. It may be the only $30 safari in the world.

Tips   Denali Changes

A massive round of changes to the main Denali National Park visitor area is complete, but work farther inside the park continues. The Eielson Visitor Center, 65 miles within the park, is closed for reconstruction. A larger building is scheduled to open in 2008. During the project, shuttle buses that formerly turned around at Eielson will turn around a few miles short of there, at Fish Creek Turnaround, at Mile 63. An information center, bookstore, and bus dispatch will all operate out of tents at Toklat Visitor Contact Center, Mile 53, where all buses will stop for a 30-minute break.

What's even more unique is that you can get off the bus pretty much whenever you want to, walk across the tundra, out of sight of the road, and be alone in this primeval wilderness. Unfortunately, many Denali visitors never take the opportunity, which normally would cost a lot of money or require a lot of muscle and outdoor skill. Being alone under God's big sky makes many people nervous. Most people have never been entirely away from other people, much less apart from anything people have made. But that's the essence of Alaska—learning, deep down, how big creation is and how small you are, one more mammal on the tundra under the broad sky. At Denali, you can experience that wonder, and then, when you're ready to return to civilization, you can just walk to the road and catch the next bus—they come every half-hour.

The Denali experience spreads beyond the park. After all, the park boundary is an artificial line—the wildlife and the scenery of the Alaska Range don't observe its significance. To the east, the **Denali Highway** runs through the same extraordinary terrain, with opportunities for hiking over the tundra and canoeing on the lakes managed by the Bureau of Land Management. To the south, **Denali State Park** and the town of **Talkeetna** provide another vantage on Mount McKinley, with the advantage of salmon fishing in the rivers. The construction of comfortable new lodges

and a variety of good outdoor guides have helped make Talkeetna a popular alternative gateway to Denali. Even though it's 150 miles from the park entrance by car, Talkeetna is physically closer to the mountain than is the park headquarters.

Visitors often skip the area's other attractions, however, and focus on **Mount McKinley,** which, at 20,320 feet, is the tallest mountain in North America. It is an impressive peak, but you don't need to go to the park to see it—in fact, most people who do go *don't* see it. Summer weather patterns usually sock in the mountain by midafternoon, at least as seen from the ground in the park.

Unfortunately, Denali has become a thing people feel they must do, and seeing Mount McKinley is a thing they must do when they visit Denali. Many package tours rush through the park so quickly it becomes a blur outside a window rather than an experience. If they miss the mountain, passengers may wonder why they traveled so far to stay at a hotel in the developed area near the park's entrance and ride on a bus over a bumpy road. A friend swears she overheard a tourist ask, as she boarded the train leaving Denali, "Why did they put the park way out here in the boondocks?"

The answer is there for you to find, at the bottom of the steps of the shuttle bus door.

1 Planning a Visit to the Park

ORIENTATION

Denali National Park and Preserve is rock- and ice-robed in tundra and stands of stunted black spruce, a huge slice of the Alaska Range that stands like a pivot in the center of Alaska. It encompasses 6 million acres, a roughly triangular polygon about 20% larger than Massachusetts. The only park entrance is 237 miles north of Anchorage and 120 miles south of Fairbanks on the paved George Parks Highway or the Alaska Railroad. Although **Mount McKinley** is visible from as far away as Anchorage, you can't see it at all from the park entrance (where you will find the railroad depot and all services accessible by private vehicle) because it's on the far side of the park. A mile north of the park entrance on the Parks Highway, along a cliff-sided canyon of the Nenana River, is **Glitter Gulch,** the local term for the seasonal roadside strip that's home to hotels and restaurants (boosters call it the **Nenana Canyon Area**). Other services are at **Carlo Creek,** 13 miles south on the Parks Highway; at another roadside development 7 miles south of the park entrance; and in the year-round town of **Healy,** 12 miles north of the park entrance. From the park entrance, a road accessible only by shuttle bus leads west 89 miles through the park, past a series of campgrounds and a visitor center, and ends at the **Kantishna district,** a patch of park-surrounded private land with wilderness lodges.

WHEN TO GO & HOW FAR AHEAD TO PLAN

Crowding is relative. Once you're out in the park, Denali is never crowded. The bottleneck created by the shuttle and tour bus system, which prevents vehicles from entering the heart of the park, protects it from overuse. What makes the July to mid-August season difficult is getting through that bottleneck from the crowded park entrance into the wilderness. At that time, travelers who just show up at the visitor center without any reservations might have to spend a day or two outside the park before they can get a desirable shuttle bus seat, a campground site, or a backcountry permit.

The flow of visitors varies greatly from year to year. After dropping for 4 years, it currently is quite busy. Some years, you needed to make **reservations** by March for a July visit; other years, a few weeks of advance planning has been enough. To be on the safe side, get your shuttle tickets and campsites as soon as you know the dates of your visit. Lodgings also get tight in July but are not as critical to the success of your visit. Reserve as far ahead as you can, but don't worry about getting stuck in a dive if you don't get your first choice of rooms or cabins, as there are few really bad places near the park.

Summer residents come to the park beginning in early May, when snow remains; they migrate south again in mid- to late September, when winter is closing in. In the off season, fewer than 200 residents stay in the area, and sled-dog-driving rangers patrol the backcountry. The shuttle bus system doesn't begin operation until Memorial Day, so May visits are inadvisable. The visitor season gets into high gear in mid-June and starts to wind down in mid-August. There are several weeks of relative quiet, reduced prices, and easy reservations at the end of the season, a wonderful time to go to Denali. The weather gets nippy at night, and there can be surprise snowfalls, but rain is less likely, and the trees and tundra turn wonderful colors. By early September, visitors are so few that the park no longer takes telephone reservations. By mid-September, private cars can drive on the park road for a few days—the park service holds a lottery in July to determine who will get that treat.

Another way to avoid the crowds is to book a stay in a **wilderness lodge.** Lodges in Kantishna, listed in section 11 of this chapter, have the right to carry clients to their businesses over the park road in buses and vans, avoiding the bottleneck.

SAMPLE ITINERARIES

The more you're willing to rough it, the closer you can get to the real Denali. There are no hotels inside the park.

THE HOTEL-STAY ITINERARY

Drive to the park or arrive by train and choose accommodations near the park—shuttles and courtesy vans can get you around. Visit the exhibits at the Denali Visitor Center, attend a ranger talk, see the *Cabin Nite* dinner-theater show, or go on a short **nature walk** around the park hotel in the evening. Get to bed early, and the next morning take a shuttle bus before 7am into the park to see the terrain and animals, and possibly to get a view of the mountain. By late morning you'll be at a point with a commanding view of McKinley (in good weather). Now ride partway back toward the entrance before getting off the bus at a place of your choosing for a walk and to eat the bag lunch you've brought along with you (pack out all trash, of course), or take one of the **National Park Service guided walks.** After enjoying the wilderness for a few hours, head back on the bus, finishing a long day back at the hotel. The next day, try an educational program at the Murie Science and Learning Center or take a rafting ride, a flightseeing trip, or another activity near the park entrance before driving onward or reboarding the train.

THE FAMILY CAMPING ITINERARY

Arrive at the park entrance by car with your camping gear and food for a couple of nights. (You can rent the camping gear and car in Anchorage or Fairbanks.) Camp that evening at the **Riley Creek Campground** near the visitor center. Enjoy the evening ranger program, see the exhibits at the visitor center, take a nature walk, or go straight to a campsite farther within the park (either way, you'll need to reserve well ahead). The next day, catch a shuttle bus to get deeper into the park for sightseeing and **hiking.** If you have another day after that within the park, you can do more hikes and have the cushion of a weather day. Add a rafting excursion at the park entrance before driving on, if you like, and possibly a night in a hotel with a soft bed and your very own bathroom.

THE BACKCOUNTRY CAMPING ITINERARY

Arrive by train, bus, or car with your backpack, camping gear, and food for at least several days' hiking. Go immediately to the Backcountry Information Center to orient yourself to the backcountry permit process, buy the information you need for your trek (see section 4 of this chapter), and choose the unit area that looks most promising. **Backcountry permits** cannot be reserved in advance; you can apply for them in person only 2 days in advance, and they go fast. If you're lucky, permits will be left for the day after you arrive; more likely, you'll need to camp for a night nearby and arrive at the visitor center by the 9am opening (in high season) to get your permit for the following day. Now you've got another day to wait; if you've reserved a shuttle-bus seat, you can get a preview of the park and see some wildlife. The next morning you can start your backcountry hike, taking the camper bus to your unit, and then traveling for up to 2 weeks in a huge area of wilderness reserved almost exclusively for your use.

Denali National Park

The Denali Highway: The Drivable Denali

From Cantwell, 27 miles south of the Denali National Park entrance, the Denali Highway leads 133 miles east to another tiny village, Paxson, on the Richardson Highway. The little-known road is a lesson in how labels influence people. It runs due east from the Denali National Park border, a natural extension of the park over the Alaska Range, with scenery that's equal to and in some ways more impressive than the park's. Yet without the national park name, the terrain along the Denali Highway is comparatively little used.

The Bureau of Land Management controls the land along the Denali Highway, and it's pretty much open for any recreational activity. The **Tangle Lakes** start a 3-day, 35-mile float trip (for experienced paddlers) to the Richardson Highway and host fine lake canoeing, where you can see an extraordinary variety of waterfowl, including trumpeter swans, sandhill cranes, and loons. Much of the highway passes through high, alpine terrain, with views that extend infinitely and good chances of seeing caribou, moose, and black and grizzly bears. At **Maclaren Pass,** at 4,086 feet, you stand in high Alaska Range terrain of tundra and rock, with views of Maclaren Glacier. The land invites you to walk at least a little way out across it.

Simply driving the road is an experience. If you're traveling to Denali National Park from Anchorage or Fairbanks, consider making a return trip via the Denali Highway and Richardson Highway. But check out road conditions first. The road is gravel and sometimes in poor condition. Check with the Alaska Department of Transportation's **road condition hotline** (© **511;** http://511.alaska.gov). When the road is good, you can cover its length in less than 4 hours. (Agencies that rent cars and RVs for these gravel highways are listed under "Equipped for the Back Roads" on p. 393, for Fairbanks; and "Car Wheels on Gravel Roads" on p. 210, for Anchorage. Most companies don't allow their vehicles on the Denali.) Small roadhouses are found along the way. **Biking** the road is one of the best ways to see it. Trails and remote roads from the highway offer some exceptional mountain-biking and hiking routes, especially in the Tangle Lakes National Register Archaeological District. There are **Bureau of Land Management campgrounds** along the highway at Brushkana Creek and Tangle Lakes, and you can camp anywhere you want outside a campground. **Tangle River Inn,** at Mile 20 (© **907/833-3970;** www.tangleriverinn.com), rents canoes for $4 an hour or $30 a day.

Be sure to get the BLM's *Denali Highway Points of Interest* road guide and *Trail Map and Guide to the Tangle Lakes National Register District.* They're available at the Alaska Public Lands Information Centers in Fairbanks, Anchorage, or Tok, or directly from the **Bureau of Land Management.** Their Glennallen Field Office, P.O. Box 147, Glennallen, AK 99588 (© **907/822-3217;** www.glennallen.ak.blm.gov; Mon–Fri 8am–4:30pm), manages the area, and rangers there can give you guidance on where to go.

THE WILDERNESS LODGE ITINERARY

For those who can afford it, this may be the best way to see Denali. The lodge will fly you in—or, if it's in Kantishna, drive you through the park—and you'll immediately be away from the crowds in remote territory. The lodges all have activities and guides to get you out into the wilderness. If you're staying at a lodge that's not in Kantishna, you may want to schedule a day to ride the shuttle bus into the park to see the mountain and wildlife anyway, with an evening in a hotel near the park or in Healy.

THE TALKEETNA OPTION

Drive only as far as Talkeetna, about 110 miles north of Anchorage, and board a flightseeing plane from there to the park, perhaps landing on a glacier on Mount McKinley. You'll stand a better chance of seeing the mountain than anyone else, since the weather tends to be better on the south side and you can fly above most clouds. You'll also save yourself hours of driving to the park and the bus ride into the park, and you'll have the pleasure of staying in a town with some character, unlike the park entrance area. If you want the on-the-ground wildlife-viewing opportunities that can be had only in the park, you can fly from Talkeetna for the day, for a price. (See section 10 of this chapter for more information.)

2 Park Essentials

VISITOR INFORMATION

Getting the information you need to plan your visit is especially important at Denali because of the need for advance reservations.

The most important resource for setting up a trip is the concessionaire: **Doyon/ARAMARK Joint Venture,** 241 W. Ship Creek Ave., Anchorage, AK 99501 (© **800/622-7275** or 907/272-7275; fax 907/258-3668; www.reservedenali.com). The concession is operated by a joint venture of ARAMARK, which manages affairs at many parks around the country, and the Doyon Native Corporation of Interior Alaska. They handle the reservations system for the campgrounds and shuttle buses, as well as several hotels, bus tours, a rafting operation, and a dinner theater. The best place to make in-person contact with the concessionaire is at the reservation and ticketing desks in the **Wilderness Access Center,** on the Denali Park Road, half a mile from the park entrance. The access center is open from mid-May to mid-September daily from 5am to 8pm; it's closed October through April. You can even buy an espresso inside to drink while you stand in line. Since there's no park entrance station, this center is also a good stop for the park map, a copy of the *Alpenglow* park newspaper, and other handouts. A small store offers a limited selection of conveniences and camping supplies, including hiking boots.

The **National Park Service** can be reached at P.O. Box 9, Denali National Park, AK 99755 (© **907/683-2294;** www.nps.gov/dena). Make contact in person at the spectacular **Denali Visitor Center,** near the railroad depot at Mile 1.5 of the park road on the right side. It is open summer daily 9am to 6pm. Find more on park service educational facilities under "Learning About the Park," p. 259.

Besides the centers at the park and the website, you can get park information on the way there at the interagency **Alaska Public Lands Information Centers** in Anchorage, Fairbanks, and Tok, listed in chapters 6 and 10. The park's nonprofit publishing arm is the **Alaska Natural History Association,** Denali Branch, P.O. Box 230, Denali National Park, AK 99755 (© **907/683-1272** summer, 907/683-1258 off season;

www.alaskanha.org). They operate the shops in the park visitor centers, and you can use their website to order books and maps before coming.

THE RESERVATIONS SYSTEM

Here's the system for reserving shuttle-bus tickets and sites at the developed campgrounds. This section may look long, but paying attention to the details of the reservations system greatly improves your chances of a good visit to the park. (The backcountry permit system is covered in section 4 of this chapter.)

FOR ADVANCE RESERVATIONS

Sixty-five percent of shuttle-bus seats and all campground sites (except Sanctuary and Igloo) are offered for booking by Internet, telephone, fax, or mail; the balance is held back for walk-ins up to 2 days before the trip. Use the Doyon/ARAMARK Joint Venture information above under "Visitor Information."

Reservations by Internet or mail open for the whole summer on December 1 of the preceding year. Reservations by phone open in mid-February. Lines are answered daily from 7am to 5pm Alaska time (remember, that's 4 hours earlier than Eastern Standard Time, where the hours would be 11am to 9pm). By using the Internet (www.reserve denali.com), you can get a big jump on those who call for reservations. Unfortunately, the website is poorly designed. There is no way of telling what dates are already taken, so you just have to fish for the best tickets by entering different dates. Also note that unless you enter the date in a numeric format without dashes or slashes (July 4, 2007, is 070407), the system will tell you that no space is available rather than cluing you in on the error. You will need a Visa, MasterCard, American Express, or Discover Card. You can also pay by check if you're reserving by phone or mail; payment is due within 10 days. But this option is not available within 30 days of the date you are arriving. It's also possible to reserve by fax, but I'm unable to think of a reason for doing so.

A **confirmation** should be sent out within 2 days of making the reservation. Take the confirmation to the "will call" desk at the Wilderness Access Center when you arrive to exchange it for a camping permit and bus ticket. If you'll be arriving after the center closes at 8pm, you must call © **907/683-9274** in advance to avoid losing your site or shuttle seat.

FOR WALK-INS

Internet, phone, mail, and fax orders are not accepted the day before the visit starts (in fact, they're mostly sold out weeks earlier), but walk-in reservations begin 2 days out, offering 35% of the shuttle-bus seats that are held back and any leftover car-camping sites (usually none), and all sites at Sanctuary and Igloo campgrounds. If it's a busy time of year, desirable shuttle reservations are snapped up early in the day. That means you may not get a good reservation for the day of your arrival or even the day after, only the next day after that. That's why it's so critical to reserve in advance.

On the other hand, don't despair if you arrive without reservations, as the flow of visitors rises and falls unpredictably. It's perfectly possible that you'll walk into the visitor center and get a shuttle seat on the same day.

FEES

Park entrance fees are $20 per family (up to eight) or $10 per person, good for 7 days. There is no entrance station to collect the fee, but it is automatically added to your bill when you make shuttle or campground reservations. If you have a National Parks Pass or a Golden Age or Golden Access pass, mention it when you reserve to get your discount. Entrance fees are in place year-round and are collected at the Murie Science and Learning Center during winter months.

Campground fees are $16 to $19 per night for car or RV camping, $12 for walk-in tent camping sites at Riley Creek Campground, and $9 at Sanctuary and Igloo campgrounds. A reservation fee of $4 is charged for the first night of stays in campgrounds other than Riley Creek and Savage River. (See "Where to Stay" later in the chapter for more particulars.) **Bus fees** are listed in the chart "Denali Park Road Bus Facts," in section 3 of this chapter. A $4 fee is charged for canceling or changing a campsite or bus ticket, except for free children's tickets. You can cancel until 5pm for campground reservations or 2 hours before departure for shuttle tickets. Tundra Wilderness Tour reservations can be cancelled only 7 days or more in advance.

GETTING THERE
BY TRAIN
The **Alaska Railroad** (© 800/544-0552 or 907/265-2494; www.alaskarailroad.com) pioneered tourism to the park before the George Parks Highway was built in 1972. In summer, trains leave both Anchorage and Fairbanks daily at 8:15am, arriving at the park from Anchorage at 3:45pm and from Fairbanks at noon, crossing and going on to the opposite city for arrival at 8:15pm in each. The basic fare from Anchorage to Denali is $129 one-way for adults, from Fairbanks $56, half-price for children ages 2 to 11, free under 2. First-class "Gold Star" seats are $85 more per leg, or $105 for a continuous ride on the Anchorage-Fairbanks leg (you pay the $85 twice if you stop over at Denali). Descriptions of the different classes of service are below under "Train Choices." The train also stops in Wasilla and Talkeetna; see the website for details. The full train runs only from mid-May to mid-September, with somewhat lower fares in the first and last few weeks of the season. During the winter, the Alaska Railroad runs a single passenger car from Anchorage to Fairbanks and back once a week—a truly spectacular, truly Alaskan experience.

BY CAR
Renting a car and driving from Anchorage or Fairbanks is far cheaper and far faster than taking the train. It's easy to average 65 on good two-lane highway, making the drive about 4½ hours from Anchorage and 2½ hours from Fairbanks. (The train averages 40 mph and takes 7½ hours to get from Anchorage to Denali.) Many of the views along the **Parks Highway** are equal to the views on the train, but large stretches, especially in the Matanuska and Susitna valleys, near Anchorage, have been spoiled by ugly roadside development (which you don't see from the train). A long but spectacular detour around the mess leads through **Hatcher Pass** on a mountainous gravel road open only in the summer (see "Through Hatcher Pass" in section 10 of chapter 6). Farther north from Anchorage, the Parks Highway passes through **Denali State Park.** If the weather's clear, you can see Mount McKinley from the pullouts there. The state park also contains several campgrounds, public-use cabins, hiking trails, and a veterans' memorial. Byers Lake is a nice stop with a good campground and with canoe and kayak rental from **Denali Southside River Guides** (© 907/733-7238; www.denali riverguides.com)—the company also offers guided river rafting, kayaking, and fly fishing. The park has a visitor contact station at the memorial, at Mile 147. For information before you go, contact the **Mat-Su Area Park Headquarters** (© 907/745-3975; www.alaskastateparks.org, click on "Individual Parks"). From Fairbanks, the drive is

Tips Train Choices

Alaska Railroad executives know that their fares are high for a simple ride to Denali. As one told me, "We're selling entertainment," and that's how you should judge your choices. So, to review the entertainment: All the cars are luxurious, and some are grand and highly memorable; the rail line follows a historic, unspoiled route through beautiful countryside; there's a good chance of seeing moose and caribou; the commentary by well-trained Alaska high-school students is fresh and engaging; and the food is good. There are disadvantages, too. The train is very expensive. You can rent a small car for a week for the same price as one round-trip on the train. It's slow, adding 3 hours to a trip from Anchorage to the park, and when it's late, it can be very late. And, once you arrive, you have to rely on shuttles and courtesy vans to get around outside the park.

After you decide to ride the train, you have to choose which part of the train. One set of Alaska Railroad locomotives pulls the Alaska Railroad cars and other sets of cars with full glass domes owned by cruise lines, two of which have seats for independent travelers (although 90% or more are filled with their older cruise-ship customers). **Princess Cruises and Tours** (*©* **800/426-0500;** www.princesslodges.com) has tall, all-dome cars with table seating upstairs and dining rooms downstairs; there's plenty of head room and large balconies at the ends of the cars on the lower deck where you can ride outdoors. **Gray Line of Alaska Package Tours,** a part of Holland America (*©* **800/544-2206** or 907/277-5581; www.graylinealaska.com), has newer cars that are even better than Princess's. They're huge and comfortable, with all seats facing forward upstairs—an advantage over table seating—and dining rooms below that are large enough so only two seatings are needed for each meal. (All meals are served at assigned seatings in the cruise-line cars.)

The **Alaska Railroad** offers two classes of service. The basic service is in traditional railroad cars. They're clean and have big windows and forward-facing seats. Passengers stroll around and dine when and how they please rather than at assigned seatings. Old fashioned VistaDome cars provide a limited but adequate number of shared dome seats. By paying another $85, you can upgrade to "Gold Star" service, with your own full-dome seat for the entire trip on custom-built double-decker cars like the cruise lines', with a sumptuous white-tablecloth dining room downstairs (eat when you like). These are my favorite cars on the train. They're decorated with original fine art and are very luxurious, but you still know you're on a train, not a cruise ship, and you're not treated as a herd animal. Also, the cars have large outdoor vestibules on the upper deck. The views and open air there are incredible.

All passenger seats are assigned on all the cars. You can't walk from one company's cars to another, but you can walk between cars in your own train section. Fares on all three options are similarly high, but they're more advantageously priced as part of lodging and tour packages, which you can buy from the railroad or the cruise lines.

pleasant but rarely spectacular. Allow an hour to stop in the quaint, riverside town of Nenana, where you can see an old railroad depot museum (p. 387).

BY BUS

Several van and bus services inexpensively connect Anchorage and Fairbanks to Denali. Most will carry bikes and other gear for an additional fee. **The Park Connection Motorcoach Service** (© 800/266-8625 or 907/245-0200; www.alaskacoach. com) runs big, comfortable coaches to Denali from Seward and Anchorage, with two buses daily in each direction. The Anchorage fare is $76, Seward $130. Children under 12 ride for half-price; those 4 and under need a car seat. **Alaska/Yukon Trails** (© 800/770-7275; www.alaskashuttle.com) offers twice-daily service from Anchorage, once a day from Fairbanks, with stops at any other point on the way. The one-way fare is $65 from Anchorage, $46 from Fairbanks.

BY AIR

Talkeetna Aero Services (© 888/733-2899 or 907/733-2899; www.talkeetna-aero. com) offers the only scheduled air service to Denali from their base in Talkeetna, or from Anchorage, in the summer only. The flights are sold as 1-day packages, including flight-seeing on the way, a bus tour at the park, a box lunch, and ground transfers. It's the only way to "do" Denali in a day. The package from Anchorage is $475, from Talkeetna $350.

GETTING AROUND

If you take the train or bus, you'll find that most accommodations have arrangements to get you around, although this becomes less convenient as you get farther from the park entrance. Ask how courtesy transportation works when you book your room. There are cabs available, too, but they have been a poor option because of sky-high rates. If you must rely on cabs, get a firm quote when you call. Companies include **Caribou Cab** (© 907/683-5000) and **Denali Transportation & Tours** (© 877/683-4765 or 907/683-4765). You can also take the train to Denali, rent a car there, and drop it in Fairbanks or Anchorage. **Teresa's Alaskan Car Rentals** (© 907/683-1377; www.denalicarrental.com) is in Healy.

If you drive to the park, you'll still need to take the shuttle bus, described below, to get into its heart, except under certain circumstances. You can drive past Mile 14 on the park road only if you have a 3-day camping permit at Teklanika Campground, 29 miles in; then your vehicle must remain parked at the campground for the entire 3 days. The rules loosen at the end of the season, when winners of a drawing can drive the road for a few days in late September (check with the park service for lottery details). After the permit driving is over, the road is open to anyone as far as Mile 30 until the snow flies; then it's maintained only as far as the headquarters, 3 miles from the entrance.

Bicycles have free access to the park road. For that option, see section 5 of this chapter.

FAST FACTS: Denali National Park

Banks There are no banks near the park entrance. A couple of ATMs are in the Glitter Gulch (Nenana Canyon) area, including one at the Lynx Creek Store and Deli. A couple more are at gas stations in Healy, 12 miles north of the park. Do your banking before leaving Anchorage or Fairbanks.

Emergencies ✆ **911** will work inside the park, but be sure to tell the operator you are within Denali National Park. However, cellphone coverage reaches only along the highway and there are no telephones except at the developed areas. Bus drivers on the park road are equipped with radios.

Gear Rental **Denali Mountain Morning Hostel and Lodge** (✆ **907/683-7503**), listed in full on p. 368, rents camping gear; a complete kit is $40 for the first day, $10 each additional day. Closer to the park entrance, **Denali Mountain Works** (✆ **907/683-1542;** www.akrivers.com), a clothing and outfitting shop, rents binoculars, sleeping bags, tents, backpacks, and stoves. It is right across from the McKinley Chalet Resort. Bikes are for rent at **Denali Outdoor Center** (✆ **888/303-1925** or 907/683-1925; www.denalioutdoorcenter.com); see p. 362.

Hospital The seasonal **Canyon Health Clinic Urgent Care Center** (✆ **907/683-4433**) is among the big hotels near the park entrance. In Healy, 12 miles north of the park entrance, the year-round **Community Interior Health Center** (✆ **907/683-2211**) is open 24 hours a day for emergencies, or normal office hours for nonemergencies. Neither clinic has a full-fledged doctor.

Police The **Alaska State Troopers** (✆ **907/683-2232** or 907/768-2202) have a post in Healy, 12 miles north of the park, and in Cantwell, 28 miles south.

Post Office The post office is just within the park entrance, right before the Riley Creek Campground.

Stores You should do major shopping before leaving Anchorage or Fairbanks, but there are handy little stores at Denali. **Riley Creek Mercantile** (✆ **907/683-9246**) is at the Riley Creek Campground, near the park entrance. It's open daily from 7am to 11pm in the summer. Besides convenience groceries, they have firewood, some basic camping supplies, RV supplies, a dump station, made-to-order sandwiches, Internet access, fax and copy service, binocular rentals, showers, and laundry. In the Glitter Gulch (Nenana Canyon) area across from the McKinley Chalet Resort, the locally owned **Denali General Store** (✆ **907/683-2920**) carries a variety of goods at better prices than in the hotel gift shops, and packs delicious picnics to take along on the shuttle bus ride.

Taxes The local **bed tax** is 7%. There is no sales tax.

3 Denali by Shuttle Bus

Your visit to Denali will likely revolve around a ride on the shuttle bus into the park to see the wildlife and to stop for a walk in the wilderness. Some planning will make it a more successful trip.

CHOOSING YOUR DESTINATION

You can buy shuttle tickets to the Toklat (*Toe*-klat) River, 53 miles into the park; to Fish Creek Turnaround (the stop taking the place of the Eielson Visitor Center while it is rebuilt), at around 63 miles; Wonder Lake, at 85 miles; or Kantishna, at 89 miles (fares are listed in the "Denali Park Road Bus Facts" chart that accompanies this section). On any day trip, you have to go both ways, so you're in for a long ride. If you don't get off the bus along the way, the round-trip takes 5 hours to Toklat (with a temporary visitor center), nearly 8 hours to Fish Creek Turnaround (or Eielson Visitor

Center, when it is in operation), 11 hours to Wonder Lake, and 12 hours to Kantishna. You must bring your own water and food.

In choosing your destination, you need to balance your stamina, your desire to save time for a day hike, and your desire to see wildlife. There are no firm rules about where wildlife shows up, but my own observations are that in the early morning, you can often see moose on the first part of the road; in midsummer, brown (grizzly) bears seem to appear most in the higher country, beyond Toklat, which also is the best area for caribou; in the fall berry season, the grizzlies show up all along the drive.

The best views of Mount McKinley show up beginning around Highway Pass at the east side of the causeway at about Mile 58, beyond Toklat (where the mountain cannot be seen at all). The mountain is most likely to be visible in the morning, as clouds often pile up during the day. Going all the way to Wonder Lake provides more amazing views, including the land-covered Muldrow Glacier and many classic images of Mount McKinley. There's really no reason to go as far as Kantishna unless you are headed to a lodge there (see section 11, "Denali Wilderness Lodges"). In general, I think Fish Creek Turnaround (or Eielson Visitor Center, when open) is the best destination for most people, offering them the chance to see the mountain and some wildlife while leaving them time to get out and walk (I've included ideas on where to hike later).

You won't be able to time your trip for good weather, as you need to book ahead. But don't despair if it rains—the sun may be out at the other end of the park. The best weather for wildlife sightings is cool, overcast skies without rain. One trick of the system that allows visitors to wait for sun is to stay at Teklanika Campground. If you drive to a campsite there, agreeing to stay for a minimum of 3 nights, you're eligible to buy a special shuttle ticket for $24 that's good for rides deeper into the park the entire time you're staying at the campground. Wherever you stay, you can buy a three-trip pass for the price of two.

Denali can be a challenge for families. Young children will go nuts on an 8-hour bus ride and often can't pick out the wildlife—this isn't a zoo, and most animals blend in with their surroundings. Older children also have a hard time keeping their patience on these trips, as do many adults. The only solution is to get off the bus and turn your trip into a romp in the heather. When you've had a chance to revive, catch

---

Tips Bus Concerns & Complaints

The Denali concessionaire uses only school bus–type vehicles for shuttles on the park road, which are not as comfortable as highway motorcoaches and do not have bathrooms on board. Safety concerns permit only these tough, lightweight buses to operate on the narrow, gravel park road. Some of the Tundra Wilderness Tour buses—unlike the shuttles and camper buses—are tricked out with higher-backed cloth seats and video monitors that allow the driver to zoom in on wildlife, but the basic bus is essentially the same. (I haven't been on these yet, but I have my doubts about going to the park to watch wildlife on a TV screen.) The road itself can be an issue, too. I've heard from visitors complaining of white knuckles on the ride. The buses act a bit like mountain goats on the heights of Polychrome Pass and near Eielson Visitor Center as the road climbs without guardrails. If you're afraid of heights, it might not be to your liking.

the next bus. Besides, just because you buy a ticket to Wonder Lake doesn't mean that you have to go that far. Keep in mind, too, that if your child normally needs a car seat, you must bring it along on the bus.

The park has alternatives to the shuttle bus, with commentary, more comfortable seats, and other amenities. Doyon/ARAMARK Joint Venture operates two narrated bus tours, booked mostly as part of package tours. The **Denali Natural History Tour** provides just a taste of the park, going 17 miles down the park road, but also includes a cultural component, with a film, a history talk at a cabin, and a presentation by an Alaska Native, which could include singing, storytelling, or information about living off the land. The **Tundra Wilderness Tour** goes to Toklat when the mountain is hidden by clouds, and 8 miles farther, across Highway Pass to Stony Hill, when it is visible. Programmed commentary provides background on what you are seeing. Food is provided, but you can't get off the bus along the way (that's the fatal flaw, in my opinion). Two other narrated tours are offered by privately owned lodges in the Kantishna area, at the far end of the park road. **Kantishna Wilderness Trails** (© **800/230-7275** or 907/683-1475; www.seedenali.com) and **Denali Backcountry Adventure** (© **888/ 560-2489** or 907/683-2643) each cover 190 miles in around 13 hours, with a stop halfway through, at the far end, for a meal and gold panning (with either), or a sled dog demonstration (with Kantishna), or a hike (with Denali Backcountry). Either way, it's a marathon and you can't get off the bus along the way, but there is no other choice for a 1-day, narrated tour that covers the whole road. The cost is around $130, plus the $10 park entrance fee, on either tour, with no discount for children (nor could any kid I know stay sane on a 13-hour bus ride).

GETTING READY

Reserve your shuttle ticket for as early as you can stand to get up in the morning. This strategy will give you more time for day hikes and enhance your chances of seeing the mountain and wildlife. Many animals are more active in the morning, especially on hot days. During peak season, the first bus leaves the visitor center at 5:15am and then one leaves roughly every 15 to 30 minutes in the morning. A few buses leave in the afternoon, mostly to pick up stragglers on the way back, returning late under the midnight sun.

By taking an early bus, you have more time to get off along the way for a hike, walking back to the road and getting the next bus that comes along with a spare seat. Time it right, and you could have more than 8 hours for hiking plus a tour of most of the park road before returning on a late bus. (To be on the safe side, don't push it to the very last bus.) The sun won't set until after 11pm May through July and it will be light all night. If you need to get back to the park entrance at a certain time, leave yourself plenty of time because after getting off your westbound bus, you can't reserve seats going back the other way, and you may have to wait an hour for a bus with room to take you.

Before you leave for the Wilderness Access Center to get on your shuttle bus, you'll need a packed lunch and plenty of water. You should wear sturdy walking shoes and layers of warm and lighter clothing with rain gear packed, you should have binoculars or a spotting scope at the ready, and you should have insect repellent. You may also want a copy of Kris Capps's worthwhile booklet *Denali Road Guide,* sold at the Denali Visitor Center bookstore and published by the Alaska Natural History Association (listed in section 2 under "Visitor Information"). It provides a milepost commentary you can follow as you ride. ANHA also publishes guides to Denali birds,

Denali Park Road Bus Facts

Note: WAC is Wilderness Access Center. All prices rounded to nearest dollar.

Bus	Purpose	Route	Frequency	Fare
Hotel Courtesy Shuttle	Links Denali Park Resorts hotels to park entrance	Hotels 1 mile north and 7 miles south	Continuous loop	Free, even if not staying within park at a DPR hotel
Riley Creek Loop	Links facilities within park entrance area	Visitor facilities, Riley Creek Campground, rail depot	Continuous loop	Free
Savage River Shuttle	Public transport to hiking near the Savage River, which can also be reached by car	From visitor center to Savage River day-use area, about 14 miles into the park	Peak season every hour 9am–9pm	Free
Camper Shuttle (Green Bus)	Access to campgrounds and backpacking beyond the park entrance	From the WAC to Wonder Lake Campground, 85 miles into the park	Several times a day	$24 adults, half-price ages 15–17, free 14 and younger
Shuttle bus (or just "the shuttle"; Green Bus)	General access to the park and wildlife viewing; limited commentary, depending on the driver; no food or water	From the visitor center as far as Kantishna, 91 miles away through the park	Every 30 minutes to Fish Creek, every hour to Wonder Lake, 4 times daily Kantishna	$19 to Toklat, $24 to Fish Creek, $33 to Wonder Lake, $36 to Kantishna; half-price ages 15–17, free 14 and younger
Tundra Wilderness Tour (Tan Bus)	6- to 8-hour guided bus tour with lunch provided; passengers may not get off en route	From the WAC to the Toklat River or Stony Hill, 53–61 miles into the park	Twice daily	$91 adults, half-price ages 14 and younger (includes park entrance fee)
Natural History Tour (Tan Bus)	5-hour guided bus tour at the edge of the park	From the WAC 17 miles into the park	Three times daily	$60 adults, half-price ages 14 and younger (includes park entrance fee)

Tips Shuttle-Bus Etiquette

It's common courtesy on the shuttle bus to yell out when you see wildlife so others can see it, too. The driver will stop and everyone will rush to your side of the bus. After you've had a look, give someone else a chance to look out your window or get a picture. Be quiet and don't stick yourself, your camera, or anything else out of the bus. You will scare away the animals or, worse, help habituate them to humans.

---

mammals, geology, and trails. If you'll be doing any extensive day hiking, you may also want to bring a detailed topographic map printed on waterproof plastic (published by Trails Illustrated and sold for $9.95 from the visitor center or by ordering from ANHA) as well as a compass; if you're just going to walk a short distance off the road, you won't need such preparations.

ON YOUR WAY

There are no reserved seats on the bus, but if you arrive early, you can find a place on the left side, which has the best views on the way out. Bus riders often see grizzly bears, caribou, Dall sheep, moose, and occasionally wolves, but, as one driver said, the animals aren't union workers, and it's possible that you won't see any at all. Of course, you have to stay on the bus when animals are present.

The shuttle-bus drivers often offer commentary about the sights on the road, but they aren't required to do so. Some do a great job and some don't say much. The tour bus drivers do a formal presentation, but you can't get off the bus on the way.

A ROAD LOG

Here are some of the highlights along the road (check the visitor center or the park service information handouts to confirm times of the guided walks):

MILE 9   In clear weather, this is the closest spot to the park entrance with a view of Mount McKinley. This section also is a likely place to see moose, especially in the fall rutting season.

MILE 14   At the end of the paved road at the Savage River Bridge, this is generally as far as private vehicles can go. A park service checkpoint stops anyone who doesn't have a proper permit. From the parking lot by the bridge, a simple climb over dry tundra leads to Primrose Ridge, also known as Mount Wright.

MILE 17   The portable toilets here are as far as the Natural History Tour bus goes.

MILE 29   An hour and 10 minutes into the drive, a large rest stop overlooks the Teklanika River, with flush toilets, the last plumbing on the road. The Teklanika, like many other rivers on Alaska's glacier-carved terrain, is a braided river—a stream wandering in a massive gravel streambed that's much too big for it. The braided riverbeds, sometimes miles wide, were created by water from fast-melting glaciers at the end of the last ice age. Each is kept free of vegetation by its river, which constantly changes course as it spreads the debris of rock and dust from the glaciers. Flat plains in glacial terrain usually are laid down by this mechanism.

MILE 34   Craggy Igloo Mountain is a likely place to see Dall sheep. Without binoculars, they'll just look like white dots. Manageable climbs on Igloo, Cathedral, and Sable mountains take off along the road in the section from Igloo Creek to Sable Pass.

MILES 38–43   Sable Pass, a critical habitat area for bears, is closed to people. A half-eaten sign helps explain why. Bears show up here mostly in the fall. This is the start of the road's broad alpine vistas.

MILE 46   Here you'll find the top of 5-mile-wide Polychrome Pass, the most scenic point on the ride, and a toilet break, 2 hours and 25 minutes into the trip. Caribou look like specks when they pass in the great valley below you, known as the Plain of Murie after Adolph Murie, a biologist who pioneered study here and helped develop the park service's scientific ethic (the name does not always appear on maps, however). Note how the mountains of colored rock on either side of the plain match up—they once were connected before glacial ice carved this valley. Huge rocks on its floor are glacial erratics, plucked from the bedrock by moving ice and left behind when the ice melted.

MILE 53   The Toklat River, another braided river, is a flat plain of gravel with easy walking. The glaciers that feed the river are 10 miles upstream; the river bottom is habitat for bears, caribou, and wolves, and a good place for picnics. While the Eielson Visitor Center is under construction, at least until 2008, Teklanika will be the main rest area for westbound buses, with all of them stopping for 30 minutes here. A large tent houses a station for the National Park Service and a tiny bookstore operated by the Alaska Natural History Association. Doyon/ARAMARK has a bus dispatch tent where you can ask about changing buses if you want to go back later or continue onward. There is no food or water, but there are outhouses.

MILE 58   Highway Pass is the highest point on the road. In good weather, dramatic views of Mount McKinley start here. The alpine tundra from here to the Eielson Visitor Center is inviting for walking, but beware: Tundra is soft underfoot and can conceal holes and declivities that can twist an ankle.

MILE 62   Stony Hill Overlook is a mountainous highway point with great views of McKinley, 36 miles away. The Tundra Wildlife Tour turns around here on days with good mountain viewing.

MILE 63   Fish Creek Turnaround is where the 8-hour shuttle bus trip turns around. There are no facilities.

MILE 64   Thorofare Pass, where the road becomes narrow and winding, is a good area to look for bears and caribou. Bus drivers know best where the animals are on any particular day, since they talk to fellow drivers.

MILE 66   This is the site of the **Eielson Visitor Center,** closed while under reconstruction. It is a fine vantage point for seeing McKinley. Seismic measurements here show frequent small earthquakes accompanying McKinley's prodigious growth—about an inch every 3 years. This region is a jumble of rocks pushed together by the expanding Pacific tectonic plate; the mountain and the whole Alaska Range are folding upward in that great collision.

MILE 68.5   The incredibly rugged terrain to the north is the earth and vegetation covering Muldrow Glacier. The ice extends to McKinley's peak and was an early and arduous route for climbers; these days, they fly to a base camp at a 7,200-foot elevation on the Kahiltna Glacier, on the south side. McKinley's glaciers, falling 15,000 vertical feet and extending up to 45 miles in length, are among the world's greatest. The Ruth Glacier has carved the Great Gorge on the south side, which is almost 6,000 feet deep above the ice and another 4,000 below—almost twice the depth of the

The Alaska-Ohio Name Game, Round 30

Mount McKinley is so large that Athabascan people speaking different languages had different names for it. The Koyukon, on the north and west, called it Deenaalee, while the Dena'ina and Ahtna on the far side called it Dengadh. In 1839 the name was recorded on a Russian map as Tenada. It often has been translated as "the great one," but a closer translation is the more generic "the high one." The Athabascans never named mountains after people, nor did the Denali area get much use, since fish and game are relatively sparse and the weather extreme, but they did regard high places as spiritually important.

The name McKinley became associated with the mountain in the haphazard way common of the Alaska gold rush period. A businessman and Princeton graduate named William Dickey was prospecting in the area in 1896, constantly arguing with his traveling companions about the big political issue of the day, the gold monetary standard supported by the Republicans and opposed by the Democrats. The Democratic presidential candidate, William Jennings Bryan, declared at his nomination convention that year, "You shall not crucify mankind upon a cross of gold." It was the gold standard that caused a deflationary economic disaster in those years, which was relieved only by the 1898 Klondike gold rush, which also led to Alaska's settlement. Anyway, when Dickey came out of the Bush, he published a piece about his travels in the *New York Sun* in which he reported his "discovery" and his name for North America's highest mountain—in honor of William McKinley, the Republican candidate who won the White House and was then assassinated. Dickey later admitted he chose the name only to spite his former traveling companions.

Alaskans have long believed McKinley is an irrelevant name for the mountain, especially since it already had a name. In 1975, the state of Alaska petitioned the U.S. Geographic Names Board to change the name back to Denali. In 1980, Congress changed the name of the national park to Denali, but a single congressman from Ohio has blocked changing the name of the mountain itself. McKinley was an Ohio governor and congressman before running for president. Rep. Ralph Regula, a Republican who has represented McKinley's former seat since 1972, and who even attended William McKinley Law School, found a clever maneuver to keep his name on the mountain. The names board has a policy of taking up no issue that is also being considered by Congress. In each Congress since 1977, Regula has introduced a single sentence as a budget amendment or as a standalone bill that states that McKinley is the mountain's permanent name. Although the bill never gets so much as a committee hearing, its existence is enough to invoke the board's policy and prevent it from considering the change.

Alaskans call the mountain Denali anyway and haven't given up on changing its official name. Their chief hope is persistence. Regula can't stay in Congress forever.

This box is largely based on an article from Alaska Magazine, *July 2005, by Peter Porco.*

Grand Canyon. The park road comes within a mile of the Muldrow's face, then continues through wet, rolling terrain past beaver ponds, and finally descends into a small spruce patch near Mile 82.

MILE 73   Buses to Wonder Lake may use this rest stop. Four chemical toilets are here temporarily.

MILE 86   Wonder Lake campground is the closest road point to Mount McKinley, 27 miles away. Some buses continue another half-hour to Kantishna. The fact that McKinley looks so massive from this considerable distance, dominating the sky, is testament to its stupendous size. You'll likely never see a larger object on this planet. From its base (your elevation here is only 2,000 ft.) to its top is an elevation gain greater than that of any other mountain on earth. Other mountains are taller overall, but they stand on higher ground.

4 Denali on Foot: Day Hiking & Backpacking

DAY HIKING IN THE BACKCOUNTRY

One of the unique aspects of Denali is the lack of developed trails—you really can take off in any direction. I've covered some of the best hiking areas above, in "A Road Log," including Primrose Ridge, Teklanika River, Igloo and Sable mountains, and the Toklat River. The park service long resisted building any trails, but finally gave in and recognized some trails visitors had created, including those at the Eielson Visitor Center (currently a construction site) and the 2-mile path that leads from the Wonder Lake Campground to the McKinley River Bar, which extends far to the east and west. You can drive or take a free shuttle to the Savage River Day Use Area, at Mile 15, which has a 1-mile loop trail and longer, informal routes for great alpine tundra hiking. No permit is needed for day hiking.

The broad, hard gravel flats of the **braided riverbeds,** such as the McKinley, Toklat, Teklanika, and Savage, are among the best routes for hiking in the park. **Stony Creek,** leading up a gorge to the north from the road at Mile 60, is an excellent walk into the mountains. You can also hike on the tundra, of which there are two varieties: The **wet tundra** lies on top of permanently frozen ground called permafrost; it's mushy, at best, like hiking on foam rubber laid over bowling balls. At worst, it's swamp. **Dry tundra** clothes the mountainsides and generally makes for firmer footing and easier walking. The brush and stunted forest of the region are virtually impenetrable.

The major risks of hiking here relate to the weather and rivers. It can get cold and wet in midsummer, and if you're not prepared with warm, waterproof clothing, you could suffer the spiraling chill of hypothermia. The rivers are dangerous because of their fast flow and icy-cold water. Experienced backcountry trekkers plan their routes to avoid crossing sizable rivers. See the notes on handling river crossings, managing hypothermia, and getting lost in the "Outdoor Health & Safety" section of chapter 2.

Tips **Ranger Programs in the Park**

Check the park newspaper, *The Alpenglow,* for ranger talks and slide shows that happen as often as several times a day in the front-country area (near the entrance) and at the Riley Creek, Savage River, and Teklanika campgrounds.

Bears, which people worry most about, have never killed a Denali visitor. Tips on avoiding them are in chapter 2 and are widely distributed at the park.

For a first foray beyond the trails, consider joining one of the park service guided hikes. One or two daily **Discovery Hikes** take off from the park road. One follows a route well inside the park toward the Eielson Visitor Center, and the other goes nearer to the entrance end of the park. A ranger takes only 15 hikers, leading them into wilderness while teaching them about the nature of the places they visit. Plan a 5- to 11-hour day, including the shuttle ride; actual hiking time is about 4 hours. The hikes generally are not too strenuous for families with school-age children, although it is wise to inquire how steep it will be if you have any doubts. They cost no more than the price of your shuttle ticket. You need to wear hiking shoes or boots and bring food, water, and rain gear. Reserve a place in advance, as hikes fill up in July and you'll need to know when and where to catch the special bus. Rangers lead other walks, too, although the lineup can change each year. There often is a walk on the short Savage River Loop, 15 miles into the park, and another along the Toklat River, at Mile 53. Check with the visitor center for the current offerings and crucial details about which bus to take.

DAY HIKING IN THE PARK ENTRANCE AREA

There are several trails at the park entrance, weaving through the boreal forest around small lakes. Only one strenuous trail leads from the entrance area, but it is a gem. The steep and spectacular hike to the **Mount Healy overlook** is a 5-mile round-trip. The trail breaks through the tree line to slopes of tundra and rock outcroppings, where you can see just how small the pocket of human infestation at the park entrance area is: The Alaska Range and its foothills extend far into the distance. If you continue on an all-day hike right to the top of Mount Healy, you can see all the way to McKinley on a clear day. Several new interpretive trails offer the chance to learn, stroll, or even get somewhere. A new bike and pedestrian trail connects the entrance area, near the Riley Creek Mercantile, to Glitter Gulch, allowing pedestrians to get back and forth without walking on the road. The McKinley Station, Morino, and Spruce Forest trails teach about nature and history. Get the book *Denali Walks,* mentioned in the previous section, to learn more.

BACKPACKING

Imagine backpacking over your own area of wilderness, without trails, limits, or the chance of seeing other people. There's no need to retrace your route to get back: Anywhere you meet the 91-mile Denali Park Road you can catch a bus back to the world of people. Any experienced backpacker should consider a backcountry trek at Denali.

Yes, it can be challenging. Hiking on the tundra, broken-rock mountainsides, and braided rivers is tiring, and it's easy to fall or turn an ankle. You must be prepared for river crossings and cold weather, know how to find your way with a map and compass, and know how to avoid attracting bears. But if you've done a backpacking trip in a less challenging area, you surely can manage it here, so long as you prepare and don't underestimate the additional time you'll need in trail-less terrain. Nor do you need to trek far—you can camp just a few miles off the road and still be in a place that looks like no one has ever been there before.

You must be flexible about where you're going and be prepared for any kind of terrain because you can't choose the **backcountry unit** you will explore until you arrive at the backcountry desk at the visitor center and find out what's available. This information, and a map of the units, is posted on a board behind the desk. Groups of four or more may have a hard time finding a place to hike, but there's almost always *somewhere* to go. You can reserve permits only 2 days in advance, and you're unlikely to get one for the day you arrive, but you can reserve permits for continuation of your trip for up to 14 days at the same time. The first night of a trip is the hard one to get—for one thing, you can reserve only units that are contiguous to the park road for the first night—but after that, each night gets progressively easier. A couple of rangers are there to help you through the process.

Buy the *Denali National Park and Preserve* **topographical map,** published by Trails Illustrated, available for $10 from the Alaska Natural History Association, listed earlier under "Visitor Information." Printed on plastic, the map includes the boundaries of the 43 backcountry units and much other valuable information. Also, you'll want a copy of the *Backcountry Companion* (ANHA, $9), which describes conditions and routes in each area. You'll find it at the visitor center, or you can glance at a well-thumbed copy kept at the backcountry desk.

The alpine units from the Toklat River to Eielson Visitor Center are the most popular. That's where you get broad views and can walk across heathery dry tundra in any direction. But to travel far, even there, you may have to climb over rugged, rocky terrain, and the tundra can be deceptively difficult to walk on—it's soft and hides ankle-turning holes. The wooded units are the least popular, since bushwhacking through overgrown country is anything but fun. The best routes for making time here (and anywhere in the Alaska Bush) are along the braided river valleys and streambeds. Be ready to walk in water. You'll have to take the **camper bus** to get to your backcountry unit, at a cost of $24 for each adult.

Before venturing into the backcountry, everyone is required to watch an **orientation film** covering safety and environmental issues, including how not to attract bears. I've spoken to competent backpackers who considered abandoning their trip because of the severity of the warnings they received about bears. That's unfortunate because sensible people taking normal precautions don't need to worry. The park service provides bear-resistant food containers in which you are required to carry all your food. Guns are not permitted in the park; carrying a pepper spray, such as CounterAssault, for self-defense from bears is allowed. Bear safety is covered in chapter 2 under "Outdoor Health & Safety."

Before you decide to go backpacking at Denali, however, you may want to broaden your thinking—if you're up to a cross-country hike without a trail, there are tens of millions of acres in Alaska available for backpacking that don't require a permit. Check with the Alaska Public Lands Information Center in Anchorage or Fairbanks for ideas about road-accessible dry tundra and other suitable areas on the Denali Highway (see earlier), and on the Dalton Highway and in Wrangell–St. Elias National Park (in chapter 9). I've listed some great trail hikes in chapter 7, under Chugach National Forest, and in chapter 9, in the sections on Chena Hot Springs Road and the Steese Highway.

5 Activities within the Park

LEARNING ABOUT THE PARK

The Denali experience changed significantly with the completion in 2005 of magnificent new educational facilities in the front country. What once was a rudimentary stepping-off point for journeys into the park became something of a destination in itself, with superb exhibits and opportunities to learn about nature.

First to the Top

It's the biggest. That's why climbers risk their lives on Mount McKinley. You can see the mountain from Anchorage, more than 100 miles away. On a flight across Alaska, McKinley stands out grandly over waves of other mountains. It's more than a mile taller than the tallest peak in the other 49 states. It's a great white triangle, always covered in snow, tall but also massive and strong.

The first group to try to climb Mount McKinley came in 1903, led by Judge James Wickersham, who also helped explore Washington's Olympic Peninsula before it became a national park. His group made it less than halfway up, but on the trip they found gold in the Kantishna Hills, setting off a small gold rush that led to the first permanent human settlement in the park area. Wickersham later became the Alaska Territory's nonvoting delegate to Congress and introduced the bill that created the national park, but the government was never able to get back land in the Kantishna area from the gold miners. Today that land is the site of wilderness lodges, right in the middle of the park.

On September 27, 1906, renowned world-explorer Dr. Frederick Cook announced to the world by telegraph that he had reached the summit of Mount McKinley after a lightning-fast climb, covering more than 85 miles and 19,000 vertical feet in 13 days with one other man, a blacksmith, at his side. On his return to New York, Cook was lionized as a conquering explorer and published a popular book of his summit diary and photographs.

In 1909, Cook again made history, announcing that he had beat Robert Peary to the North Pole. Both returned to civilization from their competing treks at about the same time. Again, Cook was the toast of the town. His story began to fall apart, however, when his Eskimo companions mentioned that he'd never been out of sight of land. After being paid by Peary to come forward, Cook's McKinley companion also recanted. A year later, Cook's famous summit photograph was re-created—on a peak 19 miles away and 15,000 feet lower than the real summit.

In 1910, disgusted with Cook, four prospectors from Fairbanks took a more Alaskan approach to the task. Without fanfare or special supplies— they carried doughnuts and hot chocolate on their incredible final ascent— they marched up the mountain carrying a large wooden flagpole they could

The 14,000-square-foot **Denali Visitor Center** introduces the park and its connections to the rest of the world in a building that takes stock of its surroundings. The structure is environmentally advanced, using solar power for electricity and clever design to save solar warmth. Inside, life-size models of cranes overhead lead to an enormous mural, 60 × 28 feet in size, showing the landscape types found at the park. The carpet simulates a flowing river of gray and brown, making a path to an exhibit area with recreations of Denali wildlife, including a full-scale moose stepping through deep snow. You will also find exhibits on the Athabascan people, mining, tourism, and scientific research. On the upper floor, a large topographic model of the park demonstrates the plant on top to prove they'd made it. But on arriving at the summit, they realized that they'd climbed the slightly shorter north peak. Weather closed in, so they set up the pole there and descended without attempting the south peak. Then, when they got back to Fairbanks, no one could see the pole, and they were accused of trying to pull off another hoax.

In 1913, Episcopal archdeacon Hudson Stuck organized the first successful climb to reach the real summit—and reported he saw the pole on the other peak. Harry Karstens led the climb (he would become the park's first superintendent in 1917), and the first person to stand at the summit was an Alaska Native, Walter Harper.

Although McKinley remains one of the world's most difficult climbs, about 10,000 people have made it to the top since Hudson Stuck's party. Since 1980 the number of climbers has boomed. Garbage and human waste disposal are a major problem. One recent June day, 115 climbers made it to the summit. In 1970, only 124 made the attempt all year; now more than 1,200 try to climb the peak each year, with about half making it to the summit. The cold, fast-changing weather is what usually stops people. From late April into early July, climbers fly from the town of Talkeetna to a base camp at 7,200 feet elevation on the Kahiltna Glacier. From there, it takes an average of about 18 days to get to the top, through temperatures as cold as –40°F (–40°C).

Climbers lose fingers, toes, and other parts to frostbite, or suffer other, more severe injuries. More than 90 climbers have died on the mountain, not counting plane crashes. During the season, the park service stations rescue rangers and an emergency medical clinic at the 14,200-foot level of the mountain, and keeps a high-altitude helicopter ready to go after climbers in trouble. In 2002, under pressure from Congress, the park service started charging climbers a $150-a-head fee, defraying a portion of the rescue costs. The park and the military spend about half a million dollars a year rescuing climbers, and sometimes much more. The cost in lives is high as well. Volunteer rangers and rescuers die as well as climbers. Plane crashes, falls, cold, and altitude all take a toll. Monuments to those who never returned are in the cemetery near the airstrip in Talkeetna.

arbitrary nature of its boundaries and another exhibit shows the six-continent routes of migratory birds found at Denali. An award-winning orientation film, *Heartbeats of Denali*, lasts 18 minutes. Summer hours are daily 9am to 6pm; the center is closed in the winter.

Another of the new facilities at the park entrance is the **Murie Science and Learning Center** (© **866/683-1269** or 907/683-1269; www.murieslc.org), a building intended to both support research and teach about the park. It is located about a mile in along the Park Road on the right side. Programming got off to a shaky start in the building's first year, and what I was told to predict did not occur. I can't say exactly what will be happening in 2007. The Alaska Natural History Association hopes to offer walk-in day programs and multiday field seminars. Some field courses are already happening, mostly exploring natural history topics in the park. A few are geared for families with children under 10 years old. Three-day courses are around $320 per person. Check topics and register well in advance on the website. The center is open summer 8:30am to 4:30pm, winter daily 10am to 4pm.

MOUNTAIN BIKING

A bicycle provides special freedom in the park. Bicyclists can ride past the checkpoint where cars have to turn back, at Mile 14 on the park road. Park campgrounds have bike stands, and, with a reservation or if there is space available, you can take a bike on the shuttle or camper bus, so you can get a lift when you need one, or ride one-way. (Groups larger than two may need to split up to fit on camper buses.) The longest stretch on the park road between campgrounds is 52 miles. On the downside, the buses kick up a lot of dust, and bikes are not permitted off-road. Pick up a copy of the bicycle rules from the backcountry desk before you start. **Denali Outdoor Center** (© **888/303-1925** or 907/683-1925; www.denalioutdoorcenter.com) rents front-suspension bikes for $40 for 24 hours, $25 for 6 hours, with discounts for longer rentals. The center has an office in Glitter Gulch and headquarters near Healy, at Otto Lake Road and Parks Highway mile 247. On the highway in the Nenana Canyon, you can also rent a bike at the **Denali Parks Resorts Activity Center** (© **907/683-2591**) for $15 for 4 hours, $30 for 8 hours.

SLED DOG DEMONSTRATIONS

In the winter, rangers patrol the park by dog sled, as they have for decades. In the summer, to keep the dogs active and amuse the tourists, they run a sled on wheels around the kennel, and a ranger gives a talk, normally at 10am, 2pm, and 4pm. Although it's no substitute for seeing dogs run on snow, you can get a sense of their speed and enthusiasm from the show. It was the highlight of my older son's trip to Denali when he was 3 years old. There's no parking at the kennels, near the headquarters at Mile 3.4 on the park road, so take a free bus that leaves the Denali Visitor Center 40 minutes before each show. Times are listed in the *Alpenglow* park newspaper.

FISHING

Fishing is poor at Denali. There are grayling in some rivers, but the water is too cold and silty for most fish. Those who don't care if they catch anything, however, do enjoy fishing in this wonderful scenery. You don't need a fishing license within park boundaries, but you do have to throw back everything you catch. Bring your own gear.

For a better chance of catching something—and an opportunity to learn about fly-fishing, too—go to a private lake outside the park with guide Rick McMahan of **Denali Fly Fishing Guides** (© **907/768-1127**; www.denalifishing.com). He picks up clients at their hotels and takes them lake or stream fishing, on the bank or wading, mostly for Arctic grayling but also rainbow trout. The per-person cost is $150 half-day, $260 full day, lunch included.

CLIMBING MOUNT MCKINLEY

Because of its altitude and weather, Mount McKinley is among the world's most challenging climbs. Summer temperatures at the high camp average 20° to 40°F below zero (–28° to –40°C). If you're looking here for advice, you're certainly not up to an unguided climb. A guided climb is a challenging and expensive endeavor requiring months of conditioning and most of a month on the mountain. Get names of guides from the park service's **Talkeetna Ranger Station,** P.O. Box 588, Talkeetna, AK 99676 (© **907/733-2231**). The climbing season lasts from late April or early May until the snow gets too soft, in late June or early July. Climbers fly from Talkeetna to a 7,200-foot base camp on Kahiltna Glacier. About 1,200 climbers attempt the mountain annually in about 300 parties; about half typically make it to the top each year, and usually a few die trying.

6 Attractions & Activities outside the Park

FLIGHTSEEING

Getting a good, close look at Mount McKinley itself is best accomplished by air. Frequently you can see McKinley from above the clouds even when you can't see it from the ground. Best of all, some Talkeetna operators that fly mountaineers also land visitors on the mountain, a unique and unforgettable experience (see section 10 of this chapter). Regardless of how close you approach the mountain, a flight shows how incredibly rugged the Alaska Range is.

Small planes and helicopters fly from the park airstrip, from private heliports and airstrips along the Parks Highway, and from the Healy airstrip. **Denali Air** (© **907/ 683-2261;** www.denaliair.com) has an office in the Nenana Canyon area and operates flights at Mile 229.5 of the Parks Highway. An hour-long flight going within a mile of the mountain costs $285 for adults, $145 for children ages 2 to 12. **Era Helicopters** (© **800/843-1947** or 907/683-2574; www.flightseeingtours.com) has 50-minute flights for $284, including van pickup from hotels in the area. Their heli-hikes land for a 4-hour walk on a mountain ridgeline, the difficulty tailored to the customers' ability, for $374. A 2-hour glacial hike costs $489.

Talkeetna Aero Services (© **888/733-2899** or 907/683-2899; www.talkeetnaaero. com) flies out of Healy, 10 miles north of the park entrance, and is the only operator in the area offering landings on a glacier on Mt. McKinley itself (several flight services do so from Talkeetna; p. 373). A 3-hour tour with a glacier landing costs $379.

RAFTING

Rafting on the Nenana River, bordering the park along the Parks Highway, is fun and popular. Several commercial guides float two stretches of the river: an upper portion, where the water is smoother and the guides explain passing scenery; and the lower portion, where the river roars through the rock-walled Nenana Canyon and rafts take on huge splashes of silty, glacial water through Class III and IV rapids. Guides take children as young as 5 on the slow trip (although I wouldn't let my kid go at that age); the youngest accepted for the fast portion is age 12. White-water rafting carries risks you shouldn't discount just because a lot of people do it, as a fatal accident on the supposedly easy tour confirmed in 1999. Each session takes 2 to 2½ hours, including safety briefings, suiting up, and riding to and from the put-in and take-out points. Prices vary from $69 to $99 for adults, with discounted rates for children (from $10 less to half off). **Denali Outdoor Center** (© **888/303-1925** or 907/683-1925; www. denalioutdoorcenter.com) is a professional operation, offering rafting trips and instruction in river techniques. Several other firms compete and you can shop around, but I've been impressed by DOC's strong safety ethic. The firm also offers self-paddled inflatable kayaks, popular with those who want to take an active hand in their float. It is located 2½ miles north of the park entrance at Otto Lake Road, at Mile 247 of the Parks Highway, and also has an office right in Glitter Gulch. Whoever you go with, plan a shower afterward—the silt in the river water will stick to your skin and hair.

HORSEBACK RIDING

There is no riding in the park itself, but various companies offer rides in similar terrain outside the Park's boundaries. One- to 2-hour rides cost from $65 to $95. Among the operators are **Denali Saddle Safaris** (© **907/683-1200;** www.denalisaddlesafaris. com), which also offers pack trips and extended journeys.

7 Where to Stay

PARK SERVICE CAMPGROUNDS

I've explained how to make camping reservations in section 2 of this chapter, under "The Reservations System." Note that reservation fees and entrance fees may be added to camping fees. Only Riley Creek Campground is open after September (water is off in winter). The rest reopen when the snow is gone in May, except Wonder Lake, which opens in June. I have noted where RVs are permitted in the description of each campground. There are no RV hookups at any campground in the park.

CAR-ACCESSIBLE CAMPGROUNDS

In addition to these, see **Teklanika River** under "Bus-Accessible Campgrounds," below; you can drive to it as long as your stay is at least 3 nights.

Riley Creek   This large campground right across the road from the visitor center is best for those who want to be in the middle of things. It's near the Riley Creek Mercantile, with its showers, laundry, Internet access, and sewage dump station. The free front-country shuttle connects the campground with other facilities. Reservations are relatively easy to get. Sites are wooded with small birch and spruce, and they're adequately separated, but this isn't exactly wilderness camping. Twenty-seven walk-in sites are only for tent users without vehicles.

Near the visitor center. 151 sites; RVs or tents. $19 vehicle sites; $12 walk-in sites. Campfires allowed; flush toilets.

Savage River   On the taiga—the thin spruce forest and tundra—this is a wonderful campground with unforgettable views. Campers can wander from their sites on some of the park's best hikes. This is the only campground you can readily drive to that's away from the activity at the park entrance. There is no telephone.

On Denali Park Rd., 13 miles from entrance. 33 sites; RVs and cars or tents. $18 per site. Campfires allowed; flush toilets.

Tips Keeping Clean at Denali

The only showers within the park are at **Riley Creek Mercantile,** the store near the Riley Creek Campground, which also has laundry machines and other services. You pay by the shower, so there's no coin-operated timer to feed. You can also wash your clothes and shower at **McKinley RV and Campground** in Healy, covered below under "Commercial Campgrounds." The larger park campgrounds have the typical cold-water bathrooms found in the national parks, while others have vault toilets.

BUS-ACCESSIBLE CAMPGROUNDS

To use these campgrounds, you'll need a camper ticket on the shuttle bus, which costs $24 for adults, half-price ages 15 to 17, free ages 14 and under. There are no businesses and no phones beyond the park entrance area; you must bring in everything you need. Wildlife management concerns sometimes close these campgrounds unexpectedly.

Sanctuary River & Igloo These two small, primitive campgrounds offer a back-country experience away from cars. You can't reserve sites in advance; permits are available only in person at the visitor center when you arrive. Igloo has been closed for several years, but the park hopes to reopen it someday.

On Denali Park Rd., Sanctuary River Mile 23, Igloo Mile 34. 7 sites each; tents only. $9 per site. No campfires; stoves permitted; chemical toilets.

Teklanika River This is the only car campground beyond the checkpoint on the Park Road. To hold down traffic, the park service requires campers to keep their vehicles in place for 3 nights. In the past couple of years, tents have not been allowed here because wolves in the area were showing too much interest; at this writing, that policy still stands. Sites are among the small trees of the boreal forest. The big advantage of staying here is that you begin the morning much closer to the heart of the park, cutting the time you have to spend on the bus. You can buy one bus ticket for the regular price and use it for your entire 3-night stay. That makes Teklanika a good base to really explore different areas of the park in varying kinds of weather.

On Denali Park Rd., 29 miles from entrance; access by camper bus, or drive in with a minimum 3-night stay. 53 sites; RVs only, no tents. $16 per site. Campfires allowed; flush toilets.

Wonder Lake It takes almost 6 hours to get here on the bus, but this campground by placid Wonder Lake, at the foot of Mount McKinley, puts you in the most beautiful and coveted area of the park. Set among a patch of spruce trees on the mountain side of the lake, the sites can be tough to get. The mosquitoes can be horrendous.

On Denali Park Rd., 85 miles from entrance. 28 sites; tents only. $16 per site. No campfires; stoves permitted; flush toilets.

COMMERCIAL CAMPGROUNDS

There are several commercial campgrounds in the general vicinity of the park entrance, although none in walking distance. **Denali Grizzly Bear Cabins and Campground** (© 866/583-2696 or 907/683-2696; www.denaligrizzlybear.com) is about 7 miles south of the park entrance at Mile 231.1 of the Parks Highway. Some sites sit on an exposed hillside, while others are among small trees. Small cabins and tent cabins dot the property as well; they range from $59 without a bathroom to $248 for a unit with a stove and bathroom. There are coin-operated showers. Tent sites are $20 for up to four people, with electrical and water hookups $6 more. (The hotel on the property is described on p. 368.)

A campground with birch trees and attractive sites is 10 miles north of the park, in Healy. **McKinley RV and Campground,** at Mile 248.4 on the Parks Highway (© 800/478-2562 or 907/683-2379; www.mtaonline.net/~rvcampak), has a deli and espresso bar, a gas station, a token-operated laundry, and hot showers. Basic tent sites are $20, full hookups $31. The campground is operated by Denali Park Resorts, which is owned by ARAMARK.

HOTELS

Patterns of land ownership and the uncontrolled development around Denali have led to a hodgepodge of roadside hotels, cabins, lodges, campgrounds, and restaurants in pockets arrayed along more than 20 miles of the Parks Highway. There are rooms of good quality in each of the pockets, but the going rates vary widely. The most expensive rooms, and the first booked, are in the immediate vicinity of the park entrance. Next are the hotels south of the park. Both these areas are entirely seasonal. The best deals are in **Healy,** 12 miles north of the park, where you can find a room for $50 less than a comparable room near the park entrance. You can find a few links to B&B websites through the **Healy Chamber of Commerce** (www.denalichamber.com; click "Directory"). If you don't have a car, Healy is not convenient; in that case, stay nearer the park entrance. The other choices are **Talkeetna,** the back door to the park (described in section 10 of this chapter), or a wilderness lodge in the **Kantishna** area or outside the park (see section 11 of this chapter). Despite their high prices, rooms can be hard to find at the peak of the season, and it's wise to book ahead.

NEAR THE PARK

This area, known formally as Nenana Canyon or more commonly as Glitter Gulch, extends about a mile north of the park entrance on the Parks Highway. Large, luxurious hotels dominate the area. Owned by the Princess and Holland American cruise lines, each hotel has superb rooms and public areas that were rebuilt in grand style within the last few years. Objectively the best lodgings in the area, I give them brief mention mainly because they serve package-tour passengers, nearly to the exclusion of other guests. The giants are the **Denali Princess Lodge,** Mile 238.5, Parks Highway (© **800/426-0500** reservations, 907/683-2282 local; www.princesslodges.com), and the **McKinley Chalet Resort,** Mile 239.1, Parks Highway (book through Doyon/ ARAMARK Joint Venture, under "Visitor Information," earlier). Rack rates are high at each of these places, but you usually don't have to pay them. You can stay for much less if you arrive on one of the days when the flow of cruise-ship passengers is down, or early or late in the season, or if you book one of their packages. Good deals are to be had there as packages with the Alaska Railroad, or out of peak season.

At one time, the canyon contained a variety of smaller locally owned hotels catering to independent travelers, but the extraordinary value of the property and ever-growing flow of cruise ship passengers has led to consolidation of lodgings, campgrounds, shops, restaurants, and other businesses into the hands of the two main cruise lines (which are, in reality, only two arms of the same corporation, Carnival), and ARAMARK, the park concessionaire, which operates under the name Denali Park Resorts outside park boundaries.

All of the hotels in this area are open only during the tourist season, roughly from May 15 to September 15.

Denali Bluffs Hotel ⍟ A series of 12 buildings on a steep mountainside looks down on the Nenana Canyon area from above the highway. The light, tastefully decorated rooms have two double beds and good amenities, and those on the upper floor have vaulted ceilings and balconies with great views. There's little to explain the rates, however, than the overheated Denali market. The courtesy van will take you anywhere in the area. ARAMARK manages the hotel and the 154-room **Grande Denali Lodge,** which perches impossibly high above the Nenana Canyon and charges $30 more for the view. Use caution and observe the mirrors at the switchbacks on the gravel road up from the highway. The information below is for Denali Bluffs, but the toll-free number and website are good for either.

Mile 238.4, Parks Hwy. (Mailing address: 241 W. Ship Creek Ave., Anchorage, AK 99501). © **866/683-8500** or 907/683-8500. Fax 907/258-3668. www.denalialaska.com. 112 units. $219 double. Extra person $20. AE, DISC, MC, V. **Amenities:** 2 restaurants; tour desk; courtesy van; coin-op laundry. *In room:* Satellite TV, coffeemaker.

Denali Crow's Nest Log Cabins ⚑ Perched in five tiers on the side of Sugarloaf Mountain above the canyon area, looking down on Horseshoe Lake and the other, larger hotels, the regularly updated cabins are roomy and comfortable, especially those on the 100 and 200 levels. A log cabin and the warmth of the Crofoot family create a truer Alaskan feeling than the modern, standard rooms that have filled the canyon, and the rates are quite reasonable for the area (believe it or not). You spend a lot of time climbing stairs, however, and the rooms have shower enclosures, not tubs. All rooms are nonsmoking. The restaurant, **The Overlook Bar and Grill,** is recommended separately under "Where to Dine," below.

Mile 238.5, Parks Hwy. (P.O. Box 70), Denali National Park, AK 99755. © **888/917-8130** or 907/683-2723. Fax 907/683-2323. www.denalicrowsnest.com. 39 cabins. High season $169 cabin for 2; low season $109 cabin for 2. Extra person $10. MC, V. **Amenities:** Restaurant; bar; outdoor hot tub; tour desk; courtesy van. *In room:* No phone.

IN HEALY

Healy is 10 miles north of the park entrance, but a world away. It's a year-round community with an economy based partly on a coal mine. It sits in a large, windy valley with a few patches of stunted trees and big, open spaces of tundra. There are hotels and B&Bs with rooms well below the cost of those near the park, and most businesses stay open in the winter when the rest of the region shuts down tight. They say the water tastes better, too. On the downside, you need a car to stay in Healy. Besides the lodgings listed below, **Dome Home Bed & Breakfast** (© **800/683-1239** or 907/683-1239; www.denalidomehome.com) is a neat place, a huge house in a geodesic dome. The seven rooms are $145 double in summer and have many amenities.

Denali Touch of Wilderness Bed and Breakfast Inn ⚑ This special inn has won a place in the hearts of people of this remote region, who congregate for retreats, quilting, wedding rehearsals, and the like. Visitors will find immaculate rooms, all with private bathrooms and phones, in one large building, decorated in a Victorian-tinged country theme. The common areas most memorably create the inn's warm feeling, however—large sitting rooms with expansive views on the nearby Alaska Range, a library of Alaskana, and a selection of movies for the TV. The inn has Wi-Fi and a free shared guest computer as well, and an outdoor Jacuzzi on an attractive deck. The location is away from the noisy highway, about 3 miles out in the country on Stampede Road. The hosts serve fabulous breakfasts from 7 to 9am.

Mile 2.9, Stampede Rd. (P.O. Box 397), Healy, AK 99743. © **800/683-2459** or 907/683-2459. www.touchof wildernessbb.com. 9 rooms. High season $180 double; low season $85 double. Extra person $20. AE, DISC, MC, V. Rates include full breakfast. **Amenities:** Outdoor Jacuzzi; Wi-Fi and computer; laundry service. *In room:* No phone.

Earthsong Lodge ⚑⚑ *Value* This place is well off the beaten path, but it's worth the trip to stay in an authentically Alaskan dwelling and meet interesting people, year-round residents Jon and Karin Nierenberg. Guests gather in the main lodge, with its library, living room, and piano. There's a coffeehouse, Henry's, serving breakfast and dinner and packing sack lunches. The lodge and individual cabins are all solid log construction. The cabins, with one or two bedrooms, have quilts on the beds and other cozy features, as well as private bathrooms (these are operational only in the summer; in the off season, guests use a shower house). Outside is the windy open tundra with sweeping views of the Alaska Range. In the evening, a naturalist puts on a slide show. In the winter they offer dog sledding, and in the summer, rides in a dog cart and kennel tours. The lodge is 17 miles north of Denali National Park, 4 miles down the scenic Stampede Road.

Stampede Trail, off the Parks Hwy. at Mile 251 (P.O. Box 89), Healy, AK 99743. © **907/683-2863**. Fax 907/683-2868. www.earthsonglodge.com. 12 cabins. Summer $135–$175 double; winter $75–$85 double. Extra person 19 and over $10, ages 12–18 $5, 11 and younger free. DISC, MC, V. **Amenities:** Restaurant (coffeehouse). *In room:* Wi-Fi, coffeemaker, hair dryer.

Motel Nord Haven ���� This fresh little gray hotel with a red roof has large, immaculate rooms, each with one or two queen-size beds. They're equal to the best standard rooms in the Denali Park area and a lot less expensive. Bill and Patsy Nordmark offer free continental breakfast in the summer, and newspapers, coffee, tea, hot chocolate, free Wi-Fi with a guest computer in a common area, and a sitting room with a collection of Alaska books. The rooms, decorated with Alaskan art and oak trim, all have interior entrances and have been smoke-free since their construction. Up to four people can stay in the rooms with two beds for the price of a double. There are three kitchenette units. The Nordmarks pack sack lunches for $10.

Mile 249.5, Parks Hwy. (P.O. Box 458), Healy, AK 99743. © **800/683-4501** or 907/683-4500. Fax 907/683-4503. www.motelnordhaven.com. 28 units. Summer $131–$157; spring/fall $94–$104; winter $80–$85. AE, DISC, MC, V. **Amenities:** Computer. *In room:* TV, Wi-Fi.

SOUTH OF THE PARK

Lodgings south of the park are in widely separated pockets of private land concentrated 7 and 14 miles south of the park. (Anything south of that is covered with Talkeetna, in section 10 of this chapter.) I've listed a few in detail below, but you may also want to try **Denali Cabins,** Mile 229, Parks Highway (© **877/233-6254** or 907/376-1992; www.denali-cabins.com).

Cedar Hotel at Denali Grizzly Bear Resort ��� The owner of the adjoining campground (Denali Grizzly Bear, p. 365) opened the hotel in 2006, producing comfortable, modern rooms in three buildings standing right over the Nenana River with the highway mostly out of view. You can hear the water from your bed or emerge on a small deck to enjoy the view (and the company of other guests, who are an arm's length away). Rooms are decorated in a rustic Alaskan motif with lots of cedar. They don't have phones.

Mile 231.1 Parks Hwy. (P.O. Box 7), Denali National Park, AK 99755. © **866/583-2696** or 907/683-2696. www.denali grizzlybear.com. 54 rooms. High season $179 double; low season $149 double. Extra person $10. DISC, MC, V. **Amenities:** Internet access in common area (fee). *In room:* TV, coffeemaker, no phone.

Denali Mountain Morning Hostel and Lodge *Value* ��� This exceptional hostel offers cozy accommodations in an octagonal log building, as well as support for forays into the park. The well-stocked store and equipment-rental operation offer everything needed for a backpacking trip, and their free shuttle runs to the park entrance four times a day. Accommodations include hostel bunks, private rooms, or separate private cabins, all advantageously priced. All guests use the shared bathhouse and have access to a fully equipped kitchen and the Internet, which carries an additional fee. The hostel is near McKinley Creekside Cafe and the Perch.

Mile 224.5, Parks Hwy. (P.O. Box 208), Denali National Park, AK 99755. (✆ **907/683-7503**. www.hostelalaska.com. 3 private rooms, 3 private cabins. Bunk $25 adult, $19 children 12 and under; private room $65 double; cabin $75 double. Extra adult $10; extra child ages 5–12 $5; extra child under 5 free. 2-night minimum in private rooms and cabins. DISC, MC, V. **Amenities:** Internet access in common area (for a fee); shared kitchen. *In room:* No phone.

Denali River Cabins 🐾🐾   These cedar cabins arrayed on a maze of boardwalks above the Nenana River are fresh and well appointed. Unlike some accommodations outside Denali, they have an outdoorsy, national park feel, lent in part by the riverside location. They have shower stalls, not tubs, and lack closets. They do have phones. The cabins on the river, with decks over the water, are $30 more. The sauna has a picture window overlooking the river. Ride the free Denali Park Resorts shuttle to the park entrance and rail depot. Don't confuse this place with Denali Cabins.

Mile 231.1, Parks Hwy. (P.O. Box 210), Denali National Park, AK 99755. (Winter mailing address: 1 Doyon Place, Suite 200, Fairbanks, AK 99701.) (✆ **800/230-7275** or 907/683-8000. Fax 907/683-8095. (Winter (✆ **907/459-2121**; fax 907/459-2160.) www.seedenali.com. 54 cabins. High season $149–$199 cabin for 2; low season $119–$199 cabin for 2. Extra adult $10; free for children under 11. AE, DISC, MC, V. **Amenities:** Restaurant; bar; sauna; tour desk; coinop laundry. *In room:* TV.

McKinley Creekside Cabins 🐾   These cozy cabins are right by the highway and the pleasant cafe of the same name (covered below), but you would never know it, thanks to how they are situated in the woods on the banks of Carlo Creek. Cabins are decorated in subdued tones and have decks and nice private bathrooms, and some have refrigerators and microwaves. The decoration stresses rustic, Northern themes, with log bed-posts made by a local craftsman. There are communal spots for visiting around barbecues and fire pits, some at the river's edge. Cabins have Wi-Fi but no TV or telephone.

Mile 224, Parks Hwy. (P.O. Box 89), Denali National Park, AK 99755. (✆ **888/5DENALI** or 907/683-2277. www. mckinleycreeksidecabins.com. 6 units, 24 cabins. High season $125–$199 unit for 2–4; low season $99–$159 unit for 2–4. Extra person $5. DISC, MC, V. Closed Oct–Apr. **Amenities:** Restaurant; barbecue. *In room:* Wi-Fi, fridge (in some), microwave (in some), coffeemaker, no phone.

The Perch 💰   In the trees along rushing Carlo Creek, 13 miles south of the park entrance, cabins range from large, modern units with private bathrooms to cozy, if spartan, A-frames with lofts that share a bathhouse. Two cabins have kitchens. There's a sense of privacy and of being out in the woods along the wooden and gravel walkways. The Perch is a good value, open year-round, which will be most appealing to budget travelers and those who enjoy a few rough edges when they visit an outdoor destination such as Denali. The restaurant and bar, set atop a steep hill, are described below under "Where to Dine"; down on the highway level, their Panorama Pizza Pub is a local gathering place.

Mile 224, Parks Hwy. (P.O. Box 53), Denali National Park, AK 99755. (✆ **888/322-2523** or (✆/fax 907/683-2523. www.denaliperchresort.com. 22 cabins, 8 with shared bathroom. $85 cabin for 2 with shared bathroom; $125 cabin for 2 with private bathroom. Extra adult $16. Rates include breakfast. AE, DISC, MC, V. **Amenities:** 2 restaurants; bar; tour desk. *In room:* Kitchen (in some).

WILDERNESS LODGES

For those who can afford it, a lodge allows you to experience real wilderness in complete comfort. For understandable reasons, lodges with any view of Mount McKinley or proximity to the park call themselves Denali lodges. Some are actually within the park's boundaries in the old gold-mining inholding of the Kantishna District, while others are reached only by air and lie well outside the park. In either case, a wilderness lodge experience revolves around the lodge and its immediate surroundings, not the park activities described earlier, so I've grouped them in section 11, later in this chapter.

8 Where to Dine

Since Denali is entirely seasonal, it lacks the range of inexpensive family restaurants that develop in year-round communities. While you may find reasonably priced food in Healy, to the north, or Carlo Creek, to the south (see below), near the park most meals are overpriced by 25% to 50% due to the short season and captive audience.

NEAR THE PARK ENTRANCE

You'll have no trouble finding an espresso at Denali. The large hotels in the canyon each have fine dining and casual restaurants; I've described the best in detail below. There are plenty of spots for a low-key meal or takeout. The **Courtyard Cafe** at the McKinley Chalet Resort serves a buffet and has a children's menu. **Lynx Creek Pizza** is something of a tradition but inconsistent from year to year. For takeout sandwiches and a great cheese steak, it's hard to beat **Bub's Subs,** located in the Rainbow Mall, next door to the Lynx Creek Store. You can eat and people-watch in the casual seating area.

You can't miss the homemade highway frontage of the hip **Denali Salmon Bake** (© **907/683-2733;** www.thebakerocks.com) in Glitter Gulch. Although extremely casual, the staff is friendly, led by owners who are involved in the community. It's fun and a hot spot for live music as well. Check the website for a calendar of who is playing and the amount of the cover charge. They'll also come to pick you up and drive you back to your hotel. The food is tasty and relatively inexpensive, including Tex-Mex selections, king crab, and grilled reindeer in addition to the grilled salmon.

Nenana View Bar & Grill ☆ PIZZA/STEAK/SANDWICHES   This attractive restaurant in the McKinley Chalet Resort has an open kitchen to watch the cooking and outdoor seating overlooking the river. They serve some of the best pizza in the area and great fire-grilled steaks.

Mile 238.9, Parks Hwy., in McKinley Chalet Resort. © **907/683-8200**. All items $12–$28. AE, DC, DISC, MC, V. May–Sept daily 11am–2:30pm and 5–11pm. Bar until 1am. Closed off season.

The Overlook Bar and Grill ☆ BURGERS/STEAK/SEAFOOD   This fun, noisy place has the feel of a classic bar and grill, with a vaulted ceiling of rough-cut lumber and a spectacular view of the Nenana Canyon. There are two dining rooms, one with the bar and another behind a glass partition that is quieter and has tablecloths. A huge variety of craft beers is available, with several on tap. At times, I've gotten excellent fare here. Call © **907/683-2723** for courtesy transportation from all area hotels.

Mile 238.5, Parks Hwy. © **907/683-2641**. Lunch main courses $9–$15; dinner main courses $16–$30. MC, V. Daily 11am–11pm. Bar until midnight. Closed mid-Sept to mid-May. Up the hill above the Denali Canyon area.

The Summit Restaurant ☆☆ STEAK/SEAFOOD   This is a terrific place for a special night of dining out right near the park. First, there's the dining room, perched on the edge of the Nenana Canyon, where you can watch rafters float by during your meal. Then there's the food and service, which are up to Princess Tours's excellent standards—steak and salmon, the usual choices for Alaska tourists—prepared expertly. For something a bit more casual, the Basecamp Bistro is in the same building.

In the Denali Princess Lodge, Mile 238.5, Parks Hwy. © **907/683-2282**. Reservations recommended. Dinner main courses $17–$37. AE, DC, DISC, MC, V. Summer daily 5–10:30am, 11am–2pm, and 5–10pm. Basecamp Bistro daily 11am–midnight.

IN HEALY

These places are 12 miles north of the park, so you will need a car.

Black Diamond Grill ✿✿ STEAK/SEAFOOD/ITALIAN   A unique 9-hole golf course lies amid the mountains and rolling taiga north of the park. The associated restaurant produced excellent meals from a menu mostly influenced by Northern Italian cookery. For lunch, sandwich choices include a pesto chicken hoagie for $7.50, and for dinner there is halibut in parchment with fresh rosemary and garlic for $20. Although not as perfect as at the best restaurants in Anchorage, the cuisine is memorable and satisfying. The dining room is light and cheery, with pine furniture and flowers on the table. Children will enjoy the minigolf course or wagon rides.

Mile 247, Parks Hwy. ✆ 907/683-4653. Lunch $7.50–$9; dinner main courses $14–$24. AE, DISC, MC, V. Daily 7am–11pm. Closed off season. Take the highway north 10 miles, and then turn left at Otto Lake Rd.

The Lunch Box *Value* TAKEOUT   This trailer produces good, inexpensive food in Asian, Italian, Mexican, and deli styles, with low-carb choices, to take on a picnic or eat back at the room. The teriyaki rice bowl and spicy beef salad are delicious. They're also famous for the ribs produced on Friday nights. A hearty box lunch is also available to pick up the night before for a day out in the park.

Healy Spur Rd. ✆ 907/683-6833. Lunch $3–$10. No credit cards. May–Aug Mon–Fri 11am–2pm and 4–7pm. Closed holidays and off season. Just off the Parks Hwy. across the street from the Mountain View Store.

SOUTH OF THE PARK

McKinley Creekside Cafe ✿ *Kids* STEAK/SEAFOOD/SANDWICHES   This cozy and friendly spot in the Carlo Creek area is a favorite of the locals. You can dine on steak or baked salmon with brown sugar, apples, and toasted almonds for around $20, or order a main-course salad or burger for around $9. The food is consistently good, including breakfast, and craft brews and wine are served. There is a playground outside and a kid's menu. They also pack substantial sack lunches for the park shuttle-bus ride.

Mile 224, Parks Hwy. ✆ 907/683-2277. www.mckinleycreeksidecabins.com. Lunch $6–$10; dinner $8–$21. DISC, MC, V. Summer daily 6am–10pm.

The Perch/Panorama Pizza Pub ✿ STEAK/SEAFOOD/PIZZA/DELI   An odd, knoblike hill gives the Perch its name (the attractive cabins described above sit below the restaurant). It's a friendly, family-run place serving a straightforward steak and Alaskan seafood menu—they don't try anything fancy, just good ingredients done right. The home-baked bread is noteworthy. The dining room is light, with well-spaced tables and big picture windows on three sides. Down on the highway level, the Panorama Pizza Pub is a hot spot for pizza and also includes a bakery/deli that packs lunches in cloth tote bags for the park bus. You can often hear local musicians playing there in the evening.

Mile 224, Parks Hwy., 13 miles south of the park. ✆ 888/322-2523 or 907/683-2523. www.denaliperchresort.com. The Perch: Dinner main courses $14–$40. AE, DISC, MC, V. Summer daily 6am–9pm, 5–9pm; winter hours vary. Panorama Pizza Pub: Pizza $15–$25. AE, DISC, MC, V. Summer daily 11am–midnight. Closed winter.

229 Parks Restaurant and Tavern ✿✿ ECLECTIC   The name comes from the milepost, which puts the restaurant in a quiet area about 8 miles south of the park entrance, where it occupies a beautiful post-and-beam building. The food created excitement as soon as Laura and Land Cole opened it. Laura is a professionally trained chef and veteran of the Marx Brothers Cafe, one of Alaska's best restaurants, and she cooked for 12 years at Camp Denali, the park's most famous lodge, which is owned by family. Whenever possible, she uses organic ingredients and local produce—eggs are naturally nested by free-range chickens. The menu changes daily and has included main-course items such as tenderloin filet, lemon pasta with asparagus, venison chops, and, of course, salmon. A sweet potato soup with king crab meat was fabulous. The appetizer list is long and interesting, including spring rolls second to none. Breakfast is coffeehouse fare, such as quiche, granola, and fruit. Locals keep the place busy even in the winter, but they close at 1pm on winter Sunday so everyone in the community can go play hockey on Deneki Lakes.

Mile 229, Parks Hwy. ⓒ 907/683-2567. www.229parks.com. Reservations recommended. Dinner $15–$33. MC, V. Summer daily 7–11am and 5–10pm; winter Fri–Sat 9am–10pm, Sun 9am–1pm.

9 Denali Nightlife

The main evening event is the concessionaire's **Cabin Nite Dinner Theater,** at the McKinley Chalet Resort (ⓒ **800/276-7234** or 907/683-8200), a professionally produced musical revue about a gold rush–era woman who ran a roadhouse in Kantishna. You can buy the $55 tickets (half-price ages 2–12) virtually anywhere in the area. The actors, singing throughout the evening, stay in character to serve big platters of food to diners sitting at long tables, and do a good job of building a rowdy, happy atmosphere for adults and kids.

Princess Cruises and Tours puts on its own evening show, *The Music of Denali,* at the Denali Princess Lodge. The performance lasts an hour; with dinner, it lasts 2 hours. Tickets are for sale at the hotel's tour desk (ⓒ **800/426-0500** or 907/683-2282) for $49 (half-price ages 6–12). The show without the meal is $20.

10 Talkeetna: Back Door to Denali

Talkeetna, a historic and funky little town with a sense of humor but not much happening, slept soundly from its decline around World War I until about a decade ago. Now there are paved streets (both of them), a fancy National Park Service building, a larger railroad depot, and two large luxury lodges. It seems that while Talkeetna slumbered in a time capsule, an explosion of visitors was happening at Denali National Park. Now, not entirely voluntarily, Talkeetna has been enveloped in that boom.

As a threshold to the park, Talkeetna has significant pros and cons that you should take into account. On the positive side, it's closer to Anchorage, the development is much more interesting and authentic than that at the park entrance, there's lots to do outdoors, and Mount McKinley is seen more frequently, because of both geography and weather. On the negative side, a big minus: You can't get into the park from here without a long drive or a flight. That may mean you miss the dramatic scenery, easy backcountry access, and unique wildlife viewing on the park road.

The town dates from the gold rush and has many charming log and clapboard buildings. With 15 sites of historic note, the entire downtown area has been listed on the National Register of Historic Places. You can spend several hours looking at two small museums and meeting people in the 2-block main street; then go out on the Talkeetna or Susitna rivers for rafting, a jet-boat ride, or fishing; or take a flightseeing trip to the national park.

ESSENTIALS

GETTING THERE   Talkeetna lies on a 13-mile spur road that branches from the Parks Highway 99 miles north of Anchorage and 138 miles south of the park entrance.

The **Alaska Railroad** (© 800/544-0552 or 907/265-2494; www.alaskarailroad. com) serves Talkeetna daily on its runs to Denali National Park during the summer and weekly in the winter. (See section 2 of this chapter for additional details.) The summer fare from Anchorage to Talkeetna is $80 one-way for adults, half-price for children, for basic service.

The **Talkeetna Shuttle Service** (© 907/733-1725 or 907/373-8548; www.denali central.com) runs to and from Anchorage. Fares are $65 one-way, $125 round-trip, but were expected to rise.

It's possible to stay in Talkeetna but do the Denali National Park shuttle bus ride and other park activities by flying there for the day. **Talkeetna Aero Services** (© 888/ 733-2899 or 907/733-2899; www.talkeetnaaero.com) offers daily round-trips for this purpose during the summer with a flightseeing tour circling Mt. McKinley en route. They charge $350 as a package with ground transfers, a bus tour, and a box lunch.

VISITOR INFORMATION   Built to serve people aiming to climb Mount McKinley, the **Denali National Park Talkeetna Ranger Station,** downtown Talkeetna (P.O. Box 588), Talkeetna, AK 99676 (© **907/733-2231;** www.nps.gov/dena), makes a fascinating stop for anyone curious about mountaineering. Inside the handsome structure, a large sitting room contains a river-rock fireplace, climbing books, and pictures of the mountain—it's like an old-fashioned explorers' club. Fascinating records open for inspection cover the history of McKinley climbs. Rangers are on hand to answer questions, too. It's open May through Labor Day daily from 8am to 6pm, winter Monday through Friday from 8am to 4:30pm.

The **Talkeetna/Denali Visitor Center,** with two offices, in a tiny cabin at the intersection of the Parks Highway and Talkeetna Spur Road, and on Main Street (P.O. Box 688), Talkeetna, AK 99676 (© **800/660-2688** or 907/733-2641; www.alaskan.com/ talkeetnadenali), is a commercial center belonging to a local flight service and providing brochures, information, and advice while earning commissions from bookings. It's the handiest commercial information stop in the region. The center is open daily from 8am to 8pm in summer, and they respond to inquiries year-round with free trip-planning help.

FAST FACTS: Talkeetna

Bank A local credit union is near the Parks Highway, at Mile 1 on the Talkeetna Spur Road. There is no bank in the town center, but an ATM is on Main Street at Nagley's General Store.

Hospital Sunshine Community Health Center, Mile 4.4 on the Talkeetna Spur Road (© **907/733-2273**).

Internet Access Free for up to 20 minutes at the **Talkeetna Public Library,** at Mile 13 of the Talkeetna Spur Road, just across the tracks.

Police For nonemergencies, call the **Alaska State Troopers** at © **907/733-2256.** The station is at Mile 1 of the Talkeetna Spur Road, near the highway.

Post Office Go to the town center, near the intersection of Talkeetna Spur Road and Main Street.

Taxes There is no **sales tax. Bed tax** in the area is 5%.

SPECIAL EVENTS   The **Talkeetna Moose Dropping Festival,** held over the second weekend in July, is the big community event of the year; this fair is finishing its third decade as a fundraiser for the Talkeetna Historical Society (ⓒ **907/733-2487**). The named event doesn't involve dropping moose, as an aggrieved animal lover once complained, but dropping moose droppings. Another event, the Mountain Mother Contest, open only to mothers, is a race of Bush skills, including splitting wood and diapering a baby.

EXPLORING THE TOWN

Talkeetna is famous for its laid-back atmosphere and outdoors, not for "attractions," but there are several places to stop in to get the sense of the place. One is the ranger station mentioned above under "Visitor Information." If you come in May or June, you're sure to meet many international mountain climbers; you'll have no difficulty picking them out (see "Climbing Mount McKinley" in section 5 of this chapter). Along Main Street are shops where artists and craftspeople often can be found at work.

The **Talkeetna Historical Society Museum,** in four buildings on the Village Airstrip a half-block south of Main Street (ⓒ **907/733-2487**; www.talkeetnahistory. org), is well worth a stop. The first building contains artifacts and displays on local mining history, including engaging photographs and biographies of individual characters. The second is an attempt to re-create the old railroad depot. The third holds climbing displays and a huge scale model of Mount McKinley and the nearby mountains (don't miss it if you will fly over the mountain). The fourth is a 1916 trapper's cabin. The museum also is a handy information stop. It is open daily in summer from 10am to 6pm and generally closed in winter, although you may get lucky on a weekend. Admission is $3, free for children 12 and under.

I've found the most affecting site in town to be the **mountain climbers' memorial** at the town cemetery, near the airstrip on the east side of the railroad tracks. Besides a granite memorial of plaques for lost mountaineers, there is a small garden of monuments to many individual climbers, some in Japanese. The bodies of 34 climbers who died on the mountain have never been recovered.

GETTING OUTSIDE

FLIGHTSEEING

There is no more dramatic or memorable experience available to the typical tourist in Alaska than to fly with one of the glacier pilots who support Mount McKinley climbs. Climbers typically begin with a flight from here to the 7,200-foot level of the Kahiltna Glacier. These immense mountains grow ever larger as you fly toward them until, like a tiny insect, you fly among their miles-tall folds, watching the climbers toiling on the ice below you. I was simply speechless.

Several operators with long experience offer the flights. The least expensive excursions cost around $160 and approach McKinley's south face. If at all possible—and if the weather is good—buy an extended tour that circles the mountain and flies over its glaciers, for $190 to $225 per person. Best of all, arrange a landing on the mountain itself, just as the climbers do. The Don Sheldon Amphitheater on the Ruth Glacier is a stunning spot high on McKinley; only after you stand there do you realize the incredible scale of what you have seen from above. In the past, this was not possible from mid-July through August, as the snow was too soft for the ski planes to land on the glaciers, but air taxis using different equipment and different landing areas have often been able to land all summer in recent years. These landings are usually treated as add-ons to the tours mentioned above, for an additional price of around $65 to $75 per person.

Should you reserve ahead or wait to see the weather? It used to be you could reliably walk in and grab a seat, but the popularity of these flights now makes reservations advisable. That's the best way to get a guaranteed price, too; otherwise, prices sometimes depend on the number of passengers aboard the plane. If you do decide on the walk-in approach, make your appearance early in the morning.

A number of air taxi companies offer these flights, all operating out of the Talkeetna airport, including these two: **Talkeetna Air Taxi** (© **800/533-2219** or 907/733-2218; www.talkeetnaair.com) and **Talkeetna Aero Services** (© **800/660-2688** or 907/733-2899; www.talkeetna-aero.com).

FISHING & JET BOAT TOURS

Talkeetna is at the confluence of the big Talkeetna and Big Susitna rivers. **Mahay's Riverboat Service** (© **800/736-2210** or 907/733-2223; www.mahaysriverboat.com) is a large guide service, with 2-hour tours on a unique 51-foot jet boat for $55 per person, operating several times a day from a dock near the public boat launch on the Talkeetna River. Owner Steve Mahay is legendary, the only person ever to shoot Devil's Canyon in a jet boat. He offers fishing charters as well.

RAFTING

Talkeetna River Guides, on Main Street (© **800/353-2677** or 907/733-2677; www.talkeetnariverguides.com), offers a 2-hour wildlife river-rafting tour, without white water, over 9 miles of the Talkeetna three times a day for $69 adults, $49 children 10 and under. They also offer guided longer rafting expeditions.

WHERE TO STAY & DINE

There are good restaurants at each of the lodgings listed here. One other place stands out, **Café Michele,** in a quaint little house at the corner of Talkeetna Spur Road and 2nd Street (© **907/733-5300**). It's a classy little bistro, serving sandwiches on homemade focaccia bread for lunch, and dinner entrees ranging up to $29. Save room for dessert, as the baking is exceptional—Michelle even bakes the area's wedding cakes. It's easy to find a burger or sandwich on Main Street.

A large **campground** is at the boat launch (cross the railroad tracks to the airport and then turn left).

Mt. McKinley Princess Lodge *&&* The Princess Cruise Line built the main lodge building to take advantage of a striking view of the mountain, only 42 miles away as the crow flies. The property isn't near any town—100 miles south of the park entrance and about 45 road miles from Talkeetna—but, like a resort, they offer everything you need on-site and a full set of activities, including a short network of trails. The design and decoration are an inspired modernization of the classic national park style. There are several dining choices, including a steak and seafood place, a cafe, and a pizzeria.

Mile 133.1, Parks Hwy., Denali State Park, AK 99683. ⓒ 800/426-0500 or 907/733-2900. Fax 907/733-2922. www.
princesslodges.com. 334 units. Summer $239 double, $369 suite; spring and fall $179 double, $289 suite. AE, DC,
DISC, MC, V. Closed mid-Sept to mid-May. **Amenities:** 3 restaurants; bar; exercise room; tour desk; coin-op laundry.
In room: TV, hair dryer.

Swiss-Alaska Inn *Finds*   This is the essence of Talkeetna: a family business in the
same hands for decades where guests are made to feel like old friends among the real
old friends often found sipping coffee with the proprietor in the small restaurant.
They serve good, familiar American meals, plus a few German dishes. Most of the
rooms are decorated in light colors and, although small, are clean, comfortable, and
reasonably priced. The larger rooms in the newer building are quite preferable.

F St., near the boat launch (P.O. Box 565), Talkeetna, AK 99676. ⓒ 907/733-2424. Fax 907/733-2425. www.swiss
alaska.com. 20 units. $118 double. Extra person $10. AE, DISC, MC, V. **Amenities:** Restaurant; bar; courtesy car (to
railroad station). *In room:* TV/DVD, hair dryer.

Talkeetna Alaskan Lodge *✦✦*   The Cook Inlet Region Native corporation spared
no expense building this magnificent hotel of big timbers and river rock, but it's not
a gaudy showplace. Trim of regionally harvested birch finishes rooms and hallways in
understated geometric designs, hung with Native art. Because the hotel sits atop a
high river bluff, views from common rooms and many guest rooms take in a broad-
canvas masterpiece of the Alaska Range, with McKinley towering in the center.
Although just 2 miles from the town, the hotel feels like it's out in the wilderness.
Rooms in the main building are preferable. They're somewhat larger and have either
one king- or two queen-size beds, and the hallways connect to several sumptuous lobbies with reading areas. As much as I like the hotel, however, the rates are high.

Mile 12.5, Talkeetna Spur Rd. (Mailing address: 2525 C St., Anchorage, AK 99503). ⓒ 888/959-9590 or 907/265-
4501 reservations; 907/733-9500 at lodge. Fax 907/263-5559. www.talkeetnalodge.com. 212 units. Summer $289–$389
double; off season $149–$209 double. Extra person 12 and over $15. AE, DISC, MC, V. Closed Oct–Apr. **Amenities:**
2 restaurants (international, cafe); bar; tour desk; courtesy van. *In room:* TV, dataport, coffeemaker, hair dryer.

11 Denali Wilderness Lodges

Staying in a wilderness lodge is expensive and requires a significant commitment of
time. It doesn't make sense to spend less than 3 days, and some lodges require longer
minimum stays. Here I've listed the best lodges in the Denali region; see chapter 7 for
lodges on Kachemak Bay, near Homer.

KANTISHNA DISTRICT

The Kantishna district is an inholding of private land within Denali National Park
where gold miners staked claims before the park was created. The lodge operators who
later obtained this land gained something more valuable than gold: the opportunity
to bring visitors to the far end of the park from the entrance, as near as a vehicle can
get to Mount McKinley, without using the park's shuttle system. Hosts drive visitors
to Kantishna in their own buses or vans over the 91-mile park road. These lodges are
open only in summer.

Camp Denali/North Face Lodge *✦✦✦*   At this pioneering eco-tourism establishment, you can wake to the white monolith of Mount McKinley filling your window.
The naturalist guides here have the right to use the park road free of the shuttle system for hikes, biking, lake canoeing, bird-watching, photography sessions, and other
outdoor learning activities, all included in the substantial price. During some sessions,

nationally respected academics and other experts lead the program. All arrivals and departures are on fixed session dates of 3, 4, or 7 days and start with a picnic supper on the park road on the way out to the lodges. Each of the Camp Denali cabins has its own outhouse, and all share a central bathhouse and wonderful lodge common rooms—it has the best views and would be my first choice for anyone who can get by without his or her own flush toilet. North Face Lodge has smallish traditional rooms with private bathrooms. Each lodge has its own dining room for family-style meals. A conservation ethic pervades the operation, from the homegrown vegetables to the proprietors' efforts to preserve the natural values of private land in the park.

Kantishna (P.O. Box 67), Denali National Park, AK 99755. © 907/683-2290. Fax 907/683-1568. www.campdenali. com. 17 cabins, all with shared bathroom (Camp Denali); 15 units (North Face Lodge). $435 per person per night, double occupancy. Rates include all meals and guided activities. Minimum stay 3 nights. No credit cards. No smoking in buildings or vehicles. *In room:* No phone.

Kantishna Roadhouse 🏕🏕 This well-kept property of many buildings along Moose Creek in the old Kantishna Mining District trades on both the mining history and outdoor opportunities of the area. Some rooms are large and luxurious, while others are in smaller single cabins with lofts. The log central lodge has an attractive lobby with people coming and going—it's got more of a hotel feel and might be more attractive to an older, less active set or to families than the other lodges in the Kantishna District. It's also somewhat less expensive, has a bar, and accommodates 2-night stays. Guided hikes, fishing, interpretive programs, biking, gold panning, a daily sled dog demonstration, and the bus ride from the park entrance are included in the rate.

Kantishna District, Denali National Park (Mailing address: 1 Doyon Place, Suite 300, Fairbanks, AK 99701). © 800/ 942-7420 or 907/683-1475. Fax 907/683-1449. (Winter: © 907/459-2120; fax 907/459-2160.) www.seedenali. com. 32 units. $360 per person per night, double occupancy; $275 ages 3–11. Additional adult $275. Rates include all meals and guided activities. Minimum stay 2 nights. AE, DISC, MC, V. **Amenities:** Restaurant; bar; sauna; mountain bikes. *In room:* No phone.

Skyline Lodge 🏕 (Value Run by pilot Greg Lahaie, owner of Kantishna Air Taxi, the lodge offers a unique alternative in Denali's backcountry: a place you don't have to be a millionaire to afford. With room for only eight guests and a self-serve philosophy, it's far simpler and more casual than the full-service lodges in Kantishna and costs less than a fourth as much. Also, there's no minimum stay, and you can fly there economically with Greg. It costs $30 a day to join the family-style lunch and dinner (breakfast is already included in the price). Rooms are in cabins, each with a double or queen-size bed and a loft. Large windows overlook Moose Creek. The kitchen, TV, and other amenities are in the central lodge building. The most important amenity, however, is that you are in the heart of Denali's backcountry. No smoking.

Kantishna District (P.O. Box 46), Denali Park, AK 99755. © 907/683-1223. Fax: 907/683-1223. www.katair.com. 3 units, all with shared bathroom. $175 double. Extra person age 2 and older $50. DISC, MC, V. Rates include continental breakfast. **Amenities:** Sauna; free mountain bikes; courtesy van; TV in common area. *In room:* No phone.

A FLY-IN LODGE

Caribou Lodge 🏕🏕 There's a lot to love about this place: the location above the tree line, on its own alpine lake, miles from any other structure; the unlimited dry tundra hiking and views along the rounded ridge tops; the wildlife and the quiet. But what I love best, and what I suspect will matter most to visitors, is that it's real. This is home to Mike and Pam Nickols, the couple who personally host just three parties at a time, and for a decade they've lived out here in true Bush style, year-round, far off the grid. They guide hiking, canoeing on the lake, and watching the wildlife; in the winter, they teach guests to drive a dog team over endlessly rolling hills of snow. Mainly, a visit is a chance to experience another way of life, one that exists in few places. The accommodations are simple but comfortable, each cabin with its own outhouse and a shared shower facility. Access is by small aircraft only, on skis in winter or floats in summer; in spring and fall, when the ice on the lake is soft, it's just about impossible to get there. For rough figuring, a plane from Talkeetna costs $145 to $180 per person, but inquire to get a more exact cost.

20 miles east of Talkeetna (P.O. Box 706), Talkeetna, AK 99676. ©/fax **907/733-2163.** www.cariboulodgealaska. com. 3 cabins. $285 per person per day. Rates include all meals and guiding, and are based on double occupancy. Minimum stay 2 nights. No credit cards. **Amenities:** Restaurant (family style, included in rate); guided activities included in rate; sauna. *In room:* No phone.

9

The Alaskan Interior

A warm summer evening in a campground; a slight breeze rustling the leaves of ghostly paper birches, barely keeping the mosquitoes at bay; the sounds of children playing; a perpetual sunset rolling slowly along the northern horizon—this is Interior Alaska. You know it's time to gather up the kids, separate them according to who belongs to whom, and put them to bed; it's 11 o'clock, for heaven's sake. But it's too difficult to feel that matters, or to alter the pace of a sun-baked day that never ends, meandering on like the broad, silty rivers and empty two-lane highways. Down by the boat landing, some college kids are getting ready to start on a float in the morning. An old, white-bearded prospector wanders out of the bar and, offering his flask to the strangers, tries out a joke while swatting the bugs. "There's not a single mosquito in Alaska," he declares. He waits for the loud, jocular objections and then adds, "They're all married with big, big families." Easy laughter; then they talk about outboard motors, road work, why so many rabbits live along a certain stretch of highway. Eventually, you have to go to bed and leave the world to its pointless turning as the sun rotates back around to the east. You know it'll all be there tomorrow, just the same—the same slow-flowing rivers, the same long highways, the same vast space that can never be filled.

Interior Alaska is so large—it basically includes everything that's not on the coasts or in the Arctic—you can spend a week of hard driving and not explore it all. Or you can spend all summer floating the rivers and still have years of floating left to do before you see all the riverbanks. It's something like what the great mass of America's Midwest once must have been, perhaps a century and a half ago, when the great flatlands had been explored but not completely civilized and Huckleberry Finn could float downriver into a wilderness of adventures. As it happens, I have a friend who grew up on a homestead in the Interior and ran away from home at age 15 in that exact same fashion, floating hundreds of miles on a handmade raft, past the little river villages, cargo barges, and fishermen. During an Interior summer, nature combines its immensity with a rare sense of gentleness, patiently awaiting the next thunderstorm.

Winter is another matter. Without the regulating influence of the ocean—the same reason summers are hot—winter temperatures can often drop to –30°F or –40°F (–34°C or –40°C), and during exceptional cold snaps, even lower. Now the earth is wobbling over in the other direction, away from the sun. The long, black nights sometimes make Fairbanks, the region's dominant city, feel more like an outpost on a barren planet, far off in outer space. That's when the northern lights come, spewing swirls of color across the entire dome of the sky and crackling with electricity. Neighbors get on the phone to wake each other and, rising from bed to put on their warmest parkas and insulated boots, stand in the street, gazing straight up. Visitors lucky enough to come at such times may be watching from a steaming hot-spring tub. During the short days, they can bundle up and watch sled-dog racing or race across the wilderness themselves on snowmobiles.

Fairbanks stands second in Alaska in population, with over 80,000 in the greater area, but the Interior otherwise is without any settlements large enough to be called cities. Instead, it's defined by roads, both paved and gravel, which are strands of civilization through sparsely settled, often swampy land. Before the roads, development occurred only on the rivers, which still serve as thoroughfares for the Athabascan villages of the region. In the summer, villagers travel by boat. In the winter, the frozen rivers become highways for snowmobiles and sled-dog teams. Non-Native homesteaders and gold miners live back in the woods, too. Gold-rush history is written on the land in piles of old gravel tailings and abandoned equipment, as well as in the prettier tourist attractions and historic sites. Gold mining goes on today, in small one-man operations and huge industrial works employing hundreds, but today the economy is based more on military and other government spending, the oil industry, and, of course, tourism. You'll find warm rural hospitality along with the great vistas on these highways and perhaps a sense of slow-river laziness Huck Finn would have recognized.

1 Exploring the Interior

More than anywhere else in Alaska, the Interior is the place where having your own car provides you with the freedom to find the out-of-the-way places that give the region its character. Trains and buses run between Fairbanks and Anchorage, but that approach will show you only the larger, tourist-oriented destinations.

If you have the time and money, you may enjoy driving one of the remote gravel highways or just poking along on the paved highways between the larger towns, ready to stop and investigate the roadhouses and meet the people who live out in the middle of nowhere. You'll find them mostly friendly and often downright odd—*colorful,* to use the polite term. As I drove an abandoned highway a few years ago, I saw a hand-lettered sign advertising coffee. It wasn't your typical espresso stand, just a log cabin dozens of miles from the next-nearest building. A squinting high-plains drifter stepped out of the cabin, wearing a cowboy hat on his head and a huge revolver on his hip, and asked, "Yeah?" The coffee came from a percolator warming on the woodstove, and the proprietor and I struck up a good conversation in his dark little dwelling. He was living the life of the old-time frontier. Another favorite roadside sign, sighted on the Alaska Highway, in spray paint on plywood: SALE—EEL SKINS—

⟨Finds⟩ Rollin' on the River

Floating any of the thousands of miles of the Interior's rivers opens great swaths of wilderness. Beginners will want to take a guided trip before venturing out on their own. (See the lists of operators in chapter 2.) To plan your own trip, start with the **Alaska Public Lands Information Center** in Fairbanks (p. 386), Tok (p. 418), or Anchorage (p. 211). Among the most accessible and historic rivers in the region are the Chena, Chatanika, and Yukon (see the sections on Fairbanks and Chena Hot Springs Road, and the boxes on the Steese Highway and Dawson City in this chapter).

ANVILS—BAIT. I've always wished I'd stopped in to window-shop and meet the person who came up with that business plan.

Of course, not every mile of back road is scenic, nor are all the stops interesting. Driving a car through Alaska takes a long time, including many hours spent in dull, brushy forest, and calls for a high tolerance for greasy hamburgers and a willingness to occasionally relieve yourself in the bushes. Paved highway sections can develop frost heaves in this often-frozen land—backbreaking dips and humps caused by the freeze and thaw of the road base and ground underneath. The gravel roads generate clouds of dust and quickly fatigue drivers, and windshields and headlights often succumb to their flying rocks. For information on renting a vehicle to drive on gravel roads, see "Equipped for the Back Roads," on p. 393.

2 Fairbanks: Alaska Heartland

If the story of the founding of Fairbanks had happened anywhere else, it wouldn't be told so proudly, for the city's father was a swindler and its undignified birth contained an element of chance not usually admitted in polite society. As the popular story goes (and the historians' version is fairly close), it seems that in 1901, E. T. Barnette decided to get rich by starting a gold-mining boomtown like the others that had sprouted from Dawson City to Nome where the stampeders of 1898 sloshed back and forth across the territory from one gold find to the next. He booked passage on a river-boat going up the Tanana with his supplies to build the town, having made an under-standing with the captain that, should the vessel get stuck, he would lighten the load by getting off with the materials on the nearest bank. Unfortunately, the captain got lost. Thinking he was heading up a slough on the Tanana, he got sidetracked into the relatively small Chena River. That was where the boat got stuck and where Barnette got left, and that was where he founded Fairbanks.

Fortunately for Barnette, an Italian prospector named Felix Pedro was looking for gold in the hills around the new trading post and the next summer made a strike in the Tanana Hills, north of the Chena. On that news, Barnette dispatched his Japan-ese cook, Jujiro Wada, off to Dawson City to spread the word. Wada's story showed up in a newspaper that winter after Christmas, and a stampede of hundreds of min-ers ensued, heading toward Fairbanks in weather as cold as –50°F (–46°C). Barnette's town was a success, but the cook nearly got lynched when the stampeders found out how far he'd exaggerated the truth. Much more gold was found later, however, and half the population of Dawson City came downriver to Fairbanks. Barnette had made it big.

The town's future was ensured thanks to a political deal. Barnette did a favor for the territory's judge, James Wickersham, by naming the settlement for Wickersham's hero in Congress, Sen. Charles Fairbanks of Indiana, who later became vice president. Wickersham then moved the federal courthouse to Fairbanks from Eagle—he loaded his records on his dog sled and mushed here, establishing the camp as the region's hub. Wickersham's story is interesting, too. He was a notable explorer, Alaska's first real statesman as a nonvoting delegate to Congress, and father of the Alaska Railroad. Houses he lived in are preserved at Pioneer Park (formerly known as Alaskaland) in Fairbanks and in Juneau just up the hill from the capitol building. Barnette didn't do as well in history's eyes: He was run out of the town he founded for bank fraud.

Fairbanks is Alaska's second-largest city now, with a population of about 30,000 in the city limits and 85,000 in the greater metropolitan area, but it has never learned to

Alaska's Highways a la Carte

You won't need a detailed highway map of Alaska because Alaska doesn't have detailed highways. A triangle of paved two-lane highways connects Tok, Fairbanks, and Anchorage. From this triangle, a few routes reach to discrete destinations, and gravel roads penetrate the periphery of the Bush. Beyond a few miles of freeway around Fairbanks and Anchorage, highways all are narrow strips of asphalt or gravel through the wilderness. (See "The Roster of Rural Roads," on p. 404, for a run-down of Alaska's unpaved and minor highways.) Always fill your tank before leaving town, as gas stations are far apart. A centralized report on road conditions, construction, and weather is operated by the Alaska Department of Transportation (© 511; http://511.alaska.gov). To help readers figure driving times, I have included my estimate of reasonable average speeds on each road (without stopping). These are based purely on my experience and assume dry, daylight conditions in summer.

Alaska Highway

Route 2 from the border to Delta Junction

Average speed (Alaska section): 55 to 65 mph

Running nearly 1,400 miles from Dawson Creek, British Columbia, to Delta Junction, Alaska, a couple of hours east of Fairbanks on the Richardson Highway, this World War II road today is paved and generally easy driving. Two tiny towns lie on the Alaska portion of the road, Delta Junction and Tok. The prettiest part is on the Canadian side, in the Kluane Lake area. See section 5, later in this chapter.

Glenn Highway

Route 1 from Anchorage to Tok

Average speed: 55 to 65 mph, except 45 mph on Matanuska Glacier section

From the Alaska Highway, this is how you get to Southcentral Alaska, including Anchorage, 330 miles southwest of Tok. The northern section, from Tok to Glennallen (sometimes called the "Tok Cut-Off"), borders Wrangell–St. Elias National Park, with broad tundra and taiga broken by high, craggy peaks. Glennallen to Anchorage is even more spectacular, as the road passes through high alpine terrain and then close by the Matanuska Glacier, where it winds through a deep canyon valley carved by the glacier's river. See section 6, later in this chapter.

Parks Highway

Route 3 from near Anchorage to Fairbanks

Average speed: 60 to 65 mph

The George Parks Highway goes straight from Anchorage to Fairbanks, 360 miles north, providing access on the way to Denali National Park. The best parts are the vistas of Mount McKinley from south of the park and the alpine terrain on either side of Broad Pass, where the road crosses the

Alaska Range and the park entrance. However, the Parks Highway is mostly a transportation route, less scenic than the Richardson or Glenn highways. From the northern (Fairbanks) end, the highway passes Nenana (p. 387), then Denali and Talkeetna (chapter 8), and finally the towns of the Matanuska and Susitna valleys (chapter 6). Pick up a free road guide called "The Corridor" from the Alaska Public Lands Information Center in Anchorage or Fairbanks.

Richardson Highway

Route 4 from Valdez to Delta Junction, Route 2 from Delta Junction to Fairbanks

Average speed: 50 to 60 mph, except 45 mph in Thompson Pass section

The state's first highway, leading 364 miles from tidewater in Valdez to Fairbanks, lost much of its traffic to the Parks Highway, which saves more than 90 miles between Anchorage and Fairbanks, and to the Glenn Highway, which saves about 120 miles from Glennallen to Tok. But it's still the most beautiful paved drive in the Interior. From the south, the road begins with a magnificent climb through Keystone Canyon and steep Thompson Pass, just out of Valdez (see chapter 7), and then passes the huge, distant peaks of southern Wrangell–St. Elias National Park. North of Glennallen, the road climbs into the Alaska Range, snaking along the shores of long alpine lakes. The road descends again to the forested area around Delta Junction and meets the Alaska Highway before arriving in Fairbanks. The highway is covered in section 7.

Seward Highway

Route 1 from Anchorage to Tern Lake, Route 9 from Tern Lake to Seward

Average speed: 45 to 60 mph, depending on traffic

The highway leaves Anchorage on the 127-mile drive to Seward following the rocky edge of mountain peaks above a surging ocean fjord. Abundant wildlife and unfolding views often slow cars. Later the road climbs through high mountain passes above the tree line, tracing sparkling alpine lakes. Alaska's best trail hikes are here. The section from Anchorage 50 miles south to Portage Glacier is covered in chapter 6; the remainder, to Seward, in chapter 7.

Sterling Highway

Route 1 from Tern Lake to Homer

Average speed: 50 to 60 mph, except 45 mph near Cooper Landing

Leading 142 miles from the Seward Highway to the tip of the Kenai Peninsula, the highway has some scenic ocean views on its southern section but is mostly a way to get to the Kenai River, the Kenai National Wildlife Refuge, Kachemak Bay, and the towns of Cooper Landing, Soldotna, Kenai, and Homer.

put on airs. It sprawls, broad and flat, along big highways and the Chena. It's a friendly, easygoing town, but one where people still take gold and their independence seriously. They're still prospecting and mining around here, fighting off environmental regulation and maintaining a traditional Alaskan attitude that "it's us against the world." Fairbanks is the birthplace of strange political movements, including the secessionist Alaskan Independence Party. It's an adamant, loopy, affable place; it doesn't seem to mind being a little bizarre or residing far from the center of things. And that makes it an intensely Alaskan city, for those are the qualities Alaskans most cherish in their myth of themselves.

Fairbanks can strike a visitor a couple of ways, depending on what you expect and what you like. Fairbanks can come across as a provincial outpost, a touristy cross between Kansas and Siberia. Driving one of the franchise-choked commercial strips, you can wonder why you went out of your way to come here. Or you can relax and take Fairbanks on its own terms, as a fun, unpretentious town that never lost its sense of being on the frontier.

My children love it here. There's plenty for families to do in Fairbanks, much of it at least a little corny and requiring drives to widespread sites at the university, on the Chena River, in the gold-mining area north of town, and at Pioneer Park. (You *must* have wheels in Fairbanks.) There are good opportunities for hiking and mountain biking, and great opportunities for canoeing and slow river-float trips.

ESSENTIALS

GETTING THERE **By Car or RV** Fairbanks is a transportation hub. The Richardson Highway heads east 100 miles to Delta Junction, the end point of the Alaska Highway, and then south to Glennallen and Valdez. The Parks Highway heads due south from Fairbanks to Denali National Park, 120 miles away, and Anchorage, 360 miles south.

By Van **Alaska/Yukon Trails** (② **800/770-7275** or 800/770-2267; www.alaska shuttle.com) offers daily service in summer (less frequently in winter) to and from Denali National Park and Anchorage (one-way fares are $46 and $91, respectively). In Fairbanks, the van stops at the visitor center and at Billie's Backpackers Hostel (p. 402), among other places. The shuttle also runs to Dawson City and from there to Whitehorse, Yukon. They pick up and drop off along the way on each route.

By Train The **Alaska Railroad** (② **800/544-0552;** www.alaskarailroad.com) links Fairbanks with Denali National Park and Anchorage, with tour commentary provided along the way. The high-season one-way fare is $56 to Denali and $185 to Anchorage (around twice the cost of flying between the cities).

By Air **Alaska Airlines** (② **800/252-7522;** www.alaskaair.com) connects Fairbanks to Anchorage. A bargain round-trip fare is under $250. The airport is a hub for various small carriers to Alaska's Interior and Arctic communities. A cab downtown from the airport is $16 to $18 with **Yellow Cab** (② **907/455-5555**).

VISITOR INFORMATION The **Fairbanks Log Cabin Visitor Information Center** is in a large log building with a sod roof at 550 1st Ave., on the Chena River at the center of town, at Cushman Street, Fairbanks, AK 99701 (② **800/327-5774** or 907/456-5774; fax 907/452-2867; www.explorefairbanks.com). Besides answering questions, the staff and volunteers provide useful maps and walking and driving tour pamphlets, and can help you find a room with their daily vacancy listing. Several computers are set up for free Internet access. The center is open daily in summer and

Greater Fairbanks

ACCOMMODATIONS ■

Aurora Express
Bed and Breakfast **4**
Billie's Backpackers Hostel **19**
Chena River State
Recreation Site **14**
Crestmont Manor
Bed and Breakfast **4**
Fairbanks Princess
Riverside Lodge **8**
Golden North Motel **9**
Minnie Street
Bed & Breakfast Inn **25**

Pike's Waterfront Lodge **7**
River's Edge Resort Cottages **11**
River's Edge RV Park
and Campground **10**
Sophie Station **13**
Wedgewood Resort **22**

DINING ◆

The Bakery **24**
Bun on the Run **18**
College Town Pizzeria **16**
Hot Licks Homemade
Ice Cream **17, 26**
Pike's Landing **7**

The Pump House
Restaurant and Saloon **5**
Sam's Sourdough Cafe **15**

ATTRACTIONS ●

Alaska Bird Observatory **23**
Creamer's Field **21**
Georgeson Botanical Garden **3**
Large Animal Research Station **1**
Pioneer Park **20**
Riverboat Discovery **6**
7 Bridges Boats and Bikes **12**
UA Museum of the North **2**

Information ⓘ   Post Office ⊠

385

Monday to Friday the rest of the year; exact hours could not be specified at this writing. They also have information desks at the airport and train depot.

The **Alaska Public Lands Information Center,** down the stairs at 3rd and Cushman streets (🕿 **907/456-0527;** www.nps.gov/aplic), is an indispensable stop for anyone planning to spend time in the outdoors, and an interesting one even if you're not. The staff is remarkably knowledgeable and can tell you about trips and activities based on first-hand experience. Besides providing maps and other details, the center houses a small museum about the state's regions and the gear needed to explore them. Daily free films and naturalist programs show in a small auditorium. Open in summer daily from 9am to 6pm, in winter Tuesday through Saturday from 10am to 6pm.

GETTING AROUND Fairbanks is designed around the car, and that's the practical way to get around. Without one, sticking downtown, you will leave with a low opinion of the place. The city is too spread out to use taxis much. **Avis, Hertz, Dollar, Budget, Payless, Alamo,** and **National** are located at the airport. **National** rents vehicles for gravel roads; for that, contact them at their local number (see, "Equipped for the Back Roads," p. 393).

The Fairbanks North Star Borough's **MACS bus system** (🕿 **907/459-1011;** www.co.fairbanks.ak.us, click on "Departments" and then "Transportation") links the university, downtown, the nearby North Pole community, shopping areas, and some hotels. Service is every 30 minutes at best, worse Saturday, and nonexistent Sunday. Pick up timetables at the visitor center. All buses connect at the transit park downtown, at 5th Avenue and Cushman Street. The fare is $1.50 adults; 75¢ for seniors, children, teens, and people with disabilities; free under age 5.

Fairbanks's car-oriented layout does not lend itself to using bikes as the primary means of transportation, but there are great mountain-biking opportunities (see "Getting Outside," later in this chapter).

FAST FACTS: Fairbanks

Banks Fairbanks has numerous banks with **ATMs** in the downtown area and along the commercial strips. **Key Bank** is at 100 Cushman.

Business Services **FedEx Kinko's Copy Center** is at 418 3rd St. (🕿 **907/456-7348**).

Hospital **Fairbanks Memorial** is at 1650 Cowles St. (🕿 **907/452-8181**).

Internet Access Log on for free at the **Log Cabin Visitor Information Center** on Cushman Street at the river downtown (see above).

Police For nonemergency police business, call the **Alaska State Troopers** (🕿 **907/451-5100**) or, within city limits, the **Fairbanks Police Department** (🕿 **907/459-6500**).

Post Office It's located at 315 Barnette St.

Taxes Fairbanks has no sales tax. North Pole charges 4% with a cap of $8 in tax on any one purchase. **Bed tax** is 8%.

SPECIAL EVENTS A recording of current local happenings can be reached at 🕿 **907/456-4636,** maintained by the Fairbanks Convention and Visitors Bureau, which also posts an event calendar at **www.explorefairbanks.com.**

(*Finds*) **Nenana: Tom Sawyer's Alaska**

If you are driving south from Fairbanks toward Denali National Park or Anchorage, plan a short stop in the town of Nenana, about 60 miles along your way. It's a town out of a Mark Twain novel, a sleepy, dusty riverside barge stop left over from the past. Here President Warren Harding drove the golden spike on the Alaska Railroad in 1923; it is still on display outside the memory-stirring old depot museum, although the train hasn't stopped regularly in 20 years. On the waterfront, riverboats are still loaded with cargo for villages up and down the Tanana River. That's also where you can see the cultural center, with its own little museum and Native craft shop. The oldest building in town is the picturesque 1905 log cabin church on Front Street. Stop in at the visitor center on the Parks Highway to learn more and to see the big book of guesses from the Nenana Ice Classic (www.nenanaakiceclassic.com). The contest is a drawing to guess the exact minute the ice on the Tanana will go out, with a jackpot over $300,000. Thanks to the game, this is one of the most carefully kept climate measurements in the north; scientists are using it to demonstrate long-term warming of the weather. See "Special Events," above, to learn about ice classic festivities.

The **Yukon Quest International Sled Dog Race** (© 907/452-7954; www.yukon quest.com) starts the second weekend in February 2007 in Whitehorse and ends more than a week later in Fairbanks (in even-numbered years, the direction is reversed). Mushers say this rugged 1,000-mile race is even tougher than the Iditarod.

The **Nenana Ice Classic** (© 907/832-5446; www.nenanaakiceclassic.com) is a sweepstakes held annually since 1917 based on who can guess closest to the exact minute when the ice will go out on the Tanana River. The classic starts with Tripod Days, the first weekend in March, when they set up the so-called four-legged tripod; when it moves 100 feet, it trips a clock, determining the winner. The Tripod Days celebration includes dance performances, dog mushing, and other activities.

Also in March, the **World Ice Art Championships** (© 907/451-8250; www. icealaska.com) brings carvers from all over the world to sculpt immense, clear chunks cut from a Fairbanks pond. It's worth planning a visit around. Ice sculptures stand in the Ice Park near the corner of Peger and Phillips Field roads. In 2007, carving will be February 27 to March 1 and March 4 to 9, with the best viewing of completed sculptures March 10 to 20. The park stays open until the last Sunday in March. Among ice carvers, Fairbanks' ice is famous for its clarity and the great size of the chunks. Some spectacular ice sculptures stand as tall as two-story buildings. Check the website for pictures of past winners.

The **North American Sled Dog Championships** (© 907/457-MUSH; www.sled dog.org) are the oldest running, taking place over 2 weekends in mid-March. Sprint mushers from all over the world compete with teams of as many as 24 dogs, streaking away from the starting line on 2nd Avenue or the Chena River.

Lots of events happen around the **summer solstice,** usually June 21. The **Midnight Sun Run** (© 907/452-6046; www.midnightsunrun.org) is a 10K race and walk, with winners chosen for both their times and their funny costumes. In 2007, it begins June 16 at 10pm on the university campus and ends at Pioneer Park.

The **Midnight Sun Baseball Game,** hosted by the semipro Alaska Goldpanners of Fairbanks (✆ **907/451-0095;** www.goldpanners.com), begins at 10:30pm on the solstice. The game, which began with a pair of pick-up teams in 1906, is played with no artificial lights. The 'Panners have hosted since 1960.

Also in June, the free **Fairbanks Summer Folk Fest** (✆ **907/488-0556;** www.alaskafolkmusic.org) fills a Pioneer Park lawn with music, food, and art booths; live music starts at noon and lasts late into the night.

The Fairbanks Summer Arts Festival, held the last 2 weeks in July on the University of Alaska Fairbanks campus (✆ **907/474-8869;** www.fsaf.org), brings artists of international reputation for performance and teaching. Classes are for all levels in music, dance, theater, opera, creative writing, visual arts, healing arts, and other subject areas (July 15–29, 2007).

The **Tanana Valley State Fair** (✆ **907/452-3750;** www.tananavalleyfair.org), in early August, shows off the area's agricultural production, arts and crafts, businesses, and entertainment, and includes rides and competitive exhibits.

In late August, Friends of Creamer's Field (✆ **907/459-7307**) hosts an annual **Sandhill Crane Festival,** with nature walks, lectures, and other activities, mostly at Creamer's Field (see "Special Places," later in this chapter).

The **BP Top of the World Classic,** November 15 to 18, 2007, brings NCAA Division I basketball teams to the University of Alaska Fairbanks for a weekend tournament (✆ **907/474-5977;** www.gonanooks.com, click on "Tournaments").

EXPLORING THE TOWN
STROLLING AROUND DOWNTOWN

Exploring downtown won't take more than an hour or two, but there are a few interesting spots in addition to the ice museum and community museum covered below. In addition, the log cabin visitor center at 1st and Cushman lends audio players with spoken tours (you have to leave a credit card imprint as a deposit). Among the highlights is the **Golden Heart Park,** a waterfront plaza next to the center, with a fountain and a bronze of a Native family, where community events often occur. A graceful footbridge spans the river, and on the other side is the town's most interesting building, the Roman Catholic **Church of the Immaculate Conception.** The white clapboard structure, built in 1904, has ornate gold-rush decoration inside, rare for its authenticity, including a pressed-tin ceiling and stained-glass windows—an appealing if incongruous mix of gold-rush and sacred decor. Also on this side of the river, peek into the lobby of the Doyon Native corporation offices to see Native cultural displays from all over Alaska, the traditional Athabascan tool collection, and the colorful modern art hanging from the walls and ceiling.

Back on the visitor center side of the river, at 1st Avenue between Kellum and Bonnifield streets, east from the center, **St. Matthew's Episcopal Church** is a cute old log church with a working rope-pull bell. It was founded by missionary and dog-sled explorer Hudson Stuck in 1904, who organized the first successful climb of Mount McKinley. The original church burned; the present structure dates from 1948.

At 500 2nd Ave., the **Ice Museum** ✦ (✆ **907/451-8222;** www.icemuseum.com) aims to show summer visitors what winter is like, with seven large ice displays and a freezer you can enter to feel –20°F (–29°C). A big-screen, high-tech slide show plays hourly, explaining the annual World Ice Art Championships (see "Special Events," above), and the freezers contain impressive ice tableaux. Admission is $11 for adults, $10 seniors and military, $6 ages 6 to 12, $2 ages 5 and under; except noon lunch

Moments **Seeing the Aurora Borealis**

One fall evening, I left the house of friends in Fairbanks to the sight of a swirling green glow that filled the dark sky. I knocked on the door and brought them out to see, only to have my friends laugh in my face. They informed me, with mock contempt for my Anchorage home, that in Fairbanks they don't even bother to bend their necks back for northern lights as dim as these. It's true—a bright aurora borealis is routine in Fairbanks. Some of the world's top experts on the phenomenon work here, at the University of Alaska's Geophysical Institute (their aurora predictions, in season, and extensive background on the aurora are posted at **www.gi.alaska.edu**). Hours-long displays can be incredibly spectacular and even moving.

Unfortunately, most visitors never see these wild strands of bright colors whipping across the sky because when most visitors come, the sky is never dark. Alaskans rarely see the stars from late May to early August, and to see the aurora well, you need an especially dark night sky. To improve your chances, plan your trip in the fall or winter. An early September trip offers brilliant fall foliage, dark night skies, and the remnants of summer weather. In midwinter, the sky is dark all night and most of the day. Many hotels near Fairbanks cater to travelers coming to see the aurora in winter, as well as visitors who come for such winter sports as dog mushing and snowmobiling; the best for that kind of trip is Chena Hot Springs Resort, covered in the next section.

shows, which include food and cost $18 for everyone. It's open from 10am to 9pm daily from mid-May to mid-September.

The **Fairbanks Community Museum** ⋇, in the old city hall at 410 Cushman St. (© **907/457-3669**), is well worth a stop for the charming historical exhibits and the sense of local pride it contains. A series of cramped galleries offers up old photographs, maps, newspapers, and other bric-a-brac, as well as skillfully created explanatory exhibits, mostly focusing on the area's gold-mining history and development. A new display features photographs that show how modern-day Fairbanksans entertain themselves in the winter. You could spend quite some time wandering this maze of small discoveries. The Yukon Quest International Sled Dog Race (see "Special Events," above) shares these quarters, teaching about mushing with displays of equipment and supporting the race with souvenirs sold in the tiny gift shop. The museum is open Tuesday through Saturday from 10am to 6pm (closed 2:30–3pm). It is closed during April.

PIONEER PARK ⋇⋇
Built for the Alaska purchase centennial in 1967, **Pioneer Park** (formerly **Alaskaland**) is the boiled-down essence of Fairbanks on grounds at the intersection of Airport Way and Peger Road (© **907/459-1087**; www.co.fairbanks.ak.us, click "Recreation," then "Pioneer Park"). It's called a theme park, but don't expect Disneyland or anything like it. Instead, Pioneer Park is a city park with a theme. It's relaxing and low-key, entrancing for young children and interesting for adults if you can give

in to the charm of the place. Admission to the park is free, and the tours and activities are generally inexpensive. The park is open year-round, but the attractions operate only Memorial Day weekend to Labor Day, daily from 11am to 9pm. Pick up a map and schedule when you arrive; here I've listed the highlights, but there is more to see. Depending on the pace you like to keep and the age level of your group, you can spend anything from a couple of hours to most of a day here.

The **SS *Nenana*** ⊕⊕ (*©* **907/456-8848**) is the park's centerpiece. Commissioned by the federally owned Alaska Railroad in 1933, the large sternwheeler plied the Yukon and Tanana rivers until 1952. In 1967, the *Nenana* came to what was then Alaskaland but was neglected and had nearly collapsed from rot when it was saved by a community restoration effort, completed in 1992. There are two decks of sumptuous mahogany, brass, and white-painted promenades to see, and the wheelhouse, well-preserved engine room, and the like. Self-guided entry to the entire boat is $3 (free for ages 5 and younger), or for $2 you can see the ground-floor cargo deck with its engaging set of dioramas showing all the riverside towns and villages where the boat called, modeled as they looked in its heyday.

Much of Fairbanks's history has been moved to Pioneer Park. A village of log cabins contains shops and restaurants, each marked with its original location and place in town history. **Judge Wickersham's house,** built around 1904, is kept as a museum, decorated appropriately according to the period of the town's founding. The house is less than grand—it may remind you of your grandmother's—but it's worth a stop to strike up a conversation with the historical society volunteers who keep it open. **President Warren Harding's railcar,** from which he stepped to drive the golden spike on the Alaska Railroad, sits near the park entrance. The **Pioneer Air Museum** (*©* **907/451-0037**) is housed in a geodesic dome toward the back of the park. Besides the aircraft, there are displays and artifacts of the crashes of Alaska's aviation pioneers. Admission is $2 adults, free 12 and under with parent, $5 for families. Other attractions include a gold-rush museum, an illustrated gold-rush show, kayak and bike rentals, a dance hall, and an art gallery.

If you have children, you certainly won't escape Pioneer Park without a ride on the **Crooked Creek and Whiskey Island Railroad** that circles the park twice, with a tour guide pointing out the sights; rides cost $2 for adults, $1 for children and seniors. Kids will also enjoy the large **playground,** with equipment for toddlers and older children, where lots of local families come to play, and the 36-hole miniature golf course. The only carnival ride is a nice old **merry-go-round,** which costs $1.

Tour groups generally come to Pioneer Park in the evening from mid-May to mid-September for the **Alaska Salmon Bake,** at the mining valley area (*©* **907/452-7274**), and the **Golden Heart Revue,** at the Palace Theatre (*©* **907/456-5960;** www. akvisit.com for both). Cost for all-you-can-eat prime rib and fish (halibut, cod, or salmon) is $28. Beer and wine are available. The seating area is pleasant, with indoor or outdoor dining. The revue, nightly at 8:15pm from mid-May to mid-September, covers the amusing story of the founding of Fairbanks with comedy and song in a nightclub setting; admission is $18 for adults.

UNIVERSITY OF ALASKA FAIRBANKS

The state university's main campus contains several interesting attractions and makes a point of serving tourists. The campus is on the west side of town; the main entrance is at the intersection of University Avenue and College Road. A widely distributed brochure lists tours, hours, and fees. A free 2-hour **walking tour,** led by students, meets at the museum Monday through Friday at 10am, June through August except July 4th and 5th. Call ahead (📞 **907/474-7581**) to confirm the time and any weather cancellations. A shuttle bus is provided in case of rain or visitor need. More campus attractions are listed below; for a complete list, go to **www.uaf.edu/univrel/tour** and click "Activities and Tours." The university's ski trails are covered later under "Winter Activities."

UA Museum of the North 🐾🐾🐾 This rich, interdisciplinary on-campus museum, long one of Alaska's best, recently added a spectacular new expansion. First, the original part of the museum: Alaska's best natural history collection and its most scholarly, with information presented at advanced as well as elementary levels. Some of the objects have a real wow factor, such as Blue Babe, the mummified steppe bison; a 5,400-pound copper nugget; and the state's largest public display of gold. There is an audio tour guide, or in the summer you can join free 20-minute talks offered through the day on the university's specialties. All this will remain, and it already provided enough to keep your interest for much of a day. Now the new part: a swooping combination of grand, graceful shapes, designed by Joan Soranno, a disciple of Frank Gehry; it is reminiscent of moving icebergs, or perhaps of the Northern Lights. Inside, the towering new gallery is devoted to art, with thematic presentation of contemporary art alongside Native and archeological objects, sound, crafts, and much more. Visit the auditorium for presentations on the aurora, Alaska Native games and dance, and other subjects.

907 Yukon Dr. (P.O. Box 756960), Fairbanks, AK 99775-6960. 📞 **907/474-7505**. www.uaf.edu/museum. Admission $10 adults, $9 ages 60 and older, $6 ages 7–17, free ages 6 and under. Summer daily 9am–7pm; winter Mon–Fri 9am–5pm, Sat–Sun noon–5pm.

Georgeson Botanical Garden 🐾 I really enjoy the mix of science and contemplation I find at this relaxed working garden. Plots are laid out to compare seeds and cultivation techniques, usually well posted with explanatory information on the experiment, but at the same time the flowers and vegetables are spectacular, and there are peaceful memorials and places to picnic. You don't need a tour to enjoy the garden. Nearby, the barn of the university's experimental farm is open for visitors to wander through and view the reindeer.

117 W. Tanana Dr. 📞 **907/474-1744**. www.uaf.edu/salrm/gbg. Admission $2. Open daylight hours; store open summer daily 9am–5pm; free guided tours Fri at 2pm.

Large Animal Research Station 🐾 The university studies captive musk ox, reindeer, and caribou here, on a property often called the musk ox farm. Tours are given daily in the high season, with naturalists bringing animals into an amphitheater for close-up viewing. At any time, on a walk along the fence from the parking lot on Yankovich Road, you can see the animals behaving naturally in the large pastures. Best times are the cool morning or evening hours, and binoculars help.

Yankovich Rd. 📞 **907/474-7207**. www.uaf.edu/lars. Half-hour tour $6, free ages 6 and under; 1-hour tour $10 adults, $9 seniors, $6 students, free ages 6 and under. Tours Memorial Day to Labor Day daily each hour 9:30am–4:30pm (hour-long tours only at 1:30 and 3:30pm). Call 📞 **907/474-5724** to check on tour times and changes. Drive north from campus, turn left on Ballaine Rd., left again on Yankovich.

COMMERCIAL TOURIST ATTRACTIONS

Three major for-profit attractions around Fairbanks pack in visitors by the hundreds of thousands, most of them on group tours. These places are educational and fun, as I've described below, but I think they all charge excessive prices. Whether they're worth your money depends on how much you've got and your level of interest; however, I doubt most independent budget travelers would feel they got their money's worth.

The Riverboat *Discovery* ✦✦   The *Discovery* belongs to the pioneering Binkley family, which has been in the riverboat business since the Klondike gold rush and has run this attraction since 1950. The *Discovery* is a real sternwheeler, a 156-foot steel vessel carrying 700 passengers on as many as three trips a day. There's nothing intimate or spontaneous about the 3½-hour ride, which mostly carries package-tour passengers off fleets of buses, but the Binkleys still provide a diverting outing that doesn't feel cheap or phony. After loading at a landing with shops off Dale Road, near the airport, the boat cruises down the Chena and up the Tanana past demonstrations on shore—among others, a bush plane taking off and landing, fish-cutting at a Native fish camp, and a musher's dog yard. Finally, the vessel pulls up at the bank for an hour-long tour of a mock Athabascan village.

1975 Discovery Dr., Fairbanks, AK 99709. ℂ 866/479-6673 or 907/479-6673. www.riverboatdiscovery.com. Tours $47 adults, $32 ages 3–13, free ages 2 and under. Sailings mid-May to mid-Sept daily 8:45am and 2pm.

The El Dorado Gold Mine ✦   A train such as you would find at an amusement park carries visitors though an impressively staged educational tour, including a trip through a tunnel in the permafrost. This is like a land version of the riverboat tour that's operated by the same family, the Binkleys. But the gold miners who act as hosts are the real attraction here. Visitors gather around a sluice to hear the amusing and authentic Dexter and Lynette (aka Yukon Yonda) Clark and watch a swoosh of water and gold-bearing gravel rush by. You pan the resulting pay dirt, and everyone goes home with enough gold dust to fill a plastic locket—typically $5 to $35 worth. Drive out to the mine after making reservations, or take a $2 shuttle.

Off the Elliott Hwy., 9 miles north of town. ℂ 866/479-6673 or 907/479-6673. www.eldoradogoldmine.com. Tours $30 adults, $20 ages 3–12, free ages 2 and under. Tours mid-May to mid-Sept daily; call for times.

Gold Dredge Number 8 ✦   Authenticity makes this the area's best historic gold-mining site. The centerpiece is a 1927 gold dredge, similar to machines in Dawson City and Nome, standing five decks tall on a barge in a pond it created. When it operated, huge scoops would dig from one end, the mechanism inside would digest the gold from the gravel, and then it would dump the spoils out the back—in this way, the pond and the dredge it supports crept 4½ miles across the frozen ground north of Fairbanks. Many sterile areas you see in this area were created by these earth-eaters, for nothing grows on their tailings for decades after. The tour company that bought the historic site added to the dredge with museums housed in relocated gold camp buildings, showing the harsh, colorless life lived by the miners. A 90-minute tour starts with a film, then a half-hour on the dredge, and finally a chance to pan for gold yourself, with success assured. It's a fascinating machine, but, as noted above, the price is high for what is essentially a single-subject museum.

1755 Old Steese Hwy., Fairbanks, AK 99712. ℂ 907/457-6058. www.golddredgeno8.com. Admission $19 tour only, $25 with gold panning, $35 with lunch of stew. Mid-May to mid-Sept tours start hourly 9:30am–3:30pm. Go north on the Steese Expressway from town, turn left on Goldstream Rd., turn left again on the Old Steese Hwy.

GETTING OUTSIDE

In this section, I've described the outdoor opportunities local to Fairbanks, but some other choices are barely farther afield: Check out section 3 of this chapter, on Chena Hot Springs Road, and the later feature, "The Steese Highway: Drive into the Wild."

The **Alaska Public Lands Information Center,** 250 Cushman St. (at 3rd Ave.; *©* **907/456-0527;** www.nps.gov/aplic), is a great resource. The staff will advise you on outings, outfitters, and where to find rental equipment. The center also sells the "Fairbanks Area Wildlife Watching Guide," a $6 booklet that contains thorough descriptions of the best places to go and tips for success. You can also buy it in area bookstores.

GEARING UP

You can rent most of what you need for outdoor explorations around Fairbanks and along the region's extraordinary rural highways from a set of local businesses that have grown up around the needs of adventurers. Some of the outdoor opportunities I describe require a drive on unpaved roads, including portions of the Steese Highway. Two businesses that rent vehicles you can take on these roads are listed in the feature "Equipped for the Back Roads," below. One of those, GoNorth Alaska Adventure Travel Center, also rents canoes, bikes, and camping gear, and offers a shuttle for canoeists and hikers. For ski rentals, see the appropriate sections below.

Alaska Outdoor Rentals & Guides, owned by the knowledgeable Larry Katkin, has its main location on the river bank at Pioneer Park (*©* **907/457-BIKE;** www. akbike.com). The company rents canoes, kayaks, and bikes, and offers pickup or drop-off for paddlers in town or far afield—even for trips on the great Yukon River. For an easy in-town paddle—say, from the park to Pike's Landing—you would pay $29 for the canoe and $15 for the pickup. If you want to go beyond the road system, Larry also carries foldable canoes that will fit in a Bush plane. He also offers lessons. This is a good place to start a mountain-biking outing, too. Bikes rent for $27 for an 8-hour day in summer. You can also rent from the long-established **7 Bridges Boats and Bikes,** at 7 Gables Inn, 4312 Birch Lane (*©* **907/479-0751;** www.7gablesinn.com/ 7bbb), for $35 per day or $100 per week, and they will drop you off at the river and pick you up at your destination for $2 per mile out of town, with a $15 minimum.

Tips Equipped for the Back Roads

Exploring Alaska's gravel highways—camping and fishing along the way, per-haps launching a canoe in a remote lake—has been tough for visitors to arrange because of the policies of most rental-car agencies, which don't allow clients to drive off pavement. An exception is the **Alamo/National** franchise in Fairbanks, with locations at the airport and at 4960 Dale Rd. (*©* **800/227-7368** or 907/451-7368). They rent four-door, four-wheel-drive pickup trucks for travel on gravel roads such as the Dalton, Steese, and Denali highways. Be sure to call the local franchise, not the national reservation number. **GoNorth Alaska Adventure Travel Center,** at 3500 Davis Rd. (*©* **866/236-7272** or 907/479-7272; www.gonorthalaska.com), goes a step further, renting not only SUVs and trucks, but also campers on four-wheel-drive pickups, perfect for exploring gravel roads. The firm also runs a tent-camp hostel; arranges self-guided out-door trips; rents canoes, bikes, and camping gear; and drives a shuttle for canoeists and hikers. With unlimited mileage, a pickup camper is $125 to $219 a day; insurance of $18 to $24 a day is required unless you present proof of your own coverage, so be sure to ask about what paperwork you will need when you reserve.

Guests at the inn get free rentals (same phone; www.7gablesinn.com). Street and mountain bikes go for $20 a day.

SPECIAL PLACES

CREAMER'S FIELD   At 1300 College Rd., right in Fairbanks, this 2,000-acre migratory waterfowl refuge is a former dairy farm that was saved from development in 1966 by a community fund drive. The pastures are a prime stopover point for Canada geese, pintails, and golden plovers in the spring and fall. We've seen many swans there in the spring. Sandhill cranes, shovelers, and mallards show up all summer. The **Friends of Creamers Field** (✆ **907/459-7307;** www.creamersfield.org) operates a small visitor center in the old farmhouse with displays on birds, wildlife, and history, open June through August daily from 10am to 5pm. They offer guided nature walks in summer Monday, Wednesday, and Friday at 2pm; Wednesday at 9am; and Tuesday and Thursday at 7pm. You don't need a guide, however: During migrations, use the blinds around the edge of the field; other times, explore the 3 miles of trails through forest, field, and wetland. I especially enjoy the boreal forest nature walk, interpreted by an excellent booklet you can pick up at the visitor center or from a kiosk at the trail head when the visitor center is closed. The **Alaska Bird Observatory** (✆ **907/451-7159;** www.alaskabird.org) conducts research and educational programs on the Creamer's Field refuge, including bird walks and bird banding that visitors can observe (call for times). It is the farthest-north facility of its kind in North America. The organization's building has interpretive displays, a nature store, and a library. Located just west of the refuge on the grounds of the Wedgewood Resort (see below), the observatory can be hard to find—look for the signs.

CHENA LAKE RECREATION AREA   This is a wonderful and unique place for a family camping trip. A birch-rimmed lake created for a flood-control project has been developed by the local government to provide lots of recreational possibilities: flat walking and bike trails, a swimming beach, fishing, a place to rent canoes and paddleboats, a self-guided 2.5-mile nature trail, a playground, big lawns, and the terrific campground with 80 camping sites, from pull-throughs for RVs to tent sites on a little island you can reach only by boat. In the winter, it's a popular area for cross-country skiing, ice fishing, and dog mushing. Camping prices may rise for 2007, but as of this writing, an overnight site is $10 and day use is $4. Drive 17 miles east of Fairbanks on the Richardson Highway and turn left on Laurance Road as you leave North Pole. For information, contact Fairbanks North Star Borough Chena Lake Recreation Area (✆ **907/488-1655**). Follow the same directions (drive along the dam past the recreation area) to the **Moose Creek Dam Salmon Watch,** a picnic and viewing area built by the U.S. Army Corps of Engineers atop the flood-control project, to watch spawning salmon in crystal-clear water from late June to the end of July. Use of the salmon watch is free, so tell the recreation-area gatehouse you are going there.

SUMMER ACTIVITIES

CANOEING   The rivers in and around Fairbanks are best seen by floating slowly along in a canoe. Paddling is as popular as hiking around here. See "Gearing Up," on p. 393, for companies that rent equipment and offer shuttle services.

The Chena River is slow and meandering as it flows through Fairbanks, and you have your pick of restaurants on the bank. Farther upriver, the canoeing passes wilder shores and near the headwaters becomes more challenging (covered in the "Chena Hot Springs Road" section, later). For beginners, try the wilderness section from the

Chena Lake Recreation Area downstream (described above). It's 12 to 16 hours from there all the way into town, or you can take out at one of the roads crossing the river along the way. The **U.S. Army Corp of Engineers** (✆ **907/488-2748**) produces a float map with put-in and take-out points and float times, available at the Alaska Public Lands Information Center (see "Visitor Information," earlier).

For something a bit more challenging but still manageable, the clear Class I water of the Chatanika River is perfect for day trips or relaxed expeditions of a week or more, if you know how to handle river hazards such as sweepers and snags that show up on any Alaska stream. Alaska State Parks produces a brochure covering the float from the Upper Chatanika River Campground, at Mile 39 of the Steese Highway, to another campground on the Elliott Highway. Low water and logjams requiring portages can slow down the trip so that it takes a long day; in better conditions, expert canoeists can do it in a few hours.

The Steese Highway also meets two National Wild and Scenic Rivers: Beaver Creek, for trips of a week or more over easy Class I water, and Birch Creek, for more expert paddlers. For detailed guidance, check with the Alaska Public Lands Information Center in Fairbanks. Also see "The Steese Highway: Drive into the Wild," p. 411.

BIKING & HIKING   Traffic goes fast in Fairbanks and the separated bike trails are few, but strong cyclists can get by. Mountain biking is good on many dirt roads and byways within and beyond Fairbanks and on the ski trails at Birch Hill Recreation Area and the University of Alaska Fairbanks (see "Winter Activities," below). The ski trails are also good for easy summer hikes, or go farther afield for more ambitious trail hikes off Chena Hot Springs Road (in the next section of this chapter) or the Steese Highway (p. 411). Inquire about all the options or other ideas at the Alaska Public Lands Information Center (p. 386).

FISHING   Salmon season here is brief and the fish, this far inland, have turned spawning colors and have softer, less palatable flesh compared to coastal salmon. Most fishing is in the streams for Arctic grayling, Northern pike, and burbot, and in stocked lakes for rainbow trout, Arctic char, and silver salmon. You can fish right in the Chena as it flows through town, although getting out of town and hiking away from a road yields better results. Fly-in fishing will further increase your chances and add sheefish and Dolly Varden char to your list, but the expense of around $300 a day is easier to justify from Anchorage or another coastal community, where you can find better salmon fishing to go along with the freshwater fish. The Alaska Public Lands Information Center (p. 386) offers guidance, or contact the **Alaska Department of Fish and Game,** at Creamer's Field, 1300 College Rd., Fairbanks, AK 99701 (✆ **907/459-7228;** sport fish information recording 907/459-7385; www.alaska.gov/adfg, click on "Sport Fisheries," then on the Interior region on the map, and then "Lower Tanana River Drainage").

WINTER ACTIVITIES
Fairbanks has real Jack London winters. The visitor bureau guarantees it. For the growing number of visitors who want to experience real cold, see the aurora borealis, and ride a dog sled, Fairbanks is the place. Chena Hot Springs Resort (p. 409) and A Taste of Alaska Lodge (p. 398) are the best destinations for winter immersion, but you can also have a good time in town, especially in March, when the days lighten up, the temperatures are moderate, and the town gets busy with dog mushing and the ice-carving contest (see "Special Events," earlier in this chapter).

DOG MUSHING   The long winters and vast wild lands make the Fairbanks area a center of dog sledding, for both racers and recreationists, and there are plenty of people willing to take you for a lift, which is really an experience not to be missed. I've heard good things about **Sun Dog Express Dog Sled Tours** (© 907/479-6983; www.mosquitonet.com/~sleddog), which charges $30 for a quick spin, up to $250 to learn to drive a team in a half-day. They also have summer cart tours.

During the summer, learn about mushing by taking a wonderfully intimate tour with Mary Shields, the first woman to finish the Iditarod. Rather than a tour, a visit to Mary's home on the outskirts of Fairbanks feels more like a chat with a fascinating new friend. You'll meet and pet Mary's dogs, talk about dog mushing, and hear tales of her extraordinary experiences as a musher. The tour, called **Alaskan Tails of the Trails** (© 800/770-2267 or 907/455-6469; www.maryshields.com), happens every evening in the summer. It costs $28 and lasts 2 hours.

CROSS-COUNTRY SKIING   The **Birch Hill Recreation Area,** off the Steese Expressway just north of town, has about 25km of good cross-country ski trails, most groomed for classical or skate skiing, and a warm-up building in which to change clothes. Several loops of a few kilometers each offer advanced skiing on the steep southern side of the hill; loops of up to 10km provide more level terrain to the north. Some trails are lighted. The **University of Alaska Fairbanks** offers a trail network of roughly the same length, two-thirds of it groomed for skate technique. Although I prefer Birch Hill, with its mix of ability levels, the University trails pass through lovely lands and have the advantage of a nearby source of rental equipment, the **Outdoor Adventures Program** at the Wood Student Center (© 907/474-6027; www.uaf.edu/outdoor). You can rent skis, poles, and boots for a mere $8 a day. One trail head is at the west end of campus, near the satellite dishes at the top of Tanana Loop. Another is off Farmers Loop Road at Ballaine Lake.

DOWNHILL SKIING   Fairbanks has several community-size downhill-skiing areas, including the relatively large **Moose Mountain Ski Resort** (© 907/479-4732; www.shredthemoose.com), with 1,300 vertical feet of skiing. Instead of freezing on a lift, you ride back up the hill and socialize in heated buses.

SHOPPING

Fairbanks has a few good shops downtown. **New Horizons Gallery,** at 519 1st Ave. (© 907/456-2063; www.newhorizonsgallery.com), occupies a large space with the work of some of Alaska's best in oils, inexpensive prints, and sculpture, and also carries gifts. It is open every day. The **Arctic Travelers Gift Shop,** at 201 Cushman St. (© 907/456-7080), specializes in Native art and crafts, carrying both valuable art and affordable but authentically Alaskan gifts. The staff is knowledgeable about what they sell. Right next door, at 215 Cushman, **If Only . . .** (© 907/452-6659) is a charming gift and stationary shop with items to hold locals' as well as visitors' interest—not just tourist stuff.

Near the airport, at 4630 Old Airport Rd., the **Great Alaskan Bowl Company** (© 800/770-4222 or 907/474-9663; www.woodbowl.com) makes and sells bowls of native birch—salad bowls, of course, but also bowls for many other purposes. Some of these bowls are simply amazing. They can carve up to eight nested bowls from one piece of wood and even laser-engrave a photo inside one. Through a glass wall looking into the shop, you can see workers cutting the bowls from raw logs. It's hard to depart without buying a bowl. The shop is open daily all year.

WHERE TO STAY

Going the bed-and-breakfast route is a good choice in Fairbanks. At the B&Bs I've listed below, you can save money over a hotel and get a private room just as good while staying in a unique place with interesting people. The **Fairbanks Association of Bed and Breakfasts** lists about 20 more on its website at **www.ptialaska.net/~fabb**. You also can get B&B information and up-to-date vacancy data at the Fairbanks Log Cabin Visitor Information Center (see p. 384).

EXPENSIVE

There are many more hotels in the expensive category than there is any need to describe here, so I have followed my usual practice of including one for each taste. The enormous **Fairbanks Princess Riverside Lodge** (© **800/426-0500** or 907/455-4477, fax 907/455-4476; www.princessalaskalodges.com) also merits a mention as a luxurious and well-run hotel in a pleasant setting near the airport (it's quite similar to Pike's Waterfront). However, in summer the Princess usually books fully with the owner's cruise-line clients.

Pike's Waterfront Lodge 🐾🐾   When Pike's appeared on the Chena River next to the Pike's Landing restaurant (see later in this chapter), it initially looked like a big rectangle the size and shape of innumerable chain hotels along interstates, but the local owner kept adding features until it became utterly unique, including a greenhouse, an ice cream parlor with an airplane sticking out of it, an extraordinary wildlife art collection, and 28 cabins. The main building is decorated in a mix of modern and faux-rustic, with lots of log work. Rooms, while not large, are well equipped, and many look out on the river. Several features make the hotel convenient, including its location, a stone's throw from the airport, Wi-Fi in much of the building and all public spaces, and efficient service. Some rooms have refrigerators and microwaves. The place fills on certain days in the summer with package tour guests—at this writing, Monday through Wednesday—but usually has room the rest of the week. Summer only, a steak-and-seafood restaurant operates on-site. The bar also serves casual meals.

1850 Hoselton Drive., Fairbanks, AK 99709. © **877/774-2400** or 907/456-4500. Fax 907/456-4515. www.pikeslodge.com. 208 units. High season $149–$210 double, $114–$465 suites; low season $69–$99 double, $89–$235 suites. Extra person 13 and over $10. AE, DC, DISC, MC, V. **Amenities:** Restaurant (summer); bar; exercise room; sauna; steam room; tour desk; courtesy van; business center; Wi-Fi in common areas; laundry service; coin-op laundry. *In room:* A/C, TV, pay movies, dataport, Wi-Fi (in some), fridge (in some), microwave (in some), hair dryer, coffeemaker, iron.

River's Edge Resort Cottages 🐾🐾 *(Kids)*   An afternoon on a sunny riverbank exemplifies the best of Interior Alaska; this place is built around that knowledge. Trim little cottages stand in a grassy compound along the gentle Chena River, where guests can fish for grayling. Inside each light, airy cottage is an excellent standard hotel room, with high ceilings and two queen beds. Outside they're like a little village, where guests can sit on the patio, watch the river go by, and socialize. The owners got the idea for the place from their RV park next door, when they noticed how their guests enjoyed visiting together in the open with their own private units to retreat to. It's perfect for families, as the outdoor areas are safe for playing and noise inside won't bother the neighbors. A large, summer-only restaurant sits at river's edge, with dining on a deck or inside at round, oak tables. Dinner entrees—steak, seafood, and down-home cooking—range up to $30; a burger is $8.

4200 Boat St., Fairbanks, AK 99709. (℄) 800/770-3343 or 907/474-0286. Fax 907/474-3665. www.riversedge.net. 86 cottages, 8 suites. High season $198 double; low season $139 double. Extra person 12 and over $10. AE, DISC, MC, V. Closed Oct–Apr. Take Sportsman Way off Airport Way to Boat St. **Amenities:** Restaurant; bar; tour desk; courtesy van; laundry service; ATM. *In room:* TV, dataport, coffeemaker, hair dryer.

Sophie Station ℛ This all-suite hotel, near the university and airport, is well equipped for business travelers or longer stays, with fully equipped kitchens, sitting rooms, and separate bedrooms in every suite. The decoration in the rooms is pleasantly muted. Everything is very clean, well maintained, and comfortable. Bathrooms and closets are quite large. The lobby contains a free Internet work station and all rooms have Wi-Fi. I was startled by the quality of the food and service in the hotel restaurant, called **Zach's,** which looks like it would produce typical, unmemorable hotel cafe dining. Each dish I selected was perfectly seasoned and done to a turn, servers were attentive without being annoying, and the meals came quickly. The cuisine includes Alaska seafood and familiar American dishes. Dinner main courses top out at $32, They're open year-round.

1717 University Ave., Fairbanks, Alaska 99709. (℄) 800/528-4916 reservations or 907/479-3650 and 907/456-3642. Fax 907/479-7951. www.fountainheadhotels.com. 148 units. High season $169–$205 double; low season $89–$120. Extra person $10. AE, DC, DISC, MC, V. **Amenities:** Restaurant; exercise room; courtesy van; coin-op laundry. *In room:* A/C, TV, dataport, Wi-Fi, kitchen, hair dryer, iron.

A Taste of Alaska Lodge ℛ Situated atop a grassy slope on 280 acres, facing Mount McKinley, the hand-crafted log main building feels like a wilderness lodge but is less than half an hour from Fairbanks. The family that originally homesteaded this property still lives here and runs the lodge, with the third generation now training to take over. Each family member I've met is an Alaskan original. A nearby musher offers dog-team rides in winter (but make sure that's available when you reserve if it's a priority). During the dark months, visitors come for exceptional aurora viewing. In summer, visitors can enjoy the hot tub and peer at goldfish in a manmade pond set amid a large field of hay. Rooms are decorated with handmade quilts, brass beds, and other reproductions, and an incredible array of knickknacks, collectibles, and pictures of Elizabeth Taylor (some will love all this; some may find it a little corny). Each room has a door straight onto the grounds, where moose often wander. The cabins are large and especially luxurious. They are reasonably priced, while the standard rooms are bit dear. Breakfast is served at 8am on the dot, and guests have to remove their shoes at the door.

551 Eberhardt Rd., Fairbanks, AK 99712. (℄) 907/488-7855. Fax 907/488-3772. www.atasteofalaska.com. 8 units, 2 cabins. $175 double; $195–$225 cabin. Extra person $25. Rates include full breakfast. AE, MC, V. Turn right 5⅓ miles out Chena Hot Springs Rd. **Amenities:** Hot tub. *In room:* TV, Wi-Fi ($10).

Wedgewood Resort ℛℛ Off College Road near the Creamer's Field Refuge, this well-kept hotel sprawls across a grassy 23-acre complex in eight large buildings. Seven of them are converted three-story apartment buildings, regularly refitted, without elevators but with large living rooms, separate dining areas, fully equipped kitchens, air conditioners, two TVs, balconies, and phones with voice mail in both the living room and bedroom. The main difference from home is that someone else cleans up after you. Another 157 units are large standard hotel rooms in the three-story Bear Lodge, which has its own lobby; however, those are closed mid-September to mid-May. A scheduled courtesy van runs to the airport and train depot and various tourist sites in the summer. A

Downtown Fairbanks

footbridge connects the hotel to Creamer's Field, and the Alaska Bird Observatory has opened its research and educational center on the grounds (see p. 394).

212 Wedgewood Dr., Fairbanks, AK 99701. ☏ **800/528-4916** reservations or 907/452-1442 and 907/456-3642. Fax 907/451-6376. www.fountainheadhotels.com. 157 units, 294 apts. High season $185 double, $154–$225 apt for 2; low season $75–$120 apt, regular double rooms not offered. Extra person in apt $10. AE, DC, DISC, MC, V. **Amenities:** 2 restaurants (summer only); bar; tour desk; computers in each lobby; courtesy van; coin-op laundry; dry cleaning. *In room:* A/C, TV, dataport, Wi-Fi (in some), kitchen (in some), coffeemaker, hair dryer, iron.

Westmark Fairbanks Hotel & Conference Center ✸✸✸   This Fairbanks landmark, the town's grand meeting place, declined until a few years ago, when the owner, Holland America Lines, demolished most of it and built a showplace and the city's tallest tower (not exactly a skyscraper, but you don't need to be very high for good views in Fairbanks). The decor leaped 30 years forward, and now the hotel is the city's most stylish, with a post-mod pastiche that includes fabrics and lamps from the Jetsons along with colonial woodwork; big, manly furniture; and lots of color. I liked it. The rooms are packed with all the latest amenities, including Wi-Fi throughout the new section. They built little shelves for the coffeemakers so they're not down with your toothpaste. Downstairs, the hotel has a cafe with a dining room that's a work of art and a comfortable steakhouse, as well as a large fitness center, large guest laundry,

---

Tips **Going with the Flow**

Many of the large, top-quality hotels in Fairbanks, including the Princess, West-mark, Pike's Waterfront Lodge, Sophie Station, River's Edge Resort, and Wedge-wood Resort, cater to enormous escorted tours, which flow through town on a rhythm set by the arrival of cruise ships hundreds of miles away. As a result, certain nights are booked up every week many months in advance, while others are wide open. Fortunately, this flow alternates on different nights for different companies, so when one hotel is full, another is empty. If you find your first choice is booked, just call one of the others. If they have rooms, ask for a discount, as they may have a lot of empty rooms.

---

and small business center. The company has made a good choice in eschewing the phony Alaskan motif you get so sick of if you spend much time touring here. Instead, they made a cool hotel, a fun place to stay.

813 Noble St., Fairbanks, AK 99701. © **800/544-0970** reservations, or 907/456-7722. Fax 907/451-7478. www.westmarkhotels.com. 400 units. Summer $200 double, $220–$500 suite; winter $69 double, $79–$500 suite. Extra person 19 and over $15. AE, DC, DISC, MC, V. **Amenities:** 2 restaurants; bar; fitness center; tour desk (seasonal); Wi-Fi; courtesy van; coin-op laundry; laundry service. *In room:* A/C, TV, dataport, Wi-Fi (in some rooms), coffeemaker, hair dryer, iron.

MODERATE

All Seasons Inn && This charming and comfortable country inn on a pleasant residential street a couple of blocks from the downtown core is the creation of Mary Richards, a longtime transplant from the southern United States who retains, along with a slight accent, the gentle hospitality and refined style she brought with her. Each cozy room has its own inspired decorative details in bold colors, and the housekeeping has always been perfect on our many visits. For visiting with Mary or other guests, a series of large, elegant common rooms connect downstairs, where you'll find a bar with hot drinks and a sun porch with books and games. Complimentary newspapers come with the full breakfast, and wireless Internet reaches all the rooms. Shoes are removed at the front door in winter. Smoking is not allowed.

763 Seventh Ave., Fairbanks, AK 99701. © **888/451-6649** or 907/451-6649. Fax 907/474-8448. www.allseasons inn.com. 8 units. High season $135–$160 double; low season $75–$90 double. Extra person $25. Rates include full breakfast. DC, DISC, MC, V. No smoking. **Amenities:** Computer center; coin-op laundry. *In room:* A/C, TV, Wi-Fi, hair dryer, iron.

Aurora Express Bed and Breakfast && *Finds* Susan Wilson's late grandmother appeared to her in a dream and told her there would be a train on a bank below her house, on the family's 15 acres high in the hills south of Fairbanks. So Wilson went out and got a train—a collection that includes a pair of 1956 Pullman sleepers, a dining car, a locomotive, a caboose, and a World War II hospital car—and her husband, Mike, brought it all up the mountain to install below the house, right in the spot indicated. Some cars are close to their original form, and Susan says older guests sometimes weep over the memories they bring back. Others were elaborately remodeled into small rooms on themes related to Fairbanks history. A full breakfast is served in the dining car, which also houses the common area, TV, and phone. One 85-foot-long car is good for families (children 7 and older only), with railroad-theme decor, puzzles, and toy trains. Then there's the incredible caboose, dedicated to Grandma.

They're located 6½ miles out of town, so you will need your own car if you stay here. Smoking is prohibited.

1540 Chena Ridge Rd. (P.O. Box 80128), Fairbanks, AK 99708. *©* 800/221-0073 or 907/474-0949. www.fairbanksalaskabedandbreakfast.com. 7 units. $135–$150 double. Extra person $15–$25. Rates include full breakfast. MC, V. Closed mid-Sept to mid-May. *In room:* No phone.

Bridgewater Hotel *(Value* *☆* This older building in a prime downtown location near the river contains comfortable, immaculate rooms that sacrifice little of substance to places charging as much as $40 a night more. Decoration in pastels creates a feminine, boutique tone in common areas. Rooms are bright and airy, and those on the corners have exceptional views. Most have shower stalls only, not tubs. A cafe serves breakfast, and one of Fairbanks' best restaurants, Gambardella's, is just steps away and allows guests to charge meals to the rooms. A great choice for summertime travelers who like staying in a traditional downtown hotel but don't need luxury hotel trappings.

723 1st Ave., Fairbanks, AK 99701. *©* 800/528-4916 or 907/452-6661 and 907/456-3642. Fax 907/452-6126. www.fountainheadhotels.com. 94 units. $129–149 double. Extra person $10. AE, DC, DISC, MC, V. Closed mid-Sept to mid-May. **Amenities:** Tour desk; courtesy van; laundry service. *In room:* A/C, TV, dataport, coffeemaker, hair dryer.

Minnie Street Bed & Breakfast Inn *☆☆* Just across the river from the downtown center, near the rail depot, buildings around a garden courtyard contain clean, large, brightly decorated rooms with many amenities, custom-designed carpeting, handmade quilts, and stylish furniture. The inn reflects the personality of its serene but exacting owner, Marnie Hazelaar, managing to feel both homey and polished. A full breakfast is served in a dining room with a high vaulted ceiling and continent breakfasts in some rooms. Huge one- and two-bedroom suites have kitchens, and three guest rooms have Jacuzzi tubs. An ambitious expansion project will add two outdoor Jacuzzis and a fourth building to the inn. Rooms have wireless Internet and there is an Internet-connected computer for guests in the common room as well.

345 Minnie St., Fairbanks, AK 99701. *©* 888/456-1849 or 907/456-1802. Fax 907/451-1751. www.minniestreet bandb.com. 10 units, 4 with shared bathroom. High season $115–$145 double, $155–$220 suite; low season $75 double, $125 suite. Extra person $25–$35. Rates include full breakfast. AE, DISC, MC, V. **Amenities:** Business center; massage; coin-op laundry. *In room:* TV, Wi-Fi, kitchen (in some), hair dryer, CD player, Jacuzzi (in some).

INEXPENSIVE

Besides the other inexpensive places listed below, **Cloudberry Lookout Bed and Breakfast,** off Goldhill Rd. at 351 Cloudberry Lane, Fairbanks, AK 99709 (*©* **907/479-7334;** fax 907/479-7134; www.mosquitonet.com/~cloudberry), is an exceptional place, a handcrafted house with a spiral staircase leading up to a 60-foot tower in the woods west of town and an eco-friendly couple as hosts.

Crestmont Manor Bed and Breakfast *☆* Phil and Connie Horton built this masterpiece of pale custom woodwork to be their home and inn (Phil is a builder), and filled it with handmade quilts (Connie is a quilter), splashes of bright colors, warm decorative themes, and huge impressionistic oil paintings (their son is an artist). The feel is crisp and airy, but the house is traditional, furnished with antiques and reproductions, like an old-fashioned home but more perfect. It sits on the side of Chena Ridge, overlooking the west side of town, near the university and some good restaurants. One small room with two twin beds and a separated bathroom rents for $100 in summer; the rest are typically sized with attached bathrooms with shower stalls. The full breakfast is served 7:30 to 8:30am, and massage is available on-site.

510 Crestmont Dr., Fairbanks, AK 99709. © **907/456-3831.** Fax 907/456-3841. www.mosquitonet.com/~crestmnt. 5 units. High season $100–$125 unit; low season $65–$75 unit. Rates include full breakfast. AE, DISC, MC, V. **Amenities:** Massage. *In room:* TV.

Golden North Motel *Value*   The Baer family, owners since 1971, are constantly improving the rooms in this two-story motel, making it the best bargain in town for those seeking a basic budget room. They make their money on return business from Alaskans who know this secret. The Baers are always replacing something, and where carpets and furniture are worn, they're still quite clean. You have a choice of small rooms and units that combine two of the smaller rooms; although strictly functional, they're very reasonably priced and have extras such as voice mail and VCRs or DVD players in the room or free to borrow, and many with microwaves and refrigerators. The building, on a side street near the airport, is a nondescript brown rectangle brightened by flower boxes on the outdoor walkways. Family members greet guest warmly with free pastries and coffee in the small lobby, which adjoins a business center with a broadband-connected computer and other business machines, free for guest use.

4888 Old Airport Rd., Fairbanks, AK 99709. © **800/447-1910** or 907/479-6201. Fax 907/479-5766. www.golden northmotel.com. 62 units. Summer $79–$99 double; winter $51–$56 double. Extra person 13 and over $10. Rates include continental breakfast. AE, DC, DISC, MC, V. **Amenities:** Courtesy van; business center. *In room:* TV, VCR or DVD (in some), Wi-Fi, fridge (in some), microwave (in some).

A HOSTEL & CAMPING

There are several hostels in Fairbanks. Among the best is the homey **Billie's Backpackers Hostel,** near the university, at 2895 Mack Blvd. (© **907/479-2034;** www. alaskahostel.com). It's a charming place with a charming owner—a real home, but quirky and fun. Billie assigns bunks as people arrive, and you could luck into a private room for the same $25 a night she charges everyone. The price includes all linens, coffee, and tea; the Internet; and much else. The Alaska/Yukon Trails shuttle stops out front (see "Getting There," p. 384). To find the hostel, turn south off College Road on Westwood Way, and then look for the first house on the left.

Tent camping is a good way to go in Fairbanks, with its mild summers and ample public lands, but stock up on the mosquito repellent. Right in town, the **Chena River State Recreation Site** (not to be confused with the recreation "area" of the same name described in the next section of this chapter), is located where University Avenue crosses the river. Sites are surrounded by birch, some are near the river, and there are flush toilets. Arrive early to camp close to the river instead of at one of the noisier sites nearer the road. Eleven sites have water and power hookups for RVs and cost $22 a night; another 45 drive-in sites for tent campers or RVs, without hookups, are $15; and 5 tent-only walk-in sites $10. Getting a bit out of town, there are superb public campgrounds at Chena Lake Recreation Area (see "Special Places," earlier in this chapter) and along Chena Hot Springs Road (see section 3 of this chapter).

Fairbanks has plenty of commercial RV parks, some with full service and then some. Pick up a list at the visitor center. Among the best is **River's Edge RV Park and Campground,** at a wooded riverside bend of the Chena at 4140 Boat St., off Airport Way and Sportsman Way (© **800/770-3343** or 907/474-0286; www.riversedge.net), with lots of services, including free shuttles. Full hookups are $30 and tent camping $19. The same people operate the cottage resort and restaurant next door.

WHERE TO DINE
DOWNTOWN

Gambardella's Pasta Bella ✿✿ ITALIAN   This warm, charming restaurant is right in the center of things. The chicken rustico (which sits on polenta) is tasty, they serve seafood in interesting ways, and the lasagna, made with sausage, thin noodles, and a rich, dusky tomato sauce, will improve your opinion of this abused dish. Dining rooms are narrow and segmented, so you always seem to be sitting with just a few other people, with elaborate decoration that adds to a pleasingly busy feeling. Unlike the synthetic ambience of some of Fairbanks's other fine dining places, Gambardella's feels real, a place where a family shares its cuisine. Perfect, no—but pleasant and satisfying. A second-story dining room with views and a patio wasn't quite complete on our last visit. They serve beer and wine.

706 2nd Ave. ✆ **907/456-3417.** www.nvo.com/gambardellas. Lunch $7–$12; dinner main courses $11–$22. 15% gratuity added for parties of 5 or more, or for split checks. AE, MC, V. Mon–Sat 11am–10pm; Sun 4:30–10pm; closes 1 hr. earlier daily off season.

Lavelle's Bistro ✿✿✿ ECLECTIC   In a big room of chrome, stone, and glass right downtown (at the base of the Marriott SpringHill Suites), Lavelle's has a grown-up, cosmopolitan feel that is quite welcome when you weary of the Alaskan rustic or gold-rush themes of many of the area's restaurants. It's also got the advantage of consistently superb food that is ambitious in conception and fine in execution, and expert service. The cuisine is difficult to categorize, as Southwest and Italian influences might be brought to a single dish, and Northwest, Asian, and French influences turn up variously. Main courses are mostly over $20, but you can dine economically on the ample appetizers and salads, or choose vegetarian lasagna that, for only $15, comes with soup or a salad and side dishes. The wine list is impressive and the 3,000-bottle cellar is behind glass in the middle of the dining room; the owners are on a mission to educate Fairbanks about wine, as they've already done with food by creating one of Alaska's best restaurants.

575 1st Ave. ✆ **907/450-0555.** www.lavellesbistro.com. Reservations recommended. Main courses $15–$30. AE, DC, DISC, MC, V. Mon–Sat 4:30–10pm; Sun 4:30–9pm.

Thai House ✿✿ THAI   In a small, brightly lit dining room in the downtown area, this is a simple, family-run restaurant with authentic Thai cuisine. Every time we've dined here, the food came quickly and was deftly seasoned and cooked to a turn. You

---

Quick Treats Unique to Fairbanks

A shop that makes its own delicious, natural ice cream started near the university; spread to North Pole, Denali, and Anchorage; and (who knows?) may soon be spread all over the planet, if the way people around here feel is an indicator. **Hot Licks Homemade Ice Cream,** at 3453 College Road (✆ **907/479-7813;** www.hotlicks.net), has all the standard flavors, plus some of their own, including blueberry and cranberry made in season with local wild berries. If you have children, their joy will be completed by a visit to the playground behind the Radio Shack next door. Right across from Hotlicks on College Road, summer only, a travel trailer in the parking lot of a sporting goods store contains a bakery called **Bun on the Run** that turns out fantastic cinnamon rolls and other baked treats, as well as hearty sandwiches.

The Roster of Rural Roads

Like frayed strands extending from the thicker rope of the main highways, these minor roads reach beyond the settled lines through Alaska into places where visitors can have real adventures. Due to the size of the state, I cannot cover everything to be found on these byways, but I have covered some highlights and enough information for you to explore on your own. You will find few other cars or tourists, lots of open land, friendly rural people, and limitless opportunities for solitude and discovery.

Unpaved highways can be hazardous. Plan on driving only 40 to 45 mph on gravel highways, and be aware of the risks of bouncing off the road or damaging your vehicle with rocks. Check road conditions, construction, and weather with the Alaska Department of Transportation (© **511**; http:// 511.alaska.gov). Bring at least one full-size spare tire and consider carrying extra gasoline in jugs. Most vehicles can make it from one gas station to the next, but what if the station is closed or you have to turn around short of a refill? Insect repellent is an absolute necessity. Drive with your headlights on at all times. Slow down or even stop to allow trucks to pass you either way; to save your windshield from rocks, it's always wise to slow down near other vehicles. Also, pull off for views or pictures—don't just stop in the middle of the road, as some people do. (Further safety and packing suggestions for rural highways are in "Driving Safety," p. 50).

Chena Hot Springs Road A relatively civilized road into the outdoors, this paved 57-mile highway east of Fairbanks meets hiking and river routes on the way to Chena Hot Springs. See section 3 of this chapter.

Dalton Highway (Rte. 11) Built to haul equipment to the Prudhoe Bay oil fields, about 500 miles north of Fairbanks, the supremely scenic Dalton

can rely on the servers, beautifully attired in national costumes, to help you order; just believe that when they say "hot," they really mean it. The first time I ate here, I rechecked the bill because it seemed too small. Thanks to this terrific restaurant and others, Fairbanks has gone a bit Thai crazy, and now, incongruously for such a provincial town, has at least five Thai restaurants. This one is the most centrally located and among the best, although that debate is part of the fun.

412 5th Ave. © **907/452-6123.** Lunch items $8–$9; dinner main courses $10–$15. MC, V. Mon–Sat 11am–4pm and 5–10pm.

WITHIN DRIVING DISTANCE

Besides the restaurants listed here, there's the salmon bake at Pioneer Park, described earlier, and the buffet at Ester Gold Camp, below. Also consider the excellent restaurant at Sophie Station Hotel (p. 398). Also in town, near the university at 3702 Cameron St. off University Ave., **Sam's Sourdough Cafe** (© **907/479-0523**) is a masterpiece in the art of the greasy spoon, with quick, friendly service, good burgers, great milkshakes, and breakfast all day. They're open from 6am to 10pm.

Some of the best pizza in town comes from **College Town Pizzeria,** near the intersection of College and University roads (© **907/457-2200**), an East Coast, reaches the heart of the wilderness, crossing the Brooks Range and the North Slope. Services are as much as a day's drive apart. See section 4 of this chapter.

Denali Highway (Rte. 8) This 133-mile gravel road connects the midpoints of the Parks and Richardson highways, passing stunning alpine vistas high in the Alaska Range that rival those within Denali National Park. Along the way are a rich network of trails and mountain lakes, and a good chance to see caribou, bear, moose, and waterfowl. See page 344.

Edgerton Highway & McCarthy Road (Rte. 10) Running east from the Richardson Highway south of Glennallen, the Edgerton leads to the tiny town of Chitina, where the McCarthy Road, a one-lane track, penetrates Wrangell–St. Elias National Park to the historic sites at McCarthy and Kennecott. The journey of 98 miles takes half a day. See page 427.

Steese Highway (Rte. 6) This road, paved for the first 62 miles, climbs the rounded tundra mountains 162 miles east of Fairbanks to the Native village of Circle, on the Yukon River. It's a rare road deep into Bush Alaska. See page 411.

Taylor Highway (Rte. 5) At times rough, narrow, and a little scary, this dirt road leads 161 miles from a junction on the Alaska Highway east of Tok to the fascinating Yukon River village of Eagle, an island in time. See page 416.

Top of the World Highway (Yukon Rte. 9) Connecting to the Taylor Highway and crossing the Canadian border to Dawson City, a distance of 79 miles, the road rides mountaintop to mountaintop, above the tree line nearly the entire way. See page 416.

order-at-the-counter, family place. The crust is wonderful—crisp yet chewy—and they prepare it either in the American style or as Italian gourmet pizza with pesto, spinach, and the like and without tomato sauce. A large combo is $21. They deliver within Fairbanks between noon and 5pm and are closed Sunday.

The Bakery *(Finds* DINER   There are an infinite number of old-fashioned coffee shops in and around Fairbanks—the kind of place where a truck driver or gold miner can find a hearty, down-home meal, a bottomless cup of coffee, and a motherly waitress. This is one of the better versions. The sourdough pancakes are good, the menu is long and inexpensive, portions are huge (sometimes they require two plates), the service is fast and friendly. The motherly waitress called me "Sweetie" on my last visit. Of course, you can get breakfast all day. They have no liquor license.

69 College Rd. ⓒ **907/456-8600.** Lunch items $7–$10; dinner main courses $9–$20. MC, V. Mon–Sat 6am–9pm (closing 8pm in winter); Sun 7am–4pm.

Pike's Landing *(*⚘ STEAK/SEAFOOD   The dining room of the fine-dining section overlooks the Chena River near the airport from a series of tiered levels, each with tables well separated and covered with linens. The menu includes a nice range of simple to more ambitious selections; highlights I have found included the appetizer of spicy crab-stuffed mushrooms with a thick, chowder-like sauce, and a lunch of a deftly seasoned seafood burrito. Portions are quite large. Sunday brunch is big and delicious. Service, in my experience, is not always perfect, however, and the entire restaurant is a bit dated. For an inexpensive meal, the bar serves basic food on the deck over the river from 2:30 to 10pm. It's a pleasant choice on a sunny day, less so in cool or rainy weather, when it remains in operation behind plastic.

4438 Airport Way. © 907/479-6500. Lunch items $9–$12; dinner main courses $12–$35. AE, DC, DISC, MC, V. Mon–Sat 11am–2pm, 5–9pm; Sun 10am–2pm, 5–9pm.

The Pump House Restaurant and Saloon ✿✿ STEAK/SEAFOOD The historic, rambling, corrugated tin building on the National Register is elaborately decorated and landscaped with authentic gold-rush relics. Sitting on the deck over the Chena, you can watch the riverboat paddle by or a group in canoes stop for appetizers and drinks from the full bar. For dinner, the cuisine is a cut above the area's typical steaks and seafood, and includes game you may not have tried, including reindeer and musk ox. Dishes such as the halibut Florentine and the fish chowder—hearty, creamy, and flavorful—make the most of the regional ingredients without trying to get too fancy. The food is award winning, and we were delighted on our last visit. Many of the side dishes are a la carte, so, although main courses are generous, it's expensive to order a large meal. Besides, you'll want to save room for one of the exceptional desserts. They serve a big Sunday brunch, too.

Mile 1.3, Chena Pump Rd. © 907/479-8452. www.pumphouse.com. Main courses $18–$36. AE, DISC, MC, V. Summer Mon–Sat 11:30am–2pm and 5–10pm, Sun 10am–2pm and 5–10pm; winter Mon–Sat 5–9pm, Sun 10am–2pm and 5–9pm.

The Turtle Club *Finds* ✿ BEEF/SEAFOOD Locals pack into this squat, windowless building, with its vinyl tablecloths and stackable metal chairs, for a menu with just a few famous selections: prime rib, lobster, king crab, prawns and, Tuesday through Thursday, barbecue ribs. These are simple, burly meals with roadhouse-style service, the menu is printed on the placemat, and vegetables are an afterthought from an indifferent salad bar. But when the beef comes, you know it—the middle-size prime rib cut is over an inch thick and covers a large plate, an insanely large portion—and the meat is tender and cooked right. The atmosphere is noisy and supercasual; people laugh loud and don't worry about putting their elbows on the table or spilling a little beer. You won't run into many other tourists here, north of the city in Fox, but you do need reservations, and even with them you often wait half an hour in the smoky bar or a narrow corridor. If this doesn't sound like fun, don't go; but if you get it, the place is energizing.

10 Mile Old Steese Hwy., Fox. © 907/457-3883. Reservations recommended. Main courses $20–$30. AE, DISC, MC, V. Mon–Sat 6–10pm; Sun 5–9pm.

FAIRBANKS NIGHTLIFE

Fairbanks has a lot of tourist-oriented evening activities, as well as entertainment also attended by locals. Call the 24-hour event recording of what's playing currently (© **907/456-4636**) or get a copy of the *Fairbanks Daily News-Miner*. A large multiplex **movie theater** is located on Airport Way. The evening show at the **Palace Theatre** is discussed earlier under "Pioneer Park."

The Ester Gold Camp (© **800/676-6925** or 907/479-2500; www.akvisit.com) is an 11-building historic site, an old mining town that's been turned into an evening tourist attraction. The main event is a gold-rush–themed show at the Malamute Saloon, with singing and Robert Service poetry, nightly at 9pm; admission is $18, half-price age 12 and under. A "photosymphony" slide show about the aurora takes place a couple of times a night in the summer and costs $8. Admission for children 12 and under is $4, but children under 2 are not admitted. From 5 to 9pm, the restaurant serves an all-you-can-eat buffet, including crab, with mess-hall seating; it costs $28, or $14 ages 12 and under. The camp offers simple, inexpensive rooms in the old gold mine bunkhouse and a campground.

Here are a couple of places to go out in the evening without having to hear about the gold rush (in other words, places real locals go). Downtown, **Café Alex Wine Bar,** at 310 1st Ave. (© **907/452-2539**), is a trendy and popular place to sip wine and nosh on shared plates from an all-appetizer menu of delicious food, and hear live music on Friday. They serve full meals as well and are open for lunch Monday through Friday. Or, 3 miles south of town on the Parks Highway, **The Blue Loon** (© **907/457-5666;** www.theblueloon.com) has live music—both local and famous imported acts—lots of beers on tap, and good burgers. They even show movies and call themselves the "cultural epicenter of Fairbanks."

3 Chena Hot Springs Road

The 57-mile paved road east from Fairbanks is an avenue to an enjoyable day trip or a destination for up to a week's outdoor activities and hot-spring swimming. Of all the roads radiating from Fairbanks, this short highway will be most rewarding to outdoors people, and there is a funky and relaxing resort at the end.

The road travels through the Chena River State Recreation Area, with spectacular hikes and float trips and well-maintained riverside campgrounds, and leads to the Chena Hot Springs, where there's a year-round resort perfect for soaking in hot mineral springs and for use as a base for summer or winter wilderness day trips. The resort is open to people who want to rent one of the comfortable rooms or to campers and day-trippers, and it's even more popular in the winter than in the summer (the slow seasons are spring and fall).

The paved road leads through a forest of birch, spruce, and cottonwood, first passing an area of scattered roadside development and then following the Chena River through the state recreation area. On a sunny summer weekend, the people of Fairbanks migrate to the riverside and the hiking trails; on a sunny winter weekend, they take to the hills on snowmobiles, cross-country skis, or dog sleds. It's a pleasant drive at any time, around 1¼ hours each way from Fairbanks, but not particularly scenic.

A pair of prospectors, the Swan brothers, discovered the hot springs in 1905, having heard that a U.S. Geological Survey crew had seen steam in a valley on the upper Chena. Thomas Swan suffered from rheumatism; incredibly, he and his brother poled up the Chena River from Fairbanks, found the hot springs, built a cabin and rock-floored pool, and spent the summer soaking. He was cured! More visitors followed, drawn by stories that whole groups of cripples were able to dance all night after soaking in the pools—by 1915 a resort was in operation, drawing worn-out miners and gold-rush stampeders and many others as well. It has been in constant use ever since.

ESSENTIALS

GETTING THERE   The Chena Hot Springs Road meets the Steese Expressway about 5 miles north of downtown Fairbanks. (Details on renting a car in Fairbanks can be found at the beginning of section 2 of this chapter.) The resort offers rides from anywhere in Fairbanks for $90 round-trip for one or two people, $45 for each additional person. Arrange for this at least 72 hours in advance.

VISITOR INFORMATION For outdoors information, check the Fairbanks **Alaska Public Lands Information Center,** 250 Cushman St. (at 3rd Ave.; ℭ **907/ 456-0527;** www.nps.gov/aplic). The **Alaska Division of Parks,** at 3700 Airport Way, Fairbanks, AK 99709 (ℭ **907/451-2695;** www.alaskastateparks.org, click on "Individual Parks" and choose the recreation area—not the "site"), manages the recreation area and produces trail, river, and road guides, which are also available at trail-head kiosks, from the public lands center, on the website, or in the area's *Chena Trailmarker* brochure. You can also contact the parks office with questions about the public cabins in the area (see "State Parks Cabin Reservations," p. 262, for how to reserve).

THE CHENA RIVER STATE RECREATION AREA

The recreation area takes in 254,000 acres along the river valley and over the rolling mountains of heather around it. Some of Interior Alaska's best hiking and floating are found here. As everywhere in the Interior, the mosquitoes are brutal.

ACTIVITIES

HIKING & BACKPACKING The best trail hikes in the Fairbanks area are in the Chena Hot Springs State Recreation Area. Backcountry camping requires no permit, and many of the trails go above the tree line, so it's a good area for backpackers to get into the wilderness.

The **Angel Rocks Trail** is a sometimes steep 3.5-mile loop to a group of large granite outcroppings, an impressive destination with good views of the valley below. The trail mostly stays below the tree line; the blackened areas you see are from major fires that burned through the area in 2002 and 2004. The trail head is well marked, at Mile 48.9 of the road. A side trail heads up to the ridgelines and goes all the way to Chena Hot Springs, a one-way hike of 8.3 miles.

The 15-mile loop of the **Granite Tors Trail,** starting at Mile 39 of the road, is a challenging day hike, rising through forest to rolling alpine terrain, but the towering tors on top more than reward the effort. (A short-cut loop reduces the hike to 3 miles but stays in the trees and doesn't make it near the tors.) Like surrealist experiments in perspective, these monolithic granite sentinels stand at random spots on the broad Plain of Monuments, at first confounding the eye's attempts to gauge their distance and size. Like the Angel Rocks, they were created when upwelling rock solidified in cracks in the surrounding earth, which then eroded away. Water is scarce, so bring along plenty. This is an excellent overnight hike, with the driest ground for camping right around the tors. There is also a public shelter halfway along the trail. Massive fires in 2004 burned over much of the trail, but it remains passable and the Plain of Monuments was practically unscathed.

For a longer backpacking trip, the **Chena Dome Trail** makes a 29-mile loop, beginning at Mile 50.5 and ending at Mile 49. The 3 miles nearest the road at either end pass through forest, but the remaining 23 miles are above the tree line, marked with cairns and with expansive views. The trail summits 4,421-foot Chena Dome after the 10-mile mark. The trail can be quite wet and muddy in parts, and steep and rocky elsewhere, and you must bring water with you. A public shelter is on the trail.

RIVER FLOATING The Chena is a lovely river, growing from a clear, frothy creek near the end of the road to a lazy, brown Class I river as it flows off toward Fairbanks, several days downstream. Where you choose to start depends on your expertise. Easier water is downstream from Rosehip Campground (Mile 27), with the slowest of all nearer Fairbanks, but the upper portion is more popular if you are up for something a bit more challenging. The road crosses the river several times, and the state park system has developed other access points, so it's possible to plan a float that exactly matches your time and abilities. Choose your route with the help of the river guide produced by the Alaska Division of Parks (see "Visitor Information," above).

Canoe Alaska (© 907/883-2628; www.canoealaska.net) specializes in white-water canoe instruction for beginners and intermediate paddlers, and leads guided canoe and raft outings and expeditions; a guided trip is around $100 a day. They also rent canoes and offer shuttle service. Other agencies offering such services are covered in the Fairbanks section, earlier (two are under "Gearing Up," p. 393, and one in the feature "Equipped for the Back Roads," p. 393).

FISHING   Several of the ponds in the recreation area are stocked with rainbow trout, which you can keep, subject to harvest limits. Signs along the road mark access points to the ponds and river. You can catch and release Arctic grayling in the Chena, but check current regulations and bait restrictions. Contact the **Alaska Department of Fish and Game,** 1300 College Rd., Fairbanks, AK 99701 (© 907/459-7207; www.alaska.gov/adfg, click on "Sport Fisheries," then on the Interior region on the map, and then "Lower Tanana River Drainage").

CAMPING & CABINS

Three beautiful campgrounds with water and pit toilets lie along the road by the Chena River, managed by the Alaska Division of Parks (see "Visitor Information," above). Although they can't be reserved ahead, the campgrounds are unlikely to be full. The **Rosehip Campground,** at Mile 27, has 37 sites, well separated by spruce and birch, with six suitable for RVs. Some sites are right on the river, and some are set up for more private tent camping, in the woods. The **Granite Tors Campground** is across from the trail head at Mile 39; it has 24 sites, 7 suitable for RVs. Some sites front on a river slough, and, as at Rosehip, float trips can start or end here. The **Red Squirrel Campground,** at Mile 42.8, has 12 sites and a pleasant picnic area on the grassy edge of a small, placid pond, where swimming is permitted. Camping is $10 a night at each of these campgrounds.

There are several public-use cabins in the recreation area, two of them easily accessible to summer visitors and not hard to book a month or two ahead. (See "State Parks Cabin Reservations," on p. 262, for how to get one.) These are primitive cabins; you must bring your own sleeping bags, lights, and cooking gear. The **North Fork Cabin** is at Mile 47.7 of the road, and the **Chena River Cabin** faces the river at Mile 32.2. You can get to either by car or canoe, and each costs $50 a night in the summer, $40 off-season. Other public cabins in the area primarily serve winter users and are difficult to reach when the ground thaws.

THE HOT SPRINGS

Chena Hot Springs Resort ♦♦   Several years ago, Bernie Karl, a Fairbanks recycling entrepreneur, bought the hot springs, the 440-acre valley they lie in, and the old resort there, which had perennially struggled to stay out of the red. As I walked around the grounds with him, he waved his hand here and there while outlining his audacious plans. I admit I nodded patronizingly. Each time I've gone back, however, more of his dream has been realized: an outdoor, boulder-rimmed swimming pond of hot mineral water, without chlorine or treatment; big buildings for large, modern rooms and for recreational activities; geothermal greenhouses growing produce for the restaurant; and, incredibly, a large arched building made of ice. Bernie built the ice hotel and filled it with expertly carved ice sculptures and got international publicity—then the building inspectors shut it down, citing, of all things, the lack of fire extinguishers. (Their real concern was the complete lack of engineering.) Bernie hired an engineer, got the disagreement worked out, and operated the ice hotel for a winter. That hotel melted the next summer, but Bernie rebuilt it, renamed it an ice museum, and has kept it going year-round with a unique refrigeration system that uses heated water from the hot springs. Whatever he says he will do next, I will believe him. Tours of the museum are $15 per person ($7.50 ages 4–12), and you can still rent it for a night. (For the price, $575, you also get Arctic clothing and an indoor room, in case you weary of the cold.)

Unfortunately, Bernie is not as good at maintaining as he is at dreaming and building, and those expecting the standards of service and polish of a corporate resort will be disappointed. If you stay, I would recommend renting the newest, most expensive rooms. Or camp out. Our family has enjoyed wonderful days here swimming and exploring. Soak in the pools, hike through the woods, and enjoy the sound of the wind in the trees.

The hot springs supply an indoor pool, a series of indoor and outdoor hot tubs and spas, and the outdoor hot pond (100–110°F/38–44°C). Kids are limited to the indoor swimming pool, which is kept cool enough to swim, allowing adults to escape from the noise by swimming outside. The locker rooms are tiny, so guests will want to change in their rooms (a long-promised expansion is supposedly coming). The swimming facility is open daily from 7am to midnight. Swim passes come with your room if you're staying at the resort; for campers or day-trippers, a day pass is $10 adults, $8 age 60 and older, $7 ages 6 to 17, free children 5 and under.

Winter is the high season, when the aurora viewing is exceptional, away from city lights, and you can enjoy Nordic skiing groomed for classical or skating techniques, Sno-Cat and snow-machine tours, dog-sled rides, and more. An aurora-viewing station, with a warm-up lodge, is established on a hilltop, where guests can flop back in the snow under a dizzying dome of stars and colors. In the summer, you can go horseback riding, rafting, canoeing, hiking, gold panning, mountain biking, or flightseeing (for guests only). Many activities are guided and carry extra fees. Some rental equipment is available.

The accommodations range from cabins and yurts to the large hotel rooms with televisions, phones, and coffeemakers. The newest rooms, in the Moose building, are solidly built and nicely done up, but noise can be a problem winter nights as guests come and go to look at the aurora. The cabins and yurts are basic but adequate if you want inexpensive lodgings and don't mind not having indoor plumbing. The intermediate rooms got new paint, carpet, and furniture in 2005 and 2006, but were cheaply built to start with. They have shower stalls, not tubs. The main lodge building contains the restaurant and bar. The menu and staff change fairly frequently. Overall, this is a good place to have fun in the real Alaska, but be ready for some rough spots.

Mile 56.5, Chena Hot Springs Rd. (P.O. Box 58740), Fairbanks, AK 99711. ℂ **800/478-4681** or 907/451-8104. Fax 907/451-8151. www.chenahotsprings.com. 80 units, 3 cabins. $160–$220 double, $65 cabins and yurts. Extra person $20. AE, DC, DISC, MC, V. **Amenities:** Restaurant; bar; indoor and outdoor pools; hot tubs; Jacuzzis; equipment rentals; guided activities; tour desk; massage; coin-op laundry. *In room* (excluding cabins): TV, coffeemaker.

The Steese Highway: Drive into the Wild

Driving the Steese Highway north from Fairbanks is like following a river upstream as it diminishes into its headwaters. First it's a four-lane freeway, then a two-lane highway, then the pavement gives out (at Mile 62), and then the gravel gives out. The road climbs over round tundra mountains, leaves behind the last tiny town, and then drifts through uninhabited woods before ending on the banks of the Yukon River at a tiny Athabaskan village, Circle (named for the Arctic Circle, which it isn't on). It's a rough 162-mile drive to nowhere. But if nowhere is where you want to go, the Steese Highway may be the right adventure for you. Just don't forget the mosquito repellent.

Most of the land along the Steese is controlled by the federal **Bureau of Land Management (BLM),** 1150 University Ave., Fairbanks, AK 99709 (© **800/ 437-7021** or 907/474-2200). Small- and large-scale gold mining takes place in the area, but most of the land is managed for recreation, with several campgrounds, some popular river floats, and a couple of beautiful hikes. Navigating the BLM website is confusing, but it contains a lot of good information. Start at www.blm.gov/ak and look for the Steese National Conservation Area and the White Mountains National Recreation Area, among other topics. In addition, State Parks manages the **Upper Chatanika River Campground,** at Mile 39, with 25 sites, pit toilets, a hand pump for water, and a $10 fee. This is the starting point for the most popular river float on the highway (covered, with others, in the Fairbanks section under "Canoeing," p. 394).

Without driving to the bitter end at Circle (where the only attraction is the Yukon River itself), you can make a goal of **Eagle Summit,** at Mile 107, the highest place on the highway (3,624 ft.), and a good place to be on June 21 each year, the summer solstice. Although it's still a degree of latitude below the Arctic Circle, the sun never sets here on the longest day because of the elevation and atmospheric refraction. People come out from Fairbanks and make a celebration of it. The midnight sun is visible for about 3 days before and after the solstice, too, assuming the sky is clear. The BLM has installed a toilet and a viewing deck on a 750-foot loop trail at the trail head to the 27-mile **Pinnell Mountain National Recreation Trail.** This is a challenging 3-day hike over amazing terrain of rounded, windblown, tundra-clothed mountaintops. To hike it downhill, start at Eagle Summit and end at Twelvemile Summit, Mile 86. Two emergency shelters along the trail provide protection from the ferocious weather that can sweep the mountains. Get the free BLM trail brochure before going.

The next sensible destination is the tiny town of Central, 128 miles along the highway. It's a real, old-fashioned gold-mining community where the current price of gold is posted in the bar and you can use gold dust to pay for your drinks. There are a couple of simple diners, lodgings, and a campground, and the small **Circle District Historical Museum** (© **907/520-1893**), which covers the area's natural and human history, including the gold mining that has sustained it since 1893. Admission is $1 adults, 50¢ 12 and under, free over age 70. It is open during summer daily noon to 5pm.

4 The Dalton Highway

The original purpose was utilitarian: to haul equipment north from Fairbanks for the trans-Alaska oil pipeline, which runs from Prudhoe Bay, on the Arctic Ocean, to Valdez, on the Pacific. But the experience of the Dalton Highway for a traveler is so far beyond the ordinary as to require a whole new frame of reference to take it all in. The road is so very long, so remote and free of traffic, and the scenery is so mind-boggling in its grandeur and repetition, that after a time it feels like you're living in a dream. At some point you have to swallow and say to yourself, "I guess I didn't know that much about the world after all."

Part of the wonder comes in the difficulty of the drive. There are extreme sports—throwing yourself off the side of a mountain and so forth—and this is an extreme road trip, one that dives into deep wilderness as far from help as most people ever get. In 500 miles, there are only two service stations. The road averages only 250 vehicles a day over its entire length. Driving the Dalton is not to be taken lightly or done on a whim. You need to prepare and you need to know you want to do it because you will be rumbling over gravel for many, many hours, breathing dust, and beating the crud out of your car.

The drive starts in Fairbanks (officially, you drive parts of the Steese Hwy. and Elliott Hwy. before the real Dalton Hwy. begins), crossing the rounded hills and low forest of that region before crossing the Yukon River on a high, wood-decked bridge. Over the miles that follow, trees grow sparser and the road crosses some spectacular alpine plateaus until, entering the Brooks Range, Arctic vegetation and the mountains' rocky ferocity take over. Beyond towering Atigun Pass, the Arctic Slope extends 170 miles, first through sensuous tundra foothills, and then over the broad, lake-dotted flatlands that extend to the Arctic Ocean. Arrival at the oil facilities can be a letdown, especially if you haven't made arrangements for the tour that is the only way through to the shore. More on that below.

Wildlife shows up all along the road: moose, caribou, and grizzly bears, and sport fish and songbirds. Animals far outnumber people. Two highway businesses are near the Yukon; in Coldfoot, there is a truck stop; and Wiseman is 15 miles up the road from Coldfoot, where the 2000 census counted 21 people. And that's it for another 240 miles of gravel to Prudhoe Bay. There are no ATMs, no grocery stores, no cell-phone coverage, no medical facilities—civilization just isn't there. Drive carefully.

DALTON HIGHWAY ESSENTIALS

PRACTICAL TIPS   You can drive the highway yourself, staying in the few motels along the way or in a tent or motor home. From Fairbanks, take the Steese Highway north to the Elliott Highway. The total road distance from Fairbanks to the Arctic Ocean is 497 miles. Road conditions are notorious on the gravel-and-dirt Dalton, but now much of it is kept in good condition with pavement working its way steadily north. Speeds of 50 mph are possible on some parts of the road, while doing 35 will keep you in one piece on rougher spots. The drive takes 12 hours each way, without stops. It's dusty, shoulders are soft, and flat tires are common. In the Fairbanks section, I have listed a business that rent four-wheel-drive pickup trucks and campers (See "Equipped for the Back Roads," on p. 393). Generally, other rental companies don't allow their vehicles on the Dalton.

Preparing for the drive is essential. Pick up the road guide produced by the BLM and get firsthand, personal advice (see "Visitor Information," below). Read up on the safety advice under "The Roster of Rural Roads," p. 404. For those who want to let someone else do the driving, a bus package is listed in section 9 of chapter 10, on Prudhoe Bay.

VISITOR INFORMATION   Getting up-to-date advice is critical before heading off on the Dalton Highway, and the best place to do that is the Fairbanks **Alaska Public Lands Information Center,** at 250 Cushman St. (at 3rd Ave.), Fairbanks, AK 99701 (℡ **907/456-0527;** www.nps.gov/aplic). Staffers there drive the road annually to stay on top of current conditions.

Much of the road runs through land managed by the **Bureau of Land Management,** 1150 University Ave., Fairbanks, AK 99709 (℡ **800/437-7021** or 907/474-2200). The handy *Dalton Highway Visitor Guide,* a free 24-page booklet, is available at the public lands information center or from any BLM information center, or by mail by calling the number above.

Two information stops are along the highway, both open summer only. A **contact station** at the Yukon River crossing is staffed by BLM volunteers and open daily in summer from 9am to 6pm. It has no phone. The recently constructed **Arctic Interagency Visitor Center** is at Mile 175 on the west side of the highway in Coldfoot (℡ **907/678-5209** or 907/678-2014), open late May to early September from 10am to 10pm daily. The free center has exhibits about the North, a theater for nightly educational programs, a trip-planning room, a bookstore, and knowledgeable staff. Even if you don't have any questions, it's hard to imagine not stopping at this one real tourist attraction in your many hours of driving.

ON THE ROAD

The bridge over the Yukon River at Mile 56 is the only crossing in Alaska, and many people drive the Dalton just to get to the **Arctic Circle** at Mile 115, where you'll find a sign for pictures as well as a crude camping area. Many, many places along the highway have incredible views. Among the most famous are Finger Mountain at Mile 98; Gobbler's Knob at Mile 132, which offers the first view of the Brooks Range; and 4,739-foot Atigun Pass at Mile 245, where the road crosses the Brooks Range, winding through impossibly rugged country. The pass is the highest point on the Alaska road system, and you may find summer snow. All along the highway are opportunities to see birds and animals, including rabbits, foxes, wolves, moose, Dall sheep, bears, and caribou. Sit still if you want to see the skittish caribou, as they may wander closer to an unmoving vehicle.

The road parallels the 4-foot-wide **trans-Alaska pipeline.** The line, completed in 1977, serves America's largest and second-largest oil fields, Prudhoe Bay and Kuparuk, carrying the hot crude 900 miles from the Arctic Ocean to docks in Valdez, where tankers pick it up for shipment primarily to the West Coast. The public road ends before reaching the Prudhoe Bay complex and the Arctic Ocean. The only way through the gate is with a tour operator, and you must make arrangements at least 24 hours ahead to clear security. Call the **Arctic Caribou Inn** (℡ **877/659-2368** or 907/659-2368; www.arcticcaribouinn.com). See section 9 of chapter 10, on Prudhoe Bay, for more details.

HIGHWAY SERVICES: FOOD, FUEL & LODGINGS

Among the three places offering services along the 414 miles of the Dalton, you won't find anything luxurious, or even approaching budget chains. Near the spectacular suspended bridge over the Yukon River, at Mile 56, is a decidedly unspectacular motel, restaurant, and gas station. **Yukon River Camp** (© **907/474-3557**) has a gift shop and tire repair, as well as food, gas, and lodging. The motel is a former pipeline-construction camp. Just 4 miles up the road from the river, the **Hot Spot Café** (© **907/ 451-7543**) offers dining, lodging, a gift shop, gas, and tire repair.

The **Coldfoot Camp** truck stop at Mile 175 (© **866/474-3400** or 907/474-3500; www.coldfootcamp.com) is the one big stopping place along the road. After the endless wilderness miles on the road, no one could stand to pass it by. The year-round camp includes several buildings on a large gravel pad. Most important are the gas pumps and the 24-hour restaurant where you pay for the fuel—a typical but friendly highway diner. Across the lot, the camp's inn is built of left-over construction camp modular units. The small rooms with low ceilings are perfectly comfortable, with private bathrooms, but far from grand. The camp also offers minor vehicle repairs, towing, RV hookup, laundry, a post office, a gift shop, and a saloon. They guide rafting on the Middle Fork Koyukuk River and offer flight tours to the village of Anaktuvuk Pass and shuttles for hiking. In the winter, the camp offers dog-sled rides. An air taxi, **Coyote Air** (© **800/252-0603** or 907/678-5995; www.flycoyote.com), offers flightseeing over this amazing country. There are other activities farther afield offered by **Northern Alaska Tour Company** (© **800/474-1986** or 907/474-8600; www.northernalaska.com). Don't miss the new interagency visitor center, described above. The pleasant BLM Marion Creek Campground is 5 miles north of Coldfoot.

After Coldfoot, the next service area is **Deadhorse,** at the end of the road another 240 miles north, with rooms, fuel, restaurants, a post office, vehicle maintenance, a general store, and an airport. See the Prudhoe Bay section in chapter 10.

GETTING OUT OF THE CAR
ACTIVITIES

FISHING   The streams and lakes of the Arctic are cold, poor in nutrients, and frozen much of the year; fishing is not a good reason to drive the Dalton. However, if you are taking the adventure anyway, there are fish in streams from July to mid-September and in lakes that don't freeze to the bottom. Many of the streams have Arctic grayling, but you'll want to hike farther than a quarter-mile from the road to increase your chances. A good bet is the **Jim River area** between miles 140 and 144, where the river follows the road and fishing pressure is more spread out. Most North Slope rivers have good Dolly Varden fishing in late August and early September. Many of the lakes along the road have grayling, and the deeper ones north of the Brooks Range have lake trout. Check current regulations. Contact the **Alaska Department of Fish and Game,** 1300 College Rd., Fairbanks, AK 99701 (© **907/459-7207;** www.alaska.gov/adfg); they produce a booklet called *Sportfishing Along the Dalton Highway,* which you can get on paper or on the Web (click "Sport Fish Publications" and then "Interior.")

HIKING   The road has no established hiking trails, but most of the area is open to self-reliant hikers who know how to pick their own route. Hiking brushy or marshy Interior country isn't fun, but the dry tundra of the ridgetops and mountains creates a wonderful sense of freedom. The country opens up north of the Chandalar Shelf at Mile 237. The best hiking area is the zone of dry tundra in the foothills north of the Brooks Range. But even at upper elevations, you still run into tussocks, wet ground, and stream crossings. Topographical maps and advice on hiking the Brooks Range are available at the sources listed under "Visitor Information," above. Remember, this is remote wilderness; do your research, be prepared, and tell someone where you're going and when you'll be back.

CAMPING

The Bureau of Land Management has a few campgrounds along the road, but there seems little reason to wait to reach them, as there are a number of places to pull off the road on a spot of gravel and spend the night, often in places of stunning beauty. The only requirements are for safety and the environment: Get far enough off the road to avoid the fast-moving trucks spewing rocks as far as 30 feet, read up on bear avoidance on p. 47, don't leave toilet paper or anything else behind, and stay no longer than 14 days in one spot. I have listed the BLM's developed areas along the road, which include campgrounds and spots where you can park for a while and obtain water. Unless the description mentions a formal campground, these are just pull-outs where you can park and camp or sleep in your car (add 83 miles to the mileposts to get the distance from Fairbanks):

- **Mile 60** (Five Mile): Artesian well with potable water, outhouses, and free public dump station (this is the last dump station on the highway).
- **Mile 98** (Finger Mountain): Nice views, outhouse, and wheelchair-accessible trail with interpretive signs.
- **Mile 115** (Arctic Circle): Outhouses, picnic tables, and an interpretive display; camp only in the undeveloped campground up the hill, which has an outhouse but no water.
- **Mile 150** (Grayling Lake): Wayside with outhouse.
- **Mile 175** (Coldfoot): A private campground with hookups is part of the Coldfoot Camp truck stop described above.
- **Mile 180** (Marion Creek): A developed BLM campground with 27 campsites, 11 of them for large RVs (no hookups). The campground has a potable well and outhouses; the fee is $8.
- **Mile 235** (Arctic tree line): Outhouse; not an attractive camping site due to truck traffic on a steep grade.
- **Mile 275** (Galbraith Lake): Undeveloped campground with an outhouse but without water about 4 miles off-road; follow the access road past the state-operated landing strip, and then continue 2½ miles on an unimproved road.
- **Mile 301** (Slope Mountain): Land north of this point is managed by the Alaska Department of Natural Resources, not the BLM; however, you can use the same visitor information sources mentioned above.
- **Mile 355** (on the North Slope): Wayside with an outhouse.
- **Mile 414** (Deadhorse): The end of the road. Deadhorse has a post office, general store, hotel, and other services, and an operator offers tours through to the Arctic Ocean, which must be arranged in advance. See p. 463.

5 The Alaska Highway

Detailed coverage of the entire 2,400-mile drive to Alaska is beyond our scope, but chapter 2's "Getting There" section provides the planning basics. Here I've covered the Alaska portion of the road, the 200 miles of the Alaska Highway that run from the border with Canada to the terminus in Delta Junction. This is mostly boring driving, miles of stunted black spruce and brush, either living or burned out. It's a relief when you hit the first major town, **Tok** (rhymes with Coke), 100 miles along. But don't get your hopes up. This is the only place where I've ever walked into a visitor center and asked what there is to do in town, only to have the host hold up her fingers in the shape of a goose egg and say, "Nothing." Another 100 miles (I hope you brought

Dawson City & Eagle: Detour into History

Instead of taking the Alaska Highway directly from Whitehorse, Yukon, to Tok, consider driving north on the Klondike Highway (Yukon Hwy. 2) to Dawson City, and then west and south over the Top of the World Highway and partially unpaved Taylor Highway to rejoin the Alaska Highway just east of Tok. This represents 502 miles of driving, about 127 miles more than if you just stay on the Alaska Highway, and includes 43 miles of sometimes rough dirt road, but it's worth doing at least one way to see historic Dawson City and the fabulous mountain scenery of the Top of the World Highway. Dawson was the destination of the 1898 Klondike Gold Rush; the bed of the Klondike River near here contained thick veins of gold. The town maintains the look of those days, when it was the second-largest city on the West Coast, after San Francisco. Many buildings, a gold dredge, and a riverboat were restored as part of the Klondike National Historic Sites, managed by **Parks Canada.** Besides the buildings and their setting, there are museums, a working not-for-profit casino, a center of indigenous culture, and other attractions, easily enough for 2 days of sightseeing. The **Klondike Visitor Association** (P.O. Box 389, Dawson City, YT, Canada Y0B 1G0; © **867/993-5575;** fax 867/993-6415; www.dawsoncity.ca), offers information on local businesses, accommodations, and community events. For information on the historic sites, contact Parks Canada at P.O. Box 390, Dawson City, YT, Canada Y0B 1G0 (© **867/ 993-7200;** www.parkscanada.gc.ca, click on "National Historic Sites" and then "Yukon"). For information on the **Han Nation people** here and their cultural center, call © **867/993-7100** (www.trondek.com).

After passing into the United States on the Top of the World Highway (note this border crossing is open only during the day and only during the

plenty of music because no radio station reaches out here) and you've made it to **Delta Junction.** There's a little more to do here, but it's still not a destination. Another 100 miles and you're in Fairbanks.

The main sources of information for the drive are based in Tok, the first town you hit after you cross the border. It acts as a threshold for the entire state. To plan the journey ahead, contact them, and see "Exploring the Interior," at the beginning of this chapter. If you're headed to Anchorage or other points south, see the sections on the Glenn and Richardson highways later in this chapter; those roads branch from the Alaska Highway at Tok and Delta, respectively.

I've arranged this section in order from the border with Canada heading west.

CROSSING THE BORDER

Remember to set your watch back an hour when crossing the border in Alaska—it's an hour later in Yukon Territory. Also, if you make significant purchases or rent rooms in Canada, you may be able to get a refund on the 7% goods and services tax (GST). Ask for the form at a Canadian border station.

CUSTOMS   Crossing the U.S./Canadian border requires preparation even for U.S. citizens. Starting the first day of 2008, U.S. citizens will need passports to re-enter the summer), a further detour leads north on the Taylor Highway to the forgotten town of Eagle on the bank of the Yukon River (going south on the Taylor leads you back to the Alaska Hwy.). The trip to Eagle adds 66 miles each way on a winding, narrow dirt road; allow 2 hours each way. But if you have the time, the destination more than rewards the effort. Eagle is lost in time, a treasure of a gold-rush river town with many original buildings full of original artifacts from a century ago. It's entirely authentic and noncommercial, with few businesses other than the store, cafe, motel, and a B&B. The **Eagle Historical Society and Museums** (© 907/547-2325; www.eagleak.org) shows off the buildings and several museums of materials left behind in this eddy in the stream of history. Their 3-hour walking tour starts once a day at 9am daily Memorial Day to Labor Day and costs $5.

To plan a float trip on the Yukon River from Eagle, or for other outdoor information, contact the Eagle Field Office of the **Yukon–Charley Rivers National Preserve,** P.O. Box 167, Eagle, AK 99738 (© 907/547-2233; www.nps.gov/yuch). The office lies on the far side of the airstrip from the main part of town.

The funny little village of Chicken is the other stop on this drive (the old joke is that they wanted to name the town Ptarmigan but didn't know how to spell it). There are a couple of businesses and it's worth stopping for gold panning, a meal, or to shop for gifts. Chicken, too, is mixed up in the area's time warp: The town has never had phone service, but businesses have free Wi-Fi.

country over the road. Canadians will need passports but not visas to enter the United States on the highway. The rule is in effect for 2007 for air and water entry. (The regulations are under review, however, so these dates could change.) See chapter 2 to learn more about passports and entry requirements for international visitors. Prior to the new requirements, U.S. and Canadian citizens don't need passports or visas going either way, but if you don't have a passport, you should carry **proof of citizenship** and **proof of identity.** Practically speaking, this means you should have a piece of photo identification such as a driver's license combined with a birth certificate. A naturalized citizen should carry a copy of the naturalization certificate rather than a birth certificate. **Children** with their parents should have a birth certificate, children or youths under 18 unaccompanied by parents need a notarized letter from a parent or guardian, and children with a single parent should carry such a letter from the other parent. There are no duties on products made in the United States or Canada. For duties on items that you buy that originated in other countries or on alcohol or smoking supplies, see chapter 2. Products you buy in Alaska made of **wildlife** will probably require special permits to be taken out of the United States, and most marine mammal products cannot be exported; see p. 44. If you are a U.S. resident, send the item home by mail without trying to take it through Canada. U.S. authorities no longer let noncitizens into the country with firearms except for permanent resident aliens or foreigners holding both a special permit from the Bureau of Alcohol Tobacco and Firearms and a nonresident hunting license (see p. 43). Going into Canada, **firearms** other than hunting rifles or shotguns generally are not allowed, and you need to fill out a form and pay a $50 fee for guns that are allowed; contact the **Canadian Firearms Center** (✆ 800/731-4000; www.cfc.gc.ca) before you go to avoid problems. Entering the U.S., **dogs** more than 3 months old require a rabies certificate with an expiration date, which should have the signature of a licensed veterinarian that is dated at least 30 days prior to crossing the border. A certificate without an expiration date is honored only 12 months from the date signed. **Beef** from Canada is not allowed to enter into the U.S., even as ingredients in pet food, nor are **citrus fruits** (except fruit clearly identified as being of U.S. origin). If in doubt about any of these issues, call before you go, as the border is a long way from anywhere: **Canadian Customs** in Whitehorse (✆ 867/667-3943) or **U.S. Customs and Border Protection** on the highway (✆ 907/772-2252) or in Skagway (✆ 907/983-2325).

FROM THE BORDER TO TOK

The first 65 miles after entering the United States, the road borders the Tetlin National Wildlife Refuge. These broad wetlands and low forests are a migratory stopover in May and in the fall for thousands of songbirds, birds of prey, and waterfowl, and the summer home of trumpeter swans and lesser sandhill cranes, among 143 other species. Caribou show up along the road, especially in the early spring and late fall. The Fish and Wildlife Service's **Tetlin Refuge Visitor Center,** 8 miles past the border, at Mile 1,229, is open May 15 to September 15 daily from 8am to 4:30pm, longer when staffing allows. There are exhibits, and the observation deck has a great view. The refuge also has two small lakeside campgrounds: Deadman Lake, at Mile 1,249, with 16 sites, some okay for RVs; and Lakeview, at Mile 1,256, with eight (no RVs over 30 feet). Rangers give evening campground programs in the summer at Deadman Lake. The campgrounds do not have drinking water. The refuge headquarters is in Tok (✆ 907/883-5312; http://tetlin.fws.gov).

TOK

Born as a construction station on the highway, Tok's role in the world has never expanded much beyond being a stop on the road. With its location at the intersection of the Alaska Highway and the Glenn Highway to Anchorage and Prince William Sound (see the next section), the town has built an economy of gas stations, gift stores, cafes, and hotels to serve highway travelers. It brags of being the coldest community in North America, a dubious distinction made possible by both the latitude and the distance from the moderating influence of the ocean.

ESSENTIALS

GETTING THERE   You're surely passing through Tok with your own set of wheels. If you get stuck for some reason, one shuttle service or another can get you on your way. **Alaska Trails/Yukon** (✆ 800/770-7275; www.alaskashuttle.com) runs through Tok between Fairbanks and Dawson City. It stops at the visitor center.

VISITOR INFORMATION   Public land agencies jointly operate an informative visitor center to introduce highway travelers to Alaska's outdoors. The **Alaska Public Lands Information Center,** P.O. Box 359, Tok, AK 99780 (✆ 907/883-5667; www.nps.gov/aplic), is on the right (north) side of the road coming from the direction of

Canada on the Alaska Highway. It is open daily from 8am to 7pm in summer and from 8am to 4:30pm in winter. You can make ferry reservations on the Alaska Marine Highway System here, too.

A few doors down at the intersection of the Alaska Highway and Tok Cut-Off (also known as the Glenn Highway), the town's **Main Street Visitor Center** is operated by the Tok Chamber of Commerce, P.O. Box 389, Tok, AK 99780 (© **907/883-5775; www.tokinfoalaska.com**). The center provides information on Tok and anywhere else you may be bound on the highway. They're open from May 1 to September 15 daily from 8am to 7pm.

FAST FACTS: Tok

Bank Denali State Bank is in the Three Bears Store and has an ATM; another ATM is at the Village Gas Station across the road from Fast Eddy's restaurant.

Hospital Tok Clinic is on the Tok Cut-Off across from the fire station (© 907/ 883-5855).

Police Contact the Alaska State Troopers (© 907/883-5111), near the intersection of the Alaska Highway and Glenn Highway.

Post Office It's at the highway junction next to the Westmark Hotel.

Taxes There are none in the region.

WHERE TO STAY

The motels are numerous and competitive in Tok. There also are many B&Bs. Check at the visitor center. Be sure to get the 50¢ state highway and campground map from the public lands center (see above), which includes all the public campgrounds in Alaska. Three attractive state park campgrounds lie near Tok on the three highway links that radiate from the town. Each has a $15 self-service fee. There are lots of competitive RV parks in Tok, too. One that has wooded sites suitable for tent camping as well is the **Sourdough Campground,** 1½ miles south of town on the Glenn Highway (© **800/ 789-5543** Alaska and Yukon only, or 907/883-5543; www.sourdoughcampground. com). They charge $30 for full hookups, $17 dry. The campground serves pancake breakfasts and beef stew or reindeer chili in sourdough bread bowls in the evening for an extra charge.

Snowshoe Motel & Fine Arts and Gifts *Value* The motel is behind the gift shop. The best units are the newer nonsmoking rooms near the front, and all are reasonably priced. Each is divided into two sections by the bathroom, providing two separate bedrooms—great for families. They have phones. Outside walkways are decorated with flowers. The gift shop carries some authentic Native art as well as highway kitsch.

Across the highway from the information center (P.O. Box 559), Tok, AK 99780. © 800/478-4511 in Alaska, Yukon, and part of B.C., or 907/883-4511. Fax 907/883-4512. snowshoe@aptalaska.net. 24 units. High season $95 double; low season $62 double. Extra person $5. MC, V. *In room:* TV, fridge, microwave, coffeemaker.

Westmark Tok The central hotel in town is closed in the winter, as its clientele is primarily the package-tour bus trade. It's made up of several buildings connected by boardwalks. Rooms are comfortable and are regularly updated. After several years of hot summers, they have installed air-conditioning throughout. The newer section has larger rooms for the same price. The restaurant serves three meals a day of Mexican and standard American fare, with dinners in the $14 to $23 range.

Intersection of Alaska and Glenn highways (P.O. Box 130), Tok, AK 99780-0130. © **800/544-0970** (reservations) or 907/883-5174. Fax 907/883-5178. www.westmarkhotels.com. 93 units. $129 double. AE, DC, DISC, MC, V. Closed mid-Sept to mid-May. **Amenities:** Restaurant; bar; Internet access and Wi-Fi in lobby; coin-op laundry. *In room:* TV, coffeemaker, hair dryer, iron.

Young's Motel   Good standard motel rooms occupy three one-story structures on the parking lot behind Fast Eddy's restaurant (described below), where you check in. Eighteen newer, smoke-free rooms are the pick of the litter, but all are acceptable.

Behind Fast Eddy's Restaurant on the Alaska Hwy. (P.O. Box 482), Tok, AK 99780. © **907/883-4411.** Fax 907/883-5023. 43 units. High season $83 double; low season $67 double. Extra person $5. AE, DISC, MC, V. **Amenities:** Restaurant; bar. *In room:* TV, Wi-Fi.

WHERE TO DINE

A reliable restaurant of many years tenure, **Fast Eddy's** (© **907/883-4411**), is on the right as you enter town from the east. Begun as a typical roadside cafe, it has developed into a place where a wine list and fine-dining entrees don't seem out of place. Yet the proprietor knows that most highway travelers just want a simple, relaxing meal, and the varied menu offers anything they might have in mind. I relish the salad bar and light dishes that offer a break from the usually carnivorous greasy-spoon choices found elsewhere along the highway. The dining room is decorated in maroon, dark wood, and brass. They're open in summer from 6am to 11pm, in winter from 6am to 10pm. Wine and beer are available with meals, but there is no bar.

DELTA JUNCTION

This intersection with the Richardson Highway, which runs from Valdez to Fairbanks (see section 7, below), is the official end of the Alaska Highway. It's an earnest little roadside town set in a broad plain between the Delta and Tanana rivers. People make their livings from farming and tourism, by working at a trans-Alaska pipeline pump station south of town, and from construction at Fort Greely, a defunct Army base reborn as the "test bed" for President Bush's missile-defense system. For visitors, there are two historic roadhouse museums, several good campgrounds, and an unpredictable chance to spy a herd of bison—but not enough to hold most people's interest for more than a few hours.

ESSENTIALS

VISITOR INFORMATION   A helpful **visitor center** run by the Delta Chamber of Commerce, P.O. Box 987, Delta Junction, AK 99737 (© **877/895-5068** or 907/895-5068, 907/895-5069 summer only; www.deltachamber.org), stands at the intersection of the Alaska and Richardson highways, in the middle of town; it's open from mid-May to mid-September.

FAST FACTS: Delta Junction

Bank **Wells Fargo,** with an ATM, is next door to the IGA Food Cache on the Richardson Highway at the center of town.

Hospital The **Family Medical Center** is at Mile 267.2 Richardson Highway, 2 miles north of the visitor center (© **907/895-4879** or 907/895-5100).

Police For nonemergency calls, reach the **Alaska State Troopers** at © 907/895-4344.

Post Office On the Richardson Highway, it's 2 blocks north of the visitor center.

Taxes None of any kind.

EXPLORING THE AREA

Before construction of the first road to Fairbanks in 1917 (today's Richardson Hwy.), travelers to the Interior followed a trail on basically the same route by horse in summer and dog sled in winter, stopping at roadhouses that provided food and shelter a day apart on the 2-week trip. Two well-preserved examples of the roadhouse system survive near Delta Junction.

In 1996, the Army saved the 1905 **Sullivan Roadhouse** (© 907/895-4415), which had stood abandoned since 1922 on what became an Army bombing range. Today the log building stands near the town visitor center and is open free of charge in summer Monday through Friday 9am to 5pm. Many of the Sullivan's original belongings have been set back in their original places, giving a strong feel for frontier life, but the heart of the restoration is the authentic hospitality of the local volunteers who show off the place with great pride.

The next stop on the trail beyond Sullivan's Roadhouse was 16 miles toward Fairbanks. **Rika's Roadhouse and Landing,** 10 miles northwest of Delta at Mile 275 on the Richardson Highway (© 907/895-4201; www.rikas.com), still makes a pleasant stop on your drive. This roadhouse lasted later than the Sullivans' because drivers had to board a ferry here to cross the Tanana River until the 1940s, and the landing was the end of the line for Tanana sternwheelers. The 1906 log building, on the National Register of Historic Places, has been altered too much by its gift shop to feel authentic, but the grassy 10-acre compound completes a vivid scene of Alaska pioneer life with surviving outbuildings, including telegraph cabins, a museum, a barn, a gorgeous vegetable garden, and livestock pens. The entire site overlooks the riverbank near an impressive suspension bridge that carries the trans-Alaska pipeline over the Tanana just beyond the park. A concessionaire manages the site for the state of Alaska, including operating a restaurant that serves soups, salads, sandwiches, and pie, and a few hot breakfast choices, daily from 9am to 5pm; the grounds and museum are open from 8am to 8pm from May 15 to September 15.

WHERE TO STAY

Check at the visitor center for a referral to one of the many B&Bs. The cute, funny, and hospitable **Kelly's Alaska Country Inn,** at the intersection of Richardson and Alaska highways (© 907/895-4667; www.kellysalaskacountryinn.com), has rooms for $109 double in summer, $99 in winter, right in the middle of town. The 20 rooms have TVs, telephones, microwaves, refrigerators, and coffeemakers; most are small and ordinary, but a funky few are an in an old Quonset hut and have arched wood ceilings. This is a family-run business going way, way back. **Alaska 7 Motel,** 3548 Richardson Hwy. (© 907/895-4848; www.alaska7motel.com), is a small, low-slung building containing standard rooms with lots of amenities, including refrigerators, microwaves, coffeemakers, and satellite TV, for $80 double.

CAMPING

Alaska State Parks maintains five campgrounds on the rivers and lakes in and around Delta Junction and a couple of public cabins. Right on the highway near town, the **Delta State Recreation Area campground** lies among large spruce and birch trees, with the sites well separated, and some with walk-in privacy. It is among the most attractive campgrounds on the highway. The **Quartz Lake State Recreation Area,** 11 miles northwest of town on the Richardson Highway and down a 3-mile turnoff, has an 80-site campground on the shallow fishing lake. The camping fee at each is $10. For information, contact the **Department of Natural Resources Public Information Center,** 3700 Airport Way, Fairbanks, AK 99709 (© **907/451-2705;** www.alaska stateparks.org, click on "Individual Parks").

To park an RV, or if you're tent camping and need a shower, **Smith's Green Acres RV Park and Campground,** 1½ miles north on the Richardson Highway from the visitor center (© **800/895-4369** or 907/895-4369), has grassy RV sites and tent sites among the trees. The place also has cabins, a small playground, and laundry facilities. Full hookup sites are $27, tent sites $14.

WHERE TO DINE

For a picnic or quick, simple meal on your drive, try the **IGA Food Cache** (© **907/895-4653**), on the south side of the highway in Delta. The deli counter sells fried food, subs, and ice cream, and the store also has a bakery counter and coffee stand. You can eat in as well as carry out. They're open daily from early in the morning until at least 8pm.

Buffalo Center Diner DINER   The locals eat here, for good reason. The dining room is light and clean, decorated with wood and plants, and the menu covers everything you would hope for in a simple family restaurant—plus buffalo burgers and sausage in honor of the Delta herd. Each time I've stopped the food has been good and the atmosphere relaxing. Service has always been friendly and quick, and the waitress called me "Hon."

1680 Richardson Hwy. © **907/895-5089.** Lunch $6–$12; dinner $8–$22. MC, V. Summer daily 7am–10pm; winter daily 7am–8pm.

6 The Glenn Highway

The Glenn Highway, Alaska Route 1, leads from the Alaska Highway at Tok to Anchorage (the section from Tok to Glennallen is also called the Tok Cut-Off). It connects the most populous part of the state to the outside world, a 328-mile strip of blacktop that grows from two lanes in Tok to six or more in urban downtown Anchorage. In this section, I cover the stretch from Glennallen to Palmer. From Tok to Glennallen, the road passes through wilderness. The portion from Palmer to downtown Anchorage is all part of the greater city and encompassed in chapter 6.

GLENNALLEN

It may look like just a wide place in the road, but this little town is the commercial hub for the Copper River Country, a great, thinly settled region. Much of the public land in the Copper River Country is managed by the **Bureau of Land Management Glennallen Field Office,** with a log-cabin office in town on the north side of the Glenn Highway at Mile 186.5 (P.O. Box 147), Glennallen, AK 99588 (© **907/822-3217;** www.glennallen.ak.blm.gov), open Monday through Friday from 8am to 4:30pm.

Information also is available from the public land information centers in Anchorage, Fairbanks, and Tok. This huge area, about as large as a midsize eastern U.S. state, is more accessible than Wrangell–St. Elias National Park, an advantage for outdoor recreation, but it's still a rough, remote land with few high-quality visitor facilities. There are several large alpine lakes, two National Wild Rivers, several hiking trails, and four campgrounds (including the State Park campground just north of Glennallen), all reached on the Richardson, Glenn, and Denali highways. Guides are available for **rafting** and **fishing** in the rivers. Check at the visitor center or BLM office for a list of operators.

For commercial information, the **Copper River Chamber of Commerce and Visitor Center** is in a gray building at the intersection of the highways next to the Hub gas station and store (P.O. Box 469, Glennallen, AK 99588; © **907/822-5555;** www. traveltoalaska.com). The center operates from May 15 to September 15 daily 8am to 7pm. Besides the hotel and restaurant listed below, Glennallen has a Wells Fargo bank with an ATM, a post office, groceries, a medical center, and government offices, all centered on a strip of the Glenn Highway around Mile 187.

Good standard accommodations are at the **New Caribou Hotel,** in town at Mile 187 of the Glenn Highway (© **800/478-3302** or 907/822-3302; www.caribouhotel. com). The rooms have the amenities of a roadside chain, but the hotel as a whole has the sleepy character of its rural highway location. They book up in the summer, so reservations are important. The summer rate is $144 double. *Note:* The annex building, a former construction camp, is much less desirable. Their **Caribou Restaurant** is inexpensive but quite fancy inside, with lots of brass and booths. Choices include burgers, steak, meatloaf, pork chops, and salmon.

THE MATANUSKA GLACIER AREA

From Glennallen, the highway traverses a broad tundra area where there's a good chance of seeing caribou and other wildlife from a distance. Next, the road climbs between two mountain ranges—the coastal Chugach Mountains that hold the glaciers around Prince William Sound, and the craggy old Talkeetna Mountains to the north. The road winds through steep, rocky terrain with wonderful, scary views, including a good look at the Matanuska Glacier. In the fall, when the tundra and the birches, aspens, and cottonwoods turn yellow and red, this drive is dizzying in its beauty.

The **Matanuska Glacier State Recreation Area** overlooks the glacier and has a 1-mile interpretive nature trail and a good 12-site campground ($15 per site plus $10 per vehicle). To get closer to the glacier, you have to take a rough side road and pay a $13 per person fee to the people who own the land in front of it, who also offer camping and guided hiking under the name **Glacier Park** (© **888/253-4480;** www. matanuskaglacier.com). Turn at Mile 102. The side road is 3 miles, followed by a 15-minute walk to the glacier's face.

There are several other good trails and camping areas along the road, too. Two exceptional remote lodges lie along the highway near the glacier, about 70 miles from Glennallen or 115 miles from Anchorage. In this remote area, there is no TV, and phones are in common rooms.

Majestic Valley Wilderness Lodge ⟨ *Finds*   This friendly lodge offers basic rooms with private bathrooms and serves excellent family-style meals to guests and others who reserve in advance. Dining is in an extraordinary log lodge building with a towering ceiling and wonderful mountain views—a quintessentially Alaskan space that is understandably popular for weddings and the like. While most of the rooms are small and basic, they're set in a gorgeous, quiet spot out of sight of the highway. A 20km network of superb cross-country skiing trails in spectacular terrain is groomed with quality equipment for diagonal or skate skiing. Anchorage families, such as ours, come here for fun winter or spring weekends, skiing and sledding all day before cooking in the wood-fired sauna, playing games and cards in the evening, and generally being rambunctious. In the summer, the hiking here, mostly above the tree line, is exceptional.

Mile 114.9, Glenn Hwy. (16162 W. Glenn Hwy., Sutton, AK 99674). AK 99645. (℄ **907/746-2930.** Fax 907/746-2931. www.majesticvalleylodge.com. 10 units, 2 cabins. $115 double; $135 cabin double. Extra adult $10, extra child ages 4–12 $5. MC, V. **Amenities:** Restaurant; free-standing wood-fired sauna. *In room:* No phone.

Sheep Mountain Lodge 🐾   On a mountainside above the road, a well-loved couple, Zack and Anjanette Steer, preside at this historic log lodge. Zack is a top competitive dog musher, so the operation is mostly oriented to the summer. Guests hike and mountain-bike over spectacular trails on the tundra mountains. Cabins are large and stylishly decorated, with high ceilings and walls of rough wood to remind you of the rural location. The sitting porches have wonderful views down the mountainside. They rent a sleeping-bag bunkhouse, too, and have a guest sauna and indoor hot tub. The little cafe serves simple, healthful food in the summer. Service is very friendly.

Mile 113.5, Glenn Hwy. (17701 West Glenn Hwy., Sutton, AK 99674). (℄ **877/645-5121** or 907/745-5121. Fax 907/ 745-5120. www.sheepmountain.com. 10 cabins. Summer $135 double, extra person $15; winter $115 double, extra person $10; bunkhouse $60 for 4, extra person $5. MC, V. Closed 1 month each in spring and fall (call ahead). **Amenities:** Restaurant; Jacuzzi; sauna. *In room:* No phone.

CHICKALOON & SUTTON

Be ready for construction delays on this section of the road in 2007 and beyond. The scenery remains attractive, with country-style development cropping up along the road as you approach urban Alaska. Chickaloon is the base of Nova Raft and Adventure Tours, the river riding company listed in the Anchorage chapter; if you're already passing through here, you may want to arrange a float. Sutton is a little town left behind by a coal mine that once operated in these mountains. The charming little historic park there is worthy of a stop to stretch your legs.

7 The Richardson Highway & Copper Center

The 364-mile drive from Fairbanks to Valdez unfolds as a grand cross-section of Alaska. It begins in the broad Interior valleys at the north, rises to the tundra and lakes of the Alaska Range, descends back down to the Copper River Country, and finally climbs over the steep coastal mountains into the Prince William Sound fjord where Valdez resides. This was the first route into Alaska, but today it is little traveled and mostly free of development, an opportunity to see real wilderness by car on paved road.

Delta Junction is covered in section 5, on the Alaska Highway. The intersection with the Denali Highway (see chapter 8) comes 81 miles south of there. This section has the most extraordinary scenery—broad vistas, the Delta River, amazing alpine lakes including long Summit Lake, and many views of the trans-Alaska pipeline. Don't plan on stops or services, although there are a few widely scattered campgrounds and seasonal businesses. The spot on the map known as Paxson, the intersection with the Denali Highway, has a business called the Paxson Inn. You can fill your tanks there 24 hours a day or buy a snack, but I wouldn't recommend the restaurant or the rooms.

South from Paxson the views remain lovely, with more lakes, increasingly surrounded by trees, as latitude and elevation decrease going into the Copper River Valley. After 15 miles, you reach the only noteworthy business on this 70-mile section of road from Pax-son to Glennallen: the **Meiers Lake Roadhouse and Atwater Chateau Motel,** at Mile 170 (© **907/822-3151**). Way out here, where they have to make their own electricity, a rugged and cheerful little family has built a fine motel of 16 cozy rooms with satellite TVs and private bathrooms. They charge $100 a night regardless of the number of people in the room and have a restaurant, bar, laundromat, and hardware store.

The next town on the Richardson is Glennallen, which is covered above, in section 6. Fourteen miles south of Glennallen, **Copper Center** is a tiny Athabascan commu-nity on the old Richardson Highway. Its historic roadhouse, the **Copper Center Lodge** (© **866/330-3245** or 907/822-3245; www.coppercenterlodge.com), has long been worthy of a stop for dinner or even overnight. The history of the lodge dates from the bizarre gold-rush origins of Copper Center and Valdez, when about 4,000 stampeders to the Klondike tried a virtually impossible all-American route from Valdez over the glaciers of the Wrangell–St. Elias region. Few made it, and hundreds who died are buried in Copper Center. The original lodge was built of the stuff they left behind. The existing building dates from 1932. Double rooms are $125 to $146, and they're open year-round.

Copper River Princess Wilderness Lodge 🕏🕏   This first-class lodge built by the Princess Cruise Line brings the comforts of the outside world to this rough and iso-lated corner of the planet. Where, at one time, a room with its own toilet was a rar-ity, now you can get one with a hair dryer and with a fine restaurant down the hall. Princess has tried to capture the trim, red-and-white look of the historic Kennecott mining district. Inside, common areas are spacious and warm, with a big slate fireplace in the lobby. Rooms are in earth tones, with faux rustic furniture and art reflecting mining history, and have king- and queen-size beds. The restaurant serves three meals a day, including sophisticated cuisine for dinner; those meals are not just in another league, but a completely different game than anything else found on the highway. Main courses are $16 to $29.

1 Brenwick-Craig Rd (P.O. Box 422), Copper Center, AK 99573 (turn at Mile 102 Richardson Hwy.). © **800/426-0500** reservations or 907/822-4000. Fax 907/822-4044. www.princesslodges.com. 85 units. High season $179 double; low season $139 double. AE, DISC, MC, V. **Amenities:** Restaurant; tour desk; courtesy van to Gulkana airport and national park visitor center. *In room:* TV, hair dryer.

8 Wrangell–St. Elias National Park & Kennecott

Looking at a relief map of Alaska, you'd think the portion drained by the Copper River was so overweighted with mountains that it might topple the whole state into the Pacific. The Alaska Range, in the center of the state, has the tallest mountain, but this Gulf of Alaska region, straddling the Alaska-Yukon border, has more mass—the second- and fourth-tallest mountains in North America (Logan and St. Elias), plus 9 of the tallest 16 peaks in the United States. Four mountain ranges intersect, creating a mad jumble of terrain covering tens of millions of acres, a trackless chaos of unnamed, unconquered peaks. The Copper River and its raging tributaries slice through it all, swallowing the gray melt of innumerable glaciers that flow from the largest ice field in North America. Everything here is the largest, most rugged, most remote; words quickly fall short of the measure. But where words fail, commerce gives a little help: These mountains are so numerous and remote that one guide service makes a business of taking visitors to mountains and valleys that no one has ever explored before.

Ironically for such a wild land, the area's main attraction for visitors is its history. The richest copper deposit in the world was found here in 1900 by a group of prospectors who mistook a green mountaintop for a patch of green grass where they could feed their horses. It was a mountain of almost pure copper, with metallic nuggets the size of desks (one is at the UA Museum of the North in Fairbanks). The deposit produced trainloads of 70% pure copper. The first ore was so rich it required no processing before shipping, and then came lots more copper that did need minimal processing. Much more lower-grade ore still lies underground. The Alaska Syndicate, an investment group that included J. P. Morgan and Daniel Guggenheim, built the Kennecott Copper Corporation from this wealth (its name was a misspelling of the Kennicott River and Glacier, where the copper was found). To get the copper out, they paid for an incredible 196-mile rail line up from Cordova (see chapter 7) and created a self-contained company town deep in the wilderness, called **Kennecott.** When the high-grade ore was gone, in 1938, they pulled the plug, leaving a ghost town of extraordinary beauty that still contains machinery and even documents they left behind.

Wrangell–St. Elias National Park and Preserve now owns Kennecott and more than 13 million acres across this region of Alaska. It's the largest national park in the United States by a long shot, six times the size of Yellowstone and about 25% larger than the entire country of Switzerland. The protected land continues across the border in Canada, in **Kluane National Park,** which is similarly massive. Most of that land is impossibly remote, but Wrangell–St. Elias has two rough gravel roads that allow access to see the mountains from a car. The main route is the abandoned roadbed of the Copper River and Northwestern Railroad leading to Kennecott and the historic sites there. It's an arduous but rewarding journey by car, requiring at least 2 days to do it right. Air taxis, river guides, and remote lodges offer other ways into the park's untouched wilderness, mostly starting from **McCarthy,** a historic village near Kennecott. There are a few trails near Kennecott, but only for day hikes. This is a country where experienced outdoors people can get away from any trace of humans for weeks on end.

THE KENNECOTT & MCCARTHY AREA

This historic copper area is the only part of the park most visitors see, as it's the most accessible and has the most services, interesting sites, and paths to explore. It's not easy to get to, however—that's why it's still so appealing—and there's little point in going without adequate time. You can hit the highlights at Kennecott and McCarthy in 1 full day, but just getting there takes time. My family and I spent 3 nights and could have stayed longer.

The main event is the ghost town at **Kennecott,** whose red buildings gaze from a mountainside across the Kennicott Glacier in the valley below. Now owned by the park service, the buildings made up an isolated company town until 1938, when it abruptly shut down. Tourists coming here as late as the 1960s saw it as if frozen in time, with breakfast dishes still on the tables from the day the last train left. Most of that was looted and destroyed in the 1970s, but when I toured the company store a few years ago, old documents still remained, and the powerhouse and 14-story mill buildings still had their heavy iron and wood equipment. Besides the buildings, there are excellent hiking trails, including one that traverses the glacier. The town now has only a few year-round residents but in summer is busy with a lodge, a couple of bed-and-breakfasts, guide services, and park rangers.

Five miles down the road, Kennecott's twin town of **McCarthy** served the miners as a place to drink, gamble, and hire prostitutes on their rare days off—the company didn't allow any frivolity in Kennecott or in the bunkhouses high up on the mountain. McCarthy retains the relaxed atmosphere of its past, with businesses and residents living in false-front buildings not much changed from Wild West days. More of a year-round community, McCarthy has a restaurant, lodging, flight services, and other businesses.

Yet even this most populous part of the park is isolated and sparsely inhabited, with few services. Only about 65 people live in the greater area year-round. You will find no banking services, general stores, gas stations, clinics, police, or anything else you're used to relying on. Phones came to McCarthy and Kennecott only in the late 1990s and still are few. Bring what you need.

ESSENTIALS
GETTING THERE   By Car   The paved **Edgerton Highway** starts 17 miles south of Copper Center on the Richardson Highway and then runs east for 33 miles to the tiny, dried-up former railroad town of **Chitina** (*chit*-na), the last reliable stop for groceries, gas, and other necessities until you return here. Do fill your tank; prudence also demands a full-size spare tire. Heading east, into the park, the **McCarthy Road** continues along the roadbed of the Copper River and Northwestern Railway. This is 60 miles of narrow dirt road, muddy in wet weather and clouded with dust when it's dry. Each year it has been improved a little, and two-wheel-drive cars can normally make it. The drive is a fun adventure, passing through tunnels of alders and crossing rivers on some of the original wooden railroad trestles; one wood-decked bridge spans a canyon more than 200 feet deep. There are virtually no services, very few buildings, and little traffic on the 3-hour drive.

The road ends at a parking lot and collection of temporary businesses on the banks of the Kennicott River. You can drive no farther. A fee applies to park at the riverside lot, but you can park free for the day ($6 overnight) a little way off at Glacier View Campground (see below). Next, you walk across a footbridge or two. Late in the summer, the Kennecott Glacier releases a flood from a glacier-dammed lake, but at other times the second channel is a dry wash and the second bridge isn't needed. Handcarts are available to move your luggage across, and on the other side you can catch a van. The place where you are staying will send one, or you ride the **van** operated by **Wrangell Mountain Air** (© 907/554-4411), $2 to McCarthy or $5 per person, one-way, to Kennecott. A public telephone is near the bridge; use it to call the van or your lodgings.

By Bus   The **Backcountry Connection** (© 866/582-5292 in Alaska only, or 907/822-5292; www.alaska-backcountry-tours.com) runs vans from Glennallen and Chitina to the footbridge daily in summer. The van leaves Glennallen at 7am and Chitina at 8:30am, arriving at the bridge at 11am. The trip departs from the bridge at 4pm, getting back to Chitina at 6pm and Glennallen at 7:30pm. The fare is $99 round-trip from Chitina, $119 from Glennallen and Copper Center.

By Air   A simple way to Kennecott and McCarthy is to drive as far as you can on pavement and fly the rest of the way on one of the air taxis. Once there, get around in the vans that shuttle back and forth over 5 miles of dirt road. **Wrangell Mountain Air** (© 800/478-1160 or 907/554-4411; www.wrangellmountainair.com) offers three flights daily from Chitina to McCarthy for $195 round-trip. Using their day trip option, you can have plenty of time at Kennecott without having to spend the night there. A reputable service operating between Chitina and McCarthy on an on-demand basis is **McCarthy Air** (© **888/989-9891** or 907/554-4440; www.mccarthyair.com). Flightseeing over the national park and charters to remote valleys and lakes for backcountry trips are covered below under "Getting Outside: Hiking & Backpacking." Wednesday or Friday, it's possible to fly in a small prop plane all the way from Anchorage. A couple of flight services team up to do this: You fly on one from Anchorage to Gulkana and then on the mail plane from Gulkana to McCarthy. The fare is about $300 one-way. Contact **Ellis Air Taxi** (© **800/478-3368** in Alaska only or 907/822-3368; www.ellisair.com), which handles all the booking and flies the Gulkana-to-McCarthy leg.

VISITOR INFORMATION   The main park visitor center is on the Richardson Highway near Copper Center (© **907/822-5234;** www.nps.gov/wrst). Stop in to buy maps and publications, watch a movie, or get advice from a ranger on outdoor treks. Hours are Memorial Day to Labor Day daily from 8am to 6pm; in winter, Monday through Friday from 8am to 4:30pm. You can write for information to P.O. Box 439, Copper Center, AK 99573. The park service is restoring buildings and developing visitor services in Kennecott itself. A former train depot has become a visitor center, a good place to stop with questions for rangers, plan a backcountry trip, or join one of the daily guided activities. A ranger station for the less-visited northern area of the park is found on the Nabesna Road near its intersection with the Glenn Highway.

EXPLORING THE TOWNS

CHITINA   Chitina lost its reason to exist in 1938, when the last train ran on the Copper River line, but it lives on with 120 residents supporting themselves largely with salmon from the river, produce from their gardens, berries from the forests, and the few tourists who stop. There's a general store and a couple of gas stations (the last gas for many a mile), a wayside interpretive area at the site of the old depot, a pond where you can often see trumpeter swans, and, down by the river, lazily rotating fish wheels plucking salmon from the river. The Copper River is too turbid for angling, but clear water tributaries and stocked lakes in the area have fish. You can also explore south on the old Copper River rail line and even through the tunnels; check with a local or the park headquarters for advice and current conditions before trying it, as landslides sometimes block the way. Chitina has one business worth a special stop: **Spirit Mountain Artworks** (© **907/823-2222** or 907/235-1014 winter; www.spiritmountainalaska.com). Art Koeninger bought a remarkable historic structure in 1977 and restored it over the next 9 years into a renowned gallery out here in the boonies. Incredibly, it survives still, although Art manages it now from Homer, where he creates his own artwork.

MCCARTHY   McCarthy feels authentic as soon as you walk down the dirt main street between the false fronts. There are flight service offices to arrange a trip out, and a business offering meals and lodging. Then, a street beyond, unbroken wilderness for hundreds and perhaps thousands of miles. On a summer evening, young backpackers and locals stand in the road—there is no traffic, since there are almost no vehicles—meeting and talking, laughing loudly, walking around dogs having their own party. Visitors quickly mix in, as everyone seems eager to talk about the town and its history and their own peculiar wilderness lives. The people here know it's unique, and everyone hopes it doesn't change much.

KENNECOTT   This has got to be one of the world's greatest ghost towns, with some 40 buildings, mostly in good enough condition to be reused today—indeed, until the current park service restoration project began, the community still played basketball in one structure. Some historic buildings have become lodgings, and the park service is using others. Locals still pick rhubarb and chives from the company garden. History has the same kind of immediacy here that you get from holding an old diary in your hand, quite different from the sanitized history-through-glass that you're used to at more accessible sites.

The park service bought most of the buildings a few years ago. When we walked through, on the eve of the takeover, items remained out on the ground or on store shelves that would be in museums in many places. If Kennecott were an ordinary industrial site, that would be interesting enough, but this place was something well out of the ordinary: an outpost beyond the edge of the world where men built a self-contained city almost a century ago. The hardship of the miners' lives and the ease of the managerial families' lives also present a fascinating contrast.

You can take in some of the story by wandering around with a walking tour booklet available from the Park Service and reading signs, but it would be a big mistake to miss going inside the buildings, and to do that you need to join a **guided tour** with **St. Elias Alpine Guides** (© 888/933-5427 or 907/544-4445; full listing below under "Hiking & Backpacking"). They have an office in the old Chinese laundry right in the ghost town. Tours, which happen three times daily, last 2½ hours and go into real depth on the geology and history, climbing to the perilous 14th floor of the mill building. I've never been on another tour like it: fascinating, challenging, and even exciting; I cannot recommend it strongly enough. They operate mid-May to mid-September and charge $25 per person. Consider making a day of it by adding a glacier hiking trip with the same company (see below). The guides will arrange a custom tour, too.

GETTING OUTSIDE
HIKING & BACKPACKING   There are a few trails radiating from Kennecott, for which crude maps are available from the rangers and others around town; or buy the **Trails Illustrated** topographic map, printed on plastic, for sale from some local businesses, or order ahead (see "Fast Facts: Alaska" in chapter 2). An impressive walk continues through the ghost town up the valley, paralleling the Kennicott Glacier and then its tributary, the Root Glacier. You can climb along the Root's edge to a towering ice fall, but a much better outing is to be had by joining a group to walk on the glacier itself. St. Elias Alpine Guides, listed below, accepts walk-ins for daily glacier day hikes and other hikes and tours. A half-day on the glacier goes for $55 a person, while all-day hikes are $100 and ice-climbing lessons $110. We combined the half-day hike with the company's ghost town tour for one of the best days of Alaska tourism we've ever spent. Another fascinating hike you can do on your own leads straight up the mountain behind the Kennecott buildings to the old Bonanza Mine and bunkhouses, 3,000 feet higher on the alpine tundra.

Beyond the trails, the park is endless miles of trackless wilderness—one of Earth's last few places that really deserves that name. Fit hikers without the backcountry experience to mount their own expedition should join one of the guides who work in the area. **St. Elias Alpine Guides** (© 888/933-5427 or 907/554-4445; www.steliasguides.com) offers day hikes, rafting, backpacking trips, and alpine ascents, but specializes in guiding extended trips to unexplored territory. Bob Jacobs, the company's founder, stopped guiding on Mount McKinley years ago because of the crowds. At Wrangell–St. Elias, it's rare to encounter another party, and peaks remain that have never been climbed by anyone: The firm offers the chance to be one of the first. A 2-week trek and climb, including 4 days of mountaineering instruction, is a big commitment and costs $3,000 and up, but then, first ascents are a finite resource. The St. Elias catalog will make anyone who loves backpacking drool. Trips begin at $775 for a 4-day Donoho Peak trek. They are all-inclusive, but not without hardship and risk—nothing can take away from the severity of this wild country.

Hiking on your own in a wilderness largely without trails is a whole new kind of experience for experienced backpackers and outdoors people who are used to more crowded parts of the planet. You feel like an explorer rather than a follower. At times, there's a fairy-tale sense of the world unfolding around you, as fresh as creation. If you're not prepared to select your own route—a task only for those already experienced in trackless, backcountry traveling—there are various established ways through the park you can follow with a topographic map. You can get a trip synopsis from the visitor center or ranger station, or download from their website (www.nps.gov/wrst). Rangers can help you choose a route to suit your party, although none are easy.

Some routes start from the roads, but a better way to go is to charter a flight into a remote valley from one of the two **air services** in McCarthy, Wrangell Mountain Air or McCarthy Air (p. 427). The planes land on gravel strips, river bars, glaciers, alpine tundra, or any other flat place the pilots know about. These companies make a business of flying out backpackers, and so have established rates for different landing sites and can help you determine a route that's right for you, as well as provide a list of supplies. Wrangell Mountain Air rents bear-proof containers and two-way radios, and McCarthy Air and the Park Service lend the containers. You can charter a flight for $200 to $600 per person, with at least two passengers. Or fly in to a lake for fishing or an alpine area for exploring from a base camp, reducing the worry about how much you pack.

Note: I wouldn't want to scare off anyone who could manage one of these trips, but people do get into trouble in the Alaska wilderness every year, and some of them don't come back. Before you head out into the backcountry, you must know how to take care of yourself where help is unavailable; this includes handling river crossings, bear avoidance, hypothermia, basic first aid, and other issues. Unless you have plenty of backpacking experience in less remote areas, I don't recommend starting here.

MOUNTAIN BIKING Anywhere else, the 60-mile road that leads to this area would be considered a mountain-biking trail. You also can make good use of bikes between McCarthy, Kennecott, and the footbridge. An old **wagon road** parallels the main road that connects the two towns, 4.5 miles each way; the road itself is a one-lane dirt track. Advanced cyclists can also ride the trails around Kennecott described above under "Hiking & Backpacking."

RAFTING Many great, wild rivers drain these huge mountains, which are still being carved by enormous glaciers. The **Kennicott River,** starting at the glacier of the same name, boils with Class III rapids for some 40 minutes starting right from the footbridge at the end of the McCarthy Road. As the area lacks roads, however, most trips must include a plane ride at least one-way, and that makes white-water rafting day trips here more expensive than outings near Anchorage or Valdez. At Wrangell–St. Elias, floats punch deep into the backcountry. The Kennicott River meets the Nizina, passing through a deep, dramatic canyon; then the Nizina River flows into the Chitina River, which meets the Copper River near the town of Chitina, 60 miles from the starting point. The Copper River flows to the ocean. A float from the footbridge through the Nizina Canyon takes all day, with lunch and bush plane flightseeing back, which could include a glacier fly-over. St. Elias Alpine Guides (see "Hiking & Back-packing," above) charges $265. Other trips continue for 3 or 4 days to Chitina, for $990 to $1,290 per person; or for 10 to 13 days, 180 miles all the way to the Copper River Delta and the sea (see "Cordova" in chapter 7), for $3,700 per person. This is Alaska on its largest and most grandiose scale, accessible only from the banks of these great rivers.

WHERE TO STAY AND DINE

The closest standard hotel rooms are in Copper Center (in the previous section). In the Kennecott-McCarthy area itself, there are several attractive places to stay, all thick with the history the towns represent, but not ordinary American lodgings. Dining is mainly at the lodges. If you're not staying there, it is a good idea to check ahead to make sure they will be ready for you for a meal.

CAMPING & HOSTELLING   There is no campground on the Kennecott-McCarthy side of the Kennicott River footbridge. The park service allows camping anywhere in the park without a permit, but there are few handy spots on public land (remember, much of the land along the roads is private).

A couple of primitive private campgrounds and a hostel are at the end of McCarthy Road. **Glacier View Campground** (© **907/554-4490,** 907/243-6677 off season; www.glacierviewcampground.com) charges $18 a night for camping and has a cabin for rent. The owners also rent mountain bikes and offer showers and free day parking. Their cafe offers barbecue for lunch and dinner and serves beer and wine. Besides the backpacker's hotel mentioned in the review of the McCarthy Lodge on p. 432, **Kennicott River Lodge and Hostel** (© **907/554-4441,** 941/447-4252 off season; www. kennicottriverlodge.com), located at the end of the road 400 feet from the footbridge, offers bunks for $28 per person. Sheets and pillows are included; other bedding is extra. The lodge also rents cabins for $100 double plus $25 for each additional person. They have a common kitchen, lounge, sauna, and showers.

There are three campgrounds on the way to the footbridge. The most attractive is the state parks' **Liberty Falls Campground,** at Mile 23 on the Edgerton Highway, which is set among big trees at the foot of a crashing waterfall. Many of the sites are walk-ins, with wooden tent platforms and lots of privacy. The self-service camping fee is $10 per vehicle; the day-use fee is $1. There are pit toilets and no running water.

Kennicott Glacier Lodge ⭐⭐   This is the largest and most comfortable accommodation in the Kennecott-McCarthy area, taking the edges off the isolation. The lodge accurately re-creates an old Kennecott building, with the same red-and-white color scheme, and stands among the historic structures of the ghost town. You can't get any closer to what you want to see. Guests can sip drinks on a long, flower-hung front porch overlooking the glacier, or relax on a lawn with play equipment and the same view. Rooms in the main lodge building are not large and have bathrooms down the hall (six shower rooms and eight bathrooms, all clean but small). The 10 rooms in a 2004 annex are larger, with two queen-size beds and private bathrooms. All the bedrooms are remarkably clean and decorated with interesting mine artifacts and papers—telegrams, blueprints, and the like. All but eight overlook the glacier and ghost town, and those on the main floor have second entrances on the veranda. A brief evening tour of the ghost town is included.

Filling dinners are served family style at 7pm on long tables, with a fixed menu in the $25 to $30 range, available to nonguests by prior reservation. The food is excellent and portions are generous: One night we had Copper River salmon with sun-dried tomatoes and pine nuts, the next night prime rib; both those evenings, the bill was $30 per person. Guests linger long after dessert; it's a friendly social occasion. A large breakfast buffet is $14, continental breakfast $8. Lunch is by menu service, with sandwiches, salads, and specials ranging from $7 to $10. There's nowhere else to eat right in Kennecott, so it makes sense to book the inclusive meal package, which is $285 double in the shared-bathroom units, $345 in the newer units; a third person is $75 with the meal package, children aged 4 to 12 half-price.

P.O. Box 103940, Anchorage, AK 99510. ℂ **800/582-5128** or 907/258-2350; 907/554-4477 (in season only). Fax 907/248-7975. www.kennicottlodge.com. 35 units, 20 with shared bathroom. $189 double with shared bathroom, $249 double with private bathroom. Additional adult $30; additional child ages 4–12 $15; free age 3 and under. AE, DISC, MC, V. Closed mid-Sept to mid-May. **Amenities:** Restaurant; tour desk; courtesy van. *In room:* No phone.

McCarthy Lodge ℛ   The lodge is the center of the relaxed village of McCarthy, 5 miles from the historically more buttoned-up Kennecott. Although you are not among the mining ruins when you stay here, you are in a real community where you can meet year-round residents and the many interesting characters who spend the summer here. The owners of the lodge also own Ma Johnson's Hotel across the street, a saloon, art shop, store, Internet cafe, and backpacker lodgings. They treasure the history and take great pains with the old buildings and food, having invested $1.25 million in the project. Rooms are full of period charm, with antiques, quilts, and memorabilia. They call it a living museum. Even the soap is authentic, made by hand. The bedrooms—which are small, as always in a historic building—are in a false-front structure that you might see in an old Western movie. Every two rooms share a bathroom. In a separate building, Lancaster's Backpacker's Hotel charges $48 single, plus $20 for each additional person up to four.

The eight-table restaurant is an authentic Bush roadhouse in an unmistakably backwoods structure that was moved here from Cordova in 1916. The dining room is decorated with artifacts, early photographs, and heavy drapes. Our meals were all perfectly prepared: chicken alfredo, Cajun halibut, and, best of all, semolina-encrusted Copper River red salmon. The price range for dinner is $15 to $24, for lunch $10 to $14. Or order from the casual and reasonably priced bar menu of pizza and the like. The McCarthy Store and Erie Internet Cafe serves coffee, sandwiches, and baked goods, and has a shower and laundry.

While the lodgings and restaurant are generally open year-round, it's important to call ahead October to April.

P.O. Box MXY, McCarthy, AK 99588. ℂ **907/554-4402**. Fax 907/554-4404. www.mccarthylodge.com. 20 units, all with shared bathroom. Year-round $159 double. MC, V. Rate includes full breakfast. **Amenities:** Restaurant; bar; courtesy van. *In room:* No phone.

10

The Bush

The Bush is most of Alaska. On a map of the state, the portion with roads and cities is a smallish corner. Yet most visitors—and, indeed, most Alaskans—never make it beyond that relatively populated corner. Several years ago a lifelong Anchorage resident was elected to the legislature and appointed chair of its rural issues committee, only to admit he had never been to the Bush. It's common for children to grow to adulthood in Anchorage, Fairbanks, or Southeast Alaska without traveling to the Arctic, the Aleutians, or the vast wetlands of western Alaska. It happens for the same reason most tourists don't go to Bush Alaska—getting there is expensive, and there's not much in the way of human activity once you arrive. Bush Alaska is one of the planet's last barely inhabited areas. But that's a reason to go, not a reason to stay away. You can meet indigenous people who still interact with the environment in their traditional way and see virgin places that remain to be explored by self-reliant outdoors people.

Although there are few people in the Bush, the hospitality of those you do meet is special and warming. In Bush Alaska, where the population is overwhelmingly Alaska Native, it's not uncommon to be befriended by total strangers simply because you've taken the trouble to come to their community and are, therefore, an honored guest. Even in the larger towns, people smile as you pass in the street. If you have a questioning look on your face, they'll stop to help. Living in a small place where people

know each other and have to work together against the elements makes for a tight, friendly community.

Alaska Native culture is based more on cooperative than competitive impulses. Respect and consensus carry greater weight than in individualistic white society. Cooperation requires slowing down, listening, not taking the lead. People from our fast-paced culture can leave a village after a visit wondering why no one spoke to them, not realizing that they never shut up long enough to give anyone a chance. The cultural differences here are real, unlike the shadows of past differences we celebrate in most regions of the homogenous United States. Long pauses in conversation are normal, looking down while addressing a person demonstrates respect, punctuality is highly relative, child care is a community function, and when gifts are offered, people really mean it—turning down even a cup of coffee is gauche. (For more on the culture of Alaska's Native peoples, see the appendix, "Alaska in Depth.")

The Native people of the Bush also have terrible problems trying to live in two worlds. There's too much alcohol and too many drugs in the Bush, too much TV, but not enough of an economic base to provide for basic services in many villages. Even in some of the relatively prosperous village hubs described in this chapter, visitors will glimpse a kind of rural poverty they may not have seen before—where prices are extremely high and steady jobs scarce and difficult to hold while pursuing traditional hunting and food gathering. But if you ask why Natives stay, you're missing something. In a world where so few indigenous cultures survive, people here are working to retain traditions that give their lives meaning—a sense of place and a depth of belonging that most of us can only envy. It's a work in progress, this combination of tradition and modernity, but there's no question they're slowly succeeding. They control their own land, they're building an economic base, and Native ways are being passed on to younger generations.

The Natives' physical environment is extreme in every respect—the weather, the land, even the geography. There's a special feeling to walking along or upon the Arctic Ocean, the virtual edge of the earth. The quantity and accessibility of wildlife are extreme, too, as are the solitude and the uniqueness of what you can do. Unfortunately, the prices also are extreme. Getting to a Bush hub from Anchorage costs more than getting to Anchorage from Seattle; it's often cheaper to get to Europe from Anchorage than to the Aleutians. And once you're at the rural hub, you're not done. Getting into the outdoors can cost as much again. Many travelers can't afford a Bush sojourn, instead satisfying their curiosity about the state's unpopulated areas on Alaska's rural highways (covered in chapter 9). Most who can afford the trip usually make the most of their time and money with brief prearranged tours or trips directly to wilderness lodges. Only a few explorers head for the Bush unguided, although there are some good places to go that way—Nome, Barrow, Kodiak, and Unalaska among them.

Covering the Bush is a challenge as well for the writer of a book like this one. There are more than 200 Bush villages; many more lodges, camps, and guides; and a vast, undefined territory to describe. All that information would fill a larger book than this one. I've chosen to provide sections on those few Bush hubs that are most accessible and popular with visitors, those that have modern facilities and can be used as gateways to more of the state for visitors who want to venture beyond the fringe of civilization.

1 Exploring the Bush

Alaska's Bush is better defined by what it's like than by where it is. The most common and convenient conception says the Bush is everything beyond the road system. On a map, everything north and west of Fairbanks obviously meets that definition, but many Bush villages lie elsewhere in the Interior, in Southcentral, and in Southeast Alaska. In fact, there are some Bush villages you can drive to. No simple definition works. You know a Bush community by how it feels. It's a place where the wilderness is closer than civilization, where people still live off the land and age-old traditions survive, and where you have to make a particular effort to get in or out.

THE REGIONS
THE ARCTIC   The Arctic Circle is the official boundary of the Arctic. The line, at 66° 33' north latitude, is the southern limit of true midnight sun—south of it, at sea level, the sun rises and sets, at least a little, every day of the year. But in Alaska, people think of the Arctic as beginning at the **Brooks Range,** which is a bit north of the circle, including **Barrow** and **Prudhoe Bay.** The northwest Alaska region, which includes **Kotzebue** and, slightly

Map Pointer

To locate these towns and regions, refer to the "Alaska" map on p. 6.

south of the Arctic Circle, **Nome,** also is Arctic in climate, culture, and topography. The biggest geographic feature in Alaska's Arctic is the broad **North Slope,** the plain of tundra that stretches from the northern side of the Brooks Range to the Arctic Ocean. It's a swampy desert, with little rain or snowfall, frozen solid all but a few months a year.

WESTERN ALASKA   This is the land of the massive, wet **Yukon-Kuskokwim Delta** and the fish-rich waters of Bristol Bay. The Y-K Delta, as it's known, was never really exploited by white explorers, and its Yup'ik people live in some of Alaska's most culturally traditional villages. In places, Yup'ik is still the dominant language. **Bethel** is the main hub city of the delta but holds little attraction for visitors. **Bristol Bay** is known for massive salmon runs, and avid anglers may be interested in its wilderness lodges, using **Dillingham** as a hub.

SOUTHWEST ALASKA   Stretching from the Aleutians—really a region of their own—to the Alaska Peninsula, Kodiak Island, and the southern part of the mountainous west side of Cook Inlet, this is a maritime region, like Southeast, but far more remote. The hub of the wet, windy **Aleutians** is **Unalaska** and its port of **Dutch Harbor. Katmai National Park** and the adjoining wild lands are the main attraction of the Alaska Peninsula, although there also are fishing lodges on the salmon-rich rivers and on the lakes to the north, including areas in **Lake Clark National Park** and **Iliamna Lake.** The lakes and west side of **Cook Inlet** are accessed primarily by Kenai, Homer, and Anchorage flight services for fishermen and hunters. **Kodiak** is hardly a Bush community, but it fits better in this chapter than anywhere else, and the town is a hub for villages and bear viewing on Kodiak Island.

GETTING AROUND

With a few exceptions for strongly motivated travelers, who might take the ferry to Kodiak and Unalaska or drive to Prudhoe Bay, getting to each town in this chapter will require flying. **Alaska Airlines** (© **800/252-7522;** www.alaskaair.com) offers the only jet service to Bush hubs. Other, smaller operators serve these towns with prop aircraft. Throughout the chapter, I've listed the plane fare to various communities from Anchorage, based on flying coach and getting a significant discount for advance purchase and some restrictions. Full fares cost more. With the way airfares fluctuate, it would be unwise to use these numbers as anything more than rough guides. To get the current best fare, use a travel agent or the Internet.

Kodiak, which barely fits in a chapter on the Bush, is the most accessible of the communities in this chapter, but it still requires either a 10-hour ferry ride from Homer or a $300 round-trip plane ticket from Anchorage. This charming, historic town is similar to towns in Southeast Alaska or Prince William Sound, but it is also a hub for Native villages on the island and remote wilderness. **Unalaska/Dutch Harbor,** in the Aleutian Islands, is an interesting place to go way off the beaten path while staying in complete comfort. From Anchorage a visit requires a 3-hour flight on a turbo prop aircraft, and fares of less than $900 are rarely seen. **Barrow,** the **Pribilof Islands, Kotzebue,** and **Kaktovik** are the most purely Native of the communities in the chapter. **Nome** has the advantages of Arctic surroundings easily accessible on gravel roads but is more of a gold-rush town than a Native village. **Prudhoe Bay,** at the end of the Dalton Highway, is an industrial complex without a real town associated with it. Fares from Anchorage range from $450 to $850 for these communities. Buying an **Alaska Airlines package tour** saves money to Nome or Barrow, and gives you something to do when you arrive.

2 Kodiak: Wild Island

The habitat that makes Kodiak Island a perfect place for bears also makes it perfect for people. Runs of salmon clog unpopulated bays and innumerable, little-fished rivers; the rounded green mountains seem to beg for someone to cross them; the gravel beaches and protected rocky inlets are free of people but full of promise. But in this respect, bears are smarter than people. Brown bears own the island, growing to prodigious size and abundant numbers, but Kodiak is as yet undiscovered by human visitors. That's part of the wonder of the place. I'll never forget flying over the luxuriant verdure of Kodiak's mountains and the narrow string of glassy Raspberry Strait on a rare sunny day, seeing no sign of human presence in the most beautiful landscape I had ever beheld.

The narrow streets of the town of Kodiak are a discovery, too. Twisting over the hills in little discernible order, they were the original stomping grounds of **Lord Alexander Baranof,** the first Russian ruler of Alaska, who arrived here in 1790. Kodiak has the oldest Russian building in North America. It was nearly lost in the 1964 Good Friday earthquake, which destroyed most of the town, explaining the general lack of old buildings. The quake brought a 30-foot wave that washed to the building's doorstep. A marker near the police station on Mill Bay Road shows the wave's incredible high-water point. Before the Russians, the **Koniag** people lived off the incomparable riches of the island. They're still here, recovering their past in a fascinating little research museum.

The town looks to the sea. Along with the Coast Guard base, fishing makes Kodiak prosperous, creating a friendly, energetic, unpolished community. Kodiak is separate from the rest of Alaska, living its own commercial fishing life without often thinking of what's going on in Anchorage or anywhere else. It's off the beaten path because it doesn't really need anything the path provides.

For the visitor, Kodiak is an undiscovered gem. A few days just scratches the surface of the charming, vibrant town and the easily accessible wild places around it, yet, even in midsummer, you will see few, if any, other tourists.

There are six **Native villages** on the island. A flight to one of them and back on a clear day is a wonderful, low-cost way to see remote areas of the island and to get a taste of how Alaska Natives live. It's also popular to fly out to see the famous bears on a day trip, or stay at one of several **wilderness lodges** for wildlife watching, fishing, sea kayaking, or hunting.

ESSENTIALS

GETTING THERE   It's a 1-hour flight from Anchorage to Kodiak on **Alaska Airlines** (© 800/252-7522; www.alaskaair.com). **ERA Aviation** (© 800/866-8394; www.flyera.com) also serves the route with prop aircraft, which may save a little money. A round-trip ticket from Anchorage costs $300 or more. A **cab,** from **A&B Taxi** (© 907/486-4343), runs about $15 from the airport.

The ferries *Tustumena* and *Kennicott,* of the **Alaska Marine Highway System** (© 800/642-0066 or 907/486-3800; www.ferryalaska.com), serve Kodiak from Homer, the closest port with a road. The run takes 10 hours, but it is truly memorable. The vessels leave land behind and thread through the strange and exposed Barren Islands. The ocean can be quite rough, and when it is, lots of passengers get seasick; take Dramamine *before* boarding. A cabin is a good idea for an overnight run.

Without a cabin, the adult passenger fare from Homer is $72. Fares for children 5 to 11 are half-price on all ferries, free for those under 5.

VISITOR INFORMATION   The **Kodiak Island Convention and Visitors Bureau,** 100 Marine Way, Ste. 200, Kodiak, AK 99615 (© **800/789-4782** or 907/486-4782; fax 907/486-6545; www.kodiak.org), occupies a small building on the ferry dock. Hours vary according to the ferry schedule but essentially follow this pattern: summer Monday 8am to 8:30pm, Tuesday through Friday 8am to 5pm, Saturday 10am to 4pm, Sunday 1 to 8:30pm; winter Monday through Friday 8am to 5pm.

The **Kodiak National Wildlife Refuge Visitor Center,** Buskin River Road, near the airport 4 miles south of town (© **888/408-3514** or 907/487-2600; http:// alaska.fws.gov/nwr/kodiak), is headquarters for a 1.9-million-acre refuge that covers two-thirds of Kodiak Island and parts of other islands, the home of the famous Kodiak brown bear. There are seven remote public-use cabins around the refuge, reachable by chartered plane. Permits are $30 a night, available though a quarterly drawing of names (Jan 2 for Apr–June, Apr 1 for July–Sept). The center has exhibits and is a good place to stop for outdoors information. They're open from mid-June to August daily from 8am to 4:30pm; the balance of the year Monday through Friday only.

ORIENTATION   The Kodiak Archipelago contains Kodiak, Shuyak, and Afognak islands, and many other smaller islands. Kodiak is the nation's second-largest island (after Hawaii's Big Island). The city of Kodiak is on a narrow point on the northeast side of Kodiak Island, surrounded by tiny islands. There are six Native villages on other parts of the island. The airport and Coast Guard base are several miles southwest of town on **Rezanof Drive,** which runs through town and comes out on the other side. The center of Kodiak is a hopeless tangle of steep, narrow streets—you need the excellent map given away by the visitor center, but it's all walkable. The ferry dock is on **Marine Way,** and most of the in-town sights are right nearby. Several paved and gravel roads, totaling 100 miles, make wonderful exploring from Kodiak to deserted shorelines, gorgeous views, pastures, recreation areas, and salmon streams. The visitors guide contains a mile-by-mile guide to each drive.

GETTING AROUND   Several companies rent cars, including **Budget** (© **800/527-0700** or 907/487-2220; www.budget.com), which has offices at the airport and downtown. **Avis** is at the Kodiak airport (© **800/331-1212** or 907/487-2264; www. avis.com). If it's not raining, a bike is a great way to get around Kodiak, and strong riders can tour far beyond the town. Bikes are for rent at **Fifty-Eight Degrees North,** a full-service bike shop at 1231 Mill Bay Rd. (© **907/486-6249**). Front-suspension mountain bikes rent for $35 for 24 hours.

FAST FACTS: Kodiak

Banks Several banks downtown have ATMs, including **Key Bank** and **Wells Fargo** on the mall at the waterfront.

Hospital **Providence Kodiak Island Medical Center** is at 1915 E. Rezanof Dr. (© **907/486-3281**).

Internet Access **The Treasury** gift and bookstore, on the mall at 104 Center St., Ste. 104 (© **907/486-0373**); or the **A. Holmes Johnson Public Library,** 319 Lower Mill Bay Rd. (© **907/486-8686**).

Police Contact the **Kodiak Police Department** at © 907/486-8000.

Post Office It's at 419 Lower Mill Bay Rd., at Hemlock Street.

Taxes **Sales tax** is 6% within city limits, and the **room tax** is 5% everywhere on the island; rooms are thus taxed 11% in Kodiak city, 5% elsewhere.

SPECIAL EVENTS Russian Orthodox Christmas, January 7, includes the evening **Starring Ceremony.** A choir follows a parishioner carrying a star to sing at the homes of church members.

The late-winter **Pillar Mountain Golf Classic** (© 907/486-2931 organizer's home phone) is played on a 1-hole, par-70 course that climbs 1,400 feet from a tee next to a derelict car to a flag on a piece of 2-by-4 lumber marking the 5-gallon bucket that serves as a hole; dogs, chain saws, two-way radios, and tracking devices are prohibited, and cursing the officials carries a $25 fine. Handsaws, machetes, and hatchets are allowed. Coating balls with fluorescent spray paint before each shot is standard procedure—the paint leaves a trail in the snow to find the ball.

The 5-day **Kodiak Crab Festival** (© 907/486-5557), over Memorial Day weekend (May 24–28, 2007), is a big event, including a king crab feed, a carnival, many fun community events, the solemn blessing of the fleet, and a memorial service for fishermen and mariners lost at sea.

On Labor Day weekend, the **Kodiak State Fair and Rodeo** (© 907/486-4488) has all kinds of small-town contests and family entertainment, including bull riding and a horse show.

The visitor bureau maintains an extensive community calendar online at **www. kodiak.org**.

EXPLORING THE TOWN

The highlights downtown include the **Fishermen's Memorial,** near the harbormaster's office at the head of the St. Paul Harbor, where a soberingly long list of Kodiak fishermen who have lost their lives at sea is posted on plaques. The warship set in concrete on Mission Way is the *Kodiak Star,* the last World War II Liberty Ship built. It came here as a fish processor after the 1964 earthquake destroyed the canneries and is still in use. Along Shelikof Avenue, overlooking St. Paul Harbor, the **Kodiak Maritime Museum** has mounted 12 attractive and interesting signs explaining the parts of a boat, North Pacific crabbing and geography, and other nautical topics. In the same area, stop in at **Kodiak Island Brewing Co.,** 338 Shelikof St., where Ben Millstein brews organic beer. Unless you want to buy a growler full (a large jug you return for $5 deposit), just try a sample now and drink more in any of the local restaurants.

At Kashevarof and Mission streets, the **Holy Resurrection Russian Orthodox Church** was founded in 1794, although the present building dates only to 1945, when the original church burned.

The **Kodiak Alutiiq Dancers** give 45-minute performances Tuesday and Thursday at 2:30pm June through August at the Shoonaq' Tribal Hall, at 312 W. Marine Way (© 907/486-4449). Admission is $15 adults, $7.50 children.

Alutiiq Museum ⚐ This exceptional museum, funded and governed by Natives, seeks to document and restore the Koniag Alutiiq people's culture, which the Russians virtually wiped out in the 18th century. Besides teaching about Alutiiq culture in a single gallery, the museum manages its own archaeological digs and repatriates Native remains and artifacts, which researchers removed by the thousands in the 1930s. The archaeological repository now includes 100,000 objects.

215 Mission Rd. (℗ 907/486-7004. www.alutiiqmuseum.com. Admission $3 adults, free for kids under 12. Summer Mon–Fri 9am–5pm, Sat 10am–5pm; winter Tues–Fri 9am–5pm, Sat 10:30am–4:30pm.

The Baranov Museum 🐸 The museum occupies the oldest Russian building of only a few left standing in North America and is Alaska's oldest building of any kind. Alexander Baranof, who ruled Alaska as manager of the Russian American Company, built the log structure in 1808 as a magazine and strong house for valuable sea otter pelts—the treasure that motivated the Russians' interest here. This was his headquarters for the invasion he extended across Alaska and down the Pacific Northwest coast. The museum stands in a grassy park overlooking the water across from the ferry dock. Inside is a little museum rich with Russian and early Native artifacts. The guides know a lot of history and show educational photo albums on various topics. The gift store is exceptional, selling antique Russian items and authentic Native crafts.

101 Marine Way. (℗ **907/486-5920.** www.baranov.us. Admission $3, free for children under 13. Summer Mon–Sat 10am–4pm; winter Tues–Sat 10am–3pm. Closed Feb.

GETTING OUTSIDE
TWO RECREATION AREAS
A couple of miles north of town on Rezanof Drive, the **Fort Abercrombie State Historical Park** encompasses World War II ruins set on coastal cliffs amid huge trees. Paths lead to the beaches and good tide-pool walking, a swimming lake, and lots of other discoveries. The gun emplacements, bunkers, and other concrete buildings defended against the Japanese, who had seized islands in the outer Aleutians and were expected to come this way. A group of local World War II buffs have built a museum of war artifacts from the Alaska fighting in the ammunition bunker at Miller Point. Hours change annually but will be posted at www.kadiak.org (yes, kadiak), or the volunteers will open it any time by appointment (℗ **907/486-7015**). The website is extensive. A wonderful 13-site campground sits atop the cliffs among the trees and ruins. Camping is $15. The **Alaska Division of State Parks,** Kodiak District Office, 1400 Abercrombie Dr., Kodiak, AK 99615 (℗ **907/486-6339;** fax 907/486-3320; www.alaskastateparks.org, click on "Individual Parks," and then "Kodiak Islands"), maintains an office here where you can pick up a walking-tour brochure or, during the summer, join the Saturday-night interpretive program or a guided tide-pool walk, scheduled to coincide with low tides. Or investigate the tide pools on your own, picking up an identification guide at the park's natural history bookstore.

The **Buskin River State Recreation Site,** 4 miles south of town off Rezanof Drive near the Fish and Wildlife Service visitor center, has 15 campsites, a hiking trail, and access to fishing. Camping is $15.

OUTDOOR ACTIVITIES
BROWN BEAR VIEWING To count on seeing Kodiak's famous bears, you need to get out on a plane or boat and visit at the right time of year. The easiest way is a Kodiak-based floatplane; expect to pay at least $400 per person, with a two- or three-person minimum for a half-day trip (larger groups can get discounts). Landing on the water, you don rubber boots (provided) and walk up to half an hour to get to where bears congregate. In early July to early August, depending on salmon runs, flights land on Frazer Lake for viewing at Frazer fish pass. A .75-mile walk on a dirt lane leads to

the viewing area. The Kodiak National Wildlife Refuge (see "Visitor Information," above) controls the viewing area with a permit system, but you can rely on the flight service for that. Flights also visit Ayakulik and Karluk rivers when fish are present, good bear-viewing areas that are unregulated. At any of these sites, binoculars and tele-photo camera lenses are essential, as no responsible guide would crowd Kodiak brown bears so closely that such lenses become unnecessary (although the bears could choose to approach within 150 feet of you). Bears congregate only when salmon are running, so the timing of your visit is critical. From early July to mid-August, you have a good chance of seeing bears fishing in streams on Kodiak, sometimes in numbers. Contact the refuge for more information on timing and bear activity.

When fish aren't running on Kodiak, such as in June or late August, air services fly to the east coast of the Alaska Peninsula, often in Katmai National Park, to watch bears digging clams from the tidal flats and eating grass and greens on the coastal meadows. Landing on water, you typically watch while standing on the plane's floats. It's interesting and the flight is spectacular, but the viewing may be from a greater dis-tance than on the streams and the bears will more likely be on their own. Generally, the flight services charge their standard bear-viewing seat rate, regardless of how far they have to fly to find bears; if you charter, it may cost much more, but you will have freedom to determine where the plane goes, for added sightseeing. Several small flight services offer bear viewing, including **Sea Hawk Air** (© **800/770-4295** or 907/486-8282; www.seahawkair.com).

If a bear-viewing day trip is the whole reason you're going to Kodiak, compare your options. You can use Homer as your base (see chapter 7), or spend more money to go to Katmai National Park to see bears really close (see section 3 of this chapter). For additional money, you can see more of Kodiak's bears on a longer outing: A flight serv-ice can leave you at a lodge for an extended stay in bear habitat. Check the visitor cen-ter for a referral. Harry and Brigid Dodge host small groups at their solar-powered Aleut Island Lodge in Uyak Bay, taking an environmentally sensitive approach while spending the time to know the bears and their habitat. Accommodations are fittingly rustic and bathing is in the sauna. The business is called Kodiak Treks (© **907/487-2122;** www.kodiaktreks.com). Rates are $275 per person per night, double, including food and activities such as kayaking and fishing, but not including the cost of getting there (about $250 per person from Kodiak). See "Sea Kayaking," below, for another option.

FISHING   The 70 miles of road leading from Kodiak reach eight good-size rivers with productive fishing for salmon and Dolly Varden char. At times you can drive to places with fishing pressure as light as some fly-in locations on the mainland. Going beyond the road network puts you on some of the best and least-used fishing oppor-tunities in Alaska. The visitor center provides a list of where to fish and the names and addresses of guides for remote fishing. You can also seek advice and regulations from the **Alaska Department of Fish and Game,** 211 Mission Rd., Kodiak, AK 99615 (© **907/486-1880;** www.alaska.gov/adfg; click on "Sport Fisheries," then on the Southcentral region, and then on "Kodiak/Aleutians"). To fish the remote areas, you'll need to charter a plane, going for a day or staying at a remote public-use cabin or wilderness lodge. About 50 boats are available in the boat harbors for ocean fishing. An advantage of coming to Kodiak is that it puts you near rich halibut grounds—you don't have to take a long boat ride for excellent fishing. Trolling for silvers is good in August. Check with the visitor center for a referral.

HIKING & BIRD-WATCHING   There are good day hikes in Kodiak, some starting from downtown. The local Audubon Society publishes a *Kodiak Hiking & Birding Guide* that you can pick up at the visitor center. Audubon's guided hikes go to different place every Saturday and Sunday of the summer, meeting at the visitor center parking lot at 9:30am for carpooling. Again, the center is the best source of information.

SEA KAYAKING   The Kodiak Archipelago, with its many folded, rocky shorelines and abundant marine life, is a perfect place for sea kayaking. Kayaks were invented here and on the Aleutian Islands to the west. For beginners, it is best to start with a day trip, and the waters around the town of Kodiak are lovely for such a paddle. Several operators can arrange an outing, although most concentrate on more ambitious trips. For a half-day, expect to pay around $100 per person; for a full day, $200. One day-trip guide with a strong environmental ethic is Andy Schroeder, whose business is called **Orcas Unlimited Charters** (© 907/481-1121; www.orcasunlimited.com). Schroeder specializes in day trips but also takes clients on extended outings using a converted fishing boat as a base. Guests paddle by day and sleep and eat aboard. Others operate using the same mothership concept. **Mythos Expeditions** (© 907/ 486-5536; www.thewildcoast.com) has for years housed kayakers on a former fishing vessel for multiday bear- and whale-viewing trips on the coasts of Kodiak and Afognak islands and the Alaska Peninsula's Katmai coast. They do day trips as well.

   Shuyak Island State Park, 54 miles north of Kodiak, is famously appealing for sea-kayaking expeditions. The park is a honeycomb of islands and narrow passages in virgin Sitka spruce coastal forest. The Division of State Parks (see addresses under "Two Recreation Areas," above) distributes a free kayaking guide with route descriptions and maintains four public-use cabins, which rent for $75 a night in the summer season. These cabins can be quite hard to get in August. See "State Parks Cabin Reservations," in section 1 of chapter 7. Mythos Expeditions, mentioned in the previous paragraph, leads trips to Shuyak Island State Park and rents kayaks there for self-guided paddlers.

WHERE TO STAY

I've listed good places in town and nearby on the roads, but Kodiak has more than 30 other B&Bs. Beyond the roads, some of Alaska's best wilderness lodges are on Kodiak Island in remote areas and near Native villages. The visitor center posts links to many B&Bs and lodges on its website at www.kodiak.org. A 50-room hotel facing the airport parking lot offers some of the area's best standard rooms. The **Comfort Inn Kodiak,** 1395 Airport Way, Kodiak, AK 99615 (© 800/544-2202 or 907/487-2700), under new ownership and freshly renovated, reincarnated the Buskin River Inn. The new affiliation and other changes were still in process as I prepared this edition. The restaurant is managed by the same chef as Mill Bay Coffee, described below.

Best Western Kodiak Inn 🐾   This is the best hotel in downtown Kodiak, with attractive rooms perched on the hill overlooking the boat harbor, right in the center of things. Rooms in the wooden building vary in size and view, but all are acceptable standard rooms with good amenities, including wireless Internet.

   The **Chart Room** restaurant, specializing in seafood and with a great view of the water, is a good choice for a nice dinner out, with entrees in the $15 to $25 range.

236 W. Rezanof Dr., Kodiak, AK 99615. © **888/563-4254** or 907/486-5712. Fax 907/486-3430. www.kodiakinn.com. 81 units. High season $159 double; low season $109 double. Extra person 18 and over $15. AE, DC, DISC, MC, V. **Amenities:** Restaurant; bar; outdoor Jacuzzi; tour desk; courtesy van. *In room:* TV, Wi-Fi, fridge, microwave, coffeemaker, hair dryer, iron.

Kodiak Bed and Breakfast   Hospitable, active Mary Monroe runs this comfortable, homey place with a big, friendly dog, Austin. There is a porch where you can eat breakfast on sunny mornings, overlooking the harbor (fish is often on the morning menu). The location is convenient, right downtown, and the entry for the bedrooms and shared sitting room downstairs doesn't require you to walk through Monroe's own living quarters. A telephone and TV are shared in the sitting room, and a freezer is available for guests' fish.

308 Cope St., Kodiak, AK 99615. (*C*) 907/486-5367. 2 units, both with shared bathroom. $116 double. Rate includes full breakfast. No credit cards. *In room:* No phone.

WHERE TO DINE

Besides the hotel restaurant listed above at the Best Western Kodiak Inn, Kodiak has several restaurants catering to locals. The best restaurant in town operates in different locations, depending on the meal you seek. **Mill Bay Coffee & Pastries,** about 2 miles out of downtown at 3833 Rezanof Dr. ((*C*) **907/486-4411;** www.millbaycoffee. com), is where award-winning, Paris-trained chef Joel Chenet produces wonderful pastries and, for lunch, brilliant combinations of local seafood and international seasonings brought to inexpensive sandwiches—the Kodiak sea burger is made of salmon, crab, shrimp, and cream cheese, among other ingredients, and costs only $10. The comfortable, casual dining room, managed by Chenet's wife, Martine, is a local hub and has Wi-Fi. To dine in the evening, try their new **Mill Bay Deux** restaurant, located in the Comfort Inn Kodiak at the airport.

Another unique place to eat, this time for dinner, could be a highlight of your trip. Marty and Marion Owen serve dinner for six on their 42-foot yacht the *Sea Breeze.* The meals from **Galley Gourmet** ((*C*) **800/253-6331** or 907/486-5079; www.kodiak-alaska-dinner-cruises.com) are usually elaborate seafood creations. The evening starts at 6pm with a 45-minute cruise in the picturesque waters near Kodiak's harbor, where guests may see puffins, sea lions, and whales. Dinner is served at anchor and you're back at the dock at 9:30pm. The price is $105 per person. They'll also do a 2-hour cruise without food service for $50 per person. The couple offers day-long whale watching and 3-day cruises, too.

Harborside Coffee and Goods, at 210 B, Shelikof St. ((*C*) **907/486-5862**), on the south side of the boat harbor, is a comfortable coffeehouse with soup, bagels, and fresh pastries, popular with young people and fishermen. **Henry's Great Alaskan Restaurant,** at 512 Marine Way ((*C*) **907/486-8844**), on the waterfront mall, is a bar and grill where you will meet many commercial fishermen and other locals. The menu includes daily specials, local seafood, and good halibut sandwiches.

3 Katmai National Park

Most of the land of the Alaska Peninsula, pointing out to the Aleutian Archipelago, is in one federally protected status or another, centering on Katmai National Park. The park, pronounced "*cat*-my," lies just west of Kodiak Island, across the storm-infested Shelikof Strait. Bear and salmon are the main attractions. **Brooks Camp,** with a campground and lodge within Katmai, is probably the most comfortable place for foolproof bear viewing in Alaska during its peak season. Bears congregate thickly at the falls on the Brooks River when red salmon try to pass up the falls at the beginning of July (more on the seasons below, under "Exploring the Park"). At times, you can sit back on a deck and watch 900-pound brown bears walk by, going about their business of devouring the fish that contribute to their awesome size. (A brown bear is the genetic twin of the grizzly, but generally larger due to its coastal diet of salmon.) Staying the night will require you to reserve a place in the 16-space campground the previous winter or stay in the pricey lodge, where rooms can book up over a year ahead for the bear season. You can go for a day trip with less planning if you can stand to pay around $600 round-trip airfare from Anchorage for 2 or 3 hours at the camp (this information is covered in "Getting There," below). Bear viewing on the Katmai Coast is covered in the Kodiak section (see p. 439), where flight services and charter boats offer trips. If you're comparing, also look at the flight operators in Homer and Anchorage (see p. 303 and 208).

Katmai was set aside in 1918 for reasons unrelated to bears. The area exploded into world consciousness in 1912 with the most destructive volcanic eruption to shake the earth in 3,400 years. When Katmai's Novarupta blew, it released 10 times more energy than Mount St. Helen's eruption of 1980 and displaced twice as much matter as 1883's Krakatoa. In Kodiak, the sky was black for 3 days, and 2 feet of ash crushed houses and choked rivers. People could clearly hear the blast in Juneau; acid rain melted fabric in Vancouver, British Columbia; and the skies darkened over most of the Northern Hemisphere. At the blast site, all life within a 40-square-mile area was wiped out and buried as deep as 700 feet. But so remote was the area, then still unnamed, that not a single human being was killed. The **Valley of Ten Thousand Smokes,** the vast wasteland created by the blast, belched steam for decades after. Today Novarupta is dormant and the steam is gone, but the area is still a barren moonscape, making a fascinating day tour or hiking trip.

ESSENTIALS

GETTING THERE   Most people fly to Katmai from Anchorage by way of the village of **King Salmon,** which lies just west of the park. **Alaska Airlines** (© **800/252-7522;** www.alaskaair.com) flies to King Salmon daily in the summer, charging at least $450 round-trip. For more flight options, you can use their prop partner, **PenAir** (© **800/448-4226;** www.penair.com), which can be booked through Alaska Airlines. Air taxis carry visitors the last leg from King Salmon to **Brooks Camp** for a fare of around $165 round-trip. **Katmai Air,** operated by park concessionaire Katmailand (© **800/544-0551** or 907/243-5448; www.katmaiair.com), does these flights and offers round-trip airfare packages from Anchorage that can save a little money (total around $575) and add simplicity to your planning.

As an alternative to Brooks Camp, more and more visitors are exploring the supremely rugged wilderness on the east side of the park from the beaches along **Shelikof Strait.** Air-taxi operators make drop-offs and do bear-viewing day trips from Homer or Kodiak (see section 2 of this chapter, earlier, on Kodiak, or see the Homer section in chapter 7), and boats out of Kodiak go across for extended cruising and kayak expeditions (see p. 441). In this park, with more than 2,000 brown bears resident (the world's largest protected population), it's easy for pilots to find them digging clams on the tidal marshes, and then land on floats for a good, close look.

RESERVATIONS & FEES   No entry fee or permit applies for day trips to Katmai, but once you're there, you have to sign up for an hour on the bear-viewing platforms (see below). Camping costs $8 per person per night. Campground capacity is allocated by person, not by site, and the limit of 60 people per night is far lower than the many visitors who want to stay during the bear season in July. The crowds are smaller in September, but the bears are not quite as numerous. Camping reservations become available for the entire summer on January 5. To reserve, call or log on to the **park service national reservation system** (© **800/365-2267** or 301/722-1257; http://reservations.nps.gov). If you're using the phone system, enter **KAT#** at the prompt.

VISITOR INFORMATION   For advance planning, contact **Katmai National Park Headquarters** at P.O. Box 7, King Salmon, AK 99613 (© **907/246-3305;** www.nps.gov/katm). At Brooks Camp, the park service has a center where all visitors are required to attend a 20-minute orientation called "The Brooks Camp School of Bear Etiquette," designed to train visitors (not bears) and keep them out of trouble. In Anchorage, you can get information at the **Alaska Public Lands Information Center,** at 4th Avenue and F Street (© **907/271-2737;** see the complete listing in section 1 of chapter 6). The King Salmon **Visitor Center** is next door to the airport (© **907/246-4250**), staffed jointly by the National Park Service, the U.S. Fish and Wildlife Service, and local governments. It is open 8am to 5pm daily in summer, Monday through Friday in winter.

GETTING AROUND   Once you've made it to Brooks Camp, a **bus** carries visitors to the Valley of Ten Thousand Smokes, 23 miles by gravel road from the camp. The park concessionaire, **Katmailand,** charges $88 per person round-trip for the all-day guided excursion, plus $8 more for lunch. A ranger leads a walk down into the valley. One-way transfers for hikers are $51.

FAST FACTS: Katmai

Bank **Wells Fargo,** with an ATM, is in the King Salmon Mall on the Peninsula Highway in King Salmon.

Hospital The **Camai Clinic,** in Naknek (© **907/246-6155**), is open during normal business hours; calls to the number go to emergency dispatchers after hours.

Police In **King Salmon,** call © **907/246-4222;** elsewhere, call **Alaska State Troopers** at © **907/246-3346** or 907/246-3464. There are no phones or cellular service out in the park.

Shopping The park is remote, without businesses other than the lodge. King Salmon is the last stop for basic supplies or groceries.

EXPLORING THE PARK

Katmai's famous bear viewing occurs at **Brooks Camp** when the bears congregate near the Brooks River to catch salmon. Viewing peaks in early July but can begin in late June and last through July, with a smaller congregation in September. This is when you're assured of seeing bears from the elevated platforms near the Brooks River falls, half a mile from Brooks Camp, even on a day trip. Forty to sixty bears feed here. Indeed, bears are seen all along the trail to the falls and elsewhere—the falls are just the most concentrated spot. Rangers don't guide visitors but are on hand to manage the foot traffic. The platforms allow a good view of the bears and just enough separation. The park service recommends that people with mobility problems avoid this trail when bears are present. Considering the expense and potential difficulty, I'd advise those with trouble getting around to choose another venue for bear viewing. Due to the popularity of the experience, there is a 1-hour limit on the falls platform during the peak season (another platform is unlimited). After your turn is up, you can sign up on a waiting list to get another chance. The falls platform and trail are closed 10pm to 7am. Outside of the short salmon runs, there are better places to see bears, so don't spend the money to come here. Bears feed all summer on clams on Katmai's east shore. See "Getting There," above.

The Brooks Camp area has a small park service campground, visitor center, and lodge, located where the Brooks River flows into Naknek Lake. When the area was first developed for fishing in the 1950s, the camp was built in the middle of a major bear corridor, where it never would be allowed today, creating a unique opportunity to stay right in some of the most concentrated bear habitat on the globe. The most comfortable way is to stay at the **Brooks Lodge,** operated by Katmailand (© **800/ 544-0551** or 907/243-5448; www.brookslodge.com). The lodge has 16 units, with private bathrooms with shower stalls. To save money, book the lodge rooms as packages with air travel from Anchorage. The least expensive 1-night visit is $826 per person double occupancy, meals not included; 3 nights is $1,414. A double room without airfare is $654. Peak dates (when the bears are around) book up 12 months out or earlier; for your choice, call as soon as the reservation system opens 18 months ahead, January of the year before the visit. Three buffet-style meals are served daily for guests and visitors who aren't staying in the lodge. Breakfast is $12, lunch $18, and dinner $28. For food, they take MasterCard and Visa at the lodge. Also at Brooks Camp, there's a small store, the park service visitor center, and a campground. See "Reservations & Fees," above, for info on campground reservations, which should be made 6 months in advance. The rangers require special precautions to keep bears away from campers.

The rivers and lakes of Katmai lure human anglers as well as ursine ones. Katmailand operates two lodges within the park other than Brooks Lodge for remote fishing, the **Kulik** and **Grosvenor lodges.** Check their website at www.katmailand.com for fishing details. The park service also has a list of dozens of fishing, hiking, and air guides. There is no central clearinghouse for remote fishing, but you can find and book a good place through an agency such as **Sport Fishing Alaska,** 9310 Shorecrest Dr., Anchorage, AK 99502 (© **888/552-8674** or 907/344-8674; www.alaskatrip planners.com), listed in full under "Planning an Outdoor Vacation" in chapter 2.

Backcountry hiking in Katmai means crossing a wilderness without trails, including the hazards of river crossings. Only experienced backpackers should plan extended trips. The park service asks hikers to obtain a voluntary permit for backcountry travel, thereby clueing them in to your plans in case you need to be rescued. You will also need to store food and items with odors in bear-resistant containers, which you can check out from the park. Anyone can walk for the day without such precautions in the desolate **Valley of Ten Thousand Smokes.** This 40-square-mile plain remains a moonscape 90 years after the titanic volcanic blast that buried it, little changed except that the famous plumes of smoke are gone and rivers have sliced through the debris in places to create narrow, white-walled canyons. Although it looks like a desert and is subject to dust storms, rain is common and temperatures rarely go higher than 65°F (18°C). Katmailand operates a tour bus from Brooks Camp, mentioned above under "Getting Around." The visitors on those tours usually stay on a short trail on the valley's rim, where a visitor center is located, but a 3-mile round-trip hike descends 800 feet to the valley floor, where you can get a better look at the ash that helps create the bizarre landforms here.

4 Unalaska/Dutch Harbor: Aleutian Boomtown

After a lifetime of hearing how desolate the Aleutians (uh-*loo*-shens) were, I felt like I was leaving the edge of the earth the first time I traveled to Unalaska (oon-ah-*las*-ka). Shortly after I arrived, a storm started slinging huge raindrops horizontally through the air so hard that they stung as they splattered on my face. People went on about their business as if nothing special was happening—stormy weather constantly batters these rocks that pop up from the empty North Pacific. My expectations seemed justified.

But the next day, the storm cleared like a curtain opening on a rich operatic scene—simultaneously opening the curtain of my dark expectations. Unalaska may lack trees, but it's not a barren rock. The island is covered with heather and wildflowers. Rounded mountains that invite wandering exploration rise from the ocean like the backs of huge beasts. For sightseeing, it has barely a day's attractions, but for outdoor exploring, bird-watching, and halibut fishing, few places come close.

With the protected port of Dutch Harbor so far out in a ferocious ocean habitat rich in crab and bottom fish, Unalaska has grown in 3 decades from a tiny, forgotten Native village to the nation's largest fishing port. The pattern of growth followed the form of the early gold rushes. There was a wild, lawless time in the 1970s when crab fishermen got rich quick and partied like Old West cowboys. Then the overfished crab stocks crashed, only to be replaced, starting in the mid-1980s, by an even bigger boom, when waters within 200 miles of the U.S. shore were rid of foreign vessels and American bottom fishing took off. Big factory ships began unloading here and huge fish plants were built on flat ground chipped from the rock. Today that expansion has reached a steady state and women and families have come to town—another part of the gold rush pattern. But domestication isn't done yet. Most of the population lives in bunkhouses and flies back to Seattle, Mexico, and the Philippines when the processing plants close for the season. Unalaska may be the best current example of the American cultural phenomenon of the frontier boomtown.

Ironically, Unalaska is Alaska's oldest town as well as its newest city. The value of a good port out in the middle of the ocean was recognized from the beginning by the Aleuts. In 1759, the Russians began trading here, and fought a war with the Aleuts from 1763 to 1766, the outcome of which was slavery for the Aleut hunters and the massacre of their people. The Russians built a permanent settlement here in 1792, their first in Alaska. Unalaska also was a key refueling stop for steamers carrying gold-rush stampeders to Nome a century ago, which brought an epidemic that killed a third of the indigenous population. In 1940, Dutch Harbor—the seaport on Amaknak Island associated with the town and island of Unalaska—was taken over by the U.S. Navy to defend against Japanese attack. That attack came: In June 1942, Japanese planes bombed Unalaska, killing 43. The Aleut people were removed from the islands for the duration of the war and interned in inadequate housing in Southeast Alaska, where many died of disease. The military pulled out in 1947, but the remains of their defenses are interesting to explore, part of a unique unit of the national park system. Thanks to a 1971 act of Congress settling Native claims, the Aleut-owned Ounalashka Corporation owns much of the land around town. But the National Park Service protects and interprets the World War II historic sites on Native-owned land.

ESSENTIALS

GETTING THERE   Alaska Airlines (© **800/252-7522;** www.alaskaair.com) no longer serves the Unalaska port and airport of Dutch Harbor with jets because the bad weather and short runway made the schedule too unreliable. Instead, Alaska books flights on a smaller partner airline, **PenAir** (© **800/448-4226;** www.penair.com), which operates 30-passenger turbo props (of course, you can also book directly with PenAir). When a squall is hitting Dutch, these smaller planes can land on a different island and wait for it to clear. The flight from Anchorage takes 3 hours and a ticket is $900 or more round-trip.

The **Alaska Marine Highway System** ferry *Tustumena* (© **800/642-0066;** www.ferryalaska.com) runs once a month from Homer, leaving Tuesday and arriving in Unalaska on Saturday after stopping in Kodiak and the villages along the way. The one-way passenger fare is $340, and a two-berth outside (with windows) cabin with facilities is $314 more. Several travelers who have done this open-sea adventure have given me glowing reports of incomparable scenery and wonderful encounters with the people of the villages along the way. Since the ship is in the open ocean, sea sickness is a real concern and you should prepare with your favorite remedy (mine's Dramamine). The complicating factor is that unless you want to spend half a day in Unalaska and then make the long return trip, you'll need to fly back.

VISITOR INFORMATION   The **Unalaska/Port of Dutch Harbor Convention and Visitors Bureau,** P.O. Box 545, Unalaska, AK 99685 (© 877/581-2612 or 907/581-2612; www.unalaska.info), is at 5th Street and Broadway, in the old part of town. A visitor center for the **Aleutian WW II National Historic Area** (© **907/ 581-9944;** www.nps.gov/aleu) occupies a war-era building at the airport. The historic area encompasses World War II ruins on the island that stand on Native-owned lands. The National Park Service helped fund the improvements and interpret the history. A $4 entry fee at the visitor center also covers the permit to hike to the ruins (see "Exploring the Town," below). The website is interesting, too (click on "In Depth").

GETTING AROUND   The main historic part of the town is a tiny street grid on a narrow peninsula facing Iliuliuk Bay. The **Bridge to the Other Side** (that's the official name) leads to Amaknak Island, the site of the airport, the Grand Aleutian Hotel, and the fishing industrial area of Dutch Harbor. Traveling down the road in the other direction leads a little way up into the mountains, a starting point for walks. Van taxis are the main way of getting around town for the hordes of fishermen. One company is **Blue Checker Taxi** (© **907/581-2186**). You can rent a car or truck from **North Port Rentals** (© **907/581-3880**). Small cars rent for $40 a day.

FAST FACTS: Unalaska/Dutch Harbor

Bank **Key Bank** is attached to the Alaska Commercial Store and has an ATM.

Hospital **Iliuliuk Family and Health Services** (© **907/581-1202**) offers clinic services.

Internet Access Free at the **public library** (© **907/581-5060**).

Police **Unalaska** Department of Public Safety (© **907/581-1233**) is just above the bridge on the Unalaska side.

Post Office It's at 82 Airport Beach Road, near the bridge on the Unalaska side.

Taxes **Sales tax** is 3%; the total **tax on rooms** is 8%.

The Aleutians: The Quiet after War

Once, thousands of men died for the rocky islands of the Aleutians. What began as a Japanese military diversion became a ferocious fight for honor, one of the worst of World War II's Pacific Theater. Yet when the fighting was done, most of the islands were abandoned, littered with military ruins, for half a century. Finally, with the construction of a new National Park Service visitor center in Unalaska, the battle for the Aleutians is just beginning to enter national consciousness.

The Japanese attacked the islands of **Kiska** and **Attu** at the start of the Pacific war to divert the American navy away from what became the Battle of Midway. But the Americans had intercepted and decoded Japanese transmissions and weren't fooled. Meanwhile, the Japanese sent 24 ships, including two aircraft carriers, to bomb the new American naval base at Dutch Harbor and occupy islands in the western Aleutians. Those ships could have tipped the balance at Midway, among the most important battles of the war. Instead, the Japanese met 2 days of bombing at Dutch Harbor; although 43 Americans were killed, the base was not greatly impaired.

The Japanese then took Kiska and Attu, meeting no resistance from 10 Americans staffing a weather station or from Aleutian villagers whose 43 inhabitants were all—even the children—sent to a prison camp in Japan to mine clay for the duration of the war. About half the prisoners survived to return to Alaska.

With the Japanese attack, America depopulated the islands. All the Aleuts were rounded up and put on ships. Their villages were burned or trashed by weather and vandalism. With little thought given to their living conditions, the Aleuts were interned in abandoned summer camps and similarly inadequate facilities in Southeast Alaska. Left without the basic necessities of life or proper sanitation, 10% died. The U.S. Fish and Wildlife Service took Aleut hunters to hunt furs as virtual slaves, much as the Russians had done 200 years before.

Significant resources were committed to a largely futile air and sea battle in the fog and endless storms. The Americans couldn't spare a land invasion force and had to rely on bombing Kiska and Attu to punish the Japanese and try to deter a further advance up the chain. To that end, they built a large base at Adak, among others, so shorter-range fighter escorts could accompany the bombers. Construction in the spongy tundra was difficult, made more so by the length of supply lines.

The Japanese high command never had any intention of advancing, but saw no reason to abandon their new Kiska air base when it was causing the Americans to exert such effort. The Japanese concentrated on fortifying Kiska, which withstood constant bombing raids by the Americans.

Finally, on May 11, 1943, almost a year after the Japanese took the islands, Americans landed on Attu and a brutal 18-day battle for the rugged island began. The Japanese were massively outnumbered but heavily dug in. Finally, with only 800 soldiers left from an original force of 2,600, the Japanese mounted a banzai attack. Only 28 were taken prisoner—the rest were killed in battle or committed suicide. The Americans lost 549 killed, 1,148 wounded, and 2,132 injured by severe cold, disease, accident, or mental breakdown.

The battle for Kiska was less dramatic. The Japanese withdrew under cover of fog. After a massive bombardment of the empty island, the Americans landed to find that no one was there. Still, 105 American soldiers died in accidents and fire from their own forces.

After the Aleutian battle was over, American forces in Alaska declined drastically but never went away altogether. Before the war, little Fort William Seward, in Haines, had been the totality of Alaska's defenses, with a couple hundred men armed with Springfield rifles and no reliable means of transportation. Afterward there were large bases in several areas of the state. Military spending became the biggest economic boom the territory had ever seen, connecting it by a new road to the Lower 48 and bringing precious year-round jobs. A new wave of postwar settlers, many former GIs looking for a new opportunity, brought a population boom. The advent of the Cold War, and Alaska's prime location in defense against the Soviet Union, brought ever-greater increases in military spending. To this day, the military is one of the largest sectors of the Alaska economy. The state has been relatively unscathed in base closures except for remote outposts like Adak, which finally was turned over to an Aleut-owned corporation in 1995.

The end of the war was bitter for the Aleuts. Returning to villages they had departed hastily 3 years before, they found homes and subsistence gear ruined and even historic Russian Orthodox churches and icons severely damaged. Many survivors of the terrible period of internment never returned. Bureaucrats wiped some of the ancient villages off the map as a cost-saving measure.

Awareness of this injustice began to resurface in the 1980s, and in 1988 Congress and President Reagan formally apologized to the Aleuts and paid compensation of $12,000 to each survivor and about half the 900 who were evacuated. That act also helped fund restoration of the five historic churches, including the beautiful church in Unalaska, and construction of one replacement. That work has been completed. Today the Aleuts own their islands. It's fitting that the National Park Service's Aleutian World War II National Historic Area is their guest, on their land, and the new visitor center belongs to a Native corporation. Stop in to learn about the lives sacrificed here, and to wonder why.

To learn more, see Brian Garfield's readable *The Thousand-Mile War; World War II in Alaska and the Aleutians* (University of Alaska Press, $25).

EXPLORING THE TOWN

Unalaska's most significant historic site is the **Holy Ascension Cathedral.** Completed in 1896 on the site of churches that had stood since 1808, the white church with green onion-shaped domes contains 697 icons, artifacts, and artworks—a significant collection that has been continuously in use by the Aleut congregation. The congregation was founded by Father Ivan Veniaminov, who translated the Gospel into Aleut and has been canonized as St. Innocent. A $1.3-million restoration saved the church from collapse in 1996. It is a dignified, geometric counterpoint to the soft edge of sparkling Iliuliuk Bay.

The professionally curated **Museum of the Aleutians,** next door to the Ounalashka Corporation on Margaret Bay in Dutch Harbor (© **907/581-5150;** www.aleutians. org), contains some of the region's best artifacts, including some from North America's oldest coastal sites on Umnak and Unalaska islands. Exhibits also cover the region's 9,000-year history. Admission is $5. It's open summer Tuesday through Saturday from 9am to 5pm, Sunday from noon to 5pm; in winter Tuesday through Saturday from 11am to 5pm.

There are several **World War II military ruins** around town, including some that are still in use, such as the submarine dry dock that today fixes fishing boats. Trails lead over the island to other sites included in the Aleutian World War II National Historic Area, which preserves this evidence of war on American soil and helps tell the story of the Native people who were interned by both the Japanese and the Americans during the war (See "The Aleutians: The Quiet after War," p. 448). U.S. Army Fort Schwatka, on Mount Ballyhoo, is about an hour's hike from the airport. The fort once had over 100 buildings. Many remain, including the best-preserved gun mounts and lookouts of all the nation's coastal defenses from the war. Besides, it's a spectacular site where you can see ships returning. Stop by the historic site visitor center at the airport first; besides learning the context of the park, your $4 admission fee is your permit for access to the ruins, which belong to the Native-owned Ounalashka Corp. (All use on their land requires a permit; see "Hiking," below).

That's about it for sightseeing in Unalaska, unless you take a walk in the port. The activity there is interesting for the size of the vessels and harvest and the incredible investment in buildings and equipment.

GETTING OUTSIDE

BIRD-WATCHING   Flip through the crisp, unused pages of your bird book to find out what you may see in the Aleutians. Several rare bird species nest in the area, and Asian birds occasionally drop in as accidentals. The whiskered auklet and red-legged kittiwake are among the birds commonly found around Unalaska that you probably haven't seen. You'll have the greatest success taking a boat to a seabird colony. The Grand Aleutian Hotel (below, under "Where to Stay and Dine") offers packages; it's also possible to combine halibut fishing and bird-watching on your own chartered boat (see the next paragraph). You're also likely to encounter sea lions and other marine mammals.

FISHING   You can fly out for salmon fishing from black-sand beaches, but Unalaska has become more famous for huge **halibut.** In 1995, a local sport fisherman caught a 395-pound halibut from an 18-foot skiff within a half-mile of town; to kill the behemoth, he had to beach it and beat it over the head with a rock. The next year, Fairbanks angler Jack Tragis landed the world's record halibut here, which weighed

459 pounds. If you're having trouble imagining a fish that big, drop by City Hall, where a stuffed replica hangs in the lobby. The convention and visitor bureau can refer you to a charter boat operator and has a few links to them on its website (see above).

HIKING   The island's green heather and rounded mountains of wildflowers are inviting for a walk. You can walk pretty much in any direction. Explore the abandoned World War II defenses, make a goal of a beach or one of the small peaks around the town, or, for the ambitious, head to the top of an active volcano, Mount Makushin. There are no bears and not many bugs, but there's great berry picking and beachcombing. The weather can be a threat, however, and fox holes can trip you up. As always in remote outdoor areas, you must be suitably dressed and leave word of where you're going and when you'll be back. Hikers beyond the World War II historic area have to pay a slightly higher fee to the **Ounalashka Corp.** (© **907/581-1276;** www.ounalashka.com), the Native village corporation that owns much of the land around town. A 1-day hiking permit is $6 per person or $10 per family; permits for longer periods are available, too. Buy permits from the historic area visitor center (see p. 447).

WHERE TO STAY AND DINE

Grand Aleutian Hotel ☆☆   It's almost unreal to arrive at this big, luxurious hotel in a hard-driving Alaska Bush community. The Grand Aleutian is the best hotel in the Alaska Bush, with rooms just as good as you find in Anchorage, but minutes away from some of the best halibut fishing and bird-watching anywhere. The accommodations are well designed and comfortable, many with good water views; the lobby is grand, with a huge stone fireplace; and there's a piano bar. As you walk outside into a driving gale, it's like teleporting from a big-city hotel back to an exposed rock out in the North Pacific.

The **Chart Room** restaurant, on the second floor, allows bird-watchers to see waterfowl in the bay while dining on steak, seafood, or pasta. The menu, although brief, is Unalaska's most sophisticated. Dinner entrees range from $15 to $45. The **Margaret Bay Cafe,** downstairs, also has a good view, with grilled sandwiches and some lighter fare.

The hotel sometimes puts together birding or fishing packages or workshops. Check for current offerings.

498 Salmon Way (P.O. Box 921169), Dutch Harbor, AK 99692. © **866/581-3844** or 907/581-3844. Fax 907/581-7150. www.grandaleutian.com. 112 units. $179 double; $249 suite. Extra person $20. Packages available. AE, DC, DISC, MC, V. **Amenities:** 2 restaurants; 2 bars; activities desk; courtesy van; limited room service; laundry service. *In room:* TV, coffeemaker, hair dryer.

5 The Pribilof Islands: Birder's Paradise

The Pribilof Islands of St. Paul and St. George sit out in the middle of the Bering Sea, due north of Unalaska, teeming with marine mammals and seabirds. Some 600,000 fur seals meet at the breeding rookeries in the summer, and two million birds of more than 200 species use the rocks. Bird-watchers visit St. Paul for one of the most exotic and productive birding and wildlife-viewing opportunities anywhere. It's best during the spring migration, from mid-May to mid-June, when great numbers of birds show up, including rare Asian accidental species; the fall migration comes in late July and August. You can count on making rare sightings any time during the summer. Indeed, the National Audubon Society's *Field Guide to North American Birds* calls this "perhaps the most spectacular seabird colony in the world."

The islands are extremely remote, however, and the accommodations simple; if you're not interested in birding or in spending a lot of time watching wildlife, it's probably too much money and trouble. The **Airport Hotel** has basic rooms and shared bathrooms. Guests eat at the airport kitchen facilities, where each meal is served buffet style: Breakfast is $10, lunch $14, dinner $17. There is one restaurant on the island, **Duna's Kitchen,** serving soup and sandwiches. The island also has a grocery store, the AC Value Store, with an **ATM.**

Visitors generally come on tours, which are sold as a package with airfare and guiding by Aleuts and expert birders. With the guides' help and radio communication, your chances of seeing exotic species are much enhanced. The tours are offered by **Tanadguix Corp.,** 4300 B St., Suite 402, Anchorage, AK 99503 (© **877/424-5637;** www.alaskabirding.com). Check the website for a wealth of birding news and species details. Packages from Anchorage start at $1,361 for a 2-night visit and operate from mid-May through August. Travelers can choose to ride on a bus as a group or hike on their own. Permanent blinds are in place for watching birds and seals. Count on cool, damp weather.

6 Nome: Arctic Frontier Town

The accidents of history deposited the streets and buildings of this lusty little town on the shore of Norton Sound, just south of the Arctic Circle in Northwest Alaska, and gave it qualities that make Nome an exceptionally attractive place for a visitor. For once, the local boosters' motto—in this case, "There's no place like Nome"—is entirely accurate, and that's because Nome, although itself nothing special to look at, combines a sense of history, a hospitable and somewhat silly attitude, and an exceptional location on the water in front of a tundra wilderness that's crossed by 250 miles of road. Those roads are the truly unique thing, for Nome is the best place (really, the only place) in Arctic Alaska for a visitor to drive or bike deep into the open country, coming across musk oxen, reindeer, rarely seen birds, Native villages, undeveloped hot springs, and even an abandoned 1881 elevated train from New York City. Elsewhere, you're obliged to fly from rural hubs to get so far into the Bush or drive the endless Dalton Highway, either of which is a more ambitious undertaking for casual explorers.

The accidents of history have been rather frequent in Nome. History has been downright sloppy. Start with the name. It's essentially a clerical error, caused by a British naval officer who, in 1850, was presumably in a creative dry spell when he wrote "? Name" on a diagram rather than name the cape he was sailing past. A mapmaker interpreted that as "Cape Nome." Or so goes one widely accepted explanation. The original gold rush of 1898 was caused by prospectors in the usual way, but a much larger 1899 population explosion happened after one of the '98 stampeders, left behind in a camp on the beach because of an injury, panned the sand outside the tent—and found that it was full of gold dust. By 1900, a fourth of Alaska's white population was in Nome sifting the sand. Small-time operators and tourists are still at it. A huge floating gold dredge of the kind that makes for major historic sites in Fairbanks and Dawson City sits idle on the edge of town. In Nome, it stopped operation only in recent years. There are two other, smaller dredges in town, too. Historic structures are few, however, as fires and storms have destroyed the town several times since the gold rush.

Nome has a particular, broad sense of humor. It shows up in the *Nome Nugget* newspaper and in silly traditions like the Labor Day bathtub race, the sea ice golf tournament, and the polar bear swim. The population is half white and half Native, and the town is run largely by the white group. Some see Nome as a tolerant mixing place of different peoples, while the town strikes others as a bit colonial. Selling booze is outlawed in Kotzebue and Barrow, the Native-dominated cities to the north, but in Nome there is still a sloppy, gold-rush–style saloon scene. That sort of thing is prettier as historic kitsch than when it shows up in the form of drunks staggering down Front Street.

But you can ignore that, instead taking advantage of the great bargains to be had on Iñupiaq arts and crafts. And, most important, you can use a pleasant little inn or bed-and-breakfast as a base to get into the countryside that beckons you down one of the gravel roads. Nome is popular with bird-watchers, who find the roads especially useful.

ESSENTIALS

GETTING THERE   Flying is the only way to get to Nome. **Alaska Airlines** (℃ 800/ 252-7522; www.alaskaair.com) flies 90 minutes by jet direct from Anchorage or with a brief hop from Kotzebue. Prices are around $450 round-trip and up. Many visitors come on escorted tour packages sold by **Alaska Airlines Vacations** (℃ 800/468-2248). As a day trip, a tour package costs about the same as a round-trip ticket without a tour; staying overnight on the package costs $460 per person, double occupancy. Despite those savings, however, I think Nome is a better destination to be on your own, especially if you rent a car.

All taxis operate according to a standard price schedule you can get from the visitor center. A ride to town from the airport is $5. There are three companies, including **Louie's Cab** (℃ 907/443-6000).

VISITOR INFORMATION   The **Nome Convention and Visitors Bureau,** Front and Division streets (P.O. Box 240), Nome, AK 99762 (℃ 907/443-6624; www. nomealaska.org/vc), provides maps and detailed information for diverse interests. The office is open from late May to mid-September daily from 9am to 9pm, the balance of the year Monday through Friday from 9am to 6pm.

The **Bering Land Bridge National Preserve Headquarters,** 214 Front St. (P.O. Box 220), Nome, AK 99762 (℃ 907/443-2522; www.nps.gov/bela), is a good source of outdoors information from the rangers who staff a desk and are responsible for a rarely visited 2.8-million-acre national park unit, which covers much of the Seward Peninsula north of the Nome road system.

Also check the *Nome Nugget* website, at **www.nomenugget.com**, a real window into the community.

GETTING AROUND   The town is a street grid along the ocean. **Front Street** follows the sea wall, **First Avenue** is a block back, and so on. A harbor is at the north end of town, and the gold-bearing beach is to the south. You can mostly walk to see this area. Three roads branch out from Nome. I've described them below, under "Venturing beyond Town by Road." To get out on the roads, you need to take a tour or rent a car, or bring a bike with you. Several local car-rental agencies operate in town; the visitor center maintains a list, with rates. **Stampede Rent-A-Car,** 302 E. Front St. (℃ 800/354-4606 or 907/443-3838), charges $90 to $130 for SUVs and vans. The same people operate the Aurora Inn (see "Where to Stay," below).

FAST FACTS: Nome

Bank **Wells Fargo,** with an ATM, is at 250 Front St.

Hospital **Norton Sound Regional** is at 5th Avenue and Bering Street (© 907/ 443-3311).

Internet Access Check your e-mail at the **Nome Public Library** at 200 Front St. (© 907/443-6626).

Police Contact the police for nonemergencies at Bering Street and 4th Avenue (© 907/443-5262).

Post Office It's at Front Street and Federal Way.

Taxes The **sales tax** is 5%; the tax on **rooms** totals 8%.

SPECIAL EVENTS   The biggest event of the year is the **Iditarod Trail Sled Dog Race** (© 907/376-5155; www.iditarod.com), a marathon of more than 1,000 miles that ends in Nome in mid-March. The sled dog racers, world media, and international visitors descend on the town for a few days of madness, with lots of community events planned. The activities last most of the month; contact the Nome Convention and Visitors Bureau, or download the calendar from www.nomealaska.org/vc. See p. 41 for information about the exciting option of volunteering for the race; see p. 481 for an article on the emotional issue of the animal rights attack on the sport.

One of the March Iditarod events, showcasing Nome's well-developed sense of humor, is the **Bering Sea Ice Golf Classic** (© 907/443-6624)—six holes are set up on the sea ice. The pressure ridges constitute a bad lie. Various similar silly events take place all year (see www.nomealaska.org/vc), including the **Polar Bear Swim,** which happens around June 21 (ice permitting) as part of the **Midnight Sun Festival** (© 907/443-5535). The festival celebrates the summer solstice, when Nome gets more than 22 hours of direct sunlight. A parade, hand-made raft race, folk festival, bank holdup, and other events headline the festival. Winners of the raft race get possession for a year of the fur-lined honey bucket (known in some places as a chamber pot).

EXPLORING THE TOWN

Most of Nome's original buildings were wiped out by fires or by storms off Norton Sound that tore across the beach and washed away major portions of the business district. A sea wall, completed in 1951, now protects the town. Among the few historic sites that survive are the gold-rush–era Board of Trade Saloon, a church, and a bust of Roald Amundsen, who landed near Nome, in Teller, after crossing the North Pole from Norway in a dirigible in 1926. Below the library, at Front Street and Lanes Way, the small **Carrie M. McLain Memorial Museum** (© 907/443-6630) contains an exhibit on the town's gold rush. The museum is free and open summer daily from noon to 8pm, winter Tuesday through Saturday from noon to 6pm.

In good weather, a pleasant walk is to be had southeast of town, along the **beach.** Small-time miners may be camped there, but the gold-bearing sand extends for miles more of solitary walking. You can buy a gold pan in town and try your luck, but the sand has been sifted for nearly 100 years, so don't expect to gather any significant amount of gold. The **Swanberg Dredge** you can see from here operated until the 1950s; a large dredge north of town worked into the mid-1990s. The 38 gold dredges that once operated on the Seward Peninsula crept across the tundra, creating their own ponds to float in as they went. The **cemetery,** with white wooden crosses on top of a little hill just out of town, also is worth a look.

Several companies offer **organized tours. Nome Discovery Tours** (© 907/ 443-2814; discover@gci.net) has the asset of talented professional actor Richard Beneville as the van driver and tour guide. He'll pick you up and drive you anywhere in the area, sharing his quirky enthusiasm and extensive knowledge of the surroundings and culture built on 20 years as a resident. The highlight is the wildlife and scenery on the roads out of town, and he also visits a working gold mine. Half-days are $50 per person, full days $100.

If you're in the market for walrus ivory carvings and other **Iñupiaq arts and crafts,** you'll find low prices and an extraordinary selection on Front Street in Nome. Jim West has a legendary collection for sale, assembled in the barroom of the historic **Board of Trade Saloon** that is attached to a shop on Front Street. The **Arctic Trading Post** is more of a traditional gift shop and also has a good ivory collection, as does **Maruskiyas of Nome. Chukotka-Alaska,** at 514 Lomen St., is an importer of art and other goods from the Russian Far East. Alaska Native art you find in Nome is likely to be authentic, but still ask; see "Native Art: Finding the Real Thing" (p. 26). International visitors should see chapter 2 to find out about the special permit you need to carry ivory out of the United States.

VENTURING BEYOND TOWN BY ROAD

The modest attractions downtown would hardly justify a trip to Nome, but the city's surroundings do. The roads provide unique access to a large stretch of the Seward Peninsula. Unlike other Arctic Bush areas, where someone has to take you into the wilderness, in Nome all you have to do is rent a car and go. There are few cars in Nome (they have to be flown in or shipped by barge), so you won't see many other vehicles on a huge expanse of spectacular territory, with wildlife-viewing opportunities as good as anywhere in the state. The **Alaska Department of Transportation** (© 907/443-3444) can provide current information on road conditions around Nome. You have a good chance of seeing moose, reindeer, owls, foxes, bears, and musk ox anywhere you drive, but check in with the visitor center or the **Alaska Department of Fish and Game,** at Front and Steadman streets (© 907/443-5796), to find out the best locales to see animals. They can also give you guidance on fishing along the roads and a *Nome Roadside Fishing Guide,* or download it from www.alaska.gov/adfg (click on "Sport Fisheries," then the northern region, and then "Northwest"). Check "Getting Around," above, to find a mode of transportation.

ROAD HIGHLIGHTS   None of the three roads radiating from Nome has services of any kind—just small Native villages, a few dwellings, and some reindeer herders— so you must be prepared and bring what you need with you, including insect repellent and a good spare tire. The visitor center provides a road guide. Here are some highlights:

The **Nome-Council road** heads 72 miles to the east, about half of that on the shoreline. It turns inland at the ghost town of Solomon, an old mining town with an abandoned railroad train known locally as the Last Train to Nowhere. The engines were originally used on the New York City elevated lines in 1881 and then were shipped to Alaska in 1903 to serve the miners along this line to Nome. This is a scenic spot for bird-watching, and fishing is good in the Solomon River, all along the road. Council, near the end of the road, has a couple of dozen families in the summer. A 3-foot-deep river separates the road from the village.

The **Nome-Taylor road,** also known as the Kougarok Road, runs north of town into the Kigluaik Mountains, 85 miles from Nome, eventually petering out and becoming impassable. About 40 miles out, you reach lovely Salmon Lake, with a lakeshore campground with picnic tables, grills, and outhouses. A few miles farther, a road to the left leads to the 125°F (52°C) Pilgrim Hot Springs, near a Catholic church. Access is limited to when the caretaker is on hand, so check with the visitor center before going.

The **Nome-Teller road** leads 73 miles to the village of Teller, which has 266 residents and a store. It's an opportunity to see an authentic Arctic Native village.

MOUNTAIN BIKING   The roads of Nome are one of the world's great, undiscovered mountain-biking destinations—where else can you bike past musk oxen and reindeer? There is no bike rental in town, but for bike enthusiasts, it may be worth renting a bike in Anchorage or bringing yours from home.

BIRD-WATCHING   Bird-watchers will make many discoveries out on the Nome roads, turning to previously unused pages of their bird books. A bird list is available at the visitor center, and they can tell you where to look—each of the three roads has a different habitat. The best times to visit for birding are right around Memorial Day, and from July to mid-August. There's a chance to see Siberian birds, and you can count on bluethroats, yellow wagtails, wheatears, Arctic warblers, and Aleutian and Arctic terns. Nome is the only place to see a bristle-thighed curlew without chartering a plane. You don't need a guide, although guided field trips do come to Nome (see "Bird-Watching" in chapter 2).

SEEING THE SIGHTS IN THE AIR

Nome is a hub for Bush plane operators. Flightseeing charters are available, or you can fly on one of the scheduled routes out to the villages and spend a couple of hours touring. The way to do it is to contact a flight service, explain what you have in mind, and follow their advice. Expect to pay $175 or more. Don't plan to stay overnight in a village without advance arrangements, and don't go in bad weather—you'll see little and may get stuck in a tiny village. **Bering Air** (© **800/478-5422** in Alaska only, or 907/443-5464; www.beringair.com) has a long and illustrious reputation and serves 32 villages from Nome and Kotzebue. They offer flightseeing trips by fixed-wing aircraft or helicopter on hourly charter rates (expensive if just one or two of you are along). Or they will sell you a seat on a scheduled loop flight that visits various villages, charging the fare only to the closest village on the trip while you enjoy the entire round-trip. They even offer charters across the Bering Strait to the Russian towns of Provideniya and Anadyr.

WHERE TO STAY

There are several good B&Bs and motel rooms besides those listed in full below, including the **Nugget Inn** (© **877/443-2323** or 907/443-2323). Staying at a B&B makes sense, as your host can introduce you to the community in a less contrived way than a formal tour company. The visitor center and their website can provide information on them.

Aurora Inn Suites ⊛   Look here for the best traditional hotel rooms in town in a mock country inn on the town's main street. They're nicely furnished and even have

The Kotzebue Option

The Northwest Arctic's authentic Iñupiaq center of Kotzebue (*kotz*-eh-biew) isn't my first choice for most visitors. Those interested in Iñupiat culture should go to Barrow, while those looking for bird-watching or self-guided outdoor sightseeing should go to Nome. I used to recommend an Alaska Airlines Vacation tour to Kotzebue, but that stopped running when the NANA Native Corporation closed its museum for demolition and replacement. The new museum is expected to be completed in 2007, but these kinds of projects are often delayed.

In any event, travelers seeking real adventure should still use Kotzebue as a hub for a vast spectacular area. The National Park Service staffs the **Iñ̃aigvik Education and Information Center** at 2nd Avenue and Lake Street (P.O. Box 1029), Kotzebue, AK 99752 (✆ **907/442-3760**; www.nps.gov/nwak), providing information on the region and offering classes on Native crafts and medicinal plants. Hours are changeable, so call prior to your visit. The local headquarters of the National Park Service, open during normal business hours all year, is in the Eskimo Building with the post office on Shore Avenue (✆ **907/442-3890**).

Several remote rivers near Kotzebue have easy self-guided floating for experienced outdoors people. The great Noatak River originates in the Brooks Range and flows 450 miles through America's largest undisturbed wilderness, the Noatak National Preserve. The Selawik, Squirrel, and Kobuk rivers all have long sections of easy water. **Alaska Discovery** and **Equinox Wilderness Expeditions,** listed in chapter 2 under "Planning an Outdoor Vacation," have float trips in the area, although not necessarily every year. Expect to pay $4,000 per person, including air travel. Most river-running in the region is self-guided. Get details from *The Alaska River Guide,* by Karen Jettmar (Alaska Northwest Books). Plan ahead, arranging details well in advance with the park service and your pilot. **Bering Air** (✆ **800/478-5422** in Alaska only, or 907/443-5464; www.beringair.com) is one good operator in Kotzebue. A popular way to do a float trip is to charter to your put-in point and then fly a scheduled service from a river village at your take-out point.

Kotzebue also offers curious travelers a chance to dig deep into the Iñupiat way of life with **Arctic Circle Educational Adventures** (✆ **907/442-6013** in summer, 907/276-0976 in winter; www.fishcamp.org). The adventure takes place at a fish camp similar to where Native people gather food for the winter. You participate in set-net fishing, fish cutting, and food gathering, as well as hiking, town tours, bird-watching, and spending time with Native people. The camp on the beach 5 miles south of town is as simple as Bush life, but with a modern kitchen, dining room, shower, and sauna. Guests sleep in plywood cabins without plumbing. Rates are $125 per person per day for lodging and meals, and an additional $100 per day for tour activities. The season is from late June to mid-August.

Alaska Airlines (✆ **800/252-7522**; www.alaskaair.com) offers daily jet service to Kotzebue. Lodging and dining are at the **Nullagvik Hotel** (✆ **907/442-3331**; www.nullagvik.com), a comfortable, modern hotel on the beachfront owned by the NANA corporation. High-season rates are $189 double.

some style, a remarkable contrast to the other hotels in Nome. As another plus in this smoky town, there are lots of nonsmoking rooms here. The same company owns a car-rental operation, which is on-site.

302 E. Front St. (P.O. Box 1008), Nome, AK 99762. © 800/354-4606 or 907/443-3838. Fax 907/443-6380. www.aurorainnome.com. 56 units. $140–$240 double. Extra person 16 and over $10. AE, MC, V. **Amenities:** Sauna; car rental; coin-op laundry. *In room:* TV, dataport, hair dryer.

Sweet Dreams B&B   It's the hosts—Erna and Leo Rasmussen—who make this place special; they are deep wells of Nome history and local knowledge. Leo is a former mayor and a personable and funny man. The two-story house has a rustic, old-fashioned feel, with lots of Alaskan memorabilia and a sun room on top. A full breakfast is served when Erna has time to prepare it.

406 W. 4th St. (P.O. Box 2), Nome, AK 99762. © 907/443-2919. 3 units, all with shared bathroom. $120 double. Rate includes full breakfast. MC, V. **Amenities:** TV in common area. *In room:* No phone.

WHERE TO DINE

You wouldn't go out of your way to dine at any of the restaurants in Nome, but you can find an adequate family meal at various establishments along Front Street. Several are operated by immigrant families, who offer their national cuisine along with standard American-style fare. There sometimes is a language barrier with the servers. **Milano's Pizzeria** (© 907/443-2924), at 503 Front St., the Old Federal Building, serves Italian and Japanese meals; its pizza is recommended by the locals. The restaurant accepts Visa and MasterCard. **Twin Dragons,** on Front Street near Steadman Street (© 907/443-5552), serves Chinese food good enough to have kept them in business for many years, and pizza, too. It also takes Visa and MasterCard.

The other flavor of restaurant in Nome, and the most popular locally, is the classic American greasy spoon. **Fat Freddie's Restaurant,** attached to the Nugget Inn (© 907/443-5899) and right next to the Iditarod Trail finish line, is a local favorite. In addition to the usual sandwiches, the restaurant serves more expensive fare in the evening, such as steaks and fried fish. They take all major cards.

8 Barrow: Way North

Half-liquid land comes to an arbitrary point at the northern tip of Alaska, Point Barrow, a long tendril reaching into the Arctic Ocean where bowhead whales pass close to shore during their annual migrations. The Iñupiat settled here more than a thousand years ago because it is such a good whale-hunting spot, and that is still why they live here, dragging their skin boats miles out on the frozen ocean to wait for whales along the cracks in the ice pack. And, according to age-old tradition, here they still share the whales they catch among the entire community. Indeed, even visitors who show up on a Saturday in late June, during the Nalukataq, may be offered a piece of *maktak* (whale blubber and skin) and a chance to bounce high in the air in the blanket toss.

Barrow is the northernmost settlement on the North American continent, above the 71st parallel, but that's not all that makes it unique. The town of 4,417 is a cultural treasure. It's ancient, but it's also the seat of the North Slope Borough, a county government encompassing an area larger than the state of Nebraska, in which lies North America's largest oil field. The borough has everything money can buy for a local government, yet the people still must contend with crushing ice, snooping polar bears, and utter isolation. From these ingredients, they have concocted an extraordinary mixture of sophisticated modernity and wise tradition. Alaska's largest corporation is based here; its top executives are also subsistence hunters. At the Iñupiat Heritage Center, it has been possible to see, on successive nights, traditional dance in the Iñupiaq language and avant-garde theater in the same language.

Geography and the natural environment also make the place interesting. This is the most heavily instrumented and intensively studied scientific site anywhere in the Arctic. At the labs north of town, cutting-edge work on climate change takes place that could affect the whole world. The tundra around Barrow is dotted with lakes divided by tendrils of swampy tundra no more substantial than the edges of fine lace. On this haven for migratory waterfowl, the flat, wet land and the ocean seem to merge. Indeed, for all but a few months, it's a frozen plain of ocean and land. For 65 days in the winter, the sun never rises. In the summer, it doesn't set. Ice recedes from the shore only for a few brief months. Such extreme geography is a magnet for visitors.

ESSENTIALS

GETTING THERE   **Alaska Airlines** (© 800/252-7522; www.alaskaair.com) flies a couple of times daily to Barrow from Anchorage, by way of Fairbanks. The round-trip fare from Anchorage is $550 and up. You can save by booking their 1-day and overnight tour packages, described in "Exploring the Town & Getting Outside," below. Book them through **Alaska Airlines Vacations** (© 800/468-2248).

VISITOR INFORMATION   The City of Barrow's **visitor center,** at Momegana and Ahkovak streets, near the airport and Wiley Post & Will Rogers Monument, operates in the summer daily from 10am to 4:30pm, with a guide to talk to, maps (including a numbered walking tour map), and other publications. To obtain advance information, contact the City of Barrow, Office of the Mayor, P.O. Box 629, Barrow, AK 99723 (© 907/852-5211, ext. 221; www.cityofbarrow.org).

GETTING AROUND   Facing the Chukchi Sea, Barrow has two sections, lying on each side of Isatkoak Lagoon. **Browerville,** to the east, has the Iñupiat Heritage Center and the Stuaqpak, or big store, which contains a small food court and many services. The old part of **Barrow,** with the hotels and airport, is to the west. The northern tip of Alaska, **Point Barrow,** is north of the town on a spit. The road leads 6 miles in that direction, but the absolute end is farther out, beyond the road. Other gravel roads lead about 10 miles out of town on the tundra.

Taxis are handy and come quickly, charging a flat $5 anywhere in town, $10 beyond town, plus $1 for each additional passenger. **Arcticab** (© 907/852-2227) is one of the four cab companies.

Fun Fact **Bush Softball**

Barrow is mad for the game. You can hear the play-by-play on the radio, but to attend you will need a car: That's how the spectators watch on the chilly Arctic evenings, honking for good plays. And remember: If a ball disappears completely from view in a puddle, runners can advance no more than two bases. On the rocky, mountainous Aleutian island of Unalaska, the problem was too small a field, so home runs carried heavy penalties. Hit three in a season, and you were expelled from the league for life. But that's all in the past: They built a new, larger field, at a cost of nearly $3 million, including the cost of bringing nine shipping-van containers of sod out from Palmer.

SPECIAL EVENTS The return of the sun after 2 months below the horizon is met by traditional celebrations on **January 21.** The **Piuraagiaqta,** a spring festival, takes place in mid-April and includes many fun events, such as a tug-of-war on the lagoon pitting white men against Eskimo women. The women won so many years in a row that in 2006, the white men didn't even show up (one white contestant claimed that the women won 1 year despite the men tying their end of the rope to the bumper of a pickup—the women pulled the truck across the ice). In the tea-making contest, couples race to set up a camp stove and melt ice to make tea. If the traditional bowhead whaling season is a success, the **Nalukataq** takes place in late June, usually on a Saturday, but the actual date depends on the preference of the successful captain. It is his responsibility to feed the entire community. The Eskimo blanket toss is also a traditional element of the event (injuries are common, so don't take it lightly). In the fall, generally from early to mid-October, the whale hunt launches from the beaches of town (rather than the ice, as in spring). If you're lucky, you can be on hand as a whale is pulled ashore and butchered by the community. This usually occurs at the NARL runway, north of town; ask around, as everyone will know if a whale has been landed.

FAST FACTS: Barrow

Alcohol Legality The sale of alcohol is illegal in Barrow, and importation for personal use in your luggage is limited and controlled by a permit system. Without going through the permit process, you can bring in 1 gallon of beer, *or* 1 liter of distilled spirits, *or* 2 liters of wine. Violating these laws is bootlegging, a serious crime. For more information, call ahead to the **Barrow Alcohol Distribution** (© 907/852-5216) or the **Office of the Mayor** (© 907/852-5211, ext. 221) or check the website (www.cityofbarrow.org). I simply don't drink when I go to Barrow.

Bank **Wells Fargo** is at 1078 Kiogak St., with an ATM.

Hospital **Samuel Simmonds Memorial Hospital** is at 1296 Agvik St. (© 907/852-4611).

Internet Access Free at the **Tuzzy Library,** at the Iñupiat Heritage Center in Browerville.

Police Contact the **North Slope Borough Police Department,** 1068 Kiogak St. (© 907/852-6111).

Post Office It's at 3080 Eben Hobson St., between the lagoon and beach.

Taxes There is no sales or bed tax in Barrow.

EXPLORING THE TOWN & GETTING OUTSIDE

The **Iñupiat Heritage Center** (© 907/852-4594) is the town's main attraction and one of Alaska's most remarkable cultural institutions. It is part museum, part gathering center, and part venue for living culture. Inside is a workshop for craftspeople where hunters build the traditional boats and tools they use and where drummers build their drums; during the summer, an artist is usually in residence for visitors. There is a performance space for storytellers and dancers, and conference rooms where elders tell old stories or identify a rich store of artifacts. In the museum area, displays of artifacts change regularly, while a permanent exhibit covers Eskimo whaling and the influence of Yankee whaling on it (the quiet pride here carries a real emotional wallop). Iñupiaq dancing and drumming demonstrations, a blanket toss, games, and a crafts sale happen every afternoon in the summer from 1:30 to 3:30pm; these are the same programs that are the highlight of the escorted tours. Admission, including the program, is $15. The center is open Monday through Friday from 8:30am to 5pm (to see the program on weekends, call ahead). Regular admission is $5 adults, $2 students and over age 55, free ages 14 or younger.

The other site that's worthy of a special trip is **NARL,** as the former Navy Arctic Research Laboratory is known. This was once the world's largest Arctic research site, with scores of buildings on the narrow spit of land north of town. Today the Navy is long gone, but Barrow's Native Corporation took over the buildings and nurtured scientific research here. Once again the facilities are the nation's busiest year-round Arctic research site. It's interesting just to walk around, and the cafeteria in the Iligsavik College building serves three good meals a day. The **UIC Science Center** (© **907/ 852-3050**), at the north end of the complex, has interesting displays about Arctic science and anthropology that are open to the public. The daily escorted tours come here, or independent travelers can usually find it open Monday through Friday 8:30am to 5pm, closed noon to 1pm for lunch hour; however, the two-person staff may not be handy at times, so it could pay to call ahead.

The main tourism business in town is **Tundra Tours** (© **800/882-8478** or 907/852-3900; www.tundratours.com). Arctic Slope Regional Corp., a corporation representing the Iñupiat, owns the company and the Top of the World Hotel. Their tour (the same one sold through Alaska Airlines Vacations) introduces the town to visitors who arrive with little idea of what to expect. The 6-hour summer tour, in a small bus, drives around the town to visit an Eskimo skin boat, the cemetery, the UIC Science Center, and the Arctic Ocean, for a dip of toes. The highlight is a visit to the Heritage Center with a cultural presentation, including Eskimo dance and a chance to buy crafts made by Native artists. The day-trip tour is $415 from Fairbanks, or $465 per person, double occupancy, for the tour and a night in Barrow at the Top of the World Hotel, giving you time on your own without the tour group; both prices include airfare and save over buying a plane ticket alone. Book the tour through Alaska Airlines Vacations or with Tundra Tours at the numbers listed above. If you buy the tour separately when you are already in Barrow, it's $85. They also offer a winter tour for seeing the aurora ($99 separately), which does not include the cultural elements.

Jim Vordestrasse (© **907/852-2010**) offers a decidedly less conventional tour, by bicycle. You can even ride as a passenger on his tandem recumbent bicycle—you don't have to peddle if you don't want to. He has given Iñupiaq elders their first bike ride on this contraption. Jim's a fascinating guy, a former mayor (as is his wife, Edith), well loved in Barrow, positive, and full of knowledge. The tour is $50. He also rents bicycles for $20 a day. If you arrive when snow is on the ground, he will take you cross-country skiing for the same tour price, equipment and polar bear protection included. He even does skiing pulled by a kite.

Barrow is the only place in the U.S. with commercial polar bear–viewing tours. The bears are always around when the ice is in; they're dangerous and people take extreme care to avoid them. Barrow and other North Slope communities have minimized the danger of bears in town by setting up sites outside of the villages to dispose of gut piles and other hunting waste. It's a way of bribing the bears to leave the town alone. In

Barrow, heavy equipment hauls the leftovers from fall whale butchering—bones and a few inedible organs—out to the very end of the point. Polar bears come for an easy meal whenever the pack ice is close to shore, which is October through June. Commercial tours take visitors out to the point in all-terrain vans or Humvees that can drive on the beach gravel. Arrangements change annually and these are casual home businesses, so if polar bear viewing is your goal, be sure to make firm arrangements with someone before you go. **Arctic Tours** (© **907/852-4512** or 907/852-1462) takes visitors out in a Humvee May through September on a 2-hour tour that costs $60 per person, with a 2-person minimum. I advise going only in May and June, when the sea ice is in and polar bear sightings are much more likely than later in the summer or in the fall.

WHERE TO STAY

King Eider Inn ★★   The best rooms in town—indeed, some of the best in the Bush—are found in this like-new building near the airport. They're crisp and airy, with faux rustic furniture, and kept up well. It surely helps that shoes are not allowed in the hotel—you have to take them off at the front door every time you come in. The halls and rooms are decorated with Native art, and a teddy bear greets you in bed. A room with a kitchenette is $10 more, and the enormous and luxurious Presidential Suite (where Barrow's honeymooners and visiting celebrities stay) is $310 summer, $275 winter. The lobby is comfortable, with a stone fireplace and free Internet terminal, and good free coffee and other hot beverages are offered there around the clock. Bathrooms have large shower stalls, not tubs.

1752 Ahkovak St. (P.O. Box 1283), Barrow, AK 99723. © **888/303-4337** reservations or 907/852-4700. Fax 907/852-2025. www.kingeider.net. 19 units. Summer $205 double, $310 suite; winter $175 double, $275 suite. Extra person $25. AE, MC, V. No smoking. **Amenities:** Sauna; car rental; Internet. *In room:* TV, kitchenette (in some).

Top of the World Hotel ★   This is a good hotel with familiar standard rooms, worn in places but perfectly comfortable. The staff works to keep the place clean and quiet. Rooms have light furniture and blue carpet, desks, and refrigerators. Those on the water side have wonderful views of the Arctic Ocean, and it's only a few steps to the beach and the heart of Barrow. The lobby is a place where people pass time, somewhat cluttered with a TV and a stuffed polar bear. The hotel is owned by the Native Corporation that also operates Tundra Tours, and you stay here if you come on the package tour.

Agvik St. (P.O. Box 189), Barrow, AK 99723. © **907/852-3900.** www.topoftheworldhotel.com. 44 units. Summer $140–$210; winter $75–$125. AE, DC, DISC, MC, V. *In room:* TV, fridge.

WHERE TO DINE

There are several decent restaurants in Barrow. Generally, they stay open very late, always have a TV on, offer free delivery, and don't brew decaffeinated coffee—people around here run on lots of caffeine and sugar.

Adjoining the Top of the World Hotel, **Pepe's North of the Border,** 1204 Agvik St. (© **907/852-8200**), is the most famous place in town, thanks to an appearance owner Fran Tate made with Johnny Carson on *The Tonight Show* some 20 years ago. They serve large portions of familiar American-style Mexican food, steak, and seafood. The bus tours come here for lunch, and Tate hands out souvenirs.

Arctic Pizza, 125 Apayauq St. (© **907/852-4222**), has the only claim to fine dining in town, as well as the pizza and burgers available everywhere. One menu is offered both in the fancier upstairs dining room, which has a great view over ancient village ruins to the ocean, and in the light downstairs dining room where the TV is on and children and teens are allowed.

Brower's Restaurant, 3220 Brower's Hill (© **907/852-3456**), occupies the most historic building in town, the 19th-century whaling station and store built by Charles Brower, who introduced Yankee whaling techniques to the Iñupiat and sired one of its most illustrious families. The restaurant serves a long menu of American and Korean dishes. Big windows look out on the beach, and a famous whalebone arch is just outside.

Northern Lights Restaurant, in Browerville at 5122 Herman St. (© **907/852-3300**), has a very comfortable, clean dining room and is operated by a charming family. Their menu goes on and on, with the owner's own Chinese food, plus deli selections and burgers, and the best pizza in town.

9 Prudhoe Bay: Arctic Industry

The Prudhoe (*prew*-dough) Bay complex is more than a huge oil field; it's an amazing achievement. Massive, complex machinery must operate in winter's deep, dark cold and in summer must avoid harm to a critical habitat for migrating caribou and waterfowl, on wet, fragile tundra that permanently shows any mark made by vehicles. Workers are forbidden even to set foot on the tundra. Most places, as you look from the edge of one of the gravel pads, the heathery ground looks as undisturbed as a calm sea.

But that doesn't make it a good place to go on your vacation. The grim town of **Deadhorse,** which serves the oil facility, is really more of an industrial yard, barely deserving to be called a town; it certainly isn't anything you'd travel to see. To get beyond it to see Prudhoe Bay, you have to sign up for a tour. The tour has never gone inside the buildings, and under post–September 11, 2001, security measures, it doesn't even go close to the most interesting areas. Visitors do get to stop at the Arctic Ocean, the only way to get to the water for those who drive up on the Dalton Highway. That hardly justifies the trip, however, unless you are bent on driving the highway anyway (it is covered in chapter 9, section 4). Frankly, I can't recommend spending the time and expense required for a Prudhoe tour. If you're curious about the Arctic, a trip to Barrow or Nome makes more sense.

If you do go, you must reserve at least 24 hours ahead to clear security for the oil field tour or the ride to the ocean. Tours are operated by the **Arctic Caribou Inn,** P.O. Box 340111, Prudhoe Bay, AK 99734 (© **907/659-2368;** www.arcticcaribouinn.com). They will need your name and an identification number that British Petroleum can use to run a background check before allowing you on the oil field: A driver's license, passport, or Social Security number will work. The inn also offers the area's visitor services, including a hotel and cafeteria, open in the summer only. Rooms start at $125 double. The restaurant has a buffet for breakfast ($12) and dinner ($20), and menu service for lunch. The town is dry: Sale of alcohol is illegal, although you can bring it with you. The hotel is near the airport in Deadhorse and serves as the starting point for the tours. The tour itself lasts 2 hours, including a 20-minute video. Visitors are carried by bus among oil field buildings (which look a lot like industrial buildings anywhere) and then stop for 15 minutes at the Arctic Ocean. It costs $37 per adult, $17 ages 12 and under. There is no other way to get from the end of the road to the water.

Alaska Airlines (© **800/252-7522;** www.alaskaair.com) has a couple of flights daily to Prudhoe Bay from Anchorage or by way of Barrow. A round-trip ticket costs $750 or more from Anchorage. Several companies drive bus tours up the Dalton

464   CHAPTER 10 · THE BUSH

Seeing ANWR for Yourself

The decades-old national controversy about whether to open the Arctic National Wildlife Refuge to oil exploration created strong interest in seeing that extraordinarily remote northeast corner of Alaska, which is done best in summer on a float trip. While these floats may have started for political reasons, however, their reputation of beauty and adventure have made them an attraction in their own right. **Alaska Discovery** (see p. 40) is famous for ANWR expeditions down from the Brooks Range on either the Kongakut or Hulahula rivers. Expect to pay as much as $5,000 per person for a trip of up to 2 weeks. Fairbanks-based **Arctic Treks,** owned by Jim Campbell and Carol Kasza (© **907/455-6502;** www.arctic treksadventures.com), is a smaller company than Alaska Discovery and offers shorter base camp trips in ANWR as well as the long river floats. For those who simply want to see ANWR without a wilderness trip, it's possible to visit the Iñupiaq village of Kaktovik, which lies within the boundaries of the refuge. While I wouldn't recommend the journey for most visitors, those with strong interest in a Bush village sojourn and curiosity about ANWR may enjoy it. Lodging and meals in Kaktovik come from the **Waldo Arms Hotel** (© **907/640-6513**), a community center known for warm hospitality. Kaktovik is served 6 days a week from Fairbanks by **Frontier Flying Service** (© **800/478-6779** or 907-450-7200; www.frontierflying.com).

Highway all the way to Prudhoe, flying the other way. **Northern Alaska Tour Company** (© **800/474-1986** or 907/474-8600; www.northernalaska.com) offers these trips, with add-ons to make it more interesting: flightseeing stops, day hikes, village visits, and other choices. The basic 3-day, 2-night tour is $749.

Appendix:
Alaska in Depth

An old photo album opens, emitting a scent of dust and dried glue. Inside, pale images speak wanly of shrunken mountains and glaciers, a huge blue sky, water, and trees, a moose standing way off in the background. No family photographer can resist the urge to capture Alaska's vastness in the little box of a camera, and none, it seems, has ever managed it. Then, turning the page, there it is—not in another picture of the landscape, but reflected in a small face at the bottom of the frame: my own face, as a child. For anyone who hasn't experienced that moment, the expression is merely enigmatic—slightly dazed, happy, but abstracted. But if you've been to Alaska, that photograph captures something familiar: It's an image of discovery. I've seen it on the fresh, pale faces in photographs stamped with the dates of my family's first explorations of Alaska 40 years ago. And then, when I began researching this book, I got to see it once again, on my own young son's face. And I knew that, like me, he had discovered something important.

So what, exactly, am I talking about? Like anything worth experiencing, it's not simple to explain.

Tour guides try to get it across with statistics. Not much hope of that, although some of the numbers do give you a general idea of scale. Once you've driven across the continental United States and know how big that is, seeing a map of Alaska placed on top of the area you crossed, just about spanning it, provides some notion of size. Alaska has 627,000 residents. If you placed them an equal distance apart, each would be almost a mile from any other. Of course, that couldn't happen. No one has ever been to some parts of Alaska.

But none of that expresses what really matters. It's not just a matter of how big Alaska is or how few people it contains. It's not an intellectual conception at all. None of that crosses your mind when you see a chunk of ice the size of a building fall from a glacier and send up a huge splash and wave surging outward, or when you feel a wave lift your sea kayak from the fall of a breaching humpback whale. Or when you hike for a couple of days to stand on top of a mountain, and from there see more mountaintops, layered off as far as the horizon, in unnamed, seemingly infinite multiplicity. A realization of what Alaska means can also come in a simple moment. It can come at the end of a long day driving an Interior Alaska highway, as your car climbs into yet another mountain range, the sun still hanging high in what should be night, storm systems arranged across the landscape before you, when you realize that you haven't seen another car in an hour. Or standing on an Arctic Ocean beach, it can happen when you look around at the sea of empty tundra behind you, the sea of green water before you, and your own place on what seems to be the edge of the world.

What's the soul alchemy of such a moment? I suppose it's different for each person, but for me it has something to do with realizing my actual size in the world, how I fit in, what it means to be just another medium-size mammal, no longer armed with the illusions supplied by civilization. On returning to the city from the wilderness, there's a re-entry process, like walking from a vivid movie to the mundane, gray street outside—

it's the movie that seems more real. For a while, it's hard to take human institutions seriously after you've been deep into Alaska.

Some people never do step back across that boundary. They live their lives out in the wilderness, away from people. Others compromise, living in Alaskan cities and walking out into the mountains when they can, the rest of the time just maintaining a prickly notion of their own independence. But anyone with the courage to come to Alaska—and the time to let the place sink in—can make the same discovery. You don't have to be an outdoors enthusiast or a young person. You only have to be open to wonder and able to slow down long enough to see it. Then, in a quiet moment when you least expect it, things may suddenly seem very clear and all that you left behind oddly irrelevant.

How you find your way back to where you started is your affair.

1 Natural History: Rough Drafts & Erasures

THE SURGING ICE

In 1986, Hubbard Glacier, north of Yakutat, suddenly decided to surge forward, cutting off Russell Fjord from the rest of the Pacific Ocean. A group of warm-hearted but ill-advised wildlife lovers set out to save the marine mammals that had been trapped behind the glacier. Catching a dolphin from an inflatable boat isn't that easy—they didn't accomplish much, but they provided a lot of entertainment for the locals. Then the water burst through the dam of ice and the lake became a fjord again, releasing the animals anyway. In 2002 it happened again (no rescue this time). Ships were warned away as the 70-square-mile lake, having risen 61 feet above sea level, quickly drained through a 300-foot-wide channel with a whoosh. Geologists say it could happen again any time.

Bering Glacier, the largest in North America (about 30 by 145 miles in area), can't decide which way to go. Surging and retreating on a 20-year cycle, it reversed course in 1995 after bulldozing a wetland migratory bird stopover, and speedily contracted back up toward the mountains. Yanert Glacier surged 100 yards a day in 2000 after moving 100 yards a year since 1942. The next year Tokositna Glacier started galloping after 50 years of quiet. In 1937, surging Black Rapids Glacier almost ate the Richardson Highway. In

Prince William Sound, Meares Glacier plowed through old-growth forest. On a larger scale, all the land of Glacier Bay—mountains, forests, sea floor—is rising 1½ inches a year as it rebounds from the weight of melted glaciers that 100 years ago were a mile thick and 65 miles longer.

Yet these new and erased lands are just small corrections around the margins compared to all the earth has done in setting down, wiping out, and rewriting the natural history of Alaska. In the last Ice Age, 15,000 years ago, much of what is Alaska today was a huge glacier. Looking up at the tops of granite mountains in Southeast Alaska, especially in the Lynn Canal, you can see a sort of high-water mark—the highest point to which the glaciers came in the Ice Age.

Some 7-year-old children worry about the bogeyman or being caught in a house fire. When I was that age, living with my family in Juneau, I was worried about glacier ice. I had learned how Gastineau Channel was formed, I had seen Mendenhall Glacier, and I had heard how it was really a river of ice, advancing and retreating. I came to fear that while I slept another Ice Age would come and grind away the city of Juneau.

It's possible that a glacier *could* get Juneau—the city fronts on the huge Juneau Ice Field—but there would be at least a few centuries' warning before it hit. Glaciers are essentially just snow that doesn't get a chance to melt. The snow accumulates at higher elevations until it gets deep enough to compress into ice and starts oozing down the mountainside. When the ice reaches the ocean, or before, the melt and calving of icebergs at the leading edge attains a point of equilibrium with the snow that's still being added at the top. The glacier stops advancing, becoming a true river of ice, moving a snowflake from the top of the mountain to the bottom in a few hundred years. When conditions change—more snow or colder long-term weather, for example—the glacier gets bigger; that's called advancing, and the opposite is retreating. Sometimes something strange will happen under the glacier and it will surge. Bering Glacier started to float on a cushion of water, and Yanert Glacier slid on a cushion of mud. But most of the time, the advance or retreat is measured in inches or feet a year.

It took some time to figure out how glaciers work. The living glaciers of Alaska, like living fossils from the last Ice Age, helped show the way. In the 1830s, scientists in Switzerland found huge rocks (now called glacial erratics) that appeared to have moved miles from where they had once been a part of similar bedrock. Scientists theorized that ancient glaciers shaping the Alps must have moved the rocks. John Muir, the famous writer and naturalist, maintained in the 1870s that the granite mountains of Yosemite National Park had been rounded and polished by the passing of glaciers that melted long ago (he was only partly right). He traveled to Alaska to prove it. Here, glaciers were still carving the land—they had never finished melting at the end of the last glacial period—and Muir could see shapes like those at Yosemite in the act of being created. Glacier Bay, which Muir "discovered" when guided there by his Alaska Native friends, was a glacial work in progress, as it still is today.

When you visit, you can see for yourself how the heavy blue ice and white snow are streaked with black rock and dust that were obviously gouged from mountains and left in hills at the faces and along the flanks of the glaciers, in debris piles called moraines. At Exit Glacier, in Kenai Fjords National Park, you can stand on a moraine that wraps the leading edge of the glacier like a scarf, and feel the cold streaming off spires of clicking ice—like standing in front of a freezer with the door open. Find another hill like that, no matter where it is, and you can be pretty sure a glacier once came that way. Likewise, you can see today's glaciers scooping out valleys in the mountains.

Today, Alaska's 100,000 glaciers cover about 5% of its landmass, mostly on the southern coast. There are no glaciers in the Arctic—the climate is too dry to produce enough snow. The northernmost large glaciers are in the Alaska Range, such as those carving great chasms in the side of Mount McKinley. At that height, the mountain creates its own weather, wringing moisture out of the atmosphere and feeding its glaciers. The Kahiltna Glacier flows 45 miles from the mountain, descending 15,000 feet over its course. The Ruth Glacier has dug a canyon twice as deep as the Grand Canyon, half filled with mile-deep ice. Similarly, fjords and valleys all over Alaska were formed by the glaciers of 50 ice ages that covered North America in the last 2.5 million years.

THE TREMBLING EARTH

Despite my early glacier phobia, I never had a similar fear of earthquakes. Living in Anchorage, I'd been through enough of them that, as early as I can remember, I generally didn't bother to get out of bed when they hit. Alaska has an average of 13 earthquakes a day, or 11% of all the earthquakes in the world, including 3 of the 10 largest ever recorded. On November 3, 2002, Alaska felt the world's largest earthquake of the year and one of the largest ever in the United States. My car rocked as I drove in Anchorage. Waves slopped across the bayous of Louisiana, and geysers at Yellowstone changed their size and period of eruptions. No one died and few people were injured because the quake occurred in such a sparsely populated area, the region between Anchorage and Fairbanks in the Alaska Range east of Mount McKinley. A 140-mile-long crack appeared right across that region, running over mountains and through glaciers. The land on each side moved laterally as much as 22 feet and vertically up to 6 feet. The Glenn Highway section known as the Tok Cut-off, between Glennallen to Tok, broke into many deep cracks. A tractor-trailer fell into one of them. Where the Interior highways crossed the big fault-line crack, lanes no longer lined up and the road got a new jog where it used to be straight.

It's all part of living in a place that isn't quite done yet. Any part of Alaska could have an earthquake, but the Pacific Rim from Southcentral Alaska to the Aleutians is the shakiest. This is where Alaska is still under construction. The very rocks that make up the state are something of an ad hoc conglomeration, still in the process of being assembled. The floor of the Pacific Ocean is moving north, and as it moves, it carries islands and mountains with it. When they hit the Alaska plate, these pieces of land, called terranes, dock like ships arriving, but slowly—an island moving an inch a year takes a long time to travel thousands of miles. Geologists studying rocks near Mount McKinley have found a terrane that used to be tropical islands. In Kenai Fjords National Park, fossils have turned up that are otherwise found only in Afghanistan and China. The slowly moving crust of the earth brought them here on a terrane that makes up a large part of the south coast of Alaska.

The earth's crust is paper thin compared to the globe's forces, and, like paper, it folds where the two edges meet. Alaska's coast is bending down; farther inshore, where McKinley stands, it is bowing up. At Kenai Fjords National Park, you can see steep little rock islands flocked with birds: They are old mountaintops, shrinking down into the earth. The monolith of McKinley is a brand-new one growing higher.

Here's how it works: Near the center of the Pacific, underwater volcanoes and cracks that constantly ooze molten new rock are adding to the tectonic plate that forms the ocean floor. As it grows from the middle, the existing sea floor spreads at a rate of perhaps an inch a year. At the other side of the Pacific plate, where it bumps up against Alaska, there's not enough room for more crust, so it's forced, bending and cracking, downward into the planet's great, molten, recycling mill of magma. Landmasses that are along for the ride smash into the continent that's already there. When one hits—the so-called Yakutat block is still in the process of docking—a mountain range gets shoved up. Earthquakes and volcanoes are a byproduct.

Living in such an unsettled land is a matter of more than abstract interest. The Mount Spurr volcano, which erupted most recently in 1992, turned day to night in Anchorage, dropping a blanket of ash all over the region. A Boeing 747 full of passengers flew into the plume and lost power in all its engines, falling in darkness for several minutes before pilots were able to restart the clogged jets. After that incident, the airport was closed until aviation authorities could find a way to keep volcanic plumes and planes apart. In the winter of 2005–06, the Anchorage airport repeatedly closed due to minor eruptions of Augustine Volcano, west of Homer. More than 80 volcanoes have been active in Alaska in the last 200 years. Earthquakes between 7 and 8 on the Richter scale—larger than the 1994 Los Angeles quake—occur once a year on average, and huge quakes over 8 averaged every 13 years over the last century. The worst of the quakes, on March 27, 1964, was the strongest ever to hit North America. It ranked 9.2 on the Richter scale, twisting an entire region of the state so land to the west sank 12 feet while on the east it rose 30 feet. More land moved laterally than in any other recorded earthquake as well. The earthquake destroyed much of Anchorage and several smaller towns, and killed about 131 people, mostly in sea waves created by underwater landslides. In Valdez, the waterfront was swept clean of people. In the Prince William Sound village of Chenega, built on a hill along the water, people started running for higher ground when the wave came. About half made it.

But even that huge earthquake wasn't an unusual occurrence, at least in the earth's terms. Geologists believe the same Alaska coast sank 6 feet in an earthquake in the year 1090.

THE FROZEN TUNDRA

The northern Interior and Arctic parts of the state are less susceptible to earthquakes and, since they receive little precipitation, they don't have glaciers, either. But there's still a sense of living on a land that's not permanent, since most of northern Alaska is solid only by virtue of being frozen. When it thaws, it turns to mush. The phenomenon is caused by permafrost, a layer of earth a little below the surface that never thaws—or at least, you'd better hope it doesn't. Buildings erected on permafrost without some mechanism for dispersing their own heat—pilings, a gravel pad, or even refrigerator coils—can thaw the ground below and sink into a self-made quicksand. With the climate warming,

sections of the trans-Alaska pipeline are leaning, and many miles of highway in Interior Alaska are being rebuilt each year because the ground they traverse has turned to mush with warming climate (more on this below).

The Arctic and much of the Interior are a swampy desert. Annual precipitation measured in Barrow is the same as in Las Vegas. Most of the time, the tundra is frozen in white; snow blows around, but not much falls. It melts in the summer, but the water can't sink into the ground, which remains frozen. Liquid water on top of the permafrost layer creates huge, shallow ponds. Alaska is a land of 10 million lakes, with 3 million larger than 20 acres. Birds arrive to feed and paddle around those circles and polygons of deep green and sky blue.

Permafrost makes the land do other strange things. On a steep slope, the thawed earth on top of the ice can begin to slowly slide downhill like a blanket sliding off the side of a bed, setting the trees at crazy angles. These groves of black spruce—the only conifer that grows on this kind of ground—are called drunken forests, and you can see them in Denali National Park and elsewhere in the Interior. Permafrost also can create weird tundra, with shaky tussocks the size of basketballs that sit a foot or two apart on a wet, muddy flat. From a distance it looks smooth, but walking on real basketballs might be easier. In other places, freezing and thawing processes create ponds with straight sides and sharp corners, polygons that appear manmade.

The permafrost also preserves many things. Although few and far between, tractor tracks remain clearly delineated for decades after they're made, appearing as narrow, parallel ponds reaching from one horizon to the other. The meat of prehistoric mastodons, still intact, has been unearthed from the frozen ground. On the Arctic Coast, the sea eroded ground near

Barrow that contained ancient ancestors of the Eskimos who still inhabit the same neighborhood. In 1982, a family was found that apparently had been crushed by sea ice up to 500 years ago. Two of the bodies were well preserved, sitting in the home they had occupied and wearing the clothes they had worn the day of the disaster, perhaps around the time Columbus was sailing to America.

Sea ice is the frozen ocean that extends from northern Alaska to the other side of the world. For a few months of summer, it pulls away from the shore. Then, in October, icebergs floating toward land are cemented together by new ice forming along the beach. But even when the ice covers the whole ocean, it still moves under the immense pressure of wind and current. The clash creates towering pressure ridges—piles of broken ice that look like small mountain ranges and are about as difficult to cross.

The National Weather Service keeps track of the ice pack and issues maps and predictions you can find on the Internet (www.arh.noaa.gov). Eskimo hunters traveling on the ice by snowmobile need this information, as do crabbers who tempt disaster by fishing the south-moving ice edge in the fall, and shippers looking for the right moment in the summer to venture north with barges of fuel and other supplies for the coast of the Arctic Ocean. Sometimes there is barely time in the summer to get there and back before the ice closes in again in the fall.

THE RAINFOREST

By comparison, southern coastal Alaska is warm and biologically rich. Temperate rainforest ranges up the coast from Southeast Alaska into Prince William Sound, with bears, deer, moose, wolves, and even big cats living among the massive western hemlock, Sitka spruce, and cedar. This old-growth forest, too wet to burn in forest fires, is the last vestige of the virgin, primeval woods that seemed

so limitless to the first white settlers who arrived on the east coast of the continent in the 17th century. The trees grow on and on, sometimes rising more than 200 feet high, with diameters up to 10 feet, and falling only after hundreds or even 1,000 years. When they fall, the trees rot on the damp moss of the forest floor and return to soil to feed more trees, which grow in rows upon their nursery trunks.

Here at least, Alaska *does* seem permanent. That sense helps explain why logging the rainforest is so controversial. Just one of these trees contains thousands of dollars' worth of wood. Vast Southeast lands owned by Alaska Native corporations were stripped of their old trees for the money they brought to their owners. But the great majority of this rainforest land belongs to the federal government, and a combination of environmental campaigns and economics put a stop to large-scale logging on that land while most of it remained virgin. When the Southeast Alaska logging economy died in the 1990s, the towns there suffered heavy economic blows. Tourism is taking the place of logging (with its own environmental and cultural impacts), but deep antipathy remains against logging opponents.

The rivers of the great coastal forests bring home runs of big salmon, clogging in spawning season like a busy sidewalk at rush hour. The fish spawn only once, returning by a precisely tuned sense of smell to the streams where they were hatched as many as 7 years before. When the fertilized eggs have been left in the stream gravel, the fish conveniently die on the beach, making a smorgasbord for bears and other forest animals. The huge Kodiak brown bear, sometimes topping 1,000 pounds, owes everything to the millions of salmon that return to the island each summer. By comparison, the grizzly bears of the Interior—the same species as browns, but living on grass, berries, and an occasional ground squirrel—are mere midgets, their weight counted in the hundreds of pounds. Forest-dwelling black bears grow to only a few hundred pounds.

FORESTS OF FIRE

Rainforest covers only a small fraction of Alaska. In fact, only a third of Alaska is forested at all, and most of this is the boreal forest that covers the central part of the state, behind the rain shadow of coastal mountains that intercept moist clouds off the oceans. Ranging from the Kenai Peninsula, south of Anchorage, to the Brooks Range, where the Arctic begins, this is a taiga—a moist, subarctic forest of smaller, slower-growing, hardier trees that leave plenty of open sky between their branches. In well-drained areas, on hillsides and southern land less susceptible to permafrost, the boreal forest is a lovely, broadly spaced combination of straight, proud white spruce and pale, spectral paper birch. Along the rivers, cottonwoods grow, with deep-grained bark and branches that spread in an oaklike matrix—if they could speak, it would be as wise old men.

Forest fires tear through Alaska's boreal forest each summer. In the newly warmed climate, million-acre years have become common, and in 2004, a record 6.5 million acres burned—an area the size of Massachusetts. It's impossible to fight that much fire. Alaska has always allowed fire to take its course unless structures or certain resources are at risk. In most cases, forest managers do no more than note the occurrence on a map. Unlike the rain forest, there's little commercially valuable timber in these thin stands, and, anyway, trying to halt the process of nature's self-immolation would be like trying to hold back a river with your hands. The boreal forest regenerates through fire—it was made to burn. The wildlife that lives in and eats it needs new growth from the burns as well as the shelter of older trees. When the forest is healthiest and most productive, the dark green of the spruce is broken by streaks and patches of light-green brush in an ever-changing succession.

This is the land of the moose. They're as big as large horses, with a long, bulbous nose and huge eyes that seem to know, somehow, just how ugly they are. Their flanks look like a worn-out shag carpet draped over a sawhorse. But moose are survivors. They thrive in land that no one else wants. In the summer, they wade out into the swampy tundra ponds to eat green muck. In the winter, they like nothing better than an old burn, where summer lightning has peeled back the forest and allowed a tangle of willows to grow— a moose's all-time favorite food. Eaten by wolves, hunted and run over by man, stranded in the snows of a hard winter, the moose always come back.

In the summer, moose disperse and are not easily seen in thick vegetation. In the winter, they gather where walking is easy, along roads and in lowlands where people also like to live. Encounters happen often in the city, until, as a resident, you begin to take the moose for granted, or see them as a pest that eats decorative plantings and blocks bike trails. Then, skiing on a Nordic trail one day, you round a corner and come face to face with an animal that stands 2 feet over you. You can smell the beast's foul scent and see his stress, the ears pulled back on the head and the whites of the eyes showing, and you know that this wild creature, fighting to live till summer, could easily kill you.

LIGHT & DARKNESS

There's no escaping the stress of winter in Alaska—not for moose or people—nor any shield from the exhilaration of the summer. In summer, it never really gets dark at night. In Fairbanks in June, the sun sets in the north around midnight, but it doesn't go down far enough for real darkness to settle, instead rising again 2 hours later. It's always light enough to keep hiking or fishing, and, in clear weather, it's always light enough to read. You may not see the stars from early May until some-time in August (the climate chart in chapter 2 gives seasonal daylight for various towns). Visitors have trouble getting used to it: Falling asleep in broad daylight can be hard. Alaskans deal with it by staying up late and being active outdoors.

In the winter, on the other hand, you forget what the sun looks like. Kids go to school in the dark and come home in the dark. The sun rises in the middle of the morning and sets after lunch. At high noon in December, the sun hangs just above the southern horizon with a weak, orange light, a constant sunset. Animals and people go into hibernation.

As you go north, the change in the length of the days gets bigger. In Ketchikan, the longest day of the year, on the June 21 summer solstice, is about 17 hours, 20 minutes; in Fairbanks, 22 hours; and in Barrow, the longest day is more than 2 months. In contrast, in Seattle, the longest day is 16 hours, 15 minutes; and in Los Angeles, 14 hours, 30 minutes. On the equator, days are always the same length, 12 hours. At the North Pole and South Pole, the sun is up half the year and down the other half.

The best way to understand this is to model it with a ball and a lamp. The earth spins on its axis, the North and South poles, once a day around. When the axis is upright, one spin of the ball puts light on each point on the ball equally—that's the spring and fall equinox, March 21 and September 21, when the day is 12 hours long everywhere. In the summer, the North Pole leans toward the light and the Northern Hemisphere gets more light than darkness, so during the course of one rotation, each northern spot is lighted more than half the time. In winter, the Southern Hemisphere gets its turn, and more than half the Northern Hemisphere is in shadow, meaning shorter days. As you go farther north in winter, the shadow gets larger, and the day in any one spot shorter. But no matter how the axis leans, the equator is always half light and half dark, like the entire globe as a whole.

In the North, on a long summer evening, you can almost feel the planet leaning toward the sun. The world lies under a bright, endless dome. In the winter, darkness falls as deep as space, and you can almost feel the earth's warmth wafting away into the universe as the freeze sinks ever deeper in the land. Now the rainforest rivers and permafrost lakes are hard ice, the salmon are away at sea, and the bears are asleep. The moose and other wintering animals burn their summer fat, a finite store of provisions that may or may not last. Up in the mountains, the glaciers grow.

THE WARMING CLIMATE

In the past 2 decades, winters have warmed and shortened and summers have gotten hotter. Individual years are sometimes closer to the long-term norm, but the trend is for warming. Years of bizarrely warm weather have become common and records have been broken so often they are hardly noted. In Anchorage, where I live, that has meant ski seasons ruined by rainy weather, massive insect kills of trees, and extraordinary forest fire danger, among many other changes. My friends and I, who grew up in Anchorage, never heard thunder until our teens; now it's commonplace, even early in the summer. Starting in the summer of 2004, the ocean warmed so much we were able to swim in it in places. That's never been possible before in my 43-year life. Alaska didn't even smell like Alaska that summer. Something about how the sun heated the ground and the plants created an odor I remember from travels in the Lower 48, not here.

In Arctic Alaska, the changes are much more pronounced: Sea ice is withdrawing from shore, catastrophic erosion washing away bluffs and villages, permafrost softening and giving way, winters warming and shortening, and ecosystems becoming disrupted as plant and animal life is stressed by the new conditions. A team of 300 scientists from all the Arctic nations, including the United States, completed a 4-year Arctic Climate Impact Assessment in 2004 and 2005. The report documented the changes and said they were largely driven by human carbon dioxide emissions. It predicted more changes, most of them negative. For example, if the sea ice continues to melt at the current rate, this century will see the end of the ecosystem that lives upon it, including the likely extinction of the polar bear.

Carbon dioxide warms the earth by trapping the heat of the sun in the atmosphere, a phenomenon understood since the late 1800s. Climate records reconstructed from ancient ice show the amount of carbon dioxide in the atmosphere has closely matched average temperature and climate conditions for the last 400,000 years. Due to human burning of fossil fuels, the carbon dioxide level in the atmosphere now is higher than at any time in that period. And now Arctic temperatures are rising at a rate that appears unprecedented in thousands of years.

Does this mean adjusting your plans as a visitor? Yes and no. Tourists in recent years have enjoyed sunny weather, but also suffered through forest fire smoke and rainy skiing. But how the changes will play out in any particular year cannot be predicted, just as you cannot set your vacation dates based on a TV weather forecast. On the other hand, we may all need to adjust our plans. The amount of carbon dioxide each of us is responsible for emitting relates directly to the nonrenewable energy we use. You can help save Alaska by carpooling or turning off an extra light.

I've written a book on this subject, *The Whale and the Supercomputer; On the Northern Front of Climate Change* (North Point Press, $14), which tells the story of how Alaska's Iñupiat and scientists are experiencing and learning about the changing climate. You can read more about it on my website, at www.wohlforth.net.

2 Politics & History: Living a Frontier Myth

The occupations of prospector, trapper, and homesteader—rugged individualists relying only on themselves in a limitless land—would dominate Alaska's economy if the state's image of itself were accurate. Alaskans talk a lot about the Alaskan spirit of independence, yearn for freedom from government, and declare that people from

Dateline

- **Approximately 15,000 years ago** First human explorers arrive in Alaska from Asia.
- **1741** Vitus Bering, on a mission originally chartered by Peter the Great, finds Alaska; ship's surgeon and naturalist Georg Steller goes ashore for a few hours on Kayak Island, the first white to set foot in Alaska.

- **1743** Russian fur traders enter the Aleutian Islands; Aleuts are enslaved to hunt sea otter and massacred when they try to revolt; Aleut cultural traditions are eliminated, and over the coming decades they are relocated as far south as California for their hunting skills.
- **1772** Unalaska, in the Aleutian Islands, becomes a permanent Russian settlement.

- **1778** British Capt. James Cook makes voyages of exploration to Alaska, seeking the Northwest Passage from the Pacific to the Atlantic, and draws charts of the coast.
- **1784** Russians build a settlement at Kodiak.
- **1799** Russians establish a fort near present-day Sitka, which will later become their

continues

"Outside" just don't understand Alaskans when they insist on locking up Alaska's lands in parks and wilderness status. The bumper sticker says, simply, "We don't give a damn how they do it Outside." A state full of self-reliant frontiersmen can't be tied down and deterred from their manifest destiny by a bunch of Washington bureaucrats. At the extreme, there has even been a movement to declare independence as a separate nation so Alaskans can extend the frontier, extracting its natural resources unfettered by bunny-hugging Easterners.

But just because you wear a cowboy hat doesn't mean you know how to ride a horse. In Las Vegas you find a lot more hats than horsemen, and Alaska is full of self-reliant pioneers who spend rush hour in traffic jams and worry more about urban drug dealing and air pollution than where to catch their next meal or dig the mother lode. As for self-reliance and independence from government, Alaska has the highest per-capita state spending of any state in the nation, with no state income or sales taxes and an annual payment that has ranged in the last decade from $845 to almost $2,000 a year to every man, woman, and child just for living here. The state government provides retirement homes; it owns various businesses, including a dairy, a railroad, and a subsidized mortgage lender; it has built schools in the smallest communities; it operates a state ferry system and a radio and television network; and it owns nearly a third of the landmass of Alaska. The state government relies on the oil industry; when oil prices are high, the state spends a lot, but when they go down, budget cuts can go deep.

That conflict between perception and reality grows out of the story of a century of development of Alaska. The state is a great storehouse of minerals, oil, timber, and fish. A lot of wealth has been extracted, and many people have gotten rich. But it has always been because the federal government let them do it. Every acre of Alaska belonged to the U.S. government from the day Secretary of State William Seward bought Alaska from Russia in 1867. Since then, the frontier has never been broader than Uncle Sam made it.

Yet the whole concept of ownership didn't fit Alaska well from the start. Did the Russians really own what they sold? Alaska Natives didn't think so. They'd been living on this land for more than 100 centuries, and at the time of the purchase, most had never seen a white face. How could Russia hold title to land that no Russian had so much as explored? As Americans flooded into Alaska to search for gold at the turn of the 20th century, this conflict became obvious. Alaska

capital; Tlingits attack and destroy the fort, but are later driven off in a counterattack; the Russian-America Company receives a 20-year exclusive franchise to govern and exploit Alaska.

- **1821** Russian naval officers are placed in control of the Russian-America Company, which begins to decline in profitability.
- **1824** Boundaries roughly matching Alaska's current

borders are set by treaty between Russia, Britain, and the United States.

- **1839** The British Hudson's Bay Company, surpassing Russia in trade, begins leasing parts of Southeast Alaska and subsequently extends trading outposts into the Interior.
- **1843** First overtures are made by American officials interested in buying Alaska from the Russians so U.S.

instead of British power could expand there.

- **1848** New England whalers begin to exploit rich Arctic stocks; over the next 60 years, they transform Native cultures and severely reduce marine mammal numbers.
- **1865** A Confederate navy ship attacks the whaling fleet, destroying 20 ships and capturing 4 more.
- **1867** In need of money and fearful that Russia couldn't

Natives, never conquered by war or treaty, soon began their legal and political fight to recover their land—a fight they would eventually win.

The concept of ownership has changed in other ways, too. For the first 100 years after the United States bought Alaska, it maintained the vast majority of the territory as "public domain," with federal land and its mineral resources free for the taking, as in the Old West of frontier lore. Each piece of Alaska belonged to everyone until someone showed up to lay private claim. Today, amid deep conflict over whether to develop such areas as the Arctic National Wildlife Refuge (known as ANWR), federal control stands out far more clearly than it did during the gold rush, when the land's wealth was free to anyone with strength enough to take it. Alaskans who want to keep receiving the good things that a rich state government brings equate the frontier spirit of the past with their own financial well-being, whether that means working at a mining claim or at a desk in a glass office tower. But other Americans feel they own Alaska, too, and they don't necessarily believe in exploiting its resource treasure. They may want the frontier to stay alive in another sense—unconquered and still wild.

White colonization of the territory came in boom-and-bust waves of migrants arriving with the goal of making a quick buck and then clearing out—without worrying about the people who already lived there. Although the gold-rush pioneers are celebrated today, the Klondike rush of 1898 that opened up and populated the territory was motivated by greed and was a mass importer of crime, inhumanity, and, for the Native people, terrible epidemics of new diseases that killed off whole villages. Like the Russians 150 years before, who had made slaves of the Natives, the new white population behaved as if the indigenous people were less than human. Until Franklin Roosevelt became president, federal policy was to suppress Alaska Native cultures. Protestant missionaries had the authority of law to forbid Native people from telling their old stories or even speaking their own languages. Segregation ended only after World War II. Meanwhile, the salmon that fed the people of the territory were overfished by a powerful Outside-owned canning industry with friends in Washington, D.C. Their abuses destroyed salmon runs. Formerly rich Native villages faced famine when their primary food source was taken away.

It was only with World War II, and the Japanese invasion of the Aleutian Islands, that Alaska developed an industry that

---

hold on to Alaska anyway, Czar Alexander II sells Alaska to the United States; Secretary of State William Seward negotiates the deal for a price of $7.2 million, roughly 2¢ an acre; the American flag is raised in Sitka, and the U.S. military assumes government of Alaska.

- **1870** The Alaska Commercial Company receives a monopoly on harvesting seals in the Pribilof Islands and soon expands across the territory (the company remains a presence in the Alaska Bush today).

- **1879** Naturalist and writer John Muir explores Southeast Alaska by canoe, discovering Glacier Bay with Native guides.

- **1880** Joe Juneau and Richard Harris, guided by local Natives, find gold on Gastineau Channel and found the city of Juneau; gold strikes begin to come every few years across the state.

- **1884** Military rule ends in Alaska, but residents still have no right to elect a legislature, governor, or congressional representative, or to make laws.

- **1885** Protestant missionaries meet to divide up the territory, parceling out each region to a different religion;

continues

was not based on exploitation of natural resources: the military industry. The war brought the construction of the territory's first road to the outside world, the Alaska Highway. After the war, military activity dropped off, but only briefly. By the late 1940s, Alaska was on the front line of the Cold War. Huge Air Force and Army bases were built, and remote radar stations were installed to detect and repel Soviet bombers and missiles. To this day, the federal government remains a key industry whose removal would deal the economy a grievous blow.

The fight for Alaska statehood also began after World War II. Alaskans argued that they needed local, independent control of natural resources, pointing to the example of overfishing in the federally managed salmon industry. Opponents said that Alaska would never be able to support itself, would always require large subsidies from the federal government, and therefore should not be a state. But the advocates pointed out that Alaska's lack of self-sufficiency came about because its citizens did not control the resources—Alaska was a colony, with decisions and profits taken away by the mother country. If Alaskans could control their own land, they could use the resources to fund government. The discovery of oil on the Swanson River on the Kenai Peninsula in 1957 helped win that argument. Here was real money that could fund a state government. In 1959, Alaska finally became the 49th state. Along with the rights of entering the Union, Alaska received a dowry, an endowment of land to develop and pay for future government. The Statehood Act gave the new state the right to select 103 million acres from a total landmass of 365 million acres. Indeed, that land does pay for state government in Alaska, in the form of oil royalties and taxes—but, to this day, the federal government still spends a lot more in Alaska than it receives.

Oil revenues supported the new state as it began to extend services to the vast, undeveloped expanse of Alaska. Anchorage boomed in the 1960s in a period of buoyant optimism. Leaders believed that the age-old problems of the wide-open frontier—poverty, lack of basic services, impenetrable remoteness—would succumb to the new government and new money, while the land would remain wide open. The pace of change redoubled in 1968 with the discovery of the largest oil field in North America at Prudhoe Bay on land that had been a wise state selection in the federal land-grant entitlement. The state government received as much money in a one-day oil lease auction as it had spent in total for the previous 6 years. This was going to be the boom of all booms.

they begin to fan out across Alaska to convert Native peoples, largely suppressing their traditional ways.

- **1898** After prospectors arrive in Seattle with a ton of gold, the Klondike gold rush begins; gold rushes in Nome and Fairbanks follow within a few years; Americans begin to populate Alaska.
- **1906** Alaska's first (nonvoting) delegate in Congress

takes office; the capital moves from Sitka to Juneau.

- **1908** The Iditarod Trail, a sled dog mail route, is completed, linking trails continuously from Seward to Nome.
- **1913** The first territorial legislature convenes, although it has few powers; the first automobile drives the Richardson Highway route, from Valdez to Fairbanks.
- **1914** Federal construction of the Alaska Railroad begins;

the first tents go up in the river bottom that will be Anchorage, along the rail line.

- **1917** Mount McKinley National Park is established.
- **1920** The first flights connect Alaska to the rest of the United States; aviation quickly becomes the most important means of transportation in the territory.
- **1923** President Warren Harding drives the final spike on

The oil bonanza on the North Slope would change Alaska more than any other event since the gold rush. Once, opening the frontier meant letting a few prospectors scratch the dirt in search of a poke of gold. But getting this immense pool of oil to market from one of the most remote spots on the globe would require allowing the world's largest companies to build across Alaska a pipeline that, when completed, could credibly claim to be the largest privately financed construction project in world history. With the stakes suddenly so much higher, it came time to figure out exactly who owned which parts of Alaska. The land couldn't just be public domain any longer.

That division wouldn't be easy. Much of the state had never even been mapped, much less surveyed, and there were some large outstanding claims that had to be settled. Alaska Natives, who had lost land, culture, and health in 2 centuries of white invasion, finally saw their luck start to turn. It wouldn't be possible to resolve the land issues surrounding the pipeline until their claims to land and compensation were answered. Native leaders cannily used that leverage to ensure that they got what they wanted.

In the early 1970s, America had a new awareness of the way its first people had been treated in the settlement of the West.

When white frontiers expanded, Native traditional homelands were stolen. In Alaska, with the powerful lure of all that oil providing the impetus, Native people were able to insist on a fairer resolution. In 1971, with the support of white Alaskans, the oil companies, and President Richard Nixon, Congress passed the Alaska Native Claims Settlement Act, called ANCSA. The act transferred 44 million acres of land and $962.5 million to corporations whose shareholders were all the Native people of Alaska. The new Native corporations would be able to exploit their own land for their shareholders' profit. In later legislation, Natives also won guaranteed subsistence hunting and fishing rights on federal land. Some Natives complained that they'd received only an eighth of the land they had owned before white contact, but it was still by far the richest settlement any of the world's indigenous people had received at that time. Today the Native corporations are Alaska's largest and most powerful homegrown businesses.

It was a political deal on a grand scale. It's unlikely that Natives would have gotten their land at all but for the desire of whites to get at the oil and their need for Native support. Nor could the pipeline have overcome environmental challenges without the Natives dropping their objections. Even with Native support in place,

---

the Alaska Railroad at Nenana, and then dies on the way home, purportedly from eating bad Alaska seafood.

- **1925** Leonhard Seppala and other dog mushers relay diphtheria serum on the Iditarod Trail to fight an epidemic in Nome; Seppala and his lead dog, Balto, become national heroes.

- **1934** Federal policy of forced assimilation of Native cultures is officially discarded

and New Deal efforts to preserve Native cultures begin.

- **1935** New Deal "colonists," broke farmers from all over the United States, settle in the Matanuska Valley north of Anchorage.

- **1940** A military buildup begins in Alaska; bases built in Anchorage accelerate the city's growth into a major population center.

- **1942** Japanese invade the Aleutians, taking Attu and

Kiska islands and bombing Unalaska/Dutch Harbor (a U.S. counterattack the next year drives out the Japanese); the Alaska Highway links Alaska to the rest of the country overland for the first time but is open to civilians only after the war.

- **1949** Massive Cold War military buildup feeds fast economic growth.

continues

legislation authorizing the pipeline passed the U.S. Senate by only one vote, cast by Vice President Spiro Agnew.

But there were other side effects of the deal that white Alaskans didn't like so much. The state still hadn't received a large portion of its land entitlement, and now the Native corporations also had a right to select the land they wanted. There still remained the question of who would get what, and the question of the wild lands that Congress, influenced by a strong new environmental movement, wanted to maintain as national parks and wilderness and not give away. That issue wasn't settled until 1980, when the Alaska National Interest Lands Conservation Act passed, setting aside an additional 106 million acres for conservation, an area larger than California. Alaska's frontier-minded population screamed bloody murder over "the lockup of Alaska," but the act was only the last tangible step in a process started by the coming of big oil and the need its arrival created to draw lines on the map, tying up the frontier.

When construction of the $9 billion pipeline finally got underway in 1974, a huge influx of new people chasing the high-paying jobs put any previous gold rush to shame. The newcomers were from a different part of the country than previously, too. Alaska had been a predominantly Democratic state, but oil workers from Texas, Oklahoma, and other Bible Belt states helped shift the balance of Alaska's politics, and now it's solidly Republican. In its frontier days, Alaska had a strong Libertarian streak, but now it became more influenced by Christian conservatism. A hippie-infested legislature of the early 1970s legalized marijuana for home use. Conservatives at the time, who thought the government shouldn't butt into its citizens' private lives, went along with them. After the pipeline, times changed, and Alaska developed tough antidrug laws.

Growth also brought urban problems. As the pipeline construction boom waned in 1977, the boomtown atmosphere of gambling and street prostitution disappeared with it, but other big-city problems remained. No longer could residents of Anchorage and Fairbanks go to bed without locking their doors. Both cities were declared "nonattainment" areas by the Environmental Protection Agency because of air pollution near the ground in cold winter weather, when people leave their cars running during the day to keep them from freezing.

But the pipeline seemed to provide limitless wealth to solve these problems. For fear that too much money would be wasted, the voters altered the state

---

- **1957** Oil is found on Kenai Peninsula's Swanson River.
- **1959** Alaska becomes a state.
- **1964** The largest earthquake ever to strike North America shakes Southcentral Alaska, killing 131 people, primarily in tsunami waves.
- **1968** Largest oil field in American history is found at Prudhoe Bay, on Alaska's North Slope.

- **1970** Environmental lawsuits tie up work to build the Alaska pipeline, which is needed to link the North Slope oil field to markets.
- **1971** Congress acknowledges and pays the federal government's debt to Alaska's indigenous people with the Alaska Native Claims Settlement Act, which transfers 44 million acres of land and almost $1 billion to

new Native-owned corporations.
- **1973** The first Iditarod Trail Sled Dog Race runs more than 1,000 miles from Anchorage to Nome.
- **1974** Congress clears away legal barriers to construction of the trans-Alaska pipeline; Vice President Spiro Agnew casts the deciding vote in the U.S. Senate.
- **1977** The trans-Alaska pipeline is completed and

constitution to bank a large portion of the new riches. The new Permanent Fund would be off-limits to the politicians in Juneau, with half the annual earnings paid out to citizens as dividends. The fund now contains more than $30 billion in savings and has become one of the largest sectors of the economy simply by virtue of paying out as much as $1 billion a year in dividends to everyone who lives at least a year in the state. All major state taxes on individuals were canceled, and people got used to receiving everything free from the government.

Then, in 1985, oil prices dropped, deflating the overextended economy. Housing prices crashed and thousands of people simply walked away from their mortgages. All but a few of the banks in the state went broke. Condominiums that had sold for $100,000 went for $20,000 or less a year later. It was the bust that always goes with the boom, but it still came as a shock to many. The spending associated with the clean-up of the *Exxon Valdez* oil spill in 1989 restarted the economy, and it continues on an even keel today, but the extreme wealth of the earlier oil years never returned.

Meanwhile, the oil from Prudhoe Bay started running out. Oil revenues, an irreplaceable 85% of the state budget, started an inexorable downward trend in the early 1990s. The oil companies downsized. Without another boom on the horizon, the question became how to avoid, or at least soften, the next bust. At this writing, that question remains unanswered. Ironically, polls show that Alaskans would support a personal income tax, but so far they haven't been given the choice. Politically, it's more expedient to hope high oil prices hold until the next big project gets the good times rolling again, such as a natural gas pipeline from the North Slope to middle America or oil development in ANWR.

Culture moves slower than politics or economics, and Alaskans still see themselves as gold-rush prospectors or wildcat oil drillers, adventuring in an open land and striking it rich by their own devices. Even as the economy blends ever more smoothly into the American corporate landscape, Alaskans' myth of themselves remains strong. Today the state's future is as little in its own hands as it has ever been. Big petroleum projects will be decided in Congress and distant corporate boardrooms, not here. Ultimately, an economy based on exploiting natural resources is anything but independent.

---

begins providing up to 25% of the U.S. domestic supply of oil.

■ **1980** Congress sets aside almost a third of Alaska in new parks and other land-conservation units; awash in new oil wealth, the state legislature abolishes all taxes paid by individuals to state government.

■ **1982** Alaskans receive their first Alaska Permanent Fund dividends, interest paid on an oil-wealth savings account.

■ **1985** Declining oil prices send the Alaska economy into a tailspin; tens of thousands leave the state and most of the banks collapse.

■ **1989** The tanker *Exxon Valdez* hits Bligh Reef in Prince William Sound, spilling 11 million gallons of North Slope crude in the worst oil spill ever in North America.

■ **1994** A federal jury in Anchorage awards $5 billion to 10,000 fishermen, Natives, and others hurt by the Exxon oil spill; Exxon appeals continue today.

3 The People: Three Ways to Win an Argument in Alaska

NUMBER 1: WAIT FOR SPRING

A small town in Alaska in March. Each time it snows, you have to throw shovels of it higher over your head to dig out. The air in the house is stale and the view out the window is black, white, and gray. Everyone's going nuts with winter. It's time for a good political ruckus. No one can predict exactly what will set it off—it could just be an ill-considered letter to the editor in the local newspaper, or it could be something juicier, like a controversial development proposal. At some point, when the cabin fever gets bad enough, it almost doesn't matter what sparks the inferno. Alaskans can generate outrage about almost anything, with a ritual of charges and countercharges, conspiracy theories, and impassioned public testimony.

It's particularly amusing when some outsider is involved, thinking he's at the town council meeting in a normal political process to get some project approved, only to wind up on the receiving end of a public hearing from hell. I'll never forget a sorry businessman who was trying to lease some land from the town of Homer. He endured hours of angry public testimony one night. He was sweating, the only person in the packed city hall meeting room wearing a tie, surrounded by flannel shirts, blue jeans, and angry faces. Finally, he stood up at his chair and, in a plaintive tone of frustration near tears, declared, "You're not very professional as a community!" For once, no one could disagree.

He gave up. He didn't know that if he had only waited a couple of months, the opposition would dry up when the salmon started running. Then most of the city council meetings are canceled, and the rest are brief and sparsely attended. If anything really important comes up, the council is smart enough to postpone it till fall. In the summer, Alaskans have more important things to attend to than government.

The sun shines deep into the night so you can catch fish and tourists, not sit inside. It's the season when the money is made. The streets are full of new people, like a bird rookery refreshed by migrants. Everyone stays awake late pounding nails, playing softball, and fly-casting for reds. Office workers in Anchorage depart straight from work for a 3-hour drive down to the Kenai Peninsula, fish through the night, catch a quick nap in the car in the wee hours, and make it to work on time the next morning, with fish stories to share. Sleep is expendable—you don't seem to need it that much when the sky is light all night.

In the Native villages of the Bush, everyone has gone to fish camp. Families load everything in an aluminum riverboat and leave town, headed upriver. On the banks and beaches, they set up wall tents and spruce-log fish-drying racks, maybe a basketball hoop and campfire, too. Extended families work as a unit. Men gather in the salmon and the women gut them with a few lightning strokes of a knife and hang them to dry on the racks. Children run around in a countryside paradise, watched by whatever adults are handiest.

Suddenly, August comes. For the first time in months, you can see the stars. It comes as a shock the first time you have to use your car headlights. The mood gets even more frantic. There's never enough time in the summer to do everything that needs to get done. Construction crews can count the days now till snow and cold will shut them down. Anything that's not done now won't be done until next May. Labor Day approaches as fast as 5pm on a busy business day.

The Iditarod

The Iditarod Trail Sled Dog Race, a 1,000-mile run from Anchorage to Nome that takes place over 2 weeks in mid-March, is the biggest event of Alaska's year, not only in terms of sports, but also culturally and as a unifying event. The race is big news—TV anchors speculate on the mushers' strategies at the top of the evening news and break away live to cover the top finishers, regardless of the time of day or night. School children plot the progress of their favorite teams on maps and over the Internet. Increasingly, the world is joining in. Visitors, especially Europeans, fill hotels in Anchorage and Nome for the Iditarod. Voices speaking French and German waft through the restaurants. It's a wonderful time of year to visit, with light skies, excellent late-season skiing, and winter festivals enlivening many towns. Nome goes crazy when the mushers hit. Even if the first team crosses the finish line at 3am in −30°F (−34°C) degree weather, a huge crowd turns out to congratulate the winner. And crowds keep turning out for the also-rans, too.

Given all this, it's difficult for me to report objectively on the activities of a Miami, Florida–based animal-rights activist group that opposes the race—but my editors insist that I try. The Sled Dog Action Coalition contends the race is cruel to the dogs, with some suffering and dying on the trail or inhumanely tethered in dog lots. The group has organized boycotts against race sponsors. While the campaign doesn't seem to be affecting the race, which grows every year, it has sparked occasional media coverage and angry debate. Iditarod supporters—the universal view in Alaska—claim the coalition exaggerates and distorts its charges. Iditarod mushers insist that the dogs, which are worth thousands of dollars, receive veterinary care superior to the doctoring that most people get. Mushers who abuse dogs are kicked out of the sport.

Harmful practices probably do occur in the lower ranks of mushing. For example, uncontrolled breeding can produce too many pups and some may end up being killed—sadly, that problem is common with pets in cities all over the U.S. At least sled dogs get the regular exercise they need.

To find out more about both sides of the issue, check out the websites of the Sled Dog Action Coalition (www.helpsleddogs.org) and of an Iditarod supporter responding to the coalition's charges (www.sunhusky.com). If you want to plan your trip to coincide with the race in March, plan well in advance because the event is extremely popular and hotels (particularly in Nome) fill up quickly. For information, contact the Iditarod Trail Committee (© 907/376-5155; www.iditarod.com).

As September turns to October, the last tourists are gone and T-shirt shops are closed for the season. The commercial fishing boats are tied up back in the harbor and the fishermen prepare for vacation. Cannery workers are already back at college. For the first time in months, people can slow down long enough to look at each other and remember where they left off in the spring. It's time to catch up on sleep, make big decisions. The hills of birch turn bright yellow, the tundra goes brick red, and the sky turns gray—there's the smell of wood smoke in the air—and then, one day, it starts to snow.

It's not the velvet darkness of midwinter that gets you. December is bearable, even if the sun rises after the kids get to school, barely cruises along the horizon, and sinks before they start for home. Nowhere is Christmas more real than in Alaska, where carolers sing with cheeks tingling from the cold. January isn't so hard. You're still excited about the skiing. The phone rings in the middle of the night—it's a friend telling you to put on your boots and go outside to see the northern lights. February is a bit harder to take, but most towns have a winter carnival to divert your attention from the cold.

March is when bizarre things start to happen. People are just holding on for the end of winter, and you never know what will set them off. That's when you hunker down and lay low, watch what you say, bite your tongue when your spouse lets hang a comment you'd like to jump on like a coho hitting fresh bait. Hold on—just until the icicles start to melt, the mud shows around the snowbanks, and the cycle starts fresh.

NUMBER 2: BE HERE FIRST

There's a simple and effective way to win an argument in Alaska—state how long you've lived here. If it's longer than your adversary, he'll find it difficult to put up a fight. This is why, when speaking in public, people will often begin their remarks by stating how many years they've been in Alaska. It's a badge of authenticity and status in a place with a young, transient population that's grown fast. No one cares where you came from or who you were back there, and there's no such thing as class in Alaska—anyone who tries to act superior will quickly find that no one else notices. But if you haven't made it

through a few winters, you probably don't know what you're talking about.

It's also traditional—although, sadly, a fading tradition—to treat strangers as friends until they prove otherwise. The smaller the town you visit, the more strongly you'll find that hospitality still alive. Visitors find it pleasantly disorienting to arrive in a small town and have everyone in the street greet them with a smile. These traditions of hospitality run deep in Alaska's Native people. (Alaskans use the word *Native* to mean all the indigenous peoples of Alaska.) But instead of beginning a conversation by stating how long they've lived here, Natives—who've always been here—try to find a relation with a new person by talking about where their families are from.

Theories differ about how North America was originally populated. The traditional notion is that the first people walked across a land bridge from Asia over the dry Bering Sea around 15,000 years ago, when glacial ice sequestered enough of the earth's water to lower the sea level. The bridge, up to 1,000 miles wide, included the entire west coast of Alaska at its largest size, and lasted longest in the area between Nome and Kotzebue.

But new archaeology and geology throw doubt on that theory, suggesting a migration story that's much more complex. People who know the Arctic know the land bridge simply wasn't necessary for migration: In the winter, you can sometimes walk between Siberia and Alaska even today, and the seafaring skills of Alaska's Aleuts and Eskimos would have enabled them to travel back and forth to Asia at any time. Siberian and Alaskan Natives share language, stories, and kin. Perhaps the connection across the north was continuous and followed many routes after northern people learned to sew skin boats and clothing about 15,000 years ago. Certainly, the idea that they walked seems increasingly questionable. Geologists now believe the route south was largely impassable during the last glacial period; if migrants did use it, they must have used boats to connect coastal pockets that remained free of glacial ice.

However and whenever the first people arrived, they quickly spread through the Americas, creating cultures of incredible complexity and diversity. Most scientists believe migrants through Alaska were the ancestors of all the indigenous peoples of the hemisphere, from the Inca to the Algonquin. Those who stayed in Alaska became the Eskimos, who include the Iñupiat of the Arctic, the Yup'ik of the Southwest, and the Alutiiq of the Gulf of Alaska coastline. They also became Indians: the Athabaskans of the Interior and the Tlingit, Haida, and Tsimshian of Southeast Alaska and British Columbia. And seafaring people in the Aleutian Chain became the Aleuts, neither Eskimo nor Indian.

The Native groups of Alaska have a lot in common culturally, but before the white invasion they had well-defined boundaries and didn't mix much. They didn't farm, and the only animal they domesticated was the dog—dog teams and boats were the primary means of transportation and commerce. But they generally were not nomadic, and no one in Alaska lived in ice igloos (farther east, in Canada, igloos were used as winter dwellings on the ice pack). On the treeless Arctic coast, houses were built of sod atop supports of whalebone and driftwood; where wood was plentiful, in the rainforests, large and intricately carved houses sheltered entire villages. Typically, a family-connected tribal group would have a winter village and a summer fish camp for gathering and laying up food. Elders guided the community in important decisions. A gifted shaman led the people in religious matters, relating to the spirits of ancestors, animals, trees, and even the ice that populated their world. Stories passed on through generations explained the universe.

Those oral traditions kept Native cultures alive. Twenty distinct Native languages were spoken. A few elders still speak only their Native language today, and only one language, Eyak, is essentially extinct. The languages break into four major families: Eskimo-Aleut, Athabaskan-Eyak-Tlingit, Haida, and Tsimshian (the last two are primarily Canadian). The Eskimo-Aleut language group includes languages spoken by coastal people from the Arctic Ocean to the Gulf of Alaska, including Iñupiaq in the Arctic; Yup'ik in the Yukon-Kuskokwim and Bristol Bay region; Aleut in the Aleutian Islands; and Alutiiq on the Alaska Peninsula, Kodiak, and Prince William Sound. There are 12 Athabaskan and Eyak languages in Alaska, and more Outside, including Apache and Navajo. In Southeast Alaska, Tlingit was spoken across most of the Panhandle. Haida was spoken on southern Prince of Wales Island and southward into what's now British Columbia, where Tsimshian also was spoken.

The first arrival of whites was often violent and destructive, spanning a 100-year period that started in the 1740s with the coming of the Russian fur traders, who enslaved the Aleuts, and continued to the 1840s, when New England whalers first met the Iñupiat of the Arctic. There were pitched battles, but disease and non-violent destruction of oral traditions were more influential. Protestant missionaries, backed by government assimilation policy, drove the old stories and even Native languages underground. Lela Kiana Oman, who has published traditional Iñupiat stories to preserve them, told me of her memories of her father secretly telling the ancient tales at night to his children. She was forbidden to speak Iñupiaq in school and did not see her first traditional Native dance until age 18.

Oman's work is part of today's Native cultural renaissance. It's not a moment too soon. In some villages, children know more about Beverly Hills, which they see on television, than about their own culture. A few don't share a language with their own grandparents. But schools in many areas now require Native language classes, or even teach using language-immersion techniques. For the Aleut, whose cultural traditions were almost completely wiped out, the process of renewal involves a certain amount of invention. On the other hand, some traditional villages remain, especially deep in the country of the Yukon-Kuskokwim Delta, where Yup'ik is still the dominant language and most of the food comes from traditional subsistence hunting and gathering, altered only by the use of modern materials and guns.

Alaska Natives also are fighting destruction fueled by alcohol and other substance-abuse problems. Rates of suicide, accidents, and domestic violence are high in the Bush. Statistically, nearly every Alaska Native in prison is there because of alcohol. A sobriety movement is attacking the problem one person at a time. One of its goals is to use traditional Native culture to fill a void of rural despair where alcohol flows in. Politically, a "local option" law provides communities the choice of partial or total alcohol prohibition; it has been successfully used in many towns but remains controversial in others.

There are social and political tensions between Natives and whites on many levels and over many issues. The Alaskan city and Alaskan village have less in common than do most different nations. Although village Natives come to the city to shop, get health care, or attend meetings, urban Alaskans have no reason to go to the villages, and most never have made the trip.

The most contentious rural-urban issue concerns allocation of fish and game. Some urban outdoorsmen feel they should have the same rights to hunt and fish that the Natives do, and the state Supreme Court has interpreted Alaska's constitution to say they're correct. But rural Natives have federal law on their side, which overrules the state. A decade of political stalemate over the issue divided Alaskans until, in 2000, the feds finally stepped in and took over fish and game management in the majority of the state to protect Native subsistence. Many Natives were glad to see it happen, as humiliating as the move was for independent-minded Alaskans. Natives feel subsistence hunting and fishing are an integral part of their cultural heritage, far more important than sport, and should take priority. Darker conflicts exist, too, and it's impossible to discount the charges of racism that Native Alaskans raise in issues as diverse as school funding and public safety.

Alaska Natives have essentially become a minority in their own land. In 1880, Alaska contained 33,000 Natives and 430 whites. By 1900, with the gold rush, the numbers were roughly equal. Since then, whites have generally outnumbered Natives in ever greater numbers. Today there are about 98,000 Alaska Natives—27,000 of whom live in the cities of Anchorage and Fairbanks—out of a total state population of 627,000 people of all races. Consequently, Alaska Natives must learn to walk in two worlds. The North Slope's Iñupiat, who hunt the bowhead whale from open boats as their forefathers did, must also know how to negotiate for their take in international diplomatic meetings. And they have to use the levers of government to protect the whale's environment from potential damage by the oil industry. The Alaska Native

Claims Settlement Act created a new class, the corporate Native, responsible for representing rural needs but also obliged to function as an executive for large, far-reaching business concerns.

Non-Natives traveling to the Bush also walk in two worlds, but they may not even know it. In a Native village, a newly met friend will ask you in for a cup of coffee; it can be rude not to accept. Too much eye contact in conversation also can be rude—that's how Native elders look at younger people who owe them respect. If a Native person looks down, speaks slowly, and seems to mumble, that's not disrespect, but the reverse. Fast-talking non-Natives have to make a conscious effort to slow down and leave pauses in conversation because Natives usually don't jump in or interrupt—they listen, consider, and then respond. Of course, most Native people won't take offense at your bad manners. They're used to spanning cultures. When I was in a village a few years ago, I looked in confusion at a clock that didn't seem right. "That's Indian time," my Athabaskan companion said. Then, pointing to a clock that was working, "White man time is over there."

Urban visitors who miss cultural nuances rarely overlook the apparent poverty of many villages. Out on a remote landscape of windswept tundra, swampy in summer and frozen in winter, they may secretly wonder why Natives endure the hardships of rural Alaskan life when even the most remote villager can see on television how easy it is in Southern California. Save your pity. As Yup'ik social observer Harold Napoleon once said, "We're poor, all right, but we've got more than most people. Our most important asset is our land and our culture, and we want to protect it, come hell or high water."

NUMBER 3: BE A REAL ALASKAN

Alaska's history books are full of the stories of economic booms, the people who came, what kind of wealth they were after, and how they populated and developed the land. In a largely empty place, you can make it into history just by showing up. But every wave is followed by a trough, the bust that comes after the boom when those who came just for the money go back where they came from. Those are the times when the real Alaskans—those who live here for the love of the place, not only the money— are divided from the rest. The real Alaskans stay; the others leave. It's the perfect way to settle an argument.

Other people have other definitions of what it takes to be a real Alaskan. One definition, which I once read on a place mat in a diner in Soldotna, holds that to be a real Alaskan, you have to know how to fix a Caterpillar tractor. Similar definitions require various feats in the outdoors— hunting, fishing, or shooting—and even acts in the barroom or the bedroom. They all assume that a real Alaskan is a big, tough, white, male, bulldozer-driving type of guy. But those can be the first to leave when the economy goes down the tubes.

The first to leave were the Russians sent by the czar and the Russian-America Company. On October 18, 1867, their flag came down over Castle Hill in Sitka in a solemn ceremony, got stuck, and had to be untangled by a soldier sent up the pole. The territory was virtually empty of Russians before the check was even signed, as Congress didn't much like the idea of the purchase and took a while to pay. The gold-rush stampeders were the next to leave. The population of Nome went from 12,500 to 852 after the stampede was over. The oil years have seen the same phenomenon.

But each time the boom went bust, enough stayed that Alaska ended up with more people than before. Over the long term, the population has kept growing dramatically. And each set of migrants has been similar: young, transplanted

An Alaska Glossary

If Alaska feels like a different country from the rest of the United States, one reason may be the odd local usage that makes English slightly different here—different enough, in fact, that the Associated Press publishes a separate style-book dictionary just for Alaska. Here are some Alaskan words you may run into:

breakup When God set up the seasons in Alaska, He forgot one: spring. While the rest of the United States enjoys new flowers and baseball, Alaskans are looking at melting snowbanks and mud. Then, in May, summer miraculously arrives. Breakup officially occurs when the ice goes out in the Interior's rivers, but it stands for the time period of winter's demise and summer's initiation.

bunny boots If you see people wearing huge bulbous white rubber boots in Alaska's winter, it's not necessarily because they have enormous feet. Those are bunny boots, superinsulated footwear originally designed for Arctic air force operations—and they're the warmest things in the world.

cheechako A newcomer or greenhorn. Not used much anymore because almost everyone is one.

dry or damp Many towns and villages have invoked a state law that allows them to outlaw alcohol completely (to go dry) or to outlaw sale but not possession (to go damp).

Lower 48 The contiguous United States.

Native When capitalized, the word refers to Alaska's indigenous people. "American Indian" isn't used much in Alaska, "Alaska Native" being the preferred term.

Native corporation In 1971, Congress settled land claims with Alaska's Natives by turning over land and money; corporations were set up, with the

mostly from the West, but from other parts of the United States, too. Most people who have come to Alaska have been white—minority populations are smaller than in the nation as a whole—but there are strong minority communities in Anchorage. In Kodiak, the canneries are run by a tight Filipino community started by just a few pioneer immigrants.

The non-Native part of Alaska, 100 years old with the anniversary of the gold rush in 1998, hasn't had time to develop an Alaskan accent. It's a melting pot of the melting pot, with a population made up of odds and ends from all over the United States. Everyone arrives with a clean slate and a chance to reinvent himself or herself. On occasion, that ability to start from scratch has created some embarrassing discoveries when the past does become relevant. There have been a series of political scandals uncovered by reporters who checked the resumes of well-known politicians, only to find out they had concocted their previous lives out of thin air. One leading legislative candidate's husband found out about his wife's real background from such a news story.

Natives then alive as shareholders, to receive the property. Most of the corporations still thrive.

oosik The huge penile bone of a walrus. Knowing this word could save you from being the butt of any of a number of practical jokes people like to play on cheechakos.

Outside Anywhere that isn't Alaska. This is a widely used term in print and is capitalized, like any other proper noun.

PFD No, not personal flotation device; it stands for Permanent Fund Dividend. When Alaska's oil riches started flowing in the late 1970s, the voters set up a savings account called the Permanent Fund. Half the interest is paid annually to every man, woman, and child in the state. With more than $30 billion in investments, the fund now yields from $900 to $2,000 in dividends to each Alaskan annually.

pioneer A white settler of Alaska who has been here longer than most other people can remember—25 or 30 years usually does it.

Southeast Most people don't bother to say "Southeast Alaska." The region may be to the northwest of everyone else in the country, but it's southeast of most Alaskans, and that's all they care about.

tsunami Earthquake-caused sea waves are often called tidal waves, but that's a misnomer. The destructive waves of the 1964 Alaska earthquake were tsunamis caused by underwater landslides and such.

village A small Alaska Native settlement in the Bush, usually tightly bound by family and cultural tradition. The word *village* is roughly analogous to *tribe* elsewhere in the U.S.

Alaska's population is as mismatched and haphazard as a thrift store clothing rack, but we do have some cultural traditions, or at least accepted ways of thinking: tolerance and equality, hospitality, independence—and a propensity for violence. In the late 1980s in Homer, a gunfight over a horse left a man lying dead on a dirt road. In the newspaper the next week, the editorial called for people not to settle their differences with guns. A couple of letters to the editor shot back on the theme, "Don't you tell *us* how to settle our differences." Guns are necessary tools in Alaska. They're also a religion. I have friends who actually exchanged handguns instead of rings when they got married.

The tradition of tolerance of newcomers has made Alaska a destination for oddballs, religious cults, hippies, and people who just can't make it in the mainstream. Perhaps the most interesting of the religious groups that formed its own community is the Old Believers, who in recent decades have built villages of brightly painted houses around Kachemak Bay, near Homer. Their resistance to convention dates from Peter the Great's reforms to Russian Orthodoxy in the 18th century, which they reject. In

Alaska they've found a place where they can live without interference—in fact, they've thrived as fishermen and boat builders. You see them around town in their 18th-century Russian peasant dress. Until a few years ago, even the girls' high-school basketball team wore long dresses, with their numbers stitched to the bodice.

Nikolaevsk was the first of the Russian Old Believer villages. In the public school there, they didn't teach about dinosaurs or men landing on the moon—that was considered heresy. Yet other Old Believers rebelled, convinced that Nikolaevsk was making too many compromises and was bound to lose the next generation to decadent American ways. They broke off and formed another village, farther up the bay, unreachable except by all-terrain vehicle, and adhered to stricter rules. That village, in turn, suffered another schism and yet another village was formed, farther up the bay, virtually inaccessible and with even stricter rules. The process continues. The fight against assimilation may be hopeless, as children will ultimately do as they please, but it's the Old Believers' own struggle. No one in Homer pushes them to change. No one pays any attention at all, except to buy their fish and their top-quality boats.

After several decades, it looks as if the Old Believers are here to stay. Whether they speak English or not, I'd say they're real Alaskans.

Index

THE NEW TRAVELOCITY GUARANTEE

EVERYTHING YOU BOOK WILL BE RIGHT, OR WE'LL WORK WITH OUR TRAVEL PARTNERS TO MAKE IT RIGHT, RIGHT AWAY.

*To drive home the point,
we're going to use the word "right" in every single sentence.*

Let's get right to it. Right to the meat! Only Travelocity guarantees everything about your booking will be right, or we'll work with our travel partners to make it right, right away. Right on!

Here's a picture taken smack dab right in the middle of Antigua, where the guarantee also covers you.

The guarantee covers all but one of the items pictured to the right.

Now, you may be thinking, "Yeah, right, I'm so sure." That's OK; you have the right to remain skeptical. That is until we mention help is always right around the corner. Call us right off the bat, knowing that our customer service reps are there for you 24/7. Righting wrongs. Left and right.

For example, what if the ocean view you booked actually looks out at a downright ugly parking lot? You'd be right to call – we're there for you. And no one in their right mind would be pleased to learn the rental car place has closed and left them stranded. Call Travelocity and we'll help get you back on the right track.

Now if you're guessing there are some things we can't control, like the weather, well you're right. But we can help you with most things – to get all the details in righting,* visit **travelocity.com/guarantee**.

*Sorry, spelling things right is one of the few things not covered under the guarantee.

I'd give my right arm for a guarantee like this, although I'm glad I don't have to.

✱✱✱ travelocity
You'll never roam alone.

IF YOU BOOK IT, IT SHOULD BE THERE.

Only Travelocity guarantees it will be, or we'll work
with our travel partners to make it right, right away.
So if you're missing a balcony or anything else you
booked, just call us 24/7. **1-888-TRAVELOCITY.**

***travelocity**

You'll never roam alo